Paraguay

the Bradt Travel Guide

Margaret Hebblethwaite

edition
I

www.bradtguides.com

Bradt Travel Guides Ltd, UK
The Globe Pequot Press Inc, USA

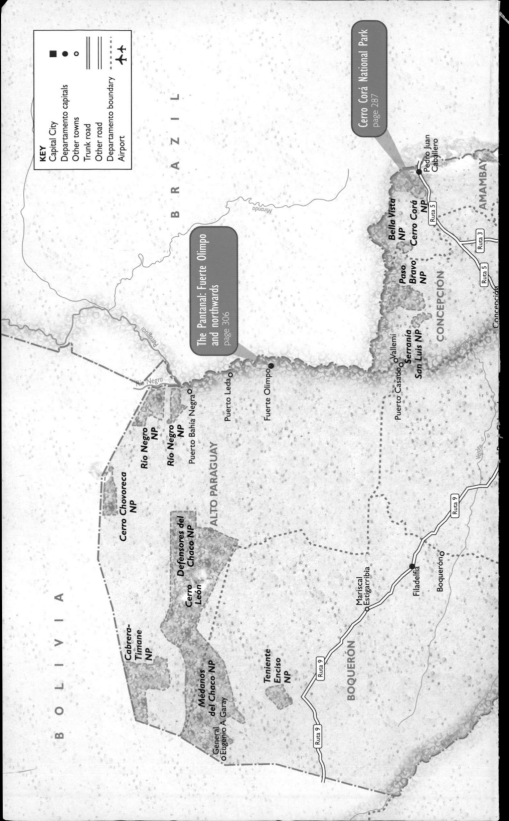

Paraguay
Don't
miss...

Paraguayan harp
The Paraguayan harp is
made entirely of wood
and has 36 strings
(LG) page ix

The *campo*
The countryside is the real
Paraguay, where national
traditions live on most strongly
(EH) page 153

Jesuit-Guaraní Reductions

Trinidad is one of the famous 'Paraguayan Reductions' which were started as missions for the Guaraní indigenous
(FA) page ix

Iguazú Falls

The Iguazú Falls make an excellent excursion from Paraguay
(SS) page 225

The craft towns

A craftswoman in Yataitý shows her handiwork in *ao po'i* lace
(FA) page x

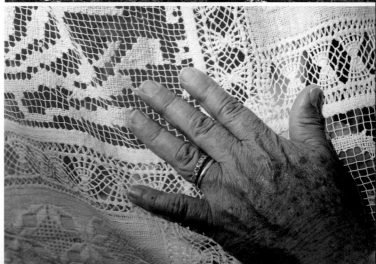

above The ornate Palacio de Gobierno, otherwise known as the Palacio de López, is the grandest building in Asunción (AS) page 94

left A journey on the steam train from the Jardín Botánico to Areguá is a delight (AS) page 98

below Asunción's Metropolitan Cathedral dominates the eastern end of the Plaza del Marzo Paraguayo (CG) page 90

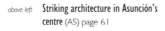

above The military cemetery at Boquerón — site of the most famous battle of the Chaco War (CM) page 302

left The unusual sandstone formations at the Kõi and Chororĩ hills near Areguá can only be found in two other places in the world (CG) page 127

below The Itaipú Dam cost US$20 billion to build (LG) page 248

AUTHOR

Margaret Hebblethwaite began her writing career as a theologian, and is the author of ten religious books in the areas of feminist theology, spirituality and Latin American liberation theology. She worked as assistant editor on *The Tablet* from 1991 to 2000, when she gave up her job to pursue her interest in Latin American liberation theology, by moving to a poor *campesino* community in South America.

She has lived in Santa María de Fe, Misiones, Paraguay since 2000, where her time has been consumed by working for a number of community projects. She founded and runs the charity Santa Maria Education Fund (*www.santamariadefe.org*); works with the sewing cooperative Taller de Hermandad to help them with their marketing (*www.santamariadefe.com*); and founded the Santa María Hotel, which is run as a community project with all profits going to the local people (*www.santamariahotel.org*). This is the first book she has written since her move to Paraguay.

AUTHOR'S STORY

When I decided to emigrate to Paraguay in the year 2000, I never imagined that one day I would be writing a guidebook. On my first visit to the country in 1996 I had fallen in love with Santa María de Fe, a small town in Misiones which had originally been a Jesuit mission (or Reduction) for the Guaraní indigenous, and I waited four years for my youngest child to grow up before I could realise my dream of moving here.

Paraguay was (and is) mercifully free of *gringos* and I wanted to keep it to myself. But there was a contradiction. I had come here to immerse myself in a poor community, inspired by the thinking of liberation theology. But as well as learning from the poor, I had to respond to the needs of the poor. They needed education, and soon the Santa María Education Fund was born (see *Chapter 2*, page 58). But education was not enough. People also needed work, they needed money.

It was clear what the untapped resource was, what Santa María – and Paraguay as a whole – had to sell to the rest of the world: tourism. The contribution I could make was not only to help bring donations into the country, but to help bring in trade, to bring in people. I had to stop being selfish about the wonderful place I had discovered. The Santa María Hotel was started; and the *Bradt Guide to Paraguay* began to be written.

PUBLISHER'S FOREWORD   *Adrian Phillips*

The first Bradt travel guide was written in 1974 by George and Hilary Bradt on a river barge floating down a tributary of the Amazon. In the 1980s and '90s the focus shifted away from hiking to broader-based guides covering new destinations – usually the first to be published about these places. In the 21st century Bradt continues to publish such ground-breaking guides, as well as others to established holiday destinations, incorporating in-depth information on culture and natural history with the nuts and bolts of where to stay and what to see.

Bradt authors support responsible travel, and provide advice not only on minimum impact but also on how to give something back through local charities. In this way a true synergy is achieved between the traveller and local communities.

* * *

They say actions speak louder than words. The actions of Margaret Hebblethwaite are certainly compelling: four years after her first visit, Margaret moved to Paraguay permanently, and in the decade since has devoted herself tirelessly to projects in support of the local community of Santa María de Fe. It's this passion and local knowledge that make her the perfect Bradt author – and her words speak pretty loudly of the merits of this wonderful country too!

First edition published July 2010
Bradt Travel Guides Ltd, 23 High Street, Chalfont St Peter, Bucks SL9 9QE, England
www.bradtguides.com
Published in the USA by The Globe Pequot Press Inc, PO Box 480, Guilford, Connecticut 06437-0480
Text copyright © 2010 Margaret Hebblethwaite
Maps copyright © 2010 Bradt Travel Guides Ltd
Illustrations copyright © 2010 Individual photographers (see below)
Margaret Hebblethwaite asserts the moral right to be identified as the author of this book.
The author and publishers have made every effort to ensure the accuracy of the information in this book at the time of going to press. However, they cannot accept any responsibility for any loss, injury or inconvenience resulting from the use of information contained in this guide.

British Library Cataloguing in Publication Data
A catalogue record for this book is available from the British Library
ISBN-13: 978 1 84162 315 3

Photographs Fernando Allen (FA), José María Blanch Cardoner (JMBC), Cecilia González (CG), Laura González (LG), Margaret Hebblethwaite (MH), Emily Horton (EH), James C Lowen (JL), Kevin Moloney/Getty Images (KM/GI), Carlos Masi (CM), Tony Morrison/South American Pictures (TM/SAP), Angela Soerensen (AS), SuperStock (SS), Rebecca Whitfield/South American Pictures (RW/SAP)
Front cover Jesuit Ruins of Trinidad (KM/GI)
Back cover Capybara (JL), Paraguayan lace (TM/SAP)
Title page Hyacinth macaw (JL), Passion of Christ statue, Santa María de Fe museum (MH), Wooden cart in the *campo* (AS)
Maps Alan Whitaker, David McCutcheon (Argentina maps), Dave Priestley (colour map)

Typeset from the author's disk by D & N Publishing, Baydon, Wiltshire
Production managed by Jellyfish Print Solutions and manufactured in India by Replika Press Pvt. Ltd.

Acknowledgements

I am indebted to the excellent work by Peter T Clark on national parks, and on wildlife; to the Paraguayan guidebook *La Magia de Nuestra Tierra* published by the En Alianza foundation (see section on guidebooks in *Appendix 4*, page 327); and to the Servicio Geográfico Militar for producing the first reliable maps of Paraguayan terrain. I acknowledge the continuing help and support of Senatur, the government tourist office, and of the group that works closely with them, Touring, who are responsible for promoting the Ruta Jesuítica. They also produce the best road maps, and the guidebook *Paraguay: Guia Túristica TACPy*.

In terms of individuals, I wish to thank the historian Ignacio Telesca, and the Jesuit linguist Bartomeu Meliá, for being constantly available on email to answer questions; the historian Margarita Durán for helping on the Franciscan Reductions, both in her published work and on the telephone; James Lowen for checking the section on fauna and supplying full, accurate names of species; and the Argentinian historian Ernesto Maeder, for reading and commenting on the section on San Ignacio Miní. I also thank Miguel del Puerto for welcoming me to his modest abode in Filadelfia and acting as a superb guide to the central Chaco; Crystian Arevalos, guide at Trinidad, for taking me to the statues of Trinidad and to the Colonias Unidas and for his prompt and informed reply to any query; Adrian Soto for updating the material on Concepción; Isabelino Martínez for being a walking encyclopaedia, particularly on Guaraní questions; María Gloria García and Ruben Dario Maidana for checking and correcting the Spanish language section; Ben Hebblethwaite for driving me around while I took notes, and for showing me some of the cheapest eating places in Asunción; and Rosa María Ortiz and Sister Margot Bremer for giving me research bases in Asunción.

I wish also to thank the English volunteers who kept the English-teaching programme in Santa María running constantly without my help, during all the period of writing and editing: Lisa Kiernan, Mollie Iggulden, Chloe Pilpel, Nicola Hardman, Katy Hardman, Richard Coombs, Dorota Sakwerda and Alice Gimblett.

FEEDBACK REQUEST

Every effort has been made to ensure that the details contained within this book are as accurate and up to date as possible. Inevitably, however, things move on. Any information regarding such changes, or relating to your experiences in Paraguay – good or bad – would be very gratefully received. Such feedback is invaluable when compiling further editions. Send your comments to Bradt Travel Guides, 23 High Street, Chalfont St Peter, Bucks SL9 9QE, UK; e info@bradtguides.com.

Contents

NOTE ABOUT MAPS

Several maps use grid lines to allow easy location of sites. Map grid references are listed in square brackets after listings in the text, with page number followed by grid number, eg: [156 C3].

Introduction

'Paraguay is fabulous. I was deeply taken with the place, the scenery, birds, people, frogs, toads and wood sprites.' Simon Barnes's comment in *The Times* of 14 June 2008 may surprise a lot of people, for whom Paraguay is a blank on the map. And it is literally a blank if you search Google maps. You find, for example, a street map of the Brazilian border town of Ponta Porã, complete up to the frontier, and then as this bi-national city crosses the line and becomes Pedro Juan Caballero, Paraguay, it turns into grey space. You come across backpackers who say, 'Don't go to Paraguay – nothing to see', but it is just that they do not know where to look.

It has been said that Paraguay is one of last holiday paradises waiting to be discovered, with 300 days of sun a year. Only two special interest groups have so far discovered Paraguay in a big way: Brazilian fishing folk, who come over in their busloads to the remotest places in the south, on the banks of the Río Paraná; and US pigeon shooters, who come over in their private-chartered-planeloads to the remotest places in the north, buried in the midst of the Paraguayan Chaco. Apart from these people, there is no tourist rush to Paraguay. It is, to a large extent, pure, virgin, undiscovered territory. You do not want to tell other people about it, for fear of spoiling it for yourself. And yet at the same time you do want to tell other people about it, because you love it so much.

When Simon Barnes came, he was taken by the wildness of the nature reserves and the richness of the bird life. That is one of Paraguay's key aspects; see *Natural History* pages 8–9. But there are other key characteristics that mark the country. If you ask people who know something about Paraguay, even if only a little, what words they associate with the country, they will come up with a list something like this:

- Poverty
- Guaraní language
- Indigenous
- Jesuit Reductions
- Harp
- Craft
- Football
- *Tereré* and *mate*

Each of these key chacteristics will be explored in turn.

KEY CHARACTERISTICS OF PARAGUAY

POVERTY Paraguay is one of the poorest countries in the poor continent of South America, generally classified as the poorest after Bolivia. Paraguay has less than half the per capita income of Brazil, and a third that of Argentina (UN figures October

2009). No-one would want to visit Paraguay who was uncomfortable with this fact. If you did not want to see barefoot children or *campesinos* (peasants) with toothless grins, you would not go to Paraguay. If you only wanted to see gleaming buildings, and travel on motorways, you would not go to Paraguay.

The people have become quite skilled at hiding their poverty, and a sense of dignity leads the majority to dress as well as they can. But scratch the surface and you find this same majority have no money in their purses to take a bus or make a phone call, they have a pile of debts at local shops to clear or reduce every time they earn a little money, and they live hand to mouth with no food in their fridge for the morrow. Nearly a quarter of the population do not have fridges, even in the sweltering heat. In Asunción there are more people with proper jobs, but in the *campo* – the real Paraguay – few people other than teachers and civil servants earn the minimum wage.

For many travellers, the poverty is a reason to come, rather than to stay away. They may come out of a desire for solidarity, in the spirit of liberation theology, in which the poor are those with special insight, who can teach the rich the message of the gospel. Or they may come out of a curiosity to see something different – the kind of culture you can no longer find in Europe or North America, the appeal of the other.

GUARANÍ LANGUAGE It is well known that Paraguay is a bilingual country: 87% of the population can speak Guaraní. In the *campo* (countryside) almost everyone speaks Guaraní as their mother tongue, but unless you go deep into the *campo*, almost everyone is fluent in Spanish as well. This gives Paraguay a unique richness among Latin American countries. There are other countries which have a strong use of indigenous languages in certain regions, but none where the country as a whole is bilingual.

While effortless bilingualism is the rule, the languages are not interchangeable. People will use Guaraní for common household matters like cooking, playing and building; and also for countryside matters like the names of animals, birds and trees. But they are unlikely to know the Guaraní words for a host of other things, particularly things that relate to education and the conceptual world.

This extends even to numbers: a Guaraní speaker is unlikely to use a Guaraní word for any number above one, and in traditional Guaraní the numbers only went up to five anyway, the word for 'five' being the same as 'hand': *po*. If you ask a *campesino* the word for 'brother' in Guaraní, he is unlikely to know, because he always says *hermano* (Spanish); in traditional Guaraní there are three words for brother, depending on whether it is an older or a younger brother and whether the speaker is male or female, and another three words for sister. But in the *mestizo* (mixed race) society, these subtleties from indigenous life have been lost.

What this means is that a mixture of Guaraní and Spanish runs right through daily life, and there is a word for this mixture: *jopará*. It will be evident throughout this guidebook, in such common terms as *sombrero pirí* (Spanish 'hat'; Guaraní 'of palm leaf') or *corredor jeré* (Spanish 'colonnade'; Guaraní 'going all around'). (See also *Appendix 1*.)

You will find that if you speak Spanish you will have no difficulty travelling all over the country, because no one will think of speaking to you, as a foreigner, in Guaraní. You will hear a lot of Guaraní spoken, but unless your Spanish is good you may not realize it because the frequency of Spanish words in Guaraní discourse may lead you to think they are talking Spanish.

THE INDIGENOUS The indigenous population (as measured in the census of 2002) is 87,000, which accounts for only 1.7% of the total population. Although this is scandalously low, it is a lot higher than in some other South American countries, and you are very aware that there is an indigenous presence as soon as you set foot in Paraguay: you see them selling their crafts in the airport, the bus terminal and on the streets of central Asunción – often wearing bright feather head-dresses to attract the tourists.

A division of the ethnic groups into different language groups is given in a table in *Chapter 1* (page 18), but here is a rough simplification. The country is divided by the Río Paraguay into the west (the Chaco) and the east (where most people live). Approximately half the indigenous live in the east and half in the west, but because the west is so sparsely populated by other groups, the indigenous are more evident there.

In the eastern half, the indigenous are Guaraní, though from different subgroups, such as the Mbyá, the Áva, the Aché and the Paĩ Tavyterã. This was the area where the Franciscans and Jesuits founded their Reductions for the Guaraní. They are in most *departamentos* (provinces), except for the southwest part of the eastern half (Central, Paraguarí, Ñeembucú and – ironically – Misiones, where they were once so strong). The Guaraní make wooden animals: different groups make them in different sizes and styles.

In the western half, the indigenous fall principally into three areas. Along the west bank of the Río Paraguay, you find the Zamuko family (of whom the Ayoreo make the fibre shoulder bags, that are a popular craft item). Along the east bank of the Río Pilcomayo and pushing a good way inland, you find the Mataco/Mataguayo family, of whom the better known groups are the Nivaclé (who are Christian and produce crucifixes) and the Maká (which is the group you can visit close to Asunción). And scattered right across the centre of the vast Chaco wilderness you find the Lengua-Maskoy group.

THE REDUCTIONS The famous 'Paraguayan Reductions' were missions for the Guaraní indigenous, distinguished by their high development of architecture, sculpture, music and other arts. The term 'Reductions' is somewhat confusing (*Reducciones* in Spanish), but it dates back to their origin and refers to a semi-nomadic people moving into fixed settlements. There were Jesuit Reductions and Franciscan Reductions, but the Jesuit Reductions are much better known: they were more pioneering in their artistic and cultural development, and bolder in the kind of independent political utopia that they established.

The Jesuit-Guaraní Reductions were far flung in the initial period, starting from 1609, and subject to destruction by slave-traders from São Paulo, but they gradually consolidated themselves and in their heyday numbered 30 towns (the 'Treinta Pueblos'). These Treinta Pueblos then formed a region stretching across three present-day countries: eight in Paraguay, seven in Brazil, and fifteen in Argentina. They are sometimes all loosely referred to as the Paraguayan Reductions, because they were all in the original Jesuit province of Paraquaria (Latin). At the time this Jesuit region was practically a nation in itself – part of the Spanish empire but independent of the jurisdiction of the other Spanish colonies in South America. (See also *Chapter 1*, page 11, and under the respective town headings throughout the book.)

Most of the Argentinian and Brazilian Reductions unfortunately fall outside the scope of this book, although San Ignacio Miní (Argentina) has been included, as a popular, nearby excursion from Paraguay (see page 204).

HARP Music came to Paraguay in a big way with the Jesuits in the early 17th century, and their Baroque compositions, principally by the Jesuit Domenico Zipoli (a contemporary of Vivaldi), were adored by the Guaraní, whose nascent musical sense had up until then been expressed in rhythmic, repetitive music to the beat of a *maraca* (gourd filled with seeds). Soon the Guaraní orchestras were the best in the continent, and their polyphonic choirs were considered by visitors to rival music in the finest cathedrals of Europe.

The Jesuit Anton Sepp, who taught the Guaraní to make musical instruments, is called the father of the Paraguayan harp. This beautiful instrument – not the classical, European harp, but the Paraguayan harp, which is different in a number of ways – is now iconic of Paraguay. It is made entirely of wood, with no metal to its frame, so is considerably lighter, and the wood of the sound box is usually carved with plant motifs. It has no pedals, so you cannot change key without retuning the whole instrument: to make a semi-tone, the player will press a string with their metal tuning key, or even with a finger. (Some new harps are now being made with a row of levers at the top of the strings, called Salvi levers.)

Today the Paraguayan harp has 36 strings, thanks to the musician who did more than anyone since Sepp to develop it, Félix Pérez Cardozo (1908–52). He added four more strings at the bass end, so as to play *Pájaro Campana* ('Bellbird') – one of the most famous pieces in the Paraguayan folk repertoire, for which he wrote the complex setting we hear today. He also wrote *Llegada* ('Arrival'), *Despedida* ('Departure') and *Tren lechero* ('The Milk Train') – one of the most exciting pieces of music for a single instrument (or a duo) that you will ever hear, full of steam shunts and whistles and clickety-clicks, produced by harp notes.

CRAFT Paraguay is also notable for its craftwork, particularly for some traditional forms of lace, meticulously done by hand and taking vast amounts of time. One of these kinds of lace is called *ñandutí* (Guaraní 'spiderweb'), because it is circular; this is particular to Paraguay, and is made in Itauguá (see *Chapter 4*, page 116). Another kind of distinctive, beautiful handiwork is called *ao po'í* (Guaraní 'cloth fine'), which can refer to the cloth itself or to the embroidery on it, and which can at times turn into a kind of lacework. This is made all over the country, but the town where the best quality *ao po'í* is made is Yataitý (see *Chapter 10*, page 225). Any self-respecting Paraguayan man who can afford it will wear a shirt embroidered with *ao po'í* for special occasions: President Lugo wore such a shirt for his investiture. A third kind of lace is called *encaje ju* (Spanish 'lace'; Guaraní 'needle'), which is made in a number of places.

Another intricate craft of great beauty that is particular to Paraguay is the *filigrana* (filigree) silver jewellery associated with Luque (see *Chapter 4*, page 125): since the amount of silver used in this meticulous work is not great, and labour is cheap in Paraguay, the brooches, ear-rings and pendants are very reasonably priced. Another craft that is enormously time-consuming is the decorative *poncho de sesenta listas* which is still made by hand, entirely out of cotton thread: this comes from Piribebúy (see *Chapter 4*, page 139).

There is a multitude of crafts with other natural materials native to the country: leather, for bags; palm leaves, for hats; rushes, for table mats; vegetable fibres, for shoulder bags; bamboo, for furniture; *palo santo* wood, for statues of saints; clay, for pottery; wool, for ponchos; cotton, for hammocks; and more besides. Each of these crafts is connected with a particular town, and often with a particular family. This makes a craft tour of Paraguay a particularly interesting, personalised experience. (See chart in *Chapter 1*, page 22.)

FOOTBALL Another key characteristic of Paraguay is football, for which it has great talent. Paraguay has qualified for the last four World Cups, which is an amazing feat for a country with such a small population, lack of infrastructure, and general level of poverty. In 2009 they even qualified ahead of Argentina, who are among the top favourites in any World Cup. The team also reached the final of the

Olympics held in Greece in 2004, winning Paraguay's first and only Olympic medal, but they then lost 0–1 to their great rivals Argentina in the final.

The Paraguayan team is renowned for its steely spirit and never-say-die approach. BBC football commentator Tim Vickery says: 'Paraguayan football has always been able to count on fighting spirit. The game brings out the warrior in the people, who knit together naturally to build teams feared all over the continent for their durability.'

This was best characterised by the 1998 side which included the eccentric José Luis Chilavert. He was generally considered to be the best goalkeeper in the world at the time, and led his team from the back – even scoring some stunning free-kicks for his country. A rock-solid defence was also the strong point of the Paraguayan side when they qualified for the 2002 and 2006 World Cups.

The 2009 team moved to a more open and attacking style of play, with three strikers where previously they would only have had one – the most famous of whom has been Roque Santa Cruz, who transferred to Manchester City in 2009 for £20 million.

In terms of local teams, Paraguay's most successful club has been Olimpia (with a black-and-white strip), who have three times won the Copa Libertadores (the South American equivalent of the Champions League in Europe).

TERERÉ You cannot think Paraguay without thinking *tereré*. If you have not been to Paraguay yet, you may not know what the word means, but you may well have heard of *mate*, because it is drunk in Argentina and Brazil as well. *Mate* is a tea made with boiling water, and *tereré* uses the same leaf, but infused in iced water.

Everywhere you go in Paraguay you will find people sitting in little groups and passing round the *tereré*. It is served in a common cup (*guampa*) and drunk through a metal straw (*bombilla*). Paraguayans really adore their *tereré*, and do not understand how other nations can live without it. (For instructions on how to participate in this ritual, see page 21.)

THE FUTURE?

Ten years ago, tourism was at a very low ebb, following the murder of a vice-president in 1999. The country teetered on the brink of a coup both in 1999 and in 2000. After that the Argentinian economic crisis hit Paraguay very hard – because every family here has relatives sending money back from Buenos Aires – and there was no money for investment in anything. Paraguay was a country in deep recession, where the poor were getting poorer and the rich were getting poorer too. Craft shops in Asunción struggled not to go bankrupt. Even professional people were saying, 'I have never known it as bad as this'. The *campesinos*, as always, suffered the most.

But from 2006 onwards the economic crisis was levelling out, and there began to be increasing movement on the tourist front, with the appointment of two good ministers of tourism (both women). There was investment in two major tourist programmes, the Ruta Jesuítica and the Camino Franciscano; the publication of local tourist materials such as guides, maps, leaflets and reviews, none of which existed five years earlier; and the sprouting up of new hotels, especially in Asunción. The number of foreign tourists rose from 388,000 in 2006, to 415,000 in 2007, and then more than doubled to 995,000 in 2008. And this is just the beginning, for Paraguay is still an undiscovered country.

The Guaraní indigenous had a dream of 'a land without evil' – *la tierra sin mal* in Spanish, or *yvý marane'ÿ* in Guaraní – 'a land without stain, without pollution'. In their semi-nomadic existence they were always looking for this paradise.

Something of the romance of the Guaraní dream under Jesuit tutelage was captured in Roland Joffé's powerful film about the Paraguayan Reductions, *The Mission*. But it was not fiction; the film recounted historical events. The historians have called the creation, and destruction, of those Jesuit-Guaraní Reductions, 'The Lost Paradise', 'The Forgotten Arcadia'.

Now that there is at last a guidebook to Paraguay – the first one published outside the country – it will be much easier for people of other cultures and other continents to come and search, nomad-like, for the land without stain, here, where it was first dreamt of, in the lost paradise of Paraguay.

ADDRESSES

This guide has not attempted to change the Paraguayan way of writing addresses, but it will not be comprehensible without some explanation. The name of the street may or may not be followed by the number, but it will almost certainly be followed by c/ or by esq or by e/...y...

c/ means *casi* ('nearly'), which means that the name is given of the nearest cross street.
esq means *esquina* ('corner'), which means that the house is on the corner of the two streets mentioned.
e/...y ... means *entre* ...*y* ... ('between ... and ...') which means that the house is between the named side streets.

For example:

Agyr 25 de mayo 1767 c/ Mayor Fleitas – means that the office of Agyr is on the street called 25 de mayo, at number 1767, which is close to the junction with the street called Mayor Fleitas.

National Yegros 501 esq Cerro Corá – means that the office of National is on the street called Yegros, at number 501, which is on the corner, at the junction with the street called Cerro Corá.

Turismo Ami Pampliega e/ Adrián Jara y Pa'í Pérez – means that the office of Turismo Ami is on the street called Pampliega, on the stretch between the side street called Adrián Jara and the side street called Pa'í Pérez.

A curiosity is that many people in the interior do not know the name of the streets in their town, sometimes not even of the street they live on. They use different points of reference.

In the interior, addresses on the main roads are often pinpointed by giving the number of kilometres from Asunción. For example:

San Ignacio Country Club Ruta 1 km230 – means that it is on Ruta 1, 230km from Asunción.

Occasionally the number of kilometres is measured from another city. For example, in the context of Ciudad del Este.

Churrasquería Interlagos Ruta 7, km5 – means that it is 5km from Ciudad del Este.

Part One

GENERAL INFORMATION

Location Paraguay is in the centre of South America, without a coastline. Its neighbours are Brazil, Argentina and Bolivia.

Area 406,752km²

Climate Sub-tropical, generally hot and humid, particularly in January, with a few cold weeks from June to August. Heavy thunderstorms are frequent, as also are months of drought. The Chaco has a rainy season and a dry season.

Status Republic with a president

Population 6,163,913

Origin of the population Indigenous from many peoples but especially Guaraní; Spanish and their *mestizo* (mixed race) descendants; more recent immigrants especially Brazilians, Argentinians, Germans and Koreans

Life expectancy 67 years

Capital Asunción, population 502,426

Other main towns Ciudad del Este, Concepción, Encarnación, Pedro Juan Caballero, Villarrica

Administrative structure 17 *departamentos* plus the capital

Principal exports Hydro-electric power, beef, soya, leather, wood, cotton, sugar, tobacco, *yerba mate*

GDP US$2,644 per capita in 2008

Official languages Spanish and Guaraní

Currency Guaraní (Gs)

Exchange rate (April 2010); US$1 = Gs4,653; £1 = Gs7,102; €1 = Gs6,275

Airport Silvio Pettirossi, Asunción

International telephone code +595

Internet domain .py

Time GMT –4 (but because the summertimes of the two hemispheres are different, Paraguay is 3 hours behind Europe and the USA from October to March, and 5 hours behind from March to October)

Voltage 220V

Weights and measures Metric; kilograms and kilometres

Flag Red, white and blue horizontal bands, with the shield of the republic in the middle on one side of the flag, and a lion in the middle on the other side

National anthem *'Paraguayos, ¡República o muerte!'* (first line of chorus)

National flower Passion flower (Guaraní *mburucuyá*)

National holidays See *Chapter 2*, page 53

National tree *Lapacho* (Guaraní *tajý*)

National bird Bellbird (*pájaro campana*)

Most successful sport Football

Most famous writer Augusto Roa Bastos

Most famous composer Agustín Pío Barrios (Mangoré)

[NB figures from *2008 Dirección General de Estadística, Encuestas y Censos (DGEEC)* and *Enciclopedia Concisa de Py*.]

Background Information

The *Introduction* has evoked the spirit of Paraguay, giving an outline of what characterises this largely undiscovered country and some of its best known features. This chapter will concentrate on some more detailed facts and figures.

GEOGRAPHY

Paraguay covers 406,752km² and is shaped like a lopsided butterfly. The eastern half is where 97% of the people live; it is a little over 150,000km² of largely fertile lowland, interrupted occasionally by wooded hills. Further to the east it rises around 400–500m into the Paraná tableland. The western part is called the Chaco, which is larger (almost 250,000km²), but has less than 3% of the population, because it is so inhospitable.

RIVERS AND LAKES The two principal rivers are the Río Paraguay, which divides the country in two (like the body of the butterfly), and the Río Paraná, which forms the frontier with Corrientes and Misiones in Argentina.

The **Río Paraguay** rises in the Brazilian Pantanal and has an average width of 500m, with numerous tributaries on both sides. They include (from north to south on the eastern side) the Río Apa (frontier with Brazil), the Aquidabán (great beaches north of Concepción), the Jejuí Guazú, the Manduvirá, the Río Salado (which runs into the great Lago Ypacaraí) and further south, on the border of Misiones, the Río Tebicuarý. The next river that flows into it from the east is the great Río Paraná.

The tributaries flowing in from the west (north to south) begin with the Río Negro of the Pantanal (which forms the boundary with Bolivia for a short distance, where the Río Paraguay comes in from the northeast and the Río Negro follows the line directly north–south). Then there are many small rivers called *riachos* along the stretch that has Brazil to the east, ending with the Riacho Mosquito just north of Puerto Casado. Then come the Río Verde, the Río Montelindo, a second Río Negro, the Río Aguaray Guazú, the Río Confuso and finally the Río Pilcomayo, which forms the boundary between the Paraguayan Chaco and the Argentinian Chaco.

The **Río Paraná** rises in the Brazilian state of Paraná, and is a swift-flowing river, 150m deep and narrow near Ciudad del Este, ranging to 15m deep and 1,500m wide near Encarnación. This is the river that has been exploited for the Itaipú and Yacyretá hydro-electric dams, and that will soon be harnessed again, for the Corpus dam (near Trinidad).

There are two principal lakes: Lago Ypacaraí and Lago Ypoá (see *Chapter 4*, pages 128 and 150).

HILLS Paraguay is generally a flat country. This is particularly so in the Chaco, where the only hill is the Cerro León (604m, though it is really a grouping of about 46 hills). In western Paraguay, there are two *cordilleras* (hill ranges). The smaller one, close to Asunción, runs through the *departamento* called Cordillera, and includes the hills to the north of Paraguarí (good for views and adventure tourism, see *Chapter 4*, page 139), the hills to the south of Areguá (of notable geological characteristics, page 127) and the hills around Tobatí and Atyrá (eg: that of Casa del Monte, page 132).

The larger *cordillera* runs from the northeast corner of Paraguay, at Cerro Corá (see *Chapter 11*, page 288), south along the Brazilian border to the reserve of Mbaracayú (page 291), where the range divides. One finger takes a turn east (and the frontier follows it) to reach Salto del Guairá on the Río Paraná. After this, the frontier follows the river southwards.

The other part of the *cordillera* goes in a southwesterly direction from Mbaracayú, through the San Joaquín area, and eventually reaches the reserve of Ybyturuzú, where Paraguay's highest hill is found: Cerro Tres Kandú, at 842m (see *Chapter 10*, page 264). From this point the *cordillera* sweeps southeast, and then southwest again, where it is named the Cordillera de San Rafael, at 455m (see *Chapter 6*, page 209).

CLIMATE

The climate of Paraguay is sub-tropical. According to the official dates, spring is 21 September to 20 December, summer is 21 December to 20 March, autumn is 21 March to 20 June and winter is 21 June to 20 September. Although there can be long periods of drought, fatal for the crops, there is generally a good level of rainfall, producing a very green landscape. The rain most typically falls in violent thunderstorms, which are not infrequent.

The average maximum temperature is 36°C in January (the hottest month) in the Chaco (Mariscal Estigarribia), and 32°C in Encarnación (the most southerly city). The average minimum in those two places in January is 23°C and 20°C respectively.

In July (the coldest month) the average maximum temperature is 26°C in Mariscal Estigarribia, and 21°C in Encarnación. The average minimum in those two places in July is 12°C and 9°C respectively.

See also *When to visit* in *Chapter 2*, page 25.

NATURAL HISTORY AND CONSERVATION

Paraguay has a very rich biodiversity, due to its being located in the subtropics, and having five distinct ecoregions – the Chaco (subdivided into dry north and wet south), the Pantanal (on the west bank of the Río Paraguay in the far north), the Pampas (or savanna or grasslands, eg: in the Misiones area), the Cerrado (mixed dry woodlands and grassland, in the north of the eastern region) and the Atlantic Forest (now largely deforested, but in the east of eastern Paraguay). There is a great extent of wetlands, encouraging a wealth of species, not only in the northern Pantanal, but also to the east of the Río Pilcomayo where there is the Tinfunque reserve, and to the east of the Río Paraguay in the *departamentos* of Ñeembucú, Paraguarí and Central.

The Chaco (which is mostly in Paraguay, with a part in Argentina and a part in Bolivia) is considered to be the world's largest natural area after the Amazon. The country is beginning to receive more attention as a tourist destination by those who want to see nature in its pristine state, in all its splendour.

FAUNA More than 398 species of fish, 171 species of mammals, 162 species of reptiles and 687 species of birds have been recorded (see *Birdwatching*, page 8) in

Paraguay. It is also extraordinarily rich in butterflies: there are at least 339 photographed species (see *www.faunaparaguay.com/butterflies.html*). Here is a brief summary of some of Paraguay's best-known animals and birds. For a selective list of fauna names in English, Latin, Spanish and Guaraní, see *Appendix 3*.

Mammals

Jaguar Without doubt Paraguay's most dramatic and handsome animal, the jaguar is the biggest feline in all America. Paraguayans commonly translate *jaguareté* (Guaraní) as *tigre*, but it is a spotted jaguar, not a striped tiger. The body length is up to 1.85m, plus the tail which can be 0.75m. Solitary and territorial, it is a dangerous hunter, feeding on capybaras, peccaries, tapirs, caimans, fish and birds. If you come across one, you should not turn around, but make a lot of noise, talking loudly, and waving your arms about holding anything you have to hand, so as to appear bigger than you are. Then withdraw slowly, but without turning your back. There are few jaguars in eastern Paraguay but in the Alto Paraguay region of the Chaco they are quite common.

Puma Another name for the puma is the mountain lion (there are many more, such as cougar). It is tawny yellow but the young have dark speckles. The end of the tail is almost black. It can grow even bigger than the jaguar, but it is a lighter cat, and feeds on smaller prey, including porcupines and vipers. It is found in both halves of the country.

Black howler monkey This is one of two kinds of monkey common in Paraguay, and there are plenty of them in both halves of the country. The males are big and black, so that they look a different species from the females, which are brown. When they howl, they make a loud repeated ululating noise somewhere between a croak and a snore. There is a family of howler monkeys that lives in the plaza of Santa María de Fe, and they are a great attraction, as they come quite close to the visitors to accept pieces of banana.

Black-striped capuchin monkey Slightly smaller than the howler monkey and the male does not have a different colouring from the female. It is only found in eastern Paraguay.

South American coati This is not quite a racoon, but almost. It has a triangular head with a long snout, and the tail has horizontal stripes all the way down. It lives in low thorn and humid forests, is a rapid climber, and eats almost anything. There are a great number at the Iguazú Falls, and their behaviour has become problematic because the visitors feed them, which changes their natural habits and makes them greedy and aggressive.

Maned wolf Known as *aguará guasú* in Guaraní, this has long reddish hair, with long ears, long, black legs and a kind of mane in a black line along its back. It is nocturnal and omnivorous, and lives in wetlands all over the country.

South American tapir A big animal that has a long snout with an extended upper lip, which almost becomes a short trunk. It has hooves and a stumpy tail, and is up to 2m in length. It is herbivorous, nocturnal and solitary, and is found in both regions of the country.

Peccary There are different types, but the Chacoan peccary – which was believed to be extinct but has been rediscovered – is like a boar with long hair that sticks up in spikes. It is herbivorous and feeds on cacti. There is also a collared peccary and a white-lipped peccary, which are found in both regions, while the Chacoan peccary lives only in the west.

Giant anteater This huge anteater is grey with a diagonal band of black, edged with white, running from its back to under the neck. The front limbs have three powerful claws, and the long, thin snout has an even longer and thinner tongue that shoots out. It has long, bristly fur and is found in both halves of the country.

Capybara Called in Spanish *carpincho* – a well-known word for what, in Paraguay, is a common animal in both regions, while few people are familiar with the term 'capybara' in English. It is herbivorous and lives where there is water, in wetlands and on riverbanks. It is more than 1m long and is a good swimmer and diver, with interdigital membranes. It is hunted by Paraguayans for its meat, and is now a protected species – not that that means anything in Paraguay. It is the world's largest rodent, with a rectangular profile to its face, and tight, reddish brown hair.

Armadillo There are different types and sizes, ranging from 25cm for the southern three-banded armadillo to 1m for the giant armadillo. It has a shell divided into little segments arranged in rows, giving the impression of armour. It feeds on ants, termites, larvae, etc, and the giant armadillo also eats honey.

Reptiles
Caiman Known by its Guaraní name *yacaré*, which in correct contemporary Guaraní should be spelt *jakaré*, though the old spelling persists. When translated into Spanish, people call it a *cocodrilo*, but strictly speaking it is a caiman, which belongs to the alligator family, rather than the crocodile. Like the capybara, the *yacaré* is a protected species which is nonetheless commonly hunted for its flesh, which tastes like a cross between meat and fish. The caiman lives on both sides of Paraguay, and there are plenty at the Iguazú Falls.

Birds
Greater rhea This bird is what many people call an ostrich but is actually subtly different, because it has three toes instead of the two that the African ostrich has. They are large, flightless, silent birds. Many rheas have been semi-domesticated because of their use in eating up pests and keeping the grass and weeds down. Unusually among birds, it is the male who sits on the eggs to incubate them and raises his brood: even more unusually, the eggs come from several different females.

Toucans One of the most famous and most colourful birds of Paraguay, the toco toucan has an enormous yellow and orange beak tipped with black. It is a big black bird (53cm) with a yellow circle round its eyes, a white bib, and a white stripe near the end of its tail. It lives in jungles and forests, in both east and west Paraguay.

Macaws Macaws are type of parrot. The red-and-green macaw is the most vividly colourful of the Paraguayan parrots. The hyacinth macaw is blue, and is the largest of the family. These magnificent birds are scarce on both sides of the country, but can be seen in several zoos, eg: Casa del Monte in Atyrá, or the Atinguý refuge outside Ayolas.

Chilean flamingo The Chilean flamingo can be observed in the Chaco without too much difficulty. This beautiful long-legged bird, which likes standing on one leg, has pink feathers, a black beak, and red knees and feet. It measures 70cm and inhabits lagoons and marshes in the western region.

Tinamous Called a *perdiz* in Spanish, which is usually translated as 'partridge' in a dictionary, but the distinctive kind of *perdiz* carved in wood and stone in the Jesuit-Guaraní Reductions has a crest on its head, and is a very regal-looking bird. This is the brushland tinamou or the quebracho crested-tinamou, found in the Chaco. There are other species of tinamou elsewhere in Paraguay; all are cryptically coloured brown and buff.

Herons and egrets These birds have long legs, usually white bodies, and they mostly eat fish. There are several kinds, and the snowy egret is common in both regions of Paraguay. They are beautiful in flight, and very distinctive, due to the retracted neck.

Southern lapwing This shorebird has a distinctive name in Spanish, *tero tero*, though is mostly known by its Guaraní name of *tetéu*. It is an elegant bird with a few purple and green highlights on its grey and white body, and a red beak. It occurs in both halves of the country.

Bare-throated bellbird The bare-throated bellbird or *pájaro campana* is particularly loved by Paraguayans because there is a famous piece of harp music named after it which evokes its song. It has been declared the 'national bird' by the Congress. The song can be heard from hundreds of metres away, and resembles the echo of a little hammer on metal (a 'bell' indeed). It is an endangered species, but can be found in the Mbaracayú reserve and in some reserves of Itaipú.

Hummingbirds Often seen in Paraguay, extracting the nectar wherever there are flowers, with its wings whirring. There are various species, but one of the most common is the glittering-bellied emerald, which is (as its name suggests) a dark emerald colour. The males have a red beak, and the females a grey beak. It is a small bird, only 9cm long, with a 2cm beak, and its name in Spanish, *picaflor*, refers to its pecking of the nectar. The *mainumbý* (to give it its Guaraní name) was regarded in old mythology as having existed before the creation of the world and having a special relationship to God, for which reason it has been used in the murals of San Ignacio to represent the Holy Spirit (instead of a dove).

FLORA The national flower of Paraguay is the *mburucuyá* which was portrayed by the artists of the Jesuit-Guaraní Reductions as their principal flower motif, in stone and wood carving: it has been captured in the logo of the Ruta Jesuítica tourist programme. The *mburucuyá* fruit – the passion fruit – has a delicious, tangy flavour: it gives a kick to any fruit salad, makes an excellent mousse and can also be turned into a fruit juice drink.

The *lapacho* (Guaraní *tajy*) is regarded as the national tree, and with its abundant pink blossom it gives a very distinctive appearance to Paraguay in springtime. The tree is tall and produces a wood which is hard and strong, and is used for pillars, door and window frames.

The *cocotero* is the distinctive and most typical tree of the *campo* in the western region – a skinny palm tree with long, sharp spines and a fragrant yellow flower that appears at Christmastime, and is customarily placed before the crib. It is very abundant. Other kinds of palm tree found in the country are the *pindó*, the *coco phoenix* and (in the Chaco) the tall *karanda'y* with its fan-like leaves, which produces an excellent hardwood used in building. For more details of the flora, see the sections on national parks and reserves in the regional chapters.

NATURE RESERVES There are a large number of nature reserves in Paraguay, some belonging to the state – the national parks – and others in private hands – the protected wild areas (*áreas silvestres protegidas*). The map shows their distribution around the country, and information on these will be found within each regional chapter.

In order to visit the national parks, you need to contact the Secretaria del Ambiente (SEAM) (❧ *021 615804/615812; www.seam.gov.py*). They can give you advice on the access roads into the reserve, on where you can stay, and can put you in touch with the park ranger (*guardaparque*), who can give you a guided tour. But visiting without prior notice is not forbidden.

There is a bilingual guide you can buy, if you can get hold of it: *Guide to Paraguay's National Parks and other Protected Wild Areas* by Peter T Clark (see *Appendix 4*). Try the Servilibro bookshop, or the Libreria Intercontinental; see *Bookshops* in *Chapter 3*, page 76, or you could try Peter Clark (❧ *021 391371;* e *petertomclark@hotmail.com*).

BIRDWATCHING Paraguay is an exceptional country for birdwatchers. It is said that expert birdwatchers can add from 400 to 450 new species to their list in just a couple of weeks in the country. The organisation Guyrá Paraguay (Guaraní 'bird') is active in developing conservation centres in remote areas, and promoting eco-tourism and birdwatching trips.

Guyrá Paraguay Gaetano Martino, fomerly José Berges, 215 esq Tte Ross; ☏ 021 229097/223567; e alistair@guyra.org.py or birding.paraguay@gmail.com; www.guyra.org.py. You can email or talk on the phone in English. See under their various biological stations that can be visited: Estación Kangue/ý in Parque San Rafael (see page 209), Campo Iris in the northern Chaco (see page 311) & Tres Gigantes in the Pantanal (see page 311).

In the Chaco, which is an arid zone with vast *estancias* (country estates), there are seven species of tinamou. This is a regular stopping place for many migratory species, including flamingoes; the time of migration is September and October. North of the tropic of Capricorn, in the uninhabited dry region of the Chaco, lucky birders find the black-legged seriema walking beside the road, or the crowned eagle flying overhead.

The Pantanal, the biggest wetland in the world, begins in the northeast of the Chaco. As you travel down the Río Paraguay towards the Río Negro, you see a great contrast to the arid western zone of the Chaco, with palm trees, gallery forests and extensive wetlands. Crossing the area on horseback, by rowing boat or on foot, you can observe aquatic species like herons, cormorants, storks, ducks, southern screamers and terns hunting the river for their next catch. The swallow-tailed hummingbird and the toco toucan are among the 280 species registered so far that inhabit the area.

In the north and centre of the eastern region you find the cerrado, which is characterised by a mixture of low forests and grassland, on nutrient-poor well-drained soils, like sand. (There is also cerrado in Brazil and Bolivia.) The national parks of Paso Bravo, Bella Vista and Cerro Corá are examples of this landscape. A little further south, the private reserves of Mbaracayú (the eastern part, see *Chapter 11*, page 291) and Laguna Blanca (dedicated to agriculture and tourism, see page 273) offer a good example of this kind of territory, and Mbaracayú additionally has a very extensive tract of Atlantic Forest. The red-legged seriema is common and, if you go exploring at night with a lamp, you may see nightbirds such as the white-winged nightjar, a globally threatened bird that was discovered in Paraguay as recently as 1995.

The principal remnant of the Atlantic Forest is found in the southeast of the country, in the San Rafael reserve. From the hilltop you can see natural grasslands with paths disappearing into the forest in the direction of the reforestation projects. Again, the bird life is stunning: in the grasslands you find a great variety of tinamous, and also endangered species like the marsh seedeater and the chestnut seedeater. In the Atlantic Forest you can see the ochre-collared piculet and the chestnut-bellied euphonia, and other colourful birds. A highlight of a night walk may be a common potoo, an extraordinary creature. By day it sits motionless on top of a dry stick, with the appearance of bark but with a long, barred tail, and at dusk it emits a long cry like a human wail. At night it metamorphoses into an agile aerial hunter.

REFORESTATION Paraguay has been massively deforested, and the illegal logging continues because it is always difficult to enforce laws in Paraguay, where the level of corruption is so high. In 1845, 55% of the eastern half of Paraguay was forested; in 1991, 15%; and in 2002, only 4%. The Atlantic Forest originally covered nine million hectares, but today only 1,300,000ha remain, and these are not continuous but scattered, which impedes the ecological function of the forest. Paraguay has been classed as the worst country in the Americas for deforestation, and the second worst in the world. Between 130 and 140 thousand hectares of woodland are cut down each year. Amazingly, however, nearly every species that has ever been recorded here still remains.

There is now a campaign, '*A todo pulmón*', to reforest the countryside, particularly in the Atlantic Forest region, with 50 million trees: *lapacho*, cedar, *yvyrapytá*, *timbó*, *kurupa'ý* and others. (See *Giving something back*, page 57.)

The best-preserved parts of the Atlantic Forest are the Bosque Mbaracayú (see *Chapter 11*, page 251) and the Reserva San Rafael (see *Chapter 6*, page 209). Both have good facilities for receiving visitors.

AQUIFER The Guaraní Aquifer, which Paraguay shares with Brazil, Uruguay and Argentina, is the third-biggest subterranean water reserve in the world, with a volume of 37 thousand million cubic metres. Out of its total extent of 1,190,000km² (an area greater than Spain, Portugal and France put together), 5.9% is in Paraguay, that is, 70,000km². The aquifer is found underneath the Atlantic Forest ecoregion, in the *departamentos* of Caaguazú and Alto Paraná, and about 200 wells in Paraguay go down deeply enough to reach it. The aquifer is replenished by rainwater.

HISTORY

The original inhabitants of what was to become Paraguay were the **indigenous**, principally the Guaraní, though there were also other peoples, including war-like tribes such as the Guaycurú. The Guaraní lived a semi-nomadic agricultural life, cultivating maize and mandioc, and hunting deer, monkey, coatí, tapirs and anteaters. They made pots and baskets, and from time to time travelled in long wooden canoes. They lived in long huts or *chozas* made of branches and adobe, with up to 60 related families in each. When they moved on, every couple of years, they dreamt that they were pursuing the *yvý marane'ÿ* (Spanish *la tierra sin mal*, 'the land without evil'). Later, when they were evangelised, this legendary paradise became identified with the reign of God.

THE CONQUEST The New World was carved up in advance by the 1494 **Treaty of Tordesillas**, that gave Portugal everything to the east and Spain everything to the west of a north–south line running 370 leagues west of the Cape Verde islands (approximately through where São Paulo is today). But the treaty could not cope with the changing situation on the ground and incursions were frequent. The first European to discover Paraguayan territory was a Portuguese, the explorer **Alejo García**, who crossed the land from Brazil to reach the Peru of the Incas with their famous gold. He filled up his boat with precious metals, but was murdered by hostile indigenous on his way down the Río Paraguay, approximately at San Pedro de Ycuamandyyú in 1525 (see *Chapter 11*, page 274).

The conquest of Paraguay began with the Spanish expedition led by Pedro de Mendoza, who established the first (short-lived) port of Buenos Aires in 1536, and sent his lieutenant **Juan de Ayolas** upriver. Ayolas stopped briefly in Lambaré (on the outskirts of the future Asunción), where he left his deputy **Domingo Martínez de Irala**, before going further north. Ayolas never returned, and Irala, who was more a politician and a diplomat than a soldier, made this area the headquarters of the invasion. Irala made a pact with the Guaraní, who were more pacific than the tribes around Buenos Aires were proving. The invaders were allowed to have relations with the Guaraní women, so laying the foundations for a *mestizo* bilingual society in which children learned Spanish from their fathers and Guaraní from their mothers.

Juan de Salazar y Espinoza is attributed as being the founder of Asunción in this period, because of the fort he established on a bend of the Río Paraguay on 15 August 1537, the feast of the Assumption. The first Buenos Aires was abandoned, to be re-founded from Asunción towards the end of the century, and the new town growing up around the fort (with its first *cabildo* or town council inaugurated in 1541) was seen as important for its strategic position on the river which led towards

Peru and its gold. The hope was that this river would become as important for silver as Peru had been for gold: hence, the Río de la Plata (river of silver).

In 1556 the *encomienda* system began, in which the initially peaceful co-existence of Spanish and Guaraní was seen in its true colours, as a cruel exploitation. The men were sent to work in the fields of the Spanish, who treated them harshly as though they were slaves, and the women cared for the homes and the sexual appetites of the Spanish in Asunción.

MISSIONS 1541 saw the arrival of the first Franciscan missionaries, who worked within the colonial system and tried to make the best of it. From 1580 onwards they formed Reductions for the Guaraní (see box on *Luis Bolaños* in *Chapter 10*, page 268).

At this stage the whole huge area south of Peru and east of the Andes was called the Provincia Gigante de Indias, and was subject to Peru, which in turn was subject to Spain. An important governor based in Asunción from 1598 to 1617 was Hernando Arias de Saavedra (known as **Hernandarias**) who was a *criollo* (son of Spaniards, born in South America) and attended to the interests of the indigenous. With his support, a group of **Jesuits** arrived from Peru in 1607 to found a new Jesuit province of Paraquaria (the origin of the name Paraguay), with the brilliant young Antonio Ruiz de Montoya (henceforth **Montoya**) among them. With them, a new era began in which the Jesuit Reductions did not work within the Spanish colonial system, but outside of it, in a territory that the Europeans were forbidden to occupy. The Spanish and Portuguese were thus deprived of slaves, and had the embarrassment of seeing those who they regarded as semi-human natives develop a civilisation of art, architecture and music superior to their own.

The resentment, jealousy and hostility this aroused was eventually to result in the order by Carlos III of Spain in 1767 for the **expulsion** of the Jesuits from South America, which was carried out the following year, in 1768. Although the Treinta Pueblos of the Jesuit-Guaraní Reductions were over-run, exploited and depopulated within only a few decades of the expulsion, those 150 years of protected life laid bases which have never been completely annihilated, most particularly in the survival of the Guaraní language in a country that is still truly bilingual.

UPRISING SUPPRESSED Before the expulsion, however, there was upheaval in Asunción, with a rebellion led by **José de Antequera**, who taught that 'the power of the commoner in any republic, city, town or village, is more powerful than the power of the king himself'. Yet again, the hunger for slaves lay at the root of the troubles, for the landowners in Asunción were seeking slaves for their estates through the capture of indigenous from the Chaco, their source of indigenous labour in the east having been denied them by the protected territory of the Treinta Pueblos. When the Jesuits obtained the ruling that the Chaco indigenous too should be handed over to them to save them from slavery, the people of Asunción wanted to rid themselves of Jesuits and of Spanish power all at the same time. Known as the **Revolución de los Comuneros** (Revolution of the Commoners) the uprising began in 1717; the first armed confrontation was at the Battle of Tebicuarý in 1724, but the uprising was suppressed at the Battle of Tabapý in 1735, with the help of Guaraní soldiers from Misiones fighting in both battles on behalf of the Spanish crown.

BUENOS AIRES The old rivalry with Buenos Aires (which had been an offspring of Asunción) continued as Asunción grew constantly stronger: in 1776 it was made capital of a new viceroyalty of Río de la Plata, with Paraguay under its jurisdiction.

When Buenos Aires declared independence in 1810, Asunción refused to go into the new republic: according to an often-repeated anecdote, the future president of Paraguay, José Gasper Rodríguez de Francia (henceforth **Dr Francia**), placed two pistols on the table in Congress, declaring, 'My arguments in favour of my ideas are these: one is destined against Fernando VII [of Spain] and the other against Buenos Aires.' The Argentinian General Manuel Belgrano invaded to try to force Paraguay into their independent republic, but was repelled in the battles of Paraguarí and Tacuarý (19 January and 9 March 1811).

INDEPENDENCE A year later, Paraguay decided to go for its independence as a separate state, and the so-called Próceres de la Independencia (agents of independence) achieved their goal in a cunning plan – with the threat of violence but without a shot being fired. The Próceres slipped out of the Casa de la Independencia on the night of 14 May 1811 to take over the army barracks in the Plaza of Asunción. The Paraguayan soldiers submitted to the leadership of the Próceres, who then released political prisoners, prepared weapons and sounded the cathedral bells. They took eight cannons to set in position in front of the house of the Spanish governor Bernardo de Valasco, who capitulated without a fight early on the morning of 15 May. (See section on the *Casa de la Independencia*, page 88, and the box on *Pedro Juan Cavallero*, page 284.)

The initial years of freedom were unsettled, as the Próceres, Fernando de la Mora, Francisco Xavier Bogarín, Fulgencio Yegros, Pedro Juan Cavallero and Dr Francia, tried to work out a regime of governance.

DR FRANCIA In 1814 Dr Francia was elected dictator, and three years later secured the position for life. He adopted a rigidly isolationist policy, closing the frontiers to all imports, in order to force the Paraguayan people to become self-sufficient – and hence stronger – and to forge a strong sense of national identity, on a more egalitarian basis than in other South American countries. He led a life of extreme and almost monkish personal austerity. (When President Fernando Lugo took power in 2008 he declared he would take Dr Francia as his model, for his witness against greed and corruption.)

THE TWO LÓPEZ PRESIDENCIES After the death of Dr Francia in 1840, a brief power vacuum was resolved when **Carlos Antonio López** became second president of the country in 1844. He ended the policy of isolationism and brought in English engineers to build a railway system, which at that date was at the cutting edge of new technology. Most of the fine buildings of Asunción were constructed under his presidency.

On the death of the obese Carlos Antonio in 1862, power was seized by Francisco Solano López (henceforth **Mariscal López**), supposedly one of his sons (although doubts have been raised on the matter). He introduced a telegraph network, began a couple of new buildings in Asunción (the Panteón and the Palacio de López), but his main passion was building up the army, which he turned into the most powerful force in Latin America. Accompanied by his Irish mistress and consort whom he met in France, Eliza Lynch (henceforth Madame Lynch), he embarked in 1864 on an ill-conceived aggression against his neighbours, in the hope of becoming some sort of an emperor in South America.

WAR OF THE TRIPLE ALLIANCE Mariscal López began the war in 1864 with an attack on Brazil, after it had intervened in Uruguayan politics. When he was refused permission to cross Argentinian territory to take his army down to Uruguay, he responded by taking the town of Corrientes in 1865. The result was that all three countries – Brazil, Uruguay and Argentina – formed a Triple Alliance against López (See section on *Piribebúy* in *Chapter 4*, page 136.)

At an early stage of the war, Mariscal López turned down the peace offer that depended on his going into exile, and his refusal to negotiate or surrender led his country into six years of utter destruction, from which Paraguay has never properly recovered. Paraguay won the next battle – that of **Curupaytý** – near the point where the rivers Paraguay and Paraná meet, in the far south (see *Chapter 7*, page 222). But inevitably the combined forces of the allies won through with time, and once Humaitá fell, after continuous bombardment over six months (see page 221), the advance of the allies was unstoppable.

Mariscal López was chased north to Asunción, then east to Piribebúy (to where he had moved his capital), and by this time his adult army had been virtually eliminated. Undeterred, he sent out an army of 3,500 children under 15 years of age, with moustaches painted on their faces to make them look like grown men, and they were wiped out in the shameful massacre of the **Battle of Acosta Ñú** in 1869.

From there on the pace of retreat quickened, and Mariscal López resorted to executing thousands of his own people for supposed treachery. Finally Mariscal López was cornered at **Cerro Corá** in the far northeast corner of the country, and with his death on 1 March 1870 the war was over. (See *Chapter 11*, page 288.) The destruction on Paraguay's side was horrific beyond words: the calculation of the numbers of Paraguayan dead varies from 58% to 75% of the population. Of males, the death toll is calculated as over 95%, and of adult males (over 20 years old) as over 99%. We owe the survival of the Paraguayan people to the children of that day, but it is not surprising that, despite a high birth rate, Paraguay is still, 140 years on, an under-populated country. (See box on *Interpretations of the Triple Alliance War*, page 288.)

COUPS In the aftermath of the war, Brazil and Argentina annexed large parts of Paraguay in compensation for war expenses, and they occupied the country until 1876. In the next stage of Paraguayan history, a constitution and an electoral system emerged, with two main parties (which persist up to the present day): the Colorados and the Liberales. But in fact power changed hands through coups, rather than through the ballot box. There were coups or assassinations of presidents in 1874, 1877, 1880, 1902, 1904 and 1911.

CHACO WAR In the 1930s another war broke out, the War of the Chaco (1932–35), against Paraguay's neighbour in the other direction, Bolivia. For a long time the boundary had been uncertain, with Paraguayans believing that all the Chaco belonged to them, and Bolivians believing that it was theirs. Until oil was mooted to be present in the Chaco, it did not much matter who it belonged to, because no one wanted to live in such inhospitable territory (see *Chapter 12*), but now a host of military outposts (*fortines*) were established by both sides. Paraguayans believe that imperialist interests from the USA and Europe, through rival petrol companies, contributed to the outbreak of the conflict.

Paraguay won the **siege of Boquerón** in 1932, against the Bolivian forces which had taken the fort three months earlier, but it took another three years to push the war to its final truce, with tragic loss of life on both sides (about 100,000 in all), either from bullets or from thirst and disease. Paraguay felt that by winning the War of the Chaco it had regained dignity after its defeat in the previous War of the Triple Alliance, but even after peace was declared the borders remained disputed, until an international commission finalised them in 1938, with both sides feeling hard done by.

It is often said, and it is a fact, that Paraguay harboured Nazis fleeing after World War II, but it can easily be blown out of proportion. There is an enormous German population in Paraguay today, with whole German areas, such as Filadelfia, Loma Plata and Neuland in the central Chaco, Nueva Germania in San Pedro, the Colonias Unidas in Itapúa, and Independencia in Guairá. Not only that, but very many of the best hotels have some element of German management. Good hotel almost equals German hotel. But it would be a great mistake to suspect all Germans in Paraguay of having a Nazi background.

Nonetheless, the first Nazi party outside of Germany was formed in Paraguay, around 1930. During World War II, the Paraguayan government distanced itself from Nazism, declaring war on Germany in 1945, three months before the defeat of Hitler. But when the dictator Stroessner (himself of German ancestry) came to power in 1954, he felt a bond with the authoritarian methods of the Nazis, and received around a dozen Nazi leaders into the country. There is even a theory (of the Paraguayan writer Mariano Llano) that Hitler did not die in his Berlin bunker but fled to Argentina in a submarine, and about ten years later passed into Paraguay incognito, but with the knowledge and consent of Stroessner, where in due course he died in anonymity.

Whatever the truth of that, there was an organisation called Odessa which helped Nazis escape to South America, and among those who did so were: Josef Mengele, the doctor who performed medical experiments on Jews in Auschwitz and subsequently obtained naturalisation in Paraguay; Edward Roschmann, commandant of the Riga concentration camp; and a number of other war criminals, including Erwin Fleiss, Marko Colak and Ante Pavelić. All these Nazis spent part of their exile in Argentina and part in Paraguay. For a hotel in a hidden-away spot that does not seem to feel it necessary to hide its interest in Nazism, see Hotel Paraíso (*Chapter 10*, page 260).

MORE COUPS Presidential power continued to change hands by coups, in 1936 and 1937. A new left-wing group called the Febreristas, took power in the aftermath of the war. It nationalised major enterprises, gave land to war veterans, and took steps to begin a social welfare programme. In 1939, the war hero, General José Félix Estigarribia, won the presidential election, and introduced the 1940 constitution, only to be killed in a plane crash the same year. He turned out to be the last non-Colorado president for 60 years, for another coup put the Colorados into power, cancelled the socialist reforms and imposed military rule. In 1947 there was a mini **civil war** as an armed uprising of Febreristas and Liberales was suppressed, and a large number of the educated classes were forced into exile, including the renowned writer Augusto Roa Bastos. (See box text, *Augusto Roa Bastos*, page 77.) There was another coup in 1949 and again in 1954.

STROESSNER DICTATORSHIP This time, in 1954, it was **Alfredo Stroessner**, the grandson of a German immigrant, and head of the armed forces, who pushed himself to the head of government. Paraguay had known dictatorships in the past – that of Dr Francia had lasted 26 years – but now this new and rather different form of dictatorship was to last as long as 34 years, during which time Stroessner was seven times 're-elected'. He established a vast network of paid spies (Guaraní *pyrague*) in every inch of the interior, and the alleged hunt for communists was the front for a savagely repressive system in which three people or more, meeting together, could constitute an illegal meeting.

A secret organisation was formed of (principally middle-class) opponents, called the **OPM** – variously deciphered as the Organización Primero de Marzo (the date of Mariscal López's death) and the Organización Politico-Militar. When the details of this organisation were discovered – principally through torturing one of its members and his pregnant wife in his presence – a full-scale repression was unleashed which swept into its path the Christian *campesino* (peasant) organisation, the **Ligas Agrarias Cristianas** (one of whose members happened to have been also a member of the OPM). Thousands of innocent *campesinos* endured long periods of imprisonment and regular, savage torture (see the Museo de las Memorias in *Chapter 3*, page 86). A dozen foreign Jesuits (the Society of Jesus having returned to Paraguay in 1927) were sent into exile on the grounds that they were subversives: virtually all returned after the end of the dictatorship.

COLORADO PRESIDENTS Stroessner's control was so absolute that only a relative of his could break it. **Andrés Rodríguez**, whose daughter was married to one of Stroessner's sons, was a senior commander in the army, and he took power in a coup of February 1989. Nine months earlier, **Pope John Paul II** had visited Paraguay, which effectively broke the ban on meetings and gave an opportunity for people to mobilise in great numbers.

Rodríguez introduced contested elections, and won the first one himself, in May 1989, standing for the same party, the Colorado party, which was in power throughout Stroessner's regime. He freed political prisoners, allowed press freedom and introduced a new constitution in 1992, under which no president could serve a second consecutive term. The second president in the newly free Paraguay was **Juan Carlos Wasmosy** (1993–98), again from the Colorado party. In his period of office a lot of banks went bankrupt, in a domino effect. In 1996 a fellow Colorado party member (or *coreligionario* as the term is), **Lino Oviedo**, mounted a coup against him, which was unsuccessful, and landed Oviedo with a ten-year prison sentence. He spent the next years being put in prison, managing to get himself released, and then being returned to prison to continue his sentence.

Lino Oviedo (still active in politics) is a populist ranter with a suspiciously huge fortune, and has won himself a large following among the *campesino* population, wooed with gifts. Barred from standing in the 1998 election, Oviedo put up a colleague as his puppet, Raúl Cubas, who won the election and released Oviedo from prison. When the Supreme Court ordered Cubas to return Oviedo to jail and the president refused, a constitutional crisis was unleashed, which was exacerbated by the murder of the vice-president, Luis María Argaña. A massive uprising in the plaza outside the Congress resulted in the events of the **Marzo Paraguayo** (see box in *Chapter 3*, page 91), and the fleeing of both Cubas and Oviedo into exile.

In the national euphoria surrounding the flight of Cubas and Oviedo, and in a situation where the vice-president had been murdered, the president of the Senate, **Luis González Macchi**, was made president by popular acclamation, and the country united for a brief time into a government of national unity. The pact was short-lived and disillusionment with González Macchi soon set in. The 2003 election was won by **Nicanor Duarte Frutos**, who made some half-hearted efforts at the beginning of his presidency to attack corruption, but was widely considered by the end of his presidency to have become as corrupt as any of his predecessors.

LUGO In 2008 a resigned bishop committed to liberation theology, from the poor diocese of San Pedro de Ycuamandyýu (see *Chapter 11*, page 274), **Fernando Lugo**, came forward to stand as a presidential candidate without a party, but supported by an alliance of most of the small parties together with the Liberales,

The national anthem (*himno nacional*) was written in 1846, in the presidency of Carlos Antonio López, ie: after independence and before the Triple Alliance War. Although it was actually written by a Uruguayan, Francisco Acuña de Figueroa, it expresses something very deep in the Paraguayan soul – pride in their independence, grief and courage in their defeats, and a sense of patriotism as the chief virtue. Paraguay is still a very formal society and the anthem is carefully taught to all school children and sung with great reverence at most public events. The first verse about the victory of independence is sung in a very slow and stately fashion, and then the chorus – which includes the catchphrase 'República o Muerte!' ('Republic or Death!') – changes to a rapid and galloping pace.

A los pueblos de América, infausto
Tres centurias un cetro oprimió,
Mas un día soberbia surgiendo,
¡Basta! dijo ... y el cetro rompió;
Nuestros padres, lidiando grandiosos,
Ilustraron su gloria marcial;
Y trozada la augusta diadema,
Enalzaron el gorro triunfal.

Paraguayos, República o Muerte!
Nuestro brío nos dio libertad;
Ni opresores, ni siervos alientan
Donde reina unión, e igualdad.

The peoples of America were sadly oppressed for three centuries by a sceptred power,
But one day pride rose up and cried, 'Enough!'... and the power was broken.
Our predecessors, great leaders, showed their martial glory:
The august diadem was shattered, and they lifted aloft the cap of triumph.

Paraguayans, Republic or Death!
Our spirit brought us freedom.
Neither oppressors, nor servants are encouraged
Where there reigns union and equality.

It does not take much of a mathematical brain to work out that if 15 May 1811 was the day of independence, then 2011 will be the bi-centenary of independence, and a year of massive celebration in Paraguay.

called the Alianza Patriótica para el Cambio (Patriotic Alliance for Change). He won, and the 60-year rule by the Colorado party, which had customarily filched national funds to bribe voters, came to an end.

GOVERNMENT AND POLITICS

The President of the Republic is directly elected by the people, for a period of five years. Under the constitution, he or she cannot stand for re-election. The term of office always begins on 15 August, the date of the foundation of Asunción, and the feast of the Assumption.

The lower house is called the Cámera de Diputados and has a minimum of 80 members. The upper house is called the Cámera de Senadores and has a minimum of 45 members. The judges of the Supreme Court are chosen by the National Congress, and there has been much complaint over the way that party interests, principally of the Colorado party, have produced corrupt judges.

The country is divided into 17 *departamentos*, each of which has a regional government known as the *gobernación*. Within each *departamento* are many *municipios*, corresponding to each small town; the local government (and its building) are called the *municipalidad*.

ECONOMY

One third of the population are classified as self-employed, and another third as private labourers. The next largest category is unpaid family workers, ie: principally mothers (10%), while domestic workers in other people's houses number 7%. The level of state employees is very high, at nearly 9%, compared to only 5% who have a private employer.

The country imports far more than it exports, particularly in the way of electrical goods. The main exports are wood, cotton, tobacco, meat, *yerba mate*, leather and hydro-electric energy from the two dams. The principal crop is soya – largely from estates owned by Brazilians, who buy up Paraguayan land to plant genetically modified crops, using toxic pesticides, and for that reason have attracted a degree of resentment from the local people. Five times as much land is used for soya plantation as is used for the next largest crop, which is maize.

Another enormous area of production is cattle-raising. There are ten million head of cattle, while the human population is only just over six million.

PEOPLE

The population of Paraguay is six million – a tiny population for a developing country, due principally to the loss of life and practical elimination of the male population in the Triple Alliance War, which ended in 1870 and from which the country is still recovering today. Just over half a million of that number live in greater Asunción.

Therefore, Paraguay has one tenth of the population of Britain, in a territory almost twice the size. Some 40% of Paraguayans are under 14, and 54% are between 15 and 64. In other words, only 6% are people who have survived beyond what would be a normal UK retirement age. This is a young country, with a rapidly expanding population, and with room for that expansion.

Under 50% of Paraguayans are on a public service of piped clean water: the rest use wells or a private network. Over 3% are still without electricity. Only 50% use a gas oven as their principal method of cooking, and less than 1% use an electric oven. More than 50% use burning as their method of waste disposal and 14% throw it into a ditch, while only 36% have it collected. Some 84% have television, and 77% have a fridge – really a necessity in a country with Paraguay's heat. (Figures from the 2002 census updated with surveys by Dirección General de Estadística, Encuestas y Censos *(Naciones Unidas esq Saavedra, Fernando de la Mora;* ↘ *021 511016;* e *info@dgeec.gov.py; www.dgeec.gov.py).*)

Only one quarter of the population of Paraguay have any form of medical insurance. However, under Lugo's presidency healthcare has been made free. Only 20% have a landline phone, but as many as 85% have a mobile phone, now slightly edging ahead of the number that have a television. In rural areas, more than 40% own a motorbike, while less than 1% have internet access at home.

Some 3% in all are without electricity, but in the *campo* that figure doubles. Cooking is done with firewood by 69% of the rural population (government figures for 2008).

LANGUAGE

In Asunción 79% of people speak Spanish as their first language, and 20% Guaraní as their first language (with only 1% having a different mother tongue). The mother tongue is Guaraní in 82.5% of rural homes, and 42.6% of urban homes, making an average of 60% of homes where Guaraní is the first language.

The survival of Guaraní owes a great deal to the Jesuits. They were responsible for turning the purely oral language into a written language, with the systematic formation of grammars and dictionaries (after some initial grammatical and vocabulary notes made by the Franciscan Luis Bolaños; see box in *Chapter 10*, page 268). This work has enabled Guaraní to take its place in the world as a survivable language. Even today, the Jesuits lead the field in this respect. For example, the leading Guaraní grammar still being used is that written by the Spaniard Antonio Guasch SJ in 1961, and the first translation of the Bible into Guaraní was done by the Diego Ortiz SJ, published in 1996.

Another reason why the Jesuits have been responsible for the survival of Guaraní is that through the Reductions (see below), in which the Jesuits did not permit Spaniards to enter for more than two or three days at a time, they created enclaves where both the Guaraní race and the Guaraní language could continue in a pure form for 150 years, until the Expulsion of the Jesuits of 1768. Meanwhile, in the rest of the continent, the process of integration of the indigenous into Spanish life began much earlier. Once the Jesuits were expelled, the Guaraní were soon assimilated through intermarriage, but the language survived.

The Guaraní indigenous are quite distinct from the *mestizo* majority (referred to by the indigenous as *los blancos* 'the whites', although European whites may sometimes have difficulty distinguishing the colour of the *mestizos* from the indigenous), and their indigenous language is purer. But increasingly the Guaraní language of the indigenous is being overtaken by the common Paraguayan Guaraní language, with all its *jopará*.

You also find the interesting phenomenon that a *campesina*, taking notes at a base community meeting, will write down notes in Spanish about a discussion held in Guaraní, and when the time comes for reading them back, will give her report in Guaraní. It is always harder for people to read and write in Guaraní than in Spanish, and the older generation cannot do it all. With the educational reforms, reading and writing in Guaraní is now taught from the first grades of primary school, all over the country, but there is no threat to the dominance of Spanish as a language of education. Although promoters of Guaraní have invented a whole new bank of Guaraní words, for days of the week, months of the year, household appliances and so forth, some people think there is something artificial about the attempt: Guaraní was not made for that.

RELIGION

Paraguay is still one of the most Catholic countries of Latin America, with an 87% Catholic population (not so far overtaken by the wave of charismatic new Protestant churches that has swept over Brazil and other nations). It is so Catholic that its three principal cities are named after three Catholic doctrines: the Assumption, the Incarnation and the (Immaculate) Conception. It has ten dioceses and one archdiocese (Asunción), and two apostolic vicariates, not yet ready to form dioceses (both in the Chaco). It is one of the few South American countries without a cardinal.

While Protestant churches are small in number, their members tend to be more active than the Catholic majority. The largest Protestant churches are Pentecostal, though Seventh-day Adventists and Mormons also have a notable presence.

The Catholic present of Paraguay is very much linked to the Catholic past, which in the case of Paraguay began with the famous Reductions (see also *Introduction*, page ix). This guide uses the term 'Jesuit-Guaraní Reductions', bearing in mind that there were Jesuit Reductions that were not for the Guaraní (in Bolivia, for example) and Guaraní Reductions that were not founded by the Jesuits (but by the Franciscans). More attention will be given to both kinds of Reduction later in this guide. Jesuit Reductions will be dealt with in *Chapter 5* (the museums) and *Chapter 6* (the Ruins); Franciscan Reductions will figure in *Chapters 4, 10* and *11*.

EDUCATION

Education is still very formal in Paraguay, despite there having been a certain level of educational reform since the dictatorship. Young school children sit at desks. A lot of emphasis is placed on the children memorising, rather than thinking for themselves. Standards of spelling and punctuation are low, even among educated people.

Many state schools now have *prescolar* (nursery) classes. Compulsory and free education runs from *Primer Grado* (at 6 years) to *Noveno Grado* (at 15 years or more). Pupils who do not pass their exams have to repeat the year. It is normal in state schools to have two shifts, so that one set of children have class in the morning (07.00–11.00) and another group in the afternoon (13.00–16.00).

After *Noveno Grado*, there are three more years of secondary schooling, at the end of which the pupils gain their *bachillerato*. With this, they can apply to university, and every university or institute of higher education has a *cursillo* (short course) followed by an entrance exam.

University education is usually in the evenings (on the assumption that people can only afford to study if they are working at the same time), and by consequence a degree usually takes about five years or more to complete. The two universities which are traditionally considered to have the best reputation are the state-run Universidad Nacional and the private Universidad Católica, both of which have branches all around the country. In recent years a plethora of private universities have opened, most of them competing with each other to offer the lowest fees, and to require the lowest number of class hours per week, in an attempt to make higher education more affordable.

The two hydroelectric dams (Itaipú and Yacyretá) fund a large number of university scholarships.

Over 5% of the population is illiterate. Only 89% of the population between six and 17 years of age attend school; no punitive or follow-up measures are taken against non-attenders.

CULTURE

MUSIC AND FOLK DANCE There are basically two types of Paraguayan popular music: the *polka* – which, though lively dance music, is not the same as the European polka – and the *guarania*, which is the nostalgic, slower version of the

---

FOLK DANCE COSTUME

WOMEN
- long, full skirt (Spanish *pollera*) with a well starched petticoat (Spanish *miriñaque* or Guaraní *saiguý*)
- blouse (Guaraní *typói*) with short sleeves made out of *encaje ju* or *ñandutí* or crochet
- shawl (Spanish *chal*) of *encaje ju* or *ñandutí* or crochet
- necklace (usually a rosary with artificial pearls)
- earrings (large costume jewellery type, to match necklace)
- a false plait of hair hanging right down the back
- artificial flowers in hair, which hide where the plait is attached
- make-up on face (originally with natural dyes from fruit)
- dance slippers (originally of leather) or bare feet
- a bottle or a water jug (Guaraní *kambuchí* or Spanish *cantero*) to carry on the head

MEN
- black trousers or breeches (Guaraní *bombacha*)
- leather boots (Spanish *botas*)
- shirt embroidered with *ao po'í*
- colourful striped woven sash as a belt (Spanish *faja*)
- neckerchief (Spanish *pañueleta*)
- hat with brim (Spanish *sombrero*) made of leather (Spanish *cuero*) or palm leaf (Guaraní *karanda'ý* or *pirí*)
- leather horse whip (Spanish *guacha*)

For *encaje ju* and *ñandutí* see page 22.

same rhythm, in a minor key. The *guarania* was invented in 1925 by another of the great figures in Paraguayan musical history, José Asunción Flores (1904–72), with the famous piece 'Jejuí'; he later wrote the famous romantic *guarania* 'India'. Both the polka and the *guarania* are syncopated: the right hand plays in 6/8 time while the left hand plays in 3/4. One of the great joys of travelling in Paraguay is hearing this fantastically lively music on harp and guitar, sometimes accompanied by accordion, played by musicians dressed in colourful *ao po'í* shirts (see below under *Craft*, and for the harp see *Introduction,* page ix). Without its distinctive music, Paraguay would lose its heart.

Another enormously enjoyable musical experience is seeing folk dance, which, particularly in the *campo*, is very much a live tradition, in which young people of both sexes eagerly take part. The dances have romantic themes, and the colourful, traditional folk costumes are very decorative. One dance has a humorous element, with people falling off chairs. Another has the girls dancing with water jugs on their heads. Some of them have the men snapping their horse whips through the air, and stamping their boots on the ground, while the girls flirt with them. There is a dance in which a girl has an ever-increasing number of bottles placed on her head, one on top of another.

There is a long training to becoming a dance teacher, as everything must be done according to time-honoured tradition. The best place to see folk dance is at a festival or a big event like the Santiago fiestas (see page 179), when there is sometimes a competition for the best dance group.

CRAFT The most typical Paraguayan crafts have already been mentioned: *ñandutí* spiderweb lace, *ao po'í* embroidery, *encaje ju* lace, *filigrana* silver jewellery, *palo santo* wooden saints and Guaraní wooden animals (see *Introduction*, page x). The chart on the following page gives fuller information on the diverse crafts and the places where each is made. Details will be found under the respective towns, most of which appear in *Chapter 4*.

The craftspeople in Paraguay are beginning to be organised at both local and national level, for better publicity. Most of the craft towns are covered in *Chapter 4*, and you generally find there is an association or co-operative for those working at the same craft, in the same town. There is an Expoferia de la Artesanía Paraguaya which takes place in the central railway station of Asunción, usually in the first two weeks of June. Then there are a couple of national networks:

Instituto Paraguayo de Artesanía (IPA) ✆ 021 614896/899; e ipa@artesania.gov.py; www.artesania.gov.py. A network organised by the government, to help small craft enterprises.

Cámara de Empresas Artesanas del Paraguay (CEAP) Mariscal López 957, PB Oficina N° 6; ✆ 021 490951; e info@ceap.org.py; www.ceap.org.py. An organisation of craftspeople making more expensive, high-quality goods.

See also the list of craft shops in *Chapter 3*, page 75.

TERERÉ AND MATE The *Introduction* has explained what *tereré* is, and how important this traditional drink is to Paraguayans (see page xi). When people from other countries have a tea break or a coffee break, Paraguayans have a *tereré* break. When Paraguayans drink *mate*, it tends to be a more solitary custom in the early morning, as a wake-up drink – unless the weather is very cold, in which case they may drink *mate* during the day as well. Unlike the Argentinians, Paraguayans never put sugar in *mate*.

Both *mate* and *tereré* are made with *yerba mate*, which means '*mate* leaf', but people usually just say *yerba* for short. The cup for the leaves is called a *guampa*, and

WHERE DIFFERENT CRAFTS ARE MADE

Places not in the *Circuito de Oro* are followed by their *departamento*.

KIND OF CRAFT	PLACE WHERE IT IS MADE
ao po'í (embroidery)	Yataitý, Guairá; and elsewhere
Appliqué embroidery	Santa María de Fe, Misiones
Bamboo souvenirs and furniture	Tañarandý (*compañía* of San Ignacio)
Banana-leaf models	Itá
Encaje ju (lace)	Yataitý, Guairá; Carapeguá (with a thicker thread); San Miguel, Misiones; and elsewhere
Fibre weaving, hats of palm leaf (*karanda'ý* or *pirí*), rush tablemats	Limpio, Tobatí, Maká indigenous
Leathercraft	Areguá; Asunción; Luque; Ypacaraí; Concepción; and elsewhere
Musical instruments (harps and guitars)	Luque
Ñandutí (spiderweb lace)	Itauguá
Poncho de 60 listas	Piribebúy (workshop of Rosa Segovia and family)
Pottery	Itá; Areguá; Tobatí
Silver filigree jewellery (*filigrana*)	Luque
Stone carving	Santa María de Fe, Misiones (workshop of the Rotela family in the *compañía* of San Gerónimo); Trinidad, Itapúa (workshop of Vicenta Morel)
Wood carving of saints	Tobatí (workshop of Zenón Páez); Capiatá (workshop of the Rodríguez family)
Wood carving	Indigenous peoples: the Nivaclé; the Mbyá Guaraní; Tobatí; Santa María de Fe, Misiones; San Ignacio, Misiones
Wooden furniture	Escuela Pa'í Pukú in the Chaco
Woollen ponchos and blankets, hammocks, tablecloths	San Miguel, Misiones; Carapeguá; and elsewhere

there are different types for *tereré* and for *mate*. For *tereré*, a cow's horn is generally used, with the point cut and filled in with a wooden stopper, so that it will stand up. For *mate*, people usually use a wooden *guampa*, because it has to be something with insulation against the heat of the water. In both cases a metal straw is used, called a *bombilla*, which has a flattened end with a strainer on it, so that the *yerba* leaves do not pass up the straw. Only one *guampa* and one *bombilla* is used, and it is passed around the group for each to drink in turn. This can be found distasteful by many foreigners, who are afraid of getting infections, but in fact that is very unlikely, although not totally unknown.

Just as there are two kinds of *guampa*, there are two kinds of vacuum flask. The one that holds hot water for *mate* is similar to the kind of Thermos you can buy in other countries. But the kind for holding iced water has to have a much broader mouth, because the ice is made in thick bars of about 4cm diameter. This fat kind of vacuum flask uses polystyrene as the insulation material, and is very light to carry. Beautiful souvenir vacuum flasks are made with a decorated leather casing, and *guampas* can have details of silverwork on them. You will see a lot of these in Luque.

The ritual of serving *tereré* is very strict, with one person acting as host, and serving the others in strict rotation. There is a lot to learn about how to serve *tereré* correctly, but all the visitor needs to know is how to respond when it is offered. If you are offered *tereré*, it is not rude to refuse, but it would be rude to wipe the *bombilla* before drinking. If you accept, you should drink all the water in the *guampa* and then return it to the host. If you do not want another turn you say '*gracias*', which in Paraguay means 'No thank you' or 'Thank you, that's enough now', rather than 'Yes thank you'.

Along with the *yerba* it is customary to add other plants, which are known as *remedios*, because they have medicinal qualities as well as enhancing the flavour. These are usually mashed in a pestle and mortar, and can be added to the *yerba* in the *guampa*, but are more often added to the iced water in the flask. Some *yerba* mixtures come ready prepared with *remedios*, usually mint and *boldo*. Other *remedios* used (some for *mate*, others for *tereré*) are *burrito*, *cedrón*, eucalyptus, aniseed, camomile, avocado leaves, sage, and other plants with untranslatable Guaraní names. When you go to somewhere like Mercado Cuatro 4 in Asunción and see a variety of strange green leaves or roots laid out near a large pestle and mortar, these are *remedios* to put in *tereré* or *mate*.

Growing *yerba* is very difficult, and depends on the right kind of soil, which is only found in this region of South America. Under the Jesuits, the Guaraní became expert at it, to the point where the major part of their export sales was for *yerba* mate – which became known as 'green gold'. Aimé Bonpland (see box on page 176) also became proficient in its production, 50 years after the Jesuits were expelled.

A plantation of *yerba* trees is called a *yerbal*. After the leaf is plucked, it has to be dried and lightly toasted, mashed into little pieces, and then stored for several years in a dry place for its flavour to develop, before finally being packeted. The Selecta *yerba mate* factory in Bella Vista welcomes visitors, to show them their production process (see page 203). *Yerba mate* is a stimulant, a digestive and a laxative. Because of its very bitter flavour, you cannot eat while drinking *tereré*, and so it also acts as a dietary aid.

2

Practical Information

WHEN TO VISIT

Visiting Paraguay at any time of year you are likely to have good, sunny weather. However, some months are a bit unpredictable, so if nothing else is determining the time of your trip, here are some factors to bear in mind.

December to February are the hottest months and June to August are the coldest ones. By the middle of September the cold weather is over. The ideal time to come, therefore, is between mid-September and November (before the fares go up for the pre-Christmas rush) or between March and May. Over Easter would be ideal if it were not the time when all the Paraguayans are enjoying their holiday of Semana Santa, which is Maundy Thursday to Easter Sunday. Easter Monday is back to work. Book your hotel ahead for those crucial three days if you want to be in Paraguay over Easter, and be prepared for everywhere to be closed.

If you cannot come in spring or autumn it is up to you to decide if you prefer to be hot or cold. Paraguayans have a long summer holiday from December to February, and in January those who can afford it tend to go to the Brazilian beaches, or to the Paraguayan beaches of San Bernardino, Villa Florida or Ayolas. They also have a short winter break in the first fortnight of July (*la quincena de julio*). The weather in July is very variable: it can be as agreeable as an English summer, but there is also the risk that it may be unpleasantly cold, and with every year's increasing climate change, the cold snaps of winter are becoming more frequent and more bitter. The old wisdom used to be that July was a good month to come, because it would not be too hot (average temperatures in Asunción in July are 10–22°C), and that if there was cold weather it would only last three or four days. With climate change, that needs to be re-assessed. June and August are generally all right, but cannot be guaranteed.

This would not matter if there was adequate heating in the buildings, but Paraguayans are not accustomed to having cold weather, and take few precautions against it. It is quite normal in the cold weather for people to sit indoors with the door and windows wide open and their overcoats on. This is a question of culture: it is what they are used to doing. Even if you are in a hotel with good-quality air conditioning, which produces either hot or cold air, you may well find that the staff do not know how to make the hot air come out, because they are not used to having heated buildings. (The trick is to adjust not just the temperature, but the mode.) In fact you may find that they automatically turn on the air conditioning when you go into your hotel room, even in the midst of winter, so making a cold room even colder, because in Paraguay, quality equals air conditioning.

In January it is always hot (average temperatures in Asunción in January are 23–33°C, but it can pass 40°C). You will need either a fan or air conditioning to get a good night's sleep, but virtually all hotels have air conditioning nowadays. The cheaper hotels, however, have the noisy kind in square boxes, rather than the long rectangular device set high in the wall which is separated from the motor that makes the noise, and is called a Split. Even the poor will have a fan going all night. People sometimes walk around under a black umbrella, which in Paraguay is not usually called *paraguas* (the word used in Spain, 'for waters') but *sombrilla* (shade).

Heavy and dramatic thunderstorms are fairly frequent, but there is no way of planning to avoid them. There can also be long spells of drought.

SUGGESTED ITINERARIES

A 'classic tour' of Paraguay might go something like this: fly into Asunción; a couple of days in Asunción; a couple of days doing part of the Circuito de Oro; a couple of days going south to visit the museums of Jesuit-Guaraní art in Misiones, perhaps stopping at a few places on the way; a couple of days to get to and visit the ruins of Itapúa; a day to get to the Iguazú Falls (ideally travelling through Argentina); a full day at the Iguazú Falls; then fly out from Foz. Alternatively, return to Asunción for the flight out, crossing over the middle of Paraguay, and perhaps taking a couple of days to visit Villarrica and Caazapá, or more towns on the Circuito de Oro.

Within the central area of the country you can stay at *estancias* (country estates): these are little paradises, and you should try to build in at least one full day at one of these (see page 50). People with an adventurous streak may want to go to Concepción, the Río Paraguay, and perhaps even the Pantanal, but that all takes time: you should allow at least a week for going to the Pantanal, and plan the dates carefully to see if it can in fact be accomplished in that time. Some will want to go overland to Bolivia, crossing the vast expanse of the Chaco desert. Those interested in the Reductions can make the excursion to the Argentinian missions (a day or two) and to the Brazilian missions (four days or more). A pleasant but more minority-interest excursion is to Pilar (and perhaps the war sites) in the extreme southwest – one to three days. A longer trip to a less frequented area would take you to the park of Cerro Corá, in the extreme northeast, taking upwards of three days, at least.

Almost everyone wants to see a little of Asunción, a little of the Circuito de Oro, a little of Misiones, the Reductions, and the Iguazú Falls. But it should be remembered that you can also do a tour of Paraguay using Foz do Iguaçu as your base, and never setting foot in Asunción. Since there are no direct flights to Paraguay from other continents, you will be making just one change at São Paulo in either case.

INTERNATIONAL TOUR OPERATORS

The best tour operators for Paraguay are the little ones, as the bigger companies do not yet have much (if any) experience of the country. In addition to the list below, Paraguay-based tour operators can be found in *Chapter 3*, page 67.

IN THE UK

Arpa Tours 111 Netherton Rd, Appleton, OX13 5LA; ☏ +44 1865 861791; e arpa.tours@paraguay.org.uk; www.paraguay.org.uk. Robert Munro, as a Paraguayan, & his wife Rosemary, as a player of the Paraguayan harp, have in-depth knowledge of the country & numerous contacts. They offer visits to all the main tourist attractions as well as opportunities to hear Paraguayan music, particularly the harp. They generally do a tour every Oct, with Robert as tour leader.

Santa Maria Hotel Lee Cottage, Blockley, Moreton-in-Marsh GL56 9HH; e info@santamariahotel.org; www.santamariahotel.org. This hotel in the Paraguayan *campo* has a base & a bank account in Britain & it is set up to receive & look after visitors from airport to airport: the service can extend to an English-speaking guide if needed, or it can just give advice & make bookings for hotels & transport. The tours are tailor-made, but they typically involve visits to Reductions & the Iguazú Falls.

Austral Tours 20 Upper Tachbrook St, London SW1V 1SH; ☎ +44 20 7233 5384;
e info@latinamerica.co.uk; www.latinamerica.co.uk. These specialists in Latin American travel focus on tailor-made trips & have the insight to say: 'Often overlooked by travellers, landlocked Paraguay is a largely unspoilt & predominantly rural nation that makes an interesting side trip from Northern Argentina or Southern Brazil.'

Audley Travel New Mill, New Mill Lane, Witney OX29 9SX; ☎ +44 1993 838650;
e mail@audleytravel.com; www.audleytravel.com; ⊕ Mon–Thu 09.00–18.00, Fri 09.00–17.30, Sat & Sun 10.00–16.00. A high-class operator specialising in quality, tailor-made journeys, & one of the few major operators ready to do trips to Paraguay, although what they offer at present is limited. The Latin America Regional Manager, Susan Owen-Evans, has lived in Paraguay.

Journey Latin America 12 & 13 Heathfield Terrace, Chiswick, London W4 4JE; ☎ +44 20 8747 8315;
e tours@journeylatinamerica.co.uk; www.journeylatinamerica.co.uk; ⊕ Mon–Fri 09.00–18.00, Sat 09.00–17.00. The great specialists in Latin American travel now offer very attractive tours all over the continent; but Paraguay currently only figures in their tour programmes *en route* from the Iguazú Falls to Bolivia. However, they do offer tailor-made ('bespoke') holidays as well as the ones in their brochures.

Condor Journeys & Adventures 2 Ferry Bank, Colintraive, Argyll PA22 3AR; ☎ +44 1700 841318;
e info@condorjourneys-adventures.com; www.condorjourneys-adventures.com. Small company based in Scotland, bilingual in French, offering tailor-made tours in South America, including the Jesuit trail, the Iguazú Falls, the Chaco & the Pantanal.

W & O Travel Welby House, 96 Wilton Rd, London SW1V 1DW; ☎ +44 845 277 3366; f +44 207 821 4001; e sales@WandOtravel.com; www.wandotravel.com; ⊕ Mon–Fri 09.00–18.00, Sat 09.00–18.30. They do tailor-made holidays, & appreciate that Paraguay 'is an under-explored region just waiting to be discovered'. The tour operator South America Experience now comes under the W & O umbrella.

Last Frontiers The Mill, Quainton Rd, Waddesdon, Bucks HP18 0LP; ☎ +44 1296 653000;
e info@lastfrontiers.com; www.lastfrontiers.com. They are specialists in tailor-made holidays all over Latin America, including Paraguay. Contact them for more information & to discuss the various options.

Tucan Travel 316 Uxbridge Rd, Acton, London W3 9QP; ☎ +44 20 8896 1600;
e uksales@tucantravel.com; www.tucantravel.com; ⊕ Mon, Tue, Thu, Fri, 09.00–17.30; Wed 10.00–17.30; Sat 09.00–13.00. This winner of a prize for best small tour operator 2009 is actually quite a big operator, offering 450 adventure tours to 72 countries. It's good to see that they include Paraguay when hardly anyone else does, but Paraguay usually only figures fleetingly alongside 5 or 6 other countries, & usually as part of a long tour (eg: one day in a tour of up to 154 days duration).

IN THE USA The USA does no better than the UK when it comes to knowledge of Paraguay, but fortunately there is one excellent small operator (as well as a couple of minority-interest pigeon-shooting companies).

Trico Tours ☎ +1 612 870 3634
e tours@tricotours.com; www.tricotours.com. This small US agency run by husband-&-wife team Tracy Gorman & Paraguayan harpist Nicolás Carter specialises in customised tours to Paraguay, Uruguay & Argentina. Family members living in Paraguay assist in guiding private tours. They can be trusted to know the country well, take you off the beaten track to experience the heart & soul of Paraguay, & to provide an attentive personal service.

Frontiers PO Box 959, Wexford PA 15090 0959; ☎ +1 800 245 1950; e info@frontierstravel; www.frontierstravel.com. Pigeon shooting in the Chaco. They say: 'A true "Mecca" of sorts for shooting at featured destinations in Argentina, Uruguay & Paraguay... These game-rich countries are teeming with high volume duck, dove, perdiz & pigeon. The absolute hunt of a lifetime awaits you.'

Wings ☎ +1 866 346 4868/803 713 9900;
e shoot@wingssafari.com; www.wingssafari.com. The company specialises in wing shooting, big game hunting (illegal in Paraguay, though the law is not observed), photo safaris & fishing. They say: 'In the Grand Chaco, the dove population approaches that of Argentina, & the area supports the largest wild pigeon population in South America. We hunt on the vast cattle ranches near the town of Filadelfia & on farms managed by the Mennonites.'

IN AUSTRALIA

Tucan Travel See above. Tucan have another branch in Australia: ✆ +61 02 9326 6633;
e ozsales@tucantravel.com

IN ARGENTINA

Exprinter Viajes Avenida R Saenz Peña 615 7º, Buenos Aires, Argentina; ✆ +54 11 4393 4160; e exprinter@exprinterviajes.com.ar; www.exprinterviajes.com.ar. A good quality

Argentinian tour operator that offers a 2-week trip through the Jesuit-Guaraní Reductions in Paraguay, Argentina & Brazil, & can offer a chaplain or spiritual companion for the group. Has experience of Misiones Paraguay.

IN BRAZIL

Missões Turismo Av dos Jesuítas, 291, sala 01, São Miguel das Missões, RS; ✆ +55 55 3381 1319; e missoesturismo@terra.com.br; www.missoesturismo.com.br; ⊕ Mon–Sat 08.00–12.00 & 13.30–18.00. Portuguese-speaking,

but a good company with much experience of doing the route of the 30 *pueblos*. As yet their Paraguayan exploration tends to stop at the Ruins of Trinidad, without penetrating into the heart of Misiones, Paraguay, with its museums.

RED TAPE

Visas are not required to enter **Paraguay** for visitors from most EU countries (including the UK), but they are required for visitors from almost anywhere else in the world (except Central and South America). But do not forget that you will probably be going to the Iguazú Falls, which are just outside the Paraguayan boundary, so you need to think about Argentina and Brazil as well. **Argentina** does not require a visa for visitors from most EU countries (including the UK), Russia, Australia, Canada, the USA or most of South America. **Brazil** does not require a visa for visitors from most EU countries (including the UK) and Canada. (However, see page 232 for relaxed rules on visiting the Iguazú Falls. See also page 226 for a way of crossing from Paraguay to Puerto Iguazú, Argentina, by ferry, without passing through Brazil.) To be sure, you should check with the Paraguayan Embassy in your country before departure.

A normal **tourist stamp** when you enter the country will last for 90 days. If you want to spend longer than this in Paraguay, you can renew the stamp quite easily by going to Migraciones in Asunción (*Caballero Nº 201 e/ Eligio Ayala;* ✆ *021 446673/446066;* ⊕ *07.00–13.00*) and paying a small fee. There is no problem at all about doing this: Paraguay likes to have foreigners in the country, who bring in money, and likes to collect fees off them. Alternatively you can make a short trip over the frontier and get a new stamp (but if you go to the Iguazú Falls make sure they actually do stamp your passport, as they will prefer to wave you through without doing so). What is not advised is to get a visa for a longer stay: it will take you time, money and frustration to assemble all the necessary documents, and when you arrive in the country the passport officer will probably give you a 90-day tourist entry stamp anyway. When you leave the country after your 90 days you will then be fined, even though you paid for a visa. At least, that has been the experience of at least one traveller. The fine for not having an appropriate entry stamp in your passport is currently Gs361,249.

If you want to stay seriously longer than 90 days, you can apply for a **resident's permit**. You must start with a temporary permit and can progress to a permanent permit after a year. Getting these permits is a long, expensive and frustrating business, but if you do want to apply for one there are certain documents you will need to bring from your country of origin, which will need to be legalised both by the Foreign Office of your country and by the Paraguayan Embassy there: birth certificate; marriage certificate, divorce or separation certificate, or death certificate of spouse (to prove if you are single, divorced, separated or widowed); and proof of employment or income and professional qualifications relevant to your work. The police certificate and health certificate can be obtained in Paraguay, and the translation of the documents must be done in Paraguay by an authorised translator: Migraciones will give you a list of these.

E EMBASSIES AND CONSULATES

These are embassies unless marked as consulates. Britain closed its embassy in Paraguay in 2005, but there is a consulate. Australia has neither embassy nor consulate: the nearest one is in Buenos Aires. All opening times are Monday to Friday.

Argentina España y Perú; ☎ 021 212320; ⏲ 07.30–14.00. Consulate: ☎ 021 442151; ⏲ 08.00–13.00
Austria (Consulate) Aviadores del Chaco 1690; ☎ 021 613323; ⏲ 07.30–12.30
Belgium (Consulate) Ruta 2 km17.5, Capiatá; ☎ 028 33326; ⏲ 10.00–13.00
Bolivia América 200; ☎ 021 660620/614984; ⏲ 09.00–13.00
Brazil Cnel Irrazabal esq Eligio Ayala; ☎ 021 2484000; ⏲ 08.00–14.30. Consulate: ☎ 021 232000
Canada Prof Ramírez c/ J de Salazar; ☎ 021 227207; ⏲ 08.00–12.30
Chile Cap Nudelman 35; ☎ 021 662756; ⏲ 08.00–13.00
China Av Mcal López 1133; ☎ 021 227168; ⏲ 07.30–12.00
Colombia Naciones Unidas 566 c/ El Dorado; ☎ 021 661131; ⏲ 08.30–12.30
Costa Rica Adolfo Riquelme 4574 e/ Torean Viera y McArthur; ☎ 021 607183; ⏲ 08.00–13.00
Cuba San Rafael 698 esq/ Nuestra Señora Del Carmen; ☎ 021 602 747; ⏲ 09.00–13.00
Denmark (Consulate) Nuestra Señora de la Asunción 766; ☎ 021 493160; ⏲ 07.30–11.30 & 15.00–18.00
Dominican Republic Cruz del Defensor 1322; ☎ 021 600088; ⏲ 08.00–13.00
Ecuador Prof Justo Román esq/ Dr Luis Maria Argaña; ☎ 021 614814; ⏲ 08.30–13.00
El Salvador Juan E O'Leary 997, Edificio El Dorado, 9th Floor; ☎ 021 490891; ⏲ 08.30–12.00
France España 893 c/ Padre Pucheu; ☎ 021 211840/213840; ⏲ 08.00–12.00
Germany Av Venezuela 241; ☎ 021 214009; ⏲ 08.00–11.00
Greece (Consulate) Félix Bogado e/ Dr Esculies y Primera; ☎ 021 331186
Honduras Cerro Corá 942; ☎ 021 447671; ⏲ 08.00–13.00

Italy Quesada 5871 c/ Bélgica; ☎ 021 615620; ⏲ 08.00–12.00
Japan Mariscal López 2364; ☎ 021 604616; ⏲ 08.00–12.00
Korea Rpca Argentina y Pacheco 678; ☎ 021 605419; ⏲ 08.30–12.00
Mexico Denis Roa 1559; ☎ 021 6182000; ⏲ 08.00–14.00
Netherlands (Consulate) Artigas 4145 c/ Teniente Delgado; ☎ 021 283657; ⏲ 15.00–18.00
Norway Teniente Delgado 527; ☎ 021 202248; ⏲ 07.30–12.00
Panama 25 de Mayo 865; ☎ 021 444534; ⏲ 08.00–12.00
Peru Agustin Barrios 852; ☎ 021 661174; ⏲ 08.30–12.30
Poland (Consulate) Palma 685; ☎ 021 448520
Portugal (Consulate) Herrera 195 c/ Yegros; ☎ 021 451950
Russia Av Artigas 1375; ☎ 021 214373; ⏲ 07.00–12.00
Spain Yegros 437, 6th Floor; ☎ 021 490686; ⏲ 08.30–13.00
Philippines General Bruguez 734; ☎ 021 202180; ⏲ 08.00–11.30
Sweden (Consulate) Artigas 1945 e/ Central y Altos; ☎ 021 214114
Switzerland O'Leary 409, esq Estrella; ☎ 021 490848; ⏲ 08.00–12.30
UK (Consulate) Eulogio Estigarribia 4846 c/Monseñor Bogarin; ☎ 021 210405/663536; ⏲ 08.00–13.00 & 15.00–17.30
Uruguay Boggiani 5832; ☎ 021 203864; ⏲ 07.30–17.30
USA Mcal Lopez 1776; ☎ 021 213715; ⏲ 08.00–12.00 & 14.00–17.00. Consulate: ⏲ 08.00–10.00
Venezuela Mariscal Estigarribia 1023; ☎ 021 444243; ⏲ 08.30–16.00

2

✈ **BY PLANE** Paraguay is a cheap country to holiday in, but is not a cheap destination to fly to, because there are no direct intercontinental flights. People usually change in São Paulo. Buenos Aires is also a possible option for changing, particularly if you are coming from Australia. The name of the international airport in Asunción is Silvio Pettirossi.

The airfare varies according to season: high season is July, August and December. At present the companies flying from São Paulo are TAM Airlines (*www.tamairlines.com*) and GOL (*www.voegol.com.br*); and from Buenos Aires, Aerolineas Argentinas (*www.aerolineas.com.ar*), Pluna (*www.flypluna.com*), TAM and GOL. GOL is a cheap-flight company, principally for online booking, with all the disadvantages of that; they also fly from Curitiba.

There are also international flights to Asunción from Santiago, with TAM Airlines; from Montevideo, with Pluna (*www.flypluna.com*); from Santa Cruz, with Aerosur (*www.aerosur.com*) and TAM Airlines; from Cochabamba, with TAM Airlines and Aerosur; and from Lima, with TACA (*www.taca.com*).

Travel agents have a history of giving bad advice over bookings to Paraguay. The specialist travel agency in the UK for Latin American flights is Journey Latin America (✆ +44 20 8747 3108; e *sales@journeylatinamerica.co.uk*), who will probably do it better than anyone else. But it is always best to check everything carefully, so here are some factors to consider.

On an intercontinental flight you get a bigger luggage allowance – usually 'two pieces' which on most journeys currently means two bags of usually 23kg each, making 46kg, in addition to hand luggage. On an international flight which is not intercontinental you usually get just 20kg in all. But if you buy the two flights at the same time from the same travel agent it counts as one ticket and your larger luggage allowance applies right through to your final destination. Your bags will be checked in all the way. If you buy the second flight separately your flight will count as two tickets, and you will have to check in your bags again at the intermediate stop (probably São Paulo). You are liable to pay a surcharge if they are overweight, and luggage surcharges are very high indeed, even though you often find that the person on the check-in desk will use their discretion to reduce it in one way or another. A luggage allowance of 20kg may be quite enough for a short holiday, but if you are going for a long time this luggage allowance question may be a key issue. Note that British Airways have recently reduced their luggage allowance on flights to South America from two bags to only one, of 23kg.

Some airlines offer very cheap rates with very low luggage allowances, including some scheduled flights, so make sure you get this information from the start. In recent years, for example, Lufthansa have been undercutting other companies in fares, but if you exceed their luggage allowance of 20kg you get hit very hard in excess luggage charges, so if you buy a few books on your trip you may find the flight has worked out more expensive than its competitors by the time you get home.

Try to avoid the travel agent booking you onto a connecting flight that lands you at Asunción airport at around midnight, unless you have chosen to do that in order to get a cheaper fare. Although you are very unlikely to have a problem, you might not feel comfortable arriving in an unknown third-world city in the middle of the night, especially when you are very tired. The morning flights from São Paulo to Asunción tend to get booked out about three weeks in advance, so you need to book ahead.

If you are flying from the UK one good option at present is to fly with TAM on both legs of the journey, a company which has its origin in the privatisation of the national airline LAP which went bust in 1996. But the flight situation is a rapidly changing scene.

If you are going to more than one place in South America, ask if you are eligible for a Mercosur airpass, which gives you reduced rates. A Mercosur airpass has to be purchased in advance overseas in conjunction with your intercontinental flight, so you need to think about this from the start.

When you arrive in São Paulo If you do not get your second boarding flight at your point of departure but have to pick it up in São Paulo, then the place to get it from is by Gate 2 in Terminal 1, and is marked 'Passageiros em Conexão'. If there is no-one there to help you, do not go and look for staff elsewhere: you will never find anyone. Just wait until the staff come, which will be in sufficient time before a flight.

By plane to Foz Another excellent route is to fly to Foz do Iguaçu, just over the Brazilian border. You will probably fly in with TAM from São Paulo, and the airport code is IGU. It makes sense to fly there because you will undoubtedly want to visit the Iguazú Falls during your visit. You can also do an 'open-jaws' flight, arriving in Foz and leaving from Asunción, or vice versa. Fuller details are given on page 231.

By plane to Posadas Less commonly done, but quite feasible, is to fly to Posadas, just over the Argentinian border. This makes sense if you want to visit Buenos Aires on the same trip, and if your interest is more focused on the Jesuit Reductions than on Asunción. You will arrive on an Aerolineas Argentinas flight from Buenos Aires, and the airport code is PSS.

🚐 BY BUS

From Buenos Aires Only one-third of the people entering Paraguay arrive at the airport. The majority are Paraguayans, coming from Buenos Aires by bus.

If you wish to do the same, you might save about £50 net on the flight – not a great deal more than that by the time you have taken into account all your extra costs. From Buenos Aires to Asunción by bus takes 18 hours and will cost you over £50 in all each way, counting taxis, tips, extra luggage charges and your lunch in Argentina, as well as the fare in a *coche cama* or *semi cama* (see below). You can do the journey out to Paraguay by spending one night on the plane and the next on the bus. But to return from Paraguay, you will almost certainly need a night in Buenos Aires to be sure that delays at the frontier do not cause you to miss your flight, so this cost also needs to be factored into your decision. If you spend a night in a hotel, you may well cancel out the savings you have made on the flight. But if you want to do it, here is how.

From Buenos Aires Ezeiza International Airport you can take the airport bus from the company Manuel Tienda León (*Av E Madero 1299;* ☎ *4315 5115; www.tiendaleon.com.ar; A$45*). Their terminal in Buenos Aires is close to the international bus terminal called Retiro: close enough to walk if you have no luggage, and a short taxi ride with luggage. Alternatively, you can take a taxi from the airport in Buenos Aires to Retiro. You want to alight from your taxi at Puente 5 (Bridge 5) to be close to the international ticket windows 179–202 on the third floor. If you need a porter, expect to pay about A$30 for the use of a trolley (*carrito*) and a tip (*propina*) on top of that. You get 30kg free luggage allowance on the bus, and for an extra 20kg you are charged about A$20. You are likely to arrive in Buenos Aires in the early morning, and to leave from Retiro in the afternoon, to arrive in Asunción the following morning, so if you need to have lunch while waiting for your bus, allow for that too: there are plenty of eating places in Retiro. On the buses food is generally provided. (This is different to the buses from São Paulo, which stop for people to get out and eat in roadside restaurants.) If you need

Timetables are always changing, but even an old timetable is some help in knowing what to expect in terms of companies, frequencies and journey times.

COMPANY	TEL NUMBER	DEPART BUENOS AIRES
Crucero del Norte	+54 11 4315 6523	12.30, 13.00, 13.30, 15.45, 17.30*, 19.00, 19.30 all daily
Encarnacena	+54 11 43132393	18.00 daily
Expreso Rio Parana	+54 11 4313 2402	16.00 daily & 20.00 Sun
Expreso Sur	+54 11 4315 6524	13.00 Wed, Fri & Sun
Godoy	+54 11 4312 3976	14.00 & 16.00 daily
N Sra de la As	+54 11 4311 7666	13.30 daily except Mon, 14.00 daily except Mon, 15.00* Sat & Sun, 16.30* Mon, 18.00* Wed & Thu, 18.30 Mon, Wed, Fri & Sun, 20.00 Tue & Sat
Santaniana	+54 11 4315 8740	17.30 Mon, Tue, Fri, Sat & Sun, 19.00 Wed & Thu
Yacyreta	+54 11 4315 3746	17.00 Mon, Fri, Sat & Sun

COMPANY	TEL NUMBER	DEPART ASUNCIÓN
Crucero del Norte	+595 21 559087	13.30 daily, 14.00 Sun, 14.30 daily except Sun, 16.30 daily, 16.45 daily, 17.00* Wed & Fri, 17.15 daily, 18.00* daily except Wed & Fri, 19.00 daily
Encarnacena	+595 21 551745	09.00 daily
Expreso Rio Parana	+595 21 551733	10.00 daily, 16.00 Mon, Fri, Sat & Sun
Expreso Sur	+595 21 557766	13.00 Tue, Thu & Sat
Godoy	+595 21 558795	15.00 & 16.00 daily
N Sra de la As	+595 21 2891000	13.30 daily except Mon, 13.40 daily except Mon, 14.00* Sun, 15.00* Tue, Wed, Thu & Sat, 16.00 Mon, Fri & Sat, 16.30 Tue, Thu & Sat
Santaniana	+595 21 551607	12.30 Sat, Sun, Mon & Thu, 14.30 Wed, 15.00 Tue & Fri
Yacyreta	+595 21 551725	12.30 Thu, Fri, Sat & Sun

* indicates a better quality service

to leave luggage, there are lockers and also a staffed left-luggage place on all three floors at Retiro.

On the way back, Manuel Tienda León can pick you up with your luggage from your hotel if you pay a bit extra.

The bus journey from Buenos Aires to Asunción will cost between A$115–270 (Gs150,000–350,000), depending on what class you choose. *Común* is also called *convencional* and has ordinary bus seats, which incline a bit; *semi cama* ('half bed') is also called *diferencial* and the seats incline more; in *coche cama* they incline more still and you get a blanket and a pillow; *cama total* is also called *ejecutivo* and the seats incline practically to the horizontal and you get a blanket and pillow.

You can pay by credit card in Buenos Aires, and in Asunción for the return journey; Nuestra Señora de la Asunción is the only company to accept credit cards and telephone bookings instead of insisting on cash, but others may follow. Retiro bus terminal is well provided with telephones, internet (middle floor near Puente 2), shops and cash machines (top floor near Puente 2 and middle floor near Puentes 1 and 3). Asunción bus terminal has a cash machine, in the middle of the ground floor, which only accepts Visa cards. It has telephones near the cash machine.

Nuestra Señora de la Asunción is the same company as Chevalier, so their buses may have either name. Nuestra Señora de la Asunción and Godoy have *depositos* where they can receive luggage earlier in the day, but Crucero del Norte does not. You will be expected to pay a small tip for each bag as it is loaded in the bus (A$1).

Accommodation near Buenos Aries airport

Posada de las Aguilas Eagle Inn; José Hernández 128, Barrio Uno, Aeropuerto Ezeiza; ✆ +54 11 4480 9637/0159; e info@posadadelasaguilas.com.ar; www.posadadelasaguilas.com.ar. If you need to spend a night in Buenos Aires on your journey, with handy access to the airport, then this is an excellent place to stay. All the comfort you could want but with the personal feel of a small family hotel. See the website (under 'Contact') for a map of how to get there: they claim it is only 1min from the airport (it cannot be more than 5) but you do not pass it on the main road. Cable television, Wi-Fi, pool, good wines, & offers tours to sites of Buenos Aires including tango shows. Transfers to & from the airport are included in the price. A place like this, once discovered, gets booked out, so reserve in advance. Prices are reasonable (though seem high compared with Paraguayan prices). Curiously, there do not seem to be any other airport hotels near Ezeiza. $$$$

From São Paulo You can also save on a flight by taking the bus from São Paulo. This has the advantage that the flight to São Paulo is often cheaper than the flight to Buenos Aires, because a lot of planes touch down in São Paulo before going on to Buenos Aires. But it is a longer bus journey – about 22 hours. As in Buenos Aires, you are likely to arrive in São Paulo by plane in the early morning (at the international airport Guarulhos), allowing you plenty of time to go to the bus terminal, Rodoviária Tietê (✆ 6221 2900/9977), and buy your ticket in good time for the bus to Paraguay, which will leave in the evening, around 18.00. Then you can put your bags in left luggage, and enjoy a day in São Paulo. The bus terminal is on the metro line so it is easy to get around.

Tietê is a 40-minute ride away in a shuttle bus. Turn right when you leave the terminal and look for the 'Airport Bus Service': they leave at least hourly. If you are penny-pinching and have your luggage on your back, there is a cheaper way to get to Tietê, by taking a bus from the airport to the metro station Tatuapé, and taking a metro from there to Tietê.

When you get to Tietê with your luggage you will find there are no trolleys, and the only lifts from the platforms to the first floor are at the far ends (before platform 1 or after platform 50). The left luggage (Guarda-Volumes) is back on the ground floor, but you have to go up to the first floor and then down again to the ground floor, but this time the lift is in the middle. There is no direct access to Guarda Volumes from the platforms, but a porter will bring your luggage to your platform 15 minutes before your bus leaves. If you are arriving by taxi, you can ask it to stop right by the Guarda-Volumes. There are luggage lockers upstairs, if your bag is not very big. There are also cash machines and internet.

The best company for the journey to Paraguay is the Brazilian Pluma (*Tietê:* ✆ 0800 6460300; *Asunción:* ✆ 021 551758). Once a week there is a *coche cama* (leaving São Paulo on Friday at 18.00) but you pay almost double for it. But every day there is a *semi cama*, which is almost as comfortable; it leaves every day at 18.30. The fare is Rs120 or Gs250,000. At the Asunción end you have to pay in cash. The other

For telephone numbers see box on page 47.

COUNTRY	CITIES	PRINCIPAL BUS COMPANIES
Argentina	Buenos Aires, Cordoba, Corrientes, etc	Crucero del Norte, Río Paraná, Encarnacena, Expreso Sur, Godoy, Nuestra Señora de la Asunción, La Santaniana, Yacyreta etc
Bolivia	Santa Cruz	Yacyretá, Pycasú, Río Paraguay, Stel Turismo
Brazil	Rio de Janeiro, São Paulo, Porto Alegre, Florianopolis, Foz, Brasilia, etc	Pluma, Brújula, Caterinense, Nuestra Señora de la Asunción, Rysa, Transcontinental etc
Chile	Santiago	Pullman del Sur (09.00 Tue & Fri; dep Santiago 13.00 Tue & Fri; 30hrs; Gs400,000)
Peru	Lima connection to Ecuador, Colombia, Venezuela	Río Paraguay
Uruguay	Montevideo	Brújula

companies making the journey are the Paraguayan companies Rysa and Brújula, which are just fractionally cheaper. They all leave São Paulo in the early evening.

The extra expenses you have to allow for are the airport bus (R$28) or taxi to Tietê (R$50), the left luggage, the metro, perhaps a map of São Paulo, a porter, your food during the day in São Paulo, and – unlike the bus from Buenos Aires – your meals on the journey, which you have to buy in the half-hour stops they give you. If your bus leaves at 18.30, you are likely to stop for supper around 22.00, for breakfast around 06.30, and reach Foz do Iguaçu around 10.00, where you may have to change buses if you are on Pluma, so that their best buses are not subjected to Paraguayan roads. It will be around midday by the time you have passed the frontier; then you stop for a late lunch in Coronel Oviedo and arrive at Asunción about 18.00. (Paraguayan time is usually one hour behind.)

Going back in the other direction, Pluma leaves the Asunción Terminal at 10.00. On Sunday there is an additional *coche cama* service that leaves at 11.00.

From Bolivia Buses from Bolivia to Asunción leave from Santa Cruz, going through Villa Montes *en route*, near the Paraguayan border. This journey is only for the hardy or the impoverished. Villa Montes is reputed to be the hottest and most mosquito-infested town in Bolivia: the hotels there are cheap and grim and the places to eat (in the main plaza) are basic. Santa Cruz is a much bigger and much more civilized place, but it is a long drive from there to Villa Montes, before you even begin on the the Chaco desert.

Stel Turismo leaves Santa Cruz daily at 20.00; Yacyreta leaves Santa Cruz at 20.00 too, but not on Sunday or Monday, and only if there are enough passengers on the other days. Pycasú leaves Santa Cruz on Wednesday at 20.00. In Asunción, the office of Stel Turismo is not in the Terminal but diagonally opposite it; however, the buses leave from the Terminal at 20.00, seven days a week. Yacyreta leaves the Asunción Terminal 20.00 on Mondays, Wednesdays and Saturdays. Pycasú leaves on Saturday at 19.30.

The quoted time to Villa Montes is 17–18 hours and to Santa Cruz 20–23 hours, but this is extremely variable. For telephone numbers of the bus companies see page 47. The fare is approximately Gs200,000 to Villa Montes, and Gs230,000 to Santa Cruz. The last stop within Paraguay is Mariscal Estigarribia, at Migraciones in that town (see *Chapter 12*, page 303).

BY BOAT

Ferries from Argentina There are a number of ways that you can cross from Argentina to Paraguay across one or other of the three river boundaries – the Río Pilcomayo, the Río Paraguay and the Río Paraná – in addition to the principal bus routes Clorinda to Falcón (see *Chapter 12*, page 295), and Encarnación to Posadas (see *Chapter 6*, page 204).

Over the Río Pilcomayo there is a bridge linking General Belgrano, Argentina, with **General Bruguez**, Paraguay; this is about 130km upriver from Asunción, in a very remote part of the Chaco.

On the Río Paraguay from Clorinda, Argentina, is a ferry that comes into **Puerto Itá Enramada** on the edge of Lambaré, just to the south of the Cerro Lambaré. The ferries leave on weekdays every half-hour between 08.00 and 18.30 from Argentina, and between 06.30 and 17.00 from Paraguay. (Note that Argentina is one hour ahead, except in the Paraguayan summertime: in 2009 Argentina decided not to change its clocks for summertime.) At weekends there are only seven crossings a day between 08.30 and 17.30 from Argentina, and between 07.00 and 16.00 from Paraguay.

On the Río Paraguay there is a well-established ferry route from Formosa, Argentina to **Alberdi**, Paraguay; this is a place where smuggling is difficult to detect, and it is also reputed to have been the route used by former politicians fleeing Argentina after the end of the military dictatorship.

Then there is Pilar to Puerto Cano (see *Chapter 7*, page 217), and Paso de Patria, Paraguay, to Paso de la Patria, Argentina (see *Chapter 7*, page 221).

On the Río Paraná there are ferries linking **Bella Vista** with Corpus (see *Chapter 6*, page 205), and linking **Presidente Franco** with Puerto Iguazú (see *Chapter 9*, page 226).

OVERLAND There are surprisingly few crossing points overland into Paraguay. Between Argentina and Paraguay there is always a river to cross, and between Bolivia and Paraguay there is the almost impassible Chaco desert (but see above on taking a bus across the Chaco).

Between Brazil and Paraguay, from Salto del Guairá southwards there is the River Paraná to cross (with bridge crossings at Foz do Iguaçu into Ciudad del Este, and at Guairá into Salto del Guairá). Continuing north from there, there is the barrier of the *cordillera*, which again makes crossing difficult. It continues until you reach Pedro Juan Caballero, where it is so easy to cross to and from Ponta Porã, Brazil, that it happens to you in the middle of the street before you have realised.

After that the frontier follows the Río Apa, but you can cross over the river from Bela Vista, Brazil, to Bella Vista, Amambay (not to be confused with Bella Vista, Hapúa). On the Río Paraguay, Paraguayan boats will stop at Porto Mortinho, Brazil, which is another easy way to get from one country to the other.

HEALTH *with Dr Felicity Nicholson*

Needless to say, **travel insurance** is important in the third world, to cover for health problems, as well as for accidents, theft, loss of luggage and mishaps generally.

For safe travelling in Paraguay you should consider visiting your GP or a travel clinic several weeks before departure. The first human cases of yellow fever for 30 years occurred in Paraguay in 2008. The World Health Organization (WHO) and Nathnac in the UK recommend yellow fever vaccination for all areas including the capital. The vaccine takes ten days to be fully effective and lasts for ten years. It may not be suitable for everyone, so make sure this is fully discussed during your consultation. A yellow fever certificate, or if the vaccine is not suitable then an exemption certificate, will be provided. The formal certificate will allow you to cross borders into other South American countries. An exemption certificate cannot guarantee entry but is usually accepted.

It is wise to be up to date on tetanus, polio and diphtheria (now given as an all-in-one vaccine, Revaxis, that lasts for ten years), and hepatitis A. Hepatitis A vaccine (Havrix Monodose or Avaxim) comprises two injections given about a year apart. The course costs about £100, but may be available on the NHS; it protects for 25 years and can be administered even close to the time of departure. Hepatitis B vaccination should be considered for longer trips (two months or more) or for those working with children or in situations where contact with blood is likely. Three injections are needed for the best protection and can be given over a three-week period if time is short for those aged 16 or over. Longer schedules give more sustained protection and are therefore preferred if time allows. Hepatitis A vaccine can also be given as a combination with hepatitis B as Twinrix, though two doses are needed at least seven days apart to be effective for the hepatitis A component, and three doses are needed for the hepatitis B. Again this schedule is only suitable for those aged 16 or over.

The newer injectable typhoid vaccines (eg: Typhim Vi) last for three years and are about 85% effective. Oral capsules (Vivotif) may also be available for those aged six and over. Three capsules over five days gives protection lasting for approximately three years but may be less effective than the injectable forms. They should be encouraged unless the traveller is leaving within a few days for a trip of a week or less, when the vaccine would not be effective in time. Rabies vaccine may also be recommended for longer trips or those working with animals.

There is a risk of **malaria**, mainly in the benign form, along the southeastern border with Brazil. The risk is much greater in rural and jungle areas. There is only minimal risk at the Iguazú Falls but for those going outside the resort into rural areas then prophylaxis will be recommended. Chloroquine is the drug of choice. It is both cheap and easy to take and has been used for many years quite safely. It is not suitable for those with epilepsy, bad psoriasis, some heart conditions, myasthenia gravis and for those with severe liver disease. When chloroquine is contraindicated then paludrine may be suitable. Preventing mosquito bites by wearing long-sleeved clothing and trousers, applying insect repellents containing 50–55% DEET to exposed skin and sleeping under impregnated bed nets will all help to prevent disease.

Dengue fever is far more common than malaria. This mosquito-borne disease may mimic malaria but there is no prophylactic medication against it. The mosquitoes that carry dengue fever bite during the daytime, so it is worth applying repellent if you see any mosquitoes around. Symptoms include strong headaches, rashes, excruciating joint and muscle pains and high fever. Viral fevers usually last about a week or so and are not normally fatal. Complete rest and paracetamol are the usual treatment; plenty of fluids also help. Some patients are given an intravenous drip to keep them from dehydrating. It is especially important to protect yourself if you have had dengue fever before, since a second infection with a different strain can result in the potentially fatal dengue haemorrhagic fever.

RABIES Rabies is carried by all mammals including bats, and is passed on to humans through a bite, scratch or a lick of an open wound. You must always assume any animal is rabid, and seek medical help as soon as possible. Meanwhile scrub the wound with soap under a running tap or while pouring water from a jug.

Find a reasonably clear-looking source of water (but at this stage the quality of the water is not important), then pour on a strong iodine or alcohol solution of gin, whisky or rum. This helps stop the rabies virus entering the body and will guard against wound infections, including tetanus.

Pre-exposure vaccination for rabies is ideally advised for everyone, but is particularly important if you intend to have contact with animals and/or are likely to be more than 24 hours away from medical help. Ideally three doses should be taken over a minimum of 21 days, though even taking one or two doses of vaccine is better than none at all. Contrary to popular belief these vaccinations are relatively painless.

If you are bitten, scratched or licked over an open wound by a sick animal, then post-exposure prophylaxis should be given as soon as possible, though it is never too late to seek help, as the incubation period for rabies can be very long. Those who have not been immunised will need a full course of injections. The vast majority of travel health advisors, including WHO, recommend rabies immunoglobulin (RIG), but this product is expensive (around US$800) and may be hard to come by – another reason why pre-exposure vaccination should be encouraged.

Tell the doctor if you have had pre-exposure vaccine, as this should change the treatment you receive. And remember that, if you do contract rabies, mortality is 100% and death from rabies is probably one of the worst ways to go.

TICKBITE FEVER Although they're uncommon in Paraguay, there are a variety of illnesses that are transmitted by ticks in the Americas. Tickbite fever is a flu-like illness that can easily be treated with doxycycline, but as there can be some serious complications it is important to visit a doctor.

Ticks should ideally be removed as soon as possible, as leaving them on the body increases the chance of infection. They should be removed with special tick tweezers that can be bought in good travel shops. Failing that you can use your fingernails: grasp the tick as close to your body as possible and pull steadily and firmly away at right angles to your skin. The tick will then come away complete, as long as you do not jerk or twist. If possible, douse the wound with alcohol (any spirit will do) or iodine. Irritants (eg: Olbas oil) or lit cigarettes are to be discouraged since they can cause the ticks to regurgitate and therefore increase the risk of disease. It is best to get a travelling companion to check you for ticks; if you are travelling with small children, remember to check their heads, and particularly behind the ears.

Spreading redness around the bite and/or fever and/or aching joints after a bite imply that you have an infection that requires antibiotic treatment, so seek advice.

PIQUE If you get little black flecks in your feet that look like dirt or a small splinter, but are irritating, then you have got *pique* - a little mite that burrows under the skin and lays eggs. It is easily treated: dig out the *pique* with a sterilised needle, but make sure you get it all out, or in a few days you will have a blister filled with a white liquid which has the eggs in it, and it will spread. You can dribble iodine (*yodo*) or clear alcohol (*alcohol rectificado*) over the wound (both easily obtainable in *farmacias*) and keep the wound covered so it does not get infected.

SNAKEBITE Snakes rarely attack unless provoked, and bites in travellers are unusual. You are less likely to get bitten if you wear stout shoes and long trousers when in the bush. Most snakes are harmless and even venomous species will dispense venom in only about half of their bites. If bitten, then, you are unlikely to have received venom; remembering this may help you to stay calm. Many so-called first-aid techniques do more harm than good: cutting into the wound is harmful; tourniquets are dangerous; suction and electrical inactivation devices do not work. The only treatment is antivenom. In case of a bite that you fear may have been from a venomous snake:

- Try to keep calm – it is likely that no venom has been dispensed.
- Prevent movement of the bitten limb by applying a splint.
- Keep the bitten limb BELOW heart height to slow the spread of any venom.
- If you have a crêpe bandage, wrap it around the whole limb (eg: all the way from the toes to the thigh), as tight as you would for a sprained ankle or a muscle pull.
- Evacuate to a hospital that has antivenom.

And remember:
NEVER give aspirin; you may take paracetamol, which is safe.
NEVER cut or suck the wound.
DO NOT apply ice packs.
DO NOT apply potassium permanganate.

If the offending snake can be captured without risk of someone else being bitten, take this to show the doctor – but beware since even a decapitated head is able to bite.

LONG-HAUL FLIGHTS, CLOTS AND DVT   *Dr Felicity Nicholson*

Any prolonged immobility, including travel by land or air, can result in deep-vein thrombosis (DVT) with the risk of embolus to the lungs. Certain factors can increase the risk and these include:

- Having a previous clot or a close relative with a history of clots
- Being over 40, with increased risk in over 80s
- Recent major operation or varicose-veins surgery
- Cancer
- Stroke
- Heart disease
- Obesity
- Pregnancy
- Hormone therapy
- Heavy smoking
- Severe varicose veins
- Being tall (over 6ft/1.8m) or short (under 5ft/1.5m)

A deep-vein thrombosis causes painful swelling and redness of the calf or sometimes the thigh. It is only dangerous if a clot travels to the lungs (pulmonary embolus). Symptoms of a pulmonary embolus (PE) – which commonly starts three to ten days after a long flight – include chest pain, shortness of breath and sometimes coughing up small amounts of blood. Anyone who thinks that they might have a DVT needs to see a doctor immediately.

PREVENTION OF DVT
Keep mobile before and during the flight; move around every couple of hours
Drink plenty of fluids during the flight
Avoid taking sleeping pills and excessive tea, coffee and alcohol
Consider wearing flight socks or support stockings (see *www.legshealth.com*)

If you think you are at increased risk of a clot, ask your doctor if it is safe to travel.

PERSONAL FIRST-AID KIT

A minimal kit contains:

- A good drying antiseptic, eg: iodine or potassium permanganate (don't take antiseptic cream)
- A few small dressings (plasters or Band-Aids)
- Suncream
- Insect repellent; anti-malarial tablets; impregnated bed-net or permethrin spray
- Aspirin or paracetamol
- Antifungal cream (eg: Canesten)
- Ciprofloxacin or norfloxacin, for severe diarrhoea
- Tinidazole for giardia or amoebic dysentery
- Antibiotic eye drops for sore, 'gritty', stuck-together eyes (conjunctivitis)
- A pair of fine pointed tweezers (to remove splinters, the thorn of the *cocotero* tree, etc)
- Alcohol-based hand rub or bar of soap in plastic box
- Condoms or femidoms
- Digital thermometer (for those going to remote areas)

TRAVEL CLINICS AND HEALTH INFORMATION

A full list of current travel clinic websites worldwide is available on www.istm.org/. For other journey preparation information, consult www.nathnac.org/ds/map_world.aspx. Information about various medications may be found on www.netdoctor.co.uk/travel.

UK

Berkeley Travel Clinic 32 Berkeley St, London W1J 8EL (near Green Park tube station); ☏ 020 7629 6233; ⊕ 10.00–18.00 Mon–Fri, 10.00–15.00 Sat

Cambridge Travel Clinic 41 Hills Rd, Cambridge CB2 1NT; ☏ 01223 367362; f 01223 368021; e enquiries@travelcliniccambridge.co.uk; www.travelcliniccambridge.co.uk; ⊕ 10.00–16.00 Mon, Tue & Sat, 12.00–19.00 Wed & Thu, 11.00–18.00 Fri

Edinburgh Travel Health Clinic 14 East Preston St, Newington, Edinburgh EH8 9QA; ☏ 0131 667 1030; www.edinburghtravelhealthclinic.co.uk; ⊕ 09.00–19.00 Mon–Wed, 09.00–18.00 Thu & Fri. Travel vaccinations & advice on all aspects of malaria prevention. All current UK-prescribed anti-malaria tablets in stock.

Fleet Street Travel Clinic 29 Fleet St, London EC4Y 1AA; ☏ 020 7353 5678; www.fleetstreetclinic.com; ⊕ 08.45–17.30 Mon–Fri. Injections, travel products & latest advice.

Hospital for Tropical Diseases Travel Clinic Mortimer Market Centre, 2nd Flr, Capper St (off Tottenham Ct Rd), London WC1E 6AU; ☏ 020 7388 9600; www.thehtd.org; ⊕ 09.00–16.00. Offers consultations & advice, & is able to provide all necessary drugs & vaccines for travellers. Runs a healthline (☏ 020

7950 7799) for country-specific information & health hazards. Also stocks nets, water purification equipment & personal protection measures. Travellers who have returned from the tropics & are unwell, with fever or bloody diarrhoea, can attend the walk-in emergency clinic at the hospital without an appointment.

MASTA (Medical Advisory Service for Travellers Abroad) London School of Hygiene & Tropical Medicine, Keppel St, London WC1 7HT; ☏ 09068 224100; e enquiries@masta.org; www.masta-travel-health.com. This is a premium-line number, charged at 60p per minute. For a fee, they will provide an individually tailored health brief, with up-to-date information on how to stay healthy, inoculations & what to take.

MASTA pre-travel clinics ☏ 01276 685040. Call or check http://www.masta-travel-health.com/travel-clinic.aspx for the nearest; there are currently 30 in Britain. They also sell malaria prophylaxis, memory cards, treatment kits, bednets, net treatment kits, etc.

NHS travel website www.fitfortravel.nhs.uk. Provides country-by-country advice on immunisation & malaria prevention, plus details of recent developments & a list of relevant health organisations.

Nomad Travel Stores Flagship store: 3–4 Wellington Terr, Turnpike Lane, London N8 0PX; ☏ 020 8889

7014; f 020 8889 9528;
e turnpike@nomadtravel.co.uk;
www.nomadtravel.co.uk; walk in or appointments
⊕ 09.15–17.00 daily with late night Thu. 6 stores
in total country wide: 3 in London, Bristol,
Southampton, Manchester. As well as dispensing health
advice, Nomad stocks mosquito nets & other anti-bug
devices, & an excellent range of adventure travel gear.
InterHealth Travel Clinic 111 Westminster Bridge Rd,
London SE1 7HR; ✆ 020 7902 9000;
e info@interhealth.org.uk; www.interhealth.org.uk;

⊕ 08.30–17.30 Mon–Fri. Competitively priced, one-
stop travel health service by appointment only.
Trailfinders Immunisation Centre 194 Kensington High
St, London W8 7RG; ✆ 020 7938 3999;
www.trailfinders.com/travelessentials/travelclinic.htm;
⊕ 09.00–17.00 Mon–Wed & Fri, 09.00–18.00 Thu,
10.00–17.15 Sat. No appointment necessary.
Travelpharm www.travelpharm.com. Their website
offers up-to-date guidance on travel-related health &
has a range of medications available through its
online mini-pharmacy.

Irish Republic
Tropical Medical Bureau Grafton St Medical Centre,
Grafton Bldgs, 34 Grafton St, Dublin 2; ✆ 1 671

9200; www.tmb.ie. Has a useful website specific to
tropical destinatisons.

USA
Centers for Disease Control 1600 Clifton Rd, Atlanta,
GA 30333; ✆ (800) 232 4636 or (800) 232 6348;
e cdcinfo@cdc.gov; www.cdc.gov/travel. The central
source of travel information in the USA. Each
summer they publish the invaluable *Health
Information for International Travel.*

IAMAT (International Association for Medical
Assistance to Travelers) 1623 Military Rd, #279
Niagara Falls, NY 14304-1745; ✆ 716 754 4883;
e info@iamat.org; www.iamat.org. A non-profit
organisation with free membership that provides lists
of English-speaking doctors abroad.

Canada
IAMAT (International Association for Medical
Assistance to Travellers) Suite 1, 1287 St Clair Av W,
Toronto, Ontario M6E 1B8; ✆ 416 652 0137;
www.iamat.org

TMVC Suite 314, 1030 W Georgia St, Vancouver, BC
V6E 2Y3; ✆ 905 648 1112; e info@tmvc.com;
www.tmvc.com. One-stop medical clinic for all your
international travel medicine & vaccination needs.

Australia, New Zealand, Thailand
TMVC (Travel Doctors Group) ✆ 1300 65 88 44;
www.tmvc.com.au. 22 clinics in Australia, New
Zealand & Thailand, including: *Auckland* Canterbury
Arcade, 170 Queen St, Auckland; ✆ 9 373 3531;
Brisbane 75a Astor Terr, Spring Hill, Brisbane QLD
4000; ✆ (07) 3815 6900;
e brisbane@traveldoctor.com.au;

Melbourne Dr Sonny Lau, 393 Little Bourke St, 2nd
Flr, Melbourne, VIC 3000; ✆ (03) 9935 8100;
e melbourne@traveldoctor.com.au; *Sydney* Dr
Mandy Hu, Dymocks Bldg, 7th Flr, 428 George St,
Sydney NSW 2000; ✆ 2 9221 7133; f 2 9221 8401
IAMAT PO Box 5049, Christchurch 5, New Zealand;
www.iamat.org

South Africa
SAA-Netcare Travel Clinics e travelinfo@netcare.co.za
www.travelclinic.co.za. 12 clinics throughout South
Africa.
TMVC NHC Health Centre, Cnr Beyers Naude &

Waugh Northcliff; ✆ 0 11 214 9030;
e traveldoctor@wtmconline.com;
www.traveldoctor.co.za. Consult the website for details
of clinics.

Switzerland
IAMAT 57 Chemin des Voirets, 1212 Grand-Lancy,
Geneva; e info@iamat.org; www.iamat.org

MOSQUITO CONTROL Mosquitoes are not usually a nuisance by day (unless you go
somewhere like the Pantanal). At night they can be a menace and stop you sleeping,
and the most common way Paraguayans deal with them is to use a **fan** or **air
conditioning**. (The mosquitoes cannot fly while the air is circulating.) Some

people have metallic netting on the windows of their houses to stop the mosquitoes getting in.

You will probably have **insect repellent** to put on the skin when needed, but this never offers complete protection. You may find it more effective to use a **plug-in** insect repellent indoors – which are readily available in Paraguay (*un enchufe contra mosquitos*) – and a **spiral** outside – which again can be easily bought locally (*un espiral contra mosquitos*). The way a spiral works is that it burns very slowly and the mosquitoes go away from the smell; so if you use it inside you should leave the window open, so that the mosquitoes can get out and the fumes can get out too. You should not sleep with either a spiral or a plug-in closer than 2m to your face.

Some Paraguayans use **mosquito nets**, but most do not. They can be bought in Paraguay in the simple form of a light circle of bamboo with nylon netting (usually in garish colours) but they are not impregnated with insecticide. Paraguayans tend to say they feel restricted inside a net, and very few hotels provide them. But there is no better protection than the barrier method, and if other methods have failed it is a great relief to be able to drop a net over you when you get bitten in the night, and so complete the night undisturbed. There is a technique to using a net: it should be tucked in all around so the mosquitoes do not get in underneath; and if your toe or arm touches the net then it is likely to be bitten through it. But a net without a means of stringing it up is useless: one of those stretchy travel clothes lines with hooks on the end might be useful here.

You can use an **insecticide spray** against mosquitoes, but it needs a bit of organisation to use it correctly. The Paraguayan sprays – usually known by the brand name Mapex – are very strong, so it is more than usually important to air the room thoroughly before sleeping in it. You should in any case close the windows of your bedroom before dusk, as that is when most mosquitoes enter, so you need to be around at the right times: spray about an hour before dusk with the window shut. Wait outside the room for at least 15 minutes. Then go in and open the window and put the fan on, to drive out the toxin and at the same time discourage mosquitoes from entering. Then close the window, before it begins to get dark, and do not open it again until it is light the next morning.

EATING, DRINKING AND HEALTH A lot of people have been put off healthy salads in Latin America by the slogan 'cook it, peel it or forget it', and are condemned to drink sugary bottled fizzy drinks when there are delicious fresh fruit juices available instead. There is no need to avoid local water when it comes from a central system where it has been treated, which is usually the case. However, it is not a good idea to drink water from wells: sometimes this can make you very unpleasantly ill, for up to a week, and if you are not sure about where the water in a fruit juice has come from, it is better to be safe than sorry. (In Paraguay, a *jugo de fruta* always has water added to the squeezed juice.) You can buy bottled mineral water all over the country, though it is not available as readily as fizzy drinks.

There are plenty of cheap foods on sale in the street and on buses which it is quite unnecessary to avoid, *empanadas* and *chipas* among them. It is up to you whether you want to accept the invitation to share *tereré* with the local people. The risk of infection from the shared *bombilla* is very small, because metal does not readily harbour germs, but the risk is not non-existent. Fresh milk – what Paraguayans call *leche de vaca* ('cow's milk') as opposed to long-life milk – must be boiled (or pasteurised) before drinking, but this is not anything you need to worry about as no-one is going to serve you milk that has not been boiled.

That said, be sensible and ensure that the food is properly cooked. Do not eat food that is lukewarm when it is meant to be piping hot. If you do get a bout of diarrhoea then it will usually settle down over 24 to 48 hours. Make sure you rehydrate yourself with plenty of fluids and rebalance salts, with rehydration sachets such as Electrolade. Alternatively you can make your own with a bottle of Coca-Cola and a three finger pinch of salt added to it. If the diarrhoea doesn't settle or you have a fever, blood and/or slime in the stool then you most often need antibiotics. Seek medical help as soon as you can. If this is not possible then ciprofloxacin or norfloxacin usually work well in this situation so if you are going to be somewhere remote then you might consider carrying them. They are only available on prescription in the UK.

SAFETY

As is well known, where there is poverty, the crime rate is higher. In Asunción and the other cities, particularly Ciudad del Este and Pedro Juan Caballero, you need to be careful, and take a few simple precautions.

Do not accept an offer of 'Taxi?' from someone who approaches you in the airport or bus terminal, and leads you to a private car. Most likely, the only harm you will come to is to find yourself with someone who does not know the city well, and will waste time looking for the address you are going to, although it could lead to a more serious assault. Some of the porters at Asunción Airport have been known to try to get work for their relatives this way, by fixing 'taxis' for the people whose bags they are carrying. Go to the taxi rank, where all the drivers are known and registered, or to a window which says 'Taxis'. In the case of Asunción Airport, the official taxis are no longer the yellow ones that you find in the rest of the city, but supposedly smarter cars that have been selected for their greater comfort, but are not recognisable as taxis. There are officials at the door who are responsible for seeing that travellers get directed to an approved taxi.

Do not go into the poorest areas of cities, even by day and even with a companion, unless that companion is someone known to the local people. This applies to the *bañados* in Asunción – the areas along the riverbank which get periodically flooded, and where there are only hovels. It also applies to a lesser extent to some of the adjacent barrios to the *bañados* such as Barrio Republicano.

Some people make a point of always travelling by taxi after dark, in the cities. This is a matter of individual decision, and others consider it excessively cautious and expensive.

Avoid crossing open spaces, especially at night: for example do not walk across the Plaza Uruguaya in Asunción at night – walk around it. It is probably better not to go for a walk in the Parque Caballero in Asunción even by day. Avoid unpopulated streets, or at least be alert to who might be following you, crossing the road to avoid other isolated male walkers. Thieves work alone sometimes, but often they operate in groups.

Be careful in public buses: a lot of theft occurs in them. There is no need to avoid taking buses, but be cautious if the bus is either very full or empty. Although it is unlikely you will have any trouble, be aware that from time to time problems can occur. Pockets can be picked, handbags can be sliced into with sharp knives, and jewellery can be snatched from your neck, so for extra safety put pendants inside your clothes. Do not expect the other passengers or driver necessarily to assist you in the case of an attempted theft: they may be at risk of reprisals.

Do not wear a money belt around your waist, unless it is well hidden and does not protrude. Otherwise all it does is announce to the thief where the valuables are, and make an assault more likely. Paraguayans will hide their money in their socks or bra rather than in a money belt.

Split up your money, so if you are robbed you have at least a little emergency money in another place. It is a good idea, also, to carry a smaller amount of money in a secondary wallet, that you can hand over with less serious loss if assaulted. Paraguayan thieves are not usually interested in credit cards and do not know how to use them: all they want is cash, jewellery, mobile phones and other electrical devices.

If you are held up at knifepoint or with a gun or by a group, do not resist. Your life and health are of more value than your money and holiday.

NOTES FOR DISABLED TRAVELLERS *Mark Davidson*

Unlike many countries in South America, Paraguay has done virtually nothing to improve the welfare of people with disabilities. As with other countries in the region, there are a large number of people lacking basic health care.

PLANNING AND BOOKING At present there are no tour operators who specifically deal with wheelchair-bound travellers wishing to visit to Paraguay. It is possible that some companies may be able to offer trips suited to your individual needs.

GETTING THERE Silvio Pettirossi International Airport at Asunción has very limited facilities for those in wheelchairs. The airport at Ciudad del Este may have a lower standard of facilities than the international airport.

ACCOMMODATION Some of the larger hotels in Asunción have facilities for those with disabilities and those in wheelchairs such as the Hotel Chaco (*Caballero;* ✆ *0 21 492 066; see page 69*).

SIGHTSEEING Many of the streets in Asunción are in need of repair so any wheelchair users will have to proceed with care when travelling around the city. Some of the walkways that allow you to view the Iguassu Falls are wheelchair accessible but it is advisable to check beforehand.

As a result of Paraguay's infrastructure, it would not be that easy for anyone with a disability to get around the country unaided. Seeking information in advance will be a necessity if you want to see some of the nation's rarer species of animal and plant life.

TRAVEL INSURANCE There are a few specialised companies that deal with travel to Paraguay. A number of operators deal with pre-existing medical conditions such as Travelbility (✆ *0845 338 1638; www.travelbility.co.uk*) and Medici Travel Insurance (✆ *0845 880 0168; www.medicitravel.com*).

The main hospitals in the country are located in the capital, such as Centro Médico Bautista, and have limited facilities for those with disabilities. Unfortunately, there is a lack of hospitals in more remote areas and those that do have medical facilities are poorly equipped in comparison to the main one due to the poor economy.

FURTHER INFORMATION The tourist information office for Paraguay may be able to provide more information for those with disabilities and they can be contacted via the website www.paraguay.gov.py.

A good website for further information on planning and booking any accessible holiday is www.able-travel.com, which provides many tips and links to travel resources worldwide.

Bradt Travel Guides' title *Access Africa – Safaris for People with Limited Mobility* is aimed at safari-goers, but is packed with advice and resources that will be useful for all disabled adventure travellers.

All of this applies to the cities. When you go to the *campo* you need have no fear of going to isolated areas or poor communities.

WOMEN TRAVELLERS There are no special rules for women travellers; although Paraguayan men are 'hotter' than European men, there is no particular safety risk for women, and it is not necessary for women to be escorted or to dress differently than they would at home.

WHAT TO TAKE

The only foreign **mobile phones** that can be relied upon to work in Paraguay are quadband. But it is easy to buy a phone when you arrive, or just a SIM card (*un chip*) for use in Paraguay. See *Telephones*, page 54.

If you are the sort of person who likes to travel with a **laptop**, there is now a huge and increasing number of hotels that have Wi-Fi. In terms of electric plugs, Paraguay uses two-pin plugs and has 220 voltage (the same as Europe, different from the USA and Brazil). A universal plug adaptor is a good idea as well as a simple adaptor to two-pin. (Some of these have pins that are just a little too thick.) In a thunderstorm you should unplug any electrical devices: computers in particular are vulnerable to being burned out, and most Paraguayans even unplug their fridges.

Some people will wish to bring **insect repellent**, long-sleeved shirts for the evening, and possibly a mosquito net, but see the section above on *Mosquito control*, page 40. If you use suncream, it is probably best to bring it with you: you cannot rely on being able to buy it in every part of Paraguay. A soft squashable **sun hat** is a good idea. Good walking sandals are necessary for most of the year.

If you are going to be here between June and August you should bring, at least as a precautionary measure, an overcoat, scarf, gloves and jerseys. Some people may also want to bring a hot water bottle, which are hard to find outside of Asunción.

$ MONEY

EXCHANGE RATE Because the guaraní is not much known outside of Paraguay, most internet currency conversion websites do not include it, but here are sites that do: www.oanda.com/currency/converter and www.xe.com/ucc/full. At the time of going to press there were just over Gs7,000 to the pound (though this has fluctuated in recent years up to Gs10,000 and down again), slightly over Gs6,000 to the euro, and a little over Gs4,500 to the dollar.

CASH MACHINES If you are coming from Argentina or Brazil you may be able to change cash for guaraníes before you arrive, but otherwise you will have to wait until you get to Paraguay to get guaraníes from a cash machine (*cajero*). You can do so straightaway at Asunción airport, where the cash machine is nearly always in working order. Or you can change dollar notes at the bank (if you arrive in banking hours).

After your passport, probably the most important single thing to bring is a **Visa card**. All cash machines accept Visa cards, whether credit or debit cards, with the exception of the machines of the Banco Nacional de Fomento, which are designed to enable Paraguayan state employees to withdraw their salaries. But only a minority of cash machines (for example, those of the Banco Continental, Interbanco, BBVA and ABN Amro) accept MasterCard, Maestro, Cirrus and other cards. Do not be misled by the notice telling you that all those cards are accepted:

when you try the machine you will find the notice is often wrong. While you will always be able to find a cash machine for the other cards in Asunción, when you are travelling in the interior it can be a problem.

Sometimes travellers have found that their bank blocks their card as soon as they attempt to use it in South America, so try to check with your bank that this will not happen before you travel. In fact, you should take a phone number for your bank with you that works from abroad (ie: not an 0845 number) because you may find that, despite your prior notification, your card still gets blocked and the only way to unblock it is to ring up. There are currently about 500 cash machines in Paraguay, three-quarters of them in the Asunción area, and they are increasing at the rate of 20% a year. They are limited in the amount of money you can take out at a time: currently the maximum is Gs1,000,000, but you can take that out three times in immediate succession on the same day, and that is plenty to keep you going for a while.

CASH It is always advisable to bring more than one way of accessing money, in case of theft: the best backup to your credit card (apart from another credit card) is cash, in **US dollars**. These can be changed all over the country, and for that reason people will usually accept payment in dollars if you do not have enough guaraníes, if you round the figure up to allow for loss on the exchange. If you bring euros or pounds these can be exchanged too, in banks or *financieras*. The euro is well respected, but people are less familiar with the pound, so you might have trouble exchanging sterling outside Asunción. However, there is no problem in changing pounds in Asunción at a place like Maxi Cambios (Shopping del Sol/Shopping Multiplaza/Shopping Mariscal López/Super Centro) or Cambios Chaco (at the airport/Palma 364/Shopping Villa Morra).

It is a good idea to bring a couple of **one-dollar notes** for tipping the porter at the airport who is likely to grab your bags, leaving you with little choice but to tip him. (You probably will not have guaraníes until you have entered the country, certainly not in small denominations.) Remember that he has to struggle to make a living, and is not allowed to work every day as a porter because of the competition for places.

Banking hours are 08.30–13.30, Monday to Friday.

TRAVELLERS' CHEQUES Travellers' cheques (*cheques viajeros*) are almost useless, since banks will only accept them for paying into a bank account, not for changing into cash. Maxi Cambios say they will change them if they are issued by American Express, but outside of Asunción and Ciudad del Este you are likely to be completely stuck. **American Express** closed their office in Paraguay recently, but Interbanco are acting as their representatives (*Edificio Citycenter, Citibank, Cruz del Chaco y Quesada;* ✆ *021 6171000;* ⏰ *08.30–15.00*).

NOTES With all those noughts it is easier to recognise notes by their colour rather than by the numbers on them. There is no note higher than Gs100,000. Here is a colour code:

Pale mauve	Gs2,000 (Adela and Celsa Speratti, educational reformers)
Red	Gs5,000 (head of Carlos Antonio López, president)
Dark brown	Gs10,000 (head of Dr Francia, president)
Slate blue	Gs20,000 (head of *la mujer paraguaya*, in folk dance costume)
Blue	Gs50,000 (head of Agustín Pio Barrios, the guitarist known as Mangoré)
Green	Gs100,000 (head of San Roque González, Jesuit saint and martyr)

The purple Gs1,000 note (head of Mariscal López) is now almost obsolete, replaced by a new coin.

The good news is that the three noughts will be removed from the currency in 2011, so instead of Gs5,000 you will just have Gs5. The colour and design of the notes will remain the same.

TIPPING The general rule in Paraguay on tipping is to do it as often as you can. A suggested tip is Gs10,000–30,000 or US$2–6 for a guide in a church or museum (depending on their knowledge); Gs5,000–10,000 or US$1–2 for a porter; Gs1,000 for a supermarket assistant carrying your bags to your car or to a street kid washing your windscreen. You can pay less if you are a backpacker, tight for money yourself, but you should pay more if you turn up leading a party of foreigners. Remember that people are very poor, and deserve to get something when they have helped others who are so much better off than themselves.

Keep in mind that the guide at a church or a museum, or the porter at the airport, may not be getting any wage for their work, and if they are it will be a very low wage. In fact, the better a guide is, the less likely it is that he or she has a wage: those who have jobs often have them through family or political connections, so those who can survive by doing a job without a wage are doing it because they are good at it.

BUDGETING

Compared to other countries – even compared to nearby Argentina, Brazil or Chile – Paraguay is cheap. Travel may be in buses of poor or indifferent quality, but you can cross the country from Asunción to Encarnación (on the southern border) or to Ciudad del Este (on the eastern border) for under US$15. You can sometimes get a cheap bed for US$7, and for US$30 you can get somewhere quite nice to stay. Backpacker survival food might cost you US$4 a day, and for US$15 you can get a good meal. If you want luxury, of course you can spend a lot, and you may be tempted to splash out on beautiful, labour-intensive craft work. But even so, you will be spending almost nothing on museums, which are mostly free.

Here are the costs of some basic items:

2-litre bottle of mineral water	under US$1 in a shop
Half-litre bottle of mineral water in a restaurant	US$1
Litre of beer	US$1.50
Bottle of decent wine	US$3.50
Loaf of bread	US$1
Street snack	US$0.20–0.50
Sweet snack	US$0.20
Postcard	US$1
T-shirt	US$6
Litre of petrol	US$1.20

GETTING AROUND

The *campo* (countryside) is the real Paraguay. This is where the national traditions live on most strongly, whether of food, dance, architecture, Guaraní language or cultural expectations. When you get into what they call the interior you get inside the country, in more than one sense.

The word *pueblo* literally means 'people' but is used for a town or a village. Most towns in the interior are small, of the size that would be called a village in Europe, so *pueblo* captures well the sense of community, in which everyone knows everyone.

The country map on pages ii–iii of the colour section shows the different *departamentos* of the interior, with their capitals.

ASUNCIÓN TELEPHONE NUMBERS FOR BUS COMPANIES

Terminal information	☏ 021 551740
Alborada	☏ 021 551612
Beato Roque González	☏ 021 551680
Boquerón	☏ 021 551738/550880
Brújula	☏ 021 551664
Canindeyú	☏ 021 555991
Caterinense	☏ 021 551738
Chaqueña	☏ 021 422975
Citta	☏ 021 553050
Ciudad de Pilar	☏ 021 558393
Cometa Amambay	☏ 021 551657
Crucero del Este	☏ 021 555082
Crucero del Norte	☏ 021 559087
EGA (Empresa General Artigas)	☏ 021 559795
Encarnacena	☏ 021 551745/555077
Expreso Sur	☏ 021 557766
Flecha de Oro	☏ 021 551641
Godoy	☏ 021 558795/557369
Guaireña	☏ 021 551727
JC	☏ 021 553050
Mariscal López	☏ 021 551612
Misionera	☏ 021 551590
Nasa	☏ 021 551731/558451/555534
Nuestra Señora de la Asunción	☏ 021 2891000
Ñeembucú	☏ 021 551680
Ortega	☏ 021 558198
Ovetense	☏ 021 551737
Paraguaya	☏ 021 559720
Pilarense	☏ 021 551736, 551660
Pluma	☏ 021 551758
Pulqui	☏ 021 555235
Pycasú	☏ 021 557700, 551735
Río Paraguay	☏ 021 555958, 551680
Río Parana	☏ 021 551733
Rysa	☏ 021 551601/2
San Jorge	☏ 021 554877, 551705
San Juan	☏ 021 555728
San Luis	☏ 021 551705
Santaniana	☏ 021 551607
Sirena del Paraná	☏ 021 553820
Sol del Paraguay	☏ 021 551763
Stel Turismo	☏ 021 551680/558051
Tigre	☏ 021 558196
TTL	☏ 021 553050
Yacyreta	☏ 021 2891000
Ybytyruzú	☏ 021 558393
Yuteña	☏ 021 555991

TRAVELLING AROUND THE INTERIOR

🚐 **By bus** As Paraguay is a poor country, where only a minority have cars, it is fair to assume that you can get to anywhere by **bus**, if you have enough time and patience. Travel by bus can be tiring and uncomfortable, but it gives you more of a feel of the country to be travelling with the local people. The website of the bus terminal in Asunción (*www.mca.gov.py/webtermi.html*) is some help with finding how to get to places, but cannot be depended on, as it has not been kept up to date. For greater convenience, there is a list of the Asunción telephone numbers of bus companies that operate all over the country on page 47. A call (in Spanish) to the general information number of the Terminal (☎ *021 551740*) will identify which bus companies go to the area you want to reach, if you have not already got that information from the relevant section of this guide.

🚗 **By taxi** If you want to travel a bit more comfortably and conserve your energy for where you are heading, there are a lot of **private transport companies** that can hire you a car or minivan with a driver (see list in *Chapter 3*, page 66). Vehicles hired from Asunción for the benefit of tourists can generally be relied upon to have air conditioning and insurance, though it is worth checking. Taxis in the interior of the country are not generally insured, and very few private cars are insured. This is illegal but it is not regarded as either shocking or abnormal – it is just one of those laws that is more honoured in the breach than the observance. The Paraguayan approach is that you do not worry about what you are never going to be able to afford to do anyway, and that if you are stopped by the police then the *coima* (bribe) will be less than the cost of the insurance.

🚗 **Car hire** If you want to go for self-drive **car hire**, there are good international companies in Asunción, and also in Ciudad del Este, and one now in Encarnación, but nowhere else in the country (see *Chapter 3*, page 66, *Chapter 9*, page 247, *Chapter 6,* page 214). You cannot, unfortunately, hire a car over the border in Posadas or in Foz do Iguaçu and bring it in; you will probably find that the small print does not allow it.

The driving rules for Paraguay that you need to know are:

- Have your headlights on even by day if you are driving on the *rutas* (main roads; but it is not necessary on small country roads or in cities). If you do not do this you are likely to be fined.
- Everyone should wear a seatbelt. (This may be surprising since people rarely put on seatbelts, but that is what the law says.)
- Carry a first-aid box, two warning triangles and a fire extinguisher.
- The simplest rule on speeds is 40km/h in towns and 80km/h on the *rutas*. But in fact some urban areas allow 50 or 60km/h, and if there is no speed limit marked on the *ruta* then you can go up to 110km/h.

Be prepared for a lack of road signs. Particularly tricky is negotiating your way out of Asunción and for this you need detailed instructions (*Chapter 4*, page 103).

✈ **By air** If you want to fly, there are hardly any **domestic flights**, as most of them were discontinued a few years ago. You can fly to Ciudad del Este by TAM (☎ *021 645500; www.tamairlines.com*), which will get you a little more quickly to the Iguazú Falls, if you are not planning to visit anywhere along the way. There is only one flight a day, leaving Asunción at 10.50 and leaving Ciudad del Este at 16.30. The flight takes 40 minutes and costs around US$50 each way (see *Chapter 9*, page 242).

There is now a new weekly – but as yet slightly irregular – service to towns on the Río Paraguay, run by the Transporte Aereo Militar (see *Chapter 12*, page 307). This, confusingly, abbreviates to TAM but should not be confused with the international airline TAM.

You can charter a plane, though you are unlikely to want to do that, even if you are rich, unless you are going to the Chaco (details are in *Chapter 12*, page 307).

MAPS It is notoriously difficult to get hold of maps in Paraguay. One reason is that there is very little distribution of any books or published materials, but another is that Paraguayans are not accustomed to using maps anyway. If you get out a map and ask to be shown where you are and where the place is you want to get to, most people will be at a loss to say. In cities in the interior, it is usually quite impossible to get hold of a map, and it is not very easy even in Asunción. However, here are some of the principal options.

Senatur (the government tourist office) produces a map of the country which can be picked up free at Turista Roga (Guaraní 'Tourists' House'), and maybe at the tourist desk at the airport too. They can also give you a free *Asunción Map Guide* and a free *Asunción Quick Guide*. These are excellent (though stuffed with advertising), and generally as good as or better than what you can buy in the *librerías*.

Touring (see page 67) do some of the best maps. They have a road map of the east of the country, a road map of the west (ie: the Chaco), and there are good maps in their guidebook (see *Appendix 4*). For their map of Asunción, see *Chapter 3*, page 67.

Ictus also do good maps, and they come in narrow packets which are easy to fit into pockets. For their map of Asunción see *Chapter 3*, page 66. They also do an excellent map of Ciudad del Este. Their map of the country is similar to, but not quite as good as, the free map distributed by Senatur.

Servicio Geográfico Militar have done a large number of detailed maps covering the whole country, and these are on sale, distributed by Meier (✆ *021 301804*). They are hard to find, but there is a newsagent's on the ground floor of the Shopping del Sol (see page 78) which stocks them. However, these maps, though of a high quality from the cartographical point of view, are so extremely out of date that they are useful only for physical features and underlying street layout. They have also done a single, whole-country map which is good, and has detailed tables of distances from town to town.

JB Ediciones is a publicity company that has started producing maps – mostly free ones of different cities, paid for by advertising.

www.jma.gov.py is a new site with a webmap of Asunción.

ACCOMMODATION

Paraguay is not provided with the kind of modern backpacker hostels you get in most other Latin American countries. But there are plenty of cheap hotels; these may be called *hotel* or *hospedaje* or *pensión* or *alojamiento*, or (more in Argentina) *residencial*, or (rarely) *hostal*. You never hear any reports of bedbugs or such things, so you can feel safe in using cheap accommodation in Paraguay.

It is important to know what the word **motel** means in Paraguay, as there are a very large number of these and they are not motels in the English sense. A *motel* is a hotel where you can hire a room by the hour to have sex with your companion. They usually have names like *amor* (love) or *bosque* (wood) or *luna* (moon) and have a discreet car park which cannot be seen from the road. Occasionally a hotel serves both purposes, but if it is called 'hotel' rather than 'motel', you can expect to be quoted a price for the night rather than a price per hour.

Most of the best hotels in Paraguay are run by Germans or have some level of German management, at least in the past. This is true not just in the German towns like Loma Plata, Independencia and Bella Vista, but all over the country.

At the other end of the scale from the country *hospedajes* are a rapidly increasing number of luxury hotels in Asunción. Because Paraguay is a cheap country, it is a good place to hold international **conferences**, for which many hotels now have ample facilities.

A continental **breakfast** means coffee or tea or *cocido* with bread and jam and probably fruit juice. An American breakfast means there is also cereal, fruit, ham, cheese, eggs, yoghurt, cakes, etc. In this guide, these terms have not been used, but 'good breakfast' indicates that more than a continental breakfast can be expected.

Although many hotels have a central water heating system, in all private houses and smaller hotels the water is heated by an electrical device in the shower-head. There is a technique to getting the maximum heat out: turn down the water flow as low as possible without cutting out the electrical device altogether. From the taps, only expect cold water, unless in a luxury hotel. There are not many plugs for basins, so you might want to consider bringing one.

Air conditioning is so common that it has not been mentioned in the guide, but if there are cheaper rooms with only fans then this has been stated. If you prefer a fan to air conditioning, some hotels have both in the same room, but most do not. **Television** and even cable television, again, is so common it has not normally been mentioned. It is common to find one double and one single bed in your room, enabling it to be used by a couple or by two sharers; quite often rooms have four beds or more. **Credit cards** are accepted in the more expensive hotels, but this has been sometimes mentioned in the case of mid-range hotels, where it might be in doubt. No **stars** have been given for hotels because there is no official rating in Paraguay, so the classification is useless. Some hotels will call themselves four-star when someone else would call them two-star. **Wi-Fi** is increasingly common in hotels, and this has generally been commented on in the mid-range hotels but not in the more expensive ones because it comes as standard.

PRICE CODES Based on a standard double room in high season.

$$$$$	Gs1,000,000+	$200+	£134+	€154+
$$$$	Gs300,000–1,000,000	$60–199	£40–134	€46–154
$$$	Gs125,000–300,000	$25–60	£17–40	€19–46
$$	Gs75,000–125,000	$15–24	£10–17	€12–19
$	<Gs75,000	<$15	<£10	<€12

ESTANCIAS What is an *estancia*? Strictly speaking, it is a large country estate, where there is a farm and a farmhouse, but out of these, some have developed their houses to receive paying guests, operating like hotels. A stay in an *estancia* involves driving into the countryside and spending at least a day enjoying the facilities. Typically they are lovely houses, well furnished, and with excellent food, so it is an enjoyable way to spend part of a holiday, in a very Paraguayan environment. You will probably be charged a daily rate for full board, and you will have access to a variety of activities, which typically include observation of farming processes such as planting, harvesting or seeing cows milked; swimming in a pool or a stream; other sports such as football, volleyball or ping pong; riding or going for a ride in a sulky or horse cart; boating or fishing; lounging in a hammock; walking, bicycling, etc. There are also hotels and country clubs which offer similar activities and are not technically *estancias*. Note that fishing is forbidden from 15 November to 20 December in Paraguayan waters, to let the fish stock recover.

PRINCIPAL *ESTANCIAS* IN THE APATUR NETWORK

Book through the Central de Reservas (☎ *021 210550; www.turismorural.org.py*).
The Asunción office is at Don Bosco c/ Piribebúy (☎ *021 497028*).

CHAPTER 4 – CIRCUITO DE ORO
Oñondivemi 27.5km; $$$; page 142
Los Manantiales 59km; $$$; page 242
La Quinta 82.5km; $$$; page 139
Mamorei 115.5km; $$$; page 149
Santa Clara 141km; $$$; page 151

CHAPTER 10 – VILLARRICA AND CENTRAL PARAGUAY
Don Emilio 138km; $$$; page 255
Loma Linda 206km; $$$; page 268
Golondrina 252km; $$$; page 254

CHAPTER 11 – CONCEPCIÓN AND THE NORTHEAST
San Guillermo 35km; $$$; page 272
Laguna Blanca 287km; $$; page 273 (This is not really an *estancia* because it is only for campers, but it is in the Atapur network.)

If you do not have a car to get to an *estancia*, the owners may be able to pick you up from the nearest bus route, so do not be deterred from asking. You will probably need to give at least one day's notice of your arrival; you cannot just turn up.

The network of *estancias* that receives visitors is called Apatur, and they have an office in Asunción at the Touring y Automóvil Club Paraguayo (*Brasil c/ 25 de mayo, 8th Floor;* ☎ *021 210550 int 126;* e *info@tacpy.com.py; www.turismorural.org.py*). If your Spanish is not up to making a phone booking, either at this number or at the *estancia* itself, take a taxi to the office, with your phrasebook in hand, as there is no-one there who speaks English. The furthest *estancias*, such as those north of Concepción, do not belong to Apatur, and for these see page 281. The *estancias* in Misiones belong to a different network, Emitur, instead of Apatur, and most of these are around Santiago (see page 181). Refer to the box above for a list of the principal Apatur *estancias*, divided according to the chapters in this book where they are featured, and in order of distance in kilometres from Asunción.

✖ EATING AND DRINKING

The concept of opening hours for **restaurants**, particularly in the smaller ones or in the interior, does not really apply. When opening hours are advertised it usually means that foreigners are running the restaurant, who are more timetabled than Paraguayans. You can assume, unless it says to the contrary, that the restaurant will be open from whenever the first member of staff turns up, probably around 07.00 in the morning, until the last person leaves, probably not before 23.00.

You can eat very well in Asunción, and even vegetarians will find plenty of good salads to fill their plates, even in the *churrasquerías* (restaurants serving roast meals). But most restaurants and bars in the interior of the country are very basic. Every town will have a bar which serves *empanadas* (like cornish pasties) and *milanesas* (escalopes), beer and fizzy drinks, and not much else. Most ordinary restaurants serve a small variety of meat dishes, accompanied by chips, rice salad, potato salad or a mixed salad (lettuce, tomato, onion). It is common to skip dessert entirely.

Practical Information EATING AND DRINKING

2

Many of the European staples are missing in Paraguay. It is not a tea country, or a coffee country, or a wine country; it is not a bread country or a cheese country. You can get good wine readily (imported from Chile and Argentina), and Hornimans do a Classic London Blend of tea. However, it is difficult to get good coffee, bread or cheese outside of good restaurants and hotels in Asunción. Instead of tea and coffee, the people drink *tereré* or *cocido*. Instead of wine they drink beer or *gaseosa* (fizzy drinks). They may drink a *jugo* (fruit juice) with their meals: these delicious mixtures blend fresh fruit with extra water and sugar, to make a longer drink in this thirsty climate. Instead of bread, *mandioc* or *sopa paraguaya* or *chipa* is eaten.

On the whole, if people go out to dinner (particularly in Asunción) they eat late: 20.00 is the earliest you should arrive at a restaurant. Lunchtime, however, happens at midday like clockwork, all over the country.

PRICE CODES Based on the average price of a main course.

$$$$$	Gs75,000+	$15+	£10+	€12+
$$$$	Gs50,000–75,000	$10–14	£7–10	€8–12
$$$	Gs30,000–50,000	$6–9	£4–7	€5–8
$$	Gs15,000–30,000	$3–5	£2–4	€2–5
$	<Gs15,000	<$3	<£2	<€2

PUBLIC HOLIDAYS AND FESTIVALS

THE PRINCIPAL FESTIVALS AND SPECIAL EVENTS Dates should be checked annually with the local *municipalidad* or other source, as they are liable to vary. For more details of these events, see under their respective towns.

Saints' days and hence patronal feast days do not vary. They are preceded by a *novena* (nine days), usually with a daily mass and some kind of evening event.

Date	Place	Event
2 January	Pilar	Fiesta Hawaiana
6 January	Capiatá, Fernando de la Mora	San Baltasar
First weekend January	Santiago	Festival de la Doma y el Folklore
January	Valenzuela	Festival de la piña
Third Sunday January	Piribebúy	Ñandejára Guasú
Weekend late January	Santiago	Fiesta de la Tradición Misionera
25 January and preceding Thursday–Sunday	Caazapá	Fiesta de Ykuá Bolaños
Up to 2 February	Areguá	Festival de Alfarería
Early February	Filadelfia	Arete Guasú
3 February	Piribebúy, Itá	San Blas
Four weekends in February/March before Lent	Encarnación	Carnaval
Thursday, Friday, Saturday of Holy Week	all over the country	Semana Santa
Good Friday	Tañarandý; Yaguarón	Procesión de Viernes Santo
Easter Saturday/Sunday	Santa María de Fe	Tupãsy Ñuvait
Second weekend June	San Miguel	Ovechá Rague
15 June and 16 July	Sapucai	train trip

29 June	Altos (*compañía* Haguazú)	Feast of St Peter and St Paul
First two weeks of July	Asunción (Mariano Roque Alonso)	Expo
31 July	San Ignacio	San Ignacio
End July to end September	Areguá (*compañía* Estanzuela)	Expo Frutilla
8 September	Santa María de Fe	Natividad de la Virgen
Last weekend September	Chaco	Transchaco Rally (motor racing)
Ten days in November or December	Yataitý	Expoferia de ao po'í
Second weekend November	Asunción (Conmebol)	Fitpar (tourism exhibition)
Late November	Asunción (Teatro Municipal)	Festival Mundial del Arpa
8 December	Caacupé	Inmaculada Concepción
18 December	Itapé	Virgen de Itapé

NATIONAL HOLIDAYS (*FERIADOS*)

1 January	Año nuevo (New Year)
1 March	Día de los héroes (Heroes' Day – anniversary of death of Mariscal López)
Variable	Maundy Thursday and Good Friday
1 May	Día del trabjador (Workers' Day)
15 May	Día de la Independencia (Independence Day)
12 June	Día de la paz del Chaco (Peace after the Chaco War)
15 August	Fundación de Asunción (The Assumption)
29 September	Aniversario de la Victoria de Boquerón (Victory of Boquerón – in the Chaco War)
8 December	Fiesta de la Virgen de Caacupé (The Immaculate Conception – feast day of Caacupé)
25 December	Navidad (Christmas)

The following are also generally celebrated nationwide:

30 July	Día de la Amistad (when people give little presents to their friends)
21 September	Día de la Juventud (when there is often a parade of floats by educational establishments)

⚑ SHOPPING

Business hours are from 08.00 (or 07.00 for manual workers or schools) until midday. Shops re-open in the afternoon, generally at 13.00, and small family shops never close. Some businesses open only in the mornings, Monday to Friday. Few people work on Sundays, apart from in family shops.

It is common to see **armed guards** outside shops and banks in the cities, with rifles or revolvers. This is supposed to make you feel safer, not more nervous.

Outside of the capital it may prove difficult to find a range of goods. Chemists (*farmacias*) are well stocked all over the country, and have long opening hours. But you may have to go to Asunción or Ciudad del Este if you want to buy, for example, a good corkscrew; a novel, even in Spanish; a pack of biological detergent; a teaspoon; a camera accessory; or a postcard (only in tourist shops in Asunción).

Traditional craft can be bought in its town of origin, but craft from all over the country can be readily bought in Asunción (see page 75); there are not many generalised craft shops outside of the capital. See page 56 and *Chapter 3*, page 79 for information on post offices.

ARTS AND ENTERTAINMENT

Festivals of music and folk dance are quite common in the *campo* but you will not find cinemas outside of the cities. Asunción has a few small theatres and a number of exhibition halls (see page 74). Pirated DVD films are readily available all over the country, to play on a laptop. For paintings and sculpture, see under *Museums* in *Chapter 3* and under San Ignacio, Santa María de Fe, Santa Rosa and Santiago in *Chapter 5* and San Cosme y Damián and Trinidad in *Chapter 6*.

VISITING MUSEUMS AND CHURCHES

Most local town **museums** in the interior of Paraguay (with the exception of the museums in the Reductions) have very predictable contents: relics from the wars such as bullets, cutlery and metal plates, rusty sables, as well as old typewriters, old telephones, old radios and the like. When you have seen one, you may feel you have seen them all. The museums of Jesuit-Guaraní art, however, are in a totally different league.

Most museums in Paraguay are free, and most of those that are not free (like the Jesuit museums of Misiones) charge only Gs5,000 entrance. If you want to visit a church or a museum and it is closed, do not just go away. Find out who has the key and go and ask them if you can visit. Usually they are more than happy to come and open up, and expect to be informed when a visitor comes, as they would waste a lot of time sitting in an empty building waiting for visitors, who may turn up only once a week or less. However, do not omit to tip them a dollar or two if they have come out specially for you, or more if they have specialised knowledge.

In Europe you are asked not to walk around during a service in **church**, but to wait until it is over. In Paraguay, however, you may sometimes need to take the opportunity to look at the church during the liturgy because when it is over the church will be locked up. In this case you should obviously be very discreet, and it is much better to do it before the mass (or funeral, or baptism) than during it.

MEDIA AND COMMUNICATIONS

TELEPHONES Outside of Asunción, it is more common to have a **mobile phone** (*celular*) than a landline (*línea baja*). A lot of telephone numbers in this guide are mobile numbers, and can be easily recognised because they begin with 09. People often change their numbers, as their mobile gets lost, or more likely stolen, but this is much less of a problem than it used to be, because it is now very inexpensive to recover your old number. People may also change their number if the signal of one network becomes better than the network they were formerly using. Some people have as many as three mobile numbers, for the different networks: 097x for Personal, 098x for Tigo and 099x for Claro. (There is also 096x for Vox, but that only works in Asunción.)

Remember that your mobile phone from home is unlikely to work in Paraguay, unless it is quadband. But it is easy to get up-and-running with a mobile phone when you arrive, even for a short period, as you will not be expected to take out a contract (*un plan*). (Nearly everyone has pay-as-you-go.) You can buy a phone for less than Gs150,000, and a *chip* to give you a number currently costs as little as

Gs15,000, which includes Gs10,000 worth of credit. Topping up is easy: everywhere you go you will find *librerías* and other shops that do a *mini carga*: you just say what your number is and how much money you want to put on it (Gs 20,000 should be more than enough at a time). This is only useful of course if you speak Spanish.

There is also a new kind of mobile in Paraguay which functions in some ways like a landline. It is run by Copaco and the service is called Copacel. These numbers begin with 0220, 0350, 0360, 0370, 0420, 0570, 0571, 0572, 0573, 0580, 0660, 0750, 0770 or 0790. It is too early to say to what extent this system will catch on.

Argentinian mobile phone numbers are confusing. (You may need these if you make the excursion to Puerto Iguazú or San Ignacio Miní.) Within the country they have two digits more than landlines, with the number 15 inserted between the area code and the phone number. If you are dialling from outside the country you drop the 15 and put in 9 earlier on, between the country code and the area code. For example:

from Argentina 03752 15 680286
from abroad +54 9 3752 680286

There have been a lot of changes in **landline codes** in Paraguay in the last few years. Every town that has been switched over to a digital network has had extra numbers added to its code. You may still come across the old numbers on printed materials, though every attempt has been made to have all the updated numbers in this book. Nearly always (but not quite always) the number after the code has six digits. Asunción numbers all begin 021, so if you find a number with that prefix in the interior of the country, it means that the people have an Asunción office, or that they live in Asunción during the week.

The national company for landline phones is called **Copaco**, but it used to be called Antelco, and you still sometimes come across the old name. Every small town has a Copaco office, where people can go to make calls, and where the operator knows the numbers of all the people in the town. These Copaco numbers, therefore, are invaluable for updating local information – whether it is for knowing if a hotel is still functioning, or to find out who is the new person responsible for opening the museum, or to ask if the road to the town has yet been asphalted. For this reason, a large number of Copaco telephone numbers have been included in this guide, under the name of the town. Also included are a large number of phone numbers for the *municipalidad* (town hall) because there will generally be someone there responsible for tourist matters. But the Copaco number is useful too, because the *municipalidad* will only be open Monday to Friday, in the mornings.

This guide includes a lot of telephone numbers so that Spanish-speakers can easily contact organisations for the latest information. As much detailed information as possible has been included, even if it is the kind of information that is liable to become out of date because even out-of-date information is better than no information. It gives you something to check, rather than leaving you in the dark as to what kind of services might be on offer. It is recommended to ask a Spanish-speaker to telephone and check on such rapidly changing details as opening times, bus fares, etc. Do not trust website information on that kind of detail as it is often outdated.

There is a large number of shops offering public telephone facilities, all over the country. These are called *cabinas* because the phones are in enclosed booths. Occasionally the booths are divided into those for landline calls, and those for different mobile networks. This makes the business of telephoning quite easy, because you can always find a quiet spot, and with someone to help you if you have a problem with the number.

The **international code** is not 00 as in other countries, but 002. The number for **directory enquiries** in Asunción is ☎ 112 or ☎ 021 2192018 or ☎ 021 2192176. They can give you other numbers for directory enquiries around the country. The word for '**extension**' is *interno*. Paraguayans write phone numbers in the form 021 645600 int 364.

ℹ️ INTERNET It is often the case that **Email addresses** and **websites** are inactive or discontinued. This is a characteristic of the poor communications of Paraguay generally. Every effort has been made to eliminate web addresses which are no longer active, even when they are advertised, and also those which are 'under construction' but have nothing on them, unless there seems a serious possibility that they may soon spring into life. Many people have email addresses but do not check their mail boxes regularly, or at all, so you may find you only get replies from the larger hotels and companies. Some Paraguayans have an email address ending yahoo.com.ar, even though they live in Paraguay and not Argentina.

Internet cafés are now very common. They are in every big shopping mall (Spanish *un shopping*) of Asunción and it generally costs Gs4,000 to use a computer for an hour (under a dollar). **Post offices**, however, are rare, even in Asunción; it is not in the culture to send letters. People are more likely to send a document by bus, as an *encomienda*, than to send it by post. Rural towns (*pueblos*) usually have a post office of sorts, but it may not be advertised as such, almost certainly will not sell stamps, and will maybe only receive correspondence for the local government office or for foreign missionaries living there. Even the word for post – *correo* – now means 'email', rather than overland post.

MEDIA The principal **newspapers** are *ABC-Color* and *Ultima Hora*, with *La Nación* coming in third place, and a couple of popular papers with scandals and pin-up girls, *Crónica* and *Popular*. However, newspapers are expensive for Paraguayans, and most people cannot afford them. They are not sold in *librerías* but in on-street *kioskos* (in Asunción and larger towns) or through individual newspaper-sellers on foot. If you have not bought one in the morning you are unlikely to get one, though the Asunción Terminal generally has them later in the day.

The Paraguayan **television** channels are Red Guaraní (2), Telefuturo (4), Paravisión (5), SNT (9), Latele (11) and Canal Trece (13). There are news programmes at 12.00 (Red Guaraní and Canal Trece), 12.30 (Telefuturo and SNT) 18.50 (Canal Trece), 20.00 (Telefuturo), 21.00 (Paravisión), 23.00 (Telefuturo) and 23.15 (Canal Trece).

The principal **radio** stations are all on AM: Radio Uno (650), Radio Caritas (680), Radio Cardinal (730), Radio 1º de Marzo (780), Radio Ñandutí (1020) and Radio Fe y Alegría (1300). The FM system is used for local radio, which is what people listen to more than the national programmes.

CULTURAL INTERACTION

When it **rains**, people assume that everything is suspended (school, social events, etc) without requiring notice of cancellation. This applies not only when the rain is heavy, but when it is a light drizzle, when it looks as though it might rain, and for quite a long time after it has stopped. This is particularly so in the *campo* where there are more dirt roads, and in state schools, where the teachers like to have a holiday as well as the pupils. In Asunción, only 9% of the capital's roads have drainage, so in times of heavy rain, you should only travel if it is essential, as some of the roads, such as Aviadores del Chaco, will turn into virtual rivers.

Paraguayans are very clean people and they regularly take a **shower** every afternoon around 16.00 or 17.00 (to wash off the sweat of the day), and you may be expected to do likewise. It is very important to know that you should not put your **toilet paper** into the toilet, but in a bin at the side; otherwise you will block the pipes.

In Asunción many people have doorbells to their houses, which are usually located outside, on the street. In the *campo*, people do not normally have either bells or door-knockers, but the method of attracting attention is by clapping your hands in the street outside. When you go into someone's house you should say 'Permiso' ('[With your] permission') as you enter, to which the reply is 'Adelante' ('Go ahead'). You should not visit people, telephone or play a radio, etc between midday and 13.00 or 14.00, which is when people are having their lunch and resting a little, though few people actually have a nap. If you are invited to eat a meal in someone's home, it is polite to say that it is 'muy rico' ('very nice').

There is plenty of sexual behaviour between unmarried couples in Paraguay, but it takes place entirely in private (at a motel or in the fields) and it is not the done thing to flaunt it. You do not see couples holding hands, let alone kissing in public places. There is a high level of homophobia but if gay couples ask for a room for two, they will often find themselves with a double and single bed anyway.

There are virtually no facilities for the disabled, and even in good hotels little effort has been made to respond to their needs. Unfortunately, it is still very rare to see someone in a wheelchair in a public place, although disabled beggars without wheelchairs may be seen crawling along the streets of Asunción.

You may be unfortunate enough to find yourself in a situation where the easiest way to extract yourself is to pay a **bribe**, although this is more likely to happen to Paraguayans than to foreigners. Resist it all you can, as giving in to expectations of bribes merely perpetuates a system, which (particularly under Lugo's government), there is a now a serious will to change. But it is understandable if people sometimes feel that they have little choice, for example if their passport has been taken away and they have a plane to catch and cannot communicate well in Spanish. Police or customs officers may make up a rule you have supposedly broken to get a bribe out of you, or you may indeed have broken one of the detailed rules that seem to exist for little purpose other than to enable bribes to be taken. The person seeking the bribe will present it as a way in which he can do you a favour, to help you get over the higher cost of a fine. The word for 'bribe' is *coima,* but it has strong negative connotations, and if you are bribing someone you would not use that word, but a euphemism like a *propina* (tip), a *colaboración* (collaboration), an *arreglo* (settling up) or *aceite* (oil). More likely there will be no discussion, but you will just be delayed until you hand over some money (Gs50,000 would be a suitable amount), perhaps tucked discreetly inside your driving licence or passport. You will know if you are being asked to bribe, rather than pay a fine, because fines are not paid to the police on the spot: they are supposed to give you a ticket, which, in the case of visitors to the country, you take to Senatur (*Secretaria Nacional de Turismo; Palma 468 c/ Alberdi;* ☎ *021 494110;* ⏰ *07.00–19.00 inc Sun*).

There are three kinds of policeman: *policia caminera* in grey shirt and brown trousers; *policia nacional* in beige shirt and trousers; and *policia municipal* in white shirt and black trousers, or light blue shirt and dark blue trousers.

GIVING SOMETHING BACK

If you would like to help with health care in the poor interior, **SOS Children's Villages** (*Asunción office: Kubitschek 1044 e/ Teodoro S Mongelós y José Asunción Flores;* ☎ *021 220189/233265/223982;* ✉ *amigos.sos@sosparaguay.org.py; www.sosparaguay.org.py*) do invaluable work running three maternity hospitals known as the Aldeas (in San

Ignacio, Hohenau and Belén). They also have other support programmes for children. You can make a donation online, or become a godparent or a friend of the Aldeas.

If you would like to help on environmental projects, the **World Wide Fund for Nature** is working on reforestation in Paraguay (*Coordinación de voluntariado, WWF Paraguay Atlantic Forest Ecoregional Office, Las Palmas 185 c/ Av Argaña, Ciudad de Lambaré, Asunción:* ☏ *+595 21 331766/21 303100;* e *voluntariado@wwf.org.py; www.wwf.org.py*). It is working on the conservation of the Atlantic Forest in Alto Paraná, and they have the aim of planting 50 million trees in a project called *A todo pulmón – Paraguay respira* ('With all its lungs, Paraguay breathes').

If you would like to help with the nutrition of poor children living in the *bañado* of Asunción, there is a daily lunch canteen run by the organisation **Ko'eju** (*15 de agosto 10, opposite the Congress;* e *info@koeju.org;* ☏ *021 445446/497333; www.koeju.org*). It began in 2002 in the Chacarita, where 350 children are fed daily, and has spread now to other areas too. It is run by Luis and Olga Manfredi, pastors of the Centro Familiar de Adoración church.

The Jesuit programme for the education of the poor in Latin America is called **Fe y Alegría**, and naturally there is a Paraguayan branch (*O'Leary 1847, c/ Séptima Proyectada;* ☏ *021 371659/390576;* e *comunicaciones@feyalegria.org.py; www.feyalegria.org.py*). It does excellent work, running schools for the poor, training programmes for community leaders, and radio schools to teach literacy, particularly in Guaraní.

A charity that works principally in giving scholarships for tertiary level education to bright students from poor homes is the **Santa Maria Education Fund** (*UK registered charity no.1105031;* e *info@santamariadefe.org; www.santamariadefe.org*). It was founded by the author of this guide, and its projects can be visited in Santa María de Fe, Misiones. It takes a limited number of volunteers as English teachers, but they must be fluent in Spanish.

If you live in England, one way of helping is via the **Anglo Paraguayan Association** (e *anglopysociety@yahoo.com or robert@munro.me.uk*). It has a very small fund which it administers, to help a number of different projects. Because the organisation is largely composed of Paraguayans who have come to live in England, they have excellent feelers for small projects that deserve aid.

If you live in the USA, you can help via the **Fundacion Ñepytyvõ Inc** (*1212 Ednor Rd, Silver Spring, MD 20905;* ☏ *+1 301 938 9395/301 476 9516;* e *vicenteaquino@hotmail.com; http://www.geocities.com/nepytyvo/*). This is a small charity founded by Vicente Aquino, a Paraguayan who went to live in the United States many years ago. The fund is administered through colleagues and relatives still in Paraguay, and works in the area of education, for example by donating computers.

Part Two

THE GUIDE

3

Asunción

Departamento: Central

Asunción is not one of Latin America's more lovely cities, though with time you come to like it.

A certain amount has been done in the last few years to clean buildings, remove over-large hoardings, widen pavements, and install pergolas, benches and period streetlamps in the key areas of the city centre. There is more to be done, a great deal more, because there are many fine 19th-century buildings in a state of near collapse, which could be magnificent if restored.

Seen at its worst, Asunción has roads and pavements in terrible condition, rubbish littering the streets, and beggars hobbling along without crutches. BBC journalist Tim Vickery wrote: 'The place and the people have a certain serene charm, but one of the abiding impressions is of mangy dogs snoozing on shattered paving stones.'

But, as the capital, Asunción brings together the best cultural, artistic and intellectual life of the country. And if you know where to go, you can find a lot of great interest and a little of great beauty. Only look at the list of museums later in this chapter to see how much this city has to offer.

HISTORY

Asunción is so named because it was founded on 15 August, the feast of the Assumption of Mary, in the year 1537, by Captain Juan de Salazar de Espinosa, whose bronze statue, with its conquistador armour and outstretched sword, stands in the centre of the Plaza del Marzo Paraguayo today. He had arrived in the ship of Don Pedro de Mendoza, in the first Spanish voyage to discover the Río de la Plata area – that is to say, going upriver from the big estuary at what is now Buenos Aires. In due course, settlers from Asunción went to found other cities, such as Buenos Aires, Corrientes, Santa Fe and Santa Cruz de la Sierra, giving rise to the tag that Asunción is 'the Mother of Cities'.

Asunción was sited on a sharp bend of the river, rendering it a good lookout post. Today the stretches of river immediately to north and south of the bulge where Juan de Salazar placed his fort, are known as Bañado Norte and Bañado Sur. They are where the poorest live – those who have come up to the capital from the poor interior in search of work, and find themselves relegated to makeshift hovels on land which is central enough but floods from time to time.

Paraguayans are proud of the fact that they gained their independence without a drop of blood being spilt. The actions of the Próceres de la Independencia are commemorated in the Casa de la Independencia. The first president, Dr José Gaspar Rodríguez de Francia (Dictator 1814–1840), began to put some town planning into what had previously been haphazard growth. Under his successor Carlos Antonio López, the railway was inaugurated, and some of the handsome 19th-century

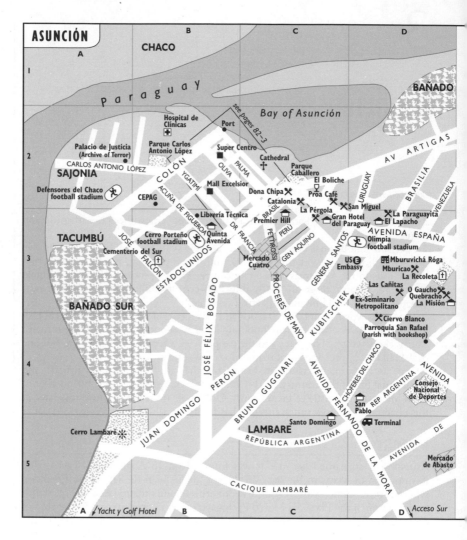

ASUNCIÓN

CHACO

Paraguay

Bay of Asunción

BAÑADO

see pages 82-3

Hospital de Clínicas

Port

Palacio de Justicia (Archive of Terror)

Parque Carlos Antonio López

Super Centro

Cathedral

CARLOS ANTONIO LÓPEZ

Parque Caballero

SAJONIA

Mall Excelsior

El Boliche

Dona Chipa

Proa Café

Defensores del Chaco football stadium

CEPAG

Catalonia

San Miguel

La Pérgola

Gran Hotel del Paraguay

La Paraguayita

El Lapacho

Librería Técnica

Premier Hill

AVENIDA ESPAÑA

TACUMBÚ

Cerro Porteño football stadium

Quinta Avenida

Olimpia football stadium

Cementerio del Sur

Mercado Cuatro

US Embassy

Mburuvichá Róga

Mburicao

La Recoleta

BAÑADO SUR

Las Cañitas

Ex-Seminario Metropolitano

O Gaucho

Quebracho

La Misión

Ciervo Blanco

Parroquia San Rafael (parish with bookshop)

Consejo Nacional de Deportes

San Pablo

Cerro Lambaré

LAMBARÉ

Santo Domingo

Terminal

Mercado de Abasto

REPÚBLICA ARGENTINA

CACIQUE LAMBARÉ

Yacht y Golf Hotel

Acceso Sur

buildings went up. The following president, Mariscal Francisco Solano López, in the short period before he embarked on his catastrophic War of the Triple Alliance, was responsible for building the grandest of the city's buildings – the Palacio de López.

In the Chaco War of 1932–35 many buildings in the city became hospitals and barracks. Since then, the city has continued to expand in population and area, until now one long, continuous urban spread unites it with what are supposedly distinct towns – Lambaré, Villa Elisa, Fernando de la Mora, San Lorenzo, Luque and Mariano Roque Alonso – to form Gran Asunción. Today there are almost a million inhabitants in the greater Asunción area, which may not sound too cumbersome, until you consider that there is no metro, and that the overcrowded buses often have to jolt their slow way over cobbled roads, making travel in the capital rather trying.

GETTING THERE

Information on how to get to Asunción can be found in *Chapter 2*, page 30.

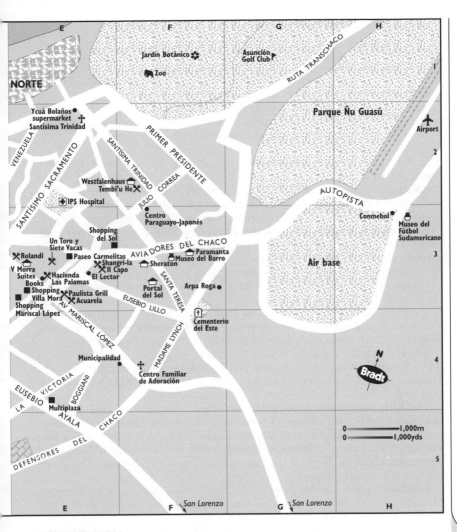

ORIENTATION

The city is like a fan, with its nub in the bend of the river where Juan de Salazar placed his fort. Or instead of a fan, you can think of the city's access roads as being like the five fingers on a hand that has its palm placed over the city centre. From north to south these five fingers are:

1 The Ruta Transchaco (the road from Argentina, from Bolivia, from the Chaco), turning into **Artigas**, which is a broad, fast road, with the Bañado Norte to one side, and the burnt-out shell of the Ycuá Bolaños supermarket to the other.
2 The Autopista (the road from the airport), turning into Aviadores del Chaco, which goes past the Sheraton Hotel, then the Shopping del Sol. It then changes its name to **España** and comes into the centre through quite a middle-class area.
3 **Mariscal López** (one of the roads from San Lorenzo), which comes in past the Shopping Villa Mora and the Shopping Mariscal López (one behind the other);

later the Mburuvichá Róga (house of the president), the US Embassy, the football club Olimpia, and so to the centre.

4 **Eusebio Ayala** (the other road from San Lorenzo), a broad street lined with buildings and household shops: plumbing supplies, furniture, lighting, domestic appliances, beds etc. Then it buries itself in Mercado Cuatro, and disappears.

5 Acceso Sur, turning into **Fernando de la Mora**, which goes past the Terminal and is lined with shops until it changes into Próceres de Mayo and goes through the thick of Mercado Cuatro. From that point on it is called Pettirossi.

The **Terminal** (⟍ *021 551740*) sits diagonally on the corner of República Argentina and Fernando de la Mora. The barrio around it is not the safest, though is not especially dangerous either. There is generally nothing to worry about if you stay alert, but think twice about walking around at night if you have opted for a cheap *hospedaje* by the bus station, unless it is on a well-frequented road.

In the **centre** the roads are one-way and run in parallel lines. When they reach the level of the east side of the Plaza de la Democracia they change their names. For example, Mariscal Estigarribia becomes Palma, 25 de mayo becomes Estrella, Cerro Corá becomes Oliva, Azara becomes General Díaz and Herrera becomes Haedo.

Continuing down the grid of these parallel streets you come to the major road Dr Francia, that becomes Ygatimí, which has the church of Cristo Rey on its far west corner, where it meets with Colón. From this point downwards, the parallel streets are popularly referred to as (**Proyectada** or **Avenida**) Primera, Segunda, Tercera, etc, even though they have other names marked on the map.

The end of many bus lines, beyond the centre, where the city hits the river, is barrio **Sajonia**, so any bus to Sajonia will be going to the centre first. South of Sajonia is Tacumbú, which is where the prison is, then the Bañado Sur, and then the Cerro Lambaré.

The **Villa Morra** area is becoming Asunción's second city centre, as can be clearly seen on the map on page 62, with a concentration of hotels and restaurants, and the three shopping centres of Mariscal López Shopping, Villa Morra Shopping and Paseo Carmelitas. Another shopping centre and more smart hotels and restaurants adjoin this barrio to the east, in the Shopping del Sol area. This area is not rich in historic buildings.

Lambaré itself is a wedge shape on the map to the southwest of the Terminal. Most maps do not show its streets because it is technically a separate town, but it juts up into Asunción and is indistinguishable from it.

A plan has been on the table for the last 15 years to build an **Avenida Costanera**, from the Botanical Gardens right into the heart of the city, as far as Colón.

GETTING AROUND

Flights to Asunción Airport have been covered in the previous chapter (see page 30). You will want to get some guaraníes before you leave the airport. The Interbanco cash machine there is nearly almost always in working order, and accepts all credit and debit cards. If you are changing money, there is a Cambios Chaco on both floors of the airport, open 24 hours.

GETTING IN FROM THE AIRPORT The airport Silvio Pettirossi [62 H2] (⟍ *021 645600/5*) is half an hour (20km) from the centre of town, in a northeasterly direction towards Limpio, down the road known as the Autopista (although it is not a motorway). To get from the airport into town, you have three choices: taxi, bus or hired car.

The people who organise the **taxis** stand by the exit door, and will make sure you get an official taxi, even though it will not have 'taxi' written on it. There are flat rates from the airport, currently Gs100,000 to the far side of the centre (the barrio Sajonia), Gs90,000 to the centre, Gs80,000 to the Terminal and Gs70,000 to the Sheraton Hotel (on Aviadores del Chaco). Ask before you get in.

To take a taxi in the other direction, from the Terminal to the airport, there is generally a set fee, currently Gs90,000, which is more than driving to anywhere else in town but is by no means excessive.

To take a **bus** from the airport is amazingly cheap, but you will need to walk a little way, down the exit road to the roundabout, where there is a bus stop. The buses come about every 20 minutes, and cost the same as any public bus anywhere in Asunción, currently Gs2,100. If you have a lot of luggage, you can have a struggle getting onto a bus, as they often have a turnstile by the driver (although this is less common with the buses from the airport). The number of the bus is 30-2 and it has a big 'A' displayed in the front window. Make sure you are on a bus going into the centre (*el centro*) and not in the other direction, to Limpio.

In the other direction, the airport bus runs from the micro-centre along España, past the Shopping del Sol on Aviadores del Chaco, and then along the Autopista.

If you **hire a car**, there are seven companies to choose from, including Avis and Hertz (see *Car hire* below). You can also return a car here if you have hired it from a central car-hire office which is closed on Sunday.

BY TAXI There is a vast network of yellow taxis, with a lot of underemployed drivers waiting for work, and innumerable taxi ranks (*paradas de taxi*). A lot of the taxis rattle as they go along or have broken door handles, etc, but if you regard that as adding to the ambience of your visit to Paraguay it should not bother you. There are no special problems of safety in taking a taxi.

A few taxis have broken meters, so check before you set off. Alternatively it can be worth making a prior agreement with the driver for a set fee for a certain period of time: eg: Gs50,000 for an hour. If you get a taxi that you like, you can also ask what they would charge for taking you on trips to the interior: a recent rate for this has been Gs3,000 per kilometre.

At night you pay a supplement over what you read on the meter; the drivers carry a written table to show what night rate corresponds to the meter reading. The *paradas* all have telephone numbers, and wherever you are in the city you can ask people to ring a taxi for you. Radio taxis include Radio Taxi Asunción (\ *021 311080*) and Radio Taxi Coop (\ *021 550116*).

See also Sudamerica Rent-a-car below for hiring a car with a driver.

BY BUS There are approximately 50 local buses, or *lineas*, run by different companies, so that each line has a slightly different coloured bus. Bus maps cannot be found. You pay when you get on, and it is a flat fare on all buses for all distances, currently Gs2,100. Try to have the change, or at least nothing bigger than a Gs10,000 note.

Here are a few of the useful lines to know:

8	from the Terminal to the centre via Fernando de la Mora
18	from the Terminal to the junction with España, via San Martín
23	from the Ruta Transchaco, IPS Hospital, España, Colón, Cuarta
30-2	from the airport to the centre
31	from the Terminal to the centre via Mariscal López
38	from the Terminal to the centre via Fernando de la Mora
48	from the Terminal to the centre via Eusebio Ayala, then Artigas

CAR HIRE Most of these have branches at the airport in addition to their central reservation offices below.

🚗 **Avis** Eligio Ayala 695 esq Antequera, Plaza Uruguaya; 📞 021 446233; e reservas@avis.com.py; www.avis.com.py

🚗 **Hertz** Av Eusebio Ayala km4.5, Camilo Recalde esq Cerafina Dávalos; 📞 021 605708; m 0971 328086; f 021 610303/611304/503921; e hertz@diesa.com.py

🚗 **Localiza** Av Santa Teresa Esq Austria 3190; 📞 021 683893; e reservation@localiza.com; www.localiza.com.py

🚗 **National** España 1009 esq Washington; 📞 021 232990/4; m 0981 622622; f 021 445890; e info@national.com.py; www.national.com.py

🚗 **Sudamerica Rent-a-car** Airport; 📞 021 645975; m 0981 163195/0971 195291; e sudamericarent@yahoo.com. Cars with or without driver.

🚗 **Touring Cars** Yegros 1045 e/ Tte Fariña y Rca de Colombia; 📞 021 375091/447945;

e wenceslao@touringcars.com.py; www.touringcars.com.py. As well as cars & 4x4, they hire out buses & motorboats.

🚗 **Touring y Automovil Club Paraguayo** 25 de mayo y Brasil; 📞 021 210550/53; www.tacpy.com.py. If you want to drive your own vehicle, & to leave the main road to go on dirt roads, then you will need to hire a 4x4. Unlike the car-hire companies, the insurance of Touring covers journeys on dirt roads – but at a price: you can expect to pay well over US$1,000 for a week of unlimited mileage on earth & asphalt.

🚗 **Trans-Guarani Rent-a-car** Denis Roa 1455; 📞 021 662071; m 0981446188; e autos@transguarani.com; www.transguarani.com

🚗 **Travel Rent-a-car** Airport; 📞 021 645600/9 int 364/021 645666; m 0981 497655/0971 276473; e travelrc@conexioncom.py; www.travelrentacar.com.py

CYCLING Do not make the mistake of the English couple who thought they would bicycle around Asunción and out into the nearby towns in December, having done this successfully in Argentina in the same month. It is much too hot and humid in Paraguay, and the roads are far too bad. After falling off seriously a few times, the couple parked their bikes with a friend and took the bus.

TRANSPORT COMPANIES The following have minibuses for small or medium-sized groups (from six–19 people). See also page 65 on taxis.

JQ Busses Moleón Andreu 1038 c/ Pizarro; 📞 021 334832; e jqbusses@hotmail.com. Run by Jorge Quintana. Has chauffeur-driven cars as well as 2 sizes of minibus, though it is an expensive company so it may not work out any cheaper.
Travel Service Mariotti, esq Pres. Santiago Leon; 📞 021 282529; e travelservice@hipuu.com.py 450207@hipuu.com.py. Very professional, reliable outfit run by Martin Molinas. Range of minibuses.

CG Transporte 📞 021 493604; e carlosgomezjara@hotmail.com. 3 sizes of minibus, & 20 years of experience.
Germán Ramos m 0982 980938; e germanramospy@gmail.com. Freelance driver of minibus, which will take 7 people. Not such a swanky vehicle but has AC & insurance & may work out cheaper.

MAPS The free map of Asunción showing hotels called *Asunción Map Guide* is good: it has amplifications of the city centre and the Villa Morra area, but lacks an index of roads. You can pick this up at Senatur (*Palma 468 e/ Alberdi y 14 de mayo*) or at the airport if the tourist desk is open there. The best map you can buy is the one by Ictus, which folds into a thin slip case, includes Lambaré (which is unusual), has a road index, and is colour-coded for ease of finding your way around; but for this very reason it is not easy to write on, if you like to mark your own places. Also, its amplification of the city centre is not nearly as good as that of the free map. You can buy the Ictus map in a lot of bookshops, including the Librería la Plaza and most of the other bookshops of the Plaza Uruguaya, and El Lector on San Martín, and not only is it the best map, but it is cheaper than its rivals too (Gs14,900). The other good map is slightly larger and is by Touring

(Gs30,000): it is comprehehnsive, has a road index, and is easy to write on as it is printed in pale pink and yellow; but it has few landmarks shown to help you locate yourself and does not include Lambaré. Also, it has no amplification of the city centre, and (at least in the first edition) had a glaring error in marking the airport on the wrong road. You can buy this in some service stations, and from the shop at the offices of Touring (*Brasil c/ 25 de mayo;* \ *021 210550;* ⊕ *08.00–17.00 Mon–Fri*). Apart from these, there is a booklet like a small A–Z called *TAP Guia Asunción*, which is probably the best for finding obscure small streets; it is published by the Hotel Westfalenhaus, and costs Gs30,000. You can buy it from the hotel (*Sgto 1° M Benitez 1577 c/ Santísima Trinidad;* \ *021 292374/292966*), which unfortunately is rather a long way from the centre. .

TOURIST INFORMATION, TOUR OPERATORS AND AGENCIES .

The website for the city of Asunción is www.mca.gov.py and it has a link to an interactive map.

A key address is that of **Senatur** (Secretaría Nacional de Turismo) which has its building Turista Róga (House of the Tourists) on the shopping street Palma in the heart of the city [82 C2] (*Palma 468 e/ Alberdi y 14 de mayo; tourist information* \ *021 494110;* f *021 491230;* e *senator@pla.net.py; www.senatur.gov.py;* ⊕ *07.00–19.00 daily inc Sun & holidays*). As well as being an excellent place to buy souvenirs (see *Craft shops*, page 75) this is the central tourist information office, and is usually able to provide free maps of the country if you ask, probably as good as or better than the maps you can buy, as well as leaflets and verbal information. Do pick up the latest monthly editions of the excellent *Asunción Map Guide* and *Asunción Quick Guide*. These can also be picked up at the airport and at the following hotels: Chaco, Crowne Plaza, Excelsior, Granados, Guaraní Esplendor, Gran Hotel del Paraguay, Las Margaritas, La Misión, Armele, Sheraton, Villa Morra Suites and Yacht y Golf Club.

Another body much involved in tourist information and publications is TACPy, usually referred to as **Touring**, which publishes a lot of materials for tourists, and generally is a good deal more than a motoring organisation [82 G2] (*Touring y Automovil Club Paraguayo, Brasil c/ 25 de mayo;* \ *021 210550;* ⊕ *08.00–17.00 Mon–Fri, 08.00–12.00 Sat*). For people organising conferences, an important contact is the Asunción Convention and Visitors' Bureau (*De las Residentas 987 c/Washington;* \ *021 200952;* e *raquel.britos@asuncionconvention.com; www.asuncionconvention.com*).

Below are the main local tour operators. If you have time to spend, you may find their tours rather rapid, with many hours sitting in a bus, before you emerge limp and weary at a wonderful place that merits more than a whistle-stop tour. But if you are pressed for time, they know how to get you to a lot of places fast.

Agyr [62 C3] 25 de mayo 1767 c/ Mayor Fleitas; \ 021 201244; e info@agyrsa.com; www.agyrsa.com. The company where the Minister of Tourism, Liz Cramer, used to work.

AMA Tours [62 C4] Av General Santos 1952 c/ Teniente Garay; \ 021 312119; e turismo@ama.com.py; www.ama.com.py. Comfortable buses & minibuses. They also have an agency in Ciudad del Este, around which their receptive tourism is mostly centred.

Amitour [62 E3] Aviadores del Chaco 1690; \ 021 612315; f 021 495430; e ami@ami.com.py; www.ami.com.py. Good tourist agency, close to Shopping del Sol.

DTP (Desarrollo Turístico Paraguayo) [62 C3] General Bruguez 353 e/ Mcal Estigarribia y 25 de Mayo; \ 021 221816; f 021 449724; e info@dtp.com.py; www.dtp.com.py. Some say this is the best tour operator.

Inter-Express [82 D3] Herrera y Yegros; \ 021 490111; f 021 449156; e iexpress@interexpress.com.py. A centrally placed travel agent with an excellent record.

Klassen Tours [62 F4] Denis Roa 1455; \ 021 612035; e info@klassentours.com; www.klassentours.com. Offer a very enticing selection of tours all over the country, attractively presented on a website that has an English version too.

Martin Travel [62 C3] Peru 436 c/ España; 𝄽 021 211747; f 021 211870; e incoming@martintravel.com.py; www.martintravel.com.py. Martin Tours is the new name for the receptive tourism wing of Intertours, a major company with a lot of experience. It has the advantages & disadvantages of a big company, ie: loads of confidence but sometimes seems in a rush.

Mavani [82 B2] Palma e/ 14 de mayo y 15 de agosto, Galería Palma, Local 38; 𝄽 021 493580/446654; f 021 441458; e mavani@mavani.com.py; www.mavani.com.py. New & making quite a mark on the market.

Paraguay Natural [62 B4] General Santos y 18 de julio; 𝄽 021 302106; e ecoturismo@paraguaynatural.com.py; www.paraguaynatural.com.py. Good for ecotourism.

Travel Service [62 E2] Mariotti esq Pres. Santiago Leon; 𝄽 021 282529; e 450207@hipuu.com.py. Primarily a transport company, run by Martin Molinas.

VIPs Tours [82 E3] Mexico 782 c/ F R Moreno; 𝄽 021 441199/497117; e vipstour@vipstour.com.py; www.vipstour.com.py. One of the major companies; can do everything from organising tours to airport pickups.

Westfalenhaus [62 F2] Sgto 1º M Benítez 1557 c/ Santísima Trinidad Asunción; 𝄽 021 280533; f 021 291241; e incoming@paraguay.lu; www.paraguay-hotels.com. Good experience & reputation.

🏠 WHERE TO STAY

Asunción has a surprisingly large and growing number of luxury hotels, not all of which can be represented here. Some are in the centre, and others scattered. (As well as the clutch of smart hotels in the Villa Morra area, there is the Yacht y Golf near the river, and the Sheraton near the airport.) In general, hotel prices are lower than those that you would expect in most other countries. At the bottom end of the scale, there is also a fair number of cheap *hospedajes*, though there is currently only one backpacker hostel of the type commonly found in other Latin American countries that caters for English speakers.

🏠 **Hotel La Misión** [62 D3] (36 rooms) San Roque González esq Eulogio Estigarribia, Villa Morra; 𝄽 021 621800/610519; e reservas@lamision.com.py; www.lamision.com.py. The most luxurious & newest of several expensive & new hotels, but this one has real style, with architecture echoing themes from the Ruins of Trinidad & Jesús, & large paintings by Nino Sotelo of Reductions life in the reception. Tucked behind the Mariscal López Shopping, it is not at all central, but this area is becoming increasingly a centre in its own right — although more of a shopping & restaurant centre than anything else. $$$$$

🏠 **Sheraton** [62 F3] (100 rooms) Av Aviadores del Chaco 2066 y Santa Teresa; 𝄽 021 6177000; f 021 6177001; e reservas.asuncion@sheraton.com; www.sheraton.com/asuncion or www.sheraton-asuncion.com.py. One of the best-known hotels, very smart, opened 2004. Not central but on busy road to airport, handy for Museo del Barro, Shopping del Sol. Hosts conferences. $$$$$

🏠 **Yacht y Golf** [62 A5] (116 rooms, 7 suites) Av del Yacht 11; 𝄽 021 906121; f 021 311807; e hotelyacht@hotelyacht.com.py; www.hotelyacht.com.py. The rooms are spacious & have a view of the river or the garden, while the luxury suites have direct access to a private beach.

Golf course, tennis courts, aquatic sports, gym, basketball, ping-pong, hockey, bicycling, Play Room Club for children. It is a long way from the centre, & is more for business people wanting the facilities of a resort, or for conferences, rather than for people wanting to explore the city. Free transfer to & from the airport. $$$$

🏠 **Granados Park Hotel** [82 B2] (71 rooms) Estrella esq 15 de agosto; 𝄽 021 497921; f 021 445324; e reservas@granadospark.com.py; www.granadospark.com.py. Directly opposite Las Margaritas, opened in the same year, with more swish but less imagination than Las Margaritas. Business centre, gym, sauna, massage room, jacuzzi, pool, Wi-Fi. Live music in piano bar. Swimming pool & hydromassage on roof terrace with views over the river. Parking for 100 cars. $$$$

🏠 **Hotel Villa Morra Suites** [62 E3] (30 rooms) Mcal López 3001 c/ Yaraví Yaraví; 𝄽 021 612715; f 021 613715; e hotelvms@villamorrasuites.com.py; www.villamorrasuites.com.py. Designed by a Uruguayan & opened in 2002, large-scale family-run business, suites all with kitchen & nearly all with lounge, some have baths. Wi-Fi, plenty of trees despite being on main road. $$$$

🏠 **Crowne Plaza** [82 F2] (74 rooms) Cerro Corá 939 e/ Tacuari y Estados Unidos; 𝄽 021 452682;

e reservas@crowneasuncion.com.py;
www.crowneasuncion.com.py. Very smart, opened
2005, looks a bit institutional on the outside but is
very nicely furnished inside. Standard, executive or
presidential rooms, & honeymoon suite. Has quiet
zones for better sleeping. Hosts conferences. $$$$

🏠 **Hotel Guaraní Esplendor** [82 C3] (110 rooms)
Oliva esq Independencia Nacional; ☎ 021 452099;
e reservas@guaraniesplendor.com;
www.guaraniesplendor.com. Recently re-opened with
'Esplendor' tagged onto the name, this tall, triangular
building was originally one of Stroessner's prestige
works, & it is a famous landmark in the very centre
of the city. The land was acquired in 1956, the
hotel completed & opened in 1961, remodelled in
1986, & closed in 1995. It fell into increasing
disrepair, but was eventually restored & reopened in
2008. The design is smartly minimalist if a bit
boring, & the AC in the rooms is noisy – no doubt
the result of being based on 50-year-old ducting.
$$$$

🏠 **Premier Hill Hotel** [82 G2] (30 rooms) 25 de
mayo y Curupayty; ☎ 021 215005; f 021 215004;
e hotel@premierhill.hotel.py;
www.premierhill.com.py. Boasts of its English style.
Each of the floors has a different name & a
different design scheme, according to different woods
used. Swimming pool, sauna, Wi-Fi. $$$$

🏠 **Hotel Paramanta** [62 F3] (28 rooms) Av
Aviadores del Chaco 3198 e/ Chacore y Capitan
Meza; ☎ 021 607053; f 021 607052;
e paramanta@paraguay-hotel.de; www.paraguay-
hotel.de. The internet suffix .de always indicates a
German-run hotel. This one is more convenient for
the airport than for the city. Next door is the
Candlewood Apart Hotel, under the same management, which has small flats with a little kitchen, at
the same price for one night, but with a monthly
rate that works out a lot cheaper pro rata. $$$$

🏠 **Hotel Chaco** [82 D2] (70 rooms) Caballero 285
esq Mariscal Estigarribia; ☎ 021 492066; f 021
444223; e info@hotelchaco.com.py;
www.hotelchaco.com.py. Ugly on the outside but is a
friendly & surprisingly cheap place that has been
constantly recommended. Internet connection in all
rooms. Gym, roof terrace, Wi-Fi, parking. It is also
conveniently situated one block from the Plaza
Uruguaya, in the right direction, & right by the best
craft shops & the Librería Intercontinental. Helpful
staff, the manager speaks English fluently. Good
reductions for groups. One free transfer to or from
airport. $$$$

🏠 **Hotel Excelsior** [82 C4] (116 rooms) Chile 980

y Manduvirá; ☎ 021 495632; f 021 496748;
e reservas@excelsior.com.py; www.excelsior.com.py.
Equipped for conferences, can host up to 800
people. Business centre, swimming pool, sauna,
massage, tennis. Rooms with striped wallpaper, deep
pile carpets, quilted bedcovers. Opposite Mall
Excelsior shopping centre, which is an irritating
10min walk from city centre. 2 restaurants, both
with separate entrances onto street: Il Pagliaccio has
recently opened with a new presentation & décor, &
Cabaña La Pascuala is a favourite with tour
agencies, for its live folk music & dance (see below
under *Where to eat*). $$$$

🏠 **Las Margaritas** [82 B2] (60 rooms) Estrella esq
15 de agosto; ☎ 021 448765;
e reservas@lasmargaritas.com.py;
www.lasmargaritas.com.py. Opened in 2000, fantastic
central location. Possibly the most tasteful of the
luxury hotels, with pleasing colour matching
(especially the green of the daisies after which the
hotel is named) & objects of Paraguayan art & craft
along the corridors & in the rooms. Fine view from
open top floor, swimming pool, sauna, gym, games
room, business centre, Wi-Fi, secure internal car park.
Recommended. $$$$

🏠 **Gran Hotel del Paraguay** [62 D3] (54 rooms)
De la Residenta y Padre Pucheau; ☎ 021
200051/52/53/021 214096/97; f 021 214098;
e granhot@pla.net.py; www.granhotel.com.py. A
famous hotel in a historic building, now
overshadowed a little by the many new modern
hotels that make this one look a bit dowdy.
Originally the house of Madame Lynch, it has been a
hotel since it was bought by an Italian immediately
after the War of the Triple Alliance, & has been
known as the Gran Hotel del Paraguay since a
German took it over in 1921. Dining room dates
from the López era & has a painted ceiling. Wi-Fi,
pool, tennis, huge & magnificent grounds full of
toucans & other birds, only a short distance from
city centre. Sat eve may have live folk music.
$$$$

🏠 **Portal del Sol** [62 F3] (50 rooms) Av Denis
Roa 1455 c/ Sta Teresa; ☎ 021 609395/607880;
f 021 662910/602349; e info@hotelportaldelsol.com;
www.portaldelsol.com. Good middle-range hotel, not
plush, but with lovely 2000m² garden with lots of
birds, shady terraces & a swimming pool. Good food
& friendly people, calls itself a 'traditional German
hotel'. Free transfers, Wi-Fi. The downside is that the
hotel is a long way from the centre, & not close to
anywhere you would want to go to except the
Museo del Barro, the Shopping del Sol & the musical

instrument shops along the road towards Luque. There are rooms & apts. Excellent value, & they have been known to be flexible on price. $$$

🏠 **Palmas del Sol Hotel** [82 F1] España 202, c/ Tacuary; 📞 021 449485; e info@hotelpalmasdelsol.com; www.hotelpalmasdelsol.com. A recently opened hotel under the same management as the popular but rather far-out Portal del Sol. Though it faces onto a rather grimy street, it is only just round the corner from the Plaza Uruguaya, so counts as central. Beautifully designed, it brings a great sense of refreshment in this hot, sweaty & polluted city: there is white everywhere, a courtyard filled with trees & plants, & a 2nd courtyard with a small swimming pool. Rooms are spacious & so are bathrooms. German run, like most of the best hotels in Paraguay. $$$

🏠 **Asunción Palace Hotel** [82 A2] (25 rooms) Colón 415, esq Estrella; 📞 021 492151/3; e aphotel@yahoo.com; www.geocities.com/aphotel. Like the Gran Hotel del Paraguay, this is another hotel in a historic building. Built in 1858, it was the house of Mariscal López's brother Venancio, & is marked by 3 rows of colonnades, one above the other, on the façade facing Colón. There are old photos in the reception showing also the time during the Triple Alliance War when it was used as a hospital by the Brazilian army. The rooms are being updated with pleasing simple colours & are quite modern in feel. It is a pity that the sizeable balconies look over such a noisy polluted road, though you can glimpse the river. One room has a real bath — very rare in Paraguay. Wi-Fi. You can negotiate a good discount if you pay cash. $$$

🏠 **Hotel Santo Domingo** [62 C5] (37 rooms) Alcides González esq O Kallsen; 📞 021 550130/555001; e hdomingo@highway.com.py; www.santodomingo.com.py. Has the merit of being close to the Terminal, though in the opposite direction from where anyone is likely to want to go. It has Wi-Fi, a garden with a swimming pool, quite a nice restaurant & they speak some English. Takes credit cards for a small supplement. $$$

🏠 **Westfalenhaus** [62 F2] Sgto 1° M Benitez 1577 c/ Santísima Trinidad; 📞 021 292374/292966; f 021 291241; e westfalenhaus@pla.net.py; www.paraguay-hotel.com. Immaculate hotel with an excellent reputation, following the rule that the best hotels are run by Germans. It looks like a whole street of houses, & has pool, honeymoon suites, rooms for people with disabilities, good conference facilities, all mod cons. Massage, reflexology & chiropractice. Russian cuisine, big buffet b/fast.

English spoken. The hotel has produced some key tourist materials: the *TAP Guía Paraguay* (see page 327) & the *TAP Guía Asunción* (see page 67). The drawback is that the hotel is inconveniently located, though in a quiet neighbourhood. $$$

🏠 **Hotel Bristol** [82 B2] 15 de agosto 472 c/ Oliva; 📞 021 494254; f 021 444221; e hotelbristol@hotelbristol.com.py; www.hotelbristol.com.py. Next door to Las Margaritas & under same management. Remodelled in the last few years. A striking painting on the wall of the lobby is practically the icon of this hotel: it shows 2 red-earth paths through the fields, a tatakuá traditional oven, & some boys playing football. Rooms are pleasantly colour co-ordinated. Wi-Fi. Excellent value. $$$

🏠 **Hotel El Lapacho** [62 D3] Republica Dominicana 543; 📞 021 210662/200721/225070; e reservas@lapacho.com.py; www.lapacho.com.py. This discreet hotel, with no sign displayed, looks like an ordinary house, but inside there is a whole separate block with a swimming pool in the midst of a quadrangle. It was the hotel most used for long stays by the many English families that adopted Paraguayan babies in the early 1990s. It is the 2nd house on the left, to the north of España. Every room has a computer with internet. $$$

🏠 **Hotel Amalfi** [82 D4] (19 rooms) Caballero 877 c/ Manuel Domínguez; 📞 021 494154/441162; e amalfi@hotelamalfi.com.py; www.hotelamalfi.com.py. A lot nicer inside than the slightly garish sign would suggest. Good standard for a modest hotel, with friendly receptionist & Wi-Fi. $$$

🏠 **Hotel Preciado** [82 F3] (18 rooms) Félix de Azara 840 c/ Tacuary; 📞 021 447661/453937; e hotelpreciado@yahoo.es; www.hotelpreciado.com.py. Economic hotel in 19th-century building, close to centre. Internal parking (entrance from the street Herrera). Wi-Fi, cable TV. A good way of combining lower mid-range quality & a central position with a building of architectural character — although there is nothing to see of the 19th-century style when you get past the façade. $$$

🏠 **City Hotel** [82 C3] (70 rooms) Nuestra Señora de la Asunción esq Humaita; 📞 021 491418/451153; f 021 491497; e hotel_city@webmail.com.py. Hideous on the outside, with grey & pink concrete cubes, but it is quite well situated for the centre, & at least has more of a Latin American clientele than most of the posher hotels. Wi-Fi, computer for use of guests. Takes credit cards for 10% surcharge. $$$

🏠 **Plaza Hotel** [82 E2] (about 40 rooms) Eligio Ayala esq Paraguarí; ✆ 021 444196/444772/448834: f 021 448834; e plazahotel@highway.com.py; www.plazahotel.com.py. On the Plaza Uruguaya, next to the disused railway station. A bit old fashioned & chipped, but with a good location. $$$

🏠 **Residencial Itapúa** [82 F3] Fulgencio R Moreno 943 c/ Estados Unidos; ✆ 021 445121. Cheap, clean & friendly, reasonably central. No sign up. Private bathrooms, fans. Priced per person so works out cheap for singles. B/fast is optional extra. $$

🏠 **Black Cat Hostel** [82 D2] Eligio Ayala 129 e/ Yegros e Independencia Nacional; ✆ 021 49827; m 0981 996033; e vcolman05@hotmail.com. New on the scene – Paraguay's first & so far, only, backpacker hostel. Dormitories, either with AC or fan. Use of sitting room, kitchen, Wi-Fi. Initial impressions are very good, helpful family, & they speak fluent English. $$

🏠 **Hotel La Española** [82 D3] Herrera 142; ✆ 021 449280/447312. A much simpler hotel, but it still offers cable TV, AC, free Wi-Fi, & takes credit cards for a small supplement. $$

🏠 **Hotel San Pablo** [62 D4] Tte Alcides González 1578 c/ Tabapý; ✆ 021 552149; f 021 550164. Cheap little place very close to the Terminal, all rooms have private bathrooms, they also do an economical monthly rate. $

🏠 **Hotel Quinta Avenida** [62 B3] (18 rooms) Parapiti 1697 c/ Quinta Av; ✆ 021 371550. Cheap but decent, most rooms have AC. $

✖ WHERE TO EAT

You can eat very well in Asunción. Most restaurants are open every day; assume this, unless otherwise specified. Key times for eating are midday for lunch, and from 20.00 for dinner. While all restaurants are marked on the maps, cafés and supermarkets are not. Those grouped under *City centre* below appear on the *City centre* map, pages 82–3; the others appear on the map on pages 62–3.

There is a surprising shortage of places where you can have lunch outside, in the hot Paraguayan weather, because Paraguayans prefer to eat indoors with air conditioning. If you are looking for a restaurant with outside space, not on a main road, try Luna Vinera and Ciervo Blanco, but note that they are open only in the evening. At lunchtime your best bet would be the Gran Hotel del Paraguay, and ask them to serve you outside, or try La Paraguayita or Il Capo near the Sheraton.

You are advised to take a long-sleeved garment as the air conditioning is often turned up high and you can be cold inside, even (and especially) when it is sweltering outside.

CITY CENTRE

✖ **Talleyrand** [82 F2] Mcal Estigarribia 932, e/ Estados Unidos y Tacury; ✆ 021 441163/661618. A 30-year-old establishment discreetly placed in the centre; excellent food but on the dear side as Paraguayan restaurants go; décor with low beams & tapestry chairs, a bit like an English pub, nice atmosphere but not a lot of customers. They also have a restaurant in the Shopping del Sol, 1st floor (✆ *021 611697*), & in Mcal López 2351 c/ Venezuela (✆ *021 214471*). $$$$$

✖ **La Preferida** [82 F2] 25 de mayo 1005 c/ EEUU; ✆ 021 210641/202222; ⏰ daily. One of the many delights in this beautiful & intimate 1st-floor restaurant is the ghostly piano that greets you with its playerless music as you walk up the stairs. Everything here is quality. Under same management as Hotel Cecilia next door. $$$$

✖ **Il Pagliaccio** [82 C4] Manduvirá esq Chile; ✆ 021 495632 int 1861; ⏰ Mon–Sat. Italian & international cuisine, part of Hotel Excelsior. $$$$

✖ **Cabaña La Pascuala** [82 C4] Manduvirá c/ Chile; ✆ 021 495632 int 1420; ⏰ Tue–Sun. The other restaurant of the Hotel Excelsior. Serves Paraguayan cuisine & a grill, with folk music & dance at 21.30 every night on a tiny stage, looking out onto a garden with a swimming pool. (A better stage for dancing is found at El Ciervo Blanco, see page 71.) $$$$

✖ **Bar San Roque** [82 E2] Eligio Ayala 792 esq Tacury; ✆ 021 446015; ⏰ Mon–Sat. This is the oldest restaurant in the country, & is recommended, for its food, its authentic Paraguayan ambience & its reasonable prices. On the corner is a bar, & the restaurant opens off there. Try the *puchero* & don't miss the mousse *mburucuyá*. $$$

✖ **Luna Vinera** [82 C5] Ygatimi 250 c/ Chile; ✆ 021 491604; ⏰ Tue–Sun, eves only from 19.00. Delightful restaurant full of character with internal courtyard open to the balmy night air & full of plants. Imaginative food, very reasonable. Attractive rooms for private dinners or events. Large chess set of Indians versus Conquistadors in the bar area. Live music sometimes. $$$

✖ **Bolsi** [82 C2] Estrella 399 esq Alberdi; ☎ 021 491841/2; ⊕ daily. Conveniently placed in the heart of the centre, Bolsi has a café & pastry shop section, & a smallish restaurant with excellent food. It is quite elegant but is surprisingly reasonable. It has been open since 1960, which in Paraguayan terms means it is an old establishment. Recommended. $$$

✖ **Café Literario** [82 D2] Mariscal Estigarribia 456; ☎ 021 491640; ⊕ 16.00–midnight Sun–Thu, 16.00–02.00 Fri & Sat. Though the service is slow, this is a place of such restful enjoyment that you may find yourself returning again & again – annoyed only by the limited opening hours. There is nothing very substantial in the way of food – sandwiches & snacks rather than full meals – but the fruit juices are splendid & the atmosphere exquisite. Not only are there papers to read, but a large & very interesting variety of books to buy, or simply to browse through while you sip your banana & strawberry juice. A wall display of writers' photos provides an education in Paraguayan literature. Upstairs in a discreet gallery are comfortable armchairs. Great place to recover your energy after footing it round town. $$$

✖ **Rodizio** [82 B2] Palma 591 e/ 14 de mayo y 15 de agosto; ☎ 021 451281; ⊕ Mon–Sat & Sun lunch. Pay by weight *churrasquería*, excellent value, packed every lunchtime. $$

✖ **Doña Chipa** [82 G1] España y Brasil; ☎ 021 228440. This is the central house of a new chain of cafés, serving a delicious range of *chipas*, with tantalising smells, to eat on the spot or take away. The *chipa a 4 quesos* ('with 4 cheeses') is particularly good, but so also are the rest of the range, which includes *mbejú*. $

✖ **Lido Bar** [82 C2] Palma y Chile; ☎ 021 446171. On the corner opposite the Panteón, this is a well-known & long-established café, always jam-packed at lunchtime, with all the customers eating around a big circular bar. Prices are cheap. The fish soup is a speciality, & there is a good variety of fruit juices. $

✖ **Via Piana** [82 C2] Estrella 330 c/ Chile; ☎ 021 453045. Small bar with character tucked in between shops close to Plaza de los Héroes, good on food & good on coffee. $

✖ **Street food** [82 C3] There are tables in the street where you can eat well enough for very little. In Palma there is one such place, though you need to be prompt at midday before the food runs out, & you might feel it inappropriate to be taking cheap food out of the mouths of the Paraguayans. In the Plaza de la Libertad, next to the craft stalls, is another open-air improvised restaurant. $

BETWEEN CITY CENTRE AND VILLA MORRA/SHOPPING DEL SOL AREA

✖ **Mburicao** [82 D3] Prof Antonio González Rioboó 737; ☎ 021 660048. Definitely expensive but high quality. Tricky to find: from Mariscal López turn down Chóferes del Chaco, then first right down Chaco Boreal, & first left down González Rioboó. Minimalist design with Scandinavian feel, wood, beige & white, bright lights, good waiters. Outside space viewed through glass walls. International menu, very big helpings. $$$$$

✖ **La Pérgola** [82 C3] Peru 240 e/ Rio de Janeiro y Jose Berges; ☎ 021 214014; ⨍ 021 212025. Smart restaurant, with upmarket cafeteria next door. On the dear side for Paraguay, but offers quality food, imaginatively presented, though the décor is angular & rather plain, & the restaurant lacks atmosphere. There is a floodlit fountain outside, but it is on the main road & you cannot sit out there. Every table gets a big basket of warm cheese-breads with a dip & a liver paste. Close to the Gran Hotel de Paraguay. $$$$

✖ **La Paraguayita** [62 D3] Brasilia y Republica Siria; ☎ 021 204497; ⊕ daily. Has a roofed outside area far enough from the main road España to make a quiet place to eat in the open air. The restaurant is frequented by Paraguayan media stars. Extensive menu, including traditional dishes, & the food comes beautifully presented. $$$

✖ **Catalonia Restaurant** [82 C2] España 560 c/ Brasil; ☎ 021 224851; ⊕ Tue–Sun lunch. Recently opened under the management of 3 partners, one of whom, Rosa Regordosa, is the mother of the Catalonian cook. Friendly service, excellent food. Recommended. $$$

✖ **San Miguel** [82 C2] España 1165 c/ Padre Cardozo; ☎ 021 200555/206047; ⊕ Mon–Sun lunch. One block before St Andrew's Anglican Church, this restaurant is famous for its *milanesas*, some of which come stuffed with vegetables. It has a garden, but it is right on the main road. Paraguayans prefer to eat inside anyway, with AC. Live music Fri 21.00. $$$

✖ [62 C2] **Proa Café** Padre Juan Pucheu 594 c/ España; ☎ 021 222456; ⊕ 08.00–23.00 Mon–Fri, 08.00–01.30 Sat & Sun. A literary & cultural café, where you can have a drink or a light meal surrounded by books & paintings by good artists. At night they may have tango. $$

✖ **El Boliche** [62 C2] Juan de Salazar 363 c/ Artigas; m 0981 444140. Bar run by Uruguayans next to Anglo language school, with rustic chairs & tables in open-air yard with roof. Homemade dishes,

VILLA MORRA/SHOPPING DEL SOL AREA

✖ **Piegari** [62 E3] Av del Chaco 2059; ✆ 021 622925; e reservas@piegari.com.py; www.piegari.com.py. Newly opened, top of the range branch of an international chain of restaurants with a pasta speciality. $$$$

✖ **Quebracho** [82 D3] Torreani Viera 343 esq Eulogio Estigarribia, barrio Villa Morra; ✆ 021 660381/663236; ⊕ for lunch daily except Sat, for dinner daily except Sun & Mon. Expensive restaurant close to Asunción's most expensive hotel, La Misión. Tasteful décor with brick-red paint balancing soft neutral colours, fish tank, huge helpings. More economical set menus at midday. $$$$

✖ **Las Cañitas** [62 D3] Carmen Soler 4105; ✆ 021 605936; ⊕ Mon–Sat. Fantastic atmosphere in the wine cellar of this excellent little wine bar & bistro. Quality food & huge wine list. They serve good wine by the glass, with good descriptions to help you choose. $$$$

✖ **Ciervo Blanco** [82 D4] Jose Asunción Flores 3870 c/Radio Operadores del Chaco; ✆ 021 214504/212918; ⊕ from 20.00, show starts at 22.00, on Fri & Sat the show goes on till the early hours, closed Sun. A great place for a night out, with a show of music & folk dance in the semi-open while you eat grilled meat; it works out a little on the pricey side, but is worth it for the ambience & entertainment. $$$$

✖ **Rolandi** [82 E3] Mcal López esq Mayor I Rivarola; ✆ 021 610447/609663; ⊕ Mon–Fri & Sat eve & Sun lunch. International & Paraguayan cuisine. Close to Hotel Villa Morra Suites. $$$$

✖ **Un Toro y Siete Vacas** [82 E3] Malutín 703 esq Eusebio Lillo; ✆ 021 600425; ⊕ daily. Excellent

OTHER AREAS

✖ **Tembi'u He** [82 F2] Francisco Fernández esq Santísima Trinidad; ✆ 021 293324. All the range of traditional Paraguayan cooking, in a restaurant with a Guaraní name ('Meal nice'). Close to Hotel Westfalenhaus & not much else. $$$

✖ **Salemma Supercenter** This huge supermarket with a monster sign saying 'S' inside 2 red circles, that

pizzas, hamburgers, etc. Hotdog (*pancho*) recommended. $

✖ **Mingo** [62 C3] Mayor Fleitas e/ Teodoro Mongeles y Herminio Giménez; ✆ 021 203580. Upstairs buffet with salad, downstairs other dishes. Near Mercado 4, this is an example of how cheaply you can eat in Asunción, & still get good quality & variety. $

cooking, good service, recommended. $$$$

✖ **Hacienda Las Palomas** [62 E3] Guido Spano 1481, esq Senador Long; ✆ 021 605111; ⊕ every eve Mon–Sat, & Sun lunch. Live music Fri & Sat. Mexican cuisine, very good, lovely décor. Recommended. Close to Shopping Villa Mora. $$$$

✖ **Paulista Grill** [82 E3] Av San Martín c/ Mariscal López; ✆ 021 608624/611501. Big churrasquería with nothing to offer in the way of décor or ambience, but the grill is excellent with an extensive selection of meats, & the parking is safe because you can sit & look at your car right outside the window. Live music Fri & Sun. $$$

✖ **Il Capo** [82 E3] Austria 1689; ✆ 021 608704. Italian cuisine, out of the centre but close to the Sheraton Hotel. Has a nice garden for eating out. Another branch of the same restaurant is opposite La Pérgola, at Perú 291 c/ José Berges; ✆ 021 213022. $$$

✖ **Shangri-la** [82 E3] Aviadores del Chaco y San Martín; ✆ 021 661618. Chinese cuisine, smart décor, out of the centre but close to the Sheraton Hotel. $$$

✖ **Acuarela** [82 E3] Mariscal López c/ San Martín; ✆ 021 605183/601750; ⊕ daily. Extensive buffet, excellent salad selection includes rocket; not a lot of ambience but very reasonable $$$

✖ **O Gaucho** [82 D3] Dr Toribio Pacheco 4444 esq Mac Arthur; ✆ 021 608596. In the small streets behind the La Recoleta cemetery, this is a Brazilian *churrasquería* which has live music, great atmosphere, packed with ordinary Paraguayans enjoying a night out. Pay Gs50,000 all inclusive & eat as much as you like. Recommended. $$$

you pass on your way into (or out of) Asunción on Eusebio Ayala, provides a handy place to eat with convenient parking on the long crawl through the suburbs of the capital, if you have missed (or cannot wait for) the Frutería in Paraguarí. It has a *churrasquería* as well as a café. $

There are **cinemas** at the Shopping del Sol [62 E3] (✆ *021 611763*), Shopping Mall Excelsior [82 C4] (✆ *021 443015*), Shopping Villa Mora [62 E3] (✆ *021 605795*), Cinecenter Hiperseis [62 E4] (*Mariscal López y Teniente Casco;* ✆ *021 613390*) and Patio Real Cines (*Acceso Sur c/ Usher Rios;* ✆ *021 525309*). See below for details of the shopping centres.

Many young people in Asunción like to stay out all night and finish the night with breakfast. If this selection of **bars, discotheques and nightclubs** is not enough for you, you will find many more at www.asunfarra.com.py/directorio.php.

☆ **Paseo Carmelitas** [62 E3] España c/ Senador Long; ⊕ till very late. New & stylish place, very much designed in the hope of finding a new cosmopolitan generation with money. Not so much a shopping centre as a complex of smart bars & restaurants.

☆ **El Sitio** [62 E4] República Argentina 1035 c/ Souza; ✆ 021 612822; ⊕ 22.00–04.00. One of the top discotheques for young people, karaoke Tue & Thu.

☆ **Pirata Bar** [82 A1] Ayolas y Benjamín Constant; ✆ 021 452953–4; www.piratabar.com.py; ⊕ 21.00–04.00 Fri & Sat. Nightclub with a pirate theme, cheaper for women than for men, gets very full. Central, near the Manzana de la Rivera.

☆ **Sargento Pimienta** [82 E1] Tacuary esq/ Mariscal López; ✆ 021 449960; ⊕ 18.30–05.00 Tue–Sat. Bar with discotheque, salsa.

☆ **Britannia Pub** [82 E2] Cerro Cora 851 c/ Tacuary; ✆ 021 43990; www.britannia-pub.com; ⊕ Tue–Sun. Bar with theme of British pub, a popular hangout, always full, sells food. Free entry except on certain nights when there is something special on.

☆ **La Mexicana** [82 A2] Presidente Franco c/ Ayolas. A bar until midnight, then they move the chairs & tables & it becomes a disco playing a mix of Latin & dance music.

CULTURAL SPACES There are a number of places around Asunción – some indoors and some outdoors – where cultural or sporting events are often held, and which are difficult to find because they are not usually marked on maps and the addresses are rarely given. You are just expected to know. The events may range from lectures to exhibitions, from films to football matches. Here is a list of relevant addresses:

Alianza Francesa [82 F2] Mariscal Estigarribia 1039 c/ EEUU; ✆ 021 210382; www.alianzafrancesa.edu.py or/ www.alfran.com. The French cultural centre. It has exhibitions & films.

Arpa Roga [62 F3] Dr Patricio Maciel 559 c/ Sinforiano Buzó; ✆ 021 672557; e info@ arparoga.com; www.arparoga.com 'The house of the harp' (Guaraní) is a venture of the Pedersen family of musicians. (Cristóbal is a guitarist & his son Kike & brother Rito are harpists.) The centre has some harps of famous musicians on display, & occasionally hosts concerts & tourist events. It is just outside the ring road & is hard to find on maps, but Buzó is the first turning off Madame Lynch to the north of the junction with Santa Teresa, & Dr Maciel is the first road parallel to Madame Lynch.

Centro Paraguayo-Japonés [62 F3] Julio Correa y Tte. Velázquez; ✆ 021 603197; www.centroparaguayojapones.blogspot.com/. The Japanese cultural centre. It has a theatre.

Cerro Porteno [62 B3] Acuña de Figueroa y Cerro León, barrio Obrero; www.clubcerro.com/historia.html. One of Asunción's two most high-profile football

clubs. Red-&-blue strip (*azulgrana*).

Club de Olimpia [62 D3] Mariscal López 1499 y Pitiantuta; ✆ 021 200680/200780; e info@olimpia.com.py; www.clubolimpia.com.py. The other high-profile football club in Asunción. Black-&-white strip. It has won the Copa Libertadores 3 times.

Conmebol [62 H3] Autopista esq Petrona Almirón de Leoz; ✆ 021 650993. The conference centre of the Confederación Suamericana de Fútbol, next to the Football Museum on the way to the airport.

Consejo Nacional de Deportes [62 D4] Eusebio Ayala e/ República Argentina y Av de la Victoria. Huge sporting area with a jockey club.

Embajada Argentina [62 C2] España esq Perú; ✆ 021 212320/4; www.embajada-argentina.org.py. It has a theatre, Leopoldo Marechal, with capacity for 300.

Estadio Defensores del Chaco [62 A2] Juan Díaz de Solis y Orihuela, barrio Carlos Antonio López, near barrio Sajonia. The principal football stadium, used for international matches & high-profile league games such as Cerro Porteño v Olimpia. Capacity for 36,000.

Ex-Seminario Metropolitano [62 D3] Kubitschek e/ 25 de mayo y Speratti. No longer used as a seminary, this is a large site that is sometimes used for other events.

Instituto Cultural Paraguayo-Alemán [62 C2] Juan de Salazar 310 c/ Artigas; ℡ 021 226242; www.icpagz.org.py. The German cultural centre.

Juan de Salazar [82 F3] Tacuary 745 c/ Herrera; ℡ 021 449921; www.juandesalazar.org.py. The Spanish cultural centre. It hosts a lot of exhibitions & films.

Municipalidad de Asunción [62 F4] Mariscal López 5556 y Capitán Bueno; ℡ 021 663311/20. The town hall of the city.

Teatro Arlequín [62 E5] Antequera 1061 y República de Colombia; ℡ 021 442152; e info@arlequin.com.py; www.arlequin.com.py. Small theatre, interesting shows.

Teatro del Banco Central del Paraguay [62 E2] Federación Rusa y Sgto Marecos (next to IPS Hospital); ℡ 021 6192243; www.bcp.gov.py. From the home page go to Aspectos Institucionales & then Complejo Edilicio. The theatre has capacity for 1,100.

Teatro Municipal [82 C2] Presidente Franco e/ Chile y Alberdi; ℡ 021 445169; e patridomi@hotmail.com; www.mca.gov.py/teatrom.html. See below, page 94.

SPECIAL EVENTS

Expo For the first two weeks of July every year, there is a large exhibition on the outskirts of Asunción, in the town of Mariano Roque Alonso, called the Expoferia Internacional de Ganadería, Industria, Agricultura, Comercio y Servicios, or the Expo for short (*Gs12.000 in 2009*). It attracts an average of 70,000 visitors. Take a bus marked 'Expo' from the Terminal, going south down Fernando de la Mora, and then north around the ring road Madame Lynch, until it passes the Expo on the right-hand side, almost an hour later.

The Expo has many special events each day, ranging from lectures to dance displays, fashion shows to motorbike displays. There are funfairs and restaurants, and almost every conceivable kind of company has a stand there. A novelty for foreign visitors is the emphasis on animals. You can observe how the typically Paraguayan Brahma (grey with a hump and floppy ears) is crossed with an Angus to produce the highly successful Brangus, which is very hardy, particularly in a hot and humid climate like Paraguay's. There are also a lot of fine horses, including Arabs, the skewbald spotted paint horse and the handsomely spotted Appaloosa.

Festival Mundial del Arpa Since 2007 there has been an annual Festival Mundial del Arpa or World Harp Festival (*www.festivalmundialdelarpa.com*) in November in Asunción, with participation of Paraguayan harpists living inside and outside of the country, as well as other international harpists who play different kinds of harps. During the day they have workshops, and on three consecutive evenings the Teatro Municipal hosts concerts.

San Baltasar Strictly speaking, Fernando de la Mora is not Asunción but a separate town, but it adjoins it in a continuous urban sprawl. In its barrio of Loma Campamento, the African-American community hold a renowned musical festival to celebrate the night of 6 January – the feast of the Epiphany and therefore of San Baltasar (traditionally the black king). The African-American dance group is called Kamba Kua. For further information contact the *municipalidad* (℡ 021 500007) or Lázaro Medina (m 0982 374736).

SHOPPING

CRAFT SHOPS See *Craft*, page x, for the varieties of Paraguayan craft.

The tourist office of **Senatur** (Secretaría Nacional de Turismo) is housed in the building called Turista Róga or 'the house of the tourists' [82 C2] (*Palma 468 e/ Alberdi y 14 de mayo;* ℡ *021 441530;* f *021 491230;* e *senator@pla.net.py; www.senatur.gov.py*). It has an excellent indoor marketplace of typical crafts, not huge but of the best quality, including silver *filigrana* jewellery, *ao po'í* embroidered clothes, carved saints, *ñandutí* lace circles and wonderful wooden and feather creations by the indigenous. This is also the central tourist information office, and is usually able to provide free maps of the country if you ask. Do pick up the latest editions of the excellent *Asunción Map Guide* and *Asunción Quick Guide*.

Another building where many of the finest crafts are gathered together in one place is **Artesano Róga** or 'the house of the artesan', on the east side of the Plaza Uruguaya, between Eligio Ayala and Mariscal Estigarribia, that is, between Avis and the Plaza bookshop. It is run by IPA, the Instituto Paraguayo de Artesanía.

There is an outdoor market of little craft stalls in the Plaza de la Libertad, **behind the Panteón**, which is enjoyable to walk through and to browse here and there.

On the other side from the centre, near the port, is a run of older craft shops under an arcade, known as La Recova. On the way to La Recova, walking down Palma, you will pass the best shops of leatherware, which sell a huge variety of bags as well as sandals, belts and other accessories. The three principal shops selling attractive Paraguayan crafts are all in the same barrio: Overall, Folklore and Bella Tierra.

Overall [82 D2] Caballero c/ Mcal Estigarribia; ✆ 021 448657; ⌚ 08.00–18.00 Mon–Fri, 8.00–12.30 Sat. Beautiful craft shop next to the Librería Intercontinental, particularly strong on Christmas cribs & tablecloths, traycloths, napkins. A branch also in the Shopping del Sol (✆ 021 611739), which does not close on Sat afternoon.
Bella Tierra [82 D2] 25 de mayo 370 c/ Iturbe; ✆ 021 447891; also Shopping Villa Morra, Local 19, PB, ✆ 021 604395; e overall@overall.com.py;

www.overall.com.py; ⌚ 08.00–18.00 Mon–Fri, 08.00–12.00 Sat. Recently renamed, this shop used to operate under the name 'Overall 25 de mayo'. It sells a tempting selection of leather, wood, silver craft, clothes & sometimes even furniture.
Folklore [82 D2] Mariscal Estigarribia esq Iturbe; ✆ 021 450148. The most visible of the craft shops because it has big wooden carvings of Guaraní mythical figures on the pavement outside.

BOOKSHOPS Most shops in Paraguay called *librería* (bookshop) are only stationers. However, in Asunción there are a number of genuine bookshops. The Plaza Uruguaya [82 E2] is the centre for **bookshops**, with several shops round about and three situated in the middle of the plaza itself: **El Lector** (✆ 021 491966/493908), and in two identical pavilions **El Libre en Su Casa** and **Servilibro**.

Librería La Plaza [82 E2] Antequera y Mcal Estigarribia; ✆ 021 440073/492853. Good secondhand stock hidden inside a discreet exterior, halfway down the side of the Plaza Uruguaya facing the taxis. They have only recently got round to putting up a shop sign.
La Oficina del Libro [82 E2] 25 de Mayo 640, entrepiso, Edificio Garantia; e laoficinadellibro@hotmail.com. Run by the dedicated and talkative Julio Rafael Aquino, & hidden away up a staircase (technically between the ground & the 1st floors) with nothing visible from the street. Tiny rooms bulging with antiquarian & secondhand books lead one into another, until you wonder where it will end.
Comuneros [82 E2] Cerro Corá 289 c/ Iturbe; ✆ 021 446176; f 021 444667; e rolon@conexion.com.py; ⌚ 07.30–12.00 & 15.30–18.00 Mon–Fri, 07.30–12.00 Mon–Sat. One of the best secondhand bookshops, also close to the Plaza Uruguaya.
Dominguez Libros [82 E2] 25 de mayo 458 c/

Caballero; ✆ 021 445459. A smaller, newer bookshop – also close to the Plaza Uruguaya. Now building up a good stock in secondhand books.
Café Literario [82 D2] Mariscal Estigarribia 456; ✆ 021 491640. A bookshop as well as a café. Have a drink while you browse, maybe flopping into an armchair in the privacy of the discreet balcony area upstairs. The walls are covered with pictures of Paraguay's leading literary figures, & not just Augusto Roa Bastos (see box opposite).
El Lector [62 E3] Av San Martin c/ Austria; ✆ 021 610639/614258/614259. The main store is in a large, modern building 5mins' walk from Shopping del Sol; another branch is in the Plaza Uruguaya, see above.
Librería Intercontinental [82 D2] Caballero 270; ✆ 021 496991/449738; e agatti@libreriaintercontinental.com.py; www.libreriaintercontinental.com.py; ⌚ 08.00–12.00 & 15.00–19.00 Mon–Fri, 08.00–12.00 Sat. One of

the best bookshops especially for academic books, the best dictionaries, & books about Paraguayan history. They take credit cards, but have to ring through first. Closed for 3hrs at lunchtime.

Librería Técnica [62 B3] Blas Garay 106 (Cuarta) c/ Independencia Nacional; ✆ 021 496778/390396; e ventas@etp.com.py or etprentas@cmm.com.py. This is hidden away, not only in its location but also in its storefront, but once you step inside, & work your way from room to room, you will find it a treasure trove – principally of academic books. There is another branch in the Shopping del Sol (*local 124;* ✆ *021 611717*).

Books [82 B2] Mariscal López 3791; ✆ 021 603722; e ventasbooks@tigo.com.py. Mostly English books, but an excellent Spanish selection too. Opposite Shopping Villa Morra, branch in Shopping del Sol, *local* 154.

Quijote [62 E3] Av San Martin 1156 c/ Agustín Barrios; ✆ 021 621551; www.quijote.com.py; ◷ 08.00–18.00 Mon–Fri, 09.00–12.00 Sat. A bookshop that reaches out more to popular tastes & to tourists, with attractive shopfronts in the most frequented shopping areas. It sells CDs as well as books & also has branches in the Shopping Mall Excelsior (*local 118;* ✆ *021 443015 int 1118*), the Shopping Mariscal López (*local 224;* ✆ *021 608455*), the Shopping del Sol (*local 160;* ✆ *021 611813*) and Estrella 691 c/ O'Leary (✆ *021 491438*).

Librería Paulinas [82 D3] Azara 279 c/ Iturbe; ✆ 021 440651; e paulinas@pla.net.py. The classic Catholic bookshop.

Parroquia San Rafael [62 D4] Cruz del Chaco 1690 c/ Alfredo Seiferheld; ✆ 021 661607; ◷ 08.00–12.00,

AUGUSTO ROA BASTOS

Undoubtedly Paraguay's most renowned literary figure, Augusto Roa Bastos (1917–2005) was born in Asunción but spent his childhood in a small village in the campo, Iturbe, and writes brilliantly about the life of campesinos in one of his most famous novels, *Hijo de Hombre* (1960). He was one of a generation of literary figures that shone in the *Grupo de 1940* (also known as the *Vy'á Ratý*, 'Nest of Joy') and regarded as the fathers of Paraguayan literature, but were then mostly forced into exile for their left-wing views in the 1947 repression, leading up to the dictatorship of Stroessner (1954–89).

Roa Bastos had to go into exile for political reasons in 1947 (after hiding in the water tank on the roof when his house was ransacked by a right-wing group), and could not permanently return until after the end of the dictatorship. In exile he wrote his most acclaimed work, *Yo El Supremo* (1974), allegedly about the dictatorship of Dr Francia (who called himself 'El Supremo') but with an implicit attack on the regime of Stroessner. This novel won the Brazilian Premio de Letras del Memorial de América Latina (1988), the highly esteemed Spanish prize Premio Cervantes (1989), and the Condecoración de la Orden Nacional del Mérito (1990) in his own country as soon as the dictatorship was ended. He was later decorated with Cuba's highest honour, the Orden José Martí (2003). He wrote five novels, and several collections of short stories (eg: *El Trueno entre las Hojas*, 1953, *El Baldío*, 1966) and of poetry (eg: *El Naranjal Ardiente*, 1960). His works have been translated into 25 languages.

A charming man who called himself 'something of an atheist' and remained deeply socialist to the end of his days, Roa Bastos returned to live in Asunción in 1996, where he died ten years later. 'Literature is capable of winning battles against adversity,' he wrote, 'with no more arms than letter and spirit, with no more power than imagination and language.'

The other literary figures of his generation include the poet Hérib Campos Cervera (1905–53), the poet Elvio Romero (1926–2004), the playwright Julio Correa (1890–1953), the novelist Gabriel Casaccia (1907–80) and the multi-skilled Josefina Plá (1909–99) – who was born in the Canary Islands but adopted Paraguay as her home in 1927, where she was prolific as an essayist, poet, journalist and academic historian, not to mention as an potter of beautiful ceramic works.

15.30–20.00 Mon–Sat. This Catholic parish bookshop specialises in books on the Jesuit Reductions written or edited by the prolific P Aldo Trento. They also sell the best postcards currently available of Jesuit–Guaraní Baroque art (which is not saying much). **Librería de Ediciones Montoya/CEPAG** [62 B2] 15 de agosto c/ 7a Proyectada. The Jesuit publishing house, which publishes a lot of important books on history, the Reductions, and the Guaraní language, as well as the Jesuit monthly *Acción*, has a bookshop here, in the building behind Fe y Alegría (which fronts onto the next street O'Leary, no. 1847).

SHOPPING CENTRES If you need quality and reliable goods of any variety, it is safest to go to one of the shopping malls, which are like palaces of the rich, with their air conditioning, escalators and conspicuous consumption. Most of them have supermarkets attached, decent eating places of an international self-service style, and clean, public toilets. All have cash machines and several have a RadioShack where you can buy reliable technology (though not cheaply – technology can be bought more cheaply in the little Korean shops found in the Galería Palma, which runs from Palma to Estrella, between 15 de agosto and O'Leary).

Super Centro [82 B3] Oliva y 14 de mayo. Less grand than the newly built malls, but is dead central, & has a lot of useful shops. Has a good salad bar in the middle, & more shops upstairs. Some useful computer shops.
Mall Excelsior [82 C4] Chile e/ Manduvirá y Piribebuy; ℡ 021 443017/8. Good range of shops, slightly south of the centre, but comfortable walking distance.
Shopping Villa Mora [62 E3] Mariscal López y General Charles de Gaulle; ℡ 021 601137/8. Some 3 blocks towards the centre from the junction with República Argentina.
Shopping Mariscal López [62 E3] Quesada y General Charles de Gaulle; ℡ 021 611272. Confusingly, the shopping mall on the road Mariscal López is called the Shopping Villa Mora, while the Shopping Mariscal López is directly behind it, in the next block.
Shopping del Sol [62 E3] Aviadores del Chaco c/ César López Moreira; ℡ 021 611780/1. Perhaps the most famous of all the shopping centres. On the road to the airport.
Multiplaza [62 E4] Eusebio Ayala 4501, c/ Av RI 18 Pitiantuta. A very large shopping centre 5km from the centre, but inside the Madame Lynch ring road. It has generally cheaper goods & is much frequented by Paraguayans, who get off their buses there on the way in from the countryside.

DEPARTMENT STORES Palma is traditionally known as the quality shopping street in Asunción, and these department stores are all on or adjacent to it.

Nueva Americana [82 D2] Mariscal Estigarribia 111 esq Independencia Nacional; ℡ 021 492021; ⊕ 9.00–20.00 Mon–Fri, 08.30–13.00 Sat
La Riojana [82 D2] Estigarribia 171 esq Yegros; ℡ 021 492211. Slightly old fashioned, more typically Paraguayan.
Unicentro [82 B2] Palma esq 15 de agosto; ℡ 021 445309/10; ⊕ 9.00–21.00 Mon–Sat, 12.00–21.00 Sun & holidays. Good shop, spread over 8 floors. They also have a branch at the Shopping del Sol, 1st floor.

MERCADO CUATRO Mercado Cuatro [62 C3] is the equivalent of a department store for ordinary Paraguayans – a vast market of little shops all jammed on top of each other, some inside and some outside, where all the shops selling the same kind of product are grouped together, eg: towels, cutlery, clothes, folk-dance accessories, CDs. Prices are very low, and it has a great buzz – a must for anyone who wants to feel the heart-throb of the city. It is located around the junction of Pettirossi, Eusebio Ayala and Próceres de Mayo.

OTHER PRACTICALITIES

MEDICAL AND EMERGENCIES For Paraguayans, there are two general **hospitals** in Asunción. IPS [62 E2] (*Instituto de Previsión Social; c/ Dr Manuel Peña, Santísimo Sacramento*) is for state employees and their families, who have a level of medical insurance. It is one of the well-known landmarks in Asunción. The other is the Hospital de Clínicas [62 B2] (*Guillermo Arias y Mazzei*) for the poor, with no insurance, and is on the other side of the centre. A recommended hospital for foreigners is the Centro Médico Bautista (*República Argentina, esq Campos Cervera;* ☎ *021 600171, appointments 021 609996, emergencies 021 607944;* f *021 602212;* e *direccionmedica@cmb.org; http://drup.cmb.org.py*). Not only is it a good hospital but it has doctors who speak English and is conveniently located in the Villa Mora area.

The telephone number for police in emergencies is 911, which is a free number; for medical emergencies ☎ 140 or ☎ 021 204800; and fire emergencies ☎ 131 (police firefighters) or ☎ 132 (volunteer firefighters: most firefighters are volunteers, all over the country). You can also supposedly ring 911 to report any malpractice or law-breaking, with the place, date and time of the offence, and your message will be recorded, though whether anyone actually ever uses this service is unclear.

BANKS The central branch of most banks is to be found on or around the street Estrella [82 B2–C2] in Asunción.

The principal banks include ABN Amro (*Estrella y Alberdi*), Amambay (*Estrella y 14 de mayo*), Continental (*Estrella c/ 15 de mayo*), HSBC (a new arrival – *Palma y O'Leary*) and Sudameris (*Cerro Corá y Independencia Nacional*). There is also Citibank (though it has closed almost all its branches), Interbanco, Banco do Brasil and Banco Regional. The Banco Nacional de Fomento is a state bank, and people say it should not be trusted. There is in fact a general distrust of banks, because a number went bankrupt in the mid-1990s, with a domino effect; and in 2002 one of the biggest banks, the Banco Alemán, also went bust, but this time without bringing down any others with it.

As well as the banking system there are *financieras* (finance companies) which change money and make loans. A number of *financieras* have recently converted into banks (eg: Visión, Itapúa, Familiar). There are also *cooperativas* (credit unions), which are much the most popular places for Paraguayans to keep their money, but are of less use to the tourist. Finally there are *casas de cambio*, specifically for changing money.

Most of the places specifically offering money-changing are on Palma [82 C2] (near the junctions with Alberdi or 14 de mayo) or on 25 de mayo [82 D2] (near the junction with Yegros). There are plenty of street money-changers too, near the corner of Estrella and the Plaza de Heroes, but with *casas de cambio* so close, which can give a proper receipt, there is little advantage in using them. One of the biggest places for changing money is Norte Cambios (*Palma 403 esq Alberdi;* ☎ *021 453277;* ⊕ *08.30–17.00 Mon–Fri, 08.30–12.00 Sat*) and they change American Express **travellers' cheques** with a 3% commission. Cambios Chaco and Maxi Cambios have already been mentioned (see page 45). Maxi Cambios (*Super Centro;* ☎ *021 494637/Shopping del Sol/Shopping Multiplaza/Shopping Mariscal López*) has facilities for receiving MoneyGram transfers, and will change travellers' cheques if they are in dollars for a US$4 commission on each cheque, and if they are in euros for a US$5 commission on each cheque. Cambios Chaco has branches in town as well as at the airport (*Palma 364;* ☎ *021 445315/Shopping Villa Morra*) but do not exchange travellers' cheques.

It has already been explained in *Chapter 2* that there is a great advantage in having a Visa card for cash machines.

POST OFFICES The central post office is at Alberdi y Paraguayo Independiente, adjoining the Plaza del Marzo Paraguayo [82 C2] (☎ *021 498112/6;* ⊕ *07.00–18.00 Mon–Fri, 07.00–12.00 Sat;* for museum see *Correo Central* below under *Museums*, page 88). There are branches at the airport, the Terminal, Shopping del Sol (rather hidden away, you may need to ask for it), Shopping Villa Mora (upstairs), the shopping Mall Excelsior and on Defensa Nacional e/ Padre

Cardozo y Washington. (*Airport & shopping centre branches* ⊕ *07.00–18.00 Mon–Fri, 09.00–21.00 Sat & Sun.*)

COURIERS There are two courier companies operating in Paraguay, though neither offer a very fast service, given the transportation difficulties. They will usually deliver only in Asunción and other big cities like Ciudad del Este and Encarnación.

DHL Brasilia 355 (head office) or Independencia Nacional 375 e/ Palma y Estrella (central office); ❱ 021 2162000; e asucs@dhl.com; www.dhl.com.py; ⊕ 08.00–18.00 Mon–Fri. 9 branches in Paraguay.

UPS Independencia Nacional 821; ❱ 021 451960; www.ups.com. Works with local courier Sky, which has an office in San Ignacio.

LANGUAGE COURSES The **Stael Ruffinelli Language Institute** [62 D2] (*Av General Santos 606, en frente de Juan de Salazar;* ❱ *021 202630;* e *info@staelenglish.com.py; www.staelenglish.com.py*) offers Spanish courses, including Business Spanish and Spanish for teaching purposes (as well as courses in English as a foreign language, for which it is better known).

Idipar [82 A4] (*Manduvirá 979–963 c/ Colon;* ❱ *021 447896;* e *idipar@cmm.com.py; www.idipar.da.ru*) offers courses in Spanish and in Guaraní, and can organise accommodation with families for US$100–150 a week. Private lessons are US$25 an hour, a 60-hour module costs US$230 and there is an enrolment fee of US$50. They do a module of either 30 or 60 hours Monday–Friday, 07.00–20.00. Courses are individual or in a group of up to six students.

WHAT TO SEE AND DO

A WALK ROUND THE CENTRE Many tour companies do a two- or three-hour 'Cititour' in a bus, with the emphasis on driving around in air-conditioned vehicles. If you find it more fun to explore on foot, here is a two- or three-hour walking tour you can make of the central area, beginning and ending at the Panteón. This is just a summary, but details of the shops and sites are given in the preceding and subsequent sections, and the route is marked on the map on pages 82–3.

Plaza de los Heroes
1 Panteón (where national heroes are buried)

2 Craft shops in Plaza de la Libertad (outdoor stalls behind Panteón)

optional extension towards Plaza Uruguaya
3 Tierra Bella (craft shop) 25 de mayo 370, near junction with Iturbe

4 Plaza Uruguaya (big square with bookshops in it; beware of thieves and prostitutes)

5 Railway station/Estación de Ferrocarril (old steam trains) ring bell round corner in Río Acaray to get in (⊕ *07.00–18.00 Mon–Fri*)

6 Café Literario (nice café for a fruit juice) Mariscal Estigarribia 456 (⊕ *16.00–midnight Sun–Thur, 16.00–02.00 Fri–Sat*)
end of optional extension

Plaza del Marzo Paraguayo
7 Cathedral (not a great deal to see inside, but good to see in the context of its surroundings)

8 Statue of Juan de Salazar with sword (founder of Asunción, 15 August 1537)

9 Monument to Marzo Paraguayo (student martyrs of 1999, demonstrating for democracy)

10 Cabildo (former Senate building, now a pleasant museum) (⊕ *Mar–Dec 09.00–19.00 Mon–Fri; Jan & Feb 10.00–17.00, 10.00–17.00 Sat & Sun*)

11 View over Bañado from first floor (slums of the poor, sometimes flooded by the river)

12 Statue of Mariscal López (who led Paraguay into Triple Alliance War, regarded as a hero)

13 Parliament (new building paid for by government of Taiwan) (⊕ *07.00–12.30 Mon–Fri; free*)

optional extension around the shopping street Palma
14 Palacio de López, also known as Palacio de Gobierno (grand design by Mariscal López, now government offices); no visits inside.

15 Manzana de la Rivera (small museum of history and art, also known as Casa Viola) (⊕ *07.00–21.00 Mon–Fri, 08.00–18.00 Sat, 09.00–18.00 Sun*)
end of optional extension

16 Casa de la Independencia (where independence was planned, colonial house/museum) 14 de mayo esq Presidente Franco (⊕ *07.00–18.30 Mon–Fri, 08.00–12.00 Sat*)

17 Turista Roga (tourist information and craft stalls) Palma 468

MUSEUMS A little mnemonic may help to remember the museums of Asunción. Five of them begin with B, four with M, three with C, two with F, and one with A.

The five Bs, in order of recommendation:
• **Museo del Barro** Definitely the top recommendation, with collections of indigenous work, Jesuit and Franciscan religious art, and modern art, and also an excellent craft shop. The only problem, apart from its obscure position in town, is its peculiar opening hours (see below).
• **Museo Bogarín** Next to the cathedral, this is easy of access and is a treasure trove of art from the Reductions, but is marred by overcrowding and unreliable opening hours.
• **Museo Boggiani** Actually in San Lorenzo, but that is practically a suburb of Asunción. This is 100% indigenous art and craft, with even more superb craft on sale than on display in the museum. (See *Chapter 4*, page 112.)
• **Museo de Bellas Artes** While not of the standard of a Museo de Bellas Artes in many other capital cities, this museum has been much improved and does contain some interesting paintings.
• **Museo Andrés Barbero** This houses ethnic and archaeological items, and is close to the railway station.

The four Ms:
• **Museo de las Memorias** A former house of torture has been converted into

a museum. Powerful and disturbing.
- **Manzana de la Rivera** An imaginatively designed museum, in easy walking distance from the centre, presenting the history of Asunción. Also sometimes known as the Casa Viola (which is the front house of the complex) or occasionally as the Museo Memoria de la Ciudad.
- **Museo Mitológico** This excellent museum is not in Asunción but at Capiatá, but it is still almost within the urban sprawl of the suburbs. (See *Chapter 4*, page 114.)
- **Museo Migliorisi** A soon-to-be-opened museum of Latin American art, both pre- and post-conquest.

The three Cs:
- **Cabildo** The former *cabildo* was more recently the Senate, but is now converted into a museum; there are only a few rooms, but they have been very well planned, covering the indigenous, the traditional crafts, the Jesuit art, the

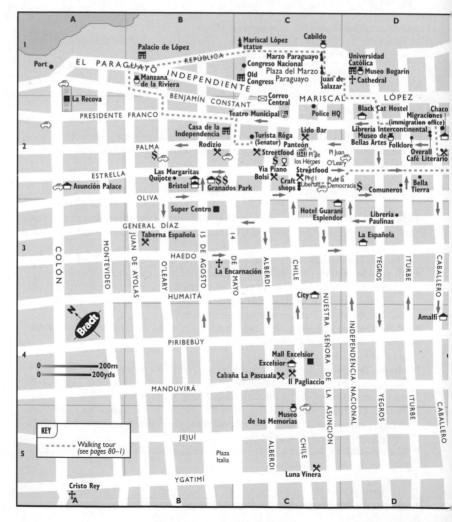

guitarist Mangoré, the López presidencies, etc. Do not miss this: it is small, central, excellently presented, covers different aspects of Paraguay and has accessible opening hours.

- **Casa de la Independencia** The house where the successful bid for independence was planned has been turned into a museum furnished in period fashion and with many items of interest both historically and artistically. Right in the centre of the city and quite small to walk around.
- The **Correo Central** has a small stamp museum.

And the two Fs:
- **Museo del Fútbol Sudamericano** A new museum near the airport, entirely devoted to football.
- **Estación de Ferrocarril** The old railway station no longer operates for actual train trips (which start at the next station along the line), but it does function as a museum. Do not miss it.

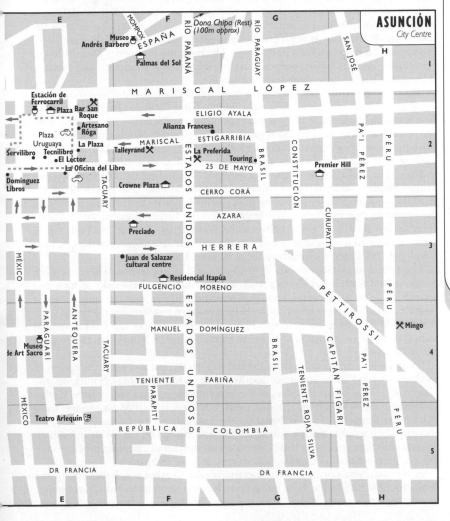

And the one A:

- **Museo de Art Sacro** A private art collection recently gone public.

Museo del Barro [62 F3] (*Grabadores del Cabichuí, entre Emeterio Miranda y Cañada;* \ *021 607996;* e *info@museodelbarro.com; www.museodelbarro.com;* ⊕ *15.30–20.00 Wed–Sat, also 09.30–12.00 Sat; adults/students Gs8,000/Gs4,000, free on Wed, Fri, Sat*)

To get to the museum take a taxi or a bus down España (28, 30-2 Aeropuerto, 44 Autopista, Luque-Aregua) to a little way past the Shopping del Sol (a big shopping complex on the left near the junction of España and San Martín) and just past the Santa Teresa fork to the right. Get off at the Farmacia Aviadores on the right-hand side, which is on the corner of Cañada, which is an unlikely looking rough road. Turn left at the first corner, and the Museo del Barro is on your right. This is five minutes' walk from the Shopping del Sol.

This is the best museum in town. Literally the 'Mud Museum', it is tucked away out of the centre and in a place so discreet that many of the taxi drivers have never heard of it. If you are in Asunción between Wednesday and Saturday, this museum, with its excellent craft shop attached, is a must. It was founded in 1972 as a travelling exhibition by a group of artists, and reached its current home after the end of the dictatorship. It is imaginatively modern with good displays, and a dose of imagination not often seen in Paraguay. The museum comprises three different collections: indigenous art, *campesino* art (mostly religious figures), and modern urban art. There are also temporary exhibitions.

Most of the permanent collection is on the first floor, and the first rooms you come to are devoted to painted wooden figures, from the Jesuit Reductions or the Franciscan Reductions, or from workshops of Guaraní artesans who moved from the Reductions after the Expulsion (see *Chapter 1*, page 11). While the museums in Misiones have large figures – life-size or nearly life-size – and there are few of these in the Museo del Barro, by far the largest number are small figures, 15cm or so high. The collection is strong in crucifixes – including the crucified woman Santa Librada – and the Niño Salvador del Mundo (the Child Saviour of the World) – a naked child Jesus holding an orb in his hand. Particularly interesting are the crucifixes that show the Holy Trinity: God the Father stretches out his arms over his crucified Son, while between the two a huge dove of the Holy Spirit breaks forth with wings outstretched. On the walls are large figures of the crucified Good and Bad Thieves – similar to those in Santa Rosa, Misiones.

The ethnic section opens out of this room and is impressive. There are fibre costumes and feather headdresses made by the Ishir, wooden masks of men and animals made by the Guaraní, huge clay pots and sculpted wooden animals, again by the Guaraní. Among a group of big-bellied wooden fish, one has tigers and birds outlined on its belly in burnt wood. There are bead necklaces and red ceremonial sashes, and a room of smaller craft works by the Ayoreo, Chamakoko, Lengua and Mbyá Guaraní.

If you go up a gentle ramp from the indigenous section you enter the rooms of modern art (and there are more rooms on the ground floor, opening off the courtyard). Some of the founders of the museum have major pieces here: Carlos Colombino has done a huge wooden panel, 9.5m x 3.4m, called *La Próxima Cena* (The Next Supper), which is based on the Last Supper by Leonardo da Vinci. Ricardo Migliorisi has made a sort of circus tent, painted on the inside in brilliant colours with dancers, circus artists, weird sea creatures and a popular procession of the Virgin: it is titled *La Carpilla Sixtina* (*carpa* is 'tent' in Spanish.)

In the shop you can buy arts and crafts similar to what you have seen in the museum: fibre bags by the Ache indigenous, lace (*encaje ju*) tablecloths, clay figures, wooden painted statues of the saints, and some prints.

Museo Bogarín [82 D1] (*Paseo Comuneros y Yegros; www.cabildoccr.gov.py/?pagina=artesacro;* ⏱ *08.00–11.00 Mon–Sat; adults/children Gs2,000/Gs1,000*) Tucked away down an alleyway beside the cathedral is one of Asunción's best (but least-known) museums, the Museo Monseñor J S Bogarín. This is packed full of items of great artistic and historical interest, even if it could do with renewed ticketing and replacement of some light bulbs. The opening times have been found to be unreliable, and staff attending the neighbouring Universidad Católica recommend aiming to arrive around 09.30, to stand the best chance of finding it open.

The alley on which the museum stands, the Paseo Comuneros, is a pleasant lane with benches, named after the revolutionary movement that led to Paraguay's independence in 1811. The historic building was originally the house of Fulgencio Yegros (one of the *Próceres* of independence, see below page 88), then during the presidency of Dr Francia it was a prison, where another of Francia's former colleagues among the *Próceres*, Pedro Juan Cavallero, was held. The building became a seminary, and later a school. At one stage it housed a laundry and even a public swimming pool, and was known as the *ykuá piscina* (Guaraní 'water hole'; Spanish 'swimming pool'). In 1960 it was taken over by the Universidad Católica and in due course was relaunched as a museum to house the magnificent personal collection of Monseñor Juan Sinforio Bogarín (1863–1949), the sixth bishop and the first archbishop of Paraguay.

Turning right when you enter, the furthest room has popular art, and includes among other treasures a beautiful crucifix in which the body of Christ emerges out of the trunk of a tree while birds sing in the branches. The second room is the Sala de Monseñor Bogarín and contains his *prie-dieu* and other fine articles of furniture, as well as his leather saddlebags. Room 3 has Jesuit-Guaraní art and has a good collection of statues, of which the Roman soldier, poised at the moment of opening the side of Christ with a lance, is of special note.

The Sala de Tesor (Room of Treasure) comes next, and contains many silver items, and the missal used by Pope John Paul II on his visit to Paraguay, with his signature dated 18 May 1988. This is the former cell of Pedro Juan Cavallero, who was imprisoned by Dr Francia for his part in a suspected plot to pass Paraguay under Argentinian control. He committed suicide here in 1821 on the eve of his planned execution, writing in his blood on the wall of his cell that he knew suicide was a sin.

The fifth room is the Room of the Passion and includes among other figures Jesus entering Jerusalem on the donkey, and a Risen Christ; there are also some fine carved wooden doors taken from the Franciscan church of Ypané (see *Chapter 4*, page 144). The sixth room is devoted to the independence and then the Triple Alliance War and displays the outspoken account of Mariscal López's killings, whippings and torturings of his own compatriots, written by his sometime chief military apothecary, George Frederick Masterman. The seventh and final room is devoted to Franciscan art, and includes the carved doors and reredos from the church of Guarambaré (see *Chapter 4*, page 144).

Museo Boggiani For this extremely interesting museum of indigenous art see the section on San Lorenzo in *Chapter 4*, page 110.

Museo de Bellas Artes [82 D2] (*Mariscal Estigarribia y Iturbe;* ☎ *021 447716;* ⏱ *07.00–17.00 Mon–Fri, 07.00–12.00 Sat, closed Sun; free*) As national art galleries go, the Museo de Bellas Artes is small and modest. It was so before it had a major theft on 29 July 2002, and might be thought to be even more so now it is denuded. The thieves had dug a tunnel 30m long to get in, and stole eight works, including a Murillo and a Tintoretto. However, the museum has some interesting paintings and if approached without high expectations is well worth visiting, especially since it is placed so centrally (between the Plaza Uruguaya and the Plaza de los Heroes) and is easy to take in on a walk around town. The core of the gallery is the collection of Juan Silvano Godoi, a wealthy politician (1850–1926) who acquired foreign art works (mostly late 19th-century paintings) in his 18 years of exile, during the political upheavals of his day. The works on display are frequently changed.

The museum is housed in a building belonging to the Archivo Nacional, which occupies the ground floor. The Archive is also open to the public wishing to do research among documents of the nation dating back to colonial times (✎ 021 447311; e archivonacpy@hotmail.com; ⊕ 07.15–12.00 & 13.30–1.30 Mon–Fri).

Museo Andrés Barbero [82 F1] (España 217 esq Mompox; ✎ 021 441696; e museobarbero@museobarbero.or.py; www.museobarbero.org.py; ⊕ 08.0–17.30 Mon–Fri, closed Jan; free) The museum is on the last bit of España before it curves round towards the station, opposite the Hotel Palmas del Sol. It is named after an early 20th-century philanthropist who founded the Paraguayan Red Cross and worked in the fields of health, archaeology and indigenous culture. A statue to him stands at the beginning of Artigas. Dr Barbero founded the ethnological museum as long ago as 1929, but it passed into the hands of a succession of other anthropologists to organise and complete: the German explorer Dr Max Schmidt, and after his death the Slovene Dr Branislava Susnik. It is now in the hands of Dr Adelina Pusineri de Madariaga.

The museum includes more than 3,000 items belonging to different tribes but most are from different branches of the Guaraní family. There are funeral pots called japepó – the Guaraní were buried in foetal position in a pot – cooking pots, stone axes, fibre hammocks, fishing nets, feather headdresses, woven cloths, lances, a hollowed-out boat and paddle, and a gallery of photographs. There is also an important library of over 20,000 specialist books.

Museo de las Memorias [82 C5] (Chile 1066 y 1072 entre Jejuí y Manduvirá; ✎ 021 493873; e msedu@rieder.net.py; ⊕ 09.00–16.00 Mon–Fri; free) The Museo de las Memorias is a new initiative to record the human rights abuses of the dictatorship, in a building that was previously the torture centre of the Stroessner regime, known then by the discreet name of Asuntos Técnicos (Technical Affairs) or La Técnica for short.

Under the umbrella of Operation Condor (which created intelligence links between a number of dictatorial regimes in the Southern Cone), and supported by the foreign policy of the USA which was intent on wiping out communism, Stroessner was able to kill, maim or exile all his opponents (very few of whom were communists) through the systematic use of savage torture methods. La Técnica was only officially closed on 23 December 1992, a day after the discovery of the Archive of Terror (police records of the imprisonment and torture of dissidents). The museum is an initiative of the Fundación Celestina Pérez de Almada, to which enquiries should be addressed (Av Carlos Antonio López 2273; ✎ 021 425345/ 425873; e fundacion@rieder.net.py).

The museum explains how systematic torture in the dictatorship began when, one year after taking power, Stroessner sent Antonio Campos Alúm to the USA in 1955 to study how to do it. La Técnica includes implements for pulling off fingernails, that were donated anonymously by a former torturer. There is a telephone used for torturing psychologically the relatives of the victims, as they heard the screams down the line. You can visit the interrogation room, and the cells. There is a bath (pileta) to illustrate the water torture, where prisoners were nearly drowned and then revived, wrapped up in chains or barbed wire, with a radio playing loudly to drown their screams. A big display board shows photographs and names of the 600 'disappeared', whose deaths have not been accounted for. It is believed that 10,000 people passed through La Técnica, of which there are written records for 3,500.

At another address, but part of the same area of interest, is the Archivo del Terror or **Archive of Terror**. This is open to the public and is now located on the ground floor of the **Palacio de Justicia** (*Testanova y Alonso;* ✆ *021 424311/15 int 2269;* e *cdya@pj.gov.py; www.unesco.org/webworld/paraguay;* ⊕ *07.00–18.00*). It is a research centre, with all the relevant police records of those detained, imprisoned and tortured under Stroessner, and has a good computer system for searching the archive.

Manzana de la Rivera [82 B1] (*Ayolas 128 esq El Paraguayo Independiente;* ✆ *021 442448/447683;* e *manzana_rivera@yahoo.com; http://museo.mca.gov.py/inicio.php;* ⊕ *07.30–19.00 Mon–Fri, 07.30–18.00 Sat & Sun; free*) The Manzana de la Rivera is the block of mostly historic interlinked houses directly opposite the Palacio de López, that operates conjointly as an art and study centre.

The Casa Viola – as you go in – is the oldest building (1750), and houses a delightfully arranged museum of the history of Asunción, with old maps, postcards, prints, newspaper cuttings and so on, all making it a most interesting and informative place to browse. This museum is sometimes called the Museo Memoria de la Ciudad, but should not be confused with the Museo de las Memorias (above).

While the Casa Viola's exhibition is permanent, the other halls in the complex are for temporary exhibitions. Casa Castelvi, built in 1804, just before independence, has two exhibition rooms. The Casa Vertúa (1898) houses a reference library. The Casa Ballario is a two-storey block with a balcony, from 1901, which has offices of Unesco. The Casa Clari is an Art Nouveau building which has a café (✆ *021 496476;* ⊕ *11.00–midnight Mon–Thu, 11.00–03.00 Fri & Sat, closed Sun*), with a fabulous view over the Palacio de López. The Casa Emasa is a modern building with offices and an art gallery called La Galería.

Museo Mitológico See section on *Capiatá* in *Chapter 4*, page 113.

Museo Migliorisi At the time of writing, a Fundación Migliorisi has been recently established, with the aim of opening a museum in the near future. Ricardo Migliorisi is one of the people who has been involved in the Museo del Barro, and his collection, which he has put together over more than 30 years, includes similar kinds of art works to those in that museum.

Cabildo [82 C1] (*Av de la República e/ Chile y Alberdi;* ✆ *021 443094/441826;* e *cabildoculturalccr@yahoo.com; www.cabildoccr.gov.py;* ⊕ *09.00–19.00 Mon–Fri except during Jan & Feb, 10.00–17.00 Sat, Sun & daily throughout Jan & Feb; free*) Another name for this museum is the Centro Cultural de la Republica. Formerly the Palacio Legislativo, where the Senate used to meet, this pink building is a distinctive symbol of the city. It was begun by Carlos Antonio López in 1842, and was then the fifth Cabildo to be built. Historic acts that took place here include the election of Mariscal López as president in 1862 (under extreme pressure), the declaration of war against Argentina in 1865 and the approval of the Constitution in various steps (1870, 1940 and 1992). The origin of the term *cabildo* is in the colonial administration, when representatives of the town, including those designated as *alcaldes* (mayors) and *regidores* (governors), would meet to organise all civil matters, including taxes, police, holidays, justice, health and the cleaning of the city.

In the most recent coup attempt (or according to some, fake coup attempt) in 2000, a tank fired a hole in the top plasterwork. The hole was there for years before it was mended. In 2004, when the new Congress building paid for by Taiwan was opened, the Cabildo was successfully converted into a pleasant museum and cultural centre.

On the ground floor to the right are three rooms beautifully laid out by the staff of the Museo del Barro (see page 84). The first has examples of intricate traditional Paraguayan craft, such as woven woollen rugs from Carapegua. The second has indigenous artefacts in feather, fibre and wood (but only a taster for the much bigger display at the Museo del Barro itself) and a big wooden canoe stood up against the wall. The third room has Jesuit-Guaraní art, in eight beautiful religious statues stunningly displayed against red walls.

To the left of the entrance are rooms devoted to temporary exhibitions of modern art. Round the corner you can see the presidential chair of the López family. There is also an interesting model of the original layout of the Plaza del Marzo Paraguayo. Upstairs are rooms devoted to Paraguayan films and music, including harps and guitars of some of the country's leading musicians such as Agustín Pío Barrios, known as 'Mangoré' (see box in *Chapter 5* on page 163). Directly above the entrance is the former Senate chamber, now used for conferences.

Stretching out behind the main building is a room used for meetings and seminars, with windows giving extensive views in all directions. To see the real Asunción, go into this room, and you will find yourself looking out directly over the hovels of the Bañado, crammed into the low-lying space between the plaza and the river. The contrast between these thousands of tumbledown shacks and the shimmering new parliament building, also visible from the window, is deeply disturbing.

Casa de la Independencia [82 B2] (*14 de mayo esq Presidente Franco;* ✎ *021 493918;* e *info@casadelaindependencia.org.py; www.casadelaindependencia.org.py;* ⊕ *07.00–18.30 Mon–Fri, 08.00–12.00 Sat; free*) This is the house where the so-called Próceres de la Independencia – Fernando de la Mora, Francisco Xavier Bogarín, Fulgencio Yegros, Pedro Juan Cavallero and Gaspar Rodríguez de Francia – secretly plotted the independence of Paraguay, which was achieved without a shot being fired. At first light on 15 May 1811 Captain Pedro Juan Cavallero led the coup.

The house was built in 1772 of adobe in classic colonial style by a Spaniard married to a Paraguayan, Antonio Martínez Sáenz. After his death it became the natural place for the plotters of independence to meet, as they were all friends of Martínez Sáenz's sons and heirs. It was acquired by the government in 1943 and declared a historic monument in 1961. In 2003 it underwent a restoration and layout improvement as a museum. There are five rooms, including an oratory, all well laid out with furniture of the period (some belonging to the Próceres), portraits of the Próceres, and art works, including statues carved in Jesuit or Franciscan workshops. Alongside the house is a restored alleyway showing what the street looked like when the Próceres slipped out of the side door there on the decisive night of 14 May 1811.

Correo Central [82 C2] (*Alberdi y Paraguayo Independiente;* ✎ *021 498112/93997;* e *filatelia@correoparaguayo.gov.py; www.correoparaguayo.gov.py;* ⊕ *07.00–18.00 Mon–Fri, 07.00–12.00 Sat; free*) The *correo central* or central post office, a grand but battered building in beige and cream plaster, occupies most of the block facing the plaza in between 14 de mayo and Alberdi. It was built at the beginning of the 20th century as the private house for a rich Italian businessman, Luiggi Patri, who also bought up and improved the rail service in Paraguay (after the Triple Alliance War). It was designed by a Swedish architect, Carlos Rehnfeldt. After the death of Patri it was aquired by the Paraguayan government, with the intention of using it as the presidential residence. Instead of that plan, however, it became the office for Post and Telegraph in 1913.

There is a central courtyard with trees, and a bust of Mariscal López who established the first national telegraph service in Latin America in 1864. A philatelic office in the far right corner sells past issues of stamps, and there is a little stamp museum. The first postage stamp in Paraguay was printed in August 1870, a few months after Mariscal López's death on 1 March 1870, and showed a lion with its paws in the air. As well as stamps, the museum has an 1896 clock, old scales for weighing letters, an old postman's uniform, and models of the little planes that used to transport the post.

(If you want to post a letter or parcel and are not near this central post office, see page 79 above.)

Museo del Fútbol Sudamericano [62 H3] (*Av Sudamericana esq Petrona Almirón de Leoz, Luque;* ✆ *021 645781;* e *museo@conmebol.com.py; www.conmebol.com*) This prestigious building, on the Autopista on the way to the airport, houses a convention centre as well as a football museum. Months of internal wrangling in the management have delayed its opening but it is hoped that it may be open to the public by the time this guide is published. The entrance fee, if there is one, will be low. Considering Paraguay's distinguished position as a footballing nation, despite its small population, it is appropriate that a museum of South American football should be sited in this country.

A huge black-and-white football forms a focus outside the museum, while inside you are met by the flags of the ten footballing countries that comprise the Confederación Sudamericana: Argentina, Bolivia, Brazil, Chile, Colombia, Ecuador, Paraguay, Peru, Uruguay and Venezuela. This leads into a hall of cups. The museum is organised with avant-garde design over two levels, and with interactive installations. On the lower level is a room of Hermanos Americanos which commemorates the symbols, history and talents of each of the ten nations. Inside the football itself is a round chamber with a multi-vision show of South American footballing history, tracing its path to the forefront of the world in this sport.

Estación de Ferrocarril [82 E2] (*México 145 esq Eligio Ayala;* ✆ *021 447848;* e *cultura@ferrocarriles.com.py; www.ferrocarriles.com.py;* ⊕ *08.00–17.00 Mon–Fri; free*) The old railway station on Plaza Uruguaya no longer functions as such, not even for the tourist train trips, which leave instead from the station at the Botanical Gardens. But it is kept open as a museum, and also an office where you can buy your ticket for the Sunday train ride (see *Excursions* below, page 98).

The railway was one of the first built in South America, and was constructed by English engineers, particularly Alonso Taylor, who was responsible for the Asunción central station. President Carlos Antonio López began it in 1854, as part of his modernisation in the days when Paraguay was great. By the time the station was finished in 1864, and the line opened as far as Paraguarí, Mariscal López was president and the Triple Alliance War was beginning. The days of glory were short-lived.

It was 1886 before the work began again to continue the line to Villarrica and beyond. In 1907 the ownership of the railway passed to an English company, and in 1913 the railway was extended to Encarnación. In 1961 the Paraguayan government bought back the railway, but it was beginning to become outdated and uneconomic to run, and it stopped functioning in 1999. The short track from the Botanical Gardens to Areguá was opened again for tourist trips in 2004.

To enter the station as such you must go round the corner to México 145, and find the door with a brass plate marked Ferro Carril Central de Paraguay

Administración. If it is not open, ring the bell. As well as buying a ticket for the train (which can also be bought at the Estación Trinidad on the day) you can walk around the station. There is enough left of old grandeur to get the sense that in its time this was something very technologically advanced and quite a classy way to travel. On the rails by the platforms are two old steam trains: it is fascinating to go inside the dining car, and the luxury sleeping car, with highly polished furniture and moulded plaster ceilings. The first train to run from here to Areguá in 1861 was the *Sapucai*, which is on display. (Sapucai is also the name of the town where the workshops are for building the trains.) You can also see the old ticket offices and a museum of old railway items – clocks, lamps, whistles, big ledgers with bills for firewood in copperplate writing, and huge drawings of the details of steam cars labelled in English. You feel you are in a time warp: nothing has changed.

Museo de Arte Sacro [82 E4] (*Villa Lina, Manuel Dominguez y Paraguarí;* ↘ *021 449439; www.museodeartesacro.com;* ⊕ *09.00–18.00 Tue–Sun; Gs25,000, free to Para-guayans*) Part of the renowned private collection of religious art belonging to Nicolás Darío Latourrete Bo was opened to the public in March 2010, as a museum of sacred art. Most of the art comes from the Reductions, and the six rooms are divided into the following themes: the Angelic Hierarchies, Christ – God made Man, the Saints – men of God, Jesuit Saints – holy Brides of Christ, the Reredos and Mary the Mother of God.

OTHER SITES TO VISIT IN THE CITY CENTRE
Cathedral [82 D1] The Metropolitan Cathedral dominates the eastern end of the long rectangular space known as the Plaza Mayor in the days of colonialisation, around which is the parliament and the former parliamentary buildings. The square does not have an official name today, but everyone can identify what is meant by the Plaza del Marzo Paraguayo (see box opposite).

The cathedral (↘ *021 449512;* ⊕ *10.00–12.00, 13.00–17.00 Mon–Sat; mass 11.00 daily inc Sun, also 19.00 Fri*) is a large but not particularly special building as cathedrals go, more chunky than ornate. It is usually closed, but the interior is undistinguished, and there is nothing at all in the way of guides, booklets or postcards. The cathedral reached its finest hour in the events of the *marzo paraguayo*, when it became a makeshift hospital for the wounded and dying demonstrators, and a banner proclaiming the names of the martyrs was soon strung up on one of towers.

The foundation stone of the cathedral was laid in 1842, in the ruins of the previous (fifth) cathedral. It was designed by an Italian architect Alejandro Ravizza (who also designed the Panteón and the church of Trinidad) and was completed in 1846 – one of the first architectural works in the presidency of Carlos Antonio López.

One of the best works is a stone bas-relief of Domingo Martínez de Irala, who led the first Spanish settlement here, embracing a group of indigenous, while a paper bearing the plan of a cathedral flutters at their feet. It was a gift of a former Spanish ambassador, Giménez Caballero, and was donated in 1965. It is outside the cathedral, so can be viewed even when the building is closed. But the message it conveys, of two races embracing, has been criticised, for the Spanish forcibly exploited the indigenous, reducing them to near slavery, and although they married the womenfolk, these had no choice in the matter.

A plaque in the porch reminds us of the important Synod of Asunción in 1603, which set the policy for evangelising the indigenous in their own language, and so laid the basis for the work of the Jesuit and Franciscan missions, with effects lasting to the present day.

Inside, two shades of green with touches of gold are the theme colours of the flat wooden roof, the pulpit and the high altar. The finest art work inside the cathedral is the altar, with its heavily worked silver panels. There is also a pleasant modern altar facing the people, with wheat and grape motifs carved into the stonework.

Universidad Católica Next door to the cathedral is the Universidad Católica – a very pleasant red-brick building of some age and distinction, with a large columned portico facing onto the plaza. In the 19th century it was the Seminario Conciliar, together with the Museo Bogarín, which nestles into the back of the building. The newly formed Universidad Católica took over the former seminary in 1960 and added the second floor in 1965. (This is one of two campuses for the Católica – the other being in the poor and somewhat dangerous area of Barrio

Republicana.) The cathedral and the university are the two buildings on the eastern end of the plaza.

House of José Asunción Flores
[82 D1] (⏰ *08.00–16.00 daily*) Behind the cathedral is the adobe house of the famous musician who created the musical form, the *guarania*. It has been recently restored and opened to the public. It is at Punto Karapá in the Chacarita Alta, and is managed by Enrique and Stela Pereira (m *0971 799790*).

Monument to the Marzo Paraguayo
[82 C1] Moving down the plaza, note the black-and-white tiles underfoot. Many of these tiles were torn up and hurled by the pro-democracy student demonstrators against their Oviedista attackers in the famous events of the Marzo Paraguayo (Paraguayan March) in 1999. The Oviedistas were aiming fireworks directly among them (the fierce rockets known as *petardos*) and later on they used gunfire. The students had no other means of self defence than to lever up the ground beneath their feet.

The demonstrators who were shot dead (six students and a *campesino* leader, with an eighth student dying from his wounds some time later) are commemorated in a composite monument of a rather do-it-yourself nature, that incorporates minor changes year by year. It is situated directly in front of the Cabildo. There is a black stone slab reading 'They gave their lives to make us free', and a wooden dove crying 'Justice! Liberty! Democracy!' There is also a cross to the memory of Luis María Argaña, the vice-president whose murder sparked off the political crisis. From this spot you can see the high-rise building with 'Whirlpool' written on the top, which is where the snipers shot from, into the crowd – though at that date the firm advertised on top was 'Marlboro'.

Directly behind the monument, but looking away from the Cabildo instead of towards it, is a **statue of Juan de Salazar y Espinoza**, with sword outstretched. He founded Asunción on 15 August 1537.

Behind the statue of Juan de Salazar is the striking pink building called the Cabildo, that used to be the Senate and is now a museum (see page 87 above). The former Congress was in the building at the western end of the plaza, next to the modern parliament. It can still be visited, via the new Congress (see below).

Facing the Cabildo, on the other side of the plaza, is another historic old building, the police headquarters, with a colonnade of yellow arches. It was built by Carlos Antonio López in 1854.

On the next block from the police headquarters is the Correo Central (see page 88 above).

At the far end of the plaza, next to the new Congress, is a striking statue of another of Paraguay's most famous figures – Mariscal Francisco Solano López, on a horse that is rearing up in dramatic fashion.

Congreso Nacional
[82 C1] It is not widely known that one can visit the new Congress building (*14 de mayo y Av República*) which was paid for by the government of Taiwan, and opened in 2003. It is on the site of the original fort established by the founder of Asunción, Juan de Salazar.

For a larger group visit, you should give notice, though individuals or small groups may be able to be shown around without prior arrangement. The Senate is reached through a side entrance facing the Plaza del Marzo Paraguayo, and has an Oficina de Relaciones Públicas (✆ *021 4145000/4145118/4145168;* e *informes@senado.gov.py; www.senado.gov.py;* ⏰ *07.00–13.00 Jan–Feb, 07.00–15.00 Mar–Dec; free*).

To visit the Cámera de Diputados, the lower house, you use the main entrance, around the corner. There is a wide stretch of steps up, and inside it is like a huge glass wigwam, set against a white background. You look for the desk marked 'Atención e Información Ciudadana'. Visits to this part of the building are organised separately from the Senate, and a good time to arrive is 09.30. They may be able to arrange an English-speaking guide, if you ask in advance (✆ *021 4144351;* e *cristinaashwell@yahoo.com;* ⊕ *07.30–13.00 year round*). The public can also attend parliamentary sessions, in the Sala de los Públicos, which generally has room.

If you cross the courtyard, you come in at the back end of the **old Congress building**, which is next door to the new one. This building, which is also known as the Casa de la Cultura, has had an extraordinarily varied history. It was originally a *colegio* opened by the Jesuits, ten years after they arrived in 1588. After the 1768 Expulsion of the Jesuits it briefly became a tobacco factory, then in 1780 the Seminario de San Carlos – the principal institution of higher education in the late colonial period. With independence it became a barracks, eventually turning into a military school. During the Chaco War it became a hospital, before becoming a military museum, a Casa de la Cultura, and then in 1996 the Cámera de Diputados.

The old Jesuit chapel has had its original floor uncovered, which dates back four centuries. This is where San Roque González was ordained priest, and where his body was brought after his martyrdom (except for his heart), and it is likely that he is actually buried here, though that is unconfirmed. On the wall is a map of 1731, drawn by a Capuchin, showing the enormous size of Paraguay at that date, occupying territory now belonging to Brazil, Argentina and Bolivia.

Plaza de los Héroes [82 C2] If you go southwest from the cathedral (away from the river), you will reach a green space after just two blocks. Apparently one large square divided into four quarters by a road, this is technically four adjoining squares: the Plaza de los Héroes (north), the Plaza Juan E O'Leary (east), the Plaza de la Democracia (south) and the Plaza de la Libertad (west). You are now as much in the centre of the city as you can get. Sometimes the group of four are referred to collectively as the Plaza de la Democracia, and sometimes as the Plaza de los Héroes, but the other two titles are used less frequently.

The **Plaza Juan E O'Leary** used to be the site of the church of La Merced until the mid-19th century, when it became the Mercado Guazú ('big market') until 1909. The square is now attractively developed as a place to sit and pass time.

The **Plaza de la Democracia** has an underground car park. On one side it faces the newly revamped and reopened Guaraní Esplendor Hotel, icon of the Stroessner era; on another, it faces the elegant 19th-century building of the Banco Nacional de Fomento.

The **Plaza de la Libertad** is one of the best places to buy craft: they have *ao po'í* clothes, *filigrana* silver jewellery, fibre bags made by the Ayoreo indigenous, hammocks, carved wood figures, *ñandutí* items, etc. The market operates all day, every day, and some people call this square the Plaza de los Artesanos. In the middle is a bronze statue called *La Razón y la Fuerza* ('Reason and Force'), which shows two struggling figures: the burly Force is unable to dominate the winged Reason.

The **Plaza de los Héroes** (properly so called, ie: one of the four squares) houses the Panteón.

Panteón [82 C2] A small circular oratory with a high dome, the Panteón houses the mortal remains of some of Paraguay's most famous people. The building was begun by Mariscal López in 1863, as an oratory dedicated to the Virgen de la Asunción, designed by the architect Alejandro Ravizza (the architect of the cathedral and the Trinidad church), but it was left incomplete with the outbreak of the Triple Alliance War. It was not completed until 1936 when, at the end of the Chaco War, it was inaugurated as a public place of honour for remains of national heroes, with the remains of Mariscal Francisco Solano López, and his son Panchito López, brought here from Cerro Corá, together with the body of an unknown soldier from the recently concluded Chaco War. The other early presidents of Paraguay also have their urns here: Dr Francia and Carlos Antonio López.

On the feast of the Assumption, 15 August, it is the statue of the Virgin from this oratory that is honoured in the public mass outside the cathedral. The building was whitewashed from head to foot a few years ago, which has covered up the attractive red tiles on the dome. There are always a couple of colourfully attired sentinels keeping guard at the door, in blue breeches, red-and-white jackets, helmets, and lances flying the Paraguayan red, white and blue flag. But do not be deterred: the building is open to the public, and you are encouraged to go inside.

Teatro Municipal [82 C2] The Teatro Municipal Ignacio A Pane, to give it its full title (*Presidente Franco e/ Chile y Alberdi;* ⟍ *021 445169*), was reopened in 2006 after extensive renovation. The enchanting 19th-century theatre was closed in 1994 because it was dangerous, and while something of its old magic has been lost, a lot of careful planning has gone into the restoration, to preserve the old while updating it to modern safety standards. One of the advantages of Paraguay having such a small population is that the principal national theatre can be contained in such an intimate space.

The Teatro Municipal is shut most of the time, with performances most weeks on Thursday, Friday, Saturday and Sunday nights at 20.30, and few people know that it can be visited outside of these times. Go to a discreet little door marked 'acceso actores y funcionarios' around the corner in Chile during the mornings (⊕ *09.00–12.00 Mon–Sat*), and a security guide will show you around the theatre. From Wednesday until Saturday you may find the box office open too, on Presidente Franco.

The first theatre in Asunción was called the Teatro Nacional, and was in the same block but not on the same site: that was the theatre that featured famously in the life of Mariscal López when he took his controversial mistress Eliza Lynch to show her off at a performance. In 1889 it was replaced with the present gem of theatrical architecture, designed by the Catalan, Baudilio Alió: the theatre is almost entirely circular, with three circles and 12 rows of stalls providing superb views of the stage.

In the foyer, the original walls have been broken in places to allow for new white marble staircases that the original building would not have had room for. But where a wall has been removed a vertical line of original bare bricks has been left to show the outline of the original building, and the new walls are constructed in glass.

Palacio de López [82 B1] If instead of going inland (south) from the cathedral to the Panteón, you instead follow the line of the river going west, along the street Paraguayo Independiente, then you come to the grandest building in the city, the huge, white and ornate Palacio de Gobierno, otherwise known as the Palacio de López, because it was begun in 1860 by Mariscal López to be his private residence. It is used for government offices – not for the parliament. On one side, towards the city, the building has an enormous flagpole, and faces the back end of the Manzana de la Rivera (see above, page 87). On the other side, it faces towards the river. In the park there, against the backdrop of the palace, a huge concert was held open to all the public, on the day President Lugo assumed office.

The Port [82 A1] A couple of blocks further along the river you reach the Port (*Puerto*). Like much in Paraguay, this has a quaint charm in its old-fashioned run-down way. You can wander down onto the quays and chat to boatmen, and may be tempted to take a river cruise, which can be done either expensively and in style, or cheaply in a boat full of local flavour (take a hammock). Details of river trips are on page 99 below and in *Chapter 11*, on page 282. On the road stretching away from the port (the beginnings of Colón) is the arcade of craft shops known as La Recova (see page 76 above.)

La Encarnación church [82 B3] (*14 de mayo e/ Haedo y Humaitá;* ⊕ *16.30–20.00 Mon–Sat, 08.00–20.00 Fri; mass: 10.00 Sun, 15.00 Fri, 19.00 Mon–Sat*) Impressive red-brick building of soaring dimensions, built in 1893 on a small hillock in the city centre. It is not in good repair, but if restored would be finer than the Cathedral.

Cristo Rey church [82 A5] For those who are coming to Paraguay with an interest in the Jesuit Reductions, a visit to the church of Cristo Rey (*Colón y Ygatimí;* ☎ *021 492870;* ⊕ *16.00–20.00 Mon–Fri*) is a must. This Jesuit church on the southwest corner of the city centre is where the (supposedly) incorrupt heart of San Roque González is held. To enquire about seeing the chapel if it is locked, or to ask for a guide, enquire at the Jesuit residence.

A small chapel to the right of the main church is dedicated to Roque González and his companions. In addition to the heart, framed in a glass case on the wall, there is another glass case containing the murder weapon: a stone axe. There is an excellent modern carved statue of the three martyrs, each with their distinctive feature: Roque González, as ever, carries the painting of *La Virgen Conquistadora*; Alonso Rodríguez is said to have nearly gone blind from weeping over the Passion, so is shown carrying a book; and Juan del Castillo carries the cord with which he was dragged by horses along the ground on the day of his martyrdom. A plaque on the wall records the names of the 26 Jesuit martyrs who lost their lives in the Reductions. Outside the chapel is a series of large wall pictures made from painted tiles that tell the life story of the saint (see box on page 96).

Cementerio de la Recoleta [62 D3] (*Mariscal López y Chóferes del Chaco;* ⊕ *07.30– 17.00 daily*) The church of La Recoleta, begun in 1853, stands at the entrance to this 13ha cemetery, which is a well-known site in the city. It has some notable monuments, such as the *art nouveau* monument *La Llorona* (*Av C, calle 57*), the tomb of Madame Lynch's baby daughter, Corinna Adelaide Lynch (*Av A, calle 9*), and the urn of Madame Lynch herself. (When you exit the church to the left, turn first right and it is the third tomb.)

SITES AWAY FROM THE CITY CENTRE
Santísima Trinidad church [62 E2] (*Santísima Sacramento y Santísima Trinidad;* ⊕ *08.00–11.00 & 15.00–19.00 Tues–Sat & 08.00–11.00 Sat; masses 07.00 Mon–Fri, 19.00 Sat, 07.30 & 10.00 sung & 19.00 Sun*) This imposing church was designed by Alejandro Ravizza (the architect of the cathedral and the Panteón). It was built in 1856 by President Carlos Antonio López, who stole for it the side altars from the beautiful old church in Yaguarón (see *Chapter 4*, page 145). It is worth going inside, and has a beautiful painted wood ceiling.

Ycuá Bolaños supermarket shrine [62 E2] On 1 August 2004 there was a horrific fire in a supermarket in which 400 people died. The principal reason for the deaths was that when the alarm was given the supermarket owner ordered his staff to lock all the fire escapes so that people could not get out. His idea was to prevent looting in the confusion, but instead hundreds of people were burned alive. Ironically the huge supermarket Ycuá Bolaños was named after the life-giving spring of water discovered by the great Franciscan in the 17th century.

Roque González de Santa Cruz (1576–1628) is Paraguay's first canonised saint, along with two other Jesuit priests martyred at the same time as him, Alonso Rodríguez and Juan del Castillo. The group is usually known as 'San Roque González and his companions', and they were canonised by Pope John Paul II during his visit to Paraguay in 1988.

San Roque González should not be confused with plain San Roque, the medieval French saint who worked with plague victims, contracted the plague himself, and is shown with a wound in his thigh and a dog bringing him food; there are innumerable statues of him in Paraguay. San Roque González, by contrast, is shown with an arrow through his exposed heart, and a picture of the Virgin in his hands, for reasons that will become apparent.

Roque González was born in 1576 of a half-indigenous Paraguayan mother, though his father was Spanish. He was ordained initially into the diocesan clergy of Asunción, and was made parish priest of the cathedral, but when he realised he was going to be made vicar general of the diocese at the young age of 33, he joined the Jesuits to escape the promotion and dedicate his life to working with the indigenous.

His first mission was to the warlike Guaicurú indigenous of the Chaco, where he succeeded in winning their trust and not getting killed by them, but for his next mission he was sent among the Guaraní. He was not the founder of San Ignacio Guasú – the first Jesuit Reduction in Paraguay, founded at the end of 1609 – but he was its chief architect, arriving there as superior in 1611. His talent and energy were summed up by his contemporary P Francisco del Valle when he wrote that he was 'carpenter, architect and builder; he does it all himself ... he wields the axe and works the wood and transports it to the construction site, yoking up the team of oxen himself'.

Roque González helped to pioneer the shape that all subsequent Reductions would take, with music, dance and theatre; carving, painting and metalwork; an economy built on shared labour rather than money; care for the sick in a mutually responsible

The huge burnt-out shell of this once ambitious supermarket is on the corner of Artigas and Santísima Trinidad, in the northeast of the city. It is a massive reddish-brown tiled building, now scrawled with graffiti with messages such as 'Silencio nunca más' ('Silence, never again'). Inside the shell, the relatives and friends have made a museum and a shrine and there is a 3m × 6m painting of the tragedy, *Agosto en llamas* ('August in flames').

Jardín Botánico y Zoológico [62 F1] (⏰ *06.00–17.00 Tue–Sun; the park itself closes at 18.00; Gs1,000*) A little further to the northeast is the 250ha Jardín Botánico, out of which 12ha are designated for the zoo. The entrance is opposite the beginning of Artigas.

The zoo has hippopotamuses, spider monkeys and peacocks, as well as the more familiar Paraguayan animals such as capybaras, peccaries, foxes, tortoises and parrots, not forgetting the magnificent Paraguayan jaguars. There is a lake for caimans and another for fish.

Within the zoo are two interesting houses, which belonged to Carlos Antonio López and his wife Juana Pabla Carrillo. The Casa Baja (Lower House) was converted into a Museum of Natural History in 1912, and houses a ghoulish collection of deformed animal foetuses in preserving jars. A little further on is the *Casa Alta* (Upper House) which is an elegant two-storey house with colonnade and balcony all around, and now is a museum of antiquities.

community; and the use of the native language of Guaraní, rather than Spanish, except for church services (which had to be in Latin).

Not content with staying in San Ignacio, he set out to build more Reductions, travelling always with a picture of Mary as la Conquistadora (the Conqueror), which represented his belief that the true rulers of the Guaraní people were Christ and his mother, who were victorious over the Europeans with their force of arms. He founded 12 Reductions in all, at the rate of about one a year, moving in a generally southeasterly direction into the region known as Tapé, to the south of both the Río Paraná and the Río Uruguay, until the year of his martyrdom in 1628. Sadly, nearly all the Tapé Reductions were overrun and destroyed by the *bandeirantes* (slave-traders) coming from São Paulo, who captured and sold half a million Guaraní in the slave markets of São Paulo, not to mention many more who were killed as being too weak to be of economic use.

It was not, however, the *bandeirantes* who were responsible for his death, but a small group of hostile *caciques* (tribal chieftains) who saw their power being eroded, notably Nesú. He sent assassins who clubbed Roque González to death as he was attaching a clapper to the bell in the new Reduction of Ca'aro, in present-day Missões, Brazil. Alonso Rodriguez heard the clamour and ran out to see what was going on, and he too was murdered, as was an elderly indigenous man who reproached the assassins, and paid for his courage with his life. The Jesuits of today are trying to secure the canonisation of this nameless Guaraní hero, to whom they have given the name Arasunú (Guaraní 'Thunder').

The heart of the dead Roque González is alleged to have reproached the assassins, and they tried unsuccessfully to silence it by piercing it with an arrow, and then throwing it into the fire. But the allegedly incorrupt heart of the saint is displayed today in the Cristo Rey church in Asunción (see page 95).

Juan del Castillo was killed two days later, in a nearby Reduction, on the orders of the same Nesú. The date of his death, 17 November, has been taken as the joint feast day of the three martyrs.

On the far side of the Jardín Botánico is the Asunción Golf Club, nestling up against the curves of the fence. There is a secondary entrance to the garden where the two meet, and opposite is the railway station of Trinidad, which Carlos Antonio López had built as close as possible to his house. Today this is where the tourist train trip starts (see *Excursions* below, page 98).

Centro Familiar de Adoración [62 F4] (*Del Maestro 3471; www.cfa.org.py; services 10.00, 16.30, 19.00 Sun*) This is not in the run of normal sightseeing, but it is a phenomenon – a simply enormous Protestant church, with seating capacity for 10,000 people, and they are talking about an expansion to take 20,000. It is located just to the north of the junction between Mariscal López and Madame Lynch. Head towards town from the junction and take the first right: the church is one block away. The Centro Familiar de Adoración began as a small Bible study group under pastors Emilio and Betania Abreu, and grew at amazing speed. Work started on the megachurch in 2004, and at the time of going to press it was still receiving finishing touches. It has four storeys plus a basement and sub-basement, and from the top gallery of seats, the preacher is so tiny that an enormous blow-up has to be projected onto the white walls.

Cerro Lambaré Mirador [62 A5] A tall monument with a cross on top, placed on a hill to the south of the Bañado Sur, occupies a position previously taken by a statue of Stroessner. Worth a brief stop if you are in a car.

Asunción is something of a dead city on a Sunday, and you may be at a loss to know what to do. Here are a few places open on a Sunday:

- The Cabildo (⏰ *10.00–17.00, see page 87*)
- The Manzana de la Rivera (⏰ *07.30–18.00, see page 87*)
- The Jardín Botánico y Zoológico (⏰ *06.00–17.00, see page 96*)
- Mercado Cuatro (*the food section at Perú y Teniente Fariña makes an interesting visit,* ⏰ *till midday, see page 78*)
- The Cathedral (⏰ *10.00–12.00, see page 90*)
- La Encarnación church (⏰ *09.30–12.00, see page 95*)
- La Santísima Trinidad church (⏰ *07.00–11.30, see page 95*)

Or you could do the train journey, see below.

EXCURSIONS

TRAIN JOURNEY It is a delight to do the tourist trip known as the Tren del Lago (✆ *021 447848*). The engine is a proper Thomas-the-Tank-Engine-style chuff-chuff, and the claim is that this is the last working steam train in the world to be fired by wood rather than coal. It travels at a stately 15km/hour, and if that seems slow, consider that it is three times as fast as walking and a lot more restful.

The train used to run from Asunción to Encarnación, but the only people who used it for getting to places were the poor, as it was so much less efficient than going by bus. The railway became more of an outing than a transport service, but some form of regular service was operated until the late 1990s, when the train fell off the rails when carrying a Sunday school outing, and a little girl was killed. All services were suspended for many years, but the train came back into operation a few years ago for Sunday excursions, setting off at 09.30 for 10.00 from Estación Trinidad (at the Jardín Botánico – not the Estación Central) via Luque to Areguá, and arriving at 11.30. After a three-hour stop for tourism, craft purchasing and lunch, the train sets off on its return journey at 14.30 for 15.00. At the time of going to press the train journeys were suspended for the repair of a bridge, but it was expected that they would resume again around June 2010.

The tickets are proper old-fashioned small rectangles of thick cardboard with slightly wonky printing. They cost US$20 for foreigners (which by Paraguayan standards is very expensive) and Gs30,000 for Paraguayans (less than a third of the price). The result is that many foreign tourists do not take the train – certainly not enough for it run more than once a week – though it has become quite popular as a Paraguayan family outing. If you have Paraguayan friends, they can buy the tickets for you, as the documents of the passengers are not checked, only the identity card of the purchaser. Children under five travel free. You can buy the tickets at the Estación Trinidad on the day, or in advance from the Estación Central on Plaza Uruguaya (see above, page 89).

You will find the Estación Trinidad for your Sunday excursion opposite the smaller entrance to the Jardín Botánico, on the Ruta Transchaco, near the junction with the Avenida Primer Presidente. The train has not been renovated as much as it could be: new paint sits over blistered old paint, and there are tiny paint splashes on the brown seats. Because of rather than despite this, the train has tremendous character. The engine is called appropriately *President C A López*, and it pulls a huge wagon of logs as well as a couple of passenger carriages. It has a shiny, shrill whistle and a shiny bell which goes dong-dong before the train sets off. You can observe from the windows how many families come out to wave at the train going past – a special once-weekly event for them. Children are kept well entertained throughout the journey, eg: by a group of comics.

The stop at Luque is too short for getting off, but at Areguá there are various options. There are a lot of craft stalls to browse through in the station itself, representing a broad range of Paraguayan artisan work, and there are indigenous stalls run by women in feather headdresses. A display of dance and harp playing awaits on the platform, with several of the most loved of the traditional songs. After this welcome, guides offer a walking tour or a bus tour of the town, or you can just wander off by yourself. (See section on *Areguá*, page 126). In short, this is far more than a train journey, it is a whole day out.

INDIAN RESERVE Visiting a village of the **Maká** indigenous, on the edges of Asunción, is easy to arrange. Basically you can just show up, and ask for Rubén Riquelme (m *0985 871116*), who is one of the Maká; then you give a voluntary donation. They will have craft to sell. It is always best to let them know in advance of a visit, but it is not strictly necessary. The village is just before the Puente Remanso (where the Ruta 9 crosses into the Chaco), on the right-hand side. To get there, ask for Mariano Roque Alonso (see map on page 104); línea 44 (from Cerro Corá in the centre), or Brújula from the Terminal, are among the buses that go there.

RIVER CRUISE

Crucero Paraguay Perú 689 c/ Juan de Salazar; \ 021 223217/232051; m 0981 520277; e crucero@cruceroparaguay.info; www.cruceroparaguay.info. Beautiful luxury cruiser with swimming pool, 5 decks, discotheque, cinema, gym. As well as longer trips, it offers w/end cruises about once a month, starting & ending in Asunción, going to Villa Hayes (with its steel industry) & to a rural *estancia* (where activities include riding & walking); cost about US$512. More info on Crucero Paraguay in *Chapter 11*, page 282.

Barco Cuñataí Club Deportivo Puerto Sajonia; \ 021 420375. This is an old boat, declared *patrimonio turístico nacional,* but it no longer makes regular trips. You can book it for Gs2,870,000, which includes the discotheque, & you buy your food & drink on board. It makes a 2½hr journey from the Club in Sajonia to the Bahía & back.

For longer journeys up the Río Paraguay from Asunción to Concepción see *Chapter 11*, page 282.

CIRCUITO DE ORO The most popular excursion from Asunción is the Circuito de Oro, which is a tour of the towns close to Asunción, noted for their craft, or for their Franciscan churches, or for both. See *Chapter 4* for details.

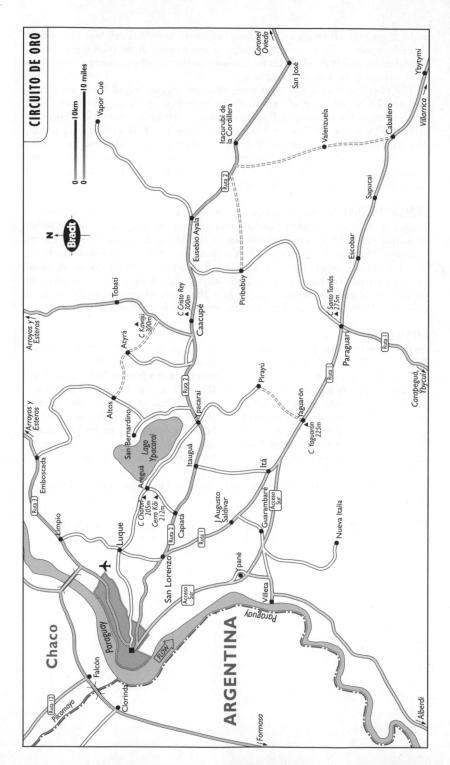

4

Circuito de Oro

Departamentos: Central, Cordillera, Paraguarí

The famous Circuito de Oro or Golden Circuit is a collection of small towns to the east and southeast of Asunción, each reachable within about an hour. The great majority of traditional Paraguayan crafts are based in one or other of these towns, so you can do a circuit that takes you from workshop to workshop, seeing (for example) the production of harps in Luque, silver *filigrana* jewellery also in Luque, pottery in Areguá, sculpture of wooden saints in Capiatá, *ñandutí* lacework in Itauguá, leatherwork in Atyrá, more sculpture of wooden saints in Tobatí, ponchos *de sesenta listas* in Piribebúy, more pottery in Itá, and so back to Asunción.

In its simplest form you do it in a day, going out on Ruta 1, crossing over to Ruta 2 on the road that goes through Piribebuy, and coming back on Ruta 2 – or vice versa. However, there are a lot of interesting places just to the north and south of Ruta 2, so with these deviations the route can become more complicated. The road through Luque and Areguá is one such loop. Another loop is San Bernardino, Altos, Atyrá. And a third is Pirayú, which provides a way of foreshortening the circuit, because it provides an earlier link between Ruta 1 and Ruta 2 – with the loss, however, of some of the most interesting places. An even more abbreviated tour can be done by making the crossover from Itá (on Ruta 1) to Itauguá (on Ruta 2). Here is an outline of the considerable number of towns covered in this chapter:

- **Towns on Ruta 2** San Lorenzo, Capiatá, Itauguá, Ypacaraí, Caacupé, Itacurubí
- **Towns to the north of Ruta 2** Luque, Areguá, San Bernardino, Altos, Emboscada, Atyrá, Tobatí, Vapor Cué
- **Towns to the south of Ruta 2** Pirayú, Piribebúy, Valenzuela, Sapucai
- **Towns on Ruta 1** Itá, Yaguarón, Paraguarí, Carapeguá, Ybycuí, San Roque González, Quiindý, Caapucú

This same area is now being promoted simultaneously under another name, the **Camino Franciscano**. This draws attention to the fact that many of the old Franciscan Reductions were sited in the same area that is now rich in craft workshops. (The Jesuit Reductions, by contrast, were a little further from Asunción, in the *departamentos* of Misiones and Itapúa). A tour of the Circuito de Oro can therefore take in both the historical art and the current craft.

For example, Capiatá has an important Franciscan church, and a famous workshop of carved wooden saints. Itauguá has a splendid museum of Jesuit and Franciscan statues, and is also the one place in Paraguay where the famous *ñandutí* lace is made. Atyrá has a Franciscan reredos in its church, and also makes leather sandals. Tobatí is known for craftwork in wood and in pottery, and also has the ancient twin statue to the Virgin of Caacupé. Piribebúy has an important Franciscan church with a fine reredos, and is also where the *poncho de sesenta listas* is made. Itá

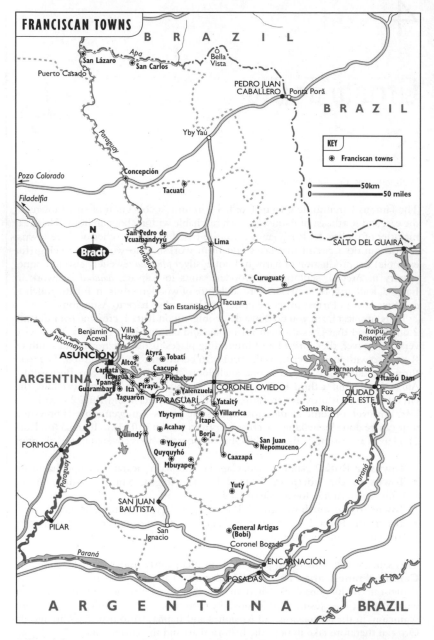

FRANCISCAN TOWNS

KEY
⊕ Franciscan towns

is famed for its pottery, and also has an old reredos in a Franciscan chuch with many original features. Its neighbouring town of Yaguarón is famed for having the most beautiful and complete church of that period to be found anywhere in Paraguay.

But two of the principal tourist attractions on this route are famed neither for their craft nor for their Franciscan heritage. San Bernardino is the most popular holiday town for Paraguayans, because of its beach on Lake Ypacaraí: in January all the hotels are full for the summer holiday, but through the rest of the year there is

The very first Franciscan Reduction was Altos in 1580 (30 years before the first Jesuit Reduction), followed in 1585 by Itá (one of the pottery towns). Soon afterwards came Yaguarón (which today has the only complete church left from the period of the Reductions) and Tobatí (which has a larger version of the Virgin of Caacupé). Next came Guarambaré, Ypané and Atyrá (reputedly 'the cleanest town' in Paraguay, and with leathercraft and a wonderful hotel, Casa del Monte).

All of these are early Franciscan foundations, though some, such as Atyrá and Tobatí, started in a different site: they moved from what is now the departmento of San Pedro to the present location in 1672 and 1699 respectively, due to attacks from other indigenous tribes. (Indeed, the origin of the twin Virgins carved by the Indio José of Tobatí was in this persecution; see box on page 119.)

Luis Bolaños went south of the Río Paraná in 1615 and left Paraguay to the Jesuits. But after a long gap, the Franciscans returned to founding Reductions in the late 18th century, with Itapé (north of Caazapá) in 1678, and San Lázaro and San Carlos by the Río Apa, along the northern frontier of present-day Paraguay. In the same period the European settlers were founding the historic cities of Concepción and San Pedro de Ycuamandyyú in the north, which inevitably were affected by Franciscan influence. The old cathedral of San Pedro, that is still standing and in good condition, is an example of a church in a Franciscan town (for Fray Pedro de Bartolomé was co-founder and first chaplain to the settlement) that was not founded as a mission for the indigenous. There is still a strong presence of Third Order Franciscans (ie: lay members) in San Pedro.

Further south, in central Paraguay, chapels began to be built in the 18th century to serve the needs of the local people who lived scattered around the region, and while these were not true Reductions (because they were not founded to gather together a group of indigenous in one place) they are rightly regarded as Franciscan towns: Capiatá, Itauguá, Pirayú, Caacupé, Piribebúy, Valenzuela and Bobí.

In 1848 the Franciscan Reductions stopped being Reductions: by order of President Carlos Antonio López, the community lands were appropriated by the state, and the indigenous were granted Paraguayan citizenship. The towns became *mestizo* (mixed race), and were absorbed into the wider Paraguayan population.

plenty of availability. And Caacupé, on Ruta 2, is the national Marian pilgrimage centre, and hundreds of thousands of Paraguayans walk to the basilica for the feast of the Immaculate Conception on 8 December. Through the rest of the year it is also well visited, and whether you are a Marian devotee or not, Caacupé represents a key feature of Paraguayan culture.

The Circuito de Oro can be done in an abbreviated form as a long day trip from Asunción, through an agency or with one of the tour companies on pages 67–8. Or you can hire a car (with or without a driver) and create your own route, with the freedom to spend nights along the way. You can also do a form of the circuit on public transport, if time is no object, and if you can stand the rattle and lurching of the buses.

GETTING OUT OF ASUNCIÓN

BY CAR If you hire a car, then getting out of Asunción is one of the biggest challenges you will face, due to the lack of road signs and a decent road map. (The maps you can buy either show the streets of Asunción or the main roads of the whole country, without anything to bridge the way between them.) Paraguayans learn to find their way by travelling first with other people: map-reading is not a

ASUNCIÓN ACCESS ROADS

traditional part of the culture. Here, then, is a beginners' guide for foreigners.

The first thing you need to know for negotiating your way out of Asunción is that there is a semi-ring road from northeast to southeast of the city, called **Madame Lynch** on its more northerly stretch, and on its more southerly stretch Defensores del Chaco – but more popularly known as **Calle Ultima** (the last road). **Cuatro Mojones** is the name of the big intersection where Calle Ultima crosses the road called Fernando de la Mora, which leads to the bus terminal.

At this point it would be useful to refresh your memory on the 'five-finger' layout of Asunción access roads (see *Chapter 3*, page 63). **To leave the city**, working from north to south around the access roads:

To go north From the centre, take Artigas, follow the edge of the Jardín Botánico, and you will then be on the **Ruta Transchaco**. Turn left to cross the Río Paraguay at Puente Remanso, after Mariano R Alonso, if you are going to the Chaco or crossing into Argentina at Clorinda: it is now called **Ruta 9**, which is another name for the Ruta Transchaco. Or carry straight on – this is now **Ruta 3** – through Limpio and onwards through Arroyos y Esteros, towards the northeast of Paraguay. Being a new highway, this is one of the few roads that have adequate road signs.

To go to the airport From the centre, take España, which will change its name to Aviadores del Chaco, and then to the **Autopista** (but it is not a real motorway –

these do not yet exist in Paraguay). After you pass the football museum on the right (very evident from its huge football outside) you will come to the airport on the left, where there is a roundabout. If you continue on the same road you will come to a junction with Ruta 3, before Limpio.

To go east From the centre do one of the following: (1) take Mariscal López from the start, which will lead you on a straight fast road into San Lorenzo, from where you turn left to get onto either Ruta 1 or Ruta 2. You want Ruta 2 to go east. Or (2) take España, but after the Shopping del Sol (on the left), take the fork right which is called Santa Teresa. This will join up with Mariscal López after crossing Madame Lynch. Then continue as above. Or (3) take Eusebio Ayala, which later changes its name to Mariscal Estigarribia, and leads you into San Lorenzo at a more southerly point. Again, you must turn left, and then you will find the road dividing into Ruta 1 and Ruta 2.

To go southeast From the centre, do one of the following: (1) take Mariscal López, which will lead you into San Lorenzo, as above. Then take Ruta 1. Or (2) take Eusebio Ayala, which later changes its name to Mariscal Estigarribia, and leads you into San Lorenzo, as above. Or (3) take the road Fernando de la Mora, which goes past the bus terminal, through Cuatro Mojones, and then straight on. Eventually it will join up with Ruta 1 on the far side of Itá, some 35km out of Asunción, where there is a big roundabout in the middle of the countryside. This route is called the **Acceso Sur**, and many car drivers prefer it, because it cuts out some of the long crawl out of the city, bypassing San Lorenzo. The difference, however, is not great. The buses take the route along Eusebio Ayala and through San Lorenzo, because it gives them more opportunities to pick up passengers on the way.

To confuse things even more, the *town* of Fernando de la Mora is between Asunción and San Lorenzo, on the roads Mariscal Estigarribia and Mariscal López, and not on the *road* Fernando de la Mora.

Finally, some clarification is needed of how to find your way through **San Lorenzo**. Nowhere is Paraguay's lack of road signs more frustrating than in San Lorenzo, when you are trying to get out of Asunción onto Ruta 1 (towards Encarnación and the south) or onto Ruta 2 (towards Ciudad del Este and the east). If you have come into San Lorenzo on Mariscal López, the secret is to turn left, two blocks after the church – which is on your right as you drive through. At this left turn – where many other cars will also be turning left – you can then see ahead of you, above the road, the signs for **Ruta 2** to the left, and **Ruta 1** to the right. From there on, it is all straight driving. If you come in on Eusebio Ayala, you also have to take a right-angle turn to the left, as shown on the map.

BY BUS If you are leaving Asunción by bus, then you avoid the problem of getting lost. If you are going to a town close to Asunción, you will probably find that the long-distance buses will not take you, even though they pass through those places. You will need to take a medium-distance bus, which you get by going down the underpass from within the Terminal building, to reach the lower level. These buses go to places like Caacupé, passing through other towns *en route*, and the fares are extremely cheap.

There are also local buses (*línea*) which you can pick up on the street, for example from the bus stop on Republica Argentina immediately outside the Terminal. The bus marked 'ITA' goes to a lot of towns on the Circuito de Oro – San Lorenzo, Capiatá, Itauguá and then Itá. However you take your bus, you will find the travelling bumpy and tiring, so you will probably not want to do more than a couple of towns in a day.

Circuito de Oro **GETTING OUT OF ASUNCIÓN**

4

If you are coming into the city on a bus on Ruta 1, and want to go out on Ruta 2 (or vice versa), then you will save an enormous amount of time if you swap roads in San Lorenzo, rather than going to the Asunción Terminal. You will need to walk one block to pick up one of the buses that go along the other road, and since it is very difficult to describe any landmark in the prolonged urban sprawl, the best is to ask the driver to show you where to get off and which direction to walk.

If you are arriving at the capital by bus, then the easiest way is to carry on to the bus terminal in Asunción, and take your bearings from there. But with more experience you can save time by getting off the bus in San Lorenzo at the point where the bus driver calls out '*Desvío Luque*' (just after you go past the cemetery, where there is a red-brick wall at the corner), walking around the corner to the right, and then taking a number 12 or a 56 local bus to the centre of Asunción, bypassing the slow drag into the southeastern quarter of Asunción where the bus terminal is. Some people get off at the Shopping Multiplaza, which is already in Asunción on the road Eusebio Ayala, and has local buses that go more directly to the centre. And vice versa, if you are confident, you can leave Asunción by the same route.

SUGGESTED CIRCUITS

CIRCUITO DE ORO TOURS OFFERED BY AGENCIES If you would like to follow a suggested route, then the easiest way to do it is on a set tour with an agency. They will know exactly where they are going, so will cover a lot more places, and will build in a presentation that includes scenery, art, traditional culture and legend.

The disadvantage of these tours is that they go at such a pace that you spend most of your time driving around in a comfortable air-conditioned vehicle, rather than exploring. The emphasis is on doing a lot of places, rather than on doing each place thoroughly. The advantage is that you get through a lot, without having to do any planning.

Mavani Palma c/ 14 de Mayo, Galería Palma, Local 38; ℡ 021 493580/446654; f 021 441458; e mavani@mavani.com.py; www.mavani.com.py. They do a very extensive tour, beginning on Ruta 2, passing to Ruta 1 by the road Itauguá-Itá, lunching at the Frutería of Paraguarí, returning to Ruta 2, & taking in some towns to the north of Ruta 2. The full programme is: San Lorenzo, Capiatá, Itauguá, Itá, Yaguarón, Paraguarí for lunch, Piribebúy, Caacupé, San Bernardino, Areguá, Luque. It sounds great, but to do 11 towns in a single day inevitably means a superficial visit in each place. The min time is 8hrs, & the cost is US$70 pp.

Travel Service Mariotti esq Presidente Santiago Leon; ℡ 021 282529; e 450207@hipuu.com.py. This excellent transport & guiding company run by Martin Molinas does a tour of Siete Pueblos más el Lago de Ypacaraí (Seven Towns plus Lake Ypacaraí) for around

US$35 (min 4 people) that includes a snatch of San Lorenzo, Capiatá, Itauguá, Ypacaraí, San Bernardino, Areguá, Luque. This omits the towns on Ruta 1 but you may feel that 7 towns is quite enough for 1 day. If you want to take in the full triangle, he will still do it in a day (around US$60, again for a min of 4 people) & will take you also to Itá, Yaguarón, the hills of Paraguarí, & Piribebúy. He can provide an English-speaking guide as an extra.

Intertours Peru 436 c/España; ℡ 021 211747; f 021 211870; e incoming@intertours.com.py; www.intertoursparaguay.com. Offer a tour from 08.30–16.00 that focuses on four towns: Itá, Yaguarón, Caacupé & San Bernardino, though towns *en route* can be stopped at too. They charge a little over US$60 pp, min 2 people.

Vips Tours Mexico 782 c/F.R.Moreno; ℡ 021 441199; e jefe@vipstour.com.py; www.vipstour.com.py

Other agencies listed in the previous chapter on pages 67–8 will offer a similar service.

ONE-, TWO- AND THREE-DAY TOURS If you prefer to be independent, the information in this chapter is sufficiently detailed for you to plan a circuit that suits you. But here are some suggested routes that you should be able to manage if you hire a car, even though more time is allowed in each place than you are generally given if you do the circuit with an agency. If you try to do the tour by public bus, you will only get half of it done because you will be more tired. Check underneath the individual town information below for details of facilities and opening times, if you want to vary from the proposed timetable. For Paraguayans the two highlights are the beach resort San Bernardino and the pilgrimage centre Caacupé, but these may not be priorities for foreigners so they do not figure in the one-day tour below.

One-day tours Here is a mini-tour that will give something of the flavour of the route, giving three craft towns, three fine Franciscan churches, four very different museums and one town with picturesque old streets. However, it still leaves out many of the best places!

08.00	Leave Asunción on Acceso Sur or Eusebio Ayala
09.00–10.00	**Itá** church with reredos; Centro Artesanal for craft
10.15–12.15	**Yaguarón** church (closes 11.00); museum
12.30–15.00	**Itauguá** lunch Jardín Alemán on road to Capiatá; return to Itauguá for old streets; museum for Reductions art; craft shops for *ñandutí*
15.15–16.15	**Capiatá** Museo Mitológico; church (opens at 16.00)
16.30–17.30	**San Lorenzo** Museo Boggiani for indigenous craft; return to Asunción

With more driving (and probably a hired driver) you can still do the full circuit through Piribebúy in a day. Here is an ideal one-day tour that may be tiring for some but takes you to what might be considered the best places.

07.30	Leave Asunción by Ruta 1
08.30–09.00	**Itá** Centro Artesanal for craft
09.00–10.00	**Yaguarón** church; museum if time
10.45–11.45	**Piribebúy** museum; church
12.30–14.30	**Atyrá** lunch in Casa del Monte; leather in Paseo San José; Casa Marianela, murals
15.00–16.00	**Itauguá** old streets; museum for Reductions art; craft shops for *ñandutí*
16.15–17.15	**Capiatá** church (opens at 16.00); Museo Mitológico
17.30–18.15	**San Lorenzo** Museo Boggiani for indigenous craft; return to Asunción

Two-day tour For many people, two days is as much time as they can devote to the Circuito de Oro. This suggested route includes many more of the important places, even though it still does not manage to take you the full circle. It takes a route via Pirayú (which has a fine reredos) to avoid the long distances to pass from Atyrá to Yaguarón via Piribebúy on the second morning (40km Atyrá to Piribebuy; 42km Piribebuy to Yaguarón). Note that the Yaguarón part of this tour will not work if day two is a Monday.

Day one

07.30	Take Avenida España to leave Asunción
08.00–08.45	**Road to Luque** harp and guitar shops on Avenida Aviadores del Chaco
09.00–10.00	**Luque** silver shops alongside Plaza General Aquino; walk down Peatonal Mariscal López for old street with colonnade

10.30–11.45	**Areguá** railway station for the craft shop; open-air craft market; road to church for colonial houses
12.00–14.00	**San Bernardino** Hotel del Lago for lunch; beach
14.30–15.30	**Caacupé** basilica; climb tower to see murals
16.00	**Atyrá** Paseo del Indio José for leather craft; church for reredos; dinner and night in Casa del Monte

Day two

08.00	Leave Casa del Monte; **Atyrá** Casa Marianela for murals
09.00–10.00	**Pirayú** church with reredos
10.45–11.45	**Yaguarón** church; museum
12.00–13.00	**Paraguarí** lunch in Frutería
13.20–14.20	**Itá** church with reredos; centro artesanal for craft
15.00–15.30	**Itauguá** old streets; museum for Reductions art; craft shops for *ñandutí*
16.30–17.30	**Capiatá** church (opens at 16.00); Museo Mitológico
17.45–18.45	**San Lorenzo** Museo Boggiani for indigenous craft; leave for Asunción

Three-day tour In three days you can do much more justice to the circuit, reaching the base line of the triangle (in the road that goes through Piribebúy) and also having sufficient time in each place to see it properly. This suggested tour covers the most important places, though it is not exhaustive. It omits, for example, Carapeguá and Valenzuela, both of which are rather far away from Asunción, but could be taken in if you were on your way to somewhere else along Ruta 1 or Ruta 2 respectively. The restaurants and hotels here have been chosen for quality rather than economy, but it is not necessary to spend the night *en route*: you can do any or all of the days using Asunción as your base. If day three is a Monday, then the Yaguarón stop will not work.

Day one

07.30	Take Avenida España to leave Asunción
08.00–08.45	**Road to Luque** harp and guitar shops on Avenida Aviadores del Chaco
09.00–10.00	**Luque** silver shops alongside Plaza General Aquino; walk down Peatonal Mariscal López for old street with colonnade
10.30–11.45	**Areguá** railway station for the craft shop; open-air craft market; road to church for colonial houses
12.00–14.00	**San Bernardino** Hotel del Lago for lunch; beach
14.30–15.30	**Altos** church for reredos; dirt road to Atyrá (Omit San Bernardino and Altos if time is short, and then you take the turning to Atyrá from Ruta 2 before Caacupé)
16.30	**Atyrá** Paseo del Indio José for leather craft; church for reredos; dinner and night in Casa del Monte

Day two

09.30	Leave Casa del Monte
10.00–11.00	**Tobatí** church for reredos; craft centre
11.15–13.30	**Caacupé** basilica; climb tower to see murals; lunch in Hotel Asunción
14.00–16.00	**Piribebúy** museum; church for reredos; workshop of *poncho de 60 listas*
16.30	Hotel Gabriela for dinner and the night

Day three

08.30	Leave Hotel Gabriela
9.00–10.00	**Yaguarón** church; museum
10.15–11.45	**Itá** church with reredos; centro artesanal for craft *or by a different road* **Pirayú** church with reredos; casa artesanal
12.00–13.30	**Ypacaraí** lunch in El Galpón
14.00–15.30	**Itauguá** old streets; museum for Reductions art; craft shops for *ñandutí*
16.00–17.30	**Capiatá** church (opens 16.00); Museo Mitológico
17.45–18.45	**San Lorenzo** Museo Boggiani for indigenous craft
18.45	Leave for Asunción, returning in on either Eusebio Ayalá or Mariscal López

BUILD YOUR OWN CIRCUIT If you have time to plan it, you can build your own circuit with the information in this chapter. Here are some hints to help.

Where to stay Most but not all places have a cheap *hospedaje* but if you are looking for a better-quality hotel, then here are some of the chief options. Remember you can use Asunción as your base, and return there each night. Remember also that if you go to an *estancia*, the idea is to spend some time there enjoying nature and the activities, and not just to get a bed for the night.

Altos – Hotel Grappa, Finca El Gaucho (page 131)
Areguá – Hotel-Restaurant Don Quijote (page 126)
Atyrá – Casa del Monte (page 132)
Capiatá – Jardín Alemán (page 113)
J Augusto Saldivar – Oñondivemí *estancia* (page 142)
Paraguarí – Hotel Gabriela (page 148)
Piribebúy – La Quinta *estancia*, Hotel Parador Chololó (page 139)
San Bernardino – Hotel del Lago and the other hotels (page 128)

Where to eat Wherever you go there will be cheap bars where you can pick up an *empanada* and a fizzy drink, but if you want something more than that there is a shortage of restaurants on this route, and you will want to plan in one of the following towns for lunchtime:

Altos – Hotel La Grappa (page 131)
Areguá – El Cántaro and the other restaurants (page 127)
Atyrá – Casa del Monte (page 132)
Capiatá – Jardín Alemán (page 113)
Luque – Rèstaurant Real (page 124)
Paraguarí – La Frutería, Hotel Gabriela (page 148)
Piribebúy – Hotel Parador Chololó (page 139)
San Bernardino – Hotel del Lago and the other hotels or Selva Negra or Café Francés (page 128)
Ypacaraí – El Galpón (page 118)

TRAVELLING ALONG RUTA 2

Ruta 2 is the highway that runs directly east until it reaches Coronel Oviedo, halfway across eastern Paraguay, on the way to Ciudad del Este. The first 100km of Ruta 2 are dotted with interesting towns, to right and left of the main road, on the Circuito de Oro.

After San Lorenzo (see below), you come to Capiatá, and from then on there are stations of the cross along the road, each bearing the picture of the Virgin of the Schoenstadt movement. When they end, you come to the little drive on the north side of the road, into the Tupãrendá retreat centre (see below page 118).

In Ypacaraí the road divides and goes around a large central island. Then you pass an ugly concrete church on the left with a strange octagonal tower. As you leave Ypacaraí you go through a *peaje* (toll station) where you will be charged Gs5,000. The next turning to come up is to San Bernardino, to the north. Between Ypacaraí and Eusebio Ayala you pass a totem pole topped with the figure of Tupã – God the Father in the traditional Guaraní religion.

A bit further on you come to a large white cross with a hollow centre, in the middle of the road, called the Kurusú Peregrino (Guaraní 'Cross'; Spanish 'Pilgrim'). This marks the final stage of the walk to Caacupé, for the annual pilgrimage of 8 December. It is also the point where you turn left if you are going to Atyrá. Carrying on towards Caacupé you pass a number of *viveros* or nursery gardens, which sell flowering plants.

At Caacupé the road divides. Eastbound traffic hugs around the town to the south, and to enter Caacupé you drive all the way round it before finding the left turn marked for the centre and the Basilica: this is the westbound carriageway of Ruta 2.

Between the Piribebúy turn and the (unmarked) Valenzuela turn, a good eating place on the road is **Viva el Sabor** (*km83;* m *0982 543605;* $). It does fast food, but is more Paraguayan than North American. It is clean, modern and tastefully designed, and has a high terrace from which can keep an eye on your car. They serve good homemade *empanadas* and hamburgers, ice cream in lots of different flavours, fresh fruit juice and crisply fresh salad.

Between the Piribebúy turn and the Eusebio Ayala turn there begins a clutch of excellent *chiperías*. The Chipería Camellito (km66) is followed by the Chipería María Ana (km69), the Chipería Leticia (km74) and the Chipería Barrero (km79). If you are driving, draw in briefly and buy one of these delicious, fresh, hot, aniseedy rolls, all soft and spongy inside from the melted cheese. The *chipas* cost only a modest Gs2,000 each. Particularly recommended is the Chipería María Ana.

In Itacurubí de la Cordillera you pass a pleasant green plaza at the side of the road and a horserace track. At the east of the town there is an excellent, popular restaurant on the south side of the road, called **La Curva** (*km88;* ℡ *0518 20064*). The staff are friendly, there are ample portions of *asado*, and there is the buzz of a successful business. They even serve breakfast.

Past Itacurubí you come to a lot of little stalls on the road selling fruit and vegetables. The next turn to the left leads to Nueva Londres (see regional map to *Chapter 10*, page 252), which was founded by British emigrants in 1893. After that you come to another toll station and shortly after it the major intersection of Coronel Oviedo (see page 253). You have now passed out of the area of the Circuito de Oro.

SAN LORENZO Copaco ℡ 021 583300; municipalidad ℡ 021 582817

San Lorenzo joins Fernando de la Mora and then Asunción in one big urban sprawl, and travelling through by bus one is tempted to curse the place for adding to the long stretch of bumpy crawl that makes arriving or leaving the capital city so unpleasant. (A bus will take at least an hour just to get onto the open road.) But the roads in San Lorenzo that the long-distance bus goes along, with their market squalor, are very different from the town centre, with its church in the middle of the plaza and its dignified houses. And the Museo Boggiani, with its accompanying

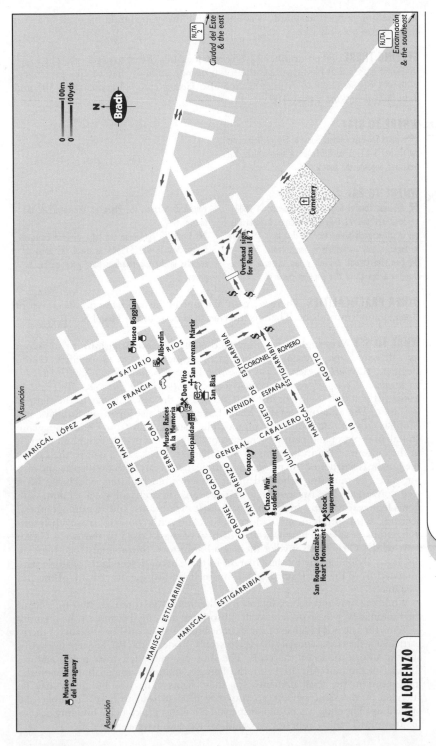

SAN LORENZO

Museo Natural
del Paraguay

Asunción

MARISCAL LÓPEZ

Asunción

MARISCAL ESTIGARRIBIA

MARISCAL ESTIGARRIBIA

1ª DE MAYO

CERRO CORÁ

DR FRANCIA

SATURIO RIOS

Museo Boggiani

Alberdín

Museo Raices
de la Memoria

Municipalidad

Don Vito

San Lorenzo Mártir

San Blas

CORONEL BOGADO

SAN LORENZO

GENERAL

CABALLERO

AVENIDA DE ESTIGARRIBIA

ESPAÑA

M CUETO

JULIA

MARISCAL

10 DE AGOSTO

CORONEL

ESTIGARRIBIA ROMERO

Copaco

Chaco War
soldier's monument

San Roque González's
Heart Monument

Stock
supermarket

Overhead sign
for Rutas 1 & 2

Cemetery

Ciudad del Este
& the east

RUTA 2

RUTA 1

Encarnación
& the southeast

0   100m
0   100yds

N

Bradt

shop selling indigenous crafts, is so interesting that you should try to fit in a visit there if you possibly can.

GETTING THERE Take a number 12, 56 or 26 local bus (*linea*) to get there. The long-distance buses that pass through the town do not generally like to take passengers who get off so close to Asunción. See also *Getting out of Asunción* page 103 and *Travelling along Ruta 2* page 109.

WHERE TO STAY

🏠 **Hotel San Blas** Coronel Romero 498 c/ Defensores del Chaco; ☎ 021 570200/576181. A simple place, but well sited opposite the church. $$

WHERE TO EAT

✖ **Alberdin** Coronel Bogado c/ Dr Francia; ☎ 0800 11 2662/021 662972. Only a hamburger & pasta bar, but it serves good-quality food at that level. There are no higher-quality restaurants in San Lorenzo. $
✖ **Don Vito** Coronel Romero y San Lorenzo. There is a branch of this popular chain of

empanada bars on the Plaza, on the corner of the square. $
✖ **Stock** Del Agrónomo esq Julia Miranda Cueto de Estigarribia; ☎ 021 575166. As usual, the patio de comidas in the supermarkets have good quality & prices. $

OTHER PRACTICALITIES There is a cash machine in the *cooperativa* on the corner of Bogado and Saturio Rios. There is internet next door to the Hotel San Blas.

WHAT TO SEE Very highly recommended is the **Museo Boggiani**, or to give it its full name, the Museo Antropológico, Arqueológico y Etnográfico Guido Boggiani (*Coronel Bogado 888, e/ Mariscal López y Saturio Ríos;* ☎ *021 584717; www.cabildoccr.gov.py/?pagina=arteindigena;* ⊕ *09.00–19.00 Tue–Sat, till 17.30 in winter*). If you find it closed, just ring the bell by the next gateway to the right of the door. The attentive curator Mari Traversi, will also open on Sundays and Mondays if you ring the bell or phone. The name comes from Guido Boggiani, an Italian explorer and painter, who was one of the first people to take an interest in the culture of the indigenous in the Chaco. A block and a half to the east of the northeast corner of the plaza, it has indigenous craft both on display and also for sale. The museum is housed in an attractive old building, which has been well converted. The museum has two sections: an archaeological section, with items from excavations, including prehistoric excavations, and an ethnographical section, with implements, adornments and cult objects from different indigenous peoples. There is a wall display of masks used in the Areté Guasú feast of the Guaraní to invoke their dead ancestors. Surprisingly, one item on display is a violin made by the Guaraní in the Chaco, descendants of those who migrated from the old Jesuit Reductions in Itatín (on the other bank of the Río Paraguay).

While the museum is very interesting, the three large rooms of craft for sale, in the building over the road, are totally absorbing, not only because of the quantity of items for sale but because of the extraordinary artistic quality of many of them, particularly the larger animals that act as stools (made by the Paî Tavyterä Guaraní), and the animal masks on the walls. The shop operates a fair-trade policy and the founder of the museum, José Antonio Perasso, continues to collaborate with the indigenous in the legal demands for their rights. The two buildings may be attended by the same person, so you may need to wait to have the other one opened up. The shop has no sign displayed but is in a pinky-beige building next to the Instituto Técnico Superior en Salud, which does have a sign.

The church of **San Lorenzo Martír** is a grand neo-Gothic building in grey and white, and is attractively set back from the road in the middle of a very pleasant green with a garden. Above the statue of St Laurence is a large painted Ascension in the apse; and there are good Stations of the Cross made out of different coloured wood blocks, with the signature 'NUMA'.

In the plaza is a **monument to the *niños mártires***, the children who died in the battle of Acosta Ñú (north of Vapor Cué) on 16 August 1869. Mariscal López had virtually no adult soldiers left, and in order to give himself time to escape, he put forward an army of 3,000 children under 15, disguised as adults with painted beards, and 500 old men and wounded, who were slaughtered by the army of the Triple Alliance, leaving just two survivors.

Around the plaza and the neighbouring streets are a good number of old **colonial houses**, with colonnades of round masonry pillars. The museum **Raíces de la Memoria** (*Coronel Bogado c/ España;* ✆ *021 582402;* m *0981 409221;* ⊕ *08.00–11.00 & 14.00–18.00 daily, but variable for lack of staff; free*) is dedicated to the history of the town. The plaque outside says 'Centro Cultural Mario Z Meyer'.

On the outskirts of town and opposite the entrance to the Universidad Nacional is the **Museo de Historia Natural del Paraguay** (⊕ *07.30–13.00 Mon–Fri*), which has collections of flora and fauna native to the country, and is run by the government Secretaría del Ambiente, SEAM. (Guided tours to groups can be arranged by ringing ✆ 021 585208.)

At San Lorenzo you can take your choice between Ruta 2, heading towards Ciudad del Este and the east, and Ruta 1, heading towards Encarnación and the southeast. This section pursues Ruta 2, while the route along the other highway, Ruta 1, begins on page 141.

CAPIATÁ Copaco ✆ 0228 634974; municipalidad ✆ 0228 634727

Capiatá is interesting on a number of counts. Most importantly, it has a fine, historic church, almost all of it original to the Franciscan Reduction. It has an interesting museum, both for Guaraní mythology and for religious art. The Rodríguez family of saint-makers (*santeros*) have their workshop here. And the folk cult of the black saint Baltasar adds a fascinating touch of popular religiosity.

GETTING THERE The journey by bus takes an hour from the Asunción Terminal, and the best place to get off is after you pass the España supermarket sign on the right-hand side of the road. The turn to the left there (Candelaria) has a taxi rank. If you want to go to the church first, this is the road that leads directly to it, just one block in from the main road.

The museum of mythology is 1km before Capiatá, on the Asunción side. If you are coming by bus and the driver does not want to drop you outside, or if you do not want to have to walk a kilometre into town afterwards, you can go on to Capiatá and take a taxi back, asking it to wait for you. You can also ask the taxi to take you to the workshop of the Rodríguez brothers, which will be the easiest way to locate it, although instructions for walkers and drivers are given below.

See also *Getting out of Asunción* page 103 and *Travelling along Ruta 2* page 109.

🏠 WHERE TO STAY AND EAT

🏠 **Hotel y Restaurant Jardín Alemán** Km24; ✆ 0228 632050/634025; e info@jardinaleman.com.py; www.jardinaleman.com.py. Outside town, almost halfway to Itauguá on Ruta 2. Pool. The restaurant

(⊕ 11.00–14.30 & 19.00–00.00, closed Mon; $$$) has a buffet service every day, & offers something better than you will find in the town itself. $$$

WHAT TO SEE The **church** of Capiatá, dedicated to Nuestra Señora de la Candelaria, is Paraguay's second most complete church of the Reduction period, after Yaguarón. It was built in the mid 18th century and completed in 1769. What we have today is nearly all original, but not quite, for the façade has been redone, the bell tower removed, the wooden pillars of the side colonnades replaced with round masonry ones, and a choir balcony removed from inside. However, the interior is magnificent, and it is surprisingly different from its contemporary Yaguarón. A restoration lasting six years was carried out at the end of the 20th century by Estela Rodríguez Cubero, who also worked on restoration in Atyrá, Yaguarón, Caazapá (both churches) and the cathedral and the Santísima Trinidad in Asunción.

Unfortunately the church is open only from 16.00 to 18.00 each day, and half of that time is taken up by mass. This is an inconvenient time for those setting off from Asunción on the Circuito de Oro, who are likely to reach Capiatá around 09.00, and equally awkward for those returning to Asunción at the end of the circuit, who have difficulty timing their arrival with such precision. It is impossible to arrange a viewing at any other time, even by arrangement and with a tip, and there is no guide. The townspeople are no more happy with this lamentable situation than the tourists are, but are unable to take over the running of the church from the parish priest.

There is not a lot of point in going to the church if you cannot get inside, as most of the original outside features have been lost. But if you do succeed in getting in, you will find a glorious extravaganza of dark red, blue and creamy beige. There are large figures of the crucified thieves (the good one and the bad one) on each side of the musicians' gallery over the entrance door. The pillars inside the church have carved details. The ceiling of the church is fairly plain, but the ceiling of the barrel vault over the chancel is painted. There is a splendid pulpit, an excellent crucifix, two side altars, and an elaborate reredos with the figure of the Candelaría in central position. It was made by the same artist who did the reredos of Yaguarón, the Portuguese José de Souza Cavadas.

The statue was removed from the church by Mariscal López during the Triple Alliance War, allegedly to prevent sacrilege, and was only identified as belonging to Capiatá many years later, when it was in the cathedral of Asunción. It was returned to its rightful place with great ceremony in 1940. The Christ Child in the Virgin's arms was subsequently stolen from the church, but it was happily recovered and replaced in 1979.

The patronal feastday is 2 February – the feast of Candlemas, or the Presentation of the Christ Child by Mary in the temple.

The **Museo Mitológico Ramón Elías** (*Ruta 2 km19;* ☏ *02286 34262;* ⊕ *08.00– 11.30 & 14.30–17.00 Mon–Sat, 07.30–12.00 Sun; Gs5,000*) is the only museum of its kind in the country, but is far more than a museum of mythology. The building itself is magnificent, having been constructed in 1976 by the artist Ramón Elías out of materials recovered from colonial buildings over the period of ten years: huge beams, heavy doors on wooden hinges, carved windows, massive roof tiles, and of course a colonnade with wooden columns and carved capitals.

Inside the museum – which is now looked after by his widow Elsa de Elías – is a gallery of monsters from traditional Paraguayan mythology, which Ramón Elías carved. According to legend, the spirit of evil, Taú, seduced a beautiful girl, Keraná, and she gave birth to seven monsters:

Tejú Jaguá was a lizard with a dog's head.
Mbói TU'Ï was a big snake with a parrot's head.
Moñái was a serpent with two spikes on his head and sharp teeth.
Jasý Jateré was a very blonde naked goblin who would whistle to attract children to lure them away during the heat of the siesta.

Kurupí had a penis so long that he had to wrap it round his waist.
Aó Aó was a fertility god looking like a sheep with sharp teeth, walking upright.
Luisõ was the most terrible of the monsters, looking like a large black dog but attacking like a tiger.

As well as these seven, Elías carved other traditional figures, including the well-known Pombero, the lord of the night, looking like a short, black, hairy man. He also included the figure of God himself, Tupã, the supreme father and source of goodness, whom the Franciscans and Jesuits identified with the God of Christians. He is portrayed by Elías (and in many subsequent sculptures) as a figure sitting on a bench with arms outstretched, one holding the sun and the other the moon, and with an enormous beard that covers his entire body in place of clothing.

But beyond this big hall of sculptures, are three further rooms. One has some old items from the Triple Alliance and the Chaco wars, but the rest of the space is devoted to art from the Reductions. There was a burglary in May 2009 when 25 statues of saints were stolen, worth over $500,000. (The guard said, somewhat implausibly, that he had gone home at 04.00 because he was feeling ill.) Though Elsa de Elías is heartbroken and says that they took all the best pieces, leaving the rooms virtually empty, she has reorganised well and the works of Jesuit art that are left are also very fine. Particularly good are three smallish crucifixes: one, in a cupboard-niche, is quite poignant; another has a twisted body with bright red blood and mauve and yellow details; and another has God the Father flying out from the top of the cross, and the dove flying out from a mitre on the head of the Father.

SAINTS AND THEIR ICONOGRAPHICAL SYMBOLS

NAME IN ENGLISH	NAME IN SPANISH	TYPICAL SYMBOL	OTHER INFORMATION
St Peter	San Pedro	keys	apostle and first pope
St Paul	San Pablo	sword	shown next to St Peter
St Antony of Padua	San Antonio	Christ Child in arms	Franciscan
St Anna (or Anne)	Santa Ana	book	mother of Virgin Mary
St Joseph	San José	Christ Child or lily	adoptive father of Jesus
St Roque	San Roque	wound in thigh and dog	medieval French
St Roque González	San Roque González	exposed heart & holding picture of Virgin	Jesuit martyr, first Paraguayan saint
St Barbara	Santa Bárbara	holding tower	early martyr
St Andrew	San Andrés	diagonal cross	apostle
St Isidore	San Isidro	hoe	patron of agriculture
St Francis of Assisi	San Francisco	stigmata	founder of Franciscans
St Blaise	San Blas	mitre	heals sore throats
St Laurence	San Lorenzo	grill	deacon, roasted alive
St Librada	Santa Librada	crucified woman	unknown in the north

On the opposite side of the road from the museum, and 50m in the direction of Asunción, is a well-presented kiosk that sells honey and related products, called **Pan de Miel**. It is just by the service station.

To reach the workshop of the **Rodríguez** *santeros* (saint-makers), take the road Santo Domingo in between the petrol station and the Tuvalu Karaoke, between the museum and the town. The shop is a pale green corner house, one block in. Cándido Rodríguez was well known when he was alive, following in his own father's footsteps as a *santero*; and now his children (Esperanza, Carlos, Justo, Maximiliano, Irenion and Juan) and his widow (Juana) carry on the practice, each with their own slightly distinct style. They employ three methods: painted, part-painted (the face, hands and feet) and unpainted. The figures are typically quite small, and each saint is easily identified by his or her symbol (see box). These little statues can also be found in the craft shops of Asunción, Overall and Bella Tierra.

The **Oratorio del Santo Rey Baltasar** (Ruta 2, km22.5) is nearly 3km after the town centre, and is thoroughly hidden from the road, so here again you may do better to take a taxi, with a driver who knows where he is going. But if you want to find it on your own, you need to look out on the right-hand side for a red and yellow sign saying 'Taller de moto' immediately after a sign saying 'Pollos Don Juan'. This is immediately opposite 'Sulmetal' on the left-hand side, before you get to the 'Toyota' sign.

Tucked in behind the car mechanic's garage, is the oratory with its five arched doorways. An oratory was built here in 1931, but it was replaced by a larger one in 1986. Red and yellow is very much the theme colour, and it sets off beautifully the black skin of King Baltasar, who traditionally was one of the three magi who visited the Christ Child in Bethlehem. Inside the oratory is a yellow altar with a red top, yellow vases with red and yellow flowers in, and the little figure of King Baltasar in a glass case, dressed in red and yellow clothes and carrying a sceptre.

The key to the oratory is held by the mechanic, but if he is not there you can see fairly well through the wrought iron gates. This is in every sense an example of popular religiosity – a shrine tucked behind a mechanic's garage, in memory of a black saint – and it is worth remembering that there were black slaves in Paraguay at least up to 1824 (see *San Roque González*, page 149). The saint's feast day is 6 January (the Epiphany) when there is mass at 08.30 and a procession to the chapel of San Francisco de Asís, down the road at km23, with the local children dressed as kings in red and yellow, and some on horseback. As is customary with patronal feast days, there is a novena for the nine days beforehand, with special prayers every evening at 20.30 at the oratory.

ITAUGUÁ Copaco ❯ 0294 221420; municipalidad ❯ 0294 220358/220252

Itauguá is an often overlooked town, but is actually one of the best places to visit on the Circuito de Oro. It is an excellent town for its craft, for its museum and for its old streets of colonial houses.

Its distinctive craft is the famous *ñandutí* lace, which is the Guaraní word for a spider's web: this is usually circular in shape, and then the circles are sewn together to make a large cloth. Its museum has two sections: one devoted to *ñandutí*, and the other devoted to art of the Reductions. The streets near the church (one block to the south of Ruta 2) are semi-pedestrianised and date from the time of Dr Francia. With their colonnades, they make the centre of Itauguá one of the most attractive towns in this part of the country.

For such an attractive town, it is a surprise to find Itauguá has no hotel, although a five-storey Olimpo Apart Hotel was under construction at the time of going to press (not perhaps an ideal kind of hotel for a visit to a small, historic, colonial town). It is sited on the corner of Cabo A Martínez, one block behind the big Stock supermarket on Ruta 2 after the traffic lights. For eating, there are a couple of simple local restaurant/bars on Ruta 2, but nowhere of higher quality. The best is probably the Guarida de Franki, near the *municipalidad* (or town hall). Stock does not have a *patio de comidas* but it does have toilets, telephones and a cash machine. There is also a Banco Visión, two blocks after Stock.

Among Paraguayans, Itauguá is well known not only for its *ñandutí* but also for having a large state hospital. This is to the east of the road that goes south to connect Itauguá with Itá, and patients come in from all over the country for specialist treatment there.

GETTING THERE See *Getting out of Asunción* page 103 and *Travelling along Ruta 2* page ·109. Any bus going to Ypacaraí or Caacupé will pass through Itauguá, but you may also pick up a bus going along Ruta 2 and then south past the hospital and on to Itá.

WHAT TO SEE The *ñandutí* shops are on Ruta 2, before the traffic lights which mark the junction with General Marcial Samaniego – the road that leads south to Itá. You begin to pass *ñandutí* shops as soon as you reach the town, and they soon come thick and fast. They are an excellent place to browse.

The traditional *ñandutí* is white, and the most delicate examples of this are exquisite. But while foreigners from the first world tend to like the whites and natural colours, Paraguayans like bright colours, so *ñandutí* has been developed into bright multi-coloured table mats and adornments. Particularly beautiful are the elaborate, long dresses made from *ñandutí*, although they are expensive because they take so long to make. Because the *ñandutí* is starched, it hangs with a good weight, and makes a superb skirt for folk dancing, with richly subtle colour variations as well as a good swing.

There is an annual Festival de Ñandutí, usually in June. Check the date with the *municipalidad*, or with the association of artisans, Asociación Tejedoras de Ñandutí de Itauguá (*Ruta 2, no 881;* ❧ *0294 22095/21255/20137;* m *0981 673617;* e *tejedorasitaugua@ceap.irg.py; www.ceap.org.py*).

Turn right after the traffic lights to reach the magnificent street of old houses and colonnades that runs parallel to Ruta 2: Teniente Esteban Martínez. On Coronel Francisco Caballero Álvarez (which joins Ruta 2 at the Banco Visión) is a little fountain set in the wall, in memory of the townspeople who have had to migrate to seek work, and one block further along is the plaza with the church.

The **Museo San Rafael** (❧ *0294 220415;* ☉ *07.00–10.50 & 14.00–17.00 Mon–Fri, 07.30–11.30 Sat; free*) was founded in the 1960s to conserve the statues from the old church and from elsewhere. (The current church was finished and inaugurated in 1908, but it incorporates the back wall of the original.) The building itself, adjoining the parish office, is old, dating back to the period of Dr Francia, and incorporates rings in the walls for hanging hammocks, just as in the Jesuit *casas de indios*.

In the *ñandutí* part of the museum, there is a display of dozens of different designs for the circular web of lace, each one only about 9cm wide and woven in fine, white cotton. Most of the designs are based on plants, insects, birds or religious symbols. There is, for example, a *ñandutí* design based on a broom, bread, clouds, bells, a star, an axe, bricks, a daisy, the beak of a toucan, a crab, fish tails, ears of wheat, and even a pregnant tummy. The museum also has on display some vestments made with *ñandutí* .

In terms of religious art, the oldest piece they have and one of the most lovely, which faces you as you go in, is a St Raphael, and it gives the name to the museum. He may have been the patron saint of the original church, but this is not known for certain. Among the most interesting of the large statues are a more-than-life-size St Stanislaus of Kostka, a St Francis which has glass eyes and is articulated (ie: the arms are hinged), and a very fine statue of Christ at the Column, which is used in the procession of Good Friday. A reredos of the original church is here too – at least the basic framework of it – with the Virgin of the Rosary in its central niche. The far room is filled with small saints, of the kind that every family once had in their home.

The **church** on the green facing the museum has a large and grand façade, and the view of its frontage is complemented by a golden fountain when you go down the Paseo José Asunción Flores that leads to it. The sacristan is often attending to the well-kept garden, and can let you inside. The Virgen del Rosario, to whom the church is dedicated, is portrayed in pink (as is the other one in the museum, and in Luque too) and with ñandutí adornment on her dress. The patronal feast day is 7 October, and on the nearest Sunday the statue is taken through the streets in a painted coach. The coach is kept behind the museum.

YPACARAÍ Copaco ➤ 0513 432270; municipalidad ➤ 0513 432267

Contrary to expectations, the town of Ypacaraí is not actually on the Lake of Yapacaraí, but it is not far off. The two towns with beaches on the lake are San Bernardino, on the east side, and Areguá, on the west side. Yapacaraí is on the south side, and a few kilometres of marshland separate it from the shore. It is one of the towns that were on the railway, when the line was still running, and the station can still be visited. Ruta 2 divides at the start of the town into separate carriageways, and joins up again after the town.

The name Ypacaraí literally means 'Water, sir?' The town is one of the points of departure used by the pilgrims who walk to Caacupé every 8 December.

GETTING THERE See *Getting out of Asunción* page 103 and *Travelling along Ruta 2* page 109. Any bus going to Caacupé will pass through Ypacaraí.

✷ WHERE TO EAT

✕ El Galpón ➤ 0513 432223. Just 3 blocks after the rather ugly church you see the notice pointing down a turn to the right. Restaurant with blue-&- white check tablecloths serving every kind of home made pasta. Only open at lunchtime. Ring in advance to be sure they make enough pasta that morning for your group. $$

WHAT TO SEE The retreat house of the Schoenstatt movement, **Tupãrenda** (➤ *021 601428/608215*), is on the north side of Ruta 2 before you reach the town of Ypacaraí. It has a beautiful chapel, adorned in excellent taste, and is used for religious conferences. The name means 'God's Place' in Guaraní. The current Bishop of Caacupé, Mons Claudio Giménez, was one of the founders of the Paraguayan branch of this German-based Marian movement, and their key date was the founding of Tupãrenda in 1981.

The city centre is to the south of the main road. The Casa de la Cultura (⏱ *07.30–12.30 Mon–Sat & 14.00–16.00 Mon–Fri*) has photographs, portraits and objects from the Triple Alliance War. Buried in Ypacaraí are Demetrio Ortiz, who wrote one of the most famous Paraguayan songs of all time, 'Recuerdos de Ypacaraí', and Teodoro Mongelós, a renowned poet who wrote in Guaraní, and was sent to fight in the Chaco War at the age of 17.

As you come into the town from Asunción you pass some places where leather goods are made. Within the town itself there is a turn that runs parallel to the lake, to Areguá, which is not clearly marked, and on this road are some manufacturers of guitars. In the opposite direction, is a turn going south to Pirayú, where, for the time being, the asphalt peters out. And just to the east of the town is the turn to San Bernardino, which is clearly marked.

CAACUPÉ Copaco ↘ 0511 243843; municipalidad ↘ 0511 242382

The Guaraní name of Paraguay's major Marian centre is a shortened form of *ka'aguy kupe* (Guaraní 'behind the wood'). Caacupé is the spiritual capital of the country, and the feast day of the Immaculate Conception on 8 December with its preceding novena brings in around a million pilgrims, known as the *promeseros*. People make a prayer-bargain with the Virgin along the lines of: if this happens to my favour, I promise to make the pilgrimage to Caacupé on 8 December. Some walk all the way from Asunción, but many take a bus part of the way (buses run all night in a constant stream), to somewhere like Ypacaraí, from where they still have to walk for several hours. Some come on bicycles from faraway towns; some make

THE LEGEND OF THE VIRGIN OF CAACUPÉ

The Indio José, who was from the Franciscan Reduction of Tobatí, was being hunted by other indigenous from the Mbayá people (a fierce tribe that no longer exists). As he hid in the forest, terrified for his life, he made a promise that if his life was saved, he would carve a statue of the Virgin from the wood of the tree behind which he was hiding. He fulfilled his promise when the danger was past, but in fact carved two identical Virgins: a larger one, 1.15m high, for the church of Tobatí, and a smaller one, 40cm high, for his personal devotion.

A second strand of legend about its origins is usually combined with the first to provide a sequel. A huge flood in 1603 from Lago Tapaicuá retreated following the prayers of Fray Luis Bolaños (the great Franciscan father of the Reductions). The Indio José (who in this version came from Atyrá – a Reduction close to Tobatí and founded around the same time) swam out to recover a small case, seen floating on the waters. Inside it was the statue of the Virgin, which the Franciscans entrusted to him to carry to the safety of his home.

In 1770 this smaller Virgin was placed in a small chapel in a little place known as Caacupé, where it received such veneration that the church was replaced by a larger one in 1783, and people built houses around it where they could stay at weekends, coming from their work in other towns to attend mass at the chapel: Caacupé began to take on the appearance of a Reduction, though it was not built to be such. A larger church was built, and consecrated in 1846, though the roof was destroyed by a lightning bolt just six years later, and one of the Virgin's fingers was damaged. This church was enlarged three times, the last time in 1856. In 1885 it was replaced by a larger building, which some still remember fondly as 'the real Basilica' although it no longer exists. Finally the present basilica was built in the 1980s. The feast of the Immaculate Conception on 8 December attracts around a million pilgrims.

The statue is similar in shape to many other statues of the Virgin in South America, that is, practically pyramidical in shape, as she is clothed in a an expansive cloak, in this case of dark blue velvet embroidered with gold. The Virgin has fairly pale skin, and brown hair falling around her shoulders in waves, and is crowned. Though carved by a Guaraní, she is far less indigenous in style and of lesser artistic quality than the great statue in the church of Santa María de Fe, also carved by a Guaraní, though anonymously. But neither the statue of Santa María de Fe, nor the larger statue by the Indio José in the church of Tobatí have much of a cult for those outside of the area, while huge crowds of pilgrims flock to the little statue of Caacupé.

their way on their knees 18km from Ypacaraí; some walk the 29km from Limpio carrying enormous heavy crosses. The walk is usually made during the night – no-one wants to walk by day in the heat of December – and the arrival is timed for the early morning mass outside the basilica. All along the road on 8 December are makeshift toilets, where the hordes of pilgrims can pay a pittance to enter a screened-off patch of field.

You pass *en route* a chapel called Pablito Róga (Guaraní 'Little Paul's house') erected in memory of a young child who died of thirst on the pilgrimage, while his mother left him to go and look for water: this is between Ypacaraí and the turn for San Bernardino.

During the novena leading up to 8 December, different bishops celebrate early morning mass and deliver sermons, which traditionally is an opportunity for them to aim a shot across the bows of the government. Caacupé is busy with pilgrims all through the year, and not only for the December feast day. It is a cultural phenomenon, and all over the country people have little copies in their homes of the Virgin of Caacupé – a small crowned figure with brown ringlets, in a full white dress decorated with gold and covered with a blue velvety cloak.

GETTING THERE See pags 103 and 109 above. Ruta 2 divides into one-way carriageways at Caacupé, with the eastward traffic making a small circle around the basilica, and the westward traffic passing through the middle of town, just one block away from the basilica.

WHERE TO STAY For a town with so many visitors, it is a surprise that there are few hotels, and that they have few rooms and limited facilities. Caacupé is very much a place for Paraguayans who have no money to stay, but go home again on the bus once their mission of reaching the pilgrimage centre is complete.

Hotel Katy Maria (15 rooms) Eligio Ayala esq Dr Pino; ☏ 0511 242860/242441. Facing the side of the Basilica. Minibars & cable TV. No internet or credit cards. $$$
Hotel Mirador (40+ rooms) Enfrente de la Basilica; ☏ 0511 242652. Exactly facing the basilica. No credit cards. $$$
Hotel Asunción (8 rooms) 8 de diciembre y Juan E O'leary; ☏ 0511 243771;

e info@asuncionhotel.com.py; www.asuncionhotel.com.py. Wi-Fi & 1 computer with internet which guests can use. Minibars, cable TV. Restaurant. No credit cards. $$
Hotel Uruguayo (10 rooms) Asunción e/ Eligio Ayala y Mariscal Estigarribia; ☏ 0511 242977/242222. The oldest established of the hotels. No internet or credit cards. Restaurant. Some cheaper rooms with fans. $

WHERE TO EAT
Hotel Asunción See above. $$
Churrasqueria Brasil Ruta 2, km52.5; ☏ 0511 243434; ⊕ daily. About 500m from the basilica in the direction of Asunción, before the 2 parts of Ruta

2 unite, opposite the supermarket Nuevo Super. $$
Hotel Uruguayo See above. Restaurant is only open for b/fast & lunch. $$

WHAT TO SEE The **basilica** is obviously the chief attraction. It is a distinctive building, with the central dome surrounded by a series of little domes, and a comparatively short nave jutting out, to end in three very high arched doorways. Above these is a space used for putting a written phrase, which changes every year, such as 'A Jesus Cristo por María Inmaculada', and above this is a large semicircular stained-glass window (where a traditional cathedral would have had a circular rose window) representing the rescue of the statue of the Virgin from the flood (see box on the Virgin of Caacupé page 119). Then a long flight of steps leads down to the plaza in front.

Inside, the little statue of the Virgin is at the far end, lifted high on a little hill, with blue light forming an atmospheric background. A stained-glass window records the blessing of the newly completed basilica by Pope John Paul II on his visit of 18 May 1988. Big though it is, for important occasions the basilica is too small, and the mass is then celebrated outside, in the very sizeable forecourt.

Entering by a side door, you can climb a high staircase to the *mirador* at the top of the basilica, and around this stairwell is a striking series of **murals by Nino Sotelo**, presenting the history of the Virgin of Caacupé. He is a marvellous artist, who specialises in large representational paintings of the Reductions. In this case he has painted a Franciscan Reduction, but he has also painted the history of the Jesuit Reductions: of San Ignacio (in the Jesuit house of studies ISEHF in Asunción), of Santa María de Fe (in the town of that name), and of Trinidad in the Hotel La Misión (in Asunción).

A short distance from the basilica, towards the north, is a well of water that is considered to have healing properties, called the **Tupãsý Ykuá** (Guaraní 'Water hole of the Mother of God'; Calle Asunción y Pozo de la Virgen), where pilgrims fill their water bottles. It is two blocks to the east and then three blocks to the north, from the basilica's forecourt. There is a model of the old basilica here, and the original altar.

There is **leather craft** and **pottery** to be bought at many little stalls, particularly around the basilica and the road that leads south from the southern side of the basilica (Dr Pino).

Outside the town to the north is the hill known as **Cerro Kavajú** (Guaraní 'Horse Hill'), which is between Atyrá, Caacupé and Tobatí. It has five natural terraces of stone that are said to have been used by the Franciscans to watch over the region. For information contact the Secretaria de Ambiente y Turismo of the *departamento* (✆ *0511 43103*), and for a guided visit, contact Alba Miranda (m *0971 314306*) or Denis Ortega (m *0971 596585*).

A smaller hill which has very steep sides, and an oratory on top, is **Cerro Cristo Rey**, a couple of kilometres from the town. For information contact the secretariate of tourism of the *municipalidad* (✆ *0511 42382*).

ITACURUBÍ DE LA CORDILLERA Copaco ✆ 0518 20370/20417; *municipalidad* ✆ 0518 20010

Though Itacurubí de la Cordillera is quite a pleasant town, the principal reason for stopping here will be either to eat or to stay the night on the drive along Ruta 2 which runs from Asunción towards Coronel Oviedo and its continuation, Ruta 7, which goes on to Ciudad del Este. (See *Travelling along Ruta 2* above, page 109.) There are two plazas: one with the church, and another shady plaza adjoining Ruta 2, with swings and slides. There are a few solid colonial-style houses.

WHERE TO STAY

Hotel San Lorenzo (14 rooms) Ruta 2 Mariscal Estigarribia c/ Antequera 324, Itacurubi; ✆ 0518 20300; m 0972 572754. The only hotel visible from the main road. Perfectly adequate but service could be more friendly. Internet places nearby but not in hotel. Car park. B/fast not inc. $$

Hotel Aguilera (10 rooms) ✆ 0518 20067. For the same modest price you can stay in this delightful hotel tucked away from the main road on the corner of the plaza that has the church. A substantial family house of character with pink colonial pillars, it has a grand sitting room & a thatched *quincho* outside where you can sit at tables to read or eat. To reach it turn north at the Petrobras petrol station for just 1 block, & you find yourself in a big grassy plaza with a football pitch & the church. As well as AC has cheaper rooms with fan. Car park. Copaco phone *cabinas* are on the same plaza. $$

Name *recommended for visit	Franciscan Reduction or Franciscan Influence	Original reredos	Distance from Asunción	Departamento	Comments
Acahay	FI		103km	Paraguarí	asphalted road on way to Ybycuí
Altos*	FR	yes	66km	Cordillera	first Reduction in Río de la Plata
Atyrá**	FR	yes	66km	Cordillera	'cleanest town'
Borja	FI	yes	198km	Guairá	difficult to access
Caacupé**	FI		54km	Cordillera	principal Marian centre
Caazapá**	FR	yes (2)	228km	Caazapá	one of the finest reredos in country
Capiatá**	FI	yes	20km	Central	second most complete church after Yaguarón
Concepción*	FI		417km	Concepción	'Pearl of the North'
Curuguaty	FR		300km	Canindeyú	asphalted Ruta 10
Emboscada*	FI	yes	39km	Cordillera	tiny gem close to Asunción
General Artigas (formerly Bobí)	FI		347km	Itapúa	difficult to access
Guarambaré	FR		31km	Central	early Reduction, off Acceso Sur
Itá*	FR	yes	36km	Central	very early Reduction
Itauguá*	FI		30km	Central	good museum of Franciscan art
Itapé*	FR		191km	Guairá	second Marian centre
Lima	FR		335km	San Pedro	on way to Concepción
Mbuyapeý	FI		182km	Paraguarí	difficult to access
Pirayú*	FI	yes	57km	Paraguarí	asphalt road from Ypacaraí

✖ WHERE TO EAT

✖ **La Curva** Ruta 2; 📞 0518 20064; 🕐 07.00–15.00 & 18.00 till last customer goes. Superb restaurant right on Ruta 2, at the west end of town, good for everything from a b/fast or a light snack to a big *asado* meal. Excellent service, lots of custom, low prices. **$**

✖ **La Casona** Burger bar on cnr facing Hotel Aguilera. **$**

TOWNS NORTH OF RUTA 2

Although we broadly think of the Circuito de Oro as out along Ruta 2, back along Ruta 1, or vice versa, some of the very best towns to visit are not on either of those two roads. The area north of Ruta 2 is particularly interesting, with the silver of

Name *recommended for visit	Franciscan Reduction or Franciscan Influence	Original reredos	Distance from Asunción	*Departamento*	Comments
Piribebúy**	FI	yes	91km	Cordillera	famous statue Ñandejára Guasú
Quiindý	FI		109km	Paraguarí	large town on Ruta 1
Quyquyhó	FI		163km	Paraguarí	difficult to access
San Carlos	FR		597km	Concepción	fort on far northern frontier, difficult to access
San Juan Nepomuceno	FR		249km	Caazapá	asphalted road from Villarrica
San Lázaro	FR		597km	Concepción	has caves
San Pedro de * Ycuamandyyú	FI	yes	348km	San Pedro	was President Lugo's diocese
Iacuati	FR		412km	San Pedro	difficult to access
Tobatí**	FR	yes	70km	Cordillera	has twin statue to Caacupé
Valenzuela**	FI	yes	100km	Cordillera	beautiful small church
Villarrica**	FI		173km	Guairá	one of most important towns in Paraguay
Yaguarón**	FR	yes	48km	Paraguarí	finest church in Paraguay
Yataitý**	FI		161km	Guairá	capital of *ao po'í*
Ybycuí*	FI		120km	Paraguarí	famous for its park and old foundry
Ybytymí	FI		101km	Paraguarí	on the old railway line
Ypané	FR	yes	32km	Central	early reduction, off Acceso Sur
Yutý	FR	yes	313km	Caazapá	difficult to access

Luque, the pottery of Areguá, the beach of San Bernardino, the church of Emboscada, the leather of Atyrá and the Virgin of Tobatí. To set off on this route you can either go north from Ruta 2 at one of several places (see map on page 100), or you can get to Luque from the road that goes towards the airport (again, consult the map on page 100).

LUQUE Copaco ☎ 021 642222; municipalidad ☎ 021 648111

Luque is famous for making harps and guitars, and for the silver *filigrana* (filigree) jewellery which is one of Paraguay's most beautiful traditional crafts.

GETTING THERE

By car If you are coming by car, take Avenida España, which turns into Avenida Aviadores del Chaco after the junction with Avenida San Martín. You will pass Shopping del Sol on your left. Keep on Aviadores del Chaco when Avenida Santa Teresa branches off to the right. You are now on the stretch of road that goes past the harp and guitar shops of what is popularly called Luque, though is in fact a musical barrio on the way to Luque proper, where there are more harp and guitar shops. See also *Getting out of Asunción*, page 103 above.

At the traffic lights the road crosses Madame Lynch (the ring road), and from then on it is known as the Autopista, though it is not a real motorway. You will not stay on this road, but rather turn first right, where there is the statue to the heroic Paraguayan woman with a child and a tattered flag ready to rebuild the country at the end of the Triple Alliance War (the Monumento a la Residenta). This road curves gently round to the left, along the edge of a green space, passing the Ñu Guazú airbase on the left and (after about five minutes) the España supermarket on the right. You pass three more harp and violin makers: Richard Sanabria, Salomon Sanabria and Dario Rojas, and then come into Luque on the Avenida General Elizardo Aquino, which goes along the side of the Plaza Elizardo Aquino and the Plaza Mariscal López, and one block later, the plaza that has the church.

You can also get to Luque by turning east off the Autopista at the junction where the Football Museum is located.

By bus If you are coming by bus, take a number 51 from Avenida Republica Argentina, just outside the Terminal, or a 30 from the centre of Asunción (but not the 30-2 with a big A in the window, that goes on to the airport rather than turning right into Luque). One block after Dario Rojas's harp shop it will turn right and shortly afterwards left, so you come into Luque slightly east of the centre. Get off at the corner where there is a taxi rank and a Sportivo Luqueño shop in the blue and yellow colours of the local football team. (They are famous, by the way, for having a pig as their mascot, which dates from the days when the fans would come into Asunción on the same train that transported pigs.) Take the road to the left, which is Dr Francia (though there is no road sign). After three blocks you will reach the plaza that has the church. You can also reach Luque by bus from Limpio and from Ypacaraí.

✗ WHERE TO EAT
Being so close to Asunción, Luque is probably not a place you will want to stay in, but it does have some good places to eat.

✗ **Restaurant Real** Peatonal Mariscal López 61; m 0981 515808/789242; ☺ daily except Sun eve & Mon lunch. 1st-class restaurant for both food & ambience, with a room for groups/events. Very pleasant to sit at a table outside in the pedestrian precinct amid all the old colonnades. Sophisticated menu which also has more economical pasta dishes. Takes credit cards. Live music Sat eve especially in summer. $$$

✗ **El Español** Mariscal López y Teniente Herrero Bueno; m 0981 719555; ☺ 11.00–midnight Tue–Sun. On the corner of the pedestrian street & the Plaza Mariscal López, this is a stylish bar that serves everything from a hamburger to a paella, from *calamares a la romana* to an *asado*. $$

✗ **Don Vito** Plaza General Aquino & also on Cerro Corá (which is the continuation of Av General Aquino). Although the photo display shows Coca-Cola and chips in every picture, Don Vito nonetheless serves good-quality *empanadas*. $

✗ **Doña Chipa** Cerro Corá c/ Dr Francia; m 0983 792174. This is part of a new chain of cafés, & they serve a delicious range of *chipas*, with tantalising smells, to eat there, take away or have delivered. The *chipa a 4 quesos* (with 4 cheeses) is particularly good, but so also are the rest of the range, which include *pastel mandió* with fillings of beef or chicken, & *mbejú*. $

WHAT TO SEE Luque is centred on three plazas. One of them has the **church**, the Virgen del Rosario, which is a tall and elegant building but not particularly old. High in the apse is a painting of the Virgin giving the rosary to St Dominic, and the Virgin is also the central of three figures in the modern reredos, together with St Joseph and St Roque González. The patronal feast day is 7 October, which also falls during the time of the Expo Luque, which is a craft festival beginning in early September.

Facing the church on the west (on Mariscal López) is the parish centre, which has within its precincts a historic house that was the site of the **printing press** for the journal *Lambaré* which was famous during the Triple Alliance War. Although the house has been preserved it is unfortunately almost completely hidden behind a high modern gate.

Two roads link this square with the other two plazas, which are adjacent to one another, separated only by a road running through the middle. One of these link roads is the **Peatonal** (that is, pedestrianised) Mariscal López, and is a most attractive street with a complete run of old colonnades along both sides. This is one of the loveliest roads in the country, and the Restaurant Real halfway along provides an opportunity to sit down at an outside table to savour the atmosphere.

The second road linking the church with the other plazas is the Avenida General Aquino, which is known as the **Avenida de los Joyeros** (Jewellers' Avenue) because of the number of shops selling the silver jewellery for which Luque is so famous. The *filigrana* jewellery is made into earrings, brooches, cufflinks, pendants and many other forms of decoration. As you go past the two plazas and beyond it, the frequency increases until every shop is a jeweller's. One might think that there would not be enough trade to support so many shops, but in fact most of them seem to have a customer in, at least on a Saturday: because Luque is so close to Asunción people can easily come here to shop. Some of the best jewellery is made in the workshop of Don Torres, between Luque and Areguá, opposite the sign to Valle Pucú. Another *filigrana* workshop between Luque and Areguá is Salvador Alvarenga's (*San Juan c/ de las Residenta;* \ *021 647244;* m *0971 615820*).

There is also **leatherwork** in some of the shops, mostly in the form of leather-covered vacuum flasks for the iced water used in *tereré*.

The square with the church is Plaza Mariscal López, and it has a big sports area and an outside stage called Rincón Cultural (Cultural Corner). There is an old colonnade along one side (Mariscal López) and a harp and guitar shop on another side (Teniente Herrero Bueno). The adjoining square is the Plaza General Aquino, and in the middle is the **mausoleum** (⊕ *07.00–13.00 Mon–Fri, 07.00–11.00 Sat*) of General Elizardo Aquino. This round, white, tall building is more interesting than it sounds, because it is really more of a museum than a mausoleum, and has many photos of the sites associated with this famous general of the Triple Alliance War (see page 12). Born in a *compañía* (outlying hamlet) of Luque in 1825, he was responsible for building the section of railway line from Areguá to Paraguarí. Under Mariscal López, he built the trench system at Humaitá that was known as the *cuadrilátero,* and led the Paraguayan defence at the battle of El Sauce. He won the battle but was mortally wounded; Mariscal López had him decorated with a gold medal, but he died on 16 July 1866, six days after his injury.

Some of the shops selling **harps and guitars** have already been mentioned, but the best-known shops are on the road running from Asunción to the airport. Most are on the south side of the road, and the majority are run by members of the Sanabria family, all sons of a famous harp maker, and each now with his own shop. All the shops sell guitars as well, but the harp may attract more interest from visitors, being such a beautiful instrument not only in its sound but also in its appearance: most are decorated with carved details (see *Harp*, page ix and *Music and* *folk dance*, page 20). The shop owners are usually happy to talk about their work, the different qualities of harps and the different woods used.

For the **Football Museum** on the Autopista, see *Chapter 3*, page 89.

AREGUÁ Copaco ☎ 0291 432457; municipalidad ☎ 0291 432410

Areguá is one of three craft towns specialising in ceramics, and is the nearest to Asunción. (The others are Itá and Tobatí.) It is a lovely town, marked by an elegant church at the top of the hill and splendid colonial-type houses on the Avenida Estigarribia leading up to it, as well as streets lined with craft shops selling ceramics. Of the pottery, there is much in the way of attractive large unglazed flowerpots and pretty small candleholders with holes for the light to shine through. However, there is also a lot of moulded clay work that is less pleasing to European and North American taste, such as garden gnomes, along with frogs, tortoises, swans and toadstools. Another variety of mass-produced moulded clay is their typical line in crib figures, which come out in force in the pre-Christmas period.

The chief founder of the pottery tradition was Ricardo Pérez, a late 19th-century potter who lived in the southern Chaco, and helped General Bernardino Caballero (war hero of the Triple Alliance War and founder of the Colorado party) to escape his enemies by hiding him in his big kiln and faking a fire inside. In gratitude Caballero gave him territory in Areguá to establish a bigger pottery business.

The *fiesta patronal* (feast day of the town's patron saint) is on 2 February, the feast of Candlemas, and Areguá has recently begun to hold a pottery fair (*feria de alfarería*) leading up to it, in late January and early February, under the auspices of the Asociación de Artesanos Aregueños. It usually begins on the last Friday of January and runs for just over two weeks, finishing on a Sunday. The other major tourist attraction of the year is the Expo Frutilla, or Strawberry Fair, which follows the strawberry season (approximately the end of July to the beginning of October) and takes place in a *compañía* of Areguá called Estanzuela, 2km from the town centre in the direction of Ypacaraí. To confirm the dates each year you can ring the *municipalidad*.

GETTING THERE One good way to reach Areguá is by **train** (see page 98). But this is a trip just to Areguá, without doing any other parts of the Circuito de Oro. **Buses** go regularly from the Asunción Terminal, and you cannot miss Areguá because you will see the craft stalls lining the roads. By **car**, take the road towards the airport, but turn right just after you leave the city for Luque. See *Getting out of Asunción*, page 103. Areguá is as far beyond Luque as Luque is beyond Asunción.

TOURIST INFORMATION The tourist centre is on Candelaria, just a little along from the El Cántaro art gallery and on the other side of the road. They do a map of the town and can provide guides, particularly for visiting the hills (see below). There is a tourist department at the *municipalidad* (☎ 0291 432501).

WHERE TO STAY

🏠 **Hotel-Restaurant Don Quijote** (5 rooms) La Candelaria 272 esq Gaspar Rodriguez de Francia; ☎ 0291 432256; m 0982 898376; e donquijote@turismo-aregua.com. On the right-hand side of the road that goes towards Luque. Art gallery, massage, spa being planned. $$$

🏠 **Hotel Restaurant Ozli** (13 rooms) Av Estigarribia; ☎ 0291 432380/432227. This has a simple café serving hamburgers & *empanadas*, very close to the station. $$

✖ **WHERE TO EAT** In addition to Don Quijote (above), there are three good restaurants, all very reasonable, as well as a number of simpler cafés such as Ozli (see above).

El Cántaro La Candelaria y Mcal Estigarribia; 0291 432954. This art gallery (see below) has a restaurant in the 2nd room inside, called La Cocina de Gulliver. Spanish food, good service, recommended. There may sometimes be live music. $$

Todo Casero Ricardo Pérez 807 c/ La Candelaria; 0291 32503. Just a little upmarket from La Palmera, which is almost opposite, this is an attractive place to eat. They serve quick snacks (pizzas, *empanadas*) as well as more substantial dishes. $$

La Palmera Mcal López 555 y Ricardo Pérez; 0291 32787; m 0991 750326. On a corner near the station. Colonial-style balcony & a pleasant roofed eating area in the garden, delicious *asados* (Sat night & Sun lunch). Friendly people, reasonably priced food. $

Don Pablo Yegros y Mariscal López; 0291 433137. The most popular restaurant in town, run by 3 German sisters, & decorated in quaint & rustic style with many art works. Excellent cheap food, good Sun buffet. $

WHAT TO SEE There is plenty of pottery to see along the streets, both inside the shops and out in open-air markets. Wandering among the shops will be the main thing you will want to do in Areguá.

El Cántaro (*La Candelaria y Mcal Estigarribia;* 0291 432954; www.el-cantaro.com) is the most important art gallery in town, run by Carlos Rolandi, with painting, sculpture and clothes. It is very welcoming, and has a restaurant attached (see above).

The **Centro Cultural del Lago** (*Yegros c/ Mariscal López;* 0291 432293/ 432633) is next door to the Don Pablo restaurant, and is a small museum with examples from the most important potters of Areguá. There is a museum shop, a cine club upstairs, and different exhibitions during the year. It is run by Ysanne Gayet (an Englishwoman) and her stepdaughter Gabriela Maldonado.

Luis Coggliolo has an art gallery on Mariscal López, just past the *policia caminera* in the direction of Ypacaraí. **Henry Centeno** is a well-known artist who has his gallery a bit further along the same road (*Mariscal López c/ Villarica;* 0291 432847). He does some paintings, but mostly curious animals in clay: toucans, giraffes, etc.

The **railway station** itself (down towards the lake, and to the left) has been turned into a craft shop, exhibiting and selling craft made in Areguá and other local towns. The **Castillo Carlota Palmerola**, on Ricardo Pérez (come out of the station and turn right), is one of the fine buildings (dating from 1911), and is now a house for Dominican nuns.

The **church** of Nuestra Señora de la Candelaria was built in 1953 and is an impressive landmark, well worth walking up the hill to see, especially since the route is lined with the town's finest colonial-style architecture. At the top there is a view of Lake Ypacaraí. Houses of architectural interest are labelled with a small sign saying 'Patrimonio cultural'. Some houses are over 300 years old. Behind the church is a little museum, the **Galería de Ña Margarita** (⏰ 07.00–12.00 & 15.00–18.00 daily).

The **Ita'o de Piedra** is a stone area with an oratory of San Miguel built on it. It is on Fray Luis Bolaños before you leave the town on the road to Luque.

Just 1km outside the town, on the road to Capiatá, are a couple of hills with an interesting geological formation of sandstone, only found in two other places in the world (South Africa and Canada). The appearance is rather like a golden-coloured beehive, with a lot of narrow channels, and it is believed the rock was formed 40 million years ago. The names of the hills are **Cerro Kõi** (just to the right of the road going southwest to Capiatá) and **Cerro Chorori** (behind the other hill). You should not attempt to go on your own as visitors' cars are regularly vandalised and broken into, but ask at the tourist centre and they will send you with guides.

Areguá has a **beach**, but be cautious as the lake water is contaminated.

San Bernardino (or San Ber for short) on Lake Yapacaraí, is the number one beach resort for Paraguayans. It nudges ahead of the two river resorts Villa Florida and Ayolas, because of its proximity to Asunción, and also perhaps because of the romance of the lake that has been immortalised in the song, 'Recuerdos de Ypacaraí'. It has developed into a fashionable place among Paraguayan towns, and a good number of people from Asunción have weekend houses there. Whatever the reason for its success, it is not for the quality of the water, as the lake is polluted, and bathing is not advised.

Founded by German immigrants in 1881, the town took the name of the then president, Bernardino Caballero. Today it has some excellent hotels. In January everywhere is booked up, but outside of the summer season the hotels can be virtually empty.

GETTING THERE Access is from Ruta 2 after Ypacaraí (reaching that point either via San Lorenzo and Itauguá, or via Luque and Areguá). See *Getting out of Asunción* page 103 and *Travelling along Ruta 2* page 109. There is also a road that goes round the other side of the lake, but it is a dirt road, with a rickety bridge over the Río Salado, and is a very long way round.

WHERE TO STAY

⌂ **Hotel Joya** [129 D7] Villa Delfina c/ Ruta General Higinio Morinigo; ✆ 0512 232872; e hotel_la_joya@hotmail.com; ☺ high season only. Expensive hotel, behind the Selva Negra restaurant. $$$$

⌂ **San Bernardino Pueblo Hotel** [129 D7] (18 rooms) Paseo del Pueblo y Mbocayá; ✆ 0512 232195; e pueblohotel@hotmail.com or pueblohotel@gmail.com. Beautifully designed, high-quality hotel with good restaurant. Tasteful terracotta colour in rooms & solid furniture. Swimming pool, volleyball, children's playground. Wi-Fi in parts. Behind the Hotel Los Alpes, before you come to the town centre. $$$

⌂ **Hotel del Lago** [129 C2] Teniente Welier c/ Carlos Antonio López; ✆ 0512 232201; e gerencia@hoteldellago.org; www.hoteldellago.org. A building of character, recently renovated with style & imagination by designer Osvaldo Codas, this now

counts as one of the leading hotels of the country. Situated on the plaza by the lake, it calls itself a hotel-museum & cultural centre, & has art exhibitions, & a big craft shop. Round towers & Gothic windows. Wi-Fi. $$$

⌂ **Hotel Acuario Country Club** [129 C7] Ruta General Morinigo km45 y Lago Ypacaraí; ✆ 0512 232375/77; e arqhotel@pla.net.py; www.hotelacuario.com.py. Grandiose round building, down on the beach before you reach the town, but not much frequented. No Wi-Fi or credit cards. $$$

⌂ **Hotel Los Alpes** [129 D7] Ruta General Morinigo km46.5; ✆ 0512 232083/232399; e losalpes@hotmail.com. Very popular middle-range hotel with a good reputation. Receives a lot of groups & conventions. Pleasant garden with pool & garden gnomes. Wi-Fi in part of hotel. At crossroads before you reach town centre. $$$

WHERE TO EAT As well as the hotels above:

✗ **Selva Negra** [129 D7] Ruta General Higinio Morinigo km 46.5; ✆ 0512 232872. Good restaurant, around corner from Hotel Joya, & part of the same conception. $$$

✗ **Café Francés** [129 C2] Av Luis Vaché 1005; ✆ 0512 232295; ☺ 09.00–22.00, closed Tue. Delightful restaurant that serves meals & snacks of a

kind you do not usually find in Paraguay, such as foie gras, *canard à l'orange* & caviar. Low beamed ceilings & lots of atmosphere. Internet place opposite. $$

✗ **Instituto Patio de Luz** [129 D7] Next to Selva Negra. Café with craft; pottery, *encaje ju* lace, hammocks. Calls itself an Espacio Cultural. $

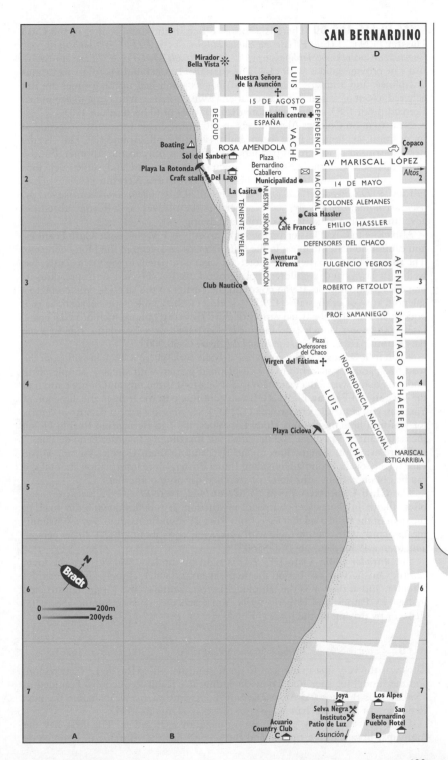

WHAT TO SEE AND DO There is a tourist office in the town centre, in the **Casa Hassler** [129 C2] (*Luis F Vaché esq Emilio Hassler;* ✎ *0512 232974;* e *sanberturismo@ hotmail.com; www.sanbernardino.gov.py;* ⏰ *08.00–16.00 Mon–Fri, & till late at w/ends*), that can provide guides with cars. The casa also has exhibitions of art in various disciplines, and a library. You may find that its published opening times are not adhered to out of season. It is named after a Swiss botanist, who came to live in San Bernardino in 1883, and stayed more than 50 years until his death in 1937.

Near to it, on Colones Alemanes, is an intriguing ancient tree that has been left in position as houses have been built carefully all around it. This is the neighbourhood of ice-cream parlours, mostly open only in the summer, but the main one, **La Casita** [129 C2], is open all year round and serves delicious homemade ices. Close to the Casa Hassler is **Aventura Xtrema** [129 C3] (*Luis F Vaché y Defensores del Chaco;* m *0981 682243;* e *info@aventuraxtrema.com.py; www.aventuraxtrema.com.py*) who advertise themselves as offering abseiling, adventure cycling, trekking, boat trips and diving.

Also close to Casa Hassler, on the same street Luis F Vaché, is the **Café Francés**. You cannot do better than eat in the Café Francés and sleep in the Hotel del Lago. The **plaza** [129 C2] where the Hotel del Lago is situated, in the town centre, has well-kept lawns and a children's playground, and a very old tree spreading its branches in the middle. If you go round the corner to the lakeside, you come to a splendid row of **craft** stalls [129 B2] selling clothes, tablecloths, *ñandutí, ao po'í,* pottery, and most of the usual variety of craft. **Boating** options include pedal boats, Gs30,000; motor launch (accompanied), Gs70,000; or a 20-minute ride in a big flat-bottom passenger boat, the *Bristol del Agua,* Gs50,000.

If you follow Luis F Vaché down towards the fork where it branches off from the road to Ypacaraí, you come to a well-planned garden with streams, simple plank bridges, good lawns and a war memorial. Next to it is the tiny and pretty church of the **Virgen del Fátima** [129 C4]. If you continue past the fork, in the direction of Ypacaraí, you come to a **crossroads** [129 D7] which is like a secondary town centre, for you find here the famous Hotel Los Alpes, the San Bernardino Pueblo Hotel, the restaurant Selva Negra, and the small but imaginative Instituto Patio de Luz.

There are a lot of nightclubs in San Ber, among them Coyote, Vulcan, Musk, Face's, La Mojada, Brahma House and Punta Prima. More information about them can be obtained from your hotel, or searched for on the internet.

The **Club Deportivo Yvytú** (✎ *021 661433;* m *0981 431972; www.yvytu.org*) offers flights in gliders and courses of instruction. It is 800m down a dirt road, to the right of the main road that leads from Ruta 2 to San Bernardino. *Yvytú* (Guaraní) means 'wind'. A 15-minute flight with a lake view costs about US$30–40 per person, a flight in a 1930s plane about US$60.

The *mirador* **Bella Vista** [129 B1] is right by the lake, and close to the town centre. On the way up, beside the steps, is an attractive church, the Virgen del Mirador, and at the top is the tall modern white statue of the Virgin, constructed in 1994 by Patricia and Roberto Ayala. You reach the top by climbing about 100 steps, or by driving up the road.

ALTOS Copaco ✎ *0512 230002; municipalidad* ✎ *0512 230030/0516 262627*

Altos was the very first Franciscan Reduction in the whole Río de La Plata region, and the model for later Reductions including the Jesuit Reductions. Founded in 1580 by Luis Bolaños and Alonso de San Buenaventura, five years before the next Reduction of Itá, it was handed over to diocesan clergy in 1599.

There are two grassy plazas, almost next to each other. The first has the municipal library in the middle and the second has the church San Lorenzo de

Altos: it dates from the end of the 19th century, but it houses a fine original reredos. Old traditions are still strong here. On Good Friday the parish commemorate the crucifixion of Christ from midday to nightfall in an outdoor Calvary they construct beside the church, with parishioners dressed as the apostles and three carved figures on the crosses.

Wooden masks called *kambá ra'angá* are made for the feast of saints Peter and Paul, 29 June, which is celebrated in the *compañía* of Itaguazú, 2km from the main town, with a simulated battle between the *kambá* and the Guaicurú indigenous.

There is a tourist route organised by the *municipalidad* called the Ruta Tukanguá which takes you on a dirt road where there are (or at least used to be) a lot of toucans.

GETTING THERE Altos is only 8km from San Bernardino. There are two dirt roads that lead across country from Altos to Atyrá, with picturesque views, because Altos is on higher ground than its surroundings.

WHERE TO STAY AND EAT

Finca El Gaucho (4 rooms, 2 dorms, 1 apt) 0516 252588; m 0971 113431; e infos@finca_el_gaucho.de; www.finca-el-gaucho.de Elegant, high-quality German-run guesthouse built in 2002 in 27ha, with landscaped garden & pool, reached by taking a turn left on the road between San Bernardino & Altos, & driving for 5km. Riding, fishing, hiking. $$$$

Punta Prima (6 rooms) m 0982 170476/0982 233760; e info@hotel-punta-prima.de; www.hotel-punta-prima.de. Lovely view of Lago Ypacaraí, on the ruta principal between San Bernardino & Altos, 3km from San Bernardino. Restaurant has good variety & quality of pizzas. $$$

La Grappa Ruta Mariscal Estigarribia 3240; 0512 230017/0516 262436; e info@paraguay-lagrappa.com; www.paraguay-lagrappa.com. Nice little hotel with lots of animals on the edge of this quiet town. There are hammocks & a toucan to greet you in the front patio & the service is friendly. Restaurant. Can organise riding & fishing, & folk music at night. Terrace with swimming pool. $$$

EMBOSCADA Copaco ✆ 0529 20297; municipalidad ✆ 0529 20025

Continuing northwards from Altos, you eventually come to Ruta 3, and the town at the junction of the two roads is called Emboscada. Here there is a little-known delight of a Franciscan-style church, dating from 1744 – tiny and precarious, with leaning door and window frames. It is complete with 70cm-thick adobe walls, wooden porticos, three reredos, a painted pulpit, carved doors and window bars, a couple of pews, and a choir loft that you can go up to if you dare; it is only the façade that is not original. The church is dedicated to St Agustine, whose statue appears at the top of the reredos, flanked by St Michael and St John the Baptist, with Saints Peter and Paul beside the Virgin on the row below. The patronal feastday is 28 August. Access to the church can be gained from the *casa parroquial* (✆ 0529 20039; ⊕ 07.30–11.30 Mon–Sat) and in the afternoons by ringing the sacristan Francisco Rojas (m 0972 897205).

ATYRÁ Copaco ✆ 0520 20192; municipalidad ✆ 0520 20188/05014

The 'cleanest town in Paraguay' is the tag that is customarily given to Atyrá, thanks to the efforts of a mayor in the 1990s, Feliciano Martínez, known as 'Nenecho', who promoted an ecological awareness. There are notices up in the streets such as 'The most hygienic town is not the one that gets the most cleaning but rather the one that the people dirty the least'. Its high standards have slipped a little, but it is still an attractive place to visit, especially if you can afford to stay in the Casa del Monte at the top of the hill, with its rural beauty.

As a Franciscan Reduction it was originally further north but it moved to its present site in 1672 because of attacks by both slave-traders and hostile indigenous tribes. The reredos of the church, San Francisco de Atyrá, is considered one of the finest in the country, and dates from the mid 18th century.

In late September/early October, there is an Expo Cuera (leather fair) in this street, and wood and basketware craft items are also put on sale.

A guide you can contact to visit the town is Gustavo Villalba (m *0981 336420*).

GETTING THERE If you are driving, you want to turn north at the huge Pilgrim Cross (Kurusú Peregrino) on Ruta 2, a little to the west of Caacupé (see *Travelling along Ruta 2* page 109). Just before you go under the entrance arch of Atyrá, you pass the dirt road that leads westward to Altos. The road into town brings you up to the Paseo Indio José – a pedestrianised lane in the centre where there are stalls of leather craft, particularly sandals. Buses from Asunción stop at this point. To reach the church, go along the Paseo Indio José, turn right, and it is facing you at the top of the hill. You will pass the *municipalidad* on your left, where there is a small tourist information centre.

WHERE TO STAY AND EAT

Casa del Monte (23 rooms) Monte Alto; ℡ 0520 20069/0516 250050; m 0981 570015/0971 150826; e info@casadelmonte.com.py; www.casadelmonte.com.py. Tourist & ecological complex, founded by a friend of Nenecho – a thoroughly Paraguayan paradise of rustic style with a little zoo. It is at the top of a hill, 2km from the town centre up a dirt road, well signed. Drive a couple of blocks past the front of the church & then turn right. If you do not have a car, they will collect you from the bus stop in the town centre for Gs25,000, or you can take a taxi. The restaurant is roofed but open at the sides, with great views. One of the bedrooms is a *choza* (round thatched hut). Little paths make fun exploration, winding around the ponds & swimming pool & among the animals, which include monkeys, macaws & peacocks, parrots & toucans, geese & grouse. Further away are pigs, sheep, goats & horses. There is sauna, massage, aromatherapy; football, volleyball, archery & ping-pong. There is a 40m^2 labyrinth – the only one in the country – & there are more than 60 species of fruit trees. They have a computer room & Wi-Fi, & they take credit cards. $$$$

Pytu'u Hostal (2 twin rooms) ℡ 0520 20021. Economical lodging, on a road where the buses from Asunción pass, 3 blocks south & 2 east from the front of the church. No b/fast, & no kitchen. $

✗ **Villa Bar** Av San Antonio y 22 de setiembre; ℡ 0520 20105. Good cheap bar serving traditional dishes. From the church, 2 blocks south & 1 east. $

WHAT TO SEE The old **reredos** of the church is beautifully decorated in red and gold, and has St Francis in the centre (above the Virgin), carrying a cross and a skull, and flanked to the left by St Roque. Above him is the seraph that brought him the stigmata. With more statues from the Reduction in the sacristy, the church effectively functions as a museum – the **Museo de Arte Sacro San Francisco de Asis** (*Casa parroquial:* ℡ *0520 20020;* ⊕ *07.30–12.00 Mon–Sat & sometimes in the afternoons; mass at 18.30 winter, 19.00 summer, Mon–Sat; 08.00 Sun*).

The Paseo Indio José takes its name from the monument to the indigenous man who carved the Virgin of Caacupé (see box on page 119). The figure of José, complete with mallet and chisel, is actually carved out of a living tree. Although in most versions of the legend José came from Tobatí, there is also a tradition that says he came from Atyrá, specifically in the story of how he rescued the Virgin from a flood.

If you want to visit the workshop where most of the **leather** goods are made, it is called J C Artesanía en Cuero (*Av Atyrá 327;* ℡ *0520 20059;* m *0981 511031*) and is run by Julio César Maidana. It is one block west and half a block south of the southern end of the Paseo Indio José. Though they do a special line in sandals, they also produce belts, coverings for vacuum flasks and *guampas*.

The barrio **Monte Alto**, up the hill on the way to Casa del Monte, has a tall Risen Christ with outstretched arms, about 8m high, standing in a garden beside the road. Also in the same compound are other religious figures, including the pregnant woman of Revelation 12 confronted by the dragon with seven heads, and a tiny stone chapel to the Divino Niño Jesús.

Outside the town to the southeast are a couple of natural sites: a waterfall called Chorro Karumbe'ý (Guaraní 'Tortoise Water Fall'), and a hill called Cerro Kavajú (Guaraní 'Horse hill'; see under Caacupé, page 121).

The **Casa Marianela** (m *0982 101933/0972 289443;* e *marianela-atyra@ gmail.com;* ☉ *07.00–12.00 & 13.00–17.00 daily*) is an extraordinary retreat and conference centre run by the Redemptorists with a capacity for 160 people; during the above visiting hours you can ask to see the house and the murals without a problem. It is located at the northeast corner of the town, five blocks from the centre. On the gate is written 'CSSR Marianela', and a long drive leads to a stunning brick building – newly built (inaugurated in 2008) but with much ornamental detail of a medieval or moorish flavour. It has 15 or more massive murals by the artist Nino Sotelo (who also did the murals on the tower of the Caacupé Basilica, see page 121). Particularly original is the chapel, raked like a lecture theatre and with huge paintings of the Last Supper and Crucifixion by Sotelo.

TOBATÍ Copaco ☎ 0516 262699; municipalidad ☎ 0516 262206

Tobatí is the furthest northeast of the little clutch of craft towns in the Circuito de Oro and is famous chiefly for wood carving and pottery. The name Tobatí in Guaraní means 'white clay', and the town also has a brick and tile industry. It is a pleasant small town with some attractive colonnades, an interesting church with some original statues from the Reductions, and a large warehouse in the Villa Artesanal which is well stocked with craft of all sorts – nearly all from Tobatí itself, showing that the town has a much broader range of craft skills than those for which it is most famous.

Tobatí is one of the oldest towns in the country, founded as a *táva* (a village for indigenous) by Domingo Martínez de Irala, in 1539 or thereabouts, some 25km to the northwest of its current position. Irala was a tough (but not ruthless) politician who consolidated the Spanish conquest throughout the Southern Cone, and is sometimes considered the founder of Paraguay. A little later, in 1583, the Franciscan Fray Luis Bolaños (see box in *Chapter 10* page 268) turned it into one of the first Christian missions, when Hernandarias entrusted all the indigenous villages around Asunción to the Franciscans for evangelisation. In the early years, Tobatí suffered many attacks from the Mbayá indigenous and in 1699 it moved to its present site. Tobatí figures importantly in the religious history of Paraguay because the Indian who carved the Virgin of Caacupé came from Tobatí and the twin statue he made is still kept in the Tobatí church (see box on page 119)

GETTING THERE AND AROUND Public **buses** leave the Asunción Terminal every ten minutes, from the lower platforms, reached by the subway. The ordinary buses with Tobatí marked as their destination are slow, bumpy, tiring and take at least two hours. However, the buses called Tobateño are even slower, very infrequent, and filled with people carrying loads of vegetables. To go by **car** takes less than half the time and is a lot more comfortable. See *Getting out of Asunción* page 103 and *Travelling along Ruta 2* page 109.

As you approach Tobatí you pass through a band of low hills with distinctive rock formations on their cliff faces: the stone has weathered to form intriguing shapes in which (with a bit of imagination) animals can be discerned: a sleeping lion, the head of a bear, and so on. There is a little chapel to the Virgen del Camino (the Virgin of the Way) at the foot of one of the cliffs. At the last cliff on the right-hand side, immediately before entering the town, is the prominent landmark of the Tres Caras de Indios (3 heads of Indians) monument, adorned with a bunch of typical Tobatí pots. Some steps wind up the side to a *mirador* on top, from where there is an extensive view to far wooded hills in all directions.

The best place to get off the **bus** is at the church. This is a small town and most places can be easily reached on foot, except for the Villa Artesanal, which is a longer walk.

There is no regular service of car-taxis in Tobatí, but there are plenty of **motorbike-taxis**, and also an excellent service of a couple of motorbike-drawn **carts** with a little canopy against the sun, which take two or three people. The cart is called a *karumbé* in Guaraní, and this is a more pleasant way of getting around town than by car, and very economical (Gs5,000 is a typical price; there are also *karumbé* in Villarrica and Encarnación). The service is run by Jose Luis Alonso (m *0972 102536*), and it is recommended.

 WHERE TO STAY AND EAT There is no hotel in Tobatí, although there are some bungalows for holiday or weekend lets (self-catering): opposite the Tres Caras de Indios (see below) is the lane leading to them. Caacupé is only 16km away and has hotels, and there is an *estancia* on the approach road.

Los Manantiales Puesto Pino \ 021 497028; m 0981 425498; e pstopino@pla.net.py; www.estancialosmanantialespuestopino.com. 4km north from Ruta 2 on the road to Tobatí you pass this *estancia* which has a fine old house built of stone. Activities on offer include riding, trips in horse carts & walking in the woods. $$$

The small and simple **Bar Kiki** (*Estrella*; \ *0516 262296;* $) is recommended by the local people as a place to eat. The staff are helpful. Blanca Rosa on the Ruta is an alternative, though again it is nothing more than a *copetín* (small cafe) and is not always open. There are bars in the Mercado Público which serve a good quality of popular Paraguayan food, and with a good local atmosphere.

FIESTAS Tobatí shares the same feast day as Caacupé, 8 December, the birthday of the Virgin. As in Itaguazú (see page 131), there is a tradition of masked figures called *kambá ra'angá* that take part in processions.

On Easter Sunday at dawn, the mass of Tupãsý Ñuvaití is celebrated (see *Chapter 5*, page 170), with a replica of the statue of the Immaculate Conception.

For a couple of weeks at the end of October and beginning of November, there is a craft fair, which means that the exhibition at the Villa Artesanal is greatly expanded, with stalls in the forecourt.

OTHER PRACTICALITIES There is no bank and no cash machine as yet in Tobatí.

WHAT TO SEE Tobatí is the home of **Zenón Páez**, the most famous sculptor of wooden saints alive in Paraguay today. He was born in 1927 to a family of *santeros* (carvers of saints/saint-makers) and his children carry on the family tradition. He takes very seriously the religious nature of his work, and was responsible for the statue of Cristo Rey (Christ the King) in the church of that name in Asunción. His shop is on the corner of Mariscal López, the road leading to the Villa Artesanal (\ *0516 262229;* e *galeriazenonpaez@hotmail.com),* and is open all day every day, if you ring the bell. The figures of saints he has in his shop, painted and plain, range from 10cm high to more than 0.5m, and prices start from Gs30,000. He also makes models of carts drawn by four or six oxen, and specialises in intricate chess sets, eg: portraying the two sides in the Triple Alliance War. Each set takes a month to carve and sells for US$1,000.

A block or two past the Páez house, away from the centre, is the house and shop of the Orego family (✆ 0516 262745; ☉ daily), who are also a family of *santeros*. It is marked 'Santería Compostura y Pinturas' and has a sculpted pillar and a yellow giraffe peering through the door. In fact Andrés Orego's wife, Nilda Páez, is Zenón's niece. All the traditional designs are continued, including the Holy Trinity cross (see pages 84 and 199) and the crucified woman Santa Librada. Wooden heads of Indians line the walls – another Tobatí traditional theme.

A third sculptor in wood, of a different style, is Ramón Ayala, whose house (*14 de mayo 847*) is near the *municipalidad* – very much the house of an artist, with carved doors, white lions outside, and a bas-relief of a group of indigenous girls. He does a line in wooden pictures of house façades, which can be bought in the Villa Artesanal.

The **pottery of Tobatí** has a very distinctive style, with unglazed faces of women moulded on the rounded side of a vase, or twigs winding across the surface in a darker brown glaze. Another variant of their work is black pots (the colouring comes from mango leaves). They are more for decoration than for use, and are all made by poor women in their own homes, so there is not any obvious place where you can go to see the potters at work.

The **Villa Artesanal** (✆ 0516 262162; ☉ 08.00–17.00 daily) is 1km away from the centre, but is very much worth getting to because of the extensive range of high-quality craft for sale in the large warehouse. It includes work by the 400 people affiliated to the local association of artisans, many of them from the *compañías*. (Zenón Páez does not exhibit here.) The sign on the main road is on the left-hand corner after you pass the CoPetrol service station on the right (coming from Asunción), and says 'Fundación Tobatí, artesanos, expo'. The range of goods includes carved chairs and tables, paintings and hammocks, *ao po'í* shirts and clothing, wooden parrots in hoops and *encaje ju* tablecloths, *filigrana* silver jewellery and leather goods, as well as pottery and wood carvings.

The **church**, set in the midst of the green, was opened in 1946 (replacing an earlier baroque church) and it has twin white towers and broad side colonnades. In theory, it is open till midday, but if closed you can call at the *casa parroquial* or parish house (✆ 0516 262552) directly behind the church, with green railings, to get access. In centre position on the reredos is the famous **statue of the Immaculate Conception** of Tobatí, which at about 1.5m high is a lot more visible than Caacupé's *Virgen de los Milagros*: the two are copies, carved by the same indigenous hand, though it is the smaller Caacupé statue that gets all the visitors and all the attention. Above it is a Christ Child Saviour of the World, on the left a Virgin of Sorrows, and on the right a fine Christ of Patience, that is, Jesus sitting to rest after his scourging. These pieces are usually described as Jesuitical in style, although Tobatí was a Franciscan town (but see *Chapter 4*, page 146.) The church has a full set of holy week statues used for processions.

The former parish priest, Teófilo Cáceres, has written a useful book on Tobatí, *Tobatí: Tava – Pueblo – Ciudad* (Asunción, 1995), which includes information about the statues. The book can be read in the public library (☉ 7.00–12.30 & 13.00–17.00) behind the *municipalidad*, on a corner adjoining the plaza, and P Cáceres himself still lives in the town, half a block behind the church on Calle Fidel Maíz (✆ 0516 262552).

VAPOR CUÉ

There is an open-air museum at Vapor Cué, 4km after the town of Caraguataý, which you reach by taking a road going northeast from Eusebio Ayala for 22km. This is a site where seven Paraguayan gunboats from the War of the Triple Alliance are kept on display, together with a monument. The boats came upriver when it was a river, but today it is nothing more than a stream. Vapor Cué is unlikely to be a particular attraction for foreign visitors, though it is of interest to Paraguayans, for whom the war is still the great scar on their souls and Mariscal López the great hero of tenacity in the midst of disaster. There is a government-run hotel and restaurant there, **Hotel Nacional de Turismo Vapor Cué** (*20 rooms;* ✆/f *0517 222395*).

On the way to Vapor Cué from Eusebio Ayala you pass a health farm called **Rubio Ñu** (*km75;* m *0981 924000/480426;*e *parquedes@hotmail.com; www.parque-de-salud; pool, sauna, gym;* $$$) where they do massage, reflexology, acupuncture, yoga and many other alternative forms of treatment.

TOWNS SOUTH OF RUTA 2

The town that forms the usual route for the crossover between Ruta 2 and Ruta 1 is Piribebúy, and it is well worth a stop for its museum and its church. But you can also go from Ypacaraí to Pirayú, which has an interesting church, and from there continue (on a stretch of dirt road) to Ruta 1 and the magnificent church of Yaguarón. Valenzuela is normally reached from Ruta 1, and Sapucai is normally reached from Ruta 1, but it is possible to go on a bit of rough road that unites these two towns, thus forming a longer circuit between the two principal Rutas (see map on page 100).

PIRAYÚ Copaco ✆ 0519 20302; municipalidad ✆ 0519 20011

Pirayú grew up under Franciscan influence from Yaguarón. The church here dates from as early as 1561 (or possibly 1567), according to a date in the choir loft. It has no fewer than five original reredos, as well as a font, confessional box and fresco of the Trinity. The church is currently undergoing some re-roofing to get rid of bat activity. Ask for access at the *Casa de las Hermanas* (the Sisters' house) on the right-hand side of the church, behind the newly restored house of the first bishop of Paraguay, Basilio López (brother of President Carlos Antonio López), which has been recently turned into a *Centro Cultural*. Profesora Gregoria Delgadillo (✆ *0519 20185/20153/20011;* m *0983 200486*) knows a lot about the town and is willing to act as a local guide.

There is also an old railway station – the only one in the country to have two towers – and a *casa artesanal* that sells *ñandutí* and hammocks.

GETTING THERE It is reachable not only from Ypacaraí (see page 118) on asphalt (12km) but also from the other direction, from Yaguarón (see page 144), on *empedrado* (10km). (A dirt road of poorer quality goes from Yaguarón to Paraguarí, see page 148.)

PIRIBEBÚY Copaco ✆ 0515 212085; municipalidad ✆ 0515 212202

Piribebúy is the town on the link road between Ruta 1 and Ruta 2, so it is strategically placed to form part of the Circuito de Oro. Though not founded as a reduction, it has a lovely church of the period and a reredos inside, that has as its centrepiece a wonderful crucifix known as Ñandejára Guasú (Guaraní 'Our great Lord'). On 21 January they celebrate their patronal feast day.

But Piribebúy is better known for having been for a brief time the capital of Paraguay, as Mariscal López fled Asunción in the Triple Alliance War. For him and for Paraguay it was the beginning of the end, that culminated with his death at Cerro Corá, in the northeast corner of the country. In Piribebúy there was a week-long battle and a massacre, and Paraguayans are proud of the heroism of the populace who fought to the death. This chapter of history is recorded in the museum.

Piribebúy is also the place where the famous *poncho de 60 listas* is made.

GETTING THERE See *Travelling along Ruta 2*, page 109. To reach Piribebúy from Ruta 2, take the turn south that is opposite the Chipería El Indio – the first of many *chiperías* on Ruta 2 – and continue for 9km. When you reach the town, signed to your right, the main road comes down towards it in a southwesterly direction but at the entrance to the town it then bends a little towards the southeasterly, before straightening out and heading directly due south. The result of this is that when you enter the town you are heading directly south, but if you then take a left turn at the museum, you hit the main road again at a right angle, the town fitting itself into an elongated wedge shape to the west of the road.

To reach Piribebúy from Ruta 1 see *Travelling along Ruta 1*, page 141. In this case you need to turn left after crossing the stream, exactly where the main road begins to bend a little leftwards, and this will bring you directly past the plaza with the church (on your left) to the museum (on the far corner of the next block, where you reach the main street of Pirebebúy).

For both routes, see *Getting out of Asunción*, page 103.

There is a **bus** (*Empresa Piribebuy;* \ *0515 212217*) that goes from Asuncíon to Piribebúy, passing through San Lorenzo, Capiatá, Itauguá, Ypacaraí and Caacupé on the way.

WHERE TO STAY AND EAT Within the town, El Galpón has probably the best food, of a simple Paraguayan style. But just outside the town, there are excellent places to stay and eat, see below.

FESTIVALS The patronal feast of Ñandejára Guasú is on the third Sunday of January, and is taken as the occasion for celebrating a festival of the *poncho de 60 listas* (see below), in the Club 12 de Agosto. But bigger and more popular in style is the feast of San Blas on 3 February. The little statue of San Blas, dressed in a long red cope, is in a sanctuary in the barrio San Blas, two blocks beyond the petrol station.

WHAT TO SEE When you approach from Ruta 2 you fork left to enter the town, and that road will lead straight ahead to the **museum**, on the corner of Mariscal Estigarribia. Its full name is the Museo Histórico Commandante Pedro Pablo Caballero (⊕ *07.00–12.00 & 14.00–17.00 Tue–Fri, 07.00–11.00 Sat, 07.00–12.00 Sun; free*) and it is named after the Paraguayan commander in the battle of Piribebúy. The museum is housed in a colonial house of the López period. It was founded by veterans of the Chaco War and has a larger section on that war, but more interest is bound to focus on the earlier war, given the particular history of Piribebúy. Although only one room is devoted to the War of the Triple Alliance, this is not a bad place to get an overview of it, with the help of the excellent guide, Miguel Ángel Romero (**m** *0971 179437*) who is also a *santero* (a carver of saints).

There are large paintings of Mariscal López and his Irish partner, Madame Lynch (known as 'Madame' because she was married to a Frenchman when the relationship with Francisco Solano López began). There is a timeline and a good map, charting the course of the war from the misconceived invasion of Mato Grosso (to the north) at the end of 1864, through the brief campaigns of Corrientes and Uruguay (to the south), to the 2½-year stand-off at Humaitá (in the southwest corner of Paraguay; see *Chapter 7*, page 221). In mid-1868 the Paraguayan army was pushed back to Pikysyrý (south of Asunción), but by mid-1869 all was defeat, as the sick and hungry vestiges of the army were dragged back by López, through Piribebúy and up to the extreme northeast corner of the country. Finally Mariscal López was killed, at Cerro Corá, on 1 March 1870, thus ending the war. See also *Chapter 11*, page 288.

In the battle of Piribebúy, of 12 August 1869, the actual Paraguayan army was not present, but was camped out at Azcurra, near Caacupé. So the battle was fought between the 20,000-strong force of the Triple Alliance, and only 1,600 defenders. The women in particular, known as the Heroines of Piribebúy, fought with rifles, swords, bottles, bones, and anything they could lay their hands on, rather than surrender. When the cannonballs ran out, they shot with coconuts. The tenacity of the Paraguayans was not predictable, but the defeat was inevitable. It was horribly followed by the burning of the hospital of Piribebúy, with the doors locked to incinerate the 600 people inside – nurses, doctors and the wounded – in one of the terrible atrocities of the war. Four days later, on 16 August, came the massacre of Acosta Ñu, in which an army of 3,000 children was slaughtered, who had been prepared for the battle by the schoolteacher, Maestro Fermín López, who taught them to paint the fake beards and moustaches on their faces as a way of making the enemy think they were older and stronger than they were (see in this chapter under San Lorenzo, page 113, and *Chapter 10*, page 262). Fermín also got the children to paint the reredos of Piribebúy yellow (see below) to preserve it from looting by the enemy.

To gain access to the **church**, ask at the museum, and the guide may take you down himself, closing the museum in the meantime. The church is one block to the east of the museum, in the middle of a green. You reach it from the back, which is the better angle from the historical point of view, because you can see the unbroken colonnade all round, supported on wooden pillars with carved capitals, and with original windows and doors. It was begun in 1733, while funds were being sought for building the larger church at Yaguarón, and when Piribebúy was finished in 1753 (according to the date on one of the roof beams) the work on the church at Yaguarón could begin. The pulpit in particular is similar to that of Yaguarón. The appearance of the Jesuit symbol IHS confirms how heavily the Franciscan churches relied on Jesuit-trained artists to build their churches. The frontage with its tower was put on later, in a different style, though the combination is quite pleasing.

There are original windows and doors, floor, pulpit, confessional boxes, niches, and a 1759 reredos. The magnificent centrepiece is the famous Ñandejára Guasú crucifix, which is articulated (it has hinged arms, so can be taken down from the cross and put in the coffin). According to some accounts, this beautiful crucifix was brought from Spain, while according to others it was brought from the Jesuit Reductions of Misiones, and it is an object of much devotion. It is flanked by the Virgin of Sorrows and the Beloved Disciple (both clothed figures), and at the top is a charming seraph – the angel that brought the stigmata to St Francis of Assisi. A modern tower over this main altar permits light to enter and show the reredos to advantage.

In 1999 there was a famous scandal, when a journalist from ABC-Color, Luis Verón, denounced the restoration done to this reredos by a foreign architect, Luis Fernando Pereira Javaloyes, who in turn sued him, and won the case. Despite that, the restoration proved so controversial that it was undone and the over-painting removed at enormous cost.

To get to the place where the famous **poncho de 60 listas** are made, you need to return to the main road, and follow it south over the little stream towards the outskirts of the town. Take the second left, where there is a sign saying 'Balneario Camping las Palmeras' and drive along the edge of the big sports ground. Then turn left down the grassy track at the edge of the field. Halfway down you will pass a house with a small notice saying 'Heladería San Cayetano'. It looks an unlikely place for a poncho workshop but it is right. Rosa Segovia and her family (*Cerro León y Capitán Cristaldo;* \ *0515 212097;* e *poncho60lista@hotmail.com*) carry on the craft that has been handed down through generations. A *poncho de 60 listas* is a kind of poncho made from cotton thread, so is very fine and ornamental, with a silky sheen, but is not made for warmth. It has 60 white stripes in it, and is enormously time-consuming to make, and for this reason the craft is in danger of extinction as a handmade product. It takes 22 days' work by one person to make the poncho, which will sell for less than US$200, of which more than half is the cost of so much cotton thread. It is said that Mariscal López had this kind of poncho, but that the tradition began even earlier, in the days of Dr Francia. Sometimes the poncho is made in black and white, sometimes in black, red and white, and sometimes in multi-coloured stripes.

If you continue on the dirt road you took when you left the asphalt, you come to Ruta 2. This is the most direct route if you want to continue travelling east.

ESTANCIAS AND ACTIVITY CENTRES OUTSIDE PIRIBEBÚY

Estancia La Aventura Ruta 2, km61.5; m 0981 441804; e estanciaaventura@hotmail.com; www.estancia-aventura.com. Close to the Piribebúy turn, but on the Asunción side of Ruta 2, this is a German-run *estancia* where you can ride with the gauchos, swim in the lake & play tennis. Tastefully designed with a good, wide colonnade to the house. Aimed at the German market & very expensive. $$$$

La Quinta Ruta Paraguarí–Piribebúy km82.5; m 0971 117444/117555; e laquinta@laquinta.com.py; www.laquinta.com.py. One of the *estancias* at the upper end of the market, used by the main tour operators. Beautifully designed & the food is gourmet cuisine & in vast quantities. All the usual activities: swimming, riding, football, volleyball, ping-pong, etc. If it can be faulted, it is for being less Paraguayan in design than other places, & also for being difficult to find. There is no sign with its name on the road, & even the sign that locates it, 'Km 82.5' (ie: from Asunción), is small. It is 10km from Piribebúy & 19km from Paraguarí, on the east side of the road, & it just a little to the Piribebúy side of the Capilla de San Juan. If you do not have your own vehicle, take a bus to Piribebúy, & then one of the hourly buses towards Chololó, or a taxi from Piribebúy or Paraguarí, or more comfortably & more expensively, let La Quinta pick you up from Asunción. Charges are for 24hrs with meals & activities, or for a day, 09.00–18.00. No credit cards. Reservations can also be made through Apatur, see Chapter 2, page 51. $$$

San Francisco Country Club Hotel Ruta Paraguarí–Piribebúy km66; \ 0516 250301; m 0981 802253; e info@francisco-country.com; www.san-francisco-country.com. Between Piribebúy & Ruta 2, on the west side of the road. Charming round thatched huts (which they call bungalows), well furnished. Pool, sports areas. $$$

Mbatoví activity centre Ruta Paraguarí–Piribebúy km72; \ 021 444844/437526; m 0971 299250; e info@mbatovi.com.py; www.mbatovi.com.py. Fantastic eco-adventure park among the hills between Piribebúy & Paraguarí. Great views of the hills from the *mirador* Mbatoví Rovetá (Guaraní, Window of Mbatoví). The tape saingo (Guaraní, hanging path) takes you abseiling & suspended on rope bridges through the treetops, with an emphasis on safety as well as excitement. The 1,700m trail Yvaropý passes through land which according to legend was the resting place of the gods. Good value for all the activities. $$$

Hotel Parador Chololó Ruta Paraguarí–Piribebúy km87; \ 0515 212766/021 553965/551207. Rooms & cabins, restaurant, 150m from the road. A paradise of streams & woods where you can spend the day or pass the night. Some cheaper rooms with fans. $$

VALENZUELA   Copaco ✆ 0516 256003; municipalidad ✆ 0516 255201/3

Valenzuela is often overlooked in the Circuito de Oro, but if you are interested in reredos from the Reductions, then it is a must. But you will have difficulty getting there without instructions.

GETTING THERE There are a few **buses** direct from the Terminal in Asunción, at least every hour. The journey takes three hours by bus, and is very much quicker by car. If you are coming by **car** on Ruta 2 (see *Travelling along Ruta 2*, page 109), then look for a turning to the south, 7km to the east of San José and 8km to the west of Itacurubí de la Cordillera. There is no road sign indicating Valenzuela, but you will know you are at the right junction when you see a café on the corner marked 'Despensa Copetín El Desvío' and a battered yellow hoarding advertising 'Cerámica Na Virginia'. You drive for 13km on this road, which is not yet asphalted, and then you reach a welcome sign announcing that Valenzuela is the town of the pineapple (*piña*): there is a festival of the pineapple in January, and it is the town's principal crop.

If you are coming on the new road that runs from Paraguarí to Villarrica, then Valenzuela is reached by a dirt road going north just before Caballero.

 WHERE TO STAY

La Cascada ✆ 021 552131/0516 255495; m 0982 215223; e oliviacantero@hotmail.com; www.lacascada.turismoparaguay.net. Just 3km beyond Valenzuela & another 1km to the right is a tourist complex with a 2km ecological reserve, waterfalls, riding, football, beach volleyball, etc. Entrance to the reserve without staying the night Gs5,000; can do B&B or full board. $$

WHAT TO SEE Valenzuela has an idyllic plaza, adorned (depending on season) with the red blossom of the *chivato* tree. Facing the church is a monument to 'P Victor Fernández Valenzuela SJ, sublime rector de la enseñanza cristiana e insigne fundador de este pueblo' (Fr Victor Fernández Valenzuela SJ, sublime rector of Christian teaching and distinguished founder of this town).

However, according to the historian Margarita Durán, the town was founded not by a Jesuit but by a diocesan priest called Antonio Fernández de Valenzuela. On his death, the private oratory he had built turned into a parish church. What we certainly know is that the relationship between Jesuit and Franciscan art, and Jesuit and Franciscan history, is a lot more intertwined than is often supposed. The date of the foundation was 24 July 1813.

The church, though small, is a gem. The keys are in the hands of Señora Amalia, who lives a block away. Ask local people to show you her house, and do not forget to tip if she comes specially to open the church for you. The church is old but has been retouched, and the general impression has been completely altered by the addition of a modern tower at centre front, quite simple but with Gothic arches. Inside, however, you find beautiful old treasures of art, notably an original reredos – not large, but ornate, and with delightful figures and still surprisingly vivid colours. In the centre of it is an unusual tabernacle with two sliding, curved doors. On the outer sides of the tabernacle are archangels with charmingly childish proportions: St Michael trampling the demon on the right-facing side; and Raphael with his fish on the left-facing side.

Above the tabernacle is St Joseph – to whom the church is dedicated – with a lily in his hand. Saints Peter and Paul, in papal tiara and mitre respectively, flank him on either side. The Virgin of the Assumption is at the summit of the reredos, standing as usual on a crescent moon adorned with cherubim heads. The pulpit is ancient (though the steps up to it are not) and it has a carved wooden pineapple hanging beneath it. Facing the altar is a choir gallery, which is modern, but in the orginal style and position. One of the notable features of this little church is the painting on the wooden bases of the pillars and the walls above them, and the arched roof above the altar, which, though simple in design, is either untouched or restored in the original style.

SAPUCAI Copaco ✆ 0539 263200/263299; municipalidad ✆ 0539 263214

The old railway line of Paraguay – one of the first in Latin America, if not the first (the claims vary) – was built with the help of English engineers and workmen, and the first stretch, from Asunción to the station Trinidad (the Botanical Gardens), was opened in 1861. Sapucai was constructed in 1887 and became not just a station on the line but the workshop where the trains were made.

GETTING THERE See *Getting out of Asunción*, page 103, and *Travelling along Ruta 1*, page 141, for getting to Paraguarí. Then take the new road that runs from Paraguarí to Villarrica (see *Chapter 10*, page 260).

WHAT TO SEE There is a well-presented **museum** (✆ 0539 263218; ⊕ 07.00–16.00 *Mon–Fri*), called the Museo Nacional Ferrocarril Presidente Carlos Antonio López after the president under whom the railway flourished, before the Triple Alliance War put an end to all development in Paraguay. Access to the museum can be arranged at weekends by prior request to the museum or the *municipalidad*. You can also obtain information about the museum from the central railway station in Asunción (✆ 021 447848).

There is also what they call the Villa Inglesa (English estate) which is where the descendants of the English workers live. About 30 of these houses are more than a century old, and in their day they had what might be called the mod cons of the period. As is the case with so much else associated with the railway, there is an air of time warp about the town, with its old houses and church, nestling into the side of the hills that run between Ruta 1 and Ruta 2 (the Cordillera). The *cementerio de los trenes* is the name they give to where the old dead trains lie.

But twice a year, on 15 June (feast of the Sacred Heart) and 16 July (anniversary of the town's foundation) one of the trains comes to life again, and runs for a kilometre before going back to sleep.

TRAVELLING ALONG RUTA I

Ruta 1 is the highway that runs from Asunción in a southeasterly direction to the border town of Encarnación, on the Río Paraná, opposite Posadas, Argentina. This is the route to Paraguay's chief tourist attraction, the Jesuit museums of Misiones and the Ruins of Itapúa, which are described in the next two chapters. For the moment, however, we are concentrating on the places that can be visited close to Asunción, in the Circuito de Oro.

All buses leaving the Asunción Terminal and heading for Encarnación go along Ruta 1, as well as those heading for Ayolas or for Pilar.

San Lorenzo is the town where the road divides into Ruta 1 and Ruta 2, but it is dealt with under Ruta 2 (on page 110 above). Remember that if you are in your own vehicle, you can take the Acceso Sur to get onto Ruta 1, as an alternative to passing through San Lorenzo (see *Getting out of Asunción*, page 103).

After passing through the craft town Itá – or after the Acceso Sur joins up with Ruta 1, if you are taking that route – you go through Yaguarón, with its famous church. The one-way system does not lead you past it, but if you are in your own vehicle it would be a great pity not to stop and visit it. It is the most beautiful church in Paraguay (see below page 144).

There is a good place to break your journey for a meal or a snack at the Frutería just before Paraguarí. All the Paraguayans with cars make it a regular stopping point (see below page 148).

After that, the next good (or at last well-known) eating place is not until you cross the Río Tebicuarý and reach Villa Florida, in Misiones (see *Chapter 5*, page 157). By then you will have left the Circuito de Oro far behind.

ITÁ   Copaco ☎ 0224 632901/632199; municipalidad ☎ 0224 632575

Itá was the second of the Franciscan Reductions, founded in 1585 by Luis Bolaños and Alonso de San Buenaventura, and its church is not only the earliest but has several interesting features, that have been lost in other Franciscan churches. Itá is also well known as one of the pottery towns: here they claim to be the capital of pottery (though the rivals would be Areguá and Tobatí).

The feast day of the patron saint San Blas is 3 February.

ORIENTATION   The town is on Ruta 1 (see *Travelling along Ruta 1*, page 141) but the town spreads to the south of the highway. The main bus stop is just before the traffic lights, which are at the junction with the road that turns off at right angles to go north to Itauguá and Ruta 2. That road is called General Caballero, and if you work westwards from there, back along Ruta 1, then the turnings are (in order) Independencia Nacional, Manuel Gamarra, Carlos Antonio López, Enrique Doldán Ibieta, Teniente Valdovinos (north side only), Curupayty, Cerro Corá, Guarambaré and San Lorenzo. This will help in locating the sites mentioned below.

There is a taxi rank on General Caballero next to the Petrobras service station by the traffic lights, and another taxi rank by a smaller Petrobras service station on Enrique D Ibieta – both on Ruta 1. The Plaza del Mercado is between Manuel Gamarra and Independencia Nacional, three blocks to the south of Ruta 1. The bus terminal is down there, next to the *municipalidad*, for those buses that end their journey at Itá.

There is not much in the way of restaurants, let alone hotels, but halfway down the Plaza del Mercado, on the west side, is a *patio de comidas* on the second floor, so obscurely signed that you may not find it unless you ask.

 **WHERE TO STAY**

 **Oñondivemi** (Guaraní 'Together') Ruta 1 km27.5; ☎ 0295 20344; m 0981 441460; e onondivemi@yahoo.com; www.onondivemi.com.py. This is one of the closest *estancias* to Asunción, not strictly speaking in Itá, but a little before it & belonging to the municipality of the previous town

J Augusto Saldivar. Activities include football, volleyball, swimming, boating, horse carts & fishing. It has a museum with about 200 stuffed animals, native to Paraguay. Book in advance – at least the day before. Reservations can also be made through Apatur (see *Chapter 2*, page 51). $$$

WHAT TO SEE   The **church** is believed to have been the first Franciscan church built in Paraguay. It is dedicated to San Blas (St Blaise in English; the 4th-century bishop who healed a boy with a fish bone stuck in his throat, and is invoked by holding two crossed candles across the throat). To reach it you take Carlos Antonio López or Enrique Doldan Ibieta from Ruta 1, and the church is between the two, three blocks from the main road.

High on the tower is a charming little figure of San Blas in his mitre, with his cope and stole painted red. A plaque in the porch acknowledges the foundation of the Reduction in 1585 by the two Franciscan friars, Bolaños and de San Buenaventura. You can gain access to the church in the mornings by calling at the parish house (*Enrique Doldán Ibieta y San Blas;* ⊕ *07.00–11.30 Mon–Fri, 14.00–16.30 Sat*). It is not marked as such but is a house on a corner of the plaza, to the southwest of the church, and next door to the Escuela Juan O'Leary. There is another chance to get into the church in the evening, as it opens at 18.30 every day for Mass at 19.00, and on Sundays there is an extra Mass at 08.00.

If you are not able to gain access, at least look in through the old wooden bars of the window near the altar on the east side, which is customarily left open. Though most of the walls are 20th century almost everything else is original: the painted roof beams (one of which bears the words 'Ec Est Domvs Domini – Firmiter Edificata – Anno 1698'), the frescoes on the walls behind the altar, the shutters, window bars, doors, statues, reredos, etc.

The reredos is very pleasing, not so much for the quality of the sculpture – for in this case the figures are clothed in material rather than being carved entirely out of wood – as for the harmonious composition of the whole, well lit, and with good use of the bright red that is typical of San Blas here. The liturgical red is picked up on the figure of St Peter, in a papal tiara, on the far left, and St Laurence the deacon, holding the grill on which he was roasted, on the far right. Between these figures and the central San Blas are two friar-saints in the brown Franciscan habit: St Francis of Assisi, with a skull and a book, and San Francisco Solano with a violin. The latter is particularly interesting, as it recalls the fact that this early Franciscan missionary, who worked in northern Argentina rather than Paraguay, was also a teacher of the violin, before the Jesuits arrived and developed the musical tradition of the Reductions to a much higher level. The three figures on the upper level of the reredos are (from left to right) St Anthony, the Virgin and St Joseph.

Over the arch above the chancel is a beautifully preserved Trinity fresco, and there are frescoes of angels all around the wall behind the reredos. Down the nave near the front entrance is a group around the crucifix – Mary and the Beloved Disciple. In the sacristy are more statues, and the original pulpit piled high on top of a large original chest of drawers.

The biggest selection of craft in Itá is in the long building called **CAPICI** (*Centro Artesanal de las Pequeñas Industrias de la Ciudad de Itá;* ⊕ *07.00–17.00 Mon–Fri, 07.00–12.00 Sat*), which is on the corner of Cerro Corá and Ruta 1. Here you can buy big garden pots, plates for hanging on the wall, cribs, banana-leaf figures, paintings, statues of San Blas, hammocks, leather bags, model dancers, crochet items, and pottery chickens. These last require some explanation, as they are traditional items to Itá. The chickens have clay feathers stuck on all round them like petals, and they come in different sizes and different colours, each colour representing a wish for good fortune in one way or another: white – love; brown – friendship; grey – health; black – abundance; blue – marriage; green – hope and orange – work.

Rosa Brítez is the most famous of the artisans in Itá, and is a delightful and dynamic person, quite used to being besieged by visitors. Her home and workshop is on Ruta 1 at the entrance to the town (from Asunción), on the south side, in between a bus shelter and a tiny canal and just before a petrol station. Her work is in black clay and is distinctive, typified by very round bodies. Of her 13 children, four work in pottery like her. She has her own plot of land, from which she can extract the clay, and she turns it black by baking it in the smoke of the *guayaiví* plant. Among her regular products are a series of 30 erotic poses as described in the *Kama Sutra*, shown in full graphic detail. This provoked the rage of one Catholic priest, who tried to have her workshop closed down. But her work appealed to the late pop singer Michael Jackson, from whom she received an order.

The **Museo Artesanal Ñande Ypykué** (Guaraní 'Our ancestors') (*Tte Rojas Silva e/ General Caballero y Independencia Nacional;* \ *0224 632244; free*) is a one-woman museum of craft made by the late Mercedes de Servín, in four rooms, that include items made out of clay, banana leaf and fabric. Her granddaughter Cristina Servín (**m** *0981 532624*) now attends. It is open at weekends, and also on request (give advance notice, or take pot luck and ring the bell: Cristina lives next door). There is craft on sale.

The best place to pick up a bus for the onward journey is by the traffic lights at the junction of Ruta 1 and General Caballero. This is where the road to Itauguá begins, but if you continue on Ruta 1, the road will swing to the right and then leave town. Immediately south of Itá is a big roundabout where the alternative route from Asunción known as Acceso Sur joins Ruta 1. (See above, page 105).

The two Franciscan Reductions of **Guarambaré** and **Ypané** are reached from the Acceso Sur. See regional map above, page 100. Ypané has had its reredos returned to the church. What remains of the reredos and the old church of Guarambaré is in the Museo Bogarín in Asunción but the modern church has an interesting statue of St Michael: call at the *casa parroquial* for access (\ *0293 932212*).

YAGUARÓN   Copaco \ *0533 232300;* municipalidad \ *0533 232296/232368*

The next town down Ruta 1 is Yaguarón, famous for being the only Reduction to have its original **church** still standing in its original form. This is a 'must-see' if you are interested in the Reductions, and although the Reduction is Franciscan, the church is on exactly the same model as in the Jesuit Reductions. If you are not in your own transport, you see it out of the window of the bus as you go through the town, travelling towards Asunción. (Travelling southwards, however, the one way system does not lead you past it.) It is highly distinctive with its simple pitched roof, massive wooden columns and separate wooden bell tower, and is clearly visible on the north side of the Ruta, which curves around it. But if you can manage to stop and go inside, do not miss the opportunity to see this gloriously harmonious extravaganza of painted and carved wood.

Fray Luis Bolaños and Fray Alonso de San Buenaventura, his missionary companion, founded Yaguarón shortly after Itá, around 1586–87. Today, Yaguarón still has an interesting band who play music of a traditional indigenous type, on old instruments such as the *turú* (cow's horn) and different sizes and shapes of drums. The band is called Peteke Peteke and it traditionally plays on 3 February (feast of San Blas), 16 August (feast of San Roque) and the first Sunday of September.

GETTING THERE See *Travelling along Ruta 1*, page 141.

WHAT TO SEE The **church** (\ *0533 232229;* ⊕ *06.00–11.00 & 13.30–17.00 Tue–Sun; mass 08.00 Sun, 18.00 Tue, Thu & Sat, 06.00 Wed & Fri*) is dedicated to St Bonaventure, the Franciscan bishop-saint after whom one of the two founders was named. There is an excellent guide, Antolín Alemán (\ *0533 232321;* **m** *0982 267978*).

The church is large and imposing, 70m long and with 30m wide colonnades all around it. At the date of its construction, the architecture of the Reductions was moving in favour of building stone churches such as Trinidad. The first metre of the walls in Yaguarón was in brick, but after some conflict the decision was made to continue the church in the traditional adobe and wood, rather than to experiment with the new techniques. According to the traditional methods of construction, this meant building the roof first, supported on massive tree trunks (of *urunde'ý* wood) up to 30m high, that were buried in the ground together with a good part of their root structure. The walls of adobe, up to 1.8m thick in places, were filled in later: they do not support the roof. The figure of Samson and the lion has been carved into one of the front doors. There is a fine choir loft over the entrance, inside.

The high, painted ceiling gives us an idea of what every church in the Reductions was like originally. (That of San Ignacio Guasú, for example, had 1,600 painted ceiling panels, before it fell into disrepair and was dismantled.) Sadly, the once painted walls were whitewashed in 1919, being considered beyond restoration.

The Franciscans called on the artistic and architectural expertise of the Jesuits in the construction of the church, and in particular for the 14m-high 6m-wide **reredos**, carved out of *peterebý* wood by a Portuguese sculptor in Buenos Aires, José de Souza Cavadas. (Later, he constructed a similar reredos for the church of Capiatá, which is still in position.) In the centre we see the Immaculate Conception, and above her the Holy Spirit. Right up at the top is God the Father, complete with orb and triangular halo to represent the Trinity. The archangel Gabriel is to his right, and the archangel Raphael to his left, carrying his usual fish. In a right-hand niche of the reredos is a third archangel, Michael, with the sword he uses to defeat the devil. The corresponding left-hand niche has St Bonaventure: he fights with the cross rather than the sword. On the door of the tabernacle is the Lamb of God .

The confessional boxes are elaborate works of art, with solomonic columns and elaborate toppings, the whole painted in meticulous detail with reds, greens and golds. The highly adorned hexagonal pulpit stands on the supportive head of a figure which could be Samson or simply an *ángel atlántico* (Atlas-like angel), and is topped with the usual dove of divine inspiration, the Holy Spirit.

In 1854, President Carlos Antonio López, removed the side altar and sent 14 cartloads of precious carvings up to adorn the new church of Trinidad that he was building in Asunción: they have not yet been returned. The church of Yaguarón benefited from some restoration in 1882 and again in the 20th century.

Behind the high altar is the **sacristy**, 12m long and so elaborately decorated that it is like a whole further chapel. It has a most ornate holy cupboard, full of drawers, for keeping the vestments and sacred vessels. The roof is painted with a *trompe l'œil* dome.

The **bell tower** outside, standing to the left of the church, is a fine example of the kind that once adorned every Reduction (with the exception of those with stone churches, where it was incorporated into the church building). Though the actual pieces of wood have been renewed over the centuries, the design is original.

Josefina Plá, the Spanish scholar and artist who married a Paraguayan and made Paraguay her home, wrote of this church, and others in the Circuito de Oro:

Of course, Yaguarón is not the only notable church in Paraguay: Piribebúy, though smaller and deprived of the framework of its original building, rivals it in elegance (and also in the mystery of its origin and realisation); Capiatá, a copy of Yaguarón, is very lovely, within its much reduced scale, and Atyrá, Tobatí and Valenzuela have original touches; Pirayú is very interesting. But Yaguarón has always attracted attention on a larger scale, perhaps for its proximity to the capital; and, apart from its undoubted value for its style and its fabrication, the plan and original features of the building are preserved. What is even more interesting for the scholar is to consider that it is one of the few churches remaining out of the 103 that the records tell us existed in the country at the beginning of the 1870 War.

On the feast of St Bonaventure, 15 June, the people bring beautiful small litters of saints or holy pictures, surrounded by pink flowers, to place in the colonnade of the church.

Though the Jesuit Reductions are much more famous than the Franciscan Reductions, it is a great mistake to ignore the latter. They were the first Reductions, and the Jesuits learned from their earlier experience. The Franciscan Luis Bolaños founded a great number of Reductions, and the two Jesuits who were most energetic in founding Reductions, Roque González and Antonio Ruiz de Montoya, built on his pioneering work.

The best-known Franciscan Reductions are close to Asunción, in the area of the Circuito de Oro ('Golden Circuit', see *Chapter 4*), but it is not generally realised that there were Franciscan missions over a much greater area, in nine different *departamentos* (Paraguarí, Cordillera, Guairá, Caazapá, Central, Canindeyú, Itapúa, San Pedro and Concepción) stretching from the northern frontier of the Río Apa to almost as far south as Jesús, in Itapúa. Some of the Franciscan towns were true Reductions, in the sense that they were founded by Franciscans as missions. Others were towns that grew up spontaneously where there was a need, in a region where Franciscan influence was strong, so that they used the same type of art, architecture and social organisation, but did not have a precise Franciscan founder. Both sorts are shown on the map on page 102.

One of the differences between the Franciscan and Jesuit Reductions is that the Franciscans, being friars, were prepared for continual movement rather than settlement in one place: when they moved on, or were asked to leave by the governor, the town found its way of continuing without them, for better or for worse. The Jesuits by contrast excluded other Europeans from the entire region, creating a pure Guaraní environment, where the language and culture of the indigenous could flourish, uncontaminated by the vices of drink, and sexual and commercial exploitation. The Franciscans believed in working within a very dirty system to ameliorate it; the Jesuits believed in pursuing the ideal.

The Jesuits were able to avoid for their Guaraní the *encomienda* system (everywhere except in San Ignacio Guasú, which was founded on the roots of a Franciscan mission, Yaguará Camigtá). The *encomienda* meant that indigenous people were sent away for hard labour for months on end, in a kind of prisoner-of-war arrangement, because they had given armed resistance to their conquerors. It was practically slavery under another name, and the *encomienda* system was not abolished until 1803. Where the Jesuits had gathered together indigenous of their own free will, in new territories where there had not been a European armed invasion, there was no basis for demanding the *encomienda*. But because the Franciscans worked alongside the secular Europeans, often evangelising settlements already established by the Spanish, they could not avoid it.

The Jesuit region of the Treinta Pueblos was more uncompromising and romantic, and has inflamed a huge historical nostalgia for a *Lost Paradise* (the title of the book by Philip Caraman SJ, 1975, Sidgwick and Jackson). But when the Jesuits were expelled the

Also in Yaguarón is the **Museo José Gaspar Rodriguez de Francia** (*Calle Pirayú 325;* ✆ *0533 232343;* ☉ *09.00–15.00 Tue–Sun; free*). It is named after Paraguay's first president, because his father originally owned the house, and Dr Francia spent his early childhood there. It is a splendid house, with a colonnade on the front side, and the display is of furniture and objects of the period, with some religious art. The curator is Rosa Acevedo (**m** *0981 912920*).

OUTSIDE YAGUARÓN The hill known as **Cerro Yaguarón** (tucked right up against the southwest corner of the town and not the one that is more visible from the Ruta when you have passed through the town) is traditionally the site of a big Good Friday procession of the Stations of the Cross. On the summit is an oratory and what are allegedly the footprints of St Thomas the Apostle, variously known in Guaraní as *Pa'i Zumé, Pa'i Tomé* and *Tumé Arandú* (Guaraní 'Thomas wise'). As you descend you pass

Reductions died and were virtually abandoned within a decade or two, as churches were looted by people from Asunción who had long been envious of their riches. The Franciscan towns, however, continued growing in a more organic way with the rest of Paraguay, and escaped the destruction that befell the Treinta Pueblos.

The Jesuits brought over from Europe some of the finest composers, writers, sculptors and architects of the era, who were themselves Jesuits, and devoted the rest of their lives to the Guaraní, in circumstances of very considerable danger: 26 lost their lives as martyrs. The Franciscans were largely dependent on the Jesuits for the development of an artistic style. Although many people contrast the simpler style of what they call 'Franciscan art' with the more flowery style of 'Jesuit art', according to Darko Sustersic, probably the leading expert on the subject, the terms are a misnomer. The real contrast, he says, is to be made between art pre-Brassanelli and post-Brassanelli. Giuseppe Brassanelli (usually written in Spanish as José Brasanelli) was a Jesuit sculptor and architect who reached South America in 1691 and changed the whole dynamic of carving. The earlier style was based on the straight tree trunk, out of which a fairly static figure was carved, solidly placed on its two feet, looking straight ahead, and symmetrical in design. There are some beautiful examples of this simple design. But Brassanelli taught by example how to make the robes seem to ripple in the wind, the body to move its weight off its centre point, the head to incline and the arms to gesture. This was the arrival of Guaraní baroque.

In terms of tourism, the Jesuit Reductions are known for their fine carved statues of saints (*imágenes*), many of which are kept in the museums of Misiones, and for their stone ruins, particularly of their great churches. But the Franciscan towns also have a beautiful artistic heritage – though a barely known one – in the form of the reredos (*retablo*), the decorative setting on the wall behind the altar, that often acts as a frame for a number of statues.

There are no extant Jesuit reredos, though there is the occasional blurry aged photograph. But if you can find someone to let you into the church of Caazapá, or Atyrá, or Piribebúy, or Tobatí, or more than half a dozen other Franciscan towns, you will find a joy to meet your eyes, as statues of saints – themselves fine works of art – are set within an exquisitely carved and painted framework of harmonious colours. Yet hardly anyone knows of the existence of these reredos, and there is no tourist infrastructure yet to present them: no books, no leaflets, no postcards, no guides, no notices, no tours. It is undiscovered territory, and all the more exciting for that. The Circuito de Oro route, as offered by the tour companies, usually focuses more on craft than on reredos. Compare this lack of attention with the proliferation of over 1,500 books and academic articles on the Jesuit Reductions – although mostly in Spanish of course.

the grotto (*gruta*) of St Thomas. Some say this was the grotto created when Pa'i Zumé destroyed seven monsters from Guaraní mythology. The neighbouring town of Paraguarí also has a hill that allegedly was connected with St Thomas (see overleaf). According to an ancient myth, the apostle Thomas came to evangelise Paraguay many centuries before the conquest. He was left unharmed by all the wild animals and insects and revered by the people, and when he left – borne away on the crystalline river waters to evangelise other countries – he left a blessing on the *yerba* used for *mate* and *tereré*. Still today, people say the first sip from the *bombilla* belongs to San Tomás.

Agua Dulce (*Ruta 1 km56;* \ *021 660784;* m *0981 221729;* e *campamento@ aguadulce.com.py; www.aguadulce.com.py*) is a recreation centre with outdoor activities and camping facilities, but with an emphasis on water: springs and waterfalls, swimming pool, football and volleyball. It is situated between Yaguarón and Paraguarí, 600m away from the main road.

PARAGUARÍ *Copaco ☎ 0531 432299; municipalidad ☎ 0531 432204*

Paraguarí is one of the larger towns within the circuit, and is useful for its facilities rather than for its sites. But it does have its own ancient tradition (rather like Yaguarón) of a cave on the hill, **Cerro Santo Tomás,** where allegedly the apostle Thomas lived (see page 147).

GETTING THERE See *Travelling along Ruta 1*, page 141. Paraguarí is the town from which to take the link road from Ruta 1 to Ruta 2, on the classic Circuito de Oro route. After Paraguarí it passes through some pretty hill country.

WHERE TO STAY

Hotel Gabriela m 0971 319219; e hotel_gabrielapy@hotmail.com; http://www.hotelgabriela.turismoparaguay.net/gabriela_pc.htm. On the road to Piribebúy, but only 3km from Paraguarí. Run by a Hungarian-German family, who breed German shepherd dogs. Very quiet, surrounded by hills. Swimming pool & games, good international food, 50ha, mini zoo. Can also go there for the day. No internet. $$$

For **La Quinta** and **Mbatoví**, see under Piribebúy, page 139.

WHERE TO EAT

Frutería Ruta 1, km61.5; ☎ 0531 432406. Outside the town on the Asunción side, on the right if you are coming from the capital, this is the place where all the Paraguayans stop for a snack or a drink or a meal. Good quality, low prices, plenty of variety, & decent toilets. Try the fruit salad; do not try the pasta. $

CARAPEGUÁ *Copaco ☎ 0532 212901/21993; municipalidad ☎ 0532 212234*

Carapeguá is the last of the craft towns on Ruta 1, until you get to San Miguel a long way south in Misiones. They make many of the same things as San Miguel: hammocks, bedcovers, ponchos and tablecloths. They specialise in a kind of cotton weave known as *ao poyví* (Guaraní 'sturdy material'), which is similar to the *ao po'í* (Guaraní 'fine material') of Yataity but with a thicker thread. They also make *encaje ju* lace, basketware and the *sombreros* with broad brims against the sun, known as *sombreros pirí*. Most of the work is done in the *compañías*, rather than in the town itself.

Carapeguá began to have an Expo Feria in 2009, around the anniversary of its foundation on 14 May. It remains to be seen whether this will prove to be an annual event.

While the Circuito de Oro is an imprecise area, Carapeguá is probably its outermost limit. But there are a few more towns on Ruta 1 before you cross the Río Tebicuarý, which fall more easily into this chapter than into the next one (Misiones).

YBYCUÍ *Copaco ☎ 0534 226500; municipalidad ☎ 0534 22396*

GETTING THERE If you want to visit the **Parque Nacional Ybycuí** (Gs5,000), take a turn to the left (southeast) from Carapeguá, and pass through the towns of Acahay, Ybycuí and La Rosada. Acahay can also be reached from Quiindý by dirt road. (For getting to Carapeguá, see page 141.) The bus Salto Cristal (☎ *021 555728*) goes there, from Asunción. The name Ybycuí means 'sand' in Guaraní.

WHERE TO STAY There is no accommodation in the park, but at holiday times the Paraguayans turn up with camping equipment. The little town of Ybycuí (which is not particularly attractive) has two small hotels.

Mamorei ✆ 021 220332/201106; e info@mamorei.com; www.mamorei.com. This *estancia*, just before the town, on the left (east) side of the road, is a better choice than either of the hotels, if you think in time to book at least one day in advance. It calls itself the 'first private farm school' and the imaginative if slow-loading website expresses the belief that 'in the country we learn to live with nature and to grow within its infinite mysteries'. Reservations can also be made through Apatur (see *Chapter 2*, page 51). $$$
Hotel Pytu'ú Rendá ✆ 0534 226364. One of two undistinguished hotels in the pueblo. $$
Hospedaje La Esperanza (✆ 0534 226320. Slightly better of the two establishments, despite costing less. Cheaper rooms have fans. $

WHAT TO SEE After going through Ybycuí, you pass on the right the house of Bernardino Caballero (a former president and founder of the Colorado party). This is worth visiting, and is open in the mornings. The Parque Ybycuí is the national park most visited by Paraguayans, for its location is within reach of Asunción. Created in 1973, it has 5,000ha with hills, woods, streams and waterfalls. There is no other national park with as many waterfalls in such a small area. The *zona histórica* of La Rosada has a well-designed museum marking the place where there was a foundry of iron, reputed to be the first in South America. It was destroyed in 1869 in the War of the Triple Alliance, but has been partially restored for tourists. The *zona recreativa* of Ybycuí, 3km away, has a visitor centre and the Salto Mina waterfall.

A bigger waterfall, the **Salto Cristal**, with a drop of 42m, is not in the park but is in the same region: it is 15km by dirt road south of the town of La Colmena – a town founded by Japanese in the 1930s, which is 25km east of Acahay.

SAN ROQUE GONZÁLEZ Copaco ✆ 0538 20000; municipalidad ✆ 0538 20151

This is the next town down from Carapeguá on Ruta 1 (see *Travelling along Ruta 1*, page 141). It is an old town founded in 1538 and until 1948 it was known as Tabapý. It was the site of the battle where the Comuneros revolution was suppressed in 1735 (see *Chapter 1*, page 11).

QUIINDÝ Copaco ✆ 0536 282599; municipalidad ✆ 0536 282553

Quiindý (the town after San Roque González, see above) grew up around a chapel dedicated to the Niño Jesús (Christ Child) in 1733, built by a certain María Peralta de Figueredo in thanksgiving for having escaped in 1743 from the indigenous who had kidnapped her. The original pulpit has been taken up to the Casa de la Independencia in Asunción. Today this is a sizeable town where leather footballs are made, and you see them displayed all along the road. It has a striking church with pointed arches that you pass in the bus.

WHERE TO STAY
Alce's Hotel km108.5; ✆ 0536 282651/282341. Set back behind the petrol station on the east side of the road, on the north side of town. A good place to stay if you are looking for a hotel on your route – pleasant & new with Wi-Fi & computer room. $$

PARQUE NACIONAL LAGO YPOÁ

The Parque Nacional Lago Ypoá is a huge area of wetlands or *humedales* (100,000ha) to the west of Quiindý, little known and barely even marked on maps, yet one of the places richest in flora and fauna in eastern Paraguay.

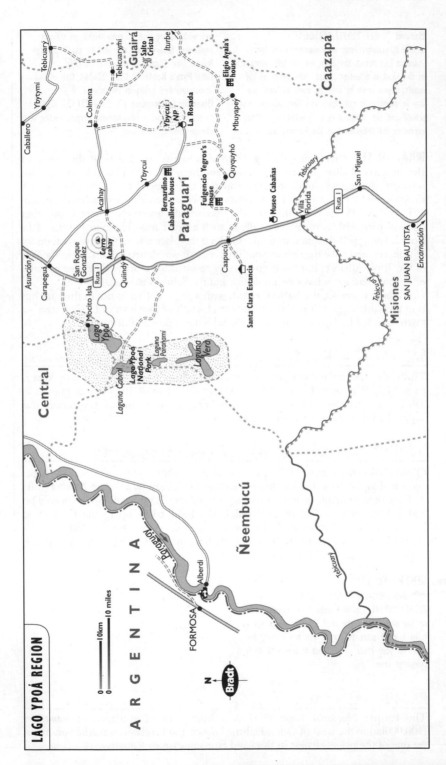

LAGO YPOÁ REGION

0 ___ 10km
0 ___ 10 miles

N
Bradt

GETTING THERE A map of the area can be studied by the roadside, opposite the Frutería of Paraguarí (see page 148). The *gobernación* of Paraguarí also has a leaflet they can give you. Their secretary for tourism is Alba de Bogado (❧ *0531 432211*) and she can give up-to-date information; a project is under way to build a passable road so people can visit this region so rich in natural beauty and fauna. Within the swamps are many islands of firm ground, or *islas*, of which Caapucú-mí is the largest. At Ykuá Ñaró Point it is said that you hear noises and see lights coming from the ghosts of the cavalry in the Triple Alliance War. You can travel through the marshes by boat, but there is nowhere to stay at present, other than a campsite.

You can get to the general area of the *humedales*, and to Mocito Isla, close to Lago Ypoá on the north side, if you take a turn 3.5km after Carapeguá, marked to 'Humedales de Ypoá'. However, this does not get you as far as the lake itself. To reach Lago Ypoá (the largest lake of the area) you have to take a track for about 20km from Ruta 1 km132, after Quiindý, and you complete the journey on a private road. But access is difficult and you can only do it with a 4×4. This is a difficult place to visit without a guide; there is a guide available, Ito Morinigo (m *0981 572720*), but he does not have a vehicle. However, this area will undoubtedly be opened up in the very near future and will be well worth a visit.

CAAPUCÚ Copaco ❧ *0531 280301/2*; municipalidad ❧ *0531 280279*

The last town on Ruta 1 before the River Tebicuarý is heralded with a striking monument of a *campesino* and a bull, on the right-hand side of Ruta 1, coming from Asunción. The town has a good-quality *estancia* and an interesting old house called the Museo Cabañas, practically on the main road.

WHERE TO STAY

Estancia Santa Clara (8 rooms); Ruta 1 km141; ❧ 021 605729; m 0981 405020; e vale@pla.net.y; www.estanciasantaclara.com.py. Only 6km to the west of Caapucú, with all the usual comforts & delights of an *estancia*, including riding, sulky horse carts, mini zoo, walks, volleyball, hammocks, pool, etc. & there is lots of homegrown produce. Reservations can also be made through Apatur (see *Chapter 2*, page 51). $$$

WHAT TO SEE Little known but not to be missed is the delightful **Museo Cabañas** (*Ruta 1 km154;* m *0971 359295;* ⊕ *09.00–16.00 Tues–Sat; free*) or to give it its full name, Museo Oratorio Prócer Manuel Anastasio Cabañas. It is 11km south of Caapucú and about 8km before the river, but the rather battered sign gives no clue of the quality of what is to be found there, barely 1km to the east of Ruta 1. The house is also known as la Alquería de Yaguarý, but the locals call it the Cabañas Guasú (the big [house] of the Cabañas). It is not actually a big house, though the original mansion of the Cabañas family had been, which was burnt down in the Triple Alliance War. What remains is a simple 17th-century outhouse of stone and adobe, and an oratory, standing separately and of similar size.

An 1886 map inside the house helps explain the history. Before the construction of Ruta 1 and the bridge over the Río Tebicuarý, travellers would cross the river by ferry at the Paso Santa María, and the road, such as it was, passed right by the Cabañas house. On the other side of the river, the road went past Santa María de Fe, instead of going past San Ignacio as it does today.

'Cavañas', as it is marked on the map, was therefore a key place through which everyone passed. In the time of the Jesuit Reductions it was a place to spend the night; the Comuneros revolutionaries led by José de Antequera, on their way from Misiones to Asunción, stopped there in 1724 and fought a battle nearby; General

Belgrano stopped there with his Argentinian troops in 1810, on the way to and from his defeat in the battles of Paraguarí y Tacuary; in the time of Dr Francia there was a covert suggestion that the dictator should be deposed and replaced with the head of the Cabañas family at that date. (For these points of history, see *Chapter 1*, page 12.)

Today the house has been beautifully furnished with period furniture, clothing and leather-thonged bed frames. There are wooden attachments in the walls for hanging hammocks, and an old hand mill for maize or *coco*. The oratory has a beautiful Cristo de la Paciencia from the Jesuit period, which is set in an original, painted niche. The well-kept garden is charming, with a well, a cooking pot over logs, tight rows of cactus plants acting as fencing, and an ancient and unusual thorn tree. The renovation was the work of the artist Carlos Colombino Lailla working with the foundation that bears his name, and the house was opened as a museum in 2002.

The guide is usually Alcides González Cabañas (m 0971 359295), a descendant of the original owners. Advance notice of a special visit can also be given to the Museo del Barro in Asunción (🕿 021 607996; ⏰ 15.30–20.00 Thu–Sat), because they were connected with the renovation, through Carlos Colombino.

5

Misiones and the Jesuit Reductions

Departamento: Misiones

If you have dozed off on the bus you may come to as you cross the bridge over the Río Tebicuarý into Misiones, because of the gentle brrm-brrm of the low speed-bumps. Stretches of cream sand extend before your eyes (depending on the river level). You are now in the famous Misiones *departamento*, or the mission territory of the Jesuit Reductions – which also continue into the next *departamento* of Itapúa. The basic rule is: museums in Misiones, Ruins in Itapúa. These two *departamentos* are Paraguay's top tourist attractions – the land of what has been called again and again 'The Lost Paradise', 'The Forgotten Arcadia', etc. Given their distance from Asunción, you need a minimum of two or three days to visit them, and five or six days (or ideally more) to do them justice.

There are four Jesuit Reductions in this *departamento*: San Ignacio, Santa María de Fe, Santa Rosa and Santiago. Passing through Misiones to the next *departamento* of Itapúa (covered in *Chapter 6*) you will find three more Reductions there: San Cosme y Damián, Trinidad and Jesús. All seven are well worth visiting, and are being promoted through the government tourist office as the Ruta Jesuítica. There were 30 such Reductions in the high days, and they were known as the Treinta Pueblos (Thirty Towns). Founded on both banks of the Río Paraná and both banks of the Río Uruguay, they stretch today from Paraguay, through Argentina and into Brazil.

HOUSES IN THE *CAMPO*

Everything in the Paraguayan countryside is strongly framed by tradition. A typical house in the *campo* will be built of brick or wood, roofed with tiles or straw, and will have two separate rooms with a roofed area between them, to give shade from the hot sun. The kitchen will be at the back – probably just a wooden hut heavily coated with smoke, with hooks to hang things from and an open log fire. There will also – always – be an outside oven called a *tatakuá*, which is like a small brick igloo sitting on the ground, with an opening at the front for access and a smaller one at the back for ventilation: a wood fire makes the bricks very hot indeed, and then the fire is taken out and the meat or *sopa paraguaya* is cooked in the residual heat of the bricks. It is much hotter than a modern oven and cooks faster. The toilet will be a latrine – called a *baño común* (common bathroom) – which will be a hole in the ground with a seat over it, within a small wooden hut with sloping corrugated iron roof, at a distance from the main building. Finally, there will typically be a well.

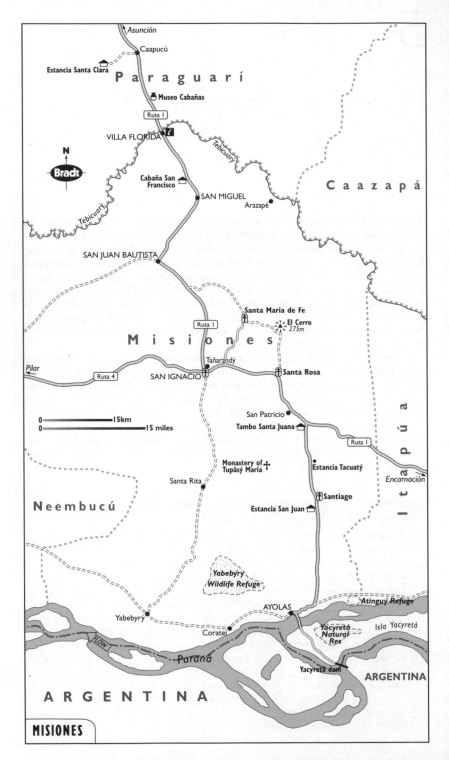

00.00	Nuestra Señora de la Asunción*	13.30	Nuestra Señora de la Asunción*
00.30	Flecha de Oro	13.45	Alborada
00.30	Encarnacena*	14.00	Ciudad de Pilar° (good bus)
01.00	Rysa*		
03.00	Flecha de Oro	14.30	Pilarense (slow, to Ayolas)
04.15	Alborada		
05.30	Flecha de Oro	15.00	Flecha de Oro
06.30	Pilarense (slow, to Ayolas)	15.30	Pilarense (slow, to Ayolas)
07.00	Alborada	15.50	Misionera
07.15	Ñeembucu	16.00	Alborada* (Fri, Sat, Sun)
07.30	Pycasú		
08.00	Misionera	16.30	Misionera (not Sun)
08.30	Encarnacena*	17.00	San Juan
08.45	Flecha de Oro	17.30	Yacyreta
09.00	Pycasú	17.30	Ortega
09.00	Encarnacena*	17.30	Encarnacena*
09.30	Alborada	17.30	Encarnacena°*
10.15	Beato Roque González	18.00	Ciudad de Pilar°* (not Sun)
10.15	Pilarense (slow)	18.45	San Juan
11.00	Yacyreta	19.00	El Tigre*
11.15	Ñeembucú	19.30	San Juan
11.30	Rysa	20.00	Ñeembucu°
11.45	Flecha de Oro	20.30	Yacyreta
11.45	Mariscal Lopez	21.00	Flecha de Oro
12.00	Encarnacena	22.30	Alborada*
12.00	Encarnacena°	22.30	Alborada* (to María Auxiliadora on Ruta 6)
12.15	Misionera		
12.20	Pycasú	22.30	Beato Roque González
12.30	Misionera (not on Sundays)	22.30	Encarnacena°*
12.50	Yacyreta	23.30	Ñeembucu°
13.00	Alborada*	23.30	Alborada
13.05	Alborada (to María Auxiliadora on Ruta 6)	23.45	Pycasú*

* Good bus but you may have to pay a higher fare; however, fares are very low anyway.
° From San Ignacio these buses go to Pilar, not to Encarnación, and in San Ignacio you must get on or off at the Hotel Arapysandú and not at the Plaza. Most of the other buses go on to Encarnación, and a few go further, past the Ruins of Trinidad to María Auxiliadora. Some go to Ayolas, which means they turn off before Encarnación.

No general timetable of this form is available from the Terminal in Asunción, except by going round every bus company and asking, or from the website www.mca.gov.py/webtermi.html by clicking on the name of every bus company in turn, but even so the timetable has not been kept up to date.

On the way to them you pass through some other attractive towns that were not Reductions, though they fell within the lands of the old Reductions and began as outposts or chapels on the *estancias*. Later they developed into urban centres in their own right. Of these, Villa Florida, with its beaches on the river, is a Paraguayan holiday town; San Miguel, with its woollen craft, is a popular tourist stop; and San Juan is the capital of the *departamento*.

From Villa Florida on, it is approximately ten minutes from town to town through Misiones.

VILLA FLORIDA   Copaco ✆ 083 240460; municipalidad ✆ 083 240216/240404

Before the bridge was built, you had to cross the Río Tebicuarý by raft: there is an old photo that shows the raft, with its sides built up with fencing. Until 1880 the place was known as Puerto Santa María or Paso Santa María, because it was the access to Santa María de Fe, which was once the largest of the Reductions (though is now only a small town).

In this country, 'Florida' is pronounced with the stress on the second, not the first syllable. Because of its extensive sandy beaches – 10km of them, weather permitting – Villa Florida is a holiday resort for Paraguayans, much in the way that San Bernardino is, but with not quite the popularity because of being that bit further from Asunción. There are a number of well-off families who have houses in Asunción, farms in the country and holiday homes in Villa Florida, a stone's throw from the beach. And the hotels are chock-a-block in the summer season, which runs from December to Semana Santa (Holy Week).

The famous *dorado* fish swims in the river – the so-called river tiger – which is considered the most delicious of the fishes, though since 2009 there has been a prohibition on fishing it for commercial purposes. The law is not always observed, though it may affect its availability in restaurants. But you should have no difficulty in ordering other fish dishes such as *chupín de surubí*, *milanesa de surubí*, *pirá caldo*, *caldo de mandi'í*, etc. (See page 183 for fish dishes).

If you penetrate beyond the main road, you will find an attractive small town that appears to be built on grass, with just a few narrow strips of asphalt where necessary for the passage of cars. Some of the houses around the plaza are well-restored old buildings – one, called Ñande Ypý Kuéra (Guaraní 'Our Ancestors'), dates back to 1872.

ORIENTATION When you cross the bridge you will pass immediately on your left a **tourist information** centre (only open in the summer season December–March) and a craft shop, next to the Parador Touring Club (see below). Then you pass through a toll (Gs5,000 for cars). Most of the facilities of the town are on Ruta 1, including all three hotels, most of the shops, the internet café Cyber K@vo, Copaco with its telephone *cabinas* or phone booths (on the corner of Boquerón or Agustín Pio Barrios, 4 blocks from the bridge), and a couple of tyre repair workshops. If you need to buy swimsuits or towels, try Bodega Florida, opposite Cyber K@vo.

Other services are on the **Avenida Tebicuarý**, which is a very broad grassy space, with a row of trees down the middle, a thin asphalt strip on one side and a volleyball pitch on the other, located one block to the northeast of Ruta 1. The post office is here (*c/ Boquerón*) and a second internet service in the Panda shop (*c/ Feliciano Orue*).

Around the **Plaza** Bernardino Caballero (which is three blocks to the south of the bridge and then two blocks to the northeast, along the asphalted Jóvenes Mártires por la Democracia) you will find the *municipalidad*, hospital, Casa de la Cultura and police station, and on its far corner is a small supermarket and a good café.

From the plaza you have a good view of the river down a couple of paths. The more westerly of these goes past the charming **church** of the Immaculate Conception, on the site of the old Jesuit chapel, but rebuilt in 1975 with help from Switzerland. In the porch is a handsome crucifix dating from the time of the Reductions.

The **taxi** driver Victor Servín (✆ *083 240374*) works principally in the summer season, but can be contacted at any time.

🏠 WHERE TO STAY

🏠 **Hotel Touring Club** (7 rooms) ✆ 083 240205. Immediately on left as you cross the bridge, the Parador Tebicuary (see below) is now a hotel with newly built rooms, opened Dec 2009. $$$$

🏠 **Hotel Nacional de Turismo Villa Florida** (20 rooms) Ruta I esq Barreiro; ✆/f 083 240207. Count 5 blocks from the bridge to find this hotel on the northeast side, set back down a driveway. One of the 2 hotels run by the government tourist office Senatur (the other is in Vapor Cué), though they have been trying for a few years to sell them to private enterprise. With 11 huge palm trees growing in the inside patio, a swimming pool & substantial dark wood furniture, this is a beautifully designed hotel which however is struggling to keep

standards up: its success in the summer does not compensate financially for its emptiness the rest of the year. $$

🏠 **Hotel La Misionera** (10 rooms) Ruta I esq 8 de diciembre; ✆ 083 240215. Just after the Parador Touring Club, on your left as you cross the bridge into Misiones. No internet. Negotiable on price. $

🏠 **Hotel Playa** (8 rooms) ✆ 083 240214. The sign for this hotel fell down, but even if it has not been replaced, you can locate the spot from the 'Expreso Río Paraná' sign (a long-distance bus company). Pleasant but simple hotel in traditional style around an inner courtyard. AC. Meals served according to the dish of the day. $

🍴 WHERE TO EAT

🍴 **Comedor Ñande Róga** ✆ 083 240582. On your right after you have left town, going south. Fish soups & *milanesas*, all dishes can be served up quickly. $$

🍴 **Parador Restaurant Tebicuary** ✆ 083 240205. The restaurant of the Hotel Touring Club. A useful stop if you are driving down from Asunción, & indeed it is used as a stop by the long-distance buses Encarnacena & Crucero del Norte. The coffee is good, & so are the toilets. The garden goes down to the river, & in the summer it is filled with animals: sheep, goats, ostriches, capybaras & many kinds of birds. $$

🍴 **Hotel Nacional de Turismo Villa Florida** See above. $$

🍴 **La Reja** Av Tebicuary, entre Bareiro y Agustín Pío Barrios; ✆ 083 240326; ⏰ every day for lunch & supper. 5 blocks along Ruta I from the bridge, & then a couple of blocks to your left. There is a sign on Ruta I. Delightful, small restaurant, full of character, lots of plants. Family atmosphere. $

🍴 **San Cayetano** ✆ 083 240319. A clean & modern café on the corner of the plaza, serving everything from sandwiches to the substantial pot roast *asado a la olla*. $

BEACHES All the beach facilities tend to be seasonal, from December until Semana Santa. Then you can expect to find fishing facilities, bars, toilets, beach volleyball, campsites, sometimes horses to ride, and from some of the beaches you can hire a boatman very cheaply to take you across the river in a rowing boat.

Caracol (Snail or conch) 5km to the east of the town. Take the 2nd turning left, when you come from Asunción.

Punta Arena Caapucú A beach on the other side of the river, belonging to the Caapucú municipality.

Paraíso (Paradise) To the west of the town. Coming from Asunción, you will see the notice pointing down a dirt road to the right – the 1st

turning after the bridge. Then turn right again at the first crossroads, & left when you reach the river. This is one of the best beaches, & the closest, with the only drawback that it gets rather full. On the 1st w/end of Feb the beach is the site for a Latin American parachuting festival. For more information contact Roland Peyrat (e *contacto@republicaflyer.com*).

Yvága (Guaraní 'Heaven') Excellent new beach, beyond Paraíso to the west of Villa Florida. Take the 2nd turning on the right after you cross the bridge (Feliciano Orué). The only disadvantage is the distance (5km).

Centú Cué As you leave town going south, there is a turning on the left (Narciso Corrales) which leads eventually to this attractive beach resort, 7km east of Villa Florida. This is the best place to fish for *dorado* (which is legal as long as it is not for commercial ends, & is within the fishing season).

SAN MIGUEL Copaco ☎ 0783 248350; municipalidad ☎ 0783 248205

San Miguel is an important place to make a brief stop, for the picturesque woollen and woven craft. This is a wonderful place to buy hammocks, blankets, rugs, bedcovers, tablecloths, jerseys, ponchos, hats and woollen socks and gloves.

The pueblo was founded in 1725 by the Jesuits, not as a Reduction but as a house for watching over cattle in the *estancia* belonging to Santa María. There is a statue of St Michael in the church that dates from this period.

Just before you enter the town you pass a monument proclaiming the town as the 'Capital de la Lana' (Capital of Wool) with a painted statue of St Michael, but it is up the bank to the right and may be above your eye level in a bus. Next to come is a roadside stall on the left, selling painted wooden toucans and parrots, made out of the natural formation of branches and twigs. This is a speciality of San Miguel, but much better known is the display of hammocks, ponchos and blankets that people hang up for sale in front of their houses, and that you pass as you go out on the southern stretch of road. This craft in wool and cotton is picturesque if you are whizzing past in a bus, but if you are in your own vehicle it will be worth your while to stop and buy something.

As you reach San Miguel, you see the turn to Arazapé 14km to the east. This small *compañía* specialises in knitted sweaters and other woollen clothes.

OTHER PRACTICALITIES San Miguel has no taxi service, no facilities for taking out or changing money, and poor or non-existent signals for Tigo mobile phones (at least at the time of going to press). There is really only one place to stay, and that is not in San Miguel but near it, on the Villa Florida side: the **Cabaña San Francisco** (*12 rooms; km173;* ☎ *083 240328;* m *0971 216171;* e *info@francisco-country.com; www.san-francisco-country.com*). This is an *estancia* 5km before the town, on Ruta 1 to the north, with sports facilities, fishing, riding, pool, *quincho*, etc. There is no restaurant, only a couple of bars – the Copetín San Cayetano and the Kiosko San Fernando – before you reach the plaza (coming from Asunción). All in all, San Miguel is a place to stop rather than a place to stay.

WHAT TO SEE In the middle of June (usually the second Thursday–Sunday, check with the *municipalidad* or Copaco for the programme of events) there is a most appealing craft festival called **Ovecha Ragué**, which in Guaraní means 'the sheep that was', in other words, wool. The grassy plaza is filled with stalls selling all the best craft products, and but there is also a singing festival, folk dance display, cycling tournament, procession of floats and of antique cars, and the sale of traditional cooked dishes. Of these, *batiburillo* is a particular treat, and is a dish specific to Misiones: it is made of beef offal, and you eat it hot in a little dish accompanied by a stick of *mandioc*.

In the middle of the plaza is the little **church** of San Miguel, with a traditional bell tower beside it: in Jesuit times, this was a chapel of the Santa María de Fe *estancia*, but today little original is left from the Jesuit period. If you climb the wooden bell tower you find two ancient bells at the top, of which the cracked one bears the words 'Santa Maria Ora Por Novis [*sic*] and A Nos L 12 4' (or possibly

1724). Inside the church in the middle of the reredos is a statue of San Miguel dating back to Jesuit times, which unfortunately has been repainted in bright colours. It is an almost exact, smaller version of one of the San Miguels (probably by Brassanelli) in the Santa María Museum (see *Chapter 5*, page 174), with outstretched wings, angled sword and squirming serpent. To the right of the reredos is a larger San Miguel – rather a fine piece, though not from the Reduction.

The first **craft shop** you come to on the road from Asunción is devoted to the craft of Arazapé. When you reach the plaza there are two good shops: Mainumby (✆ *0783 248288*), which has lots of things suitable as souvenirs, like tablecloths, clothes and little lace mats (both *encaje ju* and *ñandutí*, see *Chapter 1*, page 21), and next to it Delmia (✆ *0783 248232*), which has sheepskins hanging outside and specialises in the heavier items, like bedcovers, mats and hammocks. Next to that is the *municipalidad*.

A little further along the same road you come to a host of family-run craft shops, all with hammocks strung outside and sometimes wool hung out to dry as well. A couple of them near the end of the row – Zully (✆ *0783 248364* neighbours) and Artesanía Muñeca (✆ *0783 248214*) – have workshops behind, where you can ask to go in to see the clanking hand looms in action. Casa Irene (*last but one on the northeast side;* ✆ *0783 248225*) has a good line in blankets. El Trionfo (✆ *0783 248249*) has a lot of items hung up around a thatched workshop.

SAN JUAN BAUTISTA Copaco ✆ 081 212399; municipalidad ✆ 081 212235

San Juan Bautista is the capital of the *departamento,* though not the principal town. San Ignacio is bigger and has more facilities. The town is famed for being the birthplace of the guitarist and composer Agustín Pío Barrios, known as Mangoré (1885–1944; see box, page 163). (This claim has recently been challenged, however, by the inhabitants of Villa Florida, who maintain he was born there.)

San Juan is the see of the diocese of San Juan Bautista de las Misiones, which has historically been an important diocese for resisting the corruption and human rights abuses of successive Colorado governments. Its first bishop, Monseñor Ramón Pastor Bogarín Argaña, is the town's second most famous personage after Mangoré: his tomb and portrait have a place of special honour in the cathedral. He was courageous in opposing the Stroessner dictatorship – which wiped out the Christian Agrarian Leagues that began in this diocese – and is regarded as a quasi-martyr because he died of an untimely heart attack under the stress of the persecution, on 3 September 1976, in the year of the worst repression. It is said that from his residence he could hear the screams of those being tortured in the police cells. The present-day bishop, Monseñor Mario Melanio Medina, also has a reputation for outspoken criticism, and was the only Paraguayan bishop to support Fernando Lugo openly in his run for the presidency.

San Juan was not one of the Reductions, but it began as a chapel on the *estancia* of the Reduction of San Ignacio, and was known first as Posta San Juan and then as San Juan Capillita. It has been suggested that the first chapel may have been constructed in 1697 by the Jesuit Anton Sepp – the 'father of the Paraguayan harp' and a prolific writer about life in the Reductions. In 1893 San Juan became a *municipio* independent of San Ignacio.

It is a pretty town with two attractive plazas and cobbled streets, and Ruta 1 skims along the edge rather than cutting through the middle as it does in San Ignacio. As you reach San Juan, coming from San Miguel, you will see on the right-hand side a sign welcoming you to the 'Cuna de Mangoré' (the cradle of Mangoré), the imposing Palacio de Justicia set back from the road, and opposite the

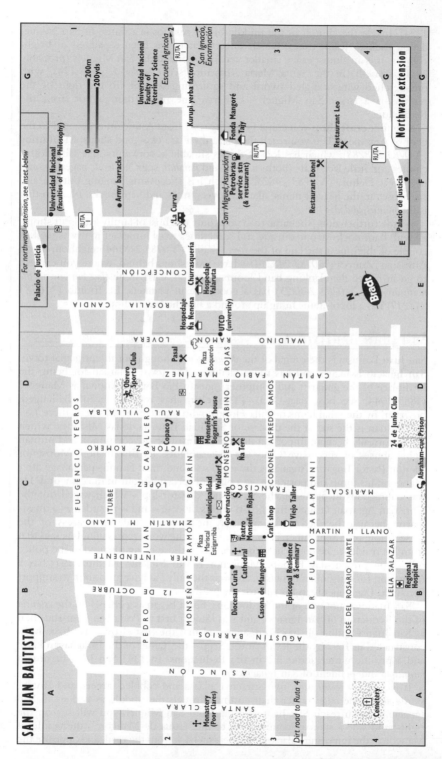

SAN JUAN BAUTISTA

0 ___ 200m
0 ___ 200yds

Northward extension

For northward extension, see inset below

Palacio de Justicia

Universidad Nacional (Faculties of Law & Philosophy)

Army barracks

Universidad Nacional Faculty of Veterinary Science

Escuela Agrícola

RUTA 1

San Ignacio, Encarnación

RUTA 1 →

Kurupi yerba factory

'La Curva'

Churrasquería
Hospedaje Yalaruta

CONCEPCIÓN

Hospedaje Ña Nenena

ROSALIA CANDIA

LOVERA

RAMÓN

UTCD (university)

WALDINO

San Miguel, Asunción / Petrobras service stn (& restaurant)

Fonda Mangoré
Tajy
RUTA 1

Restaurant Leo

Restaurant Donel
RUTA 1

Palacio de Justicia

Pasal

Plaza Boquerón

MARTÍNEZ

Obrero Sports Club

RAÚL VILLALBA

FULGENCIO YEGROS

PEDRO

ROMERO

VICTORINO CABALLERO

Copaco

Monseñor Bogarín's house

Ña Tere

MONSEÑOR GABINO E ROJAS

CAPITÁN FABIO

CORONEL ALFREDO RAMOS

Waldorf

Municipalidad

Gobernación

Teatro Monseñor Rojas

Craft shop

El Viejo Taller

FRANCISCO SOSA

LÓPEZ

ITURBE

M LLANO

JUAN MARTÍN

RAMÓN BOGARÍN

PRIMER INTENDENTE

Plaza Mariscal Estigarribia

Cathedral

Diocesan Curia

Casona de Mangoré

Episcopal Residence & Seminary

MARISCAL

MARTIN M LLANO

ALAMANNI

FULVIO

DR

JOSÉ DEL ROSARIO DIARTE M LLANO

24 de Junio Club

Abraham-cue Prison

LELIA SALAZAR

Regional Hospital

12 DE OCTUBRE

MONSEÑOR

AGUSTÍN BARRIOS

ASUNCIÓN

SANTA CLARA

Monastery (Poor Clares)

Dirt road to Ruta 4

Cemetery

N

Bradt

160

law faculty of the Universidad Nacional, with a little plaza in front of it called the Paseo de los Ilustres, with plaques to Mangoré, Monseñor Bogarín and other distinguished people from the town's past. When you reach a pronounced curve to the left (*la curva*) with a triangle of grass and the big hoarding for Kurupí *yerba*, you must turn sharp right if you want to enter the town.

WHERE TO STAY

There is a bigger selection of hotels in the next town of San Ignacio, but San Juan has one comfortable hotel and a few modest *hospedajes*:

Hotel Tajy [160 F3] Ruta 1 km195; ☎ 081 212533. On the left as you come into the town from Asunción, before you reach the Palacio de Justicia & on the other side of the road from it. This is the most comfortable hotel, which despite its unexpectedly high prices & far distance from the centre, is usually full. Wi-Fi, cheaper dormitory for groups. Meals come from the restaurant in the Petrobras service station over the road. $$$

Fonda Mangoré [160 F3] Ruta 1 km195; ☎ 081 212526. Just before the Hotel Tajy, on the outskirts of town. Restaurant. Rooms. No internet. $

Hospedaje Ña Nenena [160 E2] (17 rooms) Monseñor Bogarín 151; ☎ 081 212667. Between la curva & the 1st plaza. Simple but adequate. No b/fast, but you can get a good b/fast at Pasal on Plaza Boquerón. $

Hospedaje Valaruta [160 E2] Monseñor Bogarín c/ Concepción; ☎ 081 212039. Another small & very cheap hospedaje but with Paraguayan character, 1 block to the east of Ña Nenena. No b/fast, but you can get a good b/fast at Pasal on Plaza Boquerón. Right next door is a *churrasquería* with tempting aromas. $

WHERE TO EAT

Restaurant Donel [160 F3] ☎ 081 212135; ⊕ 10.00–22.00 daily. The entrance to the restaurant is clearly marked from Ruta 1, though the name Donel is almost illegible. On the bottom floor of a 3-storey building, this restaurant has more variety than most other local places. $

Petrobras service station [160 F3] Opposite Hotel Tajy. Has restaurant ⊕ till 22.30 daily. $

Fonda Mangoré [160 F3] See above. $

Waldorf [160 C2] Dr Victor Z Romero y Monseñor Rojas; ☎ 081 212209; ⊕ 11.45–15.00 Tue–Fri & from 19.00 Tue–Sun. A former hotel now stylishly renovated to function (for the time being) only as a restaurant, conveniently situated between the 2 plazas. $

Ña Tere [160 C3] Monseñor Rojas 499; ☎ 081 212512. Pizzas & hamburgers etc, diagonally opposite the Waldorf. Modern & clean. $

Pasal [160 D2] Monseñor Bogarín 290; ☎ 081 212026. Next door to Crisol on the Plaza Boquerón is this *confitería* & *panadería*, which serves coffee & variety of croissants with friendly service. Good for b/fast. $

OTHER PRACTICALITIES

There are two cash machines, one outside the Palacio de Justicia [160 E1], and the other at the Cooperativa San Juan Bautista [160 D2] (or Coopersanjuba for short). Both take Visa cards but no other cards (despite the notice).

Telephone *cabinas* can be found at Copaco [160 D2] (Monseñor Bogarín y Raúl Villalba).

FESTIVALS

The famous midwinter fiesta of San Juan falls on 24 June. This is dramatically celebrated all over the country with fire and dangerous games after dark, either on the eve or the day, and in San Juan this customarily takes place in the polideportivo Lucio Amarilla Leiva, otherwise known as Club 24 de junio.

In the second half of January is another fiesta in San Juan – the Festival del Batiburillo, Siriki y el Chorizo Misionero. The original Guaraní name of *siriki* is *chiringuí*, and it is a cocktail traditional to Misiones. Sometimes called the champagne of the poor, it is similar to the Brazilian *caipirinha*, made with white rum (*caña blanca*), a delicate kind of lemon (*limón sutil*) and soda water, and sometimes with grapefruit juice added. *Chorizo misionero* or *sanjuanino* is a sausage of chopped pork, and *batiburillo* is the speciality of Misiones (see above page 158).

This midwinter feast of fire, on 24 June, is one of the most important festivals in the country, and is marked by many traditional games and customs, some of them rather dangerous:

- putting a row of candles outside the house in the evening
- cooking traditional foods like *pajaguá mascada* (Guaraní 'of the Payagua indigenous'; Spanish 'bite') and *chicharõ trenzado* (Guaraní 'crackling'; Spanish 'plaited')
- kicking around a *pelota tatá* (Guaraní 'of fire'; Spanish 'ball') – a ball made out of cloth, soaked in kerosene and set alight. The game is to kick it directly at your friends, who run away screaming.
- climbing the greasy pole, or *yvyrá sỹi* (Guaraní 'tree slippery'), in search of a bag of goodies tied at the top
- *toro kandil* (Spanish 'bull torch'), another game with fire. One or two people get under a cloth representing a bull, the horns of which are set alight, and then they charge at other people, who run away screaming.
- *carrera vosá* (Spanish 'race'; Guaraní 'sack'), a sack race
- *paila jeheréi* (Spanish 'frying pan'; Guaraní 'we lick'), trying to remove a coin stuck with grease on the back of frying pan by licking it.
- *jaguá jetu'u* (Spanish 'dog'; Guaraní 'refusing to move'), two people on all fours and tied together with rope have to try to crawl in opposite directions from each other, pulling the other one behind along the floor
- *kambuchí jejoká* (Spanish 'water jar'; Guaraní 'we break'), a game where people are blindfolded and turned round to make them dizzy, and then given a stick to try to break a clay water jar filled with sweets and goodies
- *gallo ñemongaru* (Spanish 'cock'; Guaraní 'we make to eat'), a cock is starved for 24 hours and then put in a bag. Unmarried girls surround him in a circle, each holding grains of maize in the palm of the hand. The cock is released and the girl whose maize the cock eats first is the one who will get married that year.
- *casamiento koyguá* (Spanish 'wedding'; Guaraní 'from the countryside'), a dramatised comedy wedding, in which a naive and shy bride is insulted by a vulgar bridegroom
- *Judas kái* (Spanish 'Judas'; Guaraní 'burn'), the setting alight of a stuffed figure (a sort of Guy Fawkes) which has been hanged by the neck from a tree. The figure has been previously drenched in kerosene and may be stuffed with explosive fireworks.
- at the end of the night's festivities, the custom of walking barefoot across the glowing embers of the remains of the bonfire. This is called *tatapỹi ári jehasá* (Guaraní 'embers over we walk'). According to legend, the feet are protected from burns if you do this on the night of San Juan. I have seen it done and there were no burns.

WHAT TO SEE The first square (the first one you reach if you come from *la curva*) is called the **Plaza Boquerón** [160 D2] and has a monument in the form of four pyramids in memory of the Chaco War, and a mural commemorating the fiesta of San Juan. Once a month, but not on any regular day, the prisoners of the Abraham-cué jail run a stall of their craftwork in the plaza.

Five blocks on from this square is the **Plaza Mariscal Estigarribia** [160 B2–C2], which has the cathedral on the south side, and a painted statue of the

Mariscal in the centre. Another mural, commemorating Mangoré, is on the corner of Monseñor Gabino Rojas and Dr Martín Llano. On the other street that joins the two plazas is the former house of Monseñor Bogarín himself with seven columns supporting a balustraded balcony (on the southeast corner of Monseñor Bogarín y Victor Romero).

The **cathedral** [160 B3] is a splendid though unelaborate building in cream and beige, with a slightly Moorish aspect to the top of the octagonal tower. On the left as you enter is a carved wooden niche from the time of the Reductions, with a vine motif up its spiralling columns. It has been carefully repainted, and looks new. The main doors to the cathedral were carved by a local carpenter on the theme of the Lamb of God. Behind the altar to one side is a striking stained glass window of the baptism of Christ, running from floor to ceiling. The statue of St John the Baptist, which is carried in procession through the streets on the night of 24 June, is a charming old piece, with the Lamb of God at the feet of the saint.

To the right of the altar is the **tomb of Monseñor Bogarín**, with an enormous painting behind it, portraying the history of this diocese, founded in 1957.

MANGORÉ

Agustín Pío Barrios, Paraguay's great and legendary guitarist and composer, known as Mangoré, was born on 5 May 1885 in San Juan (or, according to other sources, in the neighbouring town of Villa Florida). He studied and travelled extensively with his music, visiting Belgium and Germany as well as almost every country in Latin America. He died of a heart attack in 1944 in San Salvador, where he had been directing a guitar school for the last five years of his life.

He was enormously esteemed by his pupils and disciples, and the English-Australian classical guitarist John Williams said that 'as a guitarist/composer, Barrios is the best of the lot, regardless of ear. His music is better formed, it's more poetic, it's more everything! And it's more of all those things in a timeless way.' In his work can be detected baroque influence (especially from Bach), romantic influence (especially from Chopin) and influence from Hispanic-American music (particularly Paraguayan folksong and indigenous music).

He took the professional name Nitsuga Mangoré, which is a combination of his first name spelt backwards with the name of a *cacique* of colonial times. Sometimes he wore indigenous dress to play in concerts. The photos of him, taken in many countries of the world, show a long face with thick lips and a solemn expression. He sported a moustache until the 1930s. He was a manic depressive, alternating depressed moments when he could not work with periods of hyper-intensive creativity. He wrote a sonnet 'Bohemia' in 1925, in which he said of himself:

Yo soy hermano en glorias y dolores
De aquellos medievales trovadores
Que sufrieron romántica locura!

'I am the brother in glories and sorrows
Of those medieval troubadours
Who suffered romantic madness!'

His house in San Juan, the Casona Mangoré, has been turned into a museum. One of the rooms in the Cabildo of Asunción is also dedicated to Mangoré, and his face appears on the Gs50,000 note.

Misiones and the Jesuit Reductions SAN JUAN BAUTISTA

5

Monseñor Ramón Bogarín (with the glasses) is talking to his uncle, Juan Sinforiano Bogarín, the Archbishop of Asunción, who holds the bridle of a horse. Next to him is St Luigi Orione, the Italian founder of the Sons of Divine Providence order, who prophesied to Ramón Bogarín that he would die a martyr. In the foreground, holding the hand of a child and smiling, is the bespectacled figure of P Carlos Villalba, who was to become the second bishop of the diocese. (Monseñor Medina is the third bishop.) On the left is a group of barefoot children,

LAYOUT OF A REDUCTION

The Jesuit-Guaraní Reductions (and to a lesser extent the Franciscan Reductions) were centred around a square – the plaza – which at times was very large indeed (such as in Trinidad). On three sides of the plaza were *casas de indios*, which were rows of single-storey buildings with a colonnade all around or at least on the two long sides. Each building would comprise eight or ten square rooms, with doors opening to front and back, and each room would be the home for a family. The houses consequently had more doors than windows: in some places there were windows as well as doors, and in other places not. In the old Guaraní huts, the buildings would also be long like this, but with the difference that all the families would live together: the Jesuits separated the families, in order to protect fidelity in marriage. Another difference was that the houses in the Reductions used improved building skills, passing from wood and straw, to adobe and tile, to brick, and eventually in some places to stone.

On one side of the plaza was the church, which was the most special building in the *pueblo* (town), at times quite magnificently adorned. The bell tower was a separate wooden construction to one side or the other of the church (right up until the last Reductions, when it became an integrated part of a stone church as in Europe). On one side of the church there was customarily the cemetery, behind it was the orchard, and on the other side was a group of buildings sometimes collectively referred to as the *colegio*, although they would include not only the school but also the priests' residence, rooms for guests, offices and a range of workshops. This *colegio* would be arranged around a couple of patios, with the Jesuits' house adjoining the church.

The most able boys studied in the school – mostly, but not exclusively, the sons of the *caciques*, and, inevitably for the era, boys only. They were taught to read and write in Latin, Guaraní and possibly Spanish: Spanish was not used within the Reductions but Latin was, in church. They also studied mathematics and music. The workshops of a Reduction could cover a wide variety of crafts: stone work and carpentry; carving – especially statues of saints – in stone and wood; painting – to decorate the church and colour the statues; weaving and making clothes; pottery, silverwork and goldwork, and ironwork – both for making wrought-iron railings and gates, and for making firearms. The Guaraní needed guns to use in self-defence against the *bandeirantes* who from the beginning attacked and burned down the Reductions, capturing or killing the indigenous population. Out of more than 70 Reductions that were founded for the Guaraní, more than 40 were destroyed by these slave-traders coming from São Paulo in present-day Brazil.

Close to the two patios of the college, but without a fixed, regular spot for every Reduction, was the *kotý guasú* (Guaraní 'room big') for orphans, widows and other women who needed extra help and protection. There was often a small Loreto chapel somewhere in the Reduction, and a Calvary hill, but these did not have set locations.

right   Ciudad del Este is a new city, founded as recently as 1957 (LG) page 239

below   One of the most attractive Paraguayan towns and sometimes known as the 'Pearl of the North', Concepción is quiet, picturesque and historic (RW/SAP) page 276

bottom   The Radio Guairá building in Villarrica is one of many buildings of architectural interest in the city (AS) page 257

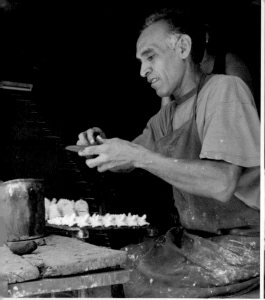

above left   Craftsman at work in Itá — the town claims to be the capital of pottery (CG) page 142

above right   A *campesino* drinking *tereré* — a national favourite, made like a tea infused in iced water (TM/SAP) page 52

left   Making *chipa* in a traditional oven — *chipa* is eaten instead of bread in Paraguay (EH) page 51

below   A typical traffic jam in the *campo* (EH)

right   Fibre weaving crafts are special to Limpio, Tobatí and the Maká indigenous (LG)

below left   Maká Indian chief — a visit to the Maká village outside Asunción is easy to arrange (CM) page 99

below right   Boy in the *campo* (JMBC)

bottom   Fisherman on the Río Paraguay (TM/SAP) page 282

top There is something almost Cistercian about the isolation and austerity of the Ruins of Jesús (SS) page 200

above Franciscan *casa de indios*, Caazapá — the houses for the indigenous, like the churches, had porticos running the length of the building (MH) page 266

left The famous carved pulpit at Trinidad (MH) page 197

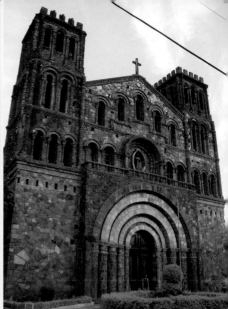

above left The figure of Mary meeting her Risen Son, carved for the procession known as Tupãsý Ñuvaitĩ, displayed at the Museo Diocesano de Artes Jesuíticas, Santa María de Fe (JMBC) page 174

above right The Ybaroty Franciscan church in Villarrica is a splendid church of Romanesque design (AS) page 261

right Yaguarón is the only original church from the Reductions to survive in its complete form, including the wooden bell tower (MH) page 144

below The imposing church in San Estanislao is built in the traditional style (AS) page 272

above left **Black howler monkey — when they howl, they make a loud repeated noise somewhere between a croak and a snore** (JL) page 5

above right **The jaguar is the biggest feline in all America** (JL) page 5

left **The South American coati lives in low thorn and humid forests** (JL) page 5

below **The caiman is known locally by its Guaraní name, *yacaré*** (JL) page 6

right The Chilean flamingo can be observed in the Chaco without too much difficulty (JL) page 6

below left Glittering-bellied emerald hummingbird — hummingbirds are often seen in Paraguay, sucking the nectar wherever there are flowers (JL) page 7

below right The toco toucan is one of the most famous and most colourful birds in Paraguay (JL) page 6

bottom Greater rheas are large, flightless, silent birds (JL) page 6

with a parrot, puppy, football, statue of the Virgin of Caacupé, folk-dance costume, and first communion dress.

Next to the cathedral is the theatre 'Monseñor Rojas', now practically unused, and on the next corner from that is the *municipalidad*. Opposite the *municipalidad* is the *gobernación* and next to it is the post office. Behind the theatre is a craft shop, and next to it, on the corner directly behind the cathedral, is the Centro Cultural **Casona de Mangoré** [160 B3] (*Coronel Alfredo Ramos y Primer Intendente;* ↘ *081 212400;* m *0995 353070;* e *ogamangore@yahoo.es;* ⊕ *08.00–13.00 & at other times on request; free, donations welcome*). This former house of Mangoré, where he lived with his parents for 14 years, has been converted into a little museum and cultural centre by the artist Gil Alegre and his wife Sebastiana Galeano, who live in part of the house and run painting workshops. Knock on the door to visit, if it is not already open. As well as mementoes of Mangoré's life and work, there is the soutane once worn by Monseñor Bogarín. The entire block with this house and the cathedral has been officially declared 'of national interest' and there are plans to renovate it, and to replace the under-used theatre with a conference hall seating 300 people.

A short distance south of the second plaza, there is a small art gallery called El Viejo Taller [160 C3] (*Dr Martín M Llano, e/ Fulvio Alamanni y Coronel Alfredo Ramos*). A bit further south is the Abraham-cué prison, infamous for having kept *campesino* members of the Christian Agrarian Leagues locked up and tortured during the Stroessner dictatorship, particularly in the year 1976 when the leagues were wiped out by the oppression.

Continuing on Ruta 1 beyond the town of San Juan, you pass the **Yerba Kurupí factory** [160 G2] (*km197;* ↘ *081 212418*) on the right, and about 10km out of San Juan, by a bus shelter, there is a turn to the left down a dirt road which is not signed but eventually comes out at Santa María de Fe.

SAN IGNACIO GUASÚ Copaco ↘ 0782 232299; municipalidad ↘ 0782 232218

San Ignacio Guasú (Guaraní 'big'; Spanish 'Saint Ignatius') is the pivotal point for the visit to the Reductions, being the largest urban centre and located right on Ruta 1. It is not only of great historical importance for being the first of the Jesuit-Guaraní Reductions, it is also an important town to visit, both for its museum and for the general cultural level of the town. (There are different spellings in use: Guasu is the correct Guaraní spelling; Guazú is the hispanicised form; but the practice of this book – see page 226 – is to use the form Guasú, though in *Chapter 8* the Argentinian practice is followed in the spelling 'Puerto Iguazú'.)

San Ignacio has some charm as a town, though it is marred by being directly on the main road Ruta 1, which runs right through the middle. Attempts have been made to reduce the traffic by making it one-way, but the side effect of this is to make the traffic go faster. As yet in Paraguay, however, there is not much traffic anyway, not even on an international highway like Ruta 1.

In 2009 San Ignacio celebrated the 400th anniversary of its foundation. Right at the end of 1609, the two Jesuit founders, Marcial de Lorenzana and Francisco de San Martín, celebrated their first mass, in the presence of the *cacique* Arapysandú, who had invited them to evangelise the area. But the Reduction was principally identified with San Roque González de Santa Cruz, who arrived the following year and forged its identity. He set a model for all subsequent Reductions, through his town planning and immense energy and organisation. (See box on San Roque González, page 96). Like most Reductions, San Ignacio moved from its original site, but in this case the move was within the same region,

5

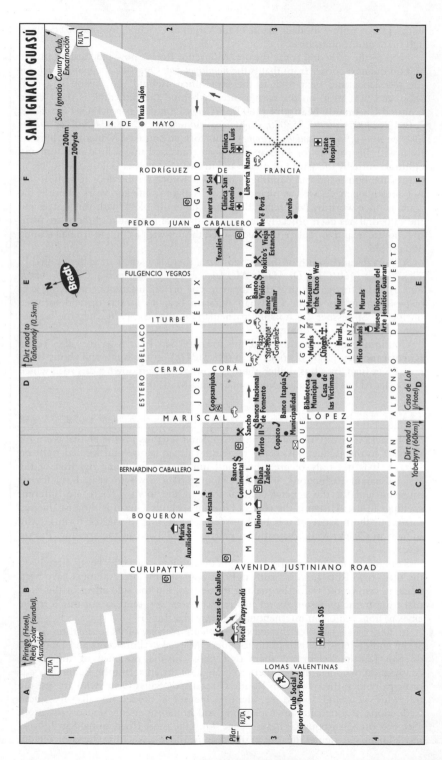

and it had settled in its final location by 1667 (when, we are told, the original church was consecrated).

After the Expulsion of 1768 the Jesuits returned to Paraguay in 1927, and to San Ignacio in 1933, so once again San Ignacio (like Santa María de Fe, and up until a few years ago Santa Rosa) is in Jesuit hands. The Jesuit residence is on the original site of the *colegio*, and so is the museum, which must be the most magnificent standing 17th-century building in Paraguay. It now houses a collection of Jesuit-Guaraní art second only to that in Santa María de Fe. There are also a number of other interesting museums and murals in the town (mostly around the old plaza), a couple of good craft shops and monuments on the outskirts of town.

WHERE TO STAY With the exception of the Country Club, none of these have internet yet for guests. There are a lot of hotels in San Ignacio but the best ones are on the edge of town and only suitable for those with cars. If you have a car, you could also consider going a little further to stay in Santa María (see page 173).

San Ignacio Country Club (6 rooms, including 1 dormitory) Ruta 1 km 230; 0782 232895; m 0975 606631; e gusjhave@hotmail.com; www.sanignaciocountryclub.com. 4km out of town on the road towards Encarnación, exactly opposite the turn to Santa María de Fe. Run by as warm & genial a host as you could find anywhere, Chilean Gustavo Jhave, this establishment provides plenty of entertainment, with horses, swimming pool, sauna, parillas, sports fields, etc. You can also bring your own food & drink & spend the day there for a modest fee, as well as staying the night. Wi-Fi. $$

Casa de Loli (c15 rooms) Mariscal López 1595; 0782 232362; e lacasadeloli@yahoo.com; www.lacasadeloli.com.py. The best hotel in town, but inconveniently placed on the furthest southern edge of town, & hidden behind a wall. Big garden, pool. $$

Hotel Piringo (10 rooms) Ruta 1 c/ Alider Vera Guillen; 0782 232913. See below under 'Practicalities'. 2nd in quality after Loli, but on the far northern outskirts of town, so neither of these are suitable if you do not have a car. It is worth visiting to see the high-quality art works on sale by local sculptors. Restaurant ⊕ all hours. Used as a stopping place by a number of long-distance bus

companies: Rysa, Nuestra Señora de la Asunción, Yacyretá & Río Paraná. (The Hotel Piringo was the old name of the Hotel Arapysandú, but these are now 2 separate hotels. Both are at the north end of town & both act as stopping places for long-distance buses, so if you go to catch a bus at Piringo, you need to be sure you are going to the right Piringo – the new one or the old one.) $$

Hotel Arapysandú Ruta 1 y Ruta 4; 0782 232213. Strategically placed in the triangular island at the junction of the road to Encarnación & the road to Pilar, & behind a service station. Taxi rank behind it, & in front is the 'horses' heads' monument (see below). Restaurant ⊕ all hours. Ciudad de Pilar bus-stop outside. $

Hotel Yexalén [166 B3] (12 rooms) Av Pedro Juan Caballero c/ José Félix Bogado; 0782 232600. Opened on this site in 2007, all new & modern, with b/fast room but no restaurant. Calls itself 5-star, but is more like good-quality 2-star. $

Hotel María Auxiliadora [166 E2] (9 rooms) Boquerón c/ José Félix Bogado; 0782 232152. A wooden plank bridge leads to this excellent shoestring option, sparsely furnished but modern & along a colonnade. Some rooms have fans, others TV & AC. Very cheap. B/fast Gs4,000 extra. $

WHERE TO EAT In addition to the hotels above:

Kandire Ruta 1 km222, Tañarandý; m 0985 181356. Outstandingly good establishment in both design & cuisine, but unfortunately closed at the time of going to press, except for the selling of craft. Expected to open again in the near future. It is on the 2nd left-hand corner in the *compañía* of

Tañarandý, 2km north of San Ignacio, reached via the road Cerro Corá that runs along the west side of the principal plaza. See *Tañarandý*, page 171. $$$

Vieja Estancia [166 E3] Mariscal Estigarribia y Pedro Juan Caballero; 0782 232297

(reservations)/0782 232366 (during open hours);
⊕ from 19.00 Thu–Sat. Huge tree trunk outside
carved into a bull's head. Slightly better quality of
restaurant than others in town, but very limited
opening hours. Advisable to book for Sat eve. Next
door, under the same management, is a discotheque,
⊕ from 23.00 or midnight onwards on Fri & Sat.
$$

✗ **Rokito's** [166 E3] Mariscal Estigarribia y Yegros;
↘ 0782 232305/232389; ⊕ all day. Pleasingly
designed café-restaurant on a corner, reasonably
priced meals. A bakery forms part of the same
establishment. **$**

✗ **Sancho** [166 D3] Ruta 1 c/ Mariscal López;
↘ 0782 232638; ⊕ all day. Small place
conveniently central & always abuzz with locals
grabbing lunch. Good value. **$**

OTHER PRACTICALITIES Although San Ignacio has four **cash machines**, only one
of them – that of the Banco Continental – receives all the cards that it says it does:
Visa, MasterCard, Maestro, Cirrus, etc. The machine of the Banco Nacional de
Fomento only works with Paraguayan cards, and the other two – at the
Coopsanjuba and at Visión – only work with Visa cards.

There are many **taxi** ranks but at night it can be difficult to find a taxi. The most
reliable places to look are on both sides of the Plaza San Roque González [166 D3
& E3] and behind the Hotel Arapysandú [166 B3] (where you can wait if need be
inside in the bar-restaurant, which is open all hours). Phone numbers of taxi ranks
are: 0782 232771/232715/232320/232812/232953.

WHAT TO SEE The square on Ruta 1 is the **Plaza San Roque González de
Santa Cruz** [166 D3]. In the centre is a stage, where a free open-air concert of
dance and folk music – Serenata Folclórica – is held every Sunday evening
(excluding January, and mid-June to mid-August). Next to it is a large, if
undistinguished, statue of San Roque González, portrayed as is customary with an
arrow through his heart. (See box on San Roque González, page 96.)

One block behind this square is the original plaza of the Reduction, with the
church [166 D4] in the middle of the green. This plaza does not have a name but
can be referred to as the old plaza. Built in the years 1928–33 the church is neither
original nor in the original position (which in a Reduction was always on one side
of the plaza and not in the middle of it), but it is nonetheless a splendid building
with both charm and dignity. Painted white, it has a high bell tower and
balustrades, and two big palm trees flanking the doorway. Inside, the reredos has St
Ignatius, St Francis Xavier and St Luis Gonzaga. There are three representations of
San Roque González: there is a statue of him (holding his painting of the Virgin)
in a side chapel; a painting by Nino Sotelo of the saint walking with the *cacique*
Arapysandú, and another painting of the martyrdom.

Six bas-relief **murals** [166 E3 & E4] in painted cement are found beside the
church and at the corner, created during the Third Meeting of Muralismo
Latinoamericano in August 1999, using Guaraní traditional mythology to portray
Christian-related themes. While the murals are the work of different artists from
different countries, they have adopted a uniform style and technique and the same
muted red, yellow and grey colour scheme. They are interesting pieces, but need
some interpretation.

Going from north to south, the first is called *Porã ypý rekávo* (Guaraní 'In search
of the primeval beauty') and shows the hummingbird – which existed before the
creation of the world – hovering Holy Spirit-like over a mother and child, in front
of a row of palm trees and next to a half-made rush basket, which evokes the
feather headdress out of which the woman was created in Guaraní mythology. The
second is called *Sãsõ* (Guaraní 'Emancipation') and shows a naked man breaking
free of the ropes that bound him to a cross, while the menacing jaguar passes by.
The third shows a Christ-figure stretching out his arms to distribute maize and the

pipe of peace, with an indigenous decorated dish in front of him, and in his other hand an armadillo, the traditional carer of the earth. This mural does not bear a name though is known locally as *La Comunión* and is the work of three local artists: Koki Ruiz, Cecilio Thompson and Teodoro Meza (see *Tañarandý*, page 171). The fourth mural is called *Itatýpe ojehái Kurusú rapykueré* (Guaraní 'Among the stones he left the track of the cross') and shows the Good Friday procession of Tañarandý (again, see below) with its crucified figure, the crowd with lanterns, and a carpet of *apepú candiles* (candles of animal fat in bitter orange skins). The fifth is called *Yvý marane'ỹ* (Guaraní 'The land without stain') and is a strong portrayal of an indigenous man attacking a conquistador, while a fierce bat – the guardian of the sacred precincts – joins in driving the evil from the land. The last, slightly smaller mural is called *Yvytú pepó ári* (Guaraní 'On the wings of the wind') and portrays the theme of protection through three symbols: the watchful hummingbird, a large hand, and a caring mother.

Two more recent painted murals by the Chilean artist Luis Marcos Enrique, known as Mico, are found on the walls of the Jesuit residence. These very colourful works of a popular, almost comic-book style, were painted in early 2009, during a week's youth mission, with the help of the young people. In the mural facing the plaza the conquistadors arrive, and attack the indigenous, who flee into the arms of the Jesuits. Together they build a church, and attend to the catechesis of the Jesuits: Roque González teaches with the help of his portrait of the Virgin, who in her turn approves and supports him. Around the corner is a bigger and more splendid mural, portraying the building of the church under Roque González's supervision.

A considerable section of **casas de indios** remain around the old plaza, on both the east and west side, with their traditional long colonnades. On the east side is the Casa de Cultura and the Museo de Semblanza de los Héroes (⊕ 07.00–12.00 & 13.30–16.00 Mon–Fri, 07.30–11.30 Sat; free). This is basically a **Museum of the Chaco War** [166 E3], with a few items from the earlier War of the Triple Alliance. The Chaco War took place from 1932–35 (see *History* in *Chapter 1*, page 13), and the museum is based on a collection donated by the local pilot Ramón Martino, who was the first aviator in South America to carry out a bombardment by night (on 22 December 1934). The names of the soldiers from San Ignacio who fought in the war and survived fill six columns on a memorial board, while the names of those who died in this tragic war fill more than three columns (ie: more than a third died). In front of the museum is a monument newly erected in 2009 to the local soldiers who fought in the war, carved in red stone by the local artist Gerardo Farias and colleagues.

Directly facing the church is an original *casa de indios* used as a private house, which, like the Casa de Cultura opposite, retains its wooden pillars. (In most original houses, when the wood has rotted it has been replaced with masonry pillars.) Next to it is the parish office, the San Luis parish centre, and then the **Casa de las Victimas** [166 D3] (✆ 0782 233000; ⊕ 07.00–11.00 & 13.00–16.00 Mon–Fri; free), which is an archive and documentation centre on the victims of Stroessner's repression: many of these were from San Ignacio, Santa Rosa and Santa María, where the Ligas Agrarias Cristianas (Christian Agrarian Leagues) had begun. The centre is generally attended by victims, who are most hospitable to guests, and some of them formed part of the Truth and Justice Commission that worked in the years 2004–08 to document the human rights' abuses of the 1954–89 dictatorship. After that in the row of houses comes the **Biblioteca Municipal** [166 D3] (⊕ 07.00–12.00 Mon–Sat; 13.00–17.00 Mon–Fri) which has a permanent exhibition of photos of the Jesuit Reductions taken by P José María Blanch SJ.

The **Museo Diocesano del Arte Jesuítico Guaraní** [166 E4] (*Iturbe 870, c/ Alfonso del Puerto;* ✆ *0782 232223;* ⊕ *14.00–17.30 daily, also 08.00–11.30 Sun & hols; Gs10,000*) is open only in the afternoons (at present), but access during the morning can often be obtained by applying to the parish office opposite the church or by telephoning in advance. From the street you can read the names of 26 Jesuit martyrs of the period of the Reductions, on a stone set high in the wall, and beginning with Roque González de Santa Cruz, followed by his two companions who were canonised along with him by Pope John Paul II on his visit to Paraguay in 1988. Alonso Rodríguez was killed as he rushed out to see what was going on as Roque González was felled with a stone axe; Juan del Castillo was killed two days later in a nearby locality as part of the same attack masterminded by Ñesú.

The museum is housed in a beautifully proportioned long building that was originally the residence of the Jesuits in the Reduction. If you go to the end of the colonnade, you can find some exposed adobe blocks which show the internal construction of the walls, almost 1m thick. On one side of the museum is the current Jesuit residence, around the other side is an old sundial, and beyond that the Jesuit retreat house, arranged around a couple of patios. Within the garden is a small area of the original floor of the church, which used to stretch down from that point to the plaza, but which was regrettably demolished in the 1920s because it was in poor repair. Destruction was cheaper than restoration. Photographs in the museum record how the church was, inside and out, immediately before it was knocked down.

The carved wooden sculptures from the Reduction underwent a restoration at the time the museum was opened, in the 1970s, under the Chilean Tito González. A second restoration a few years ago, under the direction of the Italian Donatella Salono Lippens, proved controversial. The statues in San Ignacio consequently have (for good or ill) a lucidity of colour that contrasts with the muddier tones of the old paint in a museum like that of Santa María.

Among the notable works in the first room is a huge and striking composition of Tobias and the Angel – the Angel is huge, and towers over Tobias, who is portrayed as a little boy grasping the hand of his angelic guardian – and St Michael killing the devil. You can observe a rectangle cut out of the back of the statues: all large Jesuit statues were made this way, so that the inside could be hollowed out and the weight reduced. Some also say that it removed the sappy interior that was liable to rot. A number of angel heads are set on the wall, some with and some without the two wings that are so characteristic of angel heads in the Reductions.

The next room has statues of the passion and resurrection, including a pair of statues portraying the Risen Christ meeting his mother, who greets him with arms outstretched. These two statues were originally carried in procession on Easter Sunday morning, in the ceremony known as Tupãsý Ñuvaitĩ (Guaraní 'the Encounter of the Mother of God'). (There is another statue of the Risen Christ in the church of Santa María de Fe, but the best is in the museum of Santiago. The Santa María museum also has two or three Virgins which were probably Tupãsý Ñuvaitĩ statues.) Other pieces of note are two Immaculate Conceptions (with Mary standing on the moon, see below page 175), one of which formed the centrepiece of the original reredos of the church, as can be seen in an old photograph on the wall of the museum.

The third room has a variety of saints, among them St Anna, and St Rose of Lima, and two pairs of saints from the reredos – Peter with his keys and Paul with his sword – and also the two founders of orders of friars: St Dominic holding a church, and St Francis holding a book.

Another saint from that reredos is the patron of the Reduction, St Ignatius. This statue is the triumphant central piece of the last room, with three other Jesuit saints from the reredos – St Francis Borja with his monstrance, St Francis Xavier with his crucifix and St Stanislaus Kostka with the infant Jesus. The missing piece from the reredos is San Luis (or Aloysius) Gonzaga, which went on loan to the little chapel in the *compañía* of San Luis, and has never returned.

Do not miss the little chapel, which you must enter from the side walkway. Its reredos originally belonged to one of the side altars in the old church, and its central figure is the young Jesus known as the *niño alcalde* (boy mayor). This room is still in use as a chapel.

On special occasions, a dramatisation of the original reredos of the church is put on by the Grupo La Barraca de Tañarandý (↘ *0782 22775;* m *0975 619171*). Called the *Museo Viviente*, the performance uses living actors dressed up as Jesuit statues. Brief though it is, it is a beautiful show. The feast day of St Ignatius (31 July) is also always celebrated in style.

Monuments at the west end of town If you leave the town centre behind and go to the west end of town, you can visit two modern stone monuments, both based on ideas conceived by Koki Ruiz (see below). The six **horses' heads** [166 B2] (and two horses' flanks) set on pillars outside the Hotel Arapysandú were carved by Mario Mereles, and commemorate the departure of cavalry from San Ignacio on 31 July 1932 (the feast of St Ignatius) to fight in the Chaco War.

Further out of town you come to a small hill on the south side of Ruta 1, where some stone sculptures have been set into the grass, including two tall stone slabs forming a sort of gateway. This is the **Reloj Solar** (sundial), and the idea of the piece is to compare and contrast the life of the Guaraní outside and inside the Jesuit Reductions. The sculpture is now in poor condition and some parts of it have been lost, but on one side the sundial represents the ordered daily programme that the Jesuits introduced, and on the other the leaves of *yerba mate* symbolise the unstructured life of the Guaraní in the forest.

Tañarandý Tañarandý is a *compañía* immediately to the north of San Ignacio which has gained a reputation for artistic works. The *compañía* is a charming place and should be visited if you can possibly spare the time. You can get a taxi from San Ignacio, or walk: the furthest point of Tañarandý, the chapel, is only 3km from San Ignacio. You will want to see the painted house names along the road, the craft shop Kandiré, and to go inside the chapel.

Each house along the principal dirt road, Calle Amorcito, has a colourfully painted sign outside with a picture showing the work of the owner. Most of the occupations are rural – keeping poultry, hoeing the ground and driving an ox plough – but there is also a builder, a grocer and a lorry driver. They were painted in primitive style around 2005 by a local artist Cecilio Thompson, who was tragically killed shortly afterwards when he was knocked off his bicycle. There are also carved stone owls along the road, the work of an artist called Patricio Rotela.

To get to the craft workshop of Kandire (m *0985 181356*), turn left at the second junction and it is immediately on your left. It has attractive gifts and furniture, all made out of bamboo and very professionally designed. The outstandingly good restaurant that used to be here was closed at the date of going to press, pending sale to a new owner. It is worth walking around the compound, and seeing the stone, carved Virgin and the big thatched *quincho* (roofed area), made out of bamboo.

To get to the chapel of Tañarandý keep straight on along the main access road until you reach it on the right, after the third stone owl on a pillar. Inside, it has been converted from a basically simple building into a flight of art and imagination, with painted pillars, mouldings, panels and angels, covering every inch of the walls and ceiling. The paintings were done in 2007 and 2008 by Teodoro Meza, Macarena Ruiz and Koki Ruiz. Particularly good is a *trompe l'œil* door that makes the church seem bigger than it is, and a striking deposition from the cross, painted by Koki Ruiz behind the altar. The keyholder, Seferino Corvalán, lives exactly opposite the church and will show you round if you clap your hands outside his door (the usual way of attracting attention when there is not a bell, though you can knock on the door if you prefer). Do not forget a small tip.

At dusk every Good Friday evening there is a torchlit procession of a statue of the Virgen Dolorosa (Sorrowful Virgin) accompanied by Guaraní chant. The event is free, and attracts thousands of visitors from all over the country. At the end there is customarily the deposition from the cross of a bust of Christ crucified, followed by the illumination of 'living pictures' (*cuadros vivientes*), in which people dress up and pose in the position of famous works of classical religious art, each group delineated within a frame. It is an extraordinarily beautiful and touching event, the initiative of Koki Ruiz, who lives in La Barraca, on the edge of Tañarandý, but with massive collaboration from the local people, who place on the dirt road more than ten thousand lit *candiles* in the skins of bitter oranges.

SANTA MARÍA DE FE Copaco ❭ 0781 283298; municipalidad ❭ 0781 283214

Santa María de Fe, the most northerly of the Treinta Pueblos, is a jewel. It has the best museum of any of the Reductions, including those in Argentina and Brazil, and it still operates as a living town around its historic plaza. If you only have time for one museum and one ruin from the Reductions, try to make it Santa María de Fe for the museum, and Trinidad for the Ruins. Santa María is a good place to break the journey on the way to Trinidad from Asunción, and because it is so close to San Ignacio and to Santa Rosa, there is a good chance that you may be able to see at least two if not all three of these museums, without too much expenditure of time.

Santa María was once one of the biggest of the Reductions, and the main road through Misiones used to run from Villa Florida to Santa María. But it has been saved as a tranquil, unspoilt town, little more than a village, by the fact that Ruta 1 bypasses it, and goes through San Ignacio instead. In the publicity of the Ruta Jesuítica, Santa María features as the Reduction marked by 'spirituality and calm', and visitors often speak of its special atmosphere.

Santa María de Fe was one of two Reductions (with Santiago) founded in the 1630s by the French Jesuit Jacques Ransonnier in the Itatines region to the north (in present-day Brazil). In 1647 Fr Noel Berthot consolidated the settlement after it had been dispersed by attacks from Portuguese *bandeirantes*, and in 1669 it moved again, south to its present position among the 30 Pueblos.

GETTING THERE By **car**, the journey from Asunción takes 3½ hours, and you take the signed turning to the left, 4km after San Ignacio. After 11km you arrive in the town. By **bus**, there is one direct bus each day, the Mariscal López, which leaves the Terminal in Asunción at 11.45 and arrives in Santa María about 16.30; it will drop you right at the door of the hotel or wherever else you want to go to. Or you can take one of the many buses (about two an hour) that go to San Ignacio on their way to Encarnación or to Pilar (see bus timetable at the start of this chapter), and then take a taxi, either from the Hotel Arapysandú or from the plaza: it will cost Gs30,000 and take 15 minutes.

 WHERE TO STAY AND EAT An hour may be enough to order a meal (while you visit the museum). There are also a number of bars where you can pick up an instant bite, if you only want something as simple as an *empanada*. The Santa María is the only hotel but it can arrange cheaper accommodation in home stays.

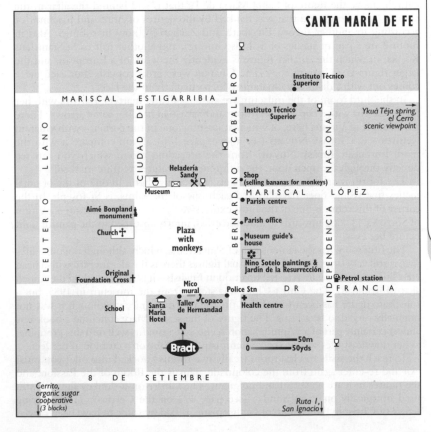 **Santa María Hotel** (3 rooms) ◊ 0781 283311; **m** 0981 861553; **e** info@santamariahotel.org; www.santamariahotel.org. On the historic plaza, a discreet little building with a carved stone sign, exactly facing the museum. Each room is adorned with a carved stone in the wall – copies from original stones in the Jesuit Ruins. Craftwork everywhere: in the leather-thonged furniture, pottery dishes, *ao po'í* tablecloths & embroidered curtains. Specialist library on the Reductions, making the hotel something of a research centre. Rustic, thatched chapel. Receptionists & guides from local families speak English. Harp & guitar music, & folk dance displays can be organised. Tours can be arranged, even to the Reductions in Argentina & Brazil; guided service in English from airport to airport. Begun in 2006 to bring work to a town with massive unemployment, the hotel specialises in introducing guests to the local people & projects. Wi-Fi. More rooms planned. Meals with a little notice. Use mobile number for 24-hour service as hotel is closed when there are no guests: you can ring from Copaco on the plaza. $$$

✘ **Heladería Sandy** ◊ 0781 283222. Bar on the same side of the plaza as the museum. Very cheap meals with a little notice. $

OTHER PRACTICALITIES There is no bank or cash machine in town (but the Banco Continental in San Ignacio accepts all cards). There is no taxi rank, but the Santa María Hotel can organise taxis.

SANTA MARÍA DE FE

MARISCAL   ESTIGARRIBIA

LLANO

CIUDAD DE HAYES

CABALLERO

NACIONAL

Instituto Técnico Superior

Instituto Técnico Superior

Ykuá Téja spring, el Cerro scenic viewpoint

Heladería Sandy

Museum

Shop (selling bananas for monkeys)

MARISCAL   LÓPEZ

BERNARDINO

Parish centre

Parish office

Museum guide's house

Nino Sotelo paintings & Jardín de la Resurrección

ELEUTERIO

Aimé Bonpland monument

Church ✝

Plaza with monkeys

Original Foundation Cross ✝

INDEPENDENCIA

Petrol station

FRANCIA

DR

School

Santa María Hotel

Taller de Hermandad

Copaco

Mico mural

Police Stn

Health centre

N

Bradt

0 ——— 50m
0 ——— 50yds

8   DE   SETIEMBRE

Cerrito, organic sugar cooperative (3 blocks)

Ruta 1, San Ignacio

5

WHAT TO SEE The most important site of Santa María is the museum. The **Museo Diocesano de Artes Jesuíticas** (*facing the Plaza; entrance Gs5,000*) is not kept open, but the guides are on constant standby to open it whenever visitors arrive (up till 17.00 when the alarm comes on). Call at the house of the guides, Isabelino Martínez and Irma Ramírez (✆ *0781 283332*), who live on the side of the plaza facing the church (see map). The museum houses 54 extraordinarily fine statues, carved out of cedar by the Guaraní in the Reduction, or by their European Jesuit teachers. The most outstanding of these was Brassanelli (see box on page 147) and the museum has a number of his works: he really changed the whole direction of Reductions art, from simple, static, face-on figures, carved out of a single tree trunk, into flowing, twisting baroque figures of great expressiveness.

The building itself is important, as it is the only original building that has retained its design. (Other original buildings along the same side of the plaza have lost their colonnade, or had the style of it changed, and are now unrecognisable as *casas de indios*; the other buildings around the plaza that look like *casas de indios* are in fact recent replicas.) The only modification to the museum has been to make connecting doors between the rooms.

The first room of the museum has some vestiges of the old church, including the wrought iron crosses that were originally on top of the church and on top of the old wooden bell tower.

The second room is devoted to Jesuit saints. The three large statues of St Ignatius, St Francis Xavier and St Francis Borgia were in the original reredos of the church, above the figure of Santa María de Fe that is still behind the altar in the church (see below), and that was flanked by the figures of Anna and Joachim (or according to another theory, Elizabeth and Zacharias), now in room 5. Also in room 2 are a pair of statues of St Luis Gonzaga, and another pair of St Stanislaus Kostka, in which the smaller figure is evidently the work of a European, and the larger figure is a Guaraní copy. The Guaraní were great copyists, but each piece comes out with a distinctly Guaraní style, particularly in the face.

In the third room of the museum are statues of early martyrs: Barbara with her tower, Cecilia with a cup of martyrdom and Sebastian holding some arrows. There are a couple of Virgins here, of which at least the one in the corner – with Guaraní features – is a Tupãsý Ñuvaitī (see above, page 170): if you compare it with the more European Tupãsý Ñuvaitī from the preceding room, which you can see directly through the open door, the difference of features is quite marked.

The fourth room has two St Michaels, and facing them, in one of the original niches that would once have housed each one of the saints, is St Joseph. In the corner of this room is one of the most expressive figures in the museum – a Virgin of Sorrows, looking upwards toward the cross, utterly absorbed in the painful sight before her eyes.

The fifth room has the famous crib of Santa María, which, although not quite life-size, is still very large. As well as the usual figures there is the elegant bird with a head crest known as the *perdiz* (crested tinamou in English – it is also carved on the ruined altar of Trinidad). The Christ Child was stolen from the museum in 1983, but a substitute figure has been found that fits the role quite nicely, although it was not originally carved to be a Jesus. The figure of the seated Mary clutching a book was almost certainly part of an Annunciation scene, but again fits well into this grouping, as her downcast eyes seem to be contemplating the baby on a cushion at her feet.

To reach the sixth and last room (really two rooms knocked into one) you must exit and re-enter again from the colonnade. This is the Room of the Passion, and the figures in it are powerful and poignant. The Christ-on-a-donkey figure is still used liturgically on Palm Sunday (see page 177 on the Cerrito). The towering figure of Christ in the Garden of Gethsemane, is said by some to have been carved by Anton Sepp, a Jesuit from the Tirol who lived in Santa María in the 1690s, during the plague that killed off 20 or 30 indigenous each day. Sepp was a prolific writer and a brilliant musician – the 'Father of the Paraguayan harp' – and was probably the best-known Jesuit of the generation following Montoya and Roque González. There is a figure of St Peter weeping as he hears the cock crow, an unusual and moving subject, and three figures of Christ at the pillar. The middle, slightly smaller piece is an extraordinarily moving and very Guaraní portrayal of Christ, with silent hurt eyes and a triangular scar on his cheek (see middle photo on title page). All in all, entering this room is a mystical experience.

Apart from the museum itself, there are many points of interest around the plaza. The great **statue of Santa María de Fe**, which gives its name to the town, is behind the altar in the church, flanked by two angels, a life-size crucifix, and a Risen Christ (see page 170 above), all from the Reduction. This large and striking statue of Mary shows the Virgin as she is spoken of in Revelation 12, clothed in the sun, standing on the moon, and with a crown of 12 stars around her head. It is a thoroughly Guaraní portrayal of an olive-skinned woman with long black hair snaking down her back, contrasting with the fair skin, blue eyes and light-brown hair of the much more famous Caacupé Madonna (even though that too was carved by an Indian, see box on page 119). The patronal feast day of Santa María de Fe is 8 September, the Birth of the Virgin (whereas that of Caacupé is 8 December, the Immaculate Conception).

The **church** itself was built in 1954 and is smaller than the double-roofed original (which fell down in 1910, according to the accounts of the local people) but it is in the original spot and is traditional in style, with a pitched roof supported on tree-trunk pillars. For access to the church ask at the parish office, in the colonnade on the opposite side of the plaza (\ 0781 283360; ⊕ 08.00–11.00 Mon–Fri). Another opportunity to get inside the church is during services. There is a community of monks, the **Comunidad San José** (\ 0781 283359), who usually sing lauds in the church daily (06.00 Mon–Fri, 06.30 Sat, Sun) and vespers on Saturdays (winter 18.00, summer 18.30 Sat) and before Sunday mass which is at 18.00 in winter and 19.00 in summer.

Outside the church is a small **monument to Aimé Bonpland** (see box on page 176), a world-famous 19th-century French botanist, who lived for ten years in Santa María de Fe.

On the next corner from the Bonpland monument, just outside the Santa María Hotel, is an original **cross** – one of four that used to stand in the four corners of the plaza. The other corners now have replica crosses, planted during youth events in 2009. On a wall next to the Copaco public telephones is a brightly coloured **mural by Mico** of Fr Noel Berthot and a group of Guaraní gathered around their statue of the Virgin. The mural was painted during a youth mission, and the artist is a Chilean whose full name is Luis Marcos Enrique (the same who did the murals in San Ignacio – see page 169). All that side of the plaza had adobe casas de indios still standing until 1943, when a cyclone knocked them down. Among the trees of the plaza lives a family of **howler monkeys**, who provide a popular tourist attraction; you can buy bananas to feed them from a greengrocer at the corner of the plaza, next to the Librería Judith. Once you have found one of them you should be able to locate another six or eight in the next tree or two – brown mothers and babies, and big black males.

Santa María has its own particular craft in the form of embroidered appliqué. The **Taller de Hermandad** (m 0985 277728; e info@santamariadefe.com; www.santamariadefe.com; ⊕ 07.00–11.00 & 13.00–16.00) is sited on the plaza between the Santa María Hotel and Copaco, in a reproduction casa de indios. The workshop is run as a co-operative of around 30 women, who work in two shifts, but the afternoon group is bigger. They always welcome visits and have a selection of craft to sell: keyrings, purses, shopping bags, T-shirts, wall hangings, etc. This is the only place in Paraguay where this colourful and intricate craftwork is done, though similar work is found in a number of other Latin American countries. Orders can be made from abroad through their website.

Another reproduction *casa de indios*, built in 2007 with substantial wooden pillars supporting a colonnade, is on the next side of the plaza (opposite the church). Though this is a private dwelling (the house of the author of this book), access can usually be arranged to see the large **paintings inside by Nino Sotelo** of the Jesuit history of Santa María de Fe: consult the Santa María Hotel or the museum guide about access. The same artist painted the history of the Virgin of Caacupé (see *Chapter 4*, page 120). Behind the house is the **Jardín de la Resurrección** (Garden of the Resurrection) where a life-size empty tomb of Christ forms the backdrop for a five-minute early-morning display of **Agua y Música**, with little irrigation fountains playing in the rays of the sun: this is made available on a regular basis to guests of the Santa Maria Hotel and sometimes on other occasions too, by arrangement.

The town has a number of interesting community projects. The **Instituto Técnico Superior,** supported by the UK charity, the Santa Maria Education Fund, offers free tertiary-level education, and English courses to a high level: the hotel receptionists have trained here.

The **organic sugar project, Tupã Mba'e** (Guaraní 'God's thing' – a term from the old Reductions), is run as a co-operative, on the west side of the town, near the Poli Deportivo: the Santa María Hotel can organise an accompanied visit.

AIMÉ BONPLAND

Aimé (in Spanish, Amado) Bonpland (1773–1858) qualified first as a medical doctor, but his passion was botany, and he travelled all over South America with his German friend, Alexander von Humboldt, producing drawings of plants and insects. He created a herbarium representing some 6,000 species, half of which he was classifying for the first time. There is a Museo de Ciencias Naturales Dr Amado Bonpland in Corrientes, Argentina.

After his initial long travels with von Humboldt (1799–1804) he became superintendent of the gardens of La Malmaison, home of Napoleon's wife, the Empress Josephine, but he returned in 1816 to Argentina and cultivated a *yerba mate* plantation. At a time when there were border disputes over what is now Misiones Argentina, Bonpland's alliance with Buenos Aires was seen as a threat by the then dictator of Paraguay, Dr Francia. He sent troops over the border to arrest Bonpland, and had him confined to Santa María de Fe for ten years (1821–31), where he married the daughter of the *cacique*, María Chirivé, and had two children (also called Amado and María). They lived at a place called the Cerrito (little hill) in the Taperã area on the edge of the village, where he opened a hospital and dedicated his time to healing the sick with natural medicines; he was seen by the local people as a *karaí arandú* (Guaraní 'man wise').

Eventually international pressure for his release resulted in him being thrown out of the country without his family. Instead of returning to Europe, he settled once more in the border area of Argentina, and continued cultivating *yerba mate*, until his death in 1857 in Santa Ana, Corrientes. He has descendants who still live in Santa María.

Liberation theology has been mentioned, and Paraguay has made a distinguished contribution to that pivotal shift in religious thinking which burgeoned out of Latin America from the 1960s and has continued until the present day – except that, as with everything else, Paraguay's contribution has been almost forgotten. Nonetheless, what is arguably the simplest, clearest, primer in liberation theology thinking was published in Spain in 1971: *Vivir como Hermanos* (Living as brothers and sisters) by José Luis Caravias (a Spanish Jesuit who has lived in Paraguay since the 1960s, with the exception of a period of forced exile when Stroessner's police threw him out, literally, onto the streets of Argentina without documents, money or spare clothing). The book was republished in Paraguay by CEPAG in 2003.

In the early 1960s, at the same time as Brazil was developing its Christian base communities – the crucible of liberation thinking among the poor – Paraguay was making a parallel development, known as the Christian Agrarian Leagues (Ligas Agrarias Cristianas), beginning in Santa Rosa in 1960. But whereas Brazil's communities survived political persecution to become world famous, the Paraguayan LACs were totally wiped out by the bloody repression unleashed by Stroessner in 1976, in what is known as the Pascua Dolorosa (Sorrowful Easter).

Today the history of the LACs is being recovered through appliqué wall hangings embroidered in Santa María de Fe, designed by the wife of one of the torture survivors. They record key moments in the life of the leagues: *mínga* (Guaraní 'working together'), *jopói* (Guaraní 'sharing'), *escuelitas campesinas* (Spanish 'little campesino schools'), biblical reflection, the repression, and torture. The sewing co-operative has a website where orders can be made (*www.santamariadefe.com*). The history of the leagues is told in a chapter by Margaret Hebblethwaite in *Unfinished Journey: The Church 40 Years after Vatican II*, ed. Austen Ivereigh, Continuum, 2003.

(See also the *Museo de las Memorias* in *Chapter 3*, page 86.)

Also at the west end of town is a small hill – the **Cerrito** – which was used as a Calvary in Jesuit times. The Cerrito is still today the site for the beginning of the Palm Sunday procession, with the figure of Christ-on-a-donkey, from the museum. On the opposite side of town, another old Jesuit site is **Ykuá Téja**, a spring of water that you pass on the cross-country way to Santa Rosa. It was once the source of water for the Reduction, and with a series of roofed pools, it is still a place where the poor go to do their washing.

A long way further down the same road, you come to the turning for the **Cerro** (or Hill), a good hour and a half's walk away. This is a traditional place of pilgrimage on Good Friday. It has an oratory at the top and a view.

SANTA ROSA *Copaco* ☎ 0858 285364; *municipalidad* ☎ 0858 285379

Today this town is smaller than San Ignacio, but bigger than Santa María de Fe, although historically it was founded in 1698 as an overflow Reduction from the then over-large Santa María. Its plaza has more original buildings than either of these two close neighbours, and although it has fewer statues, those it does have include a few remarkable pieces. It also is the only Jesuit-Guaraní Reduction in any country to have a surviving Loreto chapel – that originally many of the Reductions had, apart from the main church – and the only one to have surviving frescoes. It has an original bell tower, not of the customary wooden construction, but of stone, which accounts for it being still standing. And it has a couple of matching stone panels on the outside of its church.

In short, Santa Rosa is a jewel that should be visited if at all possible. It is easy to take in on the way to Santiago or San Cosme y Damián, or Encarnación, as it is almost on the main road: many buses enter the town before continuing down Ruta 1. There is also a dirt road that leads there from Santa María, which is in good condition, and makes a delightful country drive.

The town is named after the Peruvian St Rosa of Lima and the patronal feast day is 30 August.

🏠 WHERE TO STAY

🏠 **Dolly Palace Hotel** Presidente Franco 649 e/ Av Florida y 14 de mayo; ☎ 0858 285224; e dollyhotel@hotmail.com. New hotel half a block from the Plaza. $$$

🏠 **Hotel Parador Santa Rosa** Ruta 1 km256; ☎ 0858 285475. On the north side of Ruta 1 about 1km after Santa Rosa in the direction of San Patricio. Large dining room for special events. $$

🏠 **Hotel Avenida** Av Florida, esq Edda B de Ayala; ☎ 0858 285358. 3 blocks from Ruta 1. $

Inside the town there are bars but no obvious restaurants.

WHAT TO SEE One side of the plaza has a complete row of *casas de indios*, of which one in the middle (that of the hairdresser Don Benítez) has its original floor and wooden external door. All are actively used: most are shops, one is a small museum in the Casa de Cultura (🕑 *07.00–12.00 Mon–Sat*) and the end one is a police station. In the plaza itself are a couple of modern **stone fountains**, both of them the work of Máximo Rotela, an artist from San Gerónimo, which is a *compañia* of Santa María. One shows some stone toads and the other portrays a figure from Guaraní mythology, Kurupí (see *Chapter 4*, page 115).

The **bell tower** stands to the right of the church, and is 8m high, built out of red stone blocks. Four columns of stone have been preserved and set into the front exterior wall of the church, carved with a strong plant-based design. To gain access to the church, you pass through the parish secretary's office, which also sells the tickets to view the Loreto chapel. The original church was destroyed by fire in 1883, but the **reredos** to one of the side altars was saved and this now forms the centrepiece of the church. Delightfully, one of the cherubs perched on the top of the reredos is black, which must be one of the earliest instances of racial justice awareness expressed through art. The **saints** carved in the Jesuit period include St John the Baptist with his lamb, San Isidro with his hoe, and a figure believed to be Isidro's wife.

The little **Loreto chapel** can be visited in the mornings (☎ *0858 285221;* 🕑 *07.30–11.30 Mon–Sat; freewill donation, suggested minimum Gs5,000*), or sometimes at other times by arrangement. Before going inside, it is worth taking time to study this small and beautifully proportioned building, with its exquisitely carved door and window. Once inside you will see the **frescoes**: to your left, the Last Judgement; to the right, Joseph's carpentry workshop; and in front of you, the legendary transport of Mary's house from Nazareth, to Loreto, borne by angels through the skies. In terms of sculptures, the most famous pieces are Gabriel and Mary at the **Annunciation**, which are works by Brassanelli. One of the most wonderful pieces in this little room is the Pietà (or *Piedad* as they say in Spanish). This Mary is crazed with grief as she raises her head to howl to the heavens, her dead son in her arms notably smaller than her. It is interesting to compare this piece with the very different interpretation found in the museum in Santiago, where the *Piedad* is a classic of contemplative acceptance and breathes a spirit of enclosed tranquillity (see page 180). To either side of the door are two life-size crucifixes – not Jesus this time, but the two thieves: the good thief and the bad thief. They may have been used in an outdoor Calvary.

SANTIAGO *Copaco* ✆ *0782 20200/20393; municipalidad* ✆ *0782 20244*

Originally sited in Itatín, to the north, and called San Ignacio de Caaguazú, this Reduction changed its name to Santiago (St James) when it had to move south, because there were already two San Ignacios in the Treinta Pueblos, and one a near neighbour. It is the twin town to Santa María de Fe, founded at the same date (in the early 1630s), and moved at the same time, finally reaching its present site in 1669. One snatch from the historical records tells us that Santiago had hundreds of costumes for the opera, which was performed on the *fiesta patronal*.

Today Santiago is notable for three things: its museum and Jesuit remains, including a lot of *casas de indios* around the plaza; its two grand *fiestas* of riding skills and dance in January; and its Benedictine monastery.

To reach Santiago you take a turn right after San Patricio, which is the road going to Ayolas. After 16km you turn left to enter the town, where there is a notice proclaiming you are arriving in 'Santiago, capital de la tradición Misionera', and a white statue of a man in a sombrero on a horse.

🏠 WHERE TO STAY AND EAT

🏠 **Hotel Restaurant El Tauro** ▥ 0995 356960. A simple hotel but right on the plaza, on the far side from the church. Can take 25 people. Rooms have private bathrooms & fans (rather than AC). $
🏠 **Hospedaje Mercado** ✆ 0782 20211. Super-simple though this little hotel is – with no private bathrooms & fans (rather than AC) – it is an original house from the Reduction, in a row of *casas de indios*, right on the plaza, so the historic sense

compensates for any lack of comfort. 5 rooms, 2 bathrooms, & facilities for cooking your own *asado* in the garden, where there is a big, grassy lawn. The rate for tourists is cheap, but they take known regulars for even less, so this is definitely shoestring accommodation. $
✖ **Bar La Casona** ✆ 0782 20076. Hamburgers & *milanesas*, the most basic food. Occasionally they have rooms too. $

FIESTAS The **Festival Latinoamericano de la Doma y el Folklore** (*doma* refers to mastery over cattle) is usually held on the first weekend in January, though the date can vary. You can check the date each year with the Estancia Tacuatý that hosts it (✆ *0782 20286*), or Copaco, or the *municipalidad* (numbers above), or Emitur (see below). The festival goes on from 09.00 till sundown, and is held amidst the shady trees of the *estancia*, 7km south of Ruta 1, and 9km to the north of Santiago, on the east side of the main road. There are bucking broncos and cattle branding. There is a fine display of dancing, with many troupes, as well as those performing the traditional Paraguayan dances from neighbouring countries. There are musical groups, and a display of *caballerías* (horse teams) in their colourful uniforms, including groups from Argentina, Brazil and Uruguay. Craft is on sale from all over Paraguay, and there are traditional foods to buy, such as *asado a la estaca* (beef barbecued on near-vertical sticks, in front of an open fire) and the speciality of Misiones, *batiburillo*. (If you want to eat the *asado*, you need to take your own sharp knife, plates and cutlery.) There is sometimes another mini-festival on the same lines on Saturday of Holy Week.

Shortly afterwards, on a Friday, Saturday and Sunday in mid-January, is a very similar event, the **Fiesta de la Tradición Misionera**. It takes place on a site much closer to the town, in a big open-air stadium, which does not have the shade of the Estancia Tacuatý. It is longer established (more than 25 years old) and always very successful. Not much happens on the Friday, and on the Saturday the programme customarily begins in the evening with a procession of horse teams. The folk

5

dance, which is one of the biggest attractions, takes place very late on Saturday night, which – added to the shortage of good hotel accommodation nearby – makes it difficult for visitors to attend. Sunday is a full day, with branding of calves, castration of animals, bucking broncos, displays of riding skills, and a bullfight. (They do not kill the bull in Paraguay, or even wound it, but simply throw it to the ground.) For information ring the *municipalidad*.

WHAT TO SEE Santiago has a good number of original *casas de indios* with colonnades around the huge, historic plaza. There has been little renovation done in this town as yet, but potentially quite a lot could be restored. Next to the church is the **museum** (⊕ *08.00–11.00 & 14.00–17.00 Mon–Sat , 09.00–11.00 Sun; Gs5,000*), which is not in an old building, but in a purpose-built house constructed in reference to (but not in imitation of) the old *casas de indios*. (It has toilets.) The guide is at present Oscar Maidana (m 0975 762008).

Santiago is unique in having some brilliantly painted wooden panels. There is a charming portrayal of baby Jesus and baby John hugging a lamb together, while attendant angels offer them bunches of flowers. Sheep figure also in a painting of Jesus entrusting the keys to Peter, delightfully drawn without any sense of perspective. There is a Holy Family, a Virgin and Child, and plenty of angel heads with wings.

There is mixed quality and mixed size among the 50 or so statues of the museum, unlike Santiago's sister town Santa María where all the pieces are large masterpieces. Some of the pieces, including a crib (smaller and less complete than Santa María's) seem to show traces of Flemish influence, which is not surprising when you consider that these two Reductions were founded by Jesuits from the Belgian province. The Annunciation, too, and St Isidore and his wife, María de la Cabeza, also share in this slightly Flemish style: the popularity among the Jesuits of the 11th-century Spanish farmer saint is due to him having been canonised at the same time as St Ignatius and St Francis Xavier, in 1622. It is interesting, also, to see the first known statue of Roque González, not yet portrayed with his exposed heart, but barefoot and with one hand outstretched.

Among the statues are some works of quite outstanding quality. The best figure of the Risen Christ – for the Tupãsÿ Ñuvaitĩ procession (see *San Ignacio*, page 170) – is found here, and seems to be light as thistledown as the golden robe flies up in the wind, practically lifting Jesus into the air. There are a couple of poignant portrayals of the carrying of the cross, where the face of Christ merits careful attention. But perhaps the most marvellous of all is the Pietà (or *Piedad* in Spanish): this Mary is almost one with the flopped body that drapes across her knees, as both are enclosed by a cloak. It is supremely tragic, and peaceful at the same time.

Ask the guide for access to the church, where there is a large statue of Santiago el Matamoro (St James the Moor-killer). Santiago is riding on his horse over the dead bodies of Muslims he has slain with his sword. Odious as this conception is to a modern-day consciousness, it has to be seen in historical context: for the Guaraní, any saint victorious in battle represented for them their victory against the slave-traders – a struggle which in fact they won by force of arms in the 1641 Battle of Mbororé: from then on they were virtually safe from *bandeirantes* and an era of peace and prosperity came to the Reductions. For this reason we find portrayals of St Michael (who defeated the devil), St Sebastian (who was a Roman centurion), St Barbara (the patron saint of explosives, because a bolt of lightning killed her would-be executioner), and now Santiago el Matamoro.

The reredos of the church has a theme of baptism, with John baptising Jesus, Peter baptising the Ethiopian eunuch, and Francis Xavier baptising the eastern Christians. There is also an interesting statue of a person praying before a statue.

Monastery Though buried deep in the countryside, far from anywhere, the Benedictine monastery of Tupãsý María (Guaraní 'Mary the Mother of God') (\ *0782 20034 attended 08.00–12.00 & 15.00–18.00 Mon–Sat, 10.30–11.30 & 15.30–18.00 Sun;* e *tupasy@itacom.com.py; www.monasterio.org.ar*) belongs to the municipality of Santiago. To reach it, take a 12km dirt road that goes west from the road to Ayolas, 14km south of the junction with Ruta 1; it is well marked. There is another route via San Patricio, but it is not signed. The monastery was founded from Argentina in 1984, and is the only Benedictine monastery in the country.

The church has been built with the basic shape of the ancient Franciscan church of Yaguarón but in a much simpler style. There is a shop that sells the produce of the monks, beautifully packaged: candles, jams, yoghurts and delicious liqueurs. The public can attend the monastic hours: 07.00 lauds followed by mass (09.30 mass on Sunday); 12.15 sext; 18.15 vespers and 20.45 compline. They can also stay in a guesthouse to make retreats.

 Estancias near Santiago As well as Tacuatý (above) there are a few *estancias* near Santiago, some of which are linked to the Misiones-based Emitur network (*Emprendimiento Misionero de Turismo;* \ *0782 20286;* e *emitur@itacom.com.py*) rather than to Apatur. (See section on *estancias*, page 50.)

🏠 **San Juan** m 0985 764353. At 9km from the town, on the west side of the main road, this *estancia* has 3 rooms for guests. Riding & fishing. $$
🏠 **Tambo Santa Juana** Ruta I km256; m 0975 619669. Sited just 1km to the west of the junction of

Ruta I with the road that goes to Ayolas, this *estancia* has room for 5 or 6 guests. *Tambo* was the old word used for a guesthouse in the Reduction of Santiago. $

AYOLAS *Copaco* \ *072 222799; municipalidad* \ *072 222384*

Ayolas, on the Río Paraná, is associated with two things: fishing; and the Yacyretá dam, shared with Argentina (Paraguay's other huge hydro-electric money-earner, after the Itaipú dam, which is shared with Brazil). Huge numbers of Brazilians go to Ayolas to fish, filling the hotels in the high fishing season, which is September and October. Curiously, Ayolas has not yet developed as a general beach resort, though it could well do so. If you want a nice sandy beach, at the side of a river enormous enough to be a lake, and with a good variety of freshly caught fish for dinner, then you cannot do better than Ayolas. And you may even have the beach to yourself.

And of course, if you are a fishing devotee, Ayolas is perfect. A general price for going out in a *lancha* (motor boat) for the day is currently Gs200,000 (for up to three people) plus the fuel, which could be up to 50 litres on a long trip (currently at Gs5,500 per litre).

HISTORY The oldest part of Ayolas is the barrio San José-mí, where the present-day Hotel Ayolas is situated. It still has the best beach. The barrio San Antonio – which has nearly all the hotels – also preceded the arrival of the Entidad Binacional Yacyretá (EBY) – often known simply as '*la Entidad*', 'the Entity'.

Construction work on the project for the joint Paraguayan–Argentinian hydro-electric dam began in 1983, and at first involved building a colony for the workers: the Mil Viviendas (One Thousand Homes). In 1994 the first part of the dam was opened, and in 1998 it was completed. The former construction workers have either changed to other jobs, or moved – selling the keys to their houses to incomers. The houses themselves remain the property of EBY and form a very

5

pleasant suburb of bungalows. The staff now at Yacyretá live in another estate built by the EBY, called the Villa Permanente, which is closer to the administrative offices, but adjoins the Mil Viviendas.

As a producer of energy, Yacyretá is associated in every Paraguayan mind with money, and there is fierce competition for the jobs there, which are extremely well paid and until Lugo's presidency were distributed among Colorado party members as political favours. Many of those on the staff during the Colorado period were *planilleros*, which meant that they were paid a monthly salary but did not actually have to turn up to do any work.

GETTING THERE AND AROUND To reach Ayolas take Ruta 1 from Asunción and turn right after San Patricio. There are two bus companies that go to Ayolas from the bus terminal in Asunción: Yacyretá and Pilarense. The journey takes five hours. Both companies enter Santiago (see page 179), half an hour before reaching Ayolas.

Pilarense leaves Asunción at 03.30, 06.30, 14.15 and 15.30. For the return journey it leaves Ayolas at 04.45, 10.30, 14.10 and 22.30.

Yacyretá leaves Asunción at 04.45, 09.00, 11.00, 12.50, 17.45 and 20.30. For the return journey it leaves Ayolas at 04.15, 08.30, 12.00, 16.0, 17.00, and 23.15.

When you reach Ayolas you come to a crossroads with a sign indicating that the barrio San Antonio is straight ahead. That is the direction that you want, and the main road will swing right and take you through the Villa Permanente and past the Apart Hotel and the Hotel de Turismo before reaching the Mil Viviendas, through a series of broad avenues with green grass and trees. The barrio San Antonio, where the cheap hotels are, is towards the left, closer to the river, while the bus will pass the modern church and theatre and multi-use hall of Mil Viviendas, and will stop in due course at the Terminal – a surprisingly small building. There is a shopping centre opposite. From there the bus will continue on to its workshop, where it waits until its next journey to Asunción. There may or may not be a taxi waiting at the Terminal, but if there is not (or if it is grabbed by someone else) just sit and wait, as there is no other taxi rank in town.

The first three hotels in the list below can be reached by the bus; the others (all in the barrio San Antonio) require a taxi. If a taxi does not show up at the Terminal, you could try ringing Cristian Gómez (\ *072 222817;* m *0975 643970/0985 136055*). He and his father are both taxi drivers, and also have an eight-seater minibus. A taxi from the Terminal to your hotel may cost no more than Gs15,000 (at current prices). There is also a service of *mototaxis*, which have a little roofed trailer behind a motorbike, so they are quite adequate for journeys within the town. They charge less than half the cost of an ordinary taxi, but do not have a regular mototaxi rank, so you will need to order them through your hotel. One such *mototaxista* is Pablo Lofuente (m *0984 266377*).

 WHERE TO STAY The hotels with good riverside locations are the Hotel Nacional de Turismo, the Hotel Ayolas, the (much more modest) Hotel Leka and (if it reopens) the Apart Hotel. Most hotels in Ayolas do not include breakfast, so ask.

Hotel Nacional de Turismo (20 rooms)
\/f 072 222273; e hotel.tur.ayolaspy@gmail.com.
Was one of Senatur's hotels but recently went private, though the name has not changed. Immediately after Apart Hotel, as you come in on the main road. A driveway leads to a spacious complex, with rooms arranged along 3 colonnades facing onto a pleasant garden with palm trees. Not directly overlooking the river but has steps & a path leading through a field to the bank, making a pleasant walk. The whole hotel has been well designed & rooms have solid wood furniture. Pool & children's playground. Restaurant (see below). Takes credit cards. $$$

Hotel Ayolas (31 rooms) Plaza Juan de Ayolas; ☎ 072 222844; m 0981 456094; e emp_tur_ayolas@hotmail.com. Formerly known as Hotel El Dorado, this hotel is right on the river, with a very pleasant courtyard & a spectacular view. It is the last hotel you come to, down a cobbled road & located in the oldest barrio of the town, San José-mí, & closest to the best beach. If you come in on the Yacyretá bus, & carry on beyond the Terminal to the Yacyretá *taller* (workshop) where the bus is stationed until its next journey, then you will be only 200m away & can walk. If you come in on the Pilarense bus, then you will need a taxi from the Terminal (as for the other hotels, below). The rooms were in need of new furniture & fittings at the time of writing: they were definitely inferior to those in the Hotel de Turismo although they cost more, but potentially this could be an excellent hotel, for its location. Wi-Fi. $$

Hotel Kadel (c12 rooms) Barrio San Antonio; ☎ 072 222153; m 0971 137270. A large fish sign marks this hotel, on the north side of the road. B/fast room, thatched *quincho* at back. AC & cable TV, but also has budget rooms at less than half the price with just fans & shared bathroom. Some colour schemes rather jarring. $$

Hotel Leka (8 rooms) Barrio San Antonio; ☎ 072 222270; m 0985 115636/0975 628138. Some 500m down a dirt track & with a small sign that can be easily missed, but it is opposite 'Barcos y Rodados' & shortly after Hotel Kadel. Right on the riverbank, this modest little place is full of character & has a stunning location, perched on the cliff above a small beach. There is a big, open b/fast room, shared with the family, & you can sit & eat in the shade of trees by the riverside. There are a variety of dogs, of various sizes, but all quite friendly. Has cheaper rooms with fans. $

Hotel Mbusú (10 rooms) Barrio San Antonio; ☎ 072 222068. Next along from Kadel, on the north side of the road. Professionally orientated for fishers, organises fishing trips (*embarcación*), sells tackle & has live bait (eels & worms) in tanks. Volleyball pitch & big green area at back. $

Hospedaje Mi Abuela (10 rooms) Barrio San Antonio; ☎ 072 222568. Just off the main road, around the corner from Kadel. A very pleasant budget option, with rooms arranged a long colonnade in traditional style, brightly painted in orange & pink, all with AC & private bathroom. $

Hospedaje Orue (7 rooms) Barrio San Antonio; ☎ 072 222310; m 0972 480731. Opposite Hotel Mbusú. Very modest little place up a staircase but friendly & quite adequate. AC, TV, private bathroom but rooms are small. Pleasant airy balcony on 1st floor. There is a bell & you can come in at any time of night. $

Hotel San Antonio (10 rooms) Barrio San Antonio; ☎ 072 222518; m 0975 670428. Barrio San Antonio, on the south side of the road. Unbelievably cheap for an attractive, traditional-style row of rooms along a colonnade. Family-style hotel with shared TV. $

Apart Hotel This hotel is currently closed, but is included in case it reopens. It is a large complex of apt-style accommodation, on the left as the main road reaches the shore & swings round to the right. It is the 1st hotel you come to (by bus or by car), & potentially the most upmarket.

✖ **WHERE AND WHAT TO EAT** Fish is the recommended food in Ayolas, and there are many varieties which you will not find elsewhere in the country. Fish can be served grilled on the *parilla* (barbecue: this is also known as an *asado,* like barbecued meat); *a la plancha* (grilled); fried (*frito)*; as a *chupín* (covered with a sauce); as a *milanesa* (coated in batter); or in a *caldo* (soup).

Dorado Considered the best, and to appreciate its quality it should be cooked as an *asado*. One fish usually serves more than two people, and may cost around Gs100,000.

Surubí The only fish you will commonly find elsewhere, eg: in restaurants in Asunción. It provides good steaks of boneless white flesh, suitable for *milanesa* or *chupín*.

Pacú Suitable for *asado* or *chupín*.

Boga Suitable for *asado* or for frying.

Bagre Smaller fish, suitable for frying or *caldo*.

Mandi'í Very small fish, only suitable for *caldo*.

Most hotels, even the small ones, can serve good fish dishes if asked, even if they do not offer much else. Standard drinks on offer are limited in most places to beer (*cerveza*) and fizzy drinks (*gaseosa*) though in a few places you may be able to buy wine too, or order a fresh fruit juice (*jugo*).

✖ **Hotel Nacional de Turismo** See above. The restaurant is pleasant & large, but the AC is deafening. Under the new management improvements may be made. **$$**

✖ **Hotel Ayolas** See above. The restaurant is similar in quality to Hotel de Turismo, ie: limited in both food & service. **$$**

✖ **Restaurant Lizza** ✆ 072 2222756; ⊕ all hours daily. Set back from the road on the east side as you approach Ayolas, after the turn to Atinguyý (see below) & after you have gone under the 'Bienvenidos a Ayolas' gateway. Definitely the place to eat, packed with life & character, good variety of food & drink at very low prices. Long tables covered in white tablecloths & fascinating decorations: more to see here than in most small-town museums. Hanging from the ceiling & walls are hammocks, sombreros, bird nests, ostrich eggs, baskets, gourds, armadillos, guitars & snake skins. Also on show are two types of maize mill, an ancient chair made without nails but tied together with leather thongs, & an old iron with a cavity for putting cotton & alcohol, an air pump for fanning the flames & a dial to extinguish them. A framed certificate gives a Mención de Honor to the best restaurant in Ayolas. The food is good too – with huge portions, & the service excellent: they have even been known to get out a lounger for you if you need a kip. Unbelievable value. **$**

OTHER PRACTICALITIES Ayolas is not good on internet facilities, though there is a cyber café or two and the facilities are likely to improve.

There is only one bank, the Banco Nacional de Fomento, in the Villa Permanente, but there are a couple of cash machines that accept all cards, on the way into town, in a little cabin of Interbanco. When you are approaching Ayolas and have passed the Restaurant Lizza, you take a left fork, marked towards the Villa Permanante, and the glass cabin is almost at once, right on the road, next to the police control. Since there are two machines here, there is every chance that at least one will be working. A taxi driver can take you there quickly on the excellent roads.

Fishing is prohibited from 1 November to 20 December. The high season for fishing is before this, in September and October.

WHAT TO SEE AND DO The principal visit in Ayolas itself will obviously be to the dam, but outside of the town the excursion to the nearby Refugio Atinguý is highly recommended.

There are some attractive churches in Ayolas. The church in the old barrio of San José-mí is a good example of the traditional design. The church in Mil Viviendas is modern and is kept open. Triangular in shape, it is filled with light through its two walls of modern stained glass, with simple circular designs of pink, blue, green and yellow. There is a statue of St Francis Xavier (after whom the church is named). The church in the Villa Permanente is also modern and although this is the more expensive barrio, it is a less interesting church than that of Mil Viviendas.

Going to the beach is a must. One of the best beaches is the Playa Milenio, which you reach by taking the track round the side of the Restaurant Lizza. It has a good amount of sand and a small amount of shade (but sufficient, as you may find yourselves the only people there). The other good beach is in barrio José-mí, after the port, which is after the Hotel Ayolas. Further away is the beach of Corateí (see below). Swimming should be limited to close to the bank: the current in the Río Paraná is strong and dangerous.

The Yacyretá dam To visit the Yacyretá dam (✆ 072 222276/222141/8; e rrpp_ayolas@hotmail.com or milce.duarte@eby.gov.py; www.eby.gov.py; ⊕ visits at 08.00, 10.00, 14.00 daily; free) you must present an application with the name, nationality and passport number of each visitor. This is a simple operation that can be done by phone or email, or in person at least half an hour before each guided visit. Head for the circular hall known as Relaciones Públicas: it is a short distance to the right of the main road as you arrive in Ayolas, and there are signs. It is over the road from the *pisicultura* or fish-breeding centre.

Over 18,000 people visit Yacyretá each year. In Relaciones Públicas there is a small museum which can be seen before or after the visit (but not after the 14.00 visit, when it is already closed). It has archaeological objects, minerals and examples of the native fauna. The guides are knowledgeable but as yet there is no English-speaking guide. The visit begins with a film (again, it is only available in Spanish) and then continues with a bus journey over the bridge to the Isla Yacyretá and to the huge hall where 20 turbines work away under the floor – each one marked by a huge red circular area. At any one time, 19 turbines are functioning, permitting ongoing maintenance of all the machinery.

An interesting detail is a lift that has been constructed for the fish, particularly the *dorado*, which is migratory, so that they can be transported to the river above the dam. It appears, however, that the arrangements have not been adequate, and there has been a marked reduction in the numbers of *dorado,* and legal measures have been taken (largely ineffective) to restrict commercial fishing of *dorado* and give the fish population time to recover.

You then cross the long dam itself, which spans the strait from Paraguay's Isla Yacyretá to the Argentinian mainland. The dam is more recent than Itaipú (see page 248) and not quite so enormous. Itaipú depends on the vast power of a huge 120m drop of water (and anyone who has visited the Garganta del Diablo at the Iguazú Falls, see page 229, will know how dramatic that plunge is), whereas Yacyretá has a drop of only 15m (which will increase to 21m with the projected expansion of the lake). For reasons of the difference in water flow, the turbines at Yacyretá turn around a vertical axis, whereas those of Itaipú have a horizontal axis.

Despite its smaller size, Yacyretá represents a very major hydro-electric project, generating huge amounts of electricity, and therefore of money. The generating capacity is 19 thousand million kilowatt-hours (19,000kWh) per year. This is a lot less than Itaipú (75,000kWh) and less also than the Guri dam in Venezuela, but is more than the Aswan dam in Egypt. The Three Gorges dam recently completed in China has even more output than Itaipú (over 100,000kWh) though it is only 2,335m long, as opposed to Itaipú's 7,700m. Yacyretá is much shorter, at 808m.

There were environmental problems associated with forming the reservoir in the upper part of the river: the flooding involved relocation of populations, and loss of habitat for animals. There have also been complications such as reduced oxygen levels in the water (due to rotting vegetation) with an effect on fish population. It is estimated that 2,000 Paraguayan families live off fishing in this region, so the situation is of some concern.

On the other hand, the source of energy, being water, is perpetually renewable and is free, and the production process does not leave polluting residues. The original reservoir was established at 76m above sea level, but there are now serious plans to increase that to 83m. This will involve relocating more than 3,000 families, whereas the original level of 76m affected only 555 families.

The EBY supports environmental conservation programmes such as the Refugio Atinguý (see below), hoping in this way at least to offset the negative environmental impact of the reservoir-lake above the dam. They also use a good

5

part of the income for socially beneficial enterprises: health and education projects, and scholarships to university for the most able pupils from poor homes.

The name Yacyretá is Guaraní and means 'land of the moon' (*jasy* 'moon', *reta* 'land'). An alternative explanation of the name is that it means 'land of the turbulent water' (*y* 'water', *asy* 'difficult', *reta* 'land'). There may be something of both meanings. As will be pointed out in *Appendix 1 – The Guaraní language*, there is variety in Guaraní spelling and most place names follow the old spelling.

On the Isla Yacyretá is a house built by Stroessner and now used by President Lugo as a country retreat. There is also a nature reserve (Reserva Natural Yacyretá), but it is not open to the public. The Refugio Atinguý, however, is well worth a visit.

To the north of Ayolas, deep in the *campo*, is the Yabebyrý Wildlife Refuge, which has species preservation as its principal objective, for example of the broad-nosed caiman and marsh deer. There are no facilities for visitors.

Atinguý The Refugio Atinguý for conserving and breeding animals, particularly endangered species native to the area, is effectively a little zoo, well maintained, and should not be missed. Allow an hour for the visit, and an hour to get there and back. The 10km road, though broad and flat, is *enripiado*, not asphalted. After Atinguý the road carries on to San Cosme y Damián – a Jesuit Reduction just into the next *departamento* of Itapúa, which is reached more easily taking the turn from Ruta 1 that branches off after General Delgado.

Entrance is free, and after opening (and closing!) the gate and driving in, you find yourself in a broad grassy area with a plentiful supply of wandering greater rheas (like ostriches but they have three toes instead of two and are Latin American instead of African). There are also some southern lapwings striding masterfully around the green. There is a building to your left, and beside it you enter an attractive wooded walk, where the caged animals are to be found. Nearly all are native to the area, and many are threatened species. Atinguý has a breeding area for these species, and most are set free, with only a few examples retained in 18 large cages for the public. In all there are 84 species of mammals, 144 of birds and 15 of reptiles.

Among the mammals there are capuchin monkeys, mountain lions, jaguars (which fetch US$5,000 on the black market, when they are smuggled out of the country), anteaters with their hugely long tongues, and maned wolves (it is difficult to breed these in captivity, but Atinguý has succeeded). In a larger enclosure there are grey brocket deer. Among the birds there are examples of the mountain peacock (with black and white stripes, native to the zone, but rare), a variety of ducks and owls – all with striking colouring – not forgetting Paraguay's colourful blue-and-yellow and red-and-green macaws (which come from the Chaco, not from the local area).

The breeding zone is a larger fenced-off area with a small lake inside and offers protection to marsh deer, capybaras, and caimans. Deer, capybaras and caimans are all considered delicacies on the table. Although hunting them is illegal, in usual Paraguayan fashion this has no effect whatsoever in discouraging the practice, apart from the fact that you are unlikely to be offered them in a restaurant in Asunción. Rheas are also in this breeding enclosure, and interestingly this is one species in which the male does all the nurturing of the young, including sitting on the eggs for 42 days: the only thing the female rhea does is lay the eggs, and then abandon them.

Corateí This tiny village half an hour's journey downriver by cobbled dirt road is a pleasant place for an excursion. It has a good beach, an agreeable hotel with lots of fishing activity, and nearby is a large house that belonged to President Stroessner and that was not quite completed when he fell from power in 1989. It was restored to use in 2009 by President Lugo for official events. The roads in Corateí are broad and grassy and lead down to the river. A little wooden house marked as *copetín* (bar) oozes character, and does simple snacks but only to order. Be careful about swimming: on the curvy part of the beach it is forbidden because of the strength of the current further out in the river.

You can reach Corateí by bus from Ayolas leaving the Terminal at 06.30 or 11.00. Return buses leave Corateí at 07.00 and 15.30. If you go by taxi it may cost you Gs90,000 each way. If you are in your own vehicle, turn right when you leave Ayolas at the crossroads with a monument in the centre of the road marked Bienvenido al barrio de la Virgen de Pilar.

Where to stay

Posada Vale da Lua (11 rooms) ☏ 072 222170/021 232342; m 0975 649009/0985 708510; e valedalua_@hotmail.com or reservas@itacom.com.py or carlitos@valedalua.com. Formerly known as Posada Corateí, it changed its name to something Portuguese because its clientele is practically entirely Brazilian fishing groups. A pleasant, modest place with a buzz of fishing activity, right on the bank, with a courtyard overlooking the river, which is so broad it is like a sea. Dining room full of photos of fishing conquests, including a 16kg *dorado*. Meals are good: big selection of items for b/fast; soup, salads & fish in buffet style for dinner. Bar serves caipirinha & other cocktails. About to install internet. Good beach is 2mins' walk away. Fishing excursions. $$

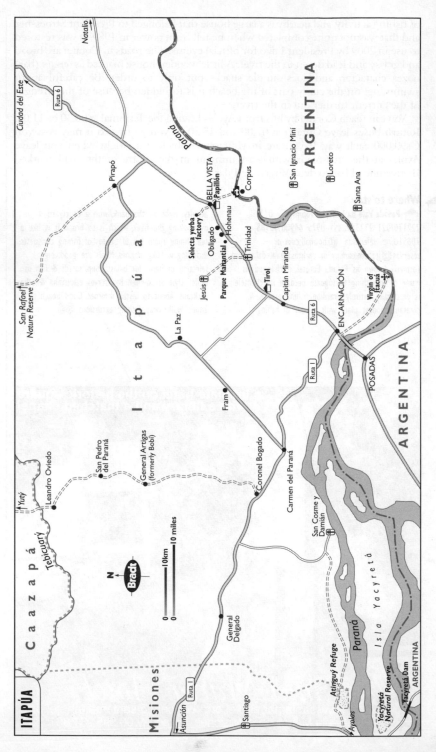

6

Southeast to Itapúa and the Ruins

Departamento: Itapúa

Though Itapúa is a different *departamento* from Misiones, it includes three old Jesuit missions: San Cosme y Damián, Trinidad and Jesús. The last two of these, and especially Trinidad, have the famous, evocative Ruins that are the icon of tourism in Paraguay. The cover picture of this book shows the watchtower and *casas de indios* of Trinidad.

There is magic in the arches of Trinidad, stepping out along the sides of the huge plaza, once athrong with activity and now inhabited only by southern lapwings with their noisy chant, and in the stone frieze of angel musicians high in the ruined church, recalling the orchestras of Guaraní musicians that once filled the building with the sweetness of their baroque music. When you add to this the quality of the carved statues now kept in the modern church, Trinidad has to be credited with being the most wonderful of all the Reductions – surpassing both San Ignacio Miní in Argentina and São Miguel in Brazil, both of which, however, are far better known and receive something like 20 times as many tourists.

Jesús, only 10km away from Trinidad, is also a romantic place, and for some people it is the favourite, with its views of palm trees framed by the windows of the abandoned church. San Cosme y Damián is also captivating – the only Reduction to have original buildings standing and in use around the best part of the plaza, including the church with original statues inside. A fourth Reduction, Itapúa, was sited at Encarnación, but nothing at all remains of it, though the city has a Jesuit museum where art work from that period is preserved.

No one should visit Paraguay without going to the Ruins of Trinidad and Jesús, if their time in the country permits it. Both have been declared World Heritage Sites by UNESCO, and all the former Reductions have now been linked in a tourist development project called the Ruta Jesuítica, which will increasingly boost the facilities offered. But travelling from Asunción to Trinidad takes about seven hours on public transport, 5½ hours in a private vehicle, so it is not comfortable to go there and back in a day. The best way to visit is to make Misiones the first stop, visiting at least some of the museums of Jesuit-Guaraní art on the way (San Ignacio, Santa María de Fe, Santa Rosa and Santiago). From there, Trinidad is a much easier journey. And from Trinidad, you can go on to reach the Iguazú Falls within a day (see *Chapter 8*), for a triumphal conclusion to a Paraguayan holiday.

Once you leave Misiones behind, you will go through two towns with very similar and rhyming names: General Delgado and Coronel Bogado. Between the two towns is the turn for San Cosme y Damián, which stands 23km south of Ruta 1, and is a historic jewel that is well worth the excursion.

San Cosme y Damián has a wonderfully peaceful atmosphere, and is unique among the Guaraní Reductions because it is more than a ruin: it has been partially restored and has the roof on the buildings that remain, which include the still functioning parish church. It is named after two early Church twin brothers who were doctors in 4th-century Sicily, and they were chosen as patrons for two reasons: the foundation of the Reduction by an Italian Jesuit, P Adriano Formoso, in the same year that a church to saints Cosmos and Damian was restored in Italy; and the danger of plagues from European illnesses made the intercession of medical saints very appropriate.

The first settlement was near Formosa in Brazil, in 1632, in the region known as Tapé, but the region was attacked by *bandeirantes* in three successive years, and like most other Reductions it had to move. It went first to what is now Argentina, in 1638, where it joined up with Candelaria – the capital of the Treinta Pueblos – and then separated again. In 1718 it moved to (present-day) Paraguay. Before the 1768 Expulsion it had over 3,000 inhabitants; 16 years after the Expulsion it had sunk to less than a third of that number.

San Cosme was famous for being an astronomical centre, under the astronomer-priest P Buenaventura Suárez, who studied Jupiter, wrote a book predicting solar eclipses and constructed a very accurate sundial that is still to be seen in position. It was Suárez who led the Reduction to this final site, and he installed in San Cosme what was only the second observatory in the continent, using local materials such as quartz crystals found on the shores of the Río Paraná, which he used as lenses.

GETTING THERE Though well worth seeing, San Cosme y Damián is a little tricky to get to. It is an awkward distance from both the museums in Misiones and the Ruins on the other side of Encarnación. If you are coming from Asunción on Ruta 1, then you reach the turn to San Cosme y Damián nearly an hour (60km) before you get to Encarnación. If you are in your own vehicle, then you only need to make a detour of 28km south to reach the remains. If you are on **public transport**, then the axis for reaching San Cosme is Coronel Bogado, 12km to the east of the turn.

Coronel Bogado is named after José Félix Bogado who fought for independence in the continent, under General San Martín. The town is famed for its *chipas* (maize rolls), and sellers may get on the bus to ply their wares from the Don Pipo Chipería (on Ruta 1 opposite the bus terminal). Paraguayans often stop for a snack or a meal at the Chipería Tatiana, on the outskirts, beyond the grassy triangular plaza to the east. Also recommended are the Chipería Tati and the Chipería Tía, both close to the Tatiana but on the other side of the road. Try the *chipas* that are filled with cheese and ham, or with chicken: they are delicious. You should also order the Paraguayan tea *cocido* to wash it down (with or without milk), rather than asking for conventional tea or coffee.

There is a Banco Regional with a cash machine at the west end of Coronel Bogado, as you arrive from the Asunción direction. Shortly afterwards you come to traffic lights and a modern, clean bus station (❯ *0741 252589*). There is a bus service from here to San Cosme throughout the day with two different companies, Perla del Sur and La San Cosmeña, that run on alternate days but follow the same timetable. They go right down to the Reduction, which is the last stop. One of the buses runs from San Cosme to Coronel Bogado (which takes almost an hour) and back again; another runs from San Cosme through Coronel Bogado to Encarnación (which takes another hour) and back again. The fare at the time of going to press was Gs8,000. You can also pick up these buses further along the Ruta, by the turn to San Cosme, and save ten minutes on the journey.

Times are a bit approximate, but the quoted departure times are: from Coronel Bogado 09.00, 10.15, 11.30, 15.00, 16.00, 17.30; from San Cosme y Damián 06.00, 07.00, 10.00, 11.00, 13.00, 16.30. There is also a Tigre bus which leaves Coronel Bogado at 19.30 (coming from Ciudad del Este) and goes to San Cosme to spend the night, leaving early in the morning at 04.30 or 05.00.

For greater comfort and speed, you can take a **taxi** and do the journey in only half an hour. There are always taxis at the terminal, and (at the time of going to press) they were charging Gs80,000–100,000 for the round trip, depending on the waiting time in San Cosme. A taxi driver called Anibal Bogado (m *0985 754292*), is recommended: he has a car with insurance and has good knowledge of San Cosme y Damián, but he is not one of the taxi drivers who wait at the terminal. There is also a taxi driver in San Cosme called Carlos (\ *073 275294*; m *0985 797378*); this is a good service to use if you only need a lift one way.

You can also take a bus north from Coronel Bogado to visit the old Franciscan church at General Artigas, on the way to Yutý, but this is dealt with in *Chapter 10*, page 268, along with the other Franciscan churches of the region.

Ramon Vilman (\ *073 275379*; m *0981 941872*) is a local man who acts as an unofficial information service for people visiting San Cosme. He is planning to open a small hotel in the future.

WHERE TO STAY AND EAT In addition to the two recommendations below, there are a number of simple *hospedajes*, some in family homes and others with dedicated rooms, and if you ring the Reduction in advance (m *0985 732956*), or even ask on the day, the guides there will organise the best for your overnight stay. With the opening of the Observatory as a night-time attraction, they are doing this more and more.

Hospedaje Aguapey Fin de la Ruta Asfáltica; \ 073 275293; m 0981 981729. The nearest thing to a proper hotel, but being at the beginning of the town (opposite the police station) it is a long way from the Reduction. $$

Residencia Cielo San Cosme e/ Mcal Estigarribia; \ 073 275309; m 0985 210393. A whole house to yourself, with modern bathroom, right next door to the Stella Mary restaurant (below) which can do breakfast. $

There are a number of small bars which will serve a simple meal at a very low price, and some family pensions will also do meals. The best **restaurant** is Stella Mary y Rafael (*Mariscal Estigarribia y San Cosme;* \ *073 275207*; m *0981 474480*; $$), half a block behind the Reduction which, however, can get so packed out at lunchtime with people from Yacyreta that you are advised to book in advance. In the evening, by contrast, it may be totally empty. As with all small places, you can expect a good service if you give a little notice, preferably the day before.

WHAT TO SEE The **Reduction** (m *0985 732956;* ☉ *winter 07.00–17.30 daily; summer 07.00–18.00 daily; foreigners Gs25,000, Paraguayans Gs15,000, local people Gs5,000; ticket is valid for Trinidad & Jesús too at no extra charge*) is the great, and indeed the only, attraction. There is no English-speaking guide and no written materials to buy, but the Spanish-speaking guides are good and helpful. Rolando Barboza does mornings (\ *073 275286*; m *0985 732956*) as does Mariela Cantero (m *0985 933532*), and Perla Machuca does afternoons (m *0985 732956*).

The splendid gateway which features the famous bat (*murcielago* in Spanish) at its peak, has been restored in two-coloured stone. (The bat was the guardian of sacred places.) The red stones are the original pieces and the white stones complete it.

The church has a new roof, faithful to the original design, but the original walls are intact. It is very long and thin, 65m x 12m, and has the choir gallery just inside the entrance that is typical of the mission churches, though in this case the staircase up to the gallery has not been replaced. The back section of the church was badly damaged by fire in 1899, and is now partitioned off, leaving the church with more workable proportions. The ancient leather chair, with carved, gilded arms and legs and the national *mburucuyá* flower painted on its back, was sat in by Pope John Paul II when he went to Encarnación on 18 May 1988. There are carved statues down both sides of the church, and though not of the quality of those in Santa María or Trinidad, there are a number of interesting pieces. Among those worthy of note are Cosmas and Damian (two big figures displayed together to the right of the altar), St Michael (a very feminine archangel, with a clearly hermaphrodite devil), the risen Christ (displayed as the central piece behind the altar, and another, more baroque figure in dark wood, which unfortunately has a broken arm) and St Isidore (with a short, flared tunic and a hoe).

The building set at right angles to the church is the complex known as the *colegio*, though it also comprises a dining room, cellar and kitchen (in the corner), workshops, grain store (on the upper storey) and 18th-century toilets (outside and at the very end, out of sight). There are original painted ceilings, one original door (and the rest restored to match), some original wrought-iron window bars, some remains of original shutters, a painted cupboard, and a stone bearing the date 1764 (four years before the Jesuits were expelled). There is access up an ancient ladder to the upper storey – this is the only building left from the Guaraní missions that has a second floor – where the huge *lapacho* floorboards, five inches thick, are impressive. You can look out from the little windows towards the River Paraná. There is a back entrance to the building, with stone steps, for people arriving from the river, some 1,800m away.

The famous sundial is marked in 15-minute sections, and does not know summer time. The slight inaccuracies that have crept in over the years are due to visitors exerting pressure on the apparatus and the metal bar distorting.

In keeping with the Reduction's history as an astronomical centre, a small planetarium was opened in March 2010, named Centro de Interpretación Astronómica Buenaventura Suárez in honour of the Jesuit astronomer. The new planetarium can accommodate 30–40 people, and there is also an observatory with a telescope suitable for star-gazing. The visit to the planetarium forms a second part to the tour of the Reduction, and the movement of the stars in different seasons is demonstrated on the domed screen. In this way, San Cosme with its planetarium, like Trinidad with its Luz y Sonido, is attracting visitors at night and not only during the day.

Extensive restoration works were carried out in 1989–91, carefully following the original design. As recently as 2008, 15 painted ceiling panels were cleaned and returned to their original position. The church is still used as the local parish church, and the weekly mass is on Saturday morning at 07.00, with a priest who travels there from Encarnación. The patronal feast day is 26 September.

A river excursion to the Isla Ybycuí is on offer from San Cosme. A dozen people will fit into the rowing boat, and life jackets and fishing rods are supplied. Details from Juan Ibarra (**m** *0983 219209*).

TRINIDAD *municipalidad* ✆ *071 270165*

The importance of the Ruins of Trinidad and Jesús has already been stressed. This is where the 'Lost Paradise' of the Jesuit-Guaraní Reductions (1609–1768) can be dreamed about, with the inspiration of so many angels carved in stone. This is the land which has inspired so many hundreds of writers all over the world to produce books and articles, plays and films. The bibliography on the Reductions runs into thousands of items, and the conference known as Jornadas Internacionales sobre las Misiones Jesuíticas attracts hundreds of scholars every time it meets.

HISTORY La Santísima Trinidad del Paraná – 'the most holy Trinity of the (River) Paraná' to give it its full title – was one of the last of the Treinta Pueblos to be founded (in 1706, by P Juan de Anaya). It was a daughter-foundation of San Carlos, in what is now Misiones Argentina. (San Carlos was also the name of Fr Gabriel's Reduction in the film *The Mission*.) Trinidad was first located near the River Uruguay, but moved to its present position in 1712, just six years after its foundation. The only Jesuit-Guaraní Reduction founded subsequently was Santo Ângelo in 1707, in present-day Brazil.

The distinctive feature of Trinidad is the use of stone for building, which has left us with the most beautiful ruins, while the earlier Reductions built in adobe and wood perished. There are two churches, and the bigger one – the *iglesia mayor* – is the triumphant work of the Italian Jesuit architect from Milan, Giovanni Battista Primoli (1643–1747), known as Juan Bautista Primoli in Paraguay. He arrived in the Río de la Plata region in 1717, and began his work by overseeing the completion of the cathedral in Córdoba, Argentina. He died at Candelaria (the capital of the Reductions, in what is now Misiones Argentina) in 1747, and it is likely that the work on the Trinidad church was then carried on by the Jesuit architects who were working in the nearby Jesús (see below, page 200), Antonio Forcada and Juan Antonio de Ribera.

The population of Trinidad reached 5,000 in its prime, and there were 30 *caciques*, and herds of 25,000 cattle. (To give meat to 5,000 people at a time they needed to slaughter 30 cattle.) The first philharmonic choir of the Río de la Plata region came from Trinidad, and was functioning in the early 1730s, a few years after the great Jesuit composer Domenico Zipoli arrived in South America (1726) and began writing masses and antiphons. There was a huge choir of 200 children.

There were only a dozen Jesuit priests in total who lived in Trinidad (four of them died there), and there were never more than two or at the most three at a time in any Reduction. The parish priest shortly before the 1768 Expulsion was Fr Pierpaolo Danesi (another Italian, like Primoli from Milan, in Trinidad 1759–63), who had an interest in clock making, sculpture and the use of precious stones: it was Danesi who completed the reconstructed dome, the frieze of angels, the bell tower of the church, and other internal decorations. He died on the journey of the expelled Jesuits back to Europe. When Trinidad was taken over by Asunción, its spiritual life was placed in the hands of the Franciscans, but the decline was immediate and rapid, and 35 years after the Expulsion, the Guaraní had abandoned the place.

There was some excavating of the church and the *colegio* as early as 1973 under the Italian-Venezuelan Graciano Gasparini, but the principal work was carried out in 1981–90 under the Italian Roberto di Stefano, when the discovery of the Ruins hit the national press. Some work was done on the friezes in 1985 by Juan Benavides.

GETTING THERE If you continue on Ruta 1 from Coronel Bogado you will arrive in Encarnación (see page 210) within an hour, and from the bus terminal there you can catch another **bus** to Trinidad, which is only 30km away on Ruta 6 – the road that ends up eventually at Ciudad del Este. Some buses are very slow and take over an hour, so ask which is the best one to take for Trinidad, and you should be there in 30 minutes. A few buses continue on from Ruta 1 to Ruta 6, passing through the terminal of Encarnación on the way. Approximate times of these from San Ignacio are: Ortega 07.00; Ñeembucú 09.00; Beato Roque Gonzalez 13.45; Alborada 16.35.

Buses leave the terminal in Encarnación at least every hour, and if you ask to be dropped at the Ruins (*las Ruinas*), you will have only a ten-minute walk up the road on the right-hand side to reach them. You cannot miss them. There is a huge sign on the main road, on the far side of the town, next to a big electricity plant with lots of pylons.

But if you are in your own **car**, there is another route to the Ruins that is slightly quicker, because it bypasses the city completely. At Carmen del Paraná (the rice capital), 12km beyond Coronel Bogado, you turn left, and drive for 28km as straight as a die through agricultural land, passing the Norwegian town of Fram (the wheat capital), and then turn right towards Ruta 6. Do not take the first turn marked to Ruta 6, which is cobbled for over 20km, because there is a better one afterwards, which is asphalted. It comes out between Capitán Miranda and Trinidad, at the Texaco service station and just before the Hotel Tirol (see opposite), which is a good place to have lunch or stop for the night.

After you have gone through Fram, if you carry straight on instead of turning right for Ruta 6, then you pass through the Japanese colonies of La Paz and Pirapó. Eventually you join up with Ruta 6 on the far side of Bella Vista. This route is sometimes called the Graneros del Sur (the Granaries of the South).

If you want to withdraw money on the way to the Ruins, then you may want to pass through Encarnación, for its banking facilities, rather than take the alternative route through Fram. But there are also **cash machines** 9km to the north of Trinidad, in the Colonias Unidas (see page 202). There are no facilities yet for exchange or cash withdrawal in either Trinidad or Jesús.

Another way of doing the journey is to take a **taxi**. This has the advantage that it takes you effortlessly to both Trinidad and Jesús, saves your energy for walking around the Ruins (which on a hot day is quite exhausting), and between the two sites whisks you away for a nice lunch at either the Hotel Tirol or the Hotel Papillón. The disadvantage is that from Encarnación it is a bit expensive – for example, around US$100 or Gs500,000 with the taxi driver from Encarnación, Miguel Benitez (**m** *0985 784634*). You can cut the cost by using a taxi from closer to the Ruins and avoiding the city prices, for example Emilio Stark (**m** *0982 223984*) or José Rojas (**m** *0985 278765; drives very fast*). If you take the bus to the Hotel Papillón (where you will probably want to spend the night anyway), and take a taxi from there – for example Juan Zang (**m** *0985 707667*) or Clemente (**m** *0985 741039*) – it will also be economical.

TOURIST INFORMATION If tourist buses come over the border from Argentina to visit the Paraguayan Reductions, then Trinidad is the place they choose, and the Ruins receive 1,000 tourists a month, or up to 2,000 in the high season (January, February, and July–October). Of these, Europeans form the biggest group, and then Latin Americans from Brazil and Argentina.

Despite being Paraguay's leading attraction, the tourist infrastructure is still very small. But the Ruta Jesuítica project (see above, page xi) is already producing some improvements and slowly the number of visitors will increase, as information spreads about the Paraguayan Reductions.

In January there is a fiesta in a village 6km behind the Ruins, to the southeast, called **Paso Güembé**, when a prize is given for the largest watermelon grown. They usually reach the 20–21kg mark, and the largest ever exhibited weighed 27kg.

WHERE TO STAY AND EAT

Hotel Papillón (40 rooms) Ruta 6 km45, Bella Vista, Itapúa; m 0767 240235/240280; e info@papillon.com.py; www.papillon.com.py. About 15km from Trinidad & despite the distance is most people's top choice for a hotel near the Ruins. It is certainly a lot busier than either the Hotel Tirol or the Hotel a las Ruinas. It is the nearest thing to a luxury hotel to be found in the Paraguayan *campo*, but at quite reasonable prices. As well as volleyball, basketball, tennis & ping-pong, the garden has a giant chess set. Excellent buffet for only Gs35,000 & even better menu à la carte. $$$

Hotel Tirol (60 rooms) Ruta 6 km20, Capitán Miranda, Itapúa; ✎ 071 202388/211053; e reservas@hoteltirol.com.py; www.hoteltirol.com.py. About 10km (& 10mins) before Trinidad, this is an enjoyable place to stay, opened in 1958 & expanded in 1970. Set in wooded park behind the brick archway that comes up on the right after you leave

Encarnación, well signed & beautifully designed, though a little dated. There are 4 swimming pools laid out on a hillside with the rooms opening onto the pool area. It is quiet, with a spectacular view & big palm trees. The main disadvantage — for the less able — is the large number of steps between the dining area & the bedroom area, though the variety of levels is fun for the young. The hotel was founded by a Belgian who fled Europe after World War II. Slightly cheaper than Papillón but not much. $$$

Hotel a las Ruinas (5 rooms, planned to increase to 7) m 0985 828563; e a.weisbach@gmx.net; www.hotel-a-las-ruinas.hola-paraguay.com. Right outside the ruins of Trinidad, used to be called Hotel León. Management has changed hands a couple of times recently & the hotel is in a transitional period. Hotels Papillón & Tirol are to be preferred at present. $$

If you ring one of the guides at the Ruins the day before, good traditional dishes can also be prepared in some of the private houses of Trinidad.

WHAT TO SEE

The Ruins of Trinidad The Ruins are on the northern edge of the town (☉ *summer 07.00–19.00 daily; winter 07.00–17.30 daily; Luz y Sonido, winter 19.00, summer 20.30 Thu–Sun; foreigners Gs25,000, Paraguayans Gs15,000, local people Gs5,000; ticket is valid for Jesús & San Cosme y Damián too at no extra charge*). There is no landline yet on site, but there are good guides with mobile phones, who you can ring for information. One of the best guides speaks English: Crystian Arevalos (m *0982 603819;* e *crystiancna@hotmail.com*). He works afternoons, but can sometimes be booked for other times on request. In the morning there is Castorina Obregón (m *0985 753997*). Others are Edgar Paredes (m *0985 772803*) and Kristina Zarza (m *0985 712979*).

Trinidad is the most evocative of the ruined Jesuit-Guaraní sites, due to its wonderful surviving stone carvings, and the magical isolation of the site. One of the advantages of the Paraguayan Mission route being less frequented than the Argentinian and Brazilian Reductions, is that it leaves more room to dream and less room for tourist tat. Brazil's tourist infrastructure in Missões is very tasteful, and Argentina's is quite pleasant, but there is nothing quite like the experience of standing alone, on the brink of Trinidad's vast plaza, and then setting off to explore. You begin walking through the arched colonnades of the *casas de indios* and crossing the huge expanse of grass towards the big church on the far side; then make your way up the nave, past the souls in the flames of purgatory on your right where the Guaraní kept night watch over their dead, past the great pulpit of the four evangelists on the left where sermons were preached in the native tongue, and into the sanctuary. There, high above your head, but clearly discernible, 46 angels play the music of heaven, just as the Guaraní had played the same instruments in the church below.

The map near the entrance shows the **typical layout** of a Reduction, with a central plaza; *casas de indios* in parallel rows on three sides of the plaza; the church opening onto the fourth side of the plaza, with a cloister on one side, including the priests' house, college and workshops; the orchard behind it; the cemetery on the other side of the church; the bell tower next to the church; and the *kotý guasú* (house for widows and orphans) close to the cloister. What is different about Trinidad is that it had two churches: the earlier church was still pretty large though not as big as the later triumphant work. The bell tower that you see (and that is shown on the cover of this book) is not the one that stood at the corner of the *iglesia mayor* but the one that was close to the *iglesia primitiva*. It is sometimes called the Torre de Atalaya, or the **watchtower**, to distinguish it from the Primoli-Danesi bell tower in the corner of the *iglesia mayor*, of which there is now only a stump. (Both were of stone, unlike the wooden constructions standing that were typical of the earlier period.)

All the Reductions were built around a large **plaza**, but the plaza of Trinidad is particularly vast, measuring 200m from east to west, and 130m from north to south. This space was used for religious processions, sporting and theatrical events, as well as for the whipping of criminals. A colonnade ran all around this long building, and in the case of Trinidad it had stone Roman (ie: round-topped) arches, with a *mburucuyá* flower carved above every junction of the arches.

The *casas de indios* are a feature of Trinidad, as they are relatively well preserved (compared with other Reductions). Originally there were 21 blocks around the Plaza Mayor, and eight still remain as ruins: the Roman arches of their colonnades are intact on a number of these. Each block comprises between six and eight square rooms, each one for a family, with a front and back door. The rooms measured 5m × 5.7m and the walls are 80cm thick. You can still see the carved stone rosette between the arches, and pick out the form, with nine separate rooms in each block – each room the home for a different family. They were originally roofed with large tiles known as *tejas coloniales* or *tejas musleras*, because they were moulded on a man's thigh, but later on the tiles were moulded on the trunk of the *cocotero* tree, to get a more uniform size. (The downside of installing the lights for the Luz y Sonido in 2009 – see below – is that these houses are now cluttered up with cables and reflectors, which reduces the magic by day, although adds to the magic by night: there are 16,000m of electrical, sound and video cables now strewn around the site.)

The great **church** (*iglesia mayor*) – Primoli's church – is on the south side, and is 85m long, 43m wide (including the colonnades) and 14m high (though originally the roof would have risen another 8m or so above this level). The discovery in 1759 of lime in a quarry 2km away enabled more ambitious architecture than had been possible earlier. This church in Trinidad was described by P Jaime Oliver (parish priest of Santa María de Fe at the time of the Expulsion) as 'the biggest and best of all the Missions; built entirely in stone, with a very beautiful dome, cupola and lantern of the dome; all done with great clarity, proportion and decoration. The façade and tower are superb. In short the whole work has turned out without equal in all that part of America and is even much to be envied in the principal cities of Europe.'

The church **bell tower** to the right of the façade – not to be confused with the watchtower that was a distance away – had a clock, according to the inventory at the time of the Expulsion, which was the work of P Danesi, in 1763. Trinidad was famous for bells, and had a foundry, which made bells from both iron and bronze. The bell tower of this main church had 12 bells of different sizes – some made here and others in San Juan Bautista (now known by its Portuguese name São João, being in Brazil).

The church originally had a **barrel vault**, 14m high, which was made of stone and brick, and on the exterior was covered with colonial tiles. The 1768 inventory records many side altars and reredos of gilded wood, which have been lost with time – either sacked, or destroyed by the elements.

The huge **dome** of this ambitious church, which was 24m high, collapsed twice. The first time was before the Expulsion, probably some time between 1750 and 1756, when it fell down one night. We know the problem was the soft, porous sandstone, and the most likely theory is that the stones fell because they filled up with rain water and doubled their weight. In the rebuild, bricks were used instead of stone, and the newly discovered lime facilitated a stronger construction. Despite this, the rebuilt dome did not last as it should have done, because after the Expulsion stones were looted from the colonnades and flying buttresses, and without this counter-tension, the dome collapsed for a second time in 1775. With the lime reinforcement it now dragged down part of the walls with it. It was never rebuilt.

The **floor** we see today is original, and beneath the centre nave were found human remains: it seems the priests were buried in the crypt – at least until their bodies could be shipped back to their home country – while the *caciques* of the *cabildo* were buried under the floor of the church, but in a foetal position in huge pots. A design of scales carved into a stone on the floor above such a grave refers to the judgement expected from God. The ordinary indigenous were buried in the cemetery to the left of the church. In a niche on the exterior is an intact stone statue of **St Paul**, with his sword, but the 12 apostles who were set in niches along the nave have been decapitated by looters who mistakenly believed that the Jesuits had hidden gold inside the soft sandstone statues.

To the right as you enter is an altar with a stone evocation of **purgatory** set above it, showing souls in flames. (In traditional Guaraní religion there was a belief in hell, which was known as *añereta*.) Dead bodies were laid out on the floor in front of this purgatory on the day before they were buried. To the left you come to the baptistery, which has a fine stone **font**, carved with the Latin baptismal formula *In nomine Patris et Filii et Spiritus Sancti* and the date 1720 (before Primoli arrived). This font was discovered buried and it is virtually intact.

As you pass up the nave you come to a beautiful, red-stone **pulpit** – all the more remarkable when you learn that this has been reconstructed out of 600 shattered fragments, though originally it had been carved out of a single stone block. It bears the symbols of the four evangelists: the angel for St Matthew, the lion for St Mark, the ox for St Luke and the eagle for St John.

At the top of the church is a large stone, carved with leaves, the *mburucuyá* flower, and large *perdiz* birds (usually translated 'partridge' but more accurately, the tinamou), which serves as the main altar: other sections of this altar, with the same design, are preserved in the cloister outside. Mass is still celebrated here on special occasions, and musicians from the Orquesta Filomúsica, together with the **Zipoli** Octet, will sometimes come from Asunción to play and sing some of the music written for the Reductions, in the context of a mass. There is no better way of experiencing the mystery of these sacred Ruins.

The church originally had three internal balconies: one over the entrance, and two at the sides where children played musical instruments. High on the wall of the transepts, above the level of the frieze, are ornate windows with flying angels carved in stone. But the most remarkable and lovely feature of this church is the **frieze of angels** playing musical instruments, high up around all the area of the altar and the transepts, silently and permanently echoing the music of the church. A line of angels symmetrically flanks the Virgin on each wall – shown either at the crib, or standing on the moon. Some angels are swinging incense, others playing violins and harps, trumpets and organs, bassoons and clavichords, and the *maraca*, which was a Guaraní rattle – a gourd filled with seeds. Both frieze and pulpit can be attributed to Danesi's direction.

The interior of the church was filled with **paintings** by the Catalan Jesuit Brother José Grimau, who also worked on the church of Jesús (see below). There were originally four side altars on each side of the church, and 24 niches with statues. While the basic construction of the church was completed in six years, with 500 workers, it continued to be worked on throughout the life of the mission, with final details being added to the interior, until the 1768 Expulsion put an end to the work, leaving some side altars still to be completed.

There are two sacristies – the one on the left for the children's choir, and the one on the right for the priests – and their doorways are also surrounded by grand carved designs of pillars and pedestals, of leaves and flying angel heads. When you enter the right-hand sacristy today you find a one-room **museum** packed full of carved stones and fragments of lettering. There is a wealth of *mburucuyá* flowers and angel heads, and a fine carved stone niche, rather like the one in the 'secondary chapel' at Jesús (see below). There is also a modern-day model of the Reduction.

Exiting the church through the sacristy you come to the **cloister** with the *colegio*, which would have had the usual cluster of priests' rooms, school and workshop buildings set out around the patio. Some of these workshop rooms had adobe walls – now reduced to just heaps of earth – but there are some good floors intact with octagonal tiles. In the central space of the cloister, some underground and overground drainage channels have been cut: the Jesuits were expert at channelling water systems.

There is a striking stone statue of a **woman with a fan** on the pavement to the right of the church – one facet of a column, with a different figure on each side, but this side is the most easily discernible. It is not known who she represents, but she is likely to be a saint. In the shadow of the colonnade here you find another fine collection of carved remains, including a gargoyle, more fragments of the high altar, and a couple of fine angel supports.

There is a second church in Trinidad, also of a good size though much simpler in design and unadorned. It was built earlier and is known as the *iglesia primitiva*. It was used while the big church was under construction, and again when the Primoli dome collapsed. The Franciscans used this church after the Expulsion.

It may be difficult to pick out the other features of this Reduction: the *kotý guasú* (next to the cloister), a reservoir for storing rainwater (in the middle of the *huerta* or orchard), a quarry (*cantera*) and a *barbacuá* (oven for drying *yerba mate*, now on private land).

A long awaited **Luz y Sonido** was inaugurated in August 2009, and operates immediately after nightfall from Thursday to Sunday. It is not really a Son et Lumiére, but a nocturnal, illuminated walk, and provides an experience of the Ruins quite different from that of daytime. The two churches, watchtower and *casas de indios* are floodlit, and 185 small lights sunk into the ground provide just enough light to find your way around, while sounds emit from 100 loudspeakers in different areas of the site – mostly music, but also birdsong and household activities – to give the effect of life going on in the Reduction, and atmospheric photographs are projected onto the walls of the *iglesia mayor*. If you are there on the right days, do not miss this beautiful experience. If its success continues, it may become a daily event before long.

The statues of Trinidad Marvellous as Trinidad is, it is still better when you discover that there are some 17 carved wooden statues of outstanding quality, kept in the modern parish church, a five-minute walk away, around the perimeter fence. The guides do not customarily mention these treasures, because it can be awkward to arrange access and the statues are in any case appallingly displayed. So if you can, give advance notice, but do not be deterred from asking on the day.

The only well-known carving here is a **painted wooden Trinity**, about 1m high, displayed in a painted niche. This piece is of considerable interest, not only because it is the icon of this place named Trinity, but also because it is the finest example of a distinctive style of portraying the three divine persons, that is typically Paraguayan and at the same time deeply theological. (There are other examples in the Museo del Barro in Asunción.) The Son stretches out his arms on the cross in total self-giving, and the Father above him stretches out his arms in a complementary and parallel movement. Between the two – fruit of the cross and at the same time springing from the Father's heart – the dove extends its wings in parallel motion. And so the persons of the Blessed Trinity are shown in perfect balance. The expressions on the faces, the painted details of wounds, and the co-ordinated colour scheme of yellow, red and brown, make this a mystical and poignant piece, despite some damage to noses, hands and feet.

In early 2006 this figure was stolen, but fortunately it was recovered a few months later, in extraordinary circumstances. The story is that there was a gang of three: after the robbery, one thief died in an accident, and then the second died too, and the third thief became so fearful of divine vengeance for the crime, that he confessed. The image was recovered from the banks of the Río Paraná, where it had been buried underground, waiting to be smuggled over the river.

All the statues in the church are of high artistic quality although, pending improved presentation, their value can easily be overlooked: they are absurdly overcrowded, and have no appropriate lighting. Some are similar to, and of at least equal quality to, statues in Santa María de Fe and San Ignacio. For example, a Virgin standing on the moon with the child Jesus at her feet (rather than in her arms); another more static Virgin whose child emerges out of the triangular shape of her robe (a more sophisticated version of the figure in the little chapel of San Ignacio); the crucifix over the altar (with a golden dove launching into flight from the top of the cross); and a Christ in the coffin with his sensitive face streaked with blood. Finally there is another work quite distinctive to Trinidad showing two very large figures from another Trinity (though this time the Spirit is missing from the group). This is the Father, with the Son seated on his right hand in heaven.

Craft It is well worth visiting the workshop of the sculptor Vicenta Morel (m *0985 726971*) who does high quality work in wood and stone – especially large stone pieces made up of several panels, and copies of the angel musicians from the frieze in the church. To reach her workshop turn sharp right immediately after you have turned off Ruta 6 by the big sign to the Ruins, and it is about the fifth house along the track that runs parallel to, and very close to, the main road.

JESÚS Copaco ✆ 071 270200; municipalidad ✆ 071 270150

The first Jesús was founded in 1685 some 200km to the east, on the banks of the River Monday. The founders were two Spanish Jesuits: P Francisco García and P Gerónimo Delfín. Its first move was in 1691 to the area of the Río Ibaretý; then it moved again to the Río Mandisoví and Capybarý. By 1731 the population had reached 2,400. But Jesús did not settle on the present site until 1758 or 1759, only ten years before the Expulsion.

The result is that Jesús was never completed – though 3,000 indigenous are said to have worked on the construction, or, according to another theory, 3,000 was the population of the town at its present site – and in fact its full name is Jesús Tavarangué, which means 'what was going to be the town of Jesús'. (In Guaraní, *táva* means 'village', -*rã* means 'going to be', and –*ngue* means 'in the past'.) It has been called (by the Jesuit historian P Bartomeu Meliá) 'the pilgrim *pueblo*'. Most of the Reductions moved once or twice, but Jesús was just beginning to settle down when the end came.

The inventory at the time of the 1768 Expulsion records fields of sugar cane, two plantations of the *yerba mate* tree and seven cotton fields.

GETTING THERE Jesús is reached from Trinidad, and is only 10km away. Allow 20 minutes for the drive, because the road is *empedrado* (cobbled), but in the process of being asphalted. Unless you are pressed for time, it would be a pity not to see both as they are so close, and although Jesús has less to explore, some people prefer it to Trinidad. If you are seeing both in the same day, you may prefer to go to Trinidad first, before you get too hot and tired, because it is generally considered the finer of the two. Or you may want to keep Trinidad for the cooler temperature of early evening, when it will be more comfortable to walk around.

For taking a **taxi** from Encarnación, see under Trinidad above (page 194). If you yourself are driving, you will see the sign to the Antigua Misión de Jesús de Tavarangué on Ruta 6, just 100m to the north of the entrance to the Trinidad Ruins, but on the opposite side of the road, right by the Petrosur service station. If you are coming from the Ruins of Trinidad, there are usually attendants with **motorbike**s who will run you down to Petrosur, to save you the ten-minute walk in the heat of the sun. If you are not in your own vehicle, or already in a taxi, you will probably be able to pick up a taxi at Petrosur. The current taxi fare is Gs45,000 to take a couple there and back, including the wait, or Gs7,000 per person each way if the group is bigger than two or three.

If there are no taxis, or if you prefer to save money, there are a number of **buses** throughout the day that run from Petrosur to the Ruins of Jesús, for Gs4,000 single (at the time of going to press). There are three bus companies that do the route: Trinidenses, Bebi and Pastoreo. Departures from Petrosur are at: 08.00, 10.00, 11.30, 12.30, 15.00, 16.00, 17.00, 17.30, 18.00 and 19.00. Departures from the Ruins of Jesús are at: 09.00, 11.00, 13.00, 14.00, 16.00, 17.00 and 18.00. On Sundays, the buses do not run, but the taxis do.

When you reach Jesús, you drive straight through the village until you reach the Ruins, and then turn right to get to the entrance.

WHAT TO SEE Though Jesús is still an active town, people only go to see one thing: the **Ruins of Jesús** (✆ *071 270038;* ⊕ *summer 07.00–19.00 daily; winter 07.00–17.30 daily; foreigners Gs25,000, Paraguayans Gs15,000, local people Gs5,000; ticket is valid for Trinidad & San Cosme y Damián too at no extra charge*).

The Ruins have a lovely situation, being on higher ground, with vistas of palm trees framed through the windows, and there is something almost Cistercian about their isolation and austerity. Guides come and go at Jesús, but one of the best informed is Lira Hein (**m** *0985 734340*). There are about 100 visitors a week to the Ruins at Jesús – around a quarter of the number that visit Trinidad.

The church and the college are the principal remains in this peaceful spot with its dramatic columns and vistas, though you can also pick out something of the whole layout of the town, according to the typical design of a Reduction. There is a plan on your left as you enter, mapping out the cemetery (to the left of the church), the orchard (behind it), and priests' house, college and workshops (to the right). The *casas de indios* were arranged in rows around the plaza, which no longer exists as a plaza, but is the long grassy space you cross before reaching the church, where you can rest halfway in the shade of some trees.

The architects were Brother José Grimau (who was also a painter), Brother Antonio Forcada (who died in 1767, the year before the Expulsion) and Brother

Juan Antonio de Ribera (who was the son of a famous Spanish architect, Pedro de Ribera). The 59m × 24m **church** is not so much a ruin as never completed. The 11m walls are intact, but it never had more than a provisional roof, as there was not time before the Expulsion to complete the work with the three vaulted roofs that had been planned. Coming from the last period of architecture in the Reductions, the church is built in stone and consequently survived, while other churches built in adobe have long since collapsed. What helped even more was the discovery of the lime quarry: the use of lime in the construction has given us walls that have remarkably withstood the battering of the elements over the centuries.

The three **doorways** into the church have a touch of Moorish influence (due to the fact that the three architects who worked on the building were all Spanish): they have a three-leaved form, similar to the mosque-cathedral in Córdoba, Spain. Two **niches** on the façade between them are beautifully adorned with plant motifs down the sides: the typical Paraguayan *mburucuyá* and the leaves of the *cocotero* palm. Above the niches you can see the papal tiara surmounting the keys of Peter, on one side, and on the other with two crossed swords – not a symbol of the gospel being spread by the sword but on the contrary of the right of this Catholic town, under the guardianship of the Pope, to carry arms in its own self defence. In short, Church protection lent the Reduction both spiritual protection (the keys to the Kingdom of Heaven) and temporal protection. Originally it is believed that the one niche held a statue of St Peter, and the other a statue of St Paul (whose symbol is the sword – the implement of his martyrdom).

There are two rows of seven **columns** down the nave, with a pulpit on both sides, placed on the fifth column. Flat against the wall are further rows of tapering columns, with capitals adorned with a palm-leaf design. The plaster on these flat columns is original, made of a mixture which included animal bones, eggshells and yellow clay. Looking out from the nave through the windows and doorways you see vistas of palm trees.

Set in the corner walls above the altar are heads of angels with wings – the very typical design of the Reductions – and below them stones with **date carvings**, one reading 'S. Fra.^{co} de Asis 1776' – a reminder that the Reduction was put in Franciscan hands after the 1768 Expulsion of the Jesuits – and on the other side 'S.^{to} Domingo de Gúzman 13 Febrero' – suggesting that Dominicans too may have had a spell in Jesús. The new regime was not successful, and within 70 years the population of the town had sunk to just 300. The church was never finished.

There are sacristies to the right and left of the main altar, where the holes for the beams can be seen, for these two rooms had their roofs in place before being abandoned. Behind the main altar is a room usually known as the **secondary chapel**. It has an attractively carved niche, topped with flying angels and with fleur de lys designs down the sides; originally this had a little sink in it for washing the sacred vessels used in the mass.

On the ground floor of the 15m **tower** that forms the right-hand front corner of the church was a baptistery with a little domed roof. An outside staircase leads up to the higher floors. You can climb to the top of the tower and there is a splendid view: on a clear day you can see as far as Trinidad. The ground floor of the tower (that the staircase bypasses) was said to be used as a storeroom or, according to another theory, as a cell for offenders: drunkenness and polygamy were some of the offences meriting punishment.

The priests' rooms, school and workshops were substantial rooms with a very wide colonnade, around what is labelled as the *plaza privada*, the patio to the side of the church, in the standard form of a Reduction.

Two rows of *casas de indios* have been excavated. The colonnade goes round all four sides, and the end rooms were larger than the others, possibly designed for the *caciques* and their families. The original floors were 50cm below the current ground level.

The work of **restoration** of Jesús began in the 1960s and continued with increasing professionalism through the rest of the past century. The walls were meticulously cleaned, and fungi, lichen and micro-organisms removed. A number of walls which were leaning or falling had to be resettled in their original positions. The tower was made safe for people to climb up and see the view. The whole site was fenced off and trees were planted around the perimeter. The gateway to the site was built in a style that echoed the doors into the church. In 1993 Jesús (along with Trinidad) was declared by UNESCO a World Heritage Site.

If you have time and sufficient interest to persist, you may be able to gain access to the current parish church, (several minutes walk away), which houses original **statues** from the Reduction, but they are not of the quality found in Trinidad or in the museums in Misiones. To do this you will need to return to the plaza in the village centre and call at the *casa parroquial* (to the left of the modern church), or ring beforehand to the ruins or to Lira Hein (numbers above) to arrange access. As always, if you have the Spanish, do not hesitate to ask – people want to help – but also do not omit to tip if someone comes out specially.

COLONIAS UNIDAS

The Colonias Unidas is the name given to three towns with a high immigrant population: Hohenau, Obligado and Bella Vista. They were all founded by Germans or by Paraguayans of German descent. Unlike European countries, where immigrants are usually poorer and struggling to establish themselves, Paraguay depends heavily on better-educated and better-off immigrants for the development of its economy. The Germans and Ukrainians, and later on the Japanese, who settled in this part of the country, have helped stimulate successful cultivation of rice, soya, wheat and cotton, through more efficient agricultural techniques and organisation, and there are a large number of food factories in this region.

HOHENAU (*Copaco* ❯ *0775 232889; municipalidad* ❯ *0775 232206*)
Hohenau ('high meadow' in German) is called the Mother of the Colonies, as it was the first of the three towns, and is now the one with most facilities, including branches of the Universidad Nacional and the Universidad Católica, and a Children's Villages hospital (Aldea SOS). It has a statue of a settler with an axe, called the monument to the Hachero de Oro (Golden axeman) on the Avenida de los Fundadores, close to the Centro Cultural Edwin Krug ($\oplus$ *07.00–11.00 Mon–Sat, 13.30–17.30 Mon–Fri; free*), where there is a small museum of things belonging to the first immigrants. These arrived in 1900 and were children of German parents, born in Mato Grosso Brazil; but after World War I there was a much greater migration from Germany. If you are looking for cheap accommodation near the Ruins (Trinidad is 8km away) then there are a couple of little hotels here on Avenida de los Fundadores that are less than half the price of Hotel Papillón but still have air conditioning and televisions (but not internet): Hotel Pillat (m *0975 603548;* $$) and Hotel Kuschel (*10 rooms; exactly opposite Casa de Cultura* ❯ *0775 232364; cheaper rooms have fans, all have TV;* $$).

Parque Manantial The Parque Manantial (*Ruta 6 km35, Hohenau;* ❯ *0775 232250/232732:* m *0985 703500;* e *manantial@tigo.com.py; www.manantial.itapua.net; Gs10,000*) is a huge nature playground, clearly signed, only just off Ruta 6 on the

Trinidad side of Hohenau, and reachable by public bus. Here you can play volleyball, ping-pong and billiards, swim and trampoline, go boating or cross the stream on a hanging bicycle, take a ride in a horse cart, tractor or lorry, visit a farm, a spring or a quarry, and if you get bored with all that then there is a Wi-Fi zone as well. You can **camp** in the park, or stay at the nearby **Hotel Papillón** (see page 195).

OBLIGADO (*Copaco* ✆ *0717 20028; municipalidad* ✆ *0717 20026*)
Obligado is set just to the west of Ruta 6, and runs on from Hohenau without any clear division. It is a German-run industrial town, founded in 1912, and now dominated by the enormous Colonias Unidas food factory. See below for information on cash machines. A good **restaurant** is Las Hermanos (*Ruta 6 km39;* ✆ *07752 32497*).

BELLA VISTA (*Copaco* ✆ *0767 240400; municipalidad* ✆ *0767 240219*)
Bella Vista is the '*yerba mate* capital', and at the crossroads of Ruta 6 with Avenida General Marcial Samaniego there is a tall monument to *yerba mate* in the form of an enormous *guampa* and *bombilla* on a white concrete support. Because the town was founded by Germans coming from the Mato Grosso region of Brazil, the *guampa* has a Brazilian shape, with a pointed bottom.

If you go left from here (northwest) for 5km, you come to the **Selecta** factory of *yerba mate* (✆ *0767 240339;* e *comercial@selecta.com.py; www.selecta.com.py*) which welcomes visits and has guides. The visit lasts about an hour, and you can follow the progress of the leaf right from the *yerba* tree (*Ilex paraguariensis*) through its drying and toasting and milling and years of maturing, to its final packeting for the market in Paraguay, Uruguay, the USA and – surprisingly – Japan. Let Selecta know of your visit beforehand if possible, so they can prepare a little pack of freebies and pass the names to the guard on the gate. Another *yerba* factory is Pajarito, to the southeast of the crossroads (*Av M Samaniego c/ Corpus;* ✆ *0767 240240;* e *info@pajarito.com.py; www.pajarito.com.py*). They too offer visits, though in practice they do not respond as readily as Selecta to such a request.

Tourist information There is a **tourist information** office at the crossroads called Mate Róga (Guaraní 'Mate House'), and the town's most knowledgeable person on tourism, Carlos Mallo of Koati Turismo (m *0985 725530;* e *koatiturismo@yahoo.com.ar*) can often be found there, or else at his pizzeria, Patio Mix, one block before the Casa de Cultura (*Av Marcial Samaniego y 12 de octubre;* ✆ *0767 240696*).

Other Practicalities Bella Vista is perhaps best known for its **Hotel Papillón**, which has been covered above under Trinidad (page 195), and has an excellent restaurant.

To find a **cash machine**, if you are coming from Trinidad, turn left at the Banco Itapúa in Hohenau (which does not yet have a cash machine) and right at the Avenida Osvaldo Tischler. When this reaches Obligado (there is no division between the two towns) it is called the Avenida Dr Francia, and on the left you will pass the Banco Regional cash machine, which takes debit as well as credit cards, and a little later on the same side the BBVA, which takes Visa. There is another Banco Regional cash machine at the crossroads in Bella Vista (five blocks beyond the Hotel Papillón).

A small local industry is that of macadamia nuts – the round light nut often found inside a chocolate coating, which is rich in Omega 3 fatty acids and reduces cholesterol. Jars under the brandname Macbella can be bought from Mate Róga.

EXCURSION TO SAN IGNACIO MINÍ

(*www.turismo.misiones.gov.ar; www.misiones-jesuiticas.com.ar; www.elbastion.com/ruinas*)
For many people, their reason for visiting Paraguay is to visit the famous
Paraguayan Reductions – the Jesuit missions for the indigenous that flourished
between 1610 and 1768, when the Jesuits were expelled. But the old area of the
Treinta Pueblos now spreads outside Paraguay, into Misiones Argentina and
Missões Brazil. In Misiones Argentina there is a much visited Reduction, San
Ignacio Miní, that has extensive ruins and is a UNESCO World Heritage Site. It
attracts some 300,000 visitors a year, and is easily reached as an excursion from
Paraguay.

Also to be taken into account is that everyone who comes to Paraguay wants to
visit the Iguazú Falls just outside the border, and these can be taken in as part of
the same excursion. They can also be done separately by taking a bus from
Asunción to Ciudad del Este and crossing into Foz (see page 226), but there are
advantages in taking the route to the waterfalls that goes through Misiones
Argentina and past San Ignacio Miní.

Misiones Argentina is the strip of land between the River Paraná (border with
Paraguay) and the River Uruguay (border with Brazil at this point, and, to the
south, with Uruguay) that you travel through from Posadas to Iguazú.

GETTING THERE There are various ways in which a visit to Paraguay can be
conveniently combined with a trip to both the Iguazú Falls and San Ignacio Miní.
You can fly into and out of Asunción, but you can also fly into and out of Foz,
Brazil. You can also do an 'open-jaws' trip, flying into one airport and out of the
other.

To get to San Ignacio Miní from Misiones Paraguay, the obvious way is to cross
from Encarnación to Posadas. From the bus terminal in Encarnación you can cross
to the bus terminal in Posadas (✆ +54 3752 456106) in three ways: in a long-
distance bus; in the little shuttle bus that goes to and fro; and by taxi. The terminal
is on the southern edge of Posadas, right on Ruta 12 which leads to San Ignacio
Miní. Do not forget that there is sometimes (not always) an hour's time difference
between Paraguay and Argentina (see page 35).

The slowest way of crossing the border is in a **long-distance bus** (a bus going
on to Buenos Aires) as it can be delayed for anything from one hour to five hours
(in high season) while Argentinian immigration and customs do their checks.
There are often Paraguayans on the bus with irregularities in their papers (such as
for having overstayed their permitted time on a previous visit) and that can hold
everyone up as fines are charged or bribes offered.

The **shuttle bus** goes regularly and is cheap (Gs5,000 or A$3 at the time of
going to press) but by contrast to the long-distance buses, is so fast you may get left
behind. The drivers have no patience in waiting for passports to be stamped: all the
Paraguayans and Argentinians have to do is flash their identity card, and while the
foreigners are waiting to have their passports vetted the bus drives off without
them and they have to wait up to half an hour for the next one.

A **taxi** is the easiest and quickest, and will cost currently about Gs60,000 or
A$50. At the taxi rank at the Encarnación bus terminal you should specify that you
want to cross into Argentina as only some of the taxis carry the necessary
paperwork. This also has the advantage that the taxi will wait while you change
your money at the *cambio* office some 100m after customs. It is a good idea to get
your money-changing done here as there are no exchange facilities in the bus
terminal of Posadas.

If you are not arriving from Paraguay but from the Iguazú Falls, then you take a
bus from the terminal in Puerto Iguazú. There is a bus about once an hour, and

the journey takes five or six hours and currently costs A$45. The quality of the buses varies: the best companies are Horianski (✆ +54 3752 455913) and A del Valle, but the latter also sells tickets on inferior quality buses. There are seven Horianski buses a day.

If you are doing a more comprehensive tour of the Reductions and want to go to San Ignacio Miní after visiting the ruins at São Miguel in Brazil, then what looks a difficult journey on the map is actually quite easy. There is one bus a day run by Reunidas (✆ *in Brazil +55 3312 1910/1495;* ✆ *in Argentina +54 3752 454795;* e *turismo@reunidas.com.br; www.reunidas.com.br*), that leaves Posadas at 12.00 every day, and reaches the Santo Ângelo terminal at 18.05 (heading for the destination Cruz Alta in Brazil). (Santo Ângelo is the nearest big town to São Miguel and was itself a Reduction.) The fare at the time of going to press was A$50 or R$40. In the other direction it leaves Santo Ângelo at 09.30 and arrives in Posadas at 15.25.

If you are **flying** to the airport at Posadas, then you will be arriving on an Aerolineas Argentinas flight from Buenos Aires. The Posadas Airport (airport code PSS) is 13km to the west of the city centre.

Once you are in Posadas, the journey of 60km to San Ignacio Miní is easy. From the bus terminal, buses leave for Puerto Iguazú approximately once an hour (20 buses in 24 hours), and most stop at San Ignacio Miní. The journey can be done in just over an hour, and currently costs A$8. Note that in Argentina they drop the Miní and speak just of San Ignacio, just as in Paraguay they talk just of San Ignacio rather than San Ignacio Guasú.

The bus will turn off the road under an arch to announce the beginning of San Ignacio, and you get off where it turns around to return to the main road. The Ruins are now a five-minute walk away to your right (northeast).

But there is also another, little known route from the Ruins of Misiones Paraguay to the Ruins of Misiones Argentina. You can take a **ferry** from the port (*puerto*) of Bella Vista over the river to Argentina, landing at Corpus, which was one of the original Reductions. Virtually nothing is left of that Reduction, and the site has not been developed for tourism, but only 15 minutes from the Port of Corpus are the famous Ruins of San Ignacio Miní. If you are staying at the Hotel Papillón in Bella Vista, then returning to Encarnación to cross the border is something of a detour and probably unnecessary.

The ferry is a raft called the *Balsa Mirlo*, run by the Argentinian company Vargas. It takes up to four cars (first come, first served) and charges A$22 if you cross with a vehicle. (At the exchange rate of Gs1,300 at the time of writing this was equivalent to less than Gs30,000, though you have to add on a fee of Gs5,000 at Argentinian customs.) The ferry starts and ends its day on the Argentinian side, and it operates from 07.00 to 11.00 and then from 13.00 to 16.00. (That is the Paraguayan timetable: Argentinian time is one hour ahead, except in the Paraguayan summertime.) Unfortunately the ferry does not run on Saturdays or Sundays, which rather significantly reduces its usefulness.

You can also cross the river in a **motorboat**, which takes about 30 passengers and charges Gs10,000. Dirt roads lead down to the ports on both sides, which are passable but difficult in rain. If you are a foot passenger, you may have to ring for a taxi on the Argentinian side: you cannot rely on there being one waiting. The ferryman Mario is helpful and his mobile number is +54 9 375 2257255. Carlos Mallo of Koati Turismo (see contacts above) can also help ensure that there will be a taxi to meet you on the other side.

A third hydro-electric dam, between the dams of Itaipú and Yacyretá, is planned for this strip of the river, near Bella Vista and Trinidad, to be called the Corpus dam. When that is built the ferry will disappear, and there may (or may not) be facilities to cross over the dam by road instead.

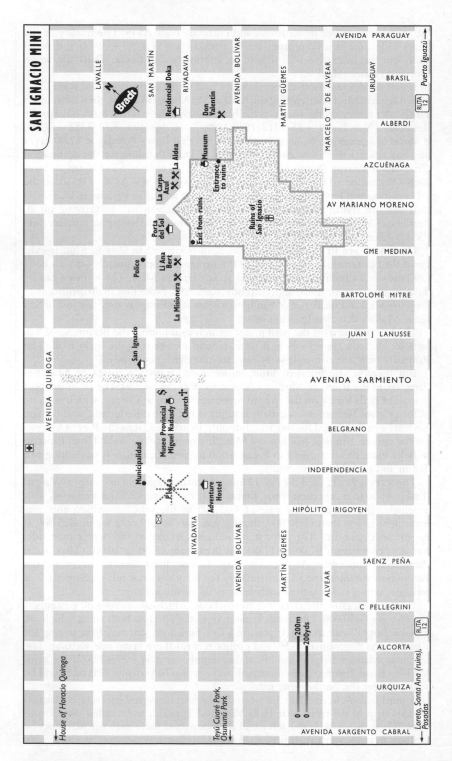

SAN IGNACIO MINÍ

AVENIDA PARAGUAY

AVENIDA BOLÍVAR

URUGUAY

BRASIL

MARTÍN GÜEMES

MARCELO T DE ALVEAR

Puerto Iguazú

RUTA 12

ALBERDI

Residencial Doka

RIVADAVIA

SAN MARTÍN

LAVALLE

Don Valentín ✕

AVENIDA BOLÍVAR

AZCUÉNAGA

Museum

La Carpa Azul ✕ ✕ La Aldea

Entrance to ruins

AV MARIANO MORENO

Porta del Sol

Ruins of San Ignacio

Exit from ruins

GME MEDINA

Police ●

Li Ana Bert ✕

BARTOLOMÉ MITRE

La Misionera ✕

JUAN J LANUSSE

San Ignacio

AVENIDA QUIROGA

AVENIDA SARMIENTO

$ Museo Provincial Miguel Nadasdy

Church ✝

BELGRANO

Municipalidad ●

INDEPENDENCIA

Plaza ╳

Adventure Hostel

HIPÓLITO IRIGOYEN

RIVADAVIA

AVENIDA BOLÍVAR

MARTÍN GÜEMES

ALVEAR

SAENZ PEÑA

C PELLEGRINI

RUTA 12

ALCORTA

200m
200yds

URQUIZA

0
0

Loreto, Santa Ana (ruins), Posadas

House of Horacio Quiroga

Teyú Cuaré Park, Osununú Park

AVENIDA SARGENTO CABRAL

HISTORY San Ignacio Miní is one of the oldest Reductions despite the fact that its name Miní means 'small', that is, 'younger', in contrast to the Paraguayan San Ignacio Guasú, the 'bigger', the 'older'. San Ignacio Guasú was founded at the end of 1609 while San Ignacio Miní was founded in 1610–11, in Guairá, the region to the northeast of the falls, in present-day Brazil. The founders were José Cataldino and Simón Masseta, and Antonio Ruiz de Montoya went to join them shortly afterwards. After persistent sackings by Portuguese slave-traders, who destroyed all the Reductions of Guairá apart from Loreto and San Ignacio Miní and carried off hundreds of thousands of Guaraní to sell in the slave markets of São Paulo, Montoya decided to move to safer territory below the waterfalls, in the region to the south of the River Paraná. Twelve thousand people set off in 1632, but only 4,000 arrived. The rest died from hunger or disease, or fled into the jungle.

The new San Ignacio Miní moved again, to settle on its present site in 1696, and over the next few decades the style of architecture began to change from adobe to stone. Thanks to the greater durability of stone, we have ruins today. Of the fifteen former Reductions in Argentina, most have disappeared and only San Ignacio Miní has a lot to see.

The town thrived until the time of the expulsion of the Jesuits in 1768, which led to the disintegration of the Reductions. By 1810 there was no population left in San Ignacio Miní, and what had not already been stolen or fallen into disrepair was burnt down by the first Paraguayan president and dictator, Dr Francia, in 1817, in a war of border disputes between Paraguay and Argentina, and again by Paraguayan troops in 1821. Today, the town is dominated by tourism.

🏠 WHERE TO STAY

🏠 **Adventure Hostel** (private rooms & dorms) Independencia 469; ☏ +54 3752 470955; e sihostel@hotmail.com; www.sihostel.com.ar. Slightly further from the Ruins; from the road on which you come in, go a couple of blocks in the opposite direction from the Ruins, & you will find it on the plaza, on the opposite side from the *municipalidad*. The design is brilliant. There is a games room & internet facilities, & they hire out kayaks & bicycles. They have facilities for short tours at reasonable prices. $$$

🏠 **Portal del Sol** (10 rooms) Rivadavia 1115; ☏ +54 3752 470005/470096; e hotelportaldelsol@gmail.com or hotelportaldelsol@hotmail.com; www.portaldelsolhotel.com. New hotel, with a touch of elegance. Swimming pool, paddle boats, volleyball, Wi-Fi, car park, central heating. $$$

🏠 **Hotel San Ignacio** (9 rooms) Sarmiento y San Martín 823; ☏ +54 3752 470422/470047/470426; e hotelsanignacio@arnet.com.ar. Right on the corner where you get off the bus. Has been modernised & the rooms are pleasantly updated, with TV, & a big en-suite bathroom. The manager Eduardo Cosgaya is very helpful. Price does not inc b/fast, but the b/fast served at the bar next door is not expensive, & is better than you get when you pay an all-inc price for B&B in a cheap hotel: you can have croissants, rolls of ham & cheese, & a fried egg. $$

🏠 **Residencial Doka** Alberdi 518; ☏ +54 3752 470131; e recidoka@yahoo.com.ar. Sited just half a block from the entrance to the Ruins. The accommodation is in a number of prefab chalets in the garden, & is clean & pleasant with all mod cons. It can be difficult to get the staff to attend the bell & let you in. $

✖ WHERE TO EAT

✖ **La Carpa Azul** Rivadavia 1295; ☏ +54 3752 470096; e lacarpaazul@hotmail.com. Facing the wall of the Ruins. Named after the capacious blue tent that houses it, with room for 350 people, behind a souvenir shop under the same management. Extensive menu. *Asado* is brought to your table on the hot grill it has been cooked on,

and they also serve grilled fish. The *empanadas* make an inexpensive starter, & are excellent. $$
✖ **Li Ana Bert** Rivadavia 1133; ☏ +54 3752 470151; e restaurant_lab@hotmail.com; www.lianabert.com.ar. Opposite the exit from the Ruins. Sells craft on the same site under the name La Negrita. They serve steaks, grilled chicken & pasta

dishes, as well as fast food of good quality – a sandwich, *milanesa* or *empanada*. The food is good as well as economical, & the location is convenient. The name comes from the 3 sisters who run the establishment: Lidia, Ana & Berta. There is a phone & internet shop next door. $$
✗ **Don Valentín** Alberdi 444; ➘ +54 3752

470284; ◷ 07.00–19.00. *Milanesas*, steaks, fast food. $$
✗ **La Aldea** Rivadavia c/ Moreno;
➘ +54 3752 470567. Small pizzeria, with character. Serves 2-course menú turístico. $
✗ **La Misionera** Rivadavia 1105; m +54 15 578895. $

WHAT TO SEE The **Ruins** of San Ignacio Miní (➘ +54 3752 470186; ◷ 07.00–19.00 daily followed by Imagen y Sonido; foreigners A$25, Latin Americans A$20, Argentinians A$15, residents of Misiones Argentina A$5, children under 12 half price) are outstanding not only for their extent and their beauty, but also for their presentation. The ticket is valid also for the other Reductions of Loreto, Santa Ana and Santa María La Mayor and lasts for two weeks. The tour begins with a Centro de Interpretación, which is a series of rooms that serve as an introduction and capture the spirit of the Guaraní. You walk through a reconstructed Guaraní house, of the kind that was used when they were still in their semi-nomadic state, through a mock-up of the jungle, and into a dark room filled with phrases from Guaraní mythology, uncannily reminiscent of biblical creation stories. Passing out into a courtyard, you are on the quay where a ship of the conquistadors has arrived.

Everyone passing out into the open air is given a guided tour, which begin every 20 minutes at busy times. There are now a few guides with just enough basic English to explain the essential points, though you cannot rely on there always being one available.

On the way to the church (designed by the Italian Jesuit architect, Brassanelli), you pass through rows of indigenous houses. They may lack their roofs, but the doorways, windows and columns of the galleries are all clear to see, and you get the feel of the huge plaza, with the 74m-long church over on the other side. The two biggest and most photographed remains are the columns on either side of the church's entrance, rising gloriously upwards and terminating in angels with flowing robes. The stonework that once united them in an arch has long since vanished.

From inside the church you can pass to the college, arranged around a courtyard and with all the basic structure still clear as well as a couple of doorways with fine sculpted details. The Jesuits' residence and the workshops were on this side, while on the other side of the church were the cemetery, the orchard and the house for widows and orphans (*kotý guasú*).

The guide will also point out trees used for different functions: *timbó* for making canoes, *hakarandá* for making bark infusions, *lapacho* for making strong columns, *cedro misionero* for making harps and creepers for making hammocks. The visit ends with a small museum containing a few archaeological remnants but it has none of the fine art statues that make the museums of the Reductions in Paraguay so remarkable.

One of the delights of San Ignacio Miní is the line of wooden street stalls that run round the outside fence of the Ruins. Here you will find wind chimes and dreamcatchers, semi-precious jewellery, hand-painted T-shirts and rough-hewn wooden buttons, hats woven from maize leaves, little animals carved by present-day Guaraní out of balsa wood and hand-rolled cigars.

After dark there is a spectacular show in the Ruins lasting 45 minutes, called **Imagen y Sonido**. This new attraction, inaugurated in July 2009, evokes the story and the life of the Reduction through projecting virtual actors onto mists of water: it begins with a personified tree, the *timbó*, and then the virtual characters of

Guaraní, priests, conquistadors and *bandeirantes* appear at eight different stations, telling the history and presenting the daily life of agriculture, schooling, music, etc. This highly imaginative and dramatic production can be experienced in English, French, German and Portuguese, as well as Spanish.

Near where the bus arrives, is the **Museo Provincial Miguel Nadasdy** (*Sarmiento 557;* ⊕ *07.00–18.00 Mon–Sat; free*), the collection of a Hungarian, with Stone Age and Jesuit remains, and a documentation centre about the Jesuit period.

While the Ruins are clearly the outstanding feature of San Ignacio Miní, it is also possible to visit the **house of Horacio Quiroga** (⊕ *07.30–19.00 daily*). Quiroga (1878–1937) was a Uruguayan writer who is attributed with having developed the story as a Latin American literary form. **Osununú** (Guaraní 'place of thunder') is a 170ha ecotourism park near the river, with seven paths, seven viewing points and trips in horse carts. A little farther away is the **Teyú Cuaré** (Guaraní 'Lizards' cave') park, so called because a huge lizard was reputed to live there. It is another nature reserve up a nearby hill by the riverside, and has a spectacular view.

The two Reductions of **Loreto** and **Santa Ana** are also easy to reach from San Ignacio Miní, and you will not be much delayed if you take them in on your journey: both are a short taxi ride away. The same ticket gets you into all three Reductions.

Taxis are to be found outside the Hotel San Ignacio, but they only look like ordinary cars. This may put off the wary, used to the rule that you never go in a car that is not an official taxi, least of all in Argentina, for fear of being assaulted and robbed; but in fact this problem is not found in a small town like San Ignacio, and it is perfectly safe. See also the Adventure Hostel above for economical tours.

EXCURSION TO SAN RAFAEL NATURE RESERVE

San Rafael is a Resource Management Reserve of Atlantic Forest, straddling the boundary of the *departamentos* Itapúa and Caazapá. It is one of the last sites in eastern Paraguay where you can still find large tracts of native forest. There are streams, waterfalls and dense forest. It was the first IBA (Important Bird Area) to be recognised in Paraguay, and it has 400 identified species – more than half the species in the whole of the country – and possibly more species not yet recognised by science. It is the only Paraguayan site to have recorded the impressive crested eagle, as well as having the harpy eagle, parrots and the famous Paraguayan bellbird, which has been immortalised in the harp piece of that name. There are tawny yellow pumas, tapirs and monkeys. The Mbyá Guaraní still lead a traditional life in this forest.

The Cerro San Rafael, just to the south of the reserve, used to figure erroneously in school textbooks as the highest hill in Paraguay. The Servicio Geográfico Militar clarified in 1988 that Tres Kandú is the highest (see *Chapter 10*, page 264).

WHERE TO STAY People wishing to visit the San Rafael reserve can contact SEAM (Secretaria del Ambiente) (✆ *021 615804/615812; www.seam.gov.py*) – see page 8 – or ring the park ranger, Gabriel Sánchez (m *0983 596775*), but best of all visit with the conservation organisation Guyrá (*Gaetano Martino, formerly José Berges, 215 esq Tte Ross;* ✆ *021 229097/223567;* e *alistair@guyra.org.py or birding.paraguay@gmail.com; www.guyra.org.py*). Their Kanguery biological station, on top of a hill with a view of the pastures, has two dormitories (six people in each), and hot water generated by solar panels. They have an excellent cook, and friendly, knowledgeable staff. It is difficult to rate the cost of this stay: it sounds very expensive (US$160 for 2 people for 2 nights) but when you take into account the difficulties of the journey, the quality of the food, and the fact that all activities are included, this all-inclusive price is less than it first appears. Alistair Kerlin who arranges the visits (from the headquarters in Asunción) is an English speaker, and at extra cost they can send an English-speaking guide from Asunción.

Excursions they offer include a guided walk through the forest, horseriding, a night ride to see foxes, owls, hares, etc, and a ride to see birds of prey. Also, there is a constant stream of interesting birds to the Kanguery station, which is a beautiful spot to relax in hammocks and read books. The staff can provide for all your needs: binoculars, books to recognise birds, etc. Be prepared for a lot of mosquitoes and other flying or creeping insects in this humid, almost tropical environment. Bring long trousers, a long-sleeved shirt, stout walking shoes, insect repellent and insecticide. But what you forget to bring, the staff will provide.

The Guyrá staff will collect you, probably from the Hotel Papillón in Bella Vista, from where the journey takes two and a half hours. After 10km on Ruta 6 in the direction of Ciudad del Este, you take a small dirt road left where there is a sign to Acá. You will be driving on a dirt road for much of the way, and from November to January it usually rains for a couple of hours in the afternoon, so you should not attempt the journey without a 4×4, and even then you are likely to get lost if you have not done the route before. An alternative route is along the Graneros del Sur road that goes through Fram (see page 194 above); before reaching Piripó you take a road north, where Alto Verá is signed.

To stay in such a beautiful and remote nature reserve, with everything made easy for you, is a special and rare kind of experience. Simon Barnes wrote (*The Times*, 14 June 2008) of his stay in the San Rafael rainforest with Guyrá: 'The place is both inhospitable and enchanting. It sucks you in, it involves you. You raise your eyes and see plants on plants on plants. Everything is soft, damp growth. If you are still enough, you can hear the trees growing.'

ENCARNACIÓN Copaco ➧ 071 208999; municipalidad ➧ 071 203982/204800

Encarnación (*www.encarnacion.gov.py*) is sometimes called the Pearl of the South, just as Concepción is known as the Pearl of the North. Both have religious names: the Incarnation and the (Immaculate) Conception. But while Concepción is a quiet, pretty town, unspoilt in its isolation, Encarnación – on the border with Argentina – is a big international thoroughfare, and one of the most important cities in Paraguay, after Asunción, Ciudad del Este and Pedro Juan Caballero.

Encarnación was the site of one of the earliest Reductions founded by Roque González in 1615, bearing the full name Nuestra Señora de la Encarnación de Itapúa, or Itapúa for short. Just three years later, it moved from the left bank (where Posadas is) to the right bank (where Encarnación is), and developed a good school of painting under the French Jesuit Louis Berger. But the once magnificent church – the work of Giuseppe Brassanelli, with three naves and a painted wooden dome – was demolished in 1848 because it had become dangerous. Today there are no remains at all. The name Itapúa has passed to the *departamento* of which Concepción is the capital. The modern bridge, nearly 3,000m long, that spans the Río Paraná to Posadas is called **Puente San Roque González** de Santa Cruz, commemorating the fact that Roque González's foundation of Itapúa began on the Argentinian side before establishing itself on the Paraguayan bank.

Encarnación is principally of interest to visitors for its **carnival**, which is the best in the country. (Until recently it was the only one, though a few places such as San Ignacio are now developing their own carnivals.) Hotels get booked out way in advance, so you need to book early. This is the reason why there are so many hotels in the city, but at other times of year you should not have a problem finding room. Other than for the carnival, tourists tend to pass through Encarnación without stopping, unless for its banking and shopping facilities, or if they want to seek out some nightlife.

For Paraguayans, there is another attraction – shopping in the Zona Baja and in La Placita, with their low prices. Encarnación is also important as a university city, with respected faculties of both the Universidad Nacional and the Universidad Católica, as well as the more minor universities. But it is not especially endowed in cultural life or in museums, though it has a few. It also has a sanctuary of the Virgin Mary at Itacuá, on the Río Paraná, that is attracting considerable crowds, like a mini-version of the country's main Marian site, Caacupé.

Encarnación is known for being the home town of President Fernando Lugo, and his sister Mercedes Lugo, the Primera Dama, still lives here, in a house on Padre Kreuser. But it is not just Paraguayans who live in Encarnación. There is also a sizeable population of descendants of immigrants – from Ukraine, Russia, Germany, Poland, China, Japan, Korea and Arab nations. There is a large Muslim population in the Zona Baja.

GETTING THERE If you are **driving** from Asunción, you will cover the 370km to Encarnación in five or six hours – six to eight by **bus**. It is straight down Ruta 1, right to the end. If you are coming from the Reductions in Misiones, allow two hours from San Ignacio by car or express bus, three by ordinary bus. If you are coming from Ciudad del Este, the journey is almost as long as coming from Asunción.

When Ruta 1 reaches the city, instead of continuing straight ahead down Avenida Dr Francia (that becomes the Sambodromo at carnival time), you follow most of the traffic in turning left. After nine blocks you come to a roundabout, where there is a shop called Luminotecnia. If you are bypassing the city to go towards the Ruins, you bear to the left here, and you will be on Ruta 6. But to enter the city you turn right, and the centre will now be on your right again. After ten blocks there are some traffic lights, on the corner of General Cabañas, which more or less marks the southern limit of the city centre. To your left you will now pass a large supermarket, Superseis, and then the Arthur Hotel, which is one of the best hotels. If you continue on, you will eventually reach the bridge into Argentina.

The **bus terminal** [212 B3] (↘ 071 202412) is the kind of third-world place awash with people trying to sell you things, where you feel you need to watch your wallet carefully. The toilets are cramped, and the facilities for changing money minimal. But it is an interesting cultural experience. If you arrive early in the morning you will find it almost impossible to get a cup of coffee, though getting a drink of *mate* is easy. All the big bus companies go from here, and there are plenty of people around to direct you to the next bus for Asunción or for Ciudad del Este, as the case may be. There are basically only two roads out of Encarnación: Ruta 1 going northwest, and Ruta 6 going northeast – as well of course as the road going south over the river to Argentina. Encarnación to Asunción currently costs around Gs60,000, and Encarnación to Ciudad del Este Gs50,000.

If you want to **cross the border** into Argentina, specify this before you get in a **taxi**, as not all of them carry the necessary paperwork. You can also get a **bus** to the terminal of Posadas for only Gs5,000. (See *San Ignacio Miní* above, page 204.)

TOURIST INFORMATION There is a **tourist information office** [212 C7] in the building with passport control, by the bridge, which can give you a copy of the latest edition of *Encarnación Quick Guide*, which has current events and a map.

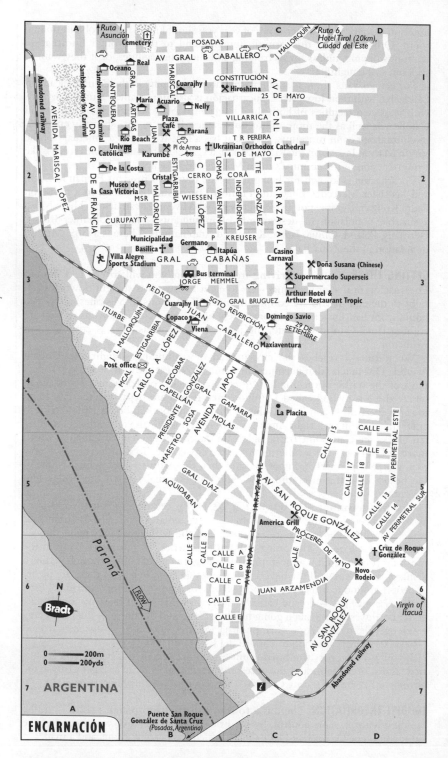

ENCARNACIÓN

WHERE TO STAY

De La Costa Hotel [212 A2] (43 rooms) Av Rodríguez de Francia 1240 c/ Cerro Corá; ↘ 071 205694/200590; e info@delacostahotel.com.py; www.delacostahotel.com.py. One of the best hotels, opened 2004, with swimming pool, minibars, Wi-Fi, restaurant, gym & view over river towards Posadas. At present it is in a rather seedy location, on the edge of town, but when the coast road is completed & the area smartens up this will be a good location. Takes credit cards. $$$

Arthur Hotel [212 C3] (60 rooms) Av Irrazábal c/ Av Japón; ↘ 071 205246/7/201823; e arthur_hotel@hotmail.com; www.arthur_hotel@hotmail.com. One of the city's top hotels: do not be put off by the faded sign. Wi-Fi, computer room, swimming pool, gym, ping-pong. Takes credit cards. $$$

Hotel Domingo Savio [212 C3] (28 rooms) 29 de setiembre e/ Av Irrazabal y Japón; ↘ 071 205800/203373; e hoteldomingosavio@hotmail.com.py. 5-storey building, swimming pool, minibars, Wi-Fi, parking. Not as nice as the Arthur round the corner, though similar price. Cramped rooms, & only continental b/fast. $$$

Hotel María [212 B1] (20 rooms) General Artigas y 25 de mayo; ↘ 071 203282/204711; e hmaria@itacom.com.py or hotelmaria@paraway.net; www.hotelmaria.com.py. Wi-Fi, takes credit cards, very decent, AC a bit noisy. $$$

Hotel Cristal [212 B2] (85 rooms) Mariscal Estigarribia 1157 c/ Cerro Corá; ↘ 071 202371/2; e hotelcristal@click.com.py. High-rise, large pool, Wi-Fi, parking, Restaurant Esmeralda. $$$

Hotel Paraná [212 B2] (38 rooms) Mariscal Estigarribia 1414 e/ Tomas Romero Pereira y Villarrica; ↘ 071 204440. Nice-looking hotel, very central, big rooms. No internet yet, neither for guests nor staff, but there is an internet place round the corner. $$$

Hotel Acuario [212 B1] (15 rooms) Juan L Mallorquín 1550 c/ Villarrica, ↘ 071 202676; e info@acuario.com.py; www.acuario.com.py. Indoor swimming pool & its own car park, internet. Won a prize (in the XXXII Premio Internacional de

Hostelería y Turismo 2007, Madrid). A couple of blocks from the plaza. Informative website. $$$

Hotel Cuarajhy I [212 B1] (25 rooms) Mariscal Estigarribia y 25 de mayo; ↘ 071 202155; e cadenacuarajhy@itacom.com.py. Has pizzeria. See next entry. $$$

Hotel Cuarajhy II [212 B3] (23 rooms) Sgto Reverchón c/ Escobar; ↘ 071 206409. The 2nd of these successful hotels, this time near the terminal. Takes credit cards. Good coffee machine in b/fast room. Internet but you pay, no Wi-Fi. $$$

Hotel Río Beach [212 B2] (8 rooms) Tomás Romero Pereira c/ Artigas; ↘ 071 206567; e riobeach@yahoo.com.ar. Internet nearby but not in hotel. Price does not include b/fast. $$$

Hotel Nelly [212 B1] (40+ rooms) 25 de mayo 448 c/ Carlos Antonio López; ↘ 071 204737. B/fast not inc. $$

Hotel Itapúa [212 B3] (50+ rooms) Carlos A López y General Cabañas; ↘ 071 205045; e contacto@hotelitapua.com.py. Close to terminal, restaurant, minibars, Wi-Fi, parking. Big & battered. Lower-priced rooms do not inc b/fast. $$

Hotel Oceano [212 A1] (20 rooms) Av Bernardino Caballero 46 c/ Ruta 1; ↘ 071 202604/202388. $$

Hotel Real [212 B1] (25 rooms) Av Bernardino Caballero 170 c/ Artigas; ↘ 071 201300. Cable TV, parking, fans. $

Hotel Viena [212 B3] (20 rooms) General Caballero 568 c/ Escobar; ↘ 071 20598; m 0985 744449. Cheap & very popular with Paraguayan commercial travellers Mon–Fri, empty at w/ends. Parking in grassy patio inside. No internet, but you can get it in the terminal, a couple of blocks away. Some rooms AC, others fans. $

Hotel Germano [212 B2] (9 rooms) General Cabañas c/ Carlos Antonio López; ↘ 071 203346; e gerstapf@hotmail.com. Ultra budget but clean & friendly family hotel, located behind the rank of white taxis. Recommended. Some budget rooms with fans rather than AC & some with shared bathrooms. Staffed 06.00–22.00 & sometimes closed on Sun, so ringing in advance is a good idea. $

WHERE TO EAT

Karumbé [212 B2] Mariscal Estigarribia y Tomas Romero Pereria; ↘ 071 201147. Popular place on corner of Plaza de Armas, stylish décor, fills up at lunchtime, recommended. $$$

Arthur Restaurant Tropic [212 C3] Av Irrazábal c/ Av Japón; ↘ 071 205245; ⏰ 11.00–14.30 &

19.00–23.00. Next door to Arthur Hotel, where Doña Susana used to be. Good buffet. Takes credit cards. $$$

Doña Susana [212 C3] General Cabañas c/ Av Irrazábal, behind the casino; ↘ 071 204915; ⏰ Wed–Mon. Excellent Chinese restaurant with

Paraguayan dishes too, which built up such a reputation in its previous good site next to the Arthur Hotel that it has taken its clientele with it to its obscure new site behind a casino, a couple of blocks away. $$
✗ **Casino Carnaval** [212 C3] Av Irrazábal y General Cabañas; ✎ 071 203836. Far more than a casino, with a snack bar, pub & restaurant, & live music every day. $$

✗ **Hiroshima** [212 B1] 25 de mayo y Lomas Valentinas; ✎ 071 206288; ⊕ 11.30–14.00 & 19.00–23.00 Mon–Fri, 19.00–midnight Sat. Japanese community centre with no sign up. Recommended. $
✗ **Supermercado Superseis** [212 C3] Irrazábal y Bruguez. Next to Arthur Hotel, has *patio de comidas.* $
✗ **La Placita** [212 C4] (open-air market) Has a lot of cheap eating places (*casillas* or *kioskos*), see below. $

Around the **terminal** are also a lot of cheap *kioskos* ($) where you can grab a bite of a typical dish with the locals. Probably best is the complex directly south, with a sign 'Bar Parrillada Comedor Valle San Pedro', next to where the *karumbé* are parked.

OTHER PRACTICALITIES You can get a **shower** for only Gs3,000 at the 'baño público con ducha' on the south side of the bus terminal [212 B3]. **Banks** are mostly clustered around the Plaza de Armas [212 B2]. **Taxis** can be found on the corner of Plaza de Armas (✎ 071 204302); radio taxis (✎ 071 200604; m 0985 700100). A **car-hire** place, Localiza, has recently opened in the city (*Ruta 6 y Petrolino Zayas;* ✎ *071 204097;* f *071 204097;* e *localiza@conexion.com.py; www.localiza.com.py;* ⊕ *07.00–12.00 & 13.30–18.00 Mon–Fri, 07.00–12.00 Sat*).

FESTIVALS Apart from the carnival, the other main festival is on 25 March, the feast of the Annunciation, which is the patronal feast day. There is an international dance festival in July, attracting visiting groups from Argentina, Brazil and Uruguay. In September there is another dance event, the Festival Nacional del Paraná, where dance teachers explain their techniques to the public.

WHAT TO SEE AND DO If you come in by bus, you will arrive close to the **Basilica of San Roque González de Santacruz** [212 B3] – in other words, the cathedral – on the block that is northeast of the terminal. There are three statues from the Reductions inside the entrance to this church. Then another five blocks north of the terminal you come to the historic grassy square of the Plaza de Armas.

The **Plaza de Armas** [212 B2] is an ancient square, nicely set out for walking and sitting, with a variety of trees and a little lake. It has a white monument in the middle like a mini Cerro Corá (see page 289) and is divided into different squares within a square, with sections devoted to children, mothers, Ukrainians, Japanese and Germans. The last section has a plaque thanking Paraguay 'for having generously accepted' their immigrants – perhaps a veiled reference to the number of Nazis who found refuge here. There is often folk dance on Saturday nights. The Ukrainian **Orthodox Cathedral** of San Jorge [212 B2] is a handsome pale green and gold building with an onion tower on the corner of Carlos Antonio López and Tomas Romero Pereira. At weekends you can hire a *karumbé* (horse cart for passengers) from the corner of the Plaza de Armas (14 de mayo y Carlos Antonio López) and do a tour of the city. These yellow, roofed vehicles, first introduced from Brazil in 1939, now have a subsidy from the *municipalidad* to continue their work, as they are regarded as something of an icon of the city. They are also found at the terminal, in the side road to the south [212 B3] (⊕ *Mon–Fri until 11.00*), next to the Hotel Río which operates as a motel (see *Appendix 2*, page 322) and so is not included in *Where to Stay* above.

From there it is three blocks west to reach the **Museo Jesuítico** at the Universidad Católica [212 A2] (*Artigas c/ Tomas Romero Pereira;* ✎ *071 201485 int 250;* ⊕ *07.00–11.30 Mon–Fri; free*). This has a collection of small carved wooden statues of saints and some construction materials. The museum was founded by historian Professor Alberto Delvalle, with items from his own collection.

In the next block south, the **Museo de la Casa Victoria** [212 B2] (*Cerro Corá c/ Artigas;* ✆ *071 203691;* ⊕ *08.00–11.00 & 14.00–17.00 Mon – Fri; free*) is a small museum with items from the Chaco War.

The *zona baja* (low zone) is so called because it is nearer the river, where the ground level is lower and where there will be more risk of flooding when the Yacyretá dam increases the depth of its reservoir (see *Chapter 5*, page 185). As with Asunción's *bañados,* the low ground is where the poor live. Just one block south of the Hotel Viena you are in the heart of the *zona baja,* with its buzz of activity, its mud and its food stalls, and a disused railway line down the middle of the street Mariscal López making transit for cars perilous.

La Placita [212 C4] (also known as La Feria) used to be the marketplace of cheap goods at the heart of the *zona baja.* But around 2006 the municipality moved La Placita to a precinct on the Avenida San Roque González, on the way to the bridge, safe from the flooding. Though some traders have resisted the move to the new purpose-made building further from their homes, it nonetheless provides plenty of atmosphere as well as convenience for buying clothes, electrics, craft, Paraguayan cheese, chickens, vegetables, etc.

A smart new **Avenida Costanera**, 27km long, will be built along the coast over the next few years. This is also part of the massive works of reconstruction to compensate for the raised river level as a result of raising the walls of the Yacyretá dam. There will then be sandy beaches, where now there is nothing but building works.

The **carnival** (✆ *071 200928; www.carnaval.com.py; Gs5,000–60,000, ranging from standing room to good seats*) has been going since 1916, when the railway reached Encarnación, which marked a watershed in the history of the city. The Encarnación Carnival is far and away the largest in Paraguay, and is held in what is called the Sambodromo on the Avenida Dr Francia, running from the Avenida Bernardino Caballero to the 14 de mayo. It takes place over three or four weekends before Lent begins, ie: in February and maybe a bit of January or March. Tickets are sold in the *municipalidad,* Banco Continental and other places, and can be bought (for a negotiable small mark-up) from private sellers outside the entrance immediately beforehand. The starting time is officially 21.00, in practice a bit later. There are about a dozen teams, and it takes at least half an hour for each to pass, with its succession of floats and radiant, energetic dancing girls, scantily dressed but harnessed into huge frameworks of brightly coloured feathers. The exuberant crowd meanwhile spray white foam out of canisters: you can buy protective glasses to keep it out of your eyes, as it has bleach in it.

The sanctuary of the **Virgin of Itacuá** is rapidly establishing itself as a new Caacupé. Near the bridge, you take a turning to the left (east) at the roundabout where there is a yellow spiral around a white pole. Then you come to a white statue of a woman carrying a fish in her hand and a basket on her head. This road, called Tupãsyrapé (Guaraní 'God's mother's road'), runs for 13km, parallel to the river, taking you through the countryside. If you do not have your own vehicle, you can reach the shrine of Itacuá by bus, taking the *línea 4.* There are also some boats that go from the port of Encarnación to the sanctuary of Itacuá, but that is more of a leisure trip.

According to the story, in 1906 a group of fishermen in a boat noticed a woman dressed in white standing among the rocks. They identified her with the Virgin Mary. A spring of water appeared, a shrine was built, and in due course miracles were noted. Today there is a large modern basilica, shaped like a ship, with a prow sticking out towards the river, and a deep-blue shell-like niche in front of the windows. If you go round the edge of the basilica you come to the little statue set in a rocky grotto. The principal feast day is 8 December, as at Caacupé, the Immaculate Conception.

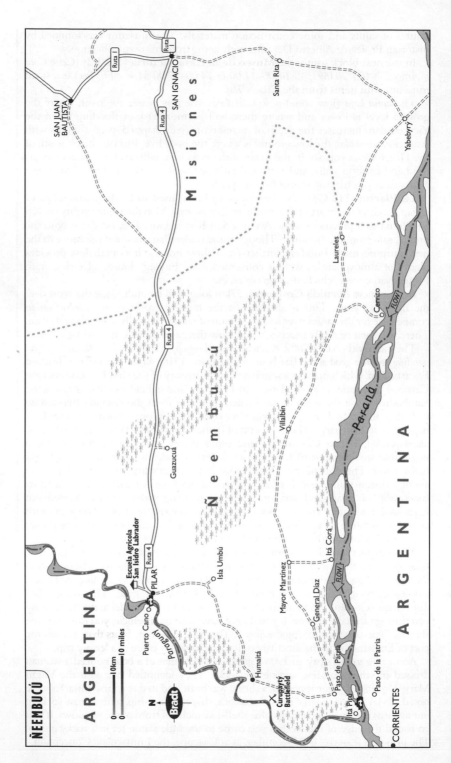

7

Southwest to Ñeembucú and the Old Battlegrounds

Departamento: Ñeembucú

Pilar is tucked right away in the southwestern tip of eastern Paraguay, a couple of hours from the international highway Ruta 1, and only recently reachable by asphalt. The access point is San Ignacio. It is truly out on a limb, and yet breathes a spirit of education that is surprising for somewhere so remote. With painted wall murals adorning street after street, it is one of Paraguay's most attractive towns. It is also the gateway to visiting the main sites from the Triple Alliance War, which figure large in Paraguay's national consciousness, especially Humaitá.

PILAR *Copaco* ☎ *0786 232300; municipalidad* ☎ *0786 231130*

Pilar was founded by Pedro Melo de Portugal y Villena on 12 October 1779, and that date is still celebrated as its *fiesta patronal*. It is a town known throughout the country for its cotton company, which also bears the name Pilar, and was founded by an Italian, Paolo Federico Alberzoni, who began to work there in 1929. The best sheets, towels and cotton fabrics come from the firm Pilar, which has a major store in Asunción as well as here in its town of origin. It is good to see the difference that a successful industry can make to a town in Paraguay: there are many attractive houses, both colonial and modern, several pleasant avenues and a lovely tree-filled plaza.

GETTING THERE

By bus Buses to Pilar run regularly from Asunción, and the journey from Asunción takes about 5½ hours (you reach San Ignacio after about 3½ hours). The bus companies are Ciudad de Pilar, which is the best (☎ *0786 232980*), la Encarnacena, Ñeembucú and la Pilarense, which is the worst. Coming by bus from the other direction, from Encarnación, you should change buses in San Ignacio. Get off at the traffic lights (*semáforo*) as you are about to leave San Ignacio, and walk a stone's throw to the left, to the Hotel Arapysandú which is behind the stone horses' heads and the service station, on the curve of the road. Ruta 4 for Pilar begins here. Or carry on a stop beyond the *semáforo* to the Hotel Piringo, where you can also pick up a bus to Pilar, crossing the road first.

By car For those travelling in their own cars, the horses' heads will also be the key landmark for turning onto Ruta 4. From there it is straight all the way. The asphalt is a little rough at first, but it improves.

By boat You can also reach Pilar by boat from Argentina or, conversely, leave Paraguay by the same route. Ferries leave Pilar at 07.00 and 13.00 every day and arrive at Puerto Cano half an hour later, from where you take a *remise* (more or less

ASUNCIÓN TO PILAR		PILAR TO ASUNCIÓN	
07.15	Ñeembucú	00.30	Encarnacena
10.15	Pilarense (slow)	01.00	Ciudad de Pilar
11.15	Ñeembucú		(semi cama, not
12.00	Encarnacena		on Sundays)
14.00	Ciudad de Pilar	07.15	Encarnacena
	(semi cama)	08.00	Ciudad de Pilar
17.30	Encarnacena	12.00	Encarnacena
18.00	Ciudad de Pilar	13.30	Pilarense
	(not on Sundays)	14.30	Ñeembucú
22.30	Encarnacena	19.00	Ñeembucú
23.30	Ñeembucú	24.00	Ñeembucú

a taxi) to Mansilla, and then a bus to Corrientes, or Resistencia, or Formosa. Of these three towns, Corrientes has the most to offer tourists, but from Pilar you cannot make the journey there and back in a day. The taxi to the ferry in Pilar costs Gs15,000, the ferry costs Gs10,000 or Gs20,000, and the bus from Puerto Cano costs A$10. Paraguayans go by boat from Pilar to Puerto Bermejo in Argentina as a day trip, to do their shopping. Ferries from Pilar leave at 07.30 and return from Puerto Bermejo at 14.00.

By air There used to be a small domestic airport at Pilar, and you will still see the signs to it, but there is no longer any air service.

WHERE TO STAY The hotels are concentrated around the bus terminal. Many of the smaller hotels in Pilar have the characteristic of not offering breakfast.

🏠 **Hotel Liza** Tacuary c/ Antequera; ☎ 0786 232944/55. Turn left & left again as you leave the terminal, & it is a block & a half away, on the left-hand side. A modern hotel, popular with visitors, so it fills up sooner than other hotels. They have a handy little map of the town they can give you. B/fast inc. $$

🏠 **Hotel Monumental I** Irala c/ Tacuary; ☎ 0786 232888/232712 & **Hotel Monumental II** Tacuary c/ Ayolas; ☎ 0786 30638. Just round the corner from each other. Smart modern signs outside, TVs, minibars & AC, usually considered Pilar's other good alternative after Liza, but very ordinary rooms. $$

🏠 **Hotel Malian** ☎ 0786 232405. Right opposite the terminal, has a bit more buzz & character,

serves food, perfectly decent modern rooms of a good size, all with private modern bathrooms. B/fast is an extra Gs5,000, parking. Cheaper rooms have fans. $

🏠 **Hotel Libra** Alberdi c/ Irala; ☎ 0786 232531. Popular & pleasant hotel with a modern feel, only half a block from the terminal. No b/fast, but can be bought just round the corner at the Malian. Cheaper rooms have fans. $

🏠 **Residencial Lucy** (9 rooms) Tacuary c/ Irala; ☎ 0786 232249. Guesthouse with a family feel, opposite Monumental II. The owner, Lucy, is chatty & always has space. Inner patio. Some rooms have bathrooms, some have AC. Rooms are a bit cramped, no b/fast. Very cheap. $

WHERE TO EAT There are not many restaurants, and not all are open at lunchtime. Fish is a speciality of the region.

✗ **Tropical Bar** 14 de mayo c/ Av Mariscal Lopez; ☎ 0786 232904; ⊕ daily except for Sun lunch. On the Plaza Mariscal Lopez, this is the top choice.

Extensive menu. The *relleno* (stuffed) with fish, cheese & ham is good. $$

✗ **Restaurant Guaraní** Tacuary c/ Antequera; ⏲ Tue–Sun from 20.00. Under same management as the Hotel Liza, just over the road. $$

✗ **Paranaense Grill** Av Irala y Mcal Estigarribia; ☎ 0786 231750; ⏲ daily. *Churrasquería* serving a variety of grilled meat with a choice of salads. A TV blares loudly from the wall. $

✗ **Restaurant Yasy** Tacuary c/ Irala; ☎ 0786 231586. Typical, modest Paraguayan restaurant/café, but good of its kind. $

OTHER PRACTICALITIES Pilar is endowed with a number of efficient **internet** places: Alberdi y Yegros; Tacuarý c/ Mcal López; Tacuarý y Tte Rene Rios; and Palma c/ Tacuarý. There are **cash machines** at the Banco Continental (*Capital Caballero c/ Tacuary*) and Cooperativa Coodeñe (*14 de mayo y Cap Caballero*). There is Western Union at the corner of the plaza (*Caballero y 14 de mayo*).

WHAT TO SEE AND DO In a covered **market** area adjoining the bus terminal, you will find a lot of typical bars, selling drinks, Paraguayan cheese and *remedios* for *mate* or *tereré*. There is a lively, friendly and thoroughly third-world feel to this area.

To reach the twin, adjoining plazas of Mariscal López and Los Héroes, turn left from the terminal for two blocks along Avenida Irala, which has palm trees down the middle of the street, and then left again down 14 de mayo. On this road, and on many others, including the plazas themselves, you will find colourful painted **murals**, generally proclaiming environmental themes. The adjoining **plazas** are a delight – filled with trees and benches and big models of local birds and animals, such as the turtle, parrot, heron and hummingbird.

The **cabildo** (*Mariscal López c/ 14 de mayo;* ☎ *0786 232078;* ⏲ *07.30–11.00 & 14.00–17.00 Tue–Fri, 09.00–11.00 Sat & Sun; free*) is an attractive colonial building with a balcony, on the Plaza Mariscal López. It dates back to 1817, in the presidency of Dr Francia. Its opening times cannot be relied on. It has a collection of relics from the Triple Alliance War, religious art, and the room that was used for government when it was a *cabildo*. At the corner of the plaza is the *gobernación* building of regional government (*14 de mayo y Av Mariscal López*) and next to it on the Avenida Mariscal López is the house of Juanita Pesoa, who was Mariscal López's first mistress and mother of three of his children: she remained a rival to Madame Lynch throughout her life.

At the far end of the adjoining Plaza de los Héroes, at the corner of Avenida Mariscal López y Mello, is a **monument to *tereré*** – the ubiquitous drink of the country – and behind is one of many picturesque old houses with a front portico. There are public toilets near this corner of the plaza. All around the plaza are educational establishments, and there is a branch of the Universidad Nacional nearer the river (*Iturbe c/ Mello*).

The largest building on the Plaza de los Héroes is the **Basilica de Nuestra Señora del Pilar**, which has a little pointed bell tower standing apart from the main building, in the style that has been typical of Paraguay from the time of the Reductions onwards. The carved wooden doors of the church show the Virgin of Guadalupe (Mexico) filling San Juan Diego's cloak with roses, and to the right of the main altar is a stained glass of San Roque González and his companions. Immediately inside the door of the church, to the left, is a striking crucifix that looks like bark peeling off a tree, and at its foot a glass coffin containing a remarkable and very bloodied Christ, articulated at the neck, shoulders and knees. Sunday masses are at 07.00 and (with rich musical accompaniment) at 19.30.

The **Avenida Mariscal López** is one of the most pleasant streets to walk down, with its central strip adorned with models of wildlife and colourful moulded pictures of the Triple Alliance War, or of the Pilar cotton factory which has brought economic survival to the town. You also pass a large statue to the founder of Pilar, Pedro Melo de Portugal y Villena.

There is a **craft** shop called Romi at Tacuary, e/ Caballero y Mcal Lopez. A little further towards the river is the shop of the famous **Pilar** cotton trade (*14 de mayo y Palma;* ☎ *0786 232386; www.pilar.com.py*), which has a big selection of rolls of fabric (all 100% cotton), sheets, towels, tablecloths and a limited selection of clothes – a good place for a browse. The Pilar factory itself is four blocks further towards the river and two to the right. Within its grounds you can visit the **Museo Paolo Federico Alberzoni** (⊕ *16.00–19.00 Thu–Sun*), which tells the story of the firm, set in the house of the company's founder. The cotton is grown more in the neighouring *departamentos* than in Ñeembucú, because the low-lying ground near the river is too wet for it.

The biggest annual event in Pilar is the **Fiesta Hawaiana** which is celebrated through the night of 2 January, down on the beach by the Club Deportivo Pilarense. Thousands of young people come to this event, filling the hotels, and there are flower garlands and lights in the river.

There is plenty of **fishing**: ask at your hotel. Damian of the Hotel Liza (m *0971 929189*) is one of the people willing to take you out on a fishing boat. He says it is an exciting experience to catch a surubi – the big, white fish most eaten in Paraguay – because it pulls hard at the fishing line 'like a cow'.

EXCURSIONS FROM PILAR

Escuela San Isidro Labrador An unusual kind of hotel, 5km out of town (turn right at the roundabout before entering Pilar), is the **Hotel de la Escuela San Isidro Labrador**, a venture begun in 2007. It is an original and interesting place to stay, where guests can be close to nature and experience the activities of the Agricultural School (e *rosasanchez009@hotmail.com* or *escuela_agricola@hotmail.com*; ☎ *0786 232177;* m *0975 171571*). There are rooms with air conditioning or fans, private or shared bathrooms, and up to 68 people can be accommodated. Activities include milking cows and goats, feeding poultry, tending pigs, growing vegetables and bathing in the stream. They also offer tours through the countryside.

Guazucuá Just 3km off Ruta 4 from San Ignacio, and 33km before you reach Pilar, is the village of Guazucuá, which has an attractive old church, La Pura y Limpia Concepción, very similar to that of Isla Umbú (below). It has statues of saints, carved wooden reredos, thick adobe walls and a ceiling made in the old traditional style of bamboo and mud. The name Guazucuá (Guaraní 'Deer hole') comes from the time when the people returned after the Triple Alliance War to find their village overrun with deer. A bus leaves Pilar at 12.30, which goes into Guazucuá, but to return you would need to find your way back to the buses on the main road. A taxi from Pilar costs around Gs150,000.

There are plans to open a tourist route by water from Guazucuá through the neighbouring lakes, where there is beautiful scenery and wildlife (fish, birds, monkeys, etc), but these plans are still in their early stages. In its low-lying marshlands, bordered on two sides of a triangle by the rivers Paraguay and Paraná, the marshlands of Ñeembucú are as important as they are unknown: there are marsh deer, pampas deer, caimans, river otters, maned wolves and parrots. For the wetlands of Lago Ypoá, which is on the borders of the three *departamentos* of Ñeembucú, Paraguarí and Central, see under *Chapter 4*, page 149.

Isla Umbú This is a delightful little place, 15km south of Pilar, and only a couple of kilometres off the road to Humaitá. It has a gem of a church built in 1862 in the time of Carlos Antonio López, in the traditional style of pitched roof and colonnade, and a separate wooden bell tower which you can climb up, (like Yaguarón). Palm trees line the path to the door, there are pine trees to the sides, and white flowers are dotted over the grass. There is a painted reredos, a brick floor, carved wooden holy water stoups, carved wooden pillars, a bamboo-lined ceiling, and a pretty choir loft.

Everything is around this plaza – the community centre, bar, police station, *municipalidad*, primary school, public library, parish office and the museum. The **Museo Histórico** (\ *0786 231441;* ⊕ *08.00–12.00 & 13.00–17.00 Tue–Fri, 08.00–10.00 Sat, 08.00–11.00 & 15.00–17.00 Sun; free*) is in the former military quarters of Mariscal López, and like so many museums focuses on relics of the Triple Alliance War. The earth down here is greyish yellow, unlike the red earth of most of eastern Paraguay.

There are local **guides**, Faustino (m *0975 663636*) and Mabel (m *0982 952086*), and there is a fledgling **information centre** for tourists next to the museum (*2 de mayo c/ José D Flecha;* \ *0786 231448;* e *islaumbu_cit@hotmail.com*).

HUMAITÁ *Copaco* \ *0786 232780; municipalidad* \ *0786 231559*

Further down towards the southwest tip, where the rivers Paraguay and Paraná join, are the chief battle sites of the Triple Alliance War in its early long campaign, and the towns to visit here, with museums, are Humaitá, and Paso de Patria (at the tip). Humaitá in Guaraní means 'ancient stone', which turned out to be an appropriate name for a remote town that came to be known chiefly – or only – for its ruin of a church, destroyed by enemy bombardment. The town was originally founded by Pedro Melo de Portugal in 1778, one year before he founded Pilar.

The journey is worth making not only for the ruin, but for the beautiful natural scenery, with herons flying, horses and cattle grazing, and white flowers blooming everywhere.

GETTING THERE The journey from Pilar is 38km and takes 1½ hours. The only access is by **dirt road** – unless you take a **boat** across the river from Paso de la Patria, Argentina, which is only half an hour from Corrientes, to Paso de Patria, Paraguay. (Ferries leave the Argentinian side at 12.00 and 15.00 on Monday, Wednesday and Friday.) When it rains, the dirt roads are impassible, though the route through General Díaz (just past the tip along the banks of the Paraná) to Isla Umbú is slightly less slippery than the coast road. (General Díaz is named after the general who led Paraguay to victory in the Battle of Curupaytý in 1866; see below.) You also have to negotiate a slightly rickety wooden bridge over the Arroyo Hondo.

Local **buses** go from the company Del Sur (\ *0786 233083*), but there are only a couple a day in each direction, so you can get to Humaitá and back in a day, but will need to stay the night somewhere if you want to go on to Paso de Patria. You are advised to buy your ticket in Pilar at 07.00 to ensure a place on the bus, even though it does not leave until 10.00. The journey all the way to Paso de Patria takes 2¼ hours. If you go by **taxi** you can expect to pay at least Gs200,000 to go as far as Humaitá,

BUS TIMETABLE: DEL SUR

PILAR	HUMAITÁ	PASO DE PATRIA
10.00	11.30	12.30
17.00	18.30	19.30

PASO DE PATRIA	HUMAITÁ	PILAR
04.00	05.00	06.30
14.00	15.00	16.30

including the wait, and Gs300,000 if you want to reach Paso de Patria. Ask around among the taxi drivers near the bus terminal, but do not be surprised if they show no enthusiasm for taking you so far on such bad roads: it really needs a 4×4.

⌂ WHERE TO STAY

⌂ **Hotel Municipal** Next to the ruin of San Carlos, looking onto the river. Nice old-fashioned feel with round pillars & an internal courtyard. You may find it deserted, & since it has no phone, bookings should be made through the neighbouring restaurant La Terraza. Alternative numbers to make a reservation at the hotel are ☎ 0786 230613, 0786 231711 & m 0985 283609. $

⌂ **Hospedaje El Bosque** Heroica Resistencia y Paso de Patria; ☎ 0786 231532. Offers fully equipped bungalow accommodation. $

✘ WHERE TO EAT

La Terraza ☎ 0786 231557; ⊕ daily. The restaurant by the Hotel Municipal, with terraces overlooking the river. $

WHAT TO SEE The church of **San Carlos de Borromeo** was one of the biggest churches in South America of its day, accommodating a congregation of up to 5,000. President Carlos Antonio López had it built, and dedicated it to his patron saint. It was inaugurated in 1861 and only five years later was bombarded continuously by the Triple Alliance, who believed it was the barracks of Mariscal López. After six months of constant cannonball fire it was left as we have it today, with fragmentary ruins of less than half the frontage. Its dramatic silhouette is one of the iconic views of Paraguay.

In the new church of Humaitá (⊕ *07.00–12.00 & 14.00–17.00*), built with bricks from the old ruin, there are a number of Jesuit-Guaraní statues, which Carlos Antonio López had ordered to be brought to adorn his building. The repainting they have suffered has not enhanced their artistic quality, and the nine statues are clumsily placed in an overcrowded row. However, there is a delightful Gabriel, with wings and arms outstretched.

At **Itá Punto**, slightly downriver of the church, Mariscal López had a barrier built across the water, with chains and dynamite, to prevent the Triple Alliance forces from sailing upriver. Vestiges of this can still be seen in the distance at low tide.

It may be surprising to find how much attention Paraguayans pay to the sites of their defeats, rather than their victories. But for them Humaitá is the 'symbol of resistance and Paraguayan heroism' (their slogan to tourists), and the sad ruins on the riverbank represent both defiance and dignity. You find the same approach in Piribebúy, Vapor Cué and Cerro Corá (see *Chapter 4*, page 136, and *Chapter 11*, page 288). The more crushing the defeat, the more is heroism seen there. What they are most proud of is that 'a Paraguayan does not surrender'.

The **Museo Histórico** (⊕ *08.00–11.00 & 14.00–17.00 Tue–Sun; free*) is in the old barracks of Mariscal López, on the old Plaza de Armas, near the ruins. Another private *museo histórico* is in the house of the Candia family (known locally as Casa Pilo). It has silver plates, coins, sables, swords and cannonballs, and also some paintings and sacred images. This is the family who run the Hospedaje El Bosque.

A teacher, Vicenta Miranda (m *0985 270690*), is a fund of knowledge on the history. Her house is on the corner behind the *colegio*, with a lot of flowers in the front patio as well as so many war remains that her house is really a museum in itself.

The site of the famous **Battle of Curupaytý**, which Paraguay won against the Triple Alliance at the start of the war in 1866, is a little to the south of Humaitá, in the *compañía* Paso Pucú, in private land belonging to the *diputado* (member of parliament) Antonio Attis. The fortifications were designed by the English colonel George Thompson and there are still trenches visible and a simple monument with a bust of General José Eduvigis Díaz, who led the Paraguayan army. The Argentinian army lost 8,000 men and the Paraguayans took only 96 casualties. If you want to make the visit, you should contract a local guide, probably by speaking to Professor Vicenta Miranda: the battlefield is 12km from Humaitá and a gate into an *estancia* needs to be unlocked to get there. But there is no tourist infrastructure and the place is likely to be more of interest to Paraguayans than to visitors.

PASO DE PATRIA Copaco ❧ 0785 202300; municipalidad ❧ 0785 20251

Further south, 20km from Humaitá (and 62km from Pilar) you come to another war town, Paso de Patria. The **museum** (*14 de mayo y Paso de Patria;* ❧ *0785 202254/202243;* **m** *0982 518915*) is housed in the former barracks of Mariscal López's army. It will be opened if you let the keyholder know, preferably in advance, that you would like to visit. It has the usual array of war relics: soldiers' plates and cutlery, cannonballs and coins, spades and spanners, spurs and swords, buckles and bottles, bullets and bayonets, etc. Statistics on the wall give the population before and after the war, showing that 75% of the Paraguayan people died: from an original population of 800,000 the survivors numbered 14,000 men, 180,000 females and 9,800 boys under ten years of age. (Bear in mind that a variety of figures have been given for casualties in the Triple Alliance War.)

This southernmost point of Ñeembucú, where the Río Paraguay and the Río Paraná join forces, is excellent for fishing, and there are herons and water birds to be seen, some of which are endangered species.

WHERE TO STAY If you want to stay, there are a few small hotels.

🏠 **Hotel Miguel Angel** ❧ 0785 202244. $ 🏠 **Hotel Robert** ❧ 0785 20244. $
🏠 **Hotel El Dorado** ❧ 0785 202231. $

MORE FISHING IN THE REMOTE SOUTH If Paso de Patria is at the tip of this southwestern corner of eastern Paraguay, Itá Pirú is at the tip of the tip, where the two rivers actually join. The name in Guaraní means 'thin stone'. You have to reach this watery point by motorboat from Paso de Patria. There is a naval base here and a hotel called **Parador Itá Pirú** (❧ *0785 202226*; $$), which caters for people keen on fishing.

Another hotel frequented by the fishing community, particularly busloads from Brazil, is in Itá Corá, 50km from Pilar, but on the Río Paraná rather than Río Paraguay. From Paso de Patria take the road east through General Díaz, and at Mayor Martínez take a little track south to Itá Corá (Guaraní 'stone'; Spanish 'circle') on the coast. The high-quality **Hotel Paranamí** (❧ *0786 231405;* **e** *richiinfo777@gmail.com;* $$$$) charges a daily rate to include bed and board, bait, boat and fuel. Just bring your fishing tackle. A much less expensive hotel is the **Hotel Itacorá** (❧ *0786 231414;* $$$).

Continuing along the dirt road that runs parallel to the coast you come to the quiet village of **Villalbín**, which has a simple *hospedaje*, and 33km further east is a turn down to **Cerrito** on the coast, which is an undiscovered paradise for fishing and bathing, with a sandy beach and several little guesthouses. The one run by the excellent Chinita is recommended (**m** *0985 135035*; $). It has a view of the sea, and her son Abel can take you out fishing.

You can continue along the same road into Misiones, until you reach Corateí and Ayolas (see *Chapter 5*). This road is very sandy, but can be done in a car if the weather is dry, or in a 4×4 if it has been raining.

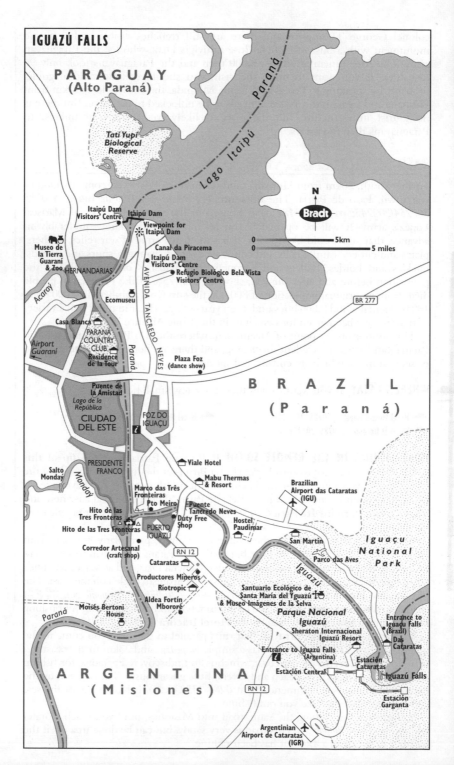

IGUAZÚ FALLS

PARAGUAY
(Alto Paraná)

Tatí Yupí Biological Reserve

Lago Itaipú

Paraná

N
Bradt

0   5km
0   5 miles

Itaipú Dam Visitors' Centre
Itaipú Dam
Viewpoint for Itaipú Dam
Canal da Piracema
Itaipú Dam Visitors' Centre
Refugio Biológico Bela Vista Visitors' Centre

Museo de la Tierra Guaraní & Zoo
HERNANDARIAS

Acaray

Ecomuseu

BR 277

Casa Blanca
PARANÁ COUNTRY CLUB
Residence de la Tour

Airport Guaraní

Paraná

AVENIDA TANCREDO NEVES

Plaza Foz (dance show)

B R A Z I L
(P a r a n á)

Puente de la Amistad
Lago de la República
CIUDAD DEL ESTE

FOZ DO IGUAÇU

PRESIDENTE FRANCO

Viale Hotel

Mabu Thermas & Resort

Brazilian Airport das Cataratas (IGU)

Salto Monday

Monday

Marco das Três Fronteiras
Pto Meiro
Puente Tancredo Neves
Duty Free Shop

Hostel Paudimar

Hito de las Tres Fronteras
Hito de las Tres Fronteras
PUERTO IGUAZÚ

San Martín

Parco das Aves

Iguaçu National Park

Corredor Artesanal (craft shop)

RN 12

Cataratas

Productores Mineros
Ríotropic
Aldea Fortín Mbororé

Iguazú

Santuario Ecológico de Santa María del Yguazú & Museo Imágenes de la Selva

Parque Nacional Iguazú

Entrance to Iguaçu Falls (Brazil)
Das Cataratas

Moisés Bertoni House

Paraná

Sheraton Internacional Iguazú Resort

Entrance to Iguazú Falls (Argentina)

Estación Cataratas

Estación Central

Iguazú Falls

A R G E N T I N A
(M i s i o n e s)

RN 12

Estación Garganta

Argentinian Airport de Cataratas (IGR)

224

8

Excursion to the Iguazú Falls

The Iguazú Falls are the eighth wonder of the world, or perhaps the first. Going to see a waterfall might not sound like a full day's occupation, but in fact that is the very minimum you need for Iguazú, and two days is still not enough for an exhaustive visit. The size, power and variety of these falls is breathtaking. They are in a region known as the Three Frontiers, where Paraguay, Argentina and Brazil meet, but the falls today are just outside Paraguayan territory, forming the border between Brazil and Argentina. No visitor to Paraguay wants, or should want, to go home without seeing them.

In the time of the President Dr Francia, there were border disputes over Misiones Argentina, but Paraguayan claims were ended by the disaster of the Triple Alliance War. Paraguayans still, however, feel a certain affinity with this territory, especially since the falls have a Guaraní name. Guaraní is still spoken as the mother tongue in Paraguay while it has been virtually lost in Argentina and Brazil as a living language, with only place names surviving.

Most people who go from Paraguay to the Iguazú Falls (or *las Cataratas* as everyone calls them) travel to the Paraguayan border city of Ciudad del Este and then cross over to Foz do Iguaçu in Brazil. This is the most direct route. But there are good reasons for preferring the alternative route through Encarnación in the south of Paraguay, to Posadas, Argentina, and then up to Puerto Iguazú, which is the town on the Argentinian side of the falls.

The advantages are as follows:

- Encarnación is a smaller and safer place than Ciudad del Este.
- Puerto Iguazú is a smaller and safer place than Foz.
- The journey on Argentinian buses up to the falls is more comfortable than the parallel journey on Paraguayan buses.
- There is more to do and explore on the Argentinian side of the falls than on the Brazilian side: most people think the Argentinian side is better.
- Travelling to Encarnación gives you the chance to visit the museums of Misiones Paraguay and the Ruins of Itapúa on the way.
- Travelling up through Misiones Argentina gives the opportunity to visit San Ignacio Miní on the way (see *Chapter 6*, page 204). (You also pass the Reductions of Loreto and Santa Ana, and the Solar del Che where Che Guevara spent his infancy, and the Minas de Wanda, which unfortunately fall outside the scope of this book.)
- There may also be a language reason for travellers to Paraguay (a Spanish-speaking country) to visit the falls in another Spanish-speaking country (Argentina) rather than a Portuguese-speaking country (Brazil).

If you have time, it is worth visiting both sides of the falls (though it is not possible to do both on the same day). If you try to come to the Argentinian side from Foz,

There are at least five different ways of spelling Iguazú. This guide uses the Argentinian form, but in Paraguay they sometimes spell it Iguasu. In English it is usually spelt Iguassu, and in Brazil they spell it Iguaçu. It is a Guaraní name, but even that does not settle the matter as there are different ways of spelling words in Guaraní. However, according to current correct practice in writing Guaraní, it would be spelt y guasú. Y means water, and guasú means big. So the name means 'big water'. To all intents and purposes, despite the distinct pronunciation of the y vowel in Guaraní, the pronunciation of the word is 'ig – wa – sue'

the journey each way will take about 1½ hours. For this reason, this chapter covers the Argentinian town of Puerto Iguazú, before moving on to the Brazilian side and Foz do Iguaçu. The next chapter then covers Ciudad del Este, which you may need to pass through if you are going from the waterfalls to Asunción.

PUERTO IGUAZÚ www.turismo.gov.ar; www.remisemisiones.com.ar

Puerto Iguazú has a population of 50,000, while Foz do Iguaçu, on the Brazilian side of the frontier, has more than 300,000. Not surprisingly, then, Puerto Iguazú is a more pleasant and manageable place, where you can walk back from a restaurant at night without feeling nervous.

GETTING THERE

By bus If you follow the suggestion to travel to the falls through Misiones Argentina, you will take a bus **from Posadas** up Argentina's Ruta RN12 – or from San Ignacio Miní, which is *en route*. They leave approximately hourly. The quality of the buses varies: the best companies are Horianski (comfortable, free drinks, terrible movies) and A del Valle, but the latter also sells tickets on inferior quality buses. The journey from Posadas to Puerto Iguazú takes four or five hours, and the cost is currently A$45 (unless you stop off at San Ignacio Miní on the way, see *Chapter 6*, page 204). If you are arriving by bus **from Buenos Aires**, the journey takes some 17 hours and you will probably come on one of the following buses, stopping at Posadas on the way: Crucero del Norte, Expreso Singer, Tigre Iguazú, Via Bariloche or Río Uruguay.

If you are travelling by bus **from Ciudad del Este**, the journey is not difficult, as there is a local bus that takes you directly through Foz to Puerto Iguazú. It costs A$3, or the equivalent in other currency, and will wait at passport control. Do not forget that there is an hour's time difference between Paraguay and Argentina, though Brazil and Argentina share the same time zone. There are also buses that go from Asunción through to Foz, but this is not necessarily a help, as they arrive at the international bus station (Rodovia) and you need to go to the local bus station (TTU) to continue your journey to Puerto Iguazú. This is also of course the bus station you must go to if you are coming by bus **from Foz** after flying into Foz Airport (busfare R$3).

Note that the planned bridge from Presidente Franco to Foz (see page 226) will also make travel easier from Ciudad del Este to Puerto Iguazú.

By ferry Another way of arriving is on the little-known ferry **crossing from Paraguay** on a *balsa* (literally, 'raft'), which leaves from the port in Presidente Franco (immediately south of Ciudad del Este, and only 8km from Puente de la Amistad). The ferry takes up to 28 cars, and begins and ends its day in Puerto Iguazú, where the port is close to the Hito de las Tres Fronteras. The first crossing is at 08.30 and the last crossing from Paraguay is at 17.15; the ferry does not run at

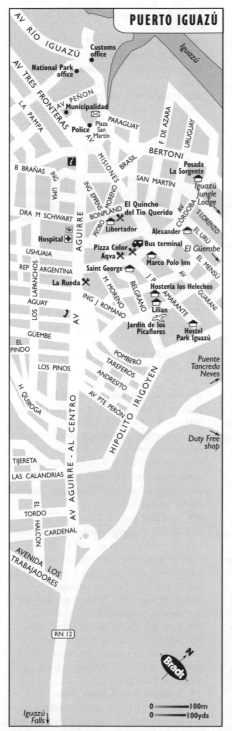

PUERTO IGUAZÚ

AV RÍO IGUAZÚ
Customs office
AV TRES FRONTERAS
National Park office
AV PEÑON
LA PAMPA
Municipalidad
PARAGUAY
Police
Plaza San Martín
B BRAÑAS
ING UMA
MISIONES
BRASIL
SAN MARTÍN
ING EPPENS
PEDRO MORENO
BONPLAND
CÓRDOBA
F DE AZARA
URUGUAY
BERTONI
Posada La Sorgente
Iguazú Jungle Lodge
El Quincho del Tío Querido
S LORENZO
DRA M SCHWART
AGUIRRE
Libertador
Alexander
EL URÚ
Hospital
Pizza Color
Aqva
Bus terminal
El Güembe
EL MENSÚ
USHUAIA
REP ARGENTINA
LOS LAPANCHOS
La Rueda
Saint George
Marco Polo Inn
AGUAY
ING J ROMANO
M MORENO
BELGRANO
AV
Hostería los Helechos
AMARANTE
GUARANI
Lilian
GÜEMBE
EL PINDO
AV AGUIRRE - AL CENTRO
Jardín de los Picaflores
Hostel Park Iguazú
H QUIROGA
LOS PINOS
POMBERO
TAREFEROS
ANDRESITO
AV PTE PERÓN
HIPOLITO IRIGOYEN
Puente Tancredo Neves
TIJERETA
LAS CALANDRIAS
Duty Free shop
EL TORDO
HALCON
CARDENAL
AVENIDA LOS TRABAJADORES
RN 12
Iguazú Falls

0 ——— 100m
0 ——— 100yds

weekends. It principally serves local people going to do their shopping in the other country, but is a great idea for tourists too, as you cross from Paraguay to Argentina in ten minutes, with none of the delays that can hit you on the Puente de la Amistad, and none of the nuisance, expense and delay of negotiating Foz. It costs only A$5 per person, and A$18 per car, and there is customs and passport control both sides of the river. There are plans to have buses go by this ferry route, but until that happens the principal difficulty with this route will be its lack of a weekend service and the need to find a taxi at either side of the river.

Puerto Iguazú has its own **airport**, the Aeropuerto Internacional Cataratas de Iguazú, 17km from the town and 12km from the waterfalls, which has flights from Buenos Aires. But though it is called International it has few if any international flights, and if you are arriving from another continent you will arrive in Foz. Both airports are called Cataratas, so the airport code is helpful to differentiate them: IGU for Foz, Brazil, and IGR for Puerto Iguazú, Argentina. For details of arriving at Foz Airport, see page 231 below.

Visas are not required to enter Argentina from holders of EU or US passports. However, you may be asked for a certificate of having had a yellow fever inoculation.

TOUR OPERATORS AND GUIDES The number of the local **Secretaría de Turismo** is +54 3757 420800. There is a tourist information office on Ruta 12 just before the junction with the road that goes to the waterfalls (see map). Here are some **tour operators**:

Venteveo Turismo Av Córdoba y Misiones; ☏ +54 3757 424062; e info@venteveoturismo.com.ar; www.venteveoturismo.com.ar. Has an office in the terminal. Helpful & efficient. Recommended.

Cuenca del Plata Paulino Amarante 76; ↘ +54 3757 421062/423330/423300; f 421458; e cuencadelplata@cuencadelplata.com. This company offers (among other attractions) a trip to a Guaraní indigenous village; see below.

Cataratas Turismo Av Tres Fronteras 301; ↘ +54 3757 420970/+54 9 3757 440809; e cataratasturismo@cataratasturismoevt.com.ar.

Another local tour operator, with cars & buses of varying sizes.

Galileo Travel Rucci 37; ↘ +54 3757 424362; e info@galileotravel.com.ar; www.galileotravel.com.ar. Does excursions & adventure holidays.

Lucas Antuña www.guassu-misted-falls-vacation.com. A freelance guide with a good website in English.

WHERE TO STAY

🏠 **Sheraton Internacional Iguazú Resort** (see map on page 224) (180 rooms) Parque Nacional; ↘ +54 3757 491800/0800 888 9180; e reservas@iguazu.sheraton.com.ar; www.sheraton.com.ar. The only hotel in the national park, looking right out over the Iguazú Falls, this light & airy building with its fabulous views offers luxury in the extreme. Some rooms face the falls & others the forest, at a lesser price. $$$$$

🏠 **Iguazú Jungle Lodge** Hipólito Irigoyen y San Lorenzo; ↘ +54 3757 420600; e info@iguazujunglelodge.com; www.iguazujunglelodge.com. 15mins from the falls, 7 blocks from town centre. Wi-Fi, games room, swimming pool, hydro-massage, balconies, a notebook in every cabin. Same company as www.iguazujunglexplorer.com. $$$$

🏠 **Hotel Saint George** Av Córdoba 148; ↘ +54 3757 420633; e reservas@hotelsaintgeorge.com; www.hotelsaintgeorge.com. On corner opposite bus terminal. Big swimming pool, & attractive rooms; lots of fruit at b/fast & the restaurant La Esquina is top class. Helpful staff, excellent English. Jacuzzi, sauna, gym, massage room, good craft & souvenir shop. Recommended. $$$$

🏠 **Hotel Cataratas** (see map on page 224) Ruta 12 km4; ↘ +54 3757 421100; f +54 3757 421090; e reservas@hotelcataratas.com; www.hotelcataratas.com Do not confuse with Hotel Das Cataratas, which is on the Brazilian side. Big rooms, extensive menu in elegant restaurant, 2 large swimming pools; jacuzzi, sauna, gym, tennis, football, musical shows. Recommended. $$$$

🏠 **Hotel Posada La Sorgente** (19 rooms) Av Córdoba 454; ↘ +54 3757 422756/424252/424072; www.lasorgentehotel.com. Italian-run hotel opened in 2005. Nice garden, 2 blocks from bus terminal. $$$$

🏠 **Hotel Riotropic** (see map on page 224) (10 rooms) Calle Montecarlo km5; ↘ +54 9 3757 405577/416764 (from within Argentina 03757 15 405577/416764); e riotropic@yahoo.com.ar; www.riotropic.com.ar. Simple but charming wooden

cabins around a pool. Turn south from RN12 at small roundabout by Productores Mineros, turn left, then right, & the last 700m is dirt road, always passable. Taxi service, & you can arrange transfer from airport when booking. Reservation must be made with a credit card, although you must then pay in cash. Recommended. $$$

🏠 **Hotel Libertador** Bonpland 110; ↘ +54 3757 420027/420570; f 3757 420984; e info@ellibertador-hotel.com.ar; www.ellibertador-hotel.com.ar. Recommended, but tends to get booked up quickly. Ask to pay a deposit when you book, if they do not ask you first: otherwise you may turn up late & find they have given your room to someone else. $$$

🏠 **Hotel Alexander** Av Córdoba 222; ↘ +54 3757 420249/420566. Opposite bus terminal. Takes credit cards. Pool. $$$

🏠 **Hostería Los Helechos** (60 rooms) Calle Paulino Amarante 76; reservations ↘ +54 3757 420829; reception ↘/f +54 3757 420338; e hosterialoshelechos@hosterialoshelechos.com.ar; www.hosterialoshelechos.com.ar. Will only take reservations Mon–Sat 09.00–13.00. Inexpensive restaurant open for dinner until 22.30 (no lunches). Swimming pool. Avoid rooms 31–45 which have no external windows. $$$

🏠 **Hotel Lilian** Fray Luis Beltran 183; ↘ +54 3757 420968; e lilian@iguazunet.com. Only 250m from the terminal. Rooms are light & attractive. Books up quickly. Will only accept reservations which are paid on a credit card. B/fast is good on bread, poor on fruit juice. No restaurant. Friendly receptionists, some speak English, & the hotel prides itself on being owner-attended. $$$

🏠 **Marco Polo** Inn Av Córdoba 158; ↘ +54 3757 425559; e iguazu@marcopoloinn.com.ar; www.marcopoloinniguazu.com. New hostel with dorms & private rooms, kitchen, tourist info, big lounge bar, Wi-Fi. $$

🏠 **El Güembe Hostel & Posada** El Urú 120; ↘ +54 3757 421035; e info@elguembe.com.ar; www.elguembe.com.ar. 2 buildings, a couple of blocks

apart, both on Fray L Beltrán. The one closer to the bus terminal has a kitchen & a pool, but the rooms are a little dingy. The second hostel has brighter rooms, a cooker & sink & outside bar. $$
🏠 **Hostel Park Iguazu** Paulino Amarante 111;

📞 +55 45 3757 424342: e hostelparkiguazu@arnet.com.ar; www.hostelparkiguazu.com.ar. Dormitories, basic but clean & modern, 2mins from the terminal, very basic b/fast. $$

✗ WHERE TO EAT

Because prices in Argentina are so much higher than in Paraguay, the classification of all these restaurants makes them sound very expensive – but this is only in comparison with Paraguay.

✗ **La Esquina** Restaurant of the Hotel Saint George (see above). Buffet with soup, fresh pasta, main dish & over 10 salads. $$$$$
✗ **Aqva** Córdoba y Carlos Thays; 📞 + 54 3757 422064; e reservas@aqvarestaurant.com; ⏲ 12.00–24.00 daily. Excellent new stylish restaurant, strong on meat & fish. $$$$$
✗ **La Toscana** Av Córdoba 454; 📞 +54 3757 422 756. Restaurant of Hotel La Sorgente, specialising in pasta. $$$$$
✗ **La Rueda** Av Córdoba 28; 📞 +54 3757 422531; e larueda1975@iguazunet.com; ⏲ lunch

& eve Wed–Sun. Excellent restaurant centrally placed, about 3 blocks from the terminal. Atmosphere, imaginative menu, well-presented food, cellar (*bodega*) where guests can choose their wine out of 350 Argentinian varieties. $$$$
✗ **El Quincho del Tio Querido** Bonpland 110; 📞 +54 3757 420151. Spacious restaurant & a good place for whiling away a long evening, as it has live musicians. $$$$
✗ **Pizza Color** Av Córdoba 135; 📞 +54 3757 420206. Right next door to the bus terminal, has decent food, at reasonable prices. $$$

IGUAZÚ FALLS

(*www.iguazuargentina.com*; *www.parquesnacionales.gov.ar*; *www.iguazujungle.com*) For the visit to the Brazilian side of these waterfalls, see page 236.

The Iguazú Falls are a natural rock formation estimated as being 150 million years old. They were first discovered by the Spanish governor of Asunción, Alvar Núñez Cabeza de Vaca, in 1542. They are so stunning that when Eleanor Roosevelt saw them she exclaimed, 'Poor Niagara!' The reason for their drama is the large lake that is formed above – swirling round to one side so that it becomes 1,200m wide – with the result that the falls run diagonally across the river, ending in a horseshoe shape. The falls have a total length of 2,700m, and the water plunges down some 70–80m to quite a narrow channel at the bottom. There are as many as 275 separate narrow waterfalls cascading over the rocks at the rate of 1,500m³ per second, with rainbows playing in the sun and a cauldron of spray that blurs visibility.

On the Argentinian side there are a lot of walkways which take you over parts of the river, giving you an ever-changing series of views. There are cliffs to climb up, and down with steps, and boat trips that take you over to San Martín island, and up as close as you can dare to the falling water, where everyone laughs and screams and gets soaked. Most dramatic of all is the Garganta del Diablo (Devil's throat) where a walkway takes you over the lake at the top until you are looking right down the 84m pit of the most thunderous fall with the spray hiding the full fearsomeness of it – a great place for photos, if you stand back. From there you can take a quiet boat ride called the *paseo ecológico*, through waters where butterflies and caimans can be seen.

There are half-hourly **buses** (A$10) from the Puerto Iguazú bus terminal to the Parque Nacional Iguazú, and you pay to get into the park when you arrive (⏲ *Oct–Mar 07.30–18.30; Apr–Sep 08.00–18.00; A$60 foreigners, A$20 residents of Misiones Argentina*). That enables you to do the walks, take the trains and visit the interpretative centre, but if you want the boat rides, or jeep rides through the forest, then there is a choice of packages with **Iguazú Jungle Explorer** that you can buy at the terminal before you set off. A green passport enables you to do all the rides, though the price seems to go up steeply every year. Many of the staff speak excellent English. You can also hire a personal guide for your group.

The peak times are Semana Santa and July (actually the coldest month, but when the South American *vacación de quince* – fortnight's holiday – coincides with the European holiday period). In 2008 there were 1.1 million visitors to the Argentinian side of the falls, of whom 60% were Argentinians and 40% foreigners. Argentina's national park was recognised by UNESCO as a World Heritage Site in 1984.

Some people recommend taking dry clothes in a rucksack, as you will get soaked in the boat tour and may end up buying them, and certainly plastic bags are advisable. A hat, water and insect repellent are recommended for those doing the 3.6km Macuco Nature Trail.

There are two places to have **lunch** – both excellent. The Restaurant La Selva is a little more expensive than the Restaurant Fortín. There are plenty of souvenir shops, and there are always Guaraní indigenous with their attractive gifts of feather headdresses, colourful bags and wooden animals. You are asked not to feed the coati (from the raccoon family) because it alters their natural behaviour and makes them aggressive.

There is so much to see and do that you can consider coming back the next day to complete the visit – and you get a 50% discount if you do. For five nights around the time of the full moon each month, you can join a visit to the Garganta del Diablo by moonlight; for dates, consult *www.iguazuargentina.com*.

A programme of eco-adventure is offered with **Iguazú Forest** (*www.iguazuforest.com*). Activities include wet-abseiling, jungle biking, trekking, climbing rope ladders, butterfly- and birdwatching and rock climbing. An information leaflet tells you what to do if you meet a jaguar: do not run away, but face the animal and make a lot of noise, clapping your hands and talking loudly. Try to appear bigger than you are, by waving your arms with any bag or item of clothing you have to hand. Do not go any closer, but withdraw slowly, without turning your back on the animal. It is very unlikely you would meet one of these large felines, but knowing what you would do if you did adds to the fun of the expedition.

WHAT ELSE TO SEE AND DO
Duty-free shop (*Ruta 12;* ✆ *+54 3757 421050;* ⊕ *10.00–21.00*) This massive

---

THE LEGEND OF IGUAZÚ

According to Guaraní myth, the land was ruled by Mbói, a mighty snake who was one of the sons of the great god Tupã. The local *cacique* Igobí had a daughter called Naipí who was so beautiful that when she stopped to look at her reflection in the river, the waters would stop in their tracks in admiration of her. This girl was promised to Mbói, but she fell in love with a young man called Tarobá, and when the day of her consecration to the God came round, while the festivities were going on, the couple escaped downriver on a canoe. When Mbói realised what had happened he was so angry that he slashed at the earth with his snake-body and caused a terrifying earthquake, so that the waterfalls of Iguazú were created as the river rushed from one level to another, and the canoe and its occupants were swallowed up. Mbói turned Tarobá into a palm tree on the upper level of the falls, while Naipí was turned into a rock at the bottom, against which the terrifying waters of the falls would pound for perpetuity, while her lover leans helplessly towards her from an unbridgeable distance above. Mbói meanwhile lives in a cave beneath the tree and watches the torment continue through endless ages. No wonder the most fearsome drop in the falls is called the Devil's Throat (Garganta del Diablo).

modern shop is in between the Tancredo Neves bridge and the Argentinian customs, with fountains playing outside. See map on page 224.

Santuario Ecológico de Santa María del Yguazú & Museo Imágenes de la Selva
(Pictures of the Forest Museum) (☉ *08.00–17.00 daily*) This little chapel and museum, in the midst of the forest on the banks of the river, are reached from Ruta 12, at 5km from the town of Puerto Iguazú. See map on page 224.

Productores Mineros (*Ruta 12, km3.5;* ☏ *+54 3757 424193;* e *info@ productoresmineros.com.ar; www.productoresmineros.com.ar.*) Interesting store of semi-precious jewellery where you can watch people work, with attentive multi-lingual staff. See map on page 224.

Jardín de los Picaflores (*Fray Luis Beltrán 150*) Three blocks from the bus terminal, almost opposite the Hotel Lilian, this is a garden of hummingbirds. In Guaraní mythology, this bird, the *mainumby* (Guaraní; Spanish *picaflor*), was the only one to have direct communication with God.

Hito de las Tres Fronteras (*Av de las 3 Fronteras*) This pyramidical obelisk looks out towards similar markers on the coasts of Brazil and Paraguay. Argentina has the best view of the three, and also has a large craft store beside it, the Corredor Artesanal. See map on page 224.

La Aldea Fortín Mbororé This is a Guaraní village which you can visit with indigenous guides, 1.5km south of RN12 (900m beyond the Hotel Riotropic, see map on page 224). There is no direct telephone line, but you can ask to arrange a tour at the bilingual Guaraní/Spanish school at the start of the village, and negotiate the price (around A$20–30 per person). You can also arrange a tour in advance through the agency Cuenca del Plata (*Paulino Amarante 76;* ☏ *+54 3757 421062/ 423330/423300;* f *421458;* e *cuencadelplata@cuencadelplata.com*).

FOZ DO IGUAÇU www.fozdoiguacu.pr.gov.br

Foz do Iguaçu is 1,065km from São Paulo, at the extreme west of the state of Paraná. It has an incredible 18,000 beds for tourists, and its principal attraction is the waterfall of Iguazú, which here is spelt Iguaçu. The city has an increasing number of increasingly smart hotels – many of them out along the Avenida das Cataratas that goes first to the airport and then to the falls.

GETTING THERE AND AROUND Travellers going to Foz may be crossing the border from Paraguay or from Argentina as part of a visit to the waterfalls, but it is also a sensible port of arrival or departure for a visit to Paraguay.

By plane Flying into Foz in order to visit Paraguay is a good idea, because it is the international airport closest to the falls, where you will undoubtedly want to go at some point in your trip. You can fly in and out of Foz instead of Asunción, or you can do an 'open-jaws' journey, into one and out of the other. You can even cut out Asunción altogether, and visit the interior of Paraguay – particularly the Jesuit-Guaraní missions – and leave again from Foz. In fact, for travellers who know they want to go to Iguazú, and are looking for other places to visit in the region to build a holiday, a trip to Paraguay is a perfect solution.

The airport (☏ *+55 45 3521 4276*) is between the town and the waterfalls, and its airport code is IGU. There are connecting flights from São Paulo, with TAM (*www.tam.com.br*), TAP Portugal, and Gol (*www.voegol.com.br*) – the South American equivalent of easyJet or Ryanair. A bus from the airport to Foz will take 45 minutes and cost R$2.80, and a taxi will cost R$40. If you are coming from Puerto Iguazú for a flight from Foz Airport, allow at least an hour for the journey.

By road To come by bus **from São Paulo** (see *Chapter 2*, page 33) Pluma (*www.pluma.com.br*) is one of the best companies. A full list of long-distance bus companies serving Foz is found under the city website (*www.fozdoiguacu.pr.gov.br*). You can also bus in from Porto Alegre.

A bus over the river **from Puerto Iguazú**, Argentina, will cost about A$6 or R$3. The bridge is called the Ponte Tancredo Neves (in Spanish, Puente Tancredo Neves).

You can get a bus **from Ciudad del Este** and go right through to Puerto Iguazú, and a taxi is quite a reasonable price. The bridge is called the Ponte da Amizade (Puente de la Amistad in Spanish). Do not forget that there is an hour's time difference between Brazil and Paraguay. Foz is quite a cut up from Paraguay. You notice the difference the moment you have crossed the border. Streets are properly asphalted, not full of holes. There is less rubbish. There are well-ordered street signs, and in the city there are proper pavements, proper buildings, proper shops. One might almost be in Europe. There can occasionally be a delay of a couple of hours in crossing the bridge from Paraguay, if the customs officials are having a drive on cutting down smuggling. To ease the delays, a new bridge is to be built to Foz from Presidente Franco (immediately south of Ciudad del Este) and work on it is due to begin in 2010.

Car hire At the airport you might just consider **renting** a car for one day to get quickly around on the Brazilian side between the waterfalls, the bird park, the Itaipú dam, the Bela Vista refuge, etc. It may work out cheaper than an all-day **taxi**, although the latter has the considerable advantage of a driver who knows where he is going. You would have to pay an extra insurance premium to take a rented car over the Argentinian border, and you will not be allowed to take it into Paraguay at all. There are a lot of car-hire firms in Foz, including Avis (e *igu@avispr.com.br*) and Hertz (e *locacao.igu@hertzsystem.com.br*) which are both at the airport as well as in the centre, and Yes – Rent a Car, which is in the centre (*Av Paraná 861 or Av Costa e Silva 3500;* e *foz@yesrentacar.com.br*). Opening hours at the airport are 09.00–19.30 Monday–Friday, 09.00–17.00 weekends. You can expect to pay about R$110 for a day in Brazil.

TOURIST INFORMATION You may have some difficulty in insisting on getting your **passport** stamped. Travellers who are just going to the waterfalls and returning do not need a stamp in their passport, and taxi drivers may be reluctant to wait while you queue. But if you are not returning by the same route after seeing the falls, you can be in trouble the next time you go through passport control. If an entry or exit stamp is missing you will be fined.

At the Rodoviária (international bus terminal) [234 D2] there is a helpful **tourist information** office, where English is spoken. There are also tourist information offices at the airport and in the city centre [234 B4] (*Av Juscelino Kubitschek aka Av J K, and Rua Rio Branco;* ✆ *+55 45 3521 1455*). To get a bus to the waterfalls, you will need to go to the local bus station or Terminal Urbana [234 A3] (*Av J K y Av Republica Argentina*).

Visas are required from holders of US, Canadian and Australian passports but not from holders of EU passports. However, if you are only entering Brazil to go to the waterfalls, passport control will wave you through without looking at or stamping your passport.

There are a large number of tour operators and agencies. A list can be found at www.fozdoiguacu.pr.gov.br.

🏠 **WHERE TO STAY** There are a huge number of hotels in Foz, and a fine selection of luxury hotels along the Rodovia das Cataratas, of which only a small selection can be covered here. More emphasis has been given to cheaper hotels, which are less easy to find details about, and to hotels near the bus terminal. But because prices are so much higher than in Paraguay, all the hotels appear comparatively expensive in the categorisation.

🏠 **Hotel das Cataratas** (see map on page 224) (195 rooms) BR 469 km28, Parque Nacional do Iguaçu; ☎ +55 45 2102 7000; e reservas@hoteldascataratas.com; www.hoteldascataratas.com. Only hotel within the national park, 25km from Foz, 15km from airport. Refreshingly, this is not a modern building, but a pale pink, elegant Portuguese colonial-style house, set back with a green between it & the beginning of the cliff walk which has all the views. $$$$$

🏠 **Mabu Thermas & Resort** (see map on page 224) Rodovia das Cataratas km3.2; ☎ +55 45 3521 2000/0800 41 7040; f 529 6361; www.hoteismabu.com.br. After the hotel in the national park itself, the Mabu, with under-lit fountain outside & its own heliport, must top the bill for expense, but it is an 'all-inclusive system' with no extra charges. Water from the Mabu spring flows fresh to the pools of the hotel & is renewed every 4hrs, maintaining a constant 36°C (body temperature) all day long & year round. $$$$$

🏠 **Viale Hotel** (see map on page 224) (152 rooms) Rodovia das Cataratas km2.5, Vila Yolanda; ☎ +54 45 2105 7200; e reservas@vialecataratas.com.br; www.vialecataratas.com.br. 10km to falls. Modern minimalist design with a chute thing like an elbow outside. $$$$

🏠 **Turrance Green Hotel** [234 C5] (96 rooms) Rua Manêncio Martins 108; ☎ +55 45 3026 4200/0800 645 2124; e turrance@turrancehotel.com.br; www.turrancehotel.com.br. On corner of the Rodovia das Cataratas. Fitness centre, home theatre, 2 swimming pools with waterfalls. $$$$

🏠 **Hotel San Martín** [234 B4] (see map on page 224) Rodovia das Cataratas; ☎ +55 45 3521 8088; f 3521 8076; e reservas@hotelsanmartin.com.br; www.hotelsanmartin.com.br. Super hotel with dark soothing wood halls, extremely close to the falls & airport. More than 2km of ecological trail in a garden of natural forest. Good English spoken. $$$$

🏠 **Hotel Rafain Centro** [234 B4] (119 rooms) Av Marechal Deodoro 984; ☎ +55 45 3521 3500; e reservas@rafaincentro.com.br; www.rafaincentro.com.br. Very good, very central, excellent b/fast. Do not confuse with Rafaín Palace or Rafaín Churrasquería. $$$$

🏠 **Mercure** [234 B3] (214 rooms) Rua Almirante Barroso, 2006; ☎ +55 45 3521 4100; f +55 45 3521 4101; e h5613-re@accor.com.br; www.mercure.com. Usual quality from the renowned Mercure chain. $$$$

🏠 **Hotel Tarobá Express** [234 A3] Rua Tarobá 1048; ☎ +55 45 2102 7770; f +45 2102 770; e reservas@hoteltaroba.com.br; www.hoteltaroba.com.br. Just over the road from bus terminal. Website has very extensive information. Sauna, business centre, Wi-Fi, etc. Small rooms with basic furniture. $$$$

🏠 **Best Western Falls Galli Hotel** [234 D2] Costa E Silva Av, 1602; ☎ +55 45 3520 1002. Large comfortable hotel offering very good value & used by a number of tour companies. $$$$

🏠 **Hotel Del Rey** [234 A3] (45 rooms) Rua Tarobá 1020; ☎ +55 45 2105 7500; e reservas@hoteldelreyfoz.com.br; www.hoteldelreyfoz.com.br. Excellent-value hotel with good facilities. Swimming pool, gym, games room, business centre, Wi-Fi, queen-size beds, safes in room. You can chat online about your reservation. $$$$

🏠 **Iguaçu Plaza Hotel** [234 B4] Rua Bartolomeu de Gusmão 859, nearly on cnr of Rua Mal Floriano Peixoto; ☎ +55 45 3523 1277; e iguacuplazahotel@purenet.com.br. Nice rooms, good for price, pay-by-hour internet, swimming pool. $$$

🏠 **Laura Pousada** [234 A3] Rua Naipi 671; ☎ +55 45 3572 4158; e reservas@pousadadalaura.com; www.pousadadalaura.com. Clean, new, 3 blocks from bus terminal, kitchen facilities, Wi-Fi, hammocks in garden, big Brazilian b/fast, English spoken. Has been well reviewed. $$$

🏠 **Pousada El Shaddai** [234 A3] Rua Engenheiro Rebouças 306; ☎ +55 45 3025 4493; e contato@pousadaelshaddai.com.br; www.pousadaelshaddai.com.br. Guesthouse/hostel. One block from bus stop to waterfalls & a few blocks

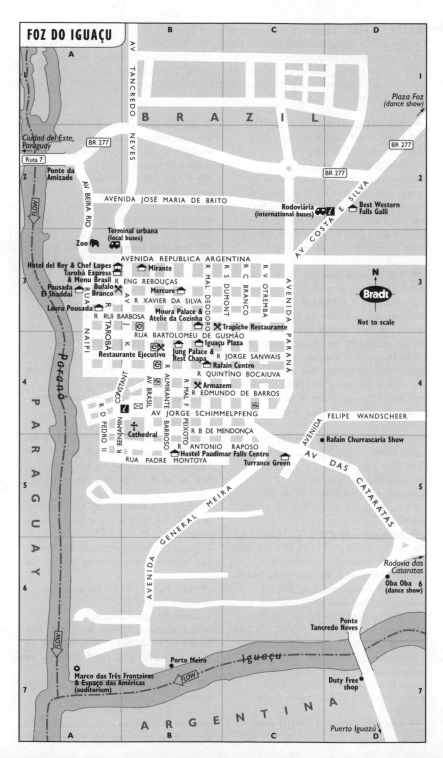

FOZ DO IGUAÇU

BRAZIL

Ciudad del Este, Paraguay

BR 277

Ruta 7

Ponte da Amizade

PARANÁ

PARAGUAY

Paraná

AV BEIRA RIO

AV TANCREDO NEVES

Zoo

Terminal urbana (local buses)

AVENIDA JOSÉ MARIA DE BRITO

Rodoviária (international buses)

BR 277

BR 277

AV COSTA E SILVA

Best Western Falls Galli

Plaza Foz (dance show)

Hotel del Rey & Chef Lopes
Tarobá Express
& Menu Brasil
Pousada
El Shaddai
Laura Pousada

Mirante

AVENIDA REPUBLICA ARGENTINA

R ENG REBOUÇAS

Bufalo Branco

R XAVIER DA SILVA

R RUI BARBOSA

Mercure

Moura Palace & Atelie da Cozinha

RUA BARTOLOMEU DE GUSMÃO

Iguaçu Plaza

Trapiche Restaurante

AVENIDA PARANÁ

R S DUMONT
R C BRANCO
R V OTREMBA
R MAL DEODORO

Restaurante Ejecutivo

Jung Palace & Rest Chapa

Rafaín Centro

R JORGE SANWAIS

R QUINTINO BOCAIUVA

Armazem

R EDMUNDO DE BARROS

AV JORGE SCHIMMELPFENG

RUA TAROBÁ

RUA NAIPI

AV CONSTANT

AV ALMIRANTE

AV BRASIL

R MAL F PEIXOTO

R BENJAMIN CONSTANT

R D PEDRO II

R BARROSO

Cathedral

R B DE MENDONÇA

R ANTONIO RAPOSO

RUA PADRE MONTOYA

Hostel Paudimar Falls Centro

Turrance Green

AVENIDA FELIPE WANDSCHEER

Rafaín Churrascaría Show

AV DAS CATARATAS

AVENIDA GENERAL MEIRA

Rodovia das Cataratas

Oba Oba (dance show)

Ponte Tancredo Neves

Iguaçu

Porto Meiro

Marco das Três Fronteiras & Espaço das Américas (auditorium)

Duty Free shop

Puerto Iguazú

ARGENTINA

Bradt

N

Not to scale

from shops & restaurants. Big Brazilian b/fast, friendly staff, pool, internet, English spoken. $$$

🏠 **Moura Palace Hotel** [234 B3] Rua Marechal Deodoro 1427, esq Bartolomeu de Gusmão; ✆ +55 45 3574 1211; f 3574 4155; e hotelmoura@ig.com.br; www.mourapalacehotel.com.br. Friendly people in this family hotel with a good Brazilian feel to it. $$$

🏠 **Hostel Paudimar** (see map on page 224) Rodovia das Cataratas km12.5, cnr Av Maria Bubiak; ✆ +55 45 3529 6061; e info@paudimar.com.br; www.paudimar.com.br. Backpackers hostel on road to the Falls, set in rural grounds, from private cabins to dormitories; good value, free internet, swimming pool, good information. Recommended. $$$

🏠 **Hostel Paudimar Falls Centro** [234 B5] Rua Antonio Raposo 820; ✆ +55 45 3028 5503; e info@paudimarfalls.com.br; www.paudimarfalls.com.br. $$$

🏠 **Jung Palace** [234 B4] Rua Bartolomeu de Gusmão 884; ✆ +55 45 3523 3267/3025 3645; e jungpalacehotel@brturbo.com.br. Cable TV in this small purpose-built hotel with big airy rooms. Cheap & good value. Does not take credit cards. Curry smells in reception but no smells in rooms. $$$

✖ **WHERE TO EAT** As with the hotels, the cheap options appear expensive here, because the prices are put in comparison with those in Paraguay.

✖ **Trapiche Restaurante** [234 B3] Rua Marechal Deodoro 1087; ✆ +55 45 3572 3951; www.trapicherestaurante.com.br; ⏱ from 17.00 Mon–Thu, from 12.00 Fri–Sun. Seafood restaurant, with great variety, & pictures to help you choose. Takes credit cards. Sometimes has live music. $$$$$

✖ **Armazem** Rua Edmundo de Barros 446; ✆ +55 45 3572 0007; ⏱ from 18.00, closed Sun. Exotic & fine meat restaurant under same management as Trapiche. Takes credit cards. $$$$

✖ **Bufalo Branco Churrascaria** [234 A3] Rua Rebouças 530; ✆ +55 45 3523 9744; www.bufalo.branco.com.br; ⏱ midday to 23.00. Close to the Hotel Del Rey & on corner of Rua Tarobá. $$$$

✖ **Chef Lópes** [234 A3] Av Rep Argentina/esq Tarobá; ✆ +55 45 3028 3531; www.cheflopes.com.br; ⏱ buffet de chef 11.30–15.00 & menu de chef 15.00–23.00. $$$$

✖ **Menu Brasil** [234 A3] Rua Tarobá 1048, corner Rua Rebouças; ✆ +55 45 3028 3355; www.menubrasilfoz.com.br. Stylish 24hr restaurant-bar. $$$$

✖ **Restaurante Chapa** [234 B4] Rua Bartolomeu de Gusmão 1014; ✆ +55 45 3572 8881; ⏱ closed Sun. Half a block from Moura Palace Hotel. $$$

✖ **Restaurante Ejecutivo** [234 B4] Sanwais, between Barroso & Brasil; ✆ +55 45 3028 1056; ⏱ closed every other Sat. Light, airy cheap eating place, fish *milanesa* every Fri, parking underneath. $$$

ENTERTAINMENT Dance shows are offered by:

Rafain Churrascaria Show [234 C5] Av das Cataratas 1749, km6.5; ✆ +55 45 3523 1177; e rafain@uol.com.br; ⏱ from 20.45 Mon–Sat. This is the best-known dance show, spanning the dance &/or music of 8 Latin American countries.
Plaza Foz [234 D2] BR 277 km726; ✆ +55 45 3526 3733; f 3526 3397; e teatroplazafoz@teatroplazafoz.com.br; www.grupocaribe.com.br; ⏱ from 21.30 Tue–Sun. Tango & samba.
Oba Oba [234 D6] Ponte Tancredo Neves, next to customs; ✆ +55 45 3529 9070; e info@obaobashow.com.br; www.obaobashow.com.br; ⏱ from 22.00 Mon–Sat. Samba & mulatas. African-Brazilian dance.

OTHER PRACTICALITIES The **Banks** in Foz include HSBC, ABN Amro and Banco do Brasil. HSBC cash machines are found at Uniamérica, Hotel das Cataratas, Vila 'A', Hipermercado Big, Bourbon Cataratas and Cataratas J L Shopping. Other 24-hour cash machines are in the service station at the east end of Avenida Schimmelpfeng, and on the corner of Avenida José Marin Toriot and Avenida Paraná.

Brasil is a major shopping street, with wide pavements and an HSBC bank with a cash machine, between Bocaiúva and E de Barros. It has at least three **internet** places: Posto Telefônico, opposite the department store Kamalito, between Rua Barbosa and Bartolomeu de Gusmão (⊕ *09.00–22.00 Mon–Sat, 09.00–13.00 & 18.00–22.00 Sun*); Galeria Brasil, between Sanwais and Gusmão; and the Cybercafé between Sanwais and Bocaiuva.

Voltage is different in Brazil, 110 volts (like the USA), unlike the 220 volts of Paraguay, Argentina and Europe. Most portable electronics these days are self-switching.

IGUAÇU FALLS

IGUAÇU FALLS (*cataratas@catarataspni.com.br; www.cataratasdoiguacu.com.br*) For the visit to the Argentinian side of these waterfalls, see page 229.

To get a bus to the Iguaçu Falls (see also page 226 above), you will need to go to the local bus station or Terminal Urbana on Avenida J K & Avenida República Argentina. The buses are marked 'Cataratas' or 'Parque Nacional' (R$2,10) and run every 20 minutes; the journey takes about 45 minutes. Then you pay to get into the national park (⊕ *summer 09.00–18.00; winter 09.00 – 17.00, last entry 1hr before closing; R$20, reduction for residents of Mercosur*). Like Argentina, Brazil receives a million visitors to the falls each year.

Brazil has a much larger national park than Argentina has around the falls: 185,000ha, as against 67,000ha in Argentina. In 1986 it was recognised by UNESCO as a World Heritage Site. But of the waterfalls themselves, Brazil owns less than Argentina: 800m, as against the 1,900m on Argentinian territory.

A visit to the Brazilian side of the Iguaçu Falls is centred on a spectacular walk along the cliffs, the Trilha das Cataratas, with amazing perspectives of the waterfalls opening in front of you, and changing as you go along. The best views of the falls are probably had from this side of the river, because they are facing you (rather than under your feet, as they are on the Argentinian side). The visit need not be as · long as the one on the Argentinian side, but you should still allow at least three hours. You may see flocks of the water-loving swifts, who build their nests just behind the falls.

The cliff walk begins from where the elegant Hotel das Cataratas is sited, discreetly set back from the cliff edge. (It is a far cry from the prominent modern Hotel Sheraton in the Argentinian national park, which is marvellous when you are on the inside looking out, but rather an eyesore for those on the Brazilian bank looking across at the view of nature.) But before you arrive, there is the option of getting off the bus for the Macuco Safari tour (*www.macucosafari.com.br*). This involves a 3km drive in a jeep, with a guide pointing out features of the trees and plants you pass. Then you continue on foot for 600m, before getting in a rubber dinghy to approach the waterfalls by river.

As in Argentina, there is a boat trip that runs you up close to the foot of a waterfall, where you get thoroughly wet. But something you do not get on the Argentinian side is the platform beneath the falls that you walk out to, mid-stream, and from where you get a stunning view of the Garganta del Diablo above and ahead of you. There is a lift up the cliff face, and when you have gone past the last waterfalls you reach a **restaurant** called Porto Canoas (excellent but not cheap). They have a big display of beautifully presented salads and you can sit on the terrace beside the lake, which here gives little indication that it is about to plunge over the edge in such a dramatic fashion.

You catch an introduction to the subtropical rainforest that comprises Brazil's national park in the first stretch of the Macuco Safari. It is a semi-deciduous seasonal forest with a great green canopy formed by big trees like fig, cinnamon and palm, and other species that can reach a height of 30m including laurel and cedar. Smaller trees include the rubber tree and varieties of palm. The ground is covered with ferns and grasses, while orchids and creepers adorn the trees. In the floodplain areas there are bamboos, palms and grasses. In the eastern area there survives the great Paraná pine, *Araucaria angustifolia*, symbol of the Paraná state.

Endangered species of animals and birds live in the forest, protected by the big trees like the *yerba mate* tree. There are 257 species of butterflies, 18 species of fish, 12 of amphibians, 41 of snakes, 8 of lizards, 45 of mammals, and 248 of birds. Among these birds you find parrots, parakeets, toucans, hawks, hummingbirds and goldfinches. Among the mammals are the jaguar and smaller wild cats, the tapir, brocket deer and capybara.

A number of longer trails are offered in the national park, by foot, bicycle or electric car, under the heading of Poço Preto or **Macuco Ecoaventura** (*www.macucoecoaventura.com.br*). Another attraction offered by the company Macuco Safari is rafting over the rapids – a 30-minute trip (*www.macucosafari.com.br*). Yet another activity is the Campo de Desafios, or Field of Challenges, which offers abseiling, rafting, tree climbing, etc, in differing degrees of difficulty, and is situated at the beginning of the Trilha das Cataratas (*www.campodedesafios.com.br*).

Helicopter trips over the falls and up to Itaipú and the Marco das 3 Fronteiras are offered by Helisul (*Rodovia das Cataratas, km16.5;* \ *+55 45 3529 7474;* f *+55 45 3529 8438;* e *helisul@helisul.com; www.helisul.com*). Some people say the trips disturb the bird life at the falls.

WHAT ELSE TO SEE

Parco das Aves (*Av das Cataratas, km17.1, next to zoo;* \ *+55 45 3529 8282; www.parquedasaves.com.br;* ⊕ *08.30–17.30 daily; US$12*) Difficult as it is to tear yourself away from the waterfalls, this bird park is well worth a visit, and is considered the best in Latin America. Over 900 birds from 150 different species are beautifully presented, along 1,000m of paths. Forest aviaries 8m high give scope for the birds to enjoy a habitat among trees. You can have direct contact with toucans, parrots and parakeets. There are also alligators, snakes and butterflies. There is a restaurant and a gift shop. See map on page 224.

Marco das Três Fronteiras (Spanish 'Hito de las Tres Fronteras') Down Rua General Meira you come to the point where the Río Iguaçu joins the Río Paraná, and three obelisks mark the meeting points of Brazil, Argentina and Paraguay. The big round building is the Espaço das Américas, a concert hall. See map on page 224.

Itaipú Dam (*Av Tancredo Neves;* \ *0800 645 4645/+55 45 3520 6676;* e *reservas@complexoitaipu.tur.br; www.complexoitaipu.tur.br*) The visit to the Itaipú dam will be covered in *Chapter 11*, page 248. Brazil and Paraguay share the same film, the same *mirador*, and the same design and infrastructure for the basic visit (what the Brazilians call the Visita Panorâmica; *lasts 1½hrs: visits at 08.00, 09.00, 10.00, 13.00, 15.00 and 15.30; R$13*). The differences are that the Brazilian side gets more visitors, because Brazil in general gets more visitors, and that you pay on the Brazilian side, while the Paraguayan side is free. Brazil also offers a longer visit, the Circuito Especial (*Circuito Especial, lasts 2½hrs; R$30*), where you get into the 1km gallery, and down a staircase to the level closer to the turbines: there are certain rules on clothing for this longer circuit, and the minimum age is 14. See map on page 224.

Ecomuseum (*Av Tancredo Neves;* \ *0800 645 4645/+55 45 3520 6676;* e *reservas@complexoitaipu.tur.br;* ⊕ *08.30–17.30 Tue–Sun; R$8*) You pass this eco-musuem on your left, on the way to the Itaipú dam, after passing the Buddhist temple. The history of the environmental projects of Itaipú is imaginatively presented, with the fauna and flora of the region, ethnography, and the details of how energy is generated by the dam. See map on page 224.

Refugio Biológico Bela Vista (*Tancredo Neves 6702;* ℡ *0800 645 4645;* f *+55 45 3520 6398;* e *reservas@complexoitaipu.tur.br; www.complexoitaipu.tur.br; R$12 & R$6*) After the Ecomuseum, you reach this down a turn to the right, before the visitors' centre of the dam. It offers five themed walks through forest, in a reserve created to house the thousands of plants and animals displaced by the dam. All the buildings were built to function on alternative energy sources. See map on page 224.

9

Ciudad del Este and the East

Departamento: Alto Paraná

Although Ciudad del Este has a reputation for crime and smuggling and is not somewhere you would normally choose to go for a holiday, you may well find yourself going there on the way to the Iguazú Falls (or the Iguaçu Falls – on the Brazilian side). If you take as much care as you normally would in a big city, there is no need to avoid the place or to feel uncomfortable there: you may even find yourself enjoying the buzz of the place. It also has more green space than most towns: it was built to be a garden city.

What is more, immediately north of Ciudad del Este are some very interesting and attractive places that really do merit a visit: the famous Itaipú dam, the Museo de la Tierra Guaraní and the Tatí Yupí. Immediately south of the city are some attractive natural sites, including the Moisés Bertoni house, the home of the esteemed Swiss naturalist, hidden in some beautiful woods. Both of these are reached via what is called the Supercarretera (or Avenida Mariscal López) which is the road that runs as straight as a die from north to south, or to be more exact, from north-northeast to south-southwest. The Supercarretera is off to the left of the map on page 243, 4km from the Puente de la Amistad, and is unmissable because there is a flyover over it.

CIUDAD DEL ESTE Copaco ↘ 061 500000; municipalidad ↘ 061 500222

This is a new city, founded as recently as 1957 in Stroessner's time, and soon named after him, Ciudad Presidente Stroessner. The name mercifully did not survive the end of the dictatorship. The city began with an airstrip, two avenues and the foundation stone of the cathedral. It subsequently grew to the point where *Forbes* magazine declared it was the third-biggest commercial city in the world after Miami and Hong Kong. For Paraguayans, it is the place you go to buy a computer, if you know where to look and what you are looking for. The commercial centre with its endless outlets selling electrical goods, grouped into big shopping centres, where everything is shiny and modern, is a phenomenon that nothing in Asunción can touch. But just a stone's throw away is the sordid, broken, dirty face of the third-world marketplace, which is what you first see when you enter Paraguay from Brazil.

As you walk down a shopping street like Adrián Jara, you find a unique blend of elegance and squalor, with a man with a rifle at every corner. There is litter in the streets, and lads lugging piles of flattened cardboard boxes on their heads, or tugging trolleys of heavy electronics uphill. And coming at you from all sides, is the *shlik* sound of packaging tape being stretched around boxes of purchases.

As a city, Ciudad del Este has severe social problems. Children as young as seven may ask you for money, and then try to steal your mobile phone; they are known

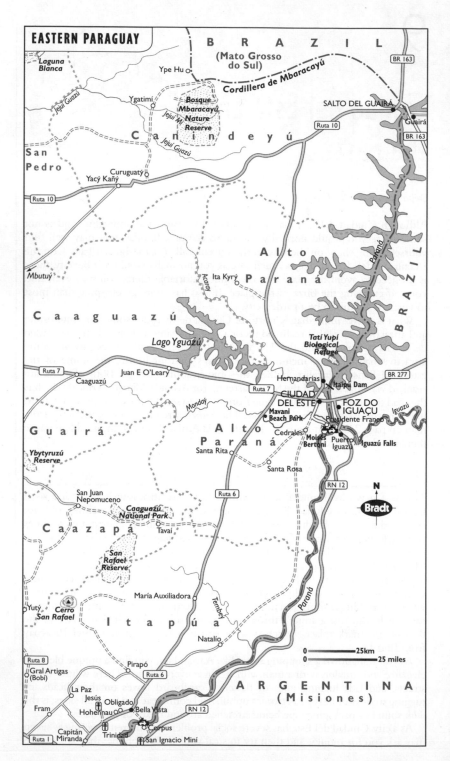

EASTERN PARAGUAY

as *pirañitas*, little sharks. There are encampments of Mbyá Guaraní – one beside the bus terminal and another beside the Centro Regional de Educación – who have come in from their ancestral grounds and resist attempts to return them there. They scrape a living in the city by begging, by collecting bottles and tins from the rubbish and selling them by the kilo, and from prostitution, organised through the taxi drivers. Watch your wallet, watch your handbag, and be prudent: at night even the Itaipú dam suffers theft of its light bulbs.

The economy of the city depends largely on cross-border smuggling. A particular phenomenon is the activity of the *sacoleiros,* the word for Brazilians who cross the bridge each day to fill their bags with cheap goods from Paraguay, and return home to sell them in Foz: goods 'for personal use' are import-free, and if they do it every day they have quite a business. From time to time the Brazilians have a drive to cut down on customs-dodging at the border, and there can be long delays in getting across the bridge, optimistically named Puente de la Amistad (Ponte da Amizade in Portuguese), the Bridge of Friendship. Taxi drivers from the terminal fortunately charge a flat rate to take you to Foz, so there are no extras if you have to wait in a queue for a couple of hours to get across the bridge.

It is not recommended to accept a supposedly cut-price offer of a taxi from someone who does not do the journey regularly. The taxi drivers from the terminal know Foz (at least to some extent) and speak Portuguese to ask for directions: without this you may find yourself having to pay for a second, Brazilian taxi, which will more than wipe out any saving you thought you were making. (See also *Chapter 8*, page 232, on crossing the border.)

GETTING THERE

By bus If you arrive in Paraguay **from Brazil**, you may be coming in a bus from São Paulo, which is a long but comfortable journey away (see *Chapter 2*, page 33).

BUS TIMETABLE: ASUNCIÓN TO CIUDAD DEL ESTE

BUS COMPANY	TELEPHONE	PRICE	DEPART ASUNCIÓN	DEPART CIUDAD DEL ESTE
Rysa	021 551601/2 061 510396	Gs75,000	approx every hour	approx every hour
Nuestra Señora de la Asunción	021 2891000 061 512095	Gs73,000	00.00, 07.30, 12.00, 13.40, 16.00, 18.40	00.00, 07.30, 11.40, 14.00, 16.00, 18.30
Crucero del Este	021 555082 061 511074	Gs50,000	05.30, 08.30, 11.30, 12.40, 15.00, 18.00	05.30, 08.30, 11.30, 12.40, 15.00,18.00
San Luis	021 551705 061 513826	Gs40,000– 50,000	approx every hour	approx every hour
Pycasú	021 557700 061 514910	Gs40,000– 73,000	approx every hour	approx every hour

Prices correct at time of going to press. It is recommended to avoid the very lowest fares of Gs40,000 as these buses can be extremely slow. The Gs50,000 service of San Luis is very little extra and has been reported as quite adequate.

Asunción Terminal Information ☎ 021 551740
Ciudad del Este Terminal Information ☎ 061 510421

(You may find that you have to change buses on the Brazilian side of the border, because the bus companies do not want their best buses to travel on Paraguayan roads.) Or you may be coming from Foz – either from the airport (which is a good way of flying to Paraguay) or from a visit to the Iguazú Falls which may have begun on the Argentinian side.

If Ciudad del Este is your first view of Paraguay, the contrast with Brazil will be a shock, particularly on this access road from the bridge. But bear in mind that this squalor is a far cry from the dignity, freshness and tradition of the Paraguayan *campo* that you will find when you leave Ciudad del Este behind.

A number of companies make the bus journey **from Asunción** to the terminal in Ciudad del Este (⟩ *061 510421*), which is 1,500m south of Avenida Monseñor Rodríguez (the southern carriageway of Ruta 7), and not far from the river. Go down General Bernardino Caballero, past Rogelio Benítez, past San Martín, and you will come to the Estadio 3 de febrero at the corner of the next road, Eugenio A Gray. The terminal is on the far side of the Estadio. There are frequent departures all day long. The journey takes five hours, and do not be misled by Crucero del Este telling you that they do it in 4½ hours. To avoid the rather exposed and sometimes dirty toilets in the terminal, go to the 'Sala VIP' where they are much better: these facilities are for travellers on international and long-distance journeys, and your journey will count as long distance.

If you are coming **from southern Paraguay** – from Encarnación – there are plenty of services, and the journey takes between four and seven hours. The bus companies include Nuestra Señora de la Encarnación, Rysa, Itapúa Poty, San Juan and Ñeembucú. The latter two go further than Encarnación, to San Ignacio and beyond. Avoid Ortega if you can: it is very slow. But if your only reason for the journey is to go to the Iguazú Falls then you might consider crossing over to Posadas and coming up to the falls through Misiones Argentina (see *Chapter 8*, page 225).

By car If you are driving, then study the instructions on page 103 for getting out of Asunción. If you get onto Ruta 2 successfully in San Lorenzo then it is straight ahead all the way, with the road changing its number to Ruta 7 at Coronel Oviedo. To cover the 327km allow five hours, plus whatever stops you make.

A suitable place to stop for **a meal** would be La Nona, next to the Hotel Bertea, just before the roundabout in Coronel Oviedo (see *Chapter 10*, page 254). If you want to do something more organised and imaginative to break your journey, and if you have that little bit of extra time, you could try ringing or emailing in advance to the *estancia* Los Manantiales (⟩ *021 497028;* m *0981 425498;* e *pstopino@pla.net.py*) just 4km north of Caacupé, or Don Emilio (⟩ *021 660791/021 603994;* m *0981 507105;* e *donemilio24@gmail.com*), 6km to the south of Ruta 2 on the road to Villarrica, and see if they can do you a lunch, or put you up overnight. An alternative way of making a reservation is through the Central de Reservas of Apatur in Asunción (*Brasil c/ 25 de mayo, 8th Floor;* ⟩ *021 210550 int 126;* e *info@tacpy.com.py; www.turismorural.org.py*). *Estancias* always require advance notice, of at least a day.

When in Ciudad del Este, try to leave the car in a guarded car park. If you cannot do that, a trick to avoid break-ins is to offer a local street kid a tip for keeping an eye on your car until you return.

By air You can fly to Ciudad del Este's Aeropuerto Guaraní (airport code AGT, from its official name of Alejo García) from Asunción and from São Paulo. But you cut down on flexibility because there is only one flight a day, with TAM Airlines (⟩ *021 645500; www.tamairlines.com*). The PZ706 departs from Asunción at 10.50 and arrives in Ciudad del Este at 11.30; then at 11.50 it continues to São Paulo, arriving at 14.30. In the other direction, the PZ707 departs from São Paulo at 15.30, arriving at Ciudad

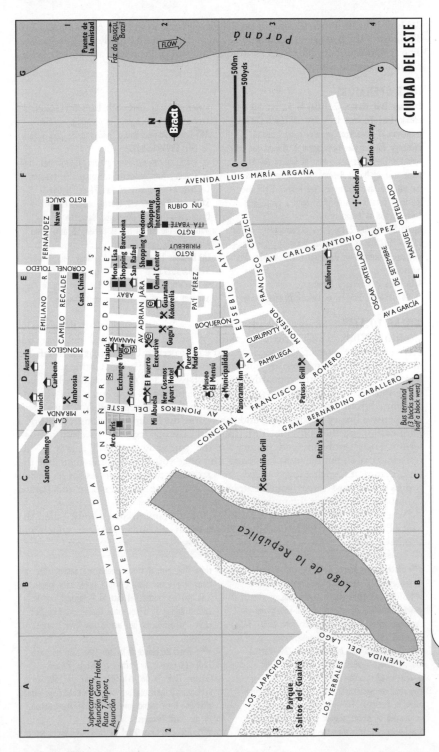

CIUDAD DEL ESTE

del Este at 16.10; it then leaves Ciudad del Este at 16.30 to arrive in Asunción at 17.10. The cost of the fare from Asunción to Ciudad del Este is currently US$76 one way. The airport is just north of Ruta 7, some 25km west of the bridge and shortly before the junction with Ruta 6.

TOUR OPERATORS

Exchange Tour/Mavani [243 D2] Av Nanawa 90 edificio Saba PB local 1; ✆ 061 500766/7/513313; e mavani@mavani.com.py; www.mavani.com.py. Exchange Tour is the travel agent & Mavani the tour operator. They offer a city-tour of Ciudad del Este; 1-day tour of Moisés Bertoni, the Monday Falls & the Hito de las 3 Fronteras (see below); flight over the local sites in a little plane with a propeller; 2-day escape to Asunción.

Aguila Edificio fuji 2, Pai Pérez c/ Curupayty; ✆ 061 502704/502705; e commercial@aguilaturismo.com; www.aguilaturismo.com. Organises tours all over the country.

AMA Tours Pa'i Pérez y Boquerón; ✆ 061 506472/506475; e turismo@ama.com.py;

www.ama.com.py. Comfortable buses & minibuses. They also have an agency in Asunción.

AGT Group Edificio Banco Unión, Adrián Jara y Abay; ✆ 061 509599/504925; e agt@agt.com.py; www.agt.com.py. Promotes itself as a young firm dedicated to sustainable tourism.

Cel Tour Av Curupaytý e/ Pa'i Pérez; ✆ 061 513116/508347; e cel_tour@hotmail.com. Organises a tour of the Itaipú dam, the Monday waterfalls, the Museo Moisés Bertoni & other sites, with all risks insurance.

Los Delfines Los Lapachos y los Guayabos; ✆ 061 514083/502730; e cdedelfines2@tigo.com.py. Can take you to the different sites of the Itaipú Tourist Complex.

WHERE TO STAY The nicest hotels are in an exclusive estate called the **Paraná Country Club**, which strictly speaking is not part of Ciudad del Este but Hernandarias. However, it is so close and easy to reach by taxi that its hotels are included here among those of Ciudad del Este. The Paraná Country Club is fiercely protected by armed guards, and you have to tell them exactly where you are going before they will let you in. You are filmed as you enter, and you are prohibited from taking photos once you are inside the compound. You pass a row of expensive luxury-goods shops, and then come the luxury mansions, every one a mini-castle, and the golf club. Entering such a protected area, so close to such serious social problems and penury in the adjoining city, will aggravate the conscience of all but the most hardened. But once you get to a somewhere like the Casa Blanca, it is such a lovely place – not so much for its luxury as for its design – that you almost forget your scruples. It is not the only hotel in the Paraná Country Club, but it is the most beautiful.

A new estate like the Paraná Country Club is being prepared now, called the Santa Elena Country y Marina Club, 28km north of Ciudad del Este, which will also have hotels.

Hotel Casino Acaray [243 F4] (50 rooms) 11 de septiembre c/ Av Luis María Argaña; ✆ 061 504250; e info@hotelcasinoacaray.com.py; www.hotelcasinoacaray.com.py. A well-known top-of-the-range hotel, right on the river front, built 1965, reopened 2009. Live shows, karaoke, casino. $$$$

Casa Blanca (see map on page 224) Paraná Country Club; ✆ 061 572121; f 061 572404; e reservas@casablancahotel.net; www.casablancahotel.net. One of the most beautiful hotels in Paraguay. Fountain in the stairwell surrounded by plants, elegant drawing rooms, big stone fireplaces, view over the slow-moving green

river. Pool, gym & sauna. Rooms are named after trees or precious stones, luxury suites very ample. 'Can this be Ciudad del Este in Paraguay?' one finds oneself asking. It is not quite Ciudad del Este, but rather Hernandarias, just across the River Acaray. $$$$

Hotel Residence de la Tour (see map on page 224) (15 rooms) Av Paraná c/ Milano, Paraná Country Club; ✆ 061 572483; f 061 573150; e latour@zipfoz.com.br; www.latourhotel.com. Named after the little round tower you enter at reception, all the usual luxuries. $$$$

Asunción Gran Hotel Av Monseñor Rodríguez c/

Roberto L Petit, km5; ☎ 061 573439/571853; www.asunciongranhotel.com. Business centre, sauna, *hidromasaje*, guarded car park. $$$$

🏠 **Hotel Panorama Inn** [243 D3] Pampliega y Eusebio Ayala; ☎ 061 500110; f 061 500958; e hpanorin@cde.rieder.net.py; www.hotelpanoramainn.com.py. On a quieter street but close to micro-centre. Spacious suites with huge mirrors, the sort of place to stay when you want to be there for a while. Lots of marble. Takes credit cards. Good restaurant. $$$

🏠 **Hotel California** [243 E4] Av Carlos Antonio López 180; ☎ 061 500350/500378; e hotelcal@hotmail.com. Almost opposite the cathedral. Minibars, TV, swimming pool, American b/fast, restaurant. $$$

🏠 **Hotel Convair** [243 D2] Av Adrián Jara y Curupayty; ☎ 061 500942/508555; f 061 500857; e reservas@hotelconvair.com. Swimming pool, internet, minibars, restaurant. Good-quality furniture but could have better design. $$$

🏠 **Hotel Munich** [243 D1] Emiliano R Fernández 71 y Capitán Miranda; ☎ 061 500347. Grand entrance, big rooms, good furniture, helpful manager, minibars, American b/fast with homemade bread. Quiet neighbourhood. Recommended. $$$

🏠 **Hotel Austria** [243 D1] (48 rooms) Emiliano R Fernández 165; ☎ 061 504213/4; www.hotelaustriarestaurante.com. Internet, parking, garden, but has seen better days. Airy b/fast room, American b/fast, quiet neighbourhood, but second choice to nearby Munich. $$$

🏠 **New Cosmos Apart Hotel** [000000] Edificio Cosmopolitan 1, Pa'i Pérez y Pampliega; ☎ 061 501232/511030. Reception on 2nd floor, every room a suite with balcony, sitting room, dining table, fridge, plates, original numbered print on wall. Includes b/fast served in your room by restaurant next door. Seems amazing value but puzzling that it also seems pretty empty – although this is probably

because it is new. $$$

🏠 **Mi Abuela Hotel** [243 D2] (24 rooms) Av Adrián Jara c/ Pioneros del Este; ☎ 061 500333/500305/500348; e miabuelahotel@hotmail.com or jaj@hotelconvair.com. Central. Under same management as Hotel Convair. Nice patio, clean, modern feel & lots of customers. B/fast room is full of historic photos, & the grandfather of the owner was Adrián Jara, one of pioneers of building Ciudad del Este. B/fast room also is a café, open to the street. Loud pop music in reception which will not suit all. $$$

🏠 **Hotel Itaipú** [243 D1] Nanawa c/ Av Rodríguez; ☎ 061 500371/508677; e hotelitaipu@hotmail.com. Rooms slightly battered but not bad, TV, phone. B/fast not inc but can be ordered from the adjoining restaurant – a simple, decent & airy café, next door to Exchange Tours (see below) & opposite Banco do Brasil. $$

🏠 **Santo Domingo Hotel** [243 D1] Emiliano Fernández y Emeterio Miranda; ☎ 061 500375/500381; f 061 513691. Plants & fountain in reception. Quiet neighbourhood. Recommended. $$

🏠 **Hotel Guarania** [243 E2] Abay 146 c/ Adrián Jara; ☎ 061 500352/510385; e hrguarania@hotmail.com. AC, cable TV, parking, American b/fast. Restaurant closes 19.00. Internet open to public 07.00–20.00. Popular budget hotel that fills up quickly, unfortunately marred by a lot of rubbish on the road outside. $$

🏠 **Hotel San Rafael** [243 E2] Av Adrián Jara y Abay; ☎ 061 500804. Wood panelling, fairly full. Cable TV, parking. Very run down, AC deafening, but helpful manager, cheap, excellent b/fast with lots of fruit, & check out at midday where many other hotels make it 10.00. $

🏠 **Caribeño** [243 D1] Emiliano R Fernández 136, e/ Capitán Miranda y Mongelos; ☎ 061 512460. Very simple & unpretentious but clean & pleasant. Quiet neighbourhood. $

✖ **WHERE TO EAT** In addition to the places below, there are excellent eating places in the shopping centres; for example, in the Mona Lisa, the Shopping Barcelona and the Shopping Vendome.

✖ **Restaurant Madame Chateau** Las Ventanas Suites Hotel, Av María de los Angeles esq Luis Bordon, Paraná Country Club; ☎ 061 574500. Smart gourmet cuisine, in a very expensive hotel. Does a lot of business lunches. $$$$$

✖ **Patussi Grill** [243 D3] Alejo García y Monseñor Cedzich; ☎ 061 502293/570621. One of the best restaurants, a *churrasquería*, with branches opposite the airport, in the Paraná Country Club & on Ruta

7 at km5. Pizza Hut is next door. $$$

✖ **Churrasquería Interlagos** Ruta 7 km5; ☎ 061 570621. This is off the map on page 243, a little further down Ruta 7, 1km past the interchange with the Supercarretera. The crude colourful sign next door to Localiza car hire does not give a hint that this is one of the best restaurants in the city, with its endless offers of juicy meats, big variety of salads, & vast number of waiters. The *mousse de* *mburucuyá* is very good. Live harp & guitar music from 20.00 on Sat, packed out as the evening wears on. Another branch of the restaurant is 1km east & around the corner, towards Hernandarias, on Supercarretera km26 (✆ *0631 22464*). $$$

✖ **El Puerto** [243 D2] Pampliega c/ Jara; �📱 0975 193375; ⏲ Mon–Fri, & Sat lunch. Calls itself a *taberna española*, small frontage leads down to cellar restaurant, great atmosphere, well patronised. Menu at lunch, evenings à la carte. Fresh fish every Wed & Thu. $$$

✖ **Hotel Panorama Inn** [243 D3] ✆ 061 500110. See above. $$$

✖ **Puerto Madero Restaurant** [243 D2] ✆ 061 511424; ⏲ 07.30–midnight daily. Next door to New Cosmos Apart Hotel, takes credit cards. Serves b/fast. $$$

✖ **Gauchiño Grill** [243 C3] Av del Lago; ✆ 061 513032; ⏲ closed Sun night & all Mon. The road it is on is also called Mariscal José Estigarribia, & it is on the corner of 12 de junio, on the east side of the lake. If you approach on Bernardino Caballero, turn right just after the *municipalidad*. Guard with rifle outside as this is a rather dark & isolated area. Big variety of excellent, tender meat; stronger on meat & desserts than on salads. Brazilian waiters. Deservedly busy. $$$

✖ **Patu's Bar** [243 D3] Bernardino Caballero 480; ✆ 061 506508; ⏲ daily. Lively, imaginative restaurant under same management as Patussi, specialising in pizzas. Across the green from the Patussi Grill, & down a little turning off Bernardino Caballero, called 12 de junio. View over lake. $$

✖ **Gugu's** [243 D2] Boquerón y Adrián Jára; ✆ 061 512494; ⏲ 10.30–21.00 Mon–Sat. Highly recommended Chinese restaurant, economical, bursting with Chinese customers, good décor, lovely bathroom. One of 3 adjacent Chinese restaurants: Restaurant Garden & Mil Mil are the others, but Gugu's is the most inviting. $$

✖ **Restaurant Kokorelia** [243 E2] Boquerón. Korean restaurant. $$

✖ **Executive Restaurant** [243 D2] Av Adrián Jara y Curupaytý; ✆ 061 500942/512215. Good snack bar underneath the rather worn Executive Hotel. $

✖ **Mi Abuela Hotel** [243 D2] See above. $

✖ **Ambrosia Restaurant** [243 D1] Edificio Santa Catalina, Salón 1 y 2, Camilo Recalde c/ Capitán Miranda (behind Oasis); ✆ 061 501667. Large clean café with AC. $

SHOPPING The principal sites in Ciudad del Este are the shops, especially the big shopping centres.

The Monalisa [243 E1] (*Carlos Antonio López e/ Av Rodríguez & Adrián Jára*) is a very smart department store. It seems to have a perfume section on every floor, and on the fourth floor is a *museo de perfumes* (just a display case with nine giant bottles). Their produce could have come straight out of a top store in Europe: L'Oréal face creams, Le Creuset saucepans, Lacoste sporting tops, Bulgari watches, and the biggest Toblerone you have ever seen in your life. They expect you to pay in dollars, not in guaraníes. Can this be Paraguay?

The Casa China [243 E1] is a smart department store, with nothing noticeably Chinese about it. But there is a big Chinese community in the city, as you become aware when you stumble across Gugu's Chinese restaurant.

Down the Avenida Rodríguez from Boquerón towards the bridge you will find it is all electronics shops, with stalls on the pavements too. (The other side of Ruta 7 is Avenida San Blas, which is all clothes shops.) Parallel to Rodríguez but one block south is Avenida Adrián Jara: this is a key street for computers and electronics. You pass in turn the Omni Center, Shopping Vendome (with its armed guards at every corner) and Shopping Internacional.

Be cautious about buying cheap computer equipment in Ciudad del Este. The price will probably not be lower than you would pay with a cheap, large company in your own country; and you occasionally hear horror stories of various tricks that a traveller may be vulnerable to: boxed products may have had internal parts changed for others of lesser quality, or may even come with only paper inside instead of the equipment.

Nave [243 F1] (*Rua Regimiento Sauce esq Emiliano Fernández;* ✆ *061 513397/513551;* e *callcenter@naveshop.com;* ⏲ *daily inc Sun; takes credit cards*) is one of the biggest and most reputable stores for computers, digital cameras, DVD players, etc. A significant indicator of its market is that its glossy leaflet is printed in Portuguese, and it is only just past the customs into Paraguay. 'Travel with peace of mind: declare your luggage' it advises.

OTHER PRACTICALITIES There is a **map** produced by J B Producciones, but much the best town plan if you can get it is by Ictus. You can get some maps of the city from Exchange Tours, upstairs (see above for address).

Cash machines are not difficult to find in Ciudad del Este and, among others, the following banks have them: Banco Continental (*Boquerón*), Banco ABN Amro (*Nanawa y Av Adrián Jara*), Interbanco (*Shopping Suni, San Blas km2,5; also Hospital Area 2, Bernardino Caballero*) and Banco Sudameris (*Pampliega y Rodríguez*)

There is **internet** at Eikkon [243 D2] (*Nanawa c/ Jara*), at a couple of places close to the junction of Jara and Curupaytý (⊕ *07.00–18.00*) and at the Hotel Guarania (see above). This central area of town is spookily empty by 19.00, even in summer when it is still light, and you would not feel comfortable taking an evening walk in the deserted streets, which are watched over by armed guards by day.

The office of the **airline** TAM is on the corner of Curupaytý and Avenida Dr Eusebio Ayala (two blocks south of Exchange Tours).

Ciudad del Este has two **car-hire** companies. You can hire from the airport, or from their offices on Ruta 7, the northern carriageway of which is called Avenida San Blas when it is inside the city.

🚗 **Localiza** Av San Blas km4.5; 📞 021 683892; airport 📞 021 683895; e localiza@ conexion.com.py; www.localiza.com.py. About 7 blocks to the west of the Supercarretera.

🚗 **Avis** Av San Blas 1294, km3.5; 📞 061 504770; airport m 0983 602825; e reservas@avis.com.py. 5 blocks to the east of the Supercarretera.

WHAT TO SEE The Lago de la República is a pleasant lake, formed by damming the Amambay stream, in parkland a little to the south of the centre. In the middle of the green is the *municipalidad* – an attractive single-storey building with colonnade (but of modern style), swarming with people paying their taxes and seeking to register their cars. To its left is the small house used as the **Museo El Mensú** [243 D2] (⊕ *07.00–13.00 Mon–Fri; free*), which, as well as the typical museum contents of old typewriters and rusty rifles, tells the history of the city, with the handwritten Acta de Fundación dated 3 February 1957. It also has photos of Moisés Bertoni, displays of bows and arrows, and skins of caimans hanging up (like Fr Gabriel comes across in the jungle in the film *The Mission*). To the other side of the *municipalidad* is a Chinese garden.

The **cathedral** [243 F4] (*Carlos Antonio López e/ Oscar Ortellado y 11 de setiembre*) is dedicated to San Blas, and was inaugurated in 1970, designed by a Bolivian architect, Javier Querejazu, and extended in 1989. This interesting and dramatic building is built to resemble a ship and is best seen from the inside: it has a broad frontage with two side towers, and the nave then narrows to the sanctuary, where round windows like portholes lead up to a tall, thin, vertical panel of brilliant red, white and blue stained glass, portraying San Blas. Most striking of all is the constant birdsong inside, from birds that live inside the building: it is said that you cannot hear the daily mass for the volume of the birdsong. To gain access, ask at the diocesan office behind the cathedral. Pope John Paul II, in his 1988 visit, gave the building a cross identical to that planted in the Dominican Republic to commemorate the fifth centenary of the evangelisation of America.

ITAIPÚ

ITAIPÚ DAM Itaipú (Guaraní) means 'the singing stone'. Visits to the Itaipú dam (☎ *061 599 8040;* e *arevalos@itaipu.gov.py; www.itaipu.gov.py;* ⊕ *visits at 08.00, 09.30, 14.00, 15.00 Mon–Sat; a 5th visit on Sat at 10.30; on Sun visits at 08.00, 09.30, 19.30; free*) last 1½ hours. (See map on page 224.) You must come with your passport and fill in a form requesting a visit. There is a good craft shop to browse in. The visit begins with a film (in English or Spanish) recounting the history of the construction. Then everyone gets in a bus, which takes them over the top of the dam to the Brazilian side, where the view is better.

The photos of Itaipú usually show it with the water thundering down the three spillways. In fact you never see this: the spillways only operate occasionally, after there has been extremely heavy rain, and even then it is unusual for more than one to be used. The water that generates the power passes over the turbines far down beneath the surface.

To see the *iluminación monumental* (*18.30 Thu, 19.30 Fri, Sat; free*) you must apply beforehand, by Thursday of the week in question, filling in a form with your full name, passport number and nationality, or sending those details by email to the address above, or by fax (f *061 599 8045*) or by phone (☎ *061 599 8040*). The illumination in itself lasts only for five minutes, but the first two hours of the evening are devoted to a musical show they put on in the auditorium. Then you are bussed over to the *mirador* on the Brazilian side. Before the illumination begins, there is a short film about the dam, then dramatic music, and then slowly, bit by bit, the dam lights up, with gathering intensity, in subtle shades of green, orange and yellow. The alcoves in the concrete, when lit up, look like a row of stone lance heads, and all in all the dam is far more lovely than it is by day.

The Itaipú project was begun with the signing of memorandum between Paraguay and Brazil in 1966. Then the formal treaty followed in 1973, and it is this that President Fernando Lugo worked so hard to renegotiate with President Lula of Brazil. He succeeded in August 2009, with the result that Paraguay will get three times as much money for the excess energy that it sells to Brazil. The problem with the treaty had been that whereas Brazil uses more energy than it produces from the dam, Paraguay, as a small country with a low population, uses much less – only 5% of its production.

For a long time Itaipú, with its 18 turbines (later increased to 20) was the largest hydro-electric dam in the world. The Three Gorges dam in China has now overtaken it, with 26 turbines, soon to increase to 32. Itaipú was also the most expensive dam ever built – largely due to the corrupt practice of *sobrefacturación*, the normal form of which is to make out a bill for an excessive amount, and to share the surplus between the two parties to the fraud. The estimate for its construction was US$3.4 billion, but in the end it cost US$20 billion.

The dam began producing energy in 1984, and the last of the 20 generators began functioning in 2007. It now has a capacity to generate 14,000 megawatts, and each one of the generators produces enough energy for a city of 2.5 million people. In 2008 Itaipú generated more than 94 million megawatt-hours. The royalties distributed to date are over US$6.6 billion – half to each country.

A 10km bypass (on the Brazilian side) called the Canal de Piracema has been created to enable fish to pass without going through the dam: they need this facility to reach their breeding areas. The lake of Itaipú is today 200km long, and holds 29 million cubic metres of water. It takes the place of the long sequence of waterfalls that formed the famous Saltos del Guairá, where the Guaraní led by Montoya lost all their statues, musical instruments and other possessions, in the great and terrible exodus from Guairá to where San Ignacio Miní is situated today (see *Chapter 11*, page 207).

ITAIPÚ'S TOURIST COMPLEX Itaipú supports (and has initiated) three tourist sites to the north of Ciudad del Este: the Museo de la Tierra Guaraní, the zoo and the Tatí Yupí Biological Refuge. Then to the south of the city are the Moisés Bertoni house and the Saltos de Mondaý.

The Museo de la Tierra Guaraní and the zoo are together in a complex 2km before Itaipú, while Tatí Yupí is a little further north, as it is on the lake above the dam. The Itaipú Tourist Complex (✆ *061 599 8040;* f *061 599 8045;* e *arevalos@itaipu.gov.py;*) is part of the Itaipú's programme of Integration, and Social and Environmental Responsibility.

To the north of Ciudad del Este

Museo de la Tierra Guaraní Do not miss the chance to visit this lovely museum (*on the Supercarretera, 2km before you reach the Itaipú dam;* ✆ *061 599 8782/8626;* ⊕ *08.00–11.30 & 14.30–17.00 Tue–Sat, 08.00–11.30 Sun; free*). (See map on page 224.) It was opened in 1975, but still has a fresh feel to it, making use of multi-media display, with touch-screen access to extensive information and interviews. It is divided into two exhibition halls. The first concentrates on the Guaraní world, and explores what we can learn from the original inhabitants, whose descendants, the Ava Guaraní of Acaray-mí and Itanara-mí, still preserve their culture. There are baskets, feather ornaments, stone tools and earthenware pots, and interesting details about the social and religious system of the Guaraní: for example, they were traditionally buried in pots, in a foetal position, and the hummingbird (*mainumby*) was considered the only bird who could communicate directly with God (*Ñandejára*).

The second hall is devoted to the World of Science, and has a lot of taxidermy. It has sections on the colonial gold hunters; the classification of species; the 18th-century naturalist Félix de Azara – who lived 20 years in Paraguay, when he was sent to delimit the boundary between Spanish and Portuguese territory; and the 19th-century naturalist Moisés Bertoni – who discovered the uses of the sweet herb *ka'a he'e* (*Stevia rebaudiana bertonii*), which is still much used in Paraguay as a sweetener, and beginning to be exported. Finally it reaches the present-day achievement of the Itaipú dam.

Zoológico The zoo (⊕ *08.00–11.30 & 14.30–17.00 Tue–Sat, 08.00–11.30 Sun; free*) has 12ha of ground, to permit reproduction of rare species. (See map on page 224.) In 2009 two baby pumas were born – which was considered a rare success. Pumas are an endangered species, as is the Chacoan peccary (Spanish *cerdo del monte;* Guaraní *taguá*), of which there are also examples in the zoo.

Surprisingly badly maintained, and with few notices, the zoo is not as good as Yacyretá's Refugio Atinguý. It has on display: deer, rodents, snakes, otters, beavers, turtles, anteaters and howler monkeys. There is a red-billed currassow bird, a yellow anaconda snake and a broad-snouted caiman. There is a huge shiny black panther, baring his teeth and flicking the end of his tail, and three jaguars, kept in separate cages, with stiff, bristly whiskers, huge yellow teeth and big tongues, growling angrily.

The two principal kinds of Paraguayan parrot can be studied here: the blue-and-yellow macaw and the red-and-green macaw.

Tatí Yupí The Biological Refuge of Tatí Yupí (⊕ *08.30–11.30 & 14.00–16.30 Tue–Sat, 08.00–12.00 Sun, 13.30–16.30 Mon; free*) was opened as recently as 2005. (See map on page 224.) To visit it, you must get authorisation from the reception desk in Itaipú, but this is easily obtained. It is 3km north of Hernandarias and you cannot reach it without a car (or taxi). The refuge covers more than 2,000ha of natural wood with streams and springs, and the area is rich in animals and birds.

The activities include rides through the woods in a sulky (horse cart), on a bicycle, on horseback or on foot. In the lunch period you can stay in the refuge and walk in the central area and on the beach, but the activities begin again at 14.00. There is a good view over the lake, where dead tree stumps stick up out of the water, stripped and whitened by sun and rain, as a reminder that this lake has been artificially created by flooding. Brazil is a long way away across the lake: you can only pick out the bigger trees. The beach is of red sand, littered with tiny shells.

There are two **dormitories** with 30 beds each, where groups (often from schools, but any group is eligible) can stay for just one night, if they bring their bedding and towels. There is a kitchen, but you must bring your plates and cutlery. Reservations need to be made at least a month beforehand (061 599 86666), and no charge is made. There are also **camping** facilities.

To the south of Ciudad del Este The **Hito de las 3 Fronteras** (see map on page 224) is the point where the three countries of Paraguay, Brazil and Argentina abut, separated only by the Río Paraná and the Río Iguazú. Each country has placed a marker with the colours of its flag. To see this from the Paraguayan side take the Avenida Bernardino Caballero which goes past the terminal, and then changes name to Mariscal Estigarribia. It is about 10km. However, the best view of the Hito is from Argentina, not from Paraguay (see *Chapter 8*, page 231).

The urban sprawl to the south of Ciudad del Este is really a separate town called Presidente Franco. A new bridge planned to cross from here to Foz, paid for by Brazil, is expected to open in 2012. Just beyond Presidente Franco, the Salto Mondaý and, a little further south, the house of Moisés Bertoni, are both now technically taken into sites promoted as the Complejo Turístico Itaipú, and information can be obtained from the usual number (061 599 8040), although they are south of Ciudad del Este and do not originate from the work of the dam.

Salto Mondaý (07.30–18.00 daily; Gs2,000) The Salto Monday (pronounced in three syllables as Mon-da-ugh) cannot begin to be compared to the Iguazú Falls, pleasant though it is, and approached through a well-kept garden. The waterfall has a drop of 40m, and there is an observation platform. It is 10km from Ciudad del Este, and is well signed, down Pioneros del Este which turns into Bernardino Caballero. Mondaý is the name of the river on the Paraguayan side that is almost opposite (but a little bit south) of the juncture of the Río Iguazú and the Río Paraná. There are plans to open a Maharishi Reserva Natural on the other side of the waterfall from its current access point.

Monumento Científico Moisés Bertoni (08.00–15.00 Tue–Sun) Dr Moisés Bertoni was an emblematic figure in the natural sciences, who did research in meteorology, agronomy, biology and cartography. His little house has been turned into a museum (see map on page 224), with his manuscripts, letters and part of his library, his Minerva printing press with pedal and guillotine, skulls of animals and a reconstruction of his laboratory. This simple two-storey wooden house with a balcony, badly maintained and insufficiently attended though it is, has nonetheless a lovely feel to it, and the Guaraní indigenous who come to sell their goods seem to feel at home. (A restoration is currently being planned.)

To reach it by car from Presidente Franco, you take the road past Salto Mondaý to Los Cedrales. It turns into cobbles so deformed it is barely passable, and there are no signs to indicate that you are on the way to the house of Moisés Bertoni. About 10km from Presidente Franco you take a turn to the left towards the Río Paraná for 5km more, followed by 16km of a much more pleasant dirt road through soya fields. From the car park there is a magical walk through the beautiful

Born in Switzerland in 1857, Moisés Santiago Bertoni was influenced by socialist ideas and studied law and botany. He set off for South America in 1884 with his family and a group of Swiss farmers to found a socialist colony. A few years later, drought impelled the colony to move from Argentina to Paraguay, where they lived in great poverty and hunger. Bertoni published works on Paraguayan geology, on the eucalyptus, cotton-growing and oranges, and had his own printing press under the imprint Ex Silvis. He studied the Guaraní people and their language, and his calendar of rainfall has only recently been outdated by global warming climate changes. For a while he directed the Escuela Nacional de Agricultura, and was contracted by the Department of Health to collect poisonous snakes for the preparation of antidotes. In 1910 he received many awards at an international exhibition in Buenos Aires for his aromatic plants, tobacco, bark, maize, coffee, vegetable dyes, bananas and other fruits, and *yerba mate*. He discovered the properties of the plant ka'á he'ē (Stevia rebaudiana bertonii), now gaining popularity as a natural sweetener. He supported his family of 13 children by selling bananas, coffee and firewood. He died of malaria in 1929.

sub-tropical forest that Bertoni enhanced and cherished around his house: the total extent of the land is 199ha. It is to be hoped that the access will soon be improved. There are paths in the woods to explore – to the stream, a little waterfall, a little bridge and an ample sandy beach. Bertoni's grave is 200m from the house, where his remains lie, at his explicit request, 'resting in majestic plenitude beneath this majestic cypress tree'.

You can expect to pay a taxi driver at least Gs200,000 for a half-day taxi ride to Moisés Bertoni, or Gs300,000 for a full day. It takes an hour to get there from central Ciudad del Este.

The Brazilians organise access by boat from across the river, from Porto Meiro, close to the Hito de las 3 Fronteras, setting off at 09.00 Brazilian time, at a cost of US$55 per person, including lunch. They can provide an English-speaking guide. (*For this tour hotel-to-hotel* e *contact@iguassufallstour.com; www.iguassufallstour.com; or for just port-to-port* e *macucosafar@foznet.com.br or comerical@macucosafari.com.br; www.macucosafari.com.br.*)

Leisure facilities The **Mavani Beach Park** (*Ruta 6 km15 from Ruta 7, left bank of Río Mondaý;* e *info@mavanibeachpark.com.py; www.mavanibeachpark.com.py*) is a soon-to-open aquatic theme park, with water chutes and slides, a lake with an artificial beach, a swimming pool with waves, etc, in a landscaped compound of 260,000m². If the Iguazú Falls have not exhausted your taste for water adventure, this promises to offer good family fun. From Ciudad del Este drive out on Ruta 7 for 30km to its junction with Ruta 6, turn left (south) for 15km and it is on your left, just before you cross the Río Monday. Accommodation planned. Information and tickets from the administrative office in the Shopping Zuni in Ciudad del Este (✆ 061 509586/9). If you are driving up from the south, there is an office in Santa Rita, about 45km to the south of the Park, on Ruta 6 (*Av 14 de mayo, esq Av de los Inmigrantes;* ✆ 0673 221345; m 0983 556434; e *mavanibeachsantarita@gmail.com*).

Paraíso Golf Ranch Resort and Spa (*Km24 Monday;* ✆ 061 514548; e *info@paraisogolf.com; www.paraisogolf.com*) This is located a turning to your left before the toll station and airport, as you drive out of Ciudad del Este. As well as a golf course, there are bungalows to stay in, a restaurant, swimming pool, riding and football.

9

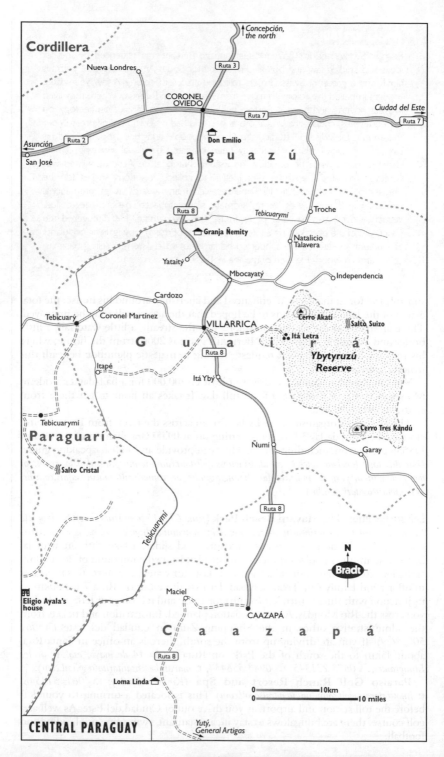

Cordillera

Nueva Londres

CORONEL OVIEDO

Concepción, the north

Ruta 3

Ruta 7

Ciudad del Este

Ruta 7

Asunción

Ruta 2

San José

Don Emilio

C a a g u a z ú

Ruta 8

Tebicuarymí

Troche

Granja Ñemity

Natalicio Talavera

Yataity

Mbocayaty

Independencia

Cardozo

Tebicuary

Coronel Martínez

VILLARRICA

G u a i r á

Cerro Akatí

Salto Suizo

Itá Letra

Ybytyruzú Reserve

Ruta 8

Itapé

Itá Yby

Tebicuarymí

Paraguarí

Cerro Tres Kándú

Ñumí

Garay

Salto Cristal

Ruta 8

Tebicuarymí

N

Bradt

Eligio Ayala's house

Maciel

CAAZAPÁ

C a a z a p á

Ruta 8

Loma Linda

0 — 10km
0 — 10 miles

Yutý, General Artigas

CENTRAL PARAGUAY

10

Villarrica and Central Paraguay

Departamentos: Caaguazú, Guairá, Caazapá

Villarrica is hidden in the very heart of Paraguay, just as Paraguay is hidden in the very heart of South America. Contrasting with the flatness of most of the country, Guairá is a region of green hills, streams and waterfalls, caves and archaeological remains. Part of the region is in the Resource Management Reserve of Ybyturuzú.

Like Cordillera (see *Chapter 4*, page 101), Guairá is an important area for Franciscan towns (see page 121, on the Franciscan Reductions): it has Yataitý, Itapé, Borja, Yutý, Villarrica itself, and most important of all, Caazapá. Bobí (now known as General Artigas) is just over the border into the *departamento* of Itapúa, but is included at the end of this chapter.

When you cross west–east on Ruta 2, from Asunción towards Ciudad del Este, the mid-point stop is Coronel Oviedo, in the *departamento* of Caaguazú. Coronel Oviedo is associated principally as a hub of road communication, with Ruta 3 leading directly north and Ruta 8 leading south to Villarrica. This has been the familiar access to the city. But there is now a new road that runs more directly from Paraguarí to Villarrica, following alongside the old railway line, and cutting about an hour off the journey. At the time of going to press the final kilometre of asphalt was being completed.

The populace of Villarrica have traditionally considered themselves a historic community, culturally a cut above the people of Asunción. They fought a publicity battle to try to have their *departamento* of Guairá, rather than Asunción, declared the Capital of the Harp. They sometimes even talk of Villarrica as the capital of the Republic of Guairá.

Going south from Villarrica you enter Caazapá, a *departamento* in the depths of the interior where asphalt reaches no further than its regional capital. Beyond are miles and miles of dirt roads, tracing their slow way until eventually they join up with the main highways of Ruta 1 and Ruta 6. Caazapá is one of the least visited *departamentos* in Paraguay, because it is so difficult to access. But the town of Caazapá itself is a jewel that well repays a visit, and it has good hotels. Its dignified avenue of palm trees leads to a church which is kept open and has what may be considered the most beautiful reredos in Paraguay. The town was the heart of the Franciscan missionary effort, founded by the great Friar Luis Bolaños, who laid crucially important foundations for the better-known work of the Jesuits.

CORONEL OVIEDO *Copaco* ☎ *0521 203099; municipalidad* ☎ *0521 203468*

There is little to be said of Coronel Oviedo from the tourist point of view, apart from it being the great crossroads at the very centre of the country. From the big roundabout, you go west to Asunción along Ruta 2; east to Ciudad del Este along Ruta 7; north to Pedro Juan Caballero on the road that is called Ruta 3 further along the route; and south to Villarrica on Ruta 8.

253

The traffic through Coronel Oviedo has been reduced a little by the new road from Paraguarí to Villarrica, and by the new stretch of Ruta 3 through Arroyos y Esteros and San Estanislao. But nothing will alter the importance of Coronel Oviedo as the mid-point on the five- or six-hour journey between Asunción and Ciudad del Este.

The **bus** station in Coronel Oviedo is set right on the big grassy roundabout, and is a busy place of hustle and bustle, with a row of orange Coca-Cola booths and as many as 13 platforms. Staff from the restaurant will rush out to hover at the windows of buses with baskets of *gaseosas* and *milanesa* buns.

WHERE TO STAY
This is a small selection from the large number of economical hotels in Coronel Oviedo.

Hotel Bertea Ruta 2 km130; 0521 202019. With a range of categories in its rooms, from very cheap up to 3 times that price for better quality. $$$

Centro Hotel Defensores del Chaco y Vicepresidente Sanchez (by the side of the Plaza de los Heroes); 0521 204610; e centrohotel@hotmail.com. Enclosed parking, cable TV. $$

Hotel San Martin Mariscal Estigarriba c/ Tajy; 0521 203208/202972. $

WHERE TO EAT AND DRINK
La Antigua Rueda *Churrasquería* by the bus station. $

La Nona 0521 202845. Recommended. An unpretentious little place, that you can easily miss, & hard to spot from the main road, unless you realise that it is next door to the large & very visible Hotel Bertea, 2km to the west of the roundabout, on the north side of the road. Used by the big bus companies, has a homely charm, being haphazardly added to. Self-service, with a choice of *asado* or hot meals, & salads. Never closes. $

EAST OF CORONEL OVIEDO
Heading east from Coronel Oviedo, after 46km you come to the town of **Caaguazú,** which gives its name to the *departamento*. It is a timber-producing town, and is noted for the large number of motorbikes ridden there. There are a couple of large international hotels, both belonging to the Sosa network (*www.sosahoteles.com*) and aimed at businesspeople rather than tourists.

César Palace Hotel (22 rooms) Av Coronel Manuel A Godoy y Roberto L Petit; 0522 43096. Costs US$1 more than the Tajy for a dbl room. $$$

Hotel Tajy (22 rooms) Ruta 7 km177; 0522 40118. $$$

About 25km beyond that, at Torín, before you reach the town of Juan E O'Leary (which is just into the *departamento* of Alto Paraná), you come to the turning south for one of the more expensive *estancias* in the Apatur network:

Golondrina Ruta 7 235km from Asunción; 026 2893/4/2238; e centralsag@gesgolondrina.com.py. If you do not mind driving 17km on a dirt road to get there, it is a beautiful place to stay, run by a Portuguese company. They have big, round bungalows, boats & fishing on the Río Monday, guided walks & riding. $$$

The largest part of the *departamento* of Caaguazú stretches to the north of Ruta 7, but is remote territory, difficult of access. Here it was that a huge underground bunker was found in February 2009, which is believed to have been built by a gang of kidnappers (kidnapping is a scourge in Paraguay).

North of Caaguazú is the former Jesuit town of **San Joaquín,** founded in 1746. You can reach it by dirt road from Caaguazú (67km) passing through Yhú; or you can take the asphalted road that goes north from Coronel Oviedo, and turn east after 50km, along the dirt road that passes through Cecilio Báez (32km). It has some original Jesuit statues in the church.

SOUTH OF CORONEL OVIEDO If instead of going east from Coronel Oviedo, you turn south towards Villarrica, then you soon pass a couple more *estancias*. Reservations at all these *estancias* can also be made through Apatur, see *Chapter 2*, page 51.

⌂ **Don Emilio** ☎ 021 660791/603994; m 0981 507105; e donemilio24@gmail.com. Just 6km to the south, & has over 1,000ha of native wood. $$$
⌂ **Granja Ecológica Ñemity** ☎ 021 512028/0549 20095; m 0971 228901;

e granjanemity@cu.com.py. This is 26km south of Coronel Oviedo on Ruta 8, & offers riding, horse carts & a swimming pool. Opposite this *estancia* is the short road that leads into the village of Yataity, just 1km to the west. $$

YATAITÝ *Copaco* ☎ *0546 20000; municipalidad* ☎ *0549 20003*

The *cuna* (cradle) of Paraguay's traditional *ao po'í* embroidery, Yataitý is an enchanting little village, with simple houses, many of which have adobe walls and thatched roofs. To reach the church and its pretty grounds, turn left off the main street.

ao po'í (Guaraní 'fine cloth') began in the presidency of Dr Francia, when his block on imports forced Paraguayans to develop their own craft. The craft is made in many places, but nowhere is it done so intensively or with such skill and dedication as in Yataitý. Typical items are beautiful natural-coloured tablecloths of all sizes with lacy panels and lines of embroidery, and clothes, especially the brightly embroidered shirts worn by Paraguayan musicians.

The real, authentic *ao po'í* is entirely handmade from start to finish, including the spinning and weaving, but for practical reasons manufactured cloth is often used as the base. This, however, will be bought from Paraguay's high-quality cotton company, Pilar, in the town of the same name (see *Chapter 7*, page 217).

All the local populace devote themselves to *ao po'í*, even the children, and it is estimated that over 2,000 in Yataitý are working at this craft. One person in the family will spin the thread, another will weave it, another will embroider and another do the lace work known as *encaje ju*. Grandmothers with failing eyesight who can no longer embroider will take part in another stage of the production process. Even the men are involved, chiefly in the ironing, which needs a strong hand after some good starching. It is all enormously delicate and time-consuming work: if one person were single-handedly to make a large tablecloth (for example), it would take her a year and a half.

Little craft shops are all along the streets, in people's houses. Digna López, known as '*la viuda de Narvajo*' (the widow of Narvajo), is one of the most highly respected craftswomen (m *0982 787572*).

For ten days in November or December, there is an Expoferia, when all the local producers have stalls in the grassy Plaza General Francisco Roa in front of the church, and the full range of products is available in one place, at amazingly reasonable prices. The local *cooperativa* decides on the dates each year, and to find out when it will be held you need to ring the *municipalidad*.

Yataitý is a place to visit, not to stay. When you leave, the southbound Ruta 8 reaches Mbocayatý after 7km. Here you have the choice of turning right for Villarrica, or left for Independencia.

Colonia Independencia is a German foundation, begun by emigrants in 1919 after the end of World War II. Recently, there has been another influx of people from German-speaking countries, and the town is so German that you can find a road called Berliner Strasse. If you have a European complexion you may well be addressed in German, by residents who speak faltering or heavily accented Spanish. The hotels typically have German websites ending in '.de', and sometimes even written in German.

There is a prettiness and order about the town, which has specialised in being a holiday place, full of hotels and not much else, on the edge of the Ybytyruzú nature reserve. It is a green and leafy place to stay, and has a municipal park of 3ha with a stream and a bathing place. Its slogan is 'the land of wine and sun', and it is indeed the only place in Paraguay with extensive vineyards and any beginnings of a serious wine culture.

You can reach Independencia from Ruta 8, turning east at Mbocaytý (a turn right if you are coming from Asunción on the new road from Paraguarí to Villarrica, but a turn left if you have come from Coronel Oviedo on Ruta 2). Or you can reach it from Ruta 7, turning south 18km after Coronel Oviedo: this takes you over a wooden bridge at Troche. The bus from Asunción is Ybyturuzú.

The town begins in a spread-out way along the entrance road, and many of the hotels are here. Then you turn right towards the town centre, heading towards the wooded hills of the Ybytyruzú park. At a mini-roundabout at the end of this road, you turn left for the Plaza Municipal, the stone church and the Centro Cultural. When you reach a petrol station the asphalt changes to *empedrado*. The next turn right is marked 'Salto Suizo' (see below), but if you carry straight on you will find your way back to the asphalt road.

Curiously, there are very few landline phones in the town: most hotels operate on mobile numbers. The internet signal is poor.

WHERE TO STAY

Hotel Independencia (16 rooms) Km180; ☏ 0548 265290; m 0981 302931; e hotel-independencia@web.de; www.hotel-independencia.de. The 4th hotel you reach. Grand entrance with a beautiful fig tree in the middle of the courtyard. Outside terrace, swimming pools, stuffed animals, internet. $$$

Hotel Tilinski (20 rooms) ☏ 0548 265240. Down a gravel side road, clearly marked from the main road. Big terrace for meals. Swimming pool. Offers lunch & swimming pool for day guests. Volleyball & football pitches, stream. Offers full board as well as a B&B price. $$$

Hotel Sport Camping (c10 rooms) m 0981 885198; e michellerickel@hotmail.com; www.hotel-sportcamping.de. The 2nd hotel you reach, on a corner opposite the (unmarked) track to Salto la Cantera. Nice big rooms in newly built thatched round bungalows. Good bathrooms. 2 swimming pools, very clean. Restaurant by pool serves simple food. Camping. $$$

Hotel Restaurant El Indio (3 rooms) m 0981 362048; e offroad@paraguay-tour.de; www.paraguay-tour.de. Enticingly tucked away a good distance down a dirt road. Opened 2005. Modern, attractive, small, personal. Restaurant (see below). Organises tours all over the country. Camping. $$$

Hotel Manantial (5 rooms) m 0981 309740. The 1st hotel you come to, on the right at the beginning of the town. A curiously sleepy place with an enormous swimming pool that is more like a lake. Homemade bread. Fierce dog behind the gate. $

WHERE TO EAT

Restaurant Austria On the left after Hotel Independencia. $$

Restaurant Freiburg On the left after you turn south towards the Ybytyruzú park, into the town centre, where you have a view of a dramatic wooded hill ahead of you. $$

El Mangal Restaurant In a turning left, just before the mini-roundabout (see above). Most dishes have German names. Outside terrace. $$

✘ **Dorf Schenke Restaurant** Near Hotel Tilinski.
⊕ Closed Mon. Pretty terrace looking onto garden.
$$

✘ **Hotel Restaurant El Indio** See above; ⊕ from
18.00 Wed–Fri, from 11.00 Sat & Sun. **$$**
✘ **Hotel Tilinski** See above. Offers lunch with use of
swimming pool. **$$**

WHAT TO SEE When you rejoin the main road, after going through the town, you come to a big map before a petrol station, which marks the 'Bodega Gerhard Bühler', just past the cemetery. This is the **Vista Alegre Winery**. It does not normally offer visits for tourists. Gerhard Bühler is bringing German expertise to help Paraguay begin a wine trade, and he says Paraguay has the perfect climate for wine production. In a number of houses in Independencia you can buy grapes, but as yet there are few vineyards elsewhere in Paraguay.

If you take the turn for **Salto Suizo** (Swiss Waterfall), you will pass the Reiterhof equestrian centre (m *0981 711874*), which offers riding lessons, hacking and trips in a horse cart. To reach the **waterfall**, carry on for 8km down this dirt road, which gets progressively worse. Eventually you can take your car no further and must walk the last stretch through the woods. When you reach the waterfall, you may be disappointed to find there is only a tiny trickle of water falling into the pool, though the drop is indeed impressive and there is a good echo. At times of heavy rainfall this would be dramatic, but then at times of heavy rainfall the road to reach it would be impassible.

Another waterfall that is more modest but closer to the main road (only 2km on foot) is the Salto la Cantera. To get there, you take a track opposite the Hotel Sport Camping. To be sure of finding it, ask for a local guide (probably a child) and pay a small tip (Gs10,000 may be enough).

The hill at this end of the Ybytyruzú reserve is called Cerro Akatí and has an excellent view (see page 264 below). There is also the Cerrito, which is a conical 'little hill' on private property, and has a quarry with natural columns of sandstone, and the Cerro de la Cruz (Hill of the Cross), which is closer to the Salto Suizo.

VILLARRICA Copaco ☎ 0541 42250; municipalidad ☎ 0541 44306/42225

Villarrica – literally the 'rich town' – is a university city and has quite a buzz to it. Pavements are adorned with colourful produce spilling out from the shops, and there is every sign of a functioning economy: there are plenty of shops of electrical equipment and mobile phones, and prices are higher here. You can pay over Gs50,000 for just wandering round town for an hour in a taxi. Many shops advertise that they change dollars and pesos – evidence of international trade – and when you go to the bus station, you seem to find more buses going to foreign destinations (São Paulo, Buenos Aires) than are going to Asunción. Villarrica has in fact a reputation for feeling itself a rival to Asunción, and for wanting to do everything differently.

But this is to give a modern interpretation to an ancient name. The town was founded by Captain Ruy Díaz de Melgarejo on 14 May 1570, and he chose the name in the belief that there were gold and silver mines in the vicinity. The original Villarrica was in the old Guairá province to the northeast, now in Brazil, before the city suffered a series of relocations to escape the Portuguese *mamelucos* or slave-traders. Its correct, full name is Villarrica del Espíritu Santo, because it was founded on the feast of the Holy Spirit (Pentecost). (See pages 207 and 292 on the Jesuit-Guaraní exodus from Guairá.)

Villarrica is known as the *ciudad andariega*, which means the city that gets up and moves. After the first two settlements in the original Guairá province to the

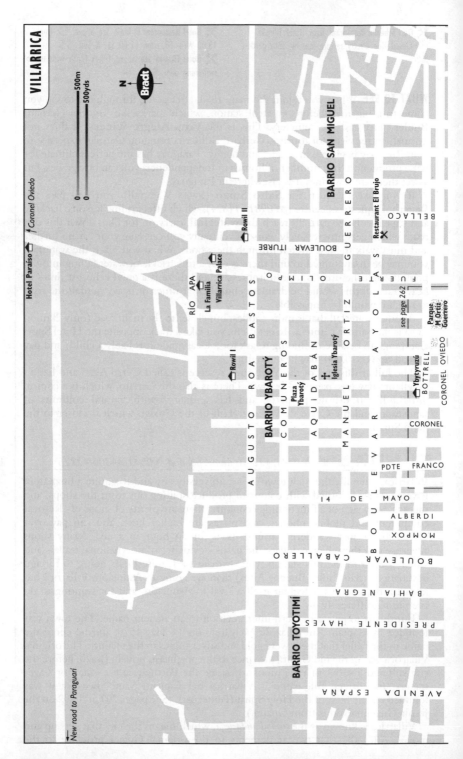

VILLARRICA

500m
500yds

N Bradt

New road to Paraguarí

Coronel Oviedo

Hotel Paraíso

Rowil II

RÍO APA
La Familia
Villarrica Palace

BOULEVAR ITURBE

BARRIO SAN MIGUEL

Restaurant El Brujo

BELLACO

G U E R R E R O

AUGUSTO ROA BASTOS
Rowil I

BARRIO YBAROTÝ

COMUNEROS
OLIMPO
OLIMPO

F U E R T E
A Y O L A S

see page 262

AQUIDABÁN
Iglesia Ybarotý
Plaza Ybarotý

MANUEL ORTIZ

A Y O L A S

Ybytyruzú
BOTTRELL
CORONEL OVIEDO

Parque
M Ortiz
Guerrero

CORONEL

PDTE FRANCO

14 DE MAYO

ALBERDI

MOMPOX

BOULEVAR CABALLERO

BAHÍA NEGRA

PRESIDENTE HAYES

BARRIO TOYOTIMÍ

AVENIDA ESPAÑA

258

BARRIO TABLADA LOMA

BARRIO SANTA LUCÍA

BARRIO SANTA LIBRADA

BARRIO ESTACIÓN

BARRIO LOMAS VALENTINAS

BELLACO

ITURBE

B O U L E V A R

Central

FUERTE   OLIMPO

AZARA

Mercado Uno

COLÓN

GRAL LÓPEZ

CORRALES

MELGAREJO

Bus terminal

GRAL BENÍTEZ

B N

Museo Maestro
Fermín López

CABALLERO

NATALICIO

Cathedral

TALAVERA

CARLOS A LÓPEZ

Municipalidad

GRAL DÍAZ

ALEJO GARCÍA

Plaza
Libertad

JUAN PABLO II

HERNANDARIAS

CURUPAYTÝ

DE

BOGADO

Gobernación

Plaza
de los
Héroes

HUMAITÁ

RUIZ

MARISCAL

MARISCAL

Mercado Dos

PDTE FRANCO

CERRO CORÁ

14 DE MAYO

ALBERDI

MOMPOX

CAPITÁN

E S T I G A R R I B I A

E S T I G A R R I B I A

J   D E M A T T E I

D O N   B O S C O

L I B E R T A D

E S T A D O S   U N I D O S

Y E G R O S

B L A S   G A R A Y

A N T E Q U E R A

J   B E R G E S

C O N S T I T U C I Ó N

B O U L E V A R

E S T A D O S   U N I D O S

BOULEVAR   CABALLERO

BAHÍA NEGRA

PRESIDENTE HAYES

RIVAROLA

ESPAÑA

A V E N I D A

Estación

La Tranquera
& internet

Old railway line

Rua
8

Caazapá

Itá Letra

Itapé

northeast, it moved in 1634 to the source of the River Jejuí (more directly north, within present-day Paraguay), and then to the present area of central Paraguay (which is now named Guairá, so the regional name moved as well as the town's name). In 1675 it was sited in Itapé (now a nearby Marian centre), moving almost at once to what is now Coronel Oviedo and in 1682 finding its final resting place on its current site, which was secured by royal permission of the King of Spain in 1701. It has had a total of seven locations.

There are two useful websites: www.villarrica.com.py and www.villarrik.com.

GETTING THERE AND AROUND Two **bus** companies run frequent services from the Terminal in Asunción: Guaireña (\ *021 551727 in Asunción;* \ *0541 42678 in Villarrica*) and Ybytyruzú. They follow Ruta 2 (the east–west highway) as far as Coronel Oviedo, and then plunge directly south for another half-hour. The total journey to Villarrica takes 2½ hours on a non-stop bus (*directo*) and 3½–4 hours on a slow bus (*removido*), of which there are a lot more. The new road through Paraguarí (see page 253 and maps on pages 100 and 292) is more direct and quicker if you are **driving**. The buses, however, are expected to continue taking the route of Ruta 2.

When you arrive you have the choice of a **taxi** – in uncharacteristically good condition for Paraguay – or a **horse cart** – which costs less than a motor taxi and is a lot more fun. The streets are full of these horse-drawn vehicles, which give considerable charm to the place. They are known as *karumbés*, which in Guaraní means 'tortoise', and they cost Gs15,000 an hour. (Encarnación is the other city famous for its *karumbés*; see *Chapter 6*, page 214.)

WHERE TO STAY

⌂ **Villarrica Palace Hotel** (68 rooms) Ruta 8 Blas Garay y Río Apa; \ 0541 43048/42832; e vph@gointernet.com.py; www.sosahoteles.com. Supposedly Villarrica's top hotel, right at the northern edge of the town, so only suitable for those travelling by car. Large complex with grand & spacious appearance, swimming pool, restaurant, sauna, gym, conference hall seating 200, enclosed parking with guard. But there have been criticisms about poor service, inadequate cleaning, worn sheets, & music from car radios late at night. Open to negotiation on price. $$$

⌂ **Hotel Ybytyruzú** (40 rooms) Carlos A López esq Dr Bottrell; \ 0541 42390/40844/41507/41598. Also a smart, modern, large hotel, & conveniently located. Has a lot of visiting conferences & is sometimes booked out. Restaurant. $$$

⌂ **Hotel Paraiso** (c6 rooms) Ruta 8 km168, Mbokayaty y 2ª División; \ 0541 40262; m 0981 243805; e info@hotel-paraiso.de; www.hotel-paraiso.de. Out of town to the north, on the west side of the road, next to an army post. German establishment (& website only in German). Model of Nazi warship complete with swastika, & of bomber planes, complete Nazi airforce uniform, newspaper cuttings from 1944 onwards all over wall. Also has cuttings about the Titanic. Good restaurant; see below. $$

⌂ **Hotel Rowil** (c20 rooms) Pa'i Anasagasti c/ Olimpo; \ 0541 42852. Situated above a music store, full of guitars & drums, on the main road into town. Rooms are basic but bright & cheery & scrupulously clean. Has another building around a more general store, 2 blocks away (\ 0541 43989). Recommended only for those with cars, as both hotels are a distance from the centre. $$

⌂ **Hotel Guairá** (25 rooms) Mcal Estigarribia y Natalicio Talavera; \ 0541 42369. Just a block & a half from the bus terminal. Rather old-fashioned with a certain traditional charm, though standards have slipped. Coffee for b/fast is almost unbearably weak, bread with no butter or jam, though freshly baked. $

⌂ **Hotel Central** (c6 rooms) Fuerte Olimpo e/Mcal Estigarribia y Alejo García; \ 0541 43765. Pay no attention to the name: it is 6 blocks from the bus terminal, but in the wrong direction for anything else, & is under-used for this reason. The rooms are big & clean & have private bathrooms. $

⌂ **Hotel La Familia** (10 rooms) Río Apa y Mayor Bullo; \ 0541 40647. Small hotel tucked away near entrance to town, b/fast not included. Budget rooms with fans available as well as with AC. $

⌂ **Bar Oasis** (3 rooms) Carlos A López, e/ Colón y Melgarejo. Small budget hostel attached to a good bar, 1 room has a private bathroom; very conveniently placed. A sweet place, but could be a touch cleaner. $

✖ WHERE TO EAT

✖ **La Tranquera** Barrio Estación; ☏ 0541 42185. Opposite the old railway station in the south of city, to the south of the railway line, this is a high-quality restaurant both for food & ambience, located in a position that may come up in the world, when the station is developed for tourism. Exposed beams, tiled floors, life-size models of indigenous where guests have their photo taken. $$$$

✖ **Restaurant El Brujo** Boulevar Iturbe y Boulevar Ayolas; m 0981 308443; ⊕ 10.00–20.00 Mon–Fri, 10.00–15.00 Sat. Pretty little restaurant with a small, leafy terrace, away from the town centre. Expensive by local standards, but quite accessible prices for foreigners. $$$

✖ **Hotel Paraíso** See above; ⊕ 12.00–22.00 Mon–Wed, 12.00–24.00 Fri & Sat, 12.00–18.00 Sun. German-run, good cooking, very extensive international menu. $$$

✖ **Restaurant Adela** ☏ 0541 43048. The restaurant of the Villarrica Palace Hotel has surprisingly economical prices if you choose the set menus. Service slow. $$

✖ **Hotel Ybyturuzú** See above; restaurant ⊕ from 18.00. $$

✖ **Restaurant Danykar** Bogado c/ Mariscal Estigarribia; ☏ 0541 41648; ⊕ 11.00–15.00, 18.00–01.00 daily. Pizza & hamburger place in good location facing Plaza de los Heroes. Smartly decorated in dark red & brown with tables inside & also over the road in the plaza itself. $$

✖ **Restaurant Noemi** Carlos Antonio López; m 0971 942788; ⊕ all day. Bright yellow new restaurant in centre, run by Argentinians, homemade pasta & bread, meals & snacks, fresh fruit juices. Recommended. $

✖ **Restaurant Pablito** Mariscal López y Natalicio Talavera; ☏ 0541 42351. On the corner facing the bus terminal, this is a pleasant little restaurant that gets plenty of local custom. $

✖ **Bar Oasis** See above. Better than most bars in the centre: they have an outdoor grill & always have some chickens turning on the grill. Other bars tend to be very basic, *empanadas* & *gaseosas* & beer & not much else. $

✖ **Supermercado Herrero** General Benítez c/ Mariscal López. As in most Paraguayan cities, the best place to pick up a good meal at a budget price, with a variety of dishes to choose from, is in the café attached to the main supermarket. $

WHAT TO SEE The *municipalidad* of Villarrica has identified at least **80 buildings of architectural interest** that need to be maintained. Heading the list are the *municipalidad* itself (1907–13), the cathedral (1883–91), the museum (1842), the Franciscan church Iglesia Ybarotý (1944–57), the Club Social El Porvenir Guaireño (1917–19) and the Banco Nacional de Fomento (c1900). All of these are marked on the city centre plan, apart from the **Ybarotý church** which is three blocks further north on Carlos Antonio López, and is marked on the plan of the whole town. It is a splendid red-stone church of Romanesque design, with two towers and 25 round-topped arches on the façade. It was begun by Fr Carlos Anasagasti in 1944, and this part of the street is named Anasagasti after him, changing its name to Carlos Antonio López as it goes south.

The **Plaza de los Heroes** is at the town centre, with the grand building of the *municipalidad* occupying one side of the square. The site was originally used by the Jesuits as a cemetery, and when the Franciscans took over they built the Convento de Santa Bárbara. The present early 20th-century building was originally one-storey and had its second floor added later. On one side of the *municipalidad* is the Salon Auditorio Municipal, built in 1911–14, which has a sizeable auditorium and hosts a lively programme of Paraguayan folk and classical dance classes.

Plaques in the Plaza de los Heroes tell the story of the battles of the Chaco War, from 1932–35. There is also a tall white monument with seven vertical slabs, representing the seven moves of the city (see introduction above). The city has now reached its final resting place 'in the region of the majestic Ybytyruzú' (announces the monument with grandiose eloquence) and 'the coquettish and constantly moving Villarrica maintains its tradition of culture and aristocratic nobility, which has rocked its cradle. It is caressed by the gentle perfumed breeze of Ybytyruzú, which lovingly lulls it as though to remind it of a century of adventures and cruel persecution.'

Hotel La Familia,
Villarrica Palace Hotel,
Hotel Paraíso

Ybytyruzú

BOTTRELL

CORONEL — BOGADO

CARLOS ANTONIO LÓPEZ

Estadio
Ykuá Pytá

Parque
Manuel Ortiz
Guerrero

CORONEL OVIEDO

Supermercado
Estrella

CURUPAYTÝ

HUMAITÁ

COLÓN

Banco de la Nación
Argentina

Banco
Regional

Bar Oasis

GENERAL BENITEZ

GENERAL BERNARDINO CABALLERO

Mercado
Uno

CORRALES

AZARA

RUIZ DE MELGAREJO

TAM Mercosur

Bus terminal

Banco Continental

CERRO CORA

PRESIDENTE FRANCO

MARISCAL LÓPEZ

Jardín
Japonés

Restaurant
Pablito

Danykar

Plaza
de los
Héroes

Municipalidad

Restaurant Noemi

Supermercado Herrero
& Patio de Comidas

MARISCAL ESTIGARRIBIA

Teatro

Visión

Guairá

N

ALEJO GARCÍA

Banco Nacional
de Fomento

Curia
Diocesano

Bradt

JUAN PABLO II

Gobernación

Plaza
Libertad

Cathedral

Museo Maestro
Fermín López

GENERAL DÍAZ

CARLOS ANTONIO LÓPEZ

NATALICIO TALAVERA

Club Social
El Porvenir

Casa de
la Juventud

0 —— 125m
0 —— 125yds

HERNANDARIAS

Mercado
Dos

ESTIGARRIBIA

   The present **cathedral** is a large cream-coloured building, which replaced a wooden building that fell down in a storm in 1877. Of the three bells in the tower, one dates back to 1781. You are unlikely to find the cathedral open unless you go at the time of a mass. A second square opens out in front – the **Plaza Libertad** – with the figure of a woman on a column in the middle, carrying a torch of liberty.

   Behind the cathedral is the jewel of Villarrica: the **Museo Maestro Fermín López** (*Natalicio Talavera esq Juan Pablo II;* \ *0541 41521;* ⏰ *7.00–12.00 & 15.00–17.00 Mon–Fri, 7.00–12.00 Sat; free*). The museum is a long single-storey traditional building built in 1842 with colonnades front and back, and was originally a school called La Patria. It takes its name from the famous schoolmaster who initiated the school and led his pupils from here and from the school of Piribebúy out to fight in the War of the Triple Alliance. He continued to run his school in the trenches, and all the children were killed in the battle of Acosta Ñu in 1869.

   In 1972 the decision was made to turn it into a museum and today it houses a charming collection of historical items. There is a useful display board about the Itá Letra carvings (see opposite) and the different theories about their origin. The first room to the left of the reception is devoted to the indigenous and houses a huge wooden canoe, 6m long, hollowed out of a single tree trunk; there are bows and arrows, woven fibre bags, a pestle and mortar, wooden sandals and a feather headdress. A couple of historical rooms follow, with old postcards and dance trophies, old printing blocks and vinyl records, old musical instruments and kerosene lamps, old coins and notes from all over the world.

Going back further to the time of President Carlos Antonio López (1844–62) there are padlocks, candlesticks and rosaries. From the Triple Alliance War (1864–70) there are rusty sabres and spurs and bayonets – and a portrait of Mariscal López on a white charger. From the more recent war of the Chaco there are rifles and photos. From the illustrious Bishop of Villarrica, Felipe Benítez, who was Paraguay's leading thinker in the Second Vatican Council (1962–65), there are dainty silk shoes and an episcopal hat adorned with green and gold tassles.

The final room is devoted to the local poet Manuel Ortiz Guerrero (1894–1933). It includes the bars of the window beside which he first declaimed one of his famous Guaraní love poems, 'Ne rendápe ajú': 'From far away I come to you, my love, to gaze at you. You have been living for a long time in my soul, my hope and faith.' Like many other poems of his, this was set to music by the famous composer José Asunción Flores. If you are lucky, you may hear sounds of a harp class drift from an adjacent room, reminding you that you are in a cultural capital.

On the corner behind the cathedral and close to the museum is the **Curia Diocesana** – a beautifully restored single-storey building in the old style, with some unusual wooden windowsills. On the next corner is another traditional building, the Casa de la Juventud.

Another building of interest is the old **railway station**, in the southwest corner of the town. At the time of writing, the model for the project to open it as a tourist attraction was housed within the old station itself. A few of these old stations have already been reopened: the central station in Asunción is now a museum, and that of Aregua is now a craft shop as well as a functioning station. There are many more stations waiting to be restored, mostly along the line of the new road from Paraguarí to Villarrica, which follows the route of the railway line constructed in the years 1884–89.

EXCURSIONS FROM VILLARRICA

ITAPÉ Day trips from Villarrica include a journey of 21km west on a dirt road to the village of Itapé, which has a Marian shrine. The Virgen del Paso (The Virgin of the Journey), as she is called, is a doll clothed in a white and gold dress and blue mantle, not dissimilar to the better-known Virgin of Caacupé. She is housed in the church, but on the eve of the annual feast day of 18 December she is taken in solemn procession to a tiny sanctuary on the shore of the River Tebicuary-mí. To reach the shrine, go straight through the village as far as you can go, bearing left at the end, and you will reach the riverbank. You go up a little staircase to gain access to the sanctuary, and in the minute room inside there are sellers of rosaries and crucifixes squashed in alongside the devotees. On the ground floor there are holders for the blue candles typical of this devotion. The Marian devotion of Itapé dates back to its foundation as a Franciscan Reduction in 1678. Today Itapé competes with Itacuá, Encarnación, for being the second Marian site of the country after Caacupé.

Buses go to Itapé from the Villarrica terminal, or you can take a taxi. On 18 December there are a lot of buses, and huge crowds go for the day. After the morning mass, people stay to bathe in the river, and there is a party atmosphere. To stay the night in Itapé, try the Hospedaje Juanita (↘ 0554 250218).

ITÁ LETRA Heading east from Villarrica, into the Ybytyruzú nature reserve, you can explore some ancient enigmatic writing in the rock, the meaning of which is not known. They are not dissimilar from the rock carvings at Gasory near Pedro Juan Caballero (see *Chapter 11*, page 290), and it is believed that the two sites are

10

related. A date of 2000–4000BC has been suggested. Incredible as it sounds, a number of people believe them to have been carved by Vikings.

Itá Letra (Spanish 'letter'; Guaraní 'stone') is at Tororõ, about 18km from Villarrica. The better of two dirt roads branches off Ruta 8 on the southern outskirts of Villarrica (see town plan), and winds a little to the north. When you come to a road junction, turn right, which will lead you up the sharply pointed hill to Tororõ. There are more than 50 inscriptions, some with parallel lines, like railway lines or like rakes, others with circles, curves and irregular shapes, all seeming to have some definite significance that has been long lost in time.

From Itá Letra you can continue through the Ybytyruzú reserve to visit the hill **Cerro Akatí**, which has an excellent view, descending to Independencia before returning by road to Villarrica. To do this as a taxi day trip could cost you Gs500,000: ask the taxi drivers at the bus terminal, or ring them (↘ *0541 42475*). A Dutchman, Nico de Joungh, who is attached to the Hotel Westfalenhaus (↘ *021 446216*) also organises visits to Itá Letra. Or ring the Asociación de Guias de Turismo de Guairá (m *0983 453821*), which can also give information on abseiling on the cliffs near Itá Letra, providing equipment and instructors.

CERRO TRES KANDÚ
An excursion to the top of Paraguay's highest hill, Cerro Tres Kandú (Spanish 'hill of three'; Guaraní 'bumps'), is well worthwhile, but needs a little organisation. Tres Kandú is 842m high, while Cerro Akatí – on the other side of the Ybytyruzú reserve; see above – is 697m high.

To reach the base point for climbing Tres Kandú you need to go to Garay, 20km southeast of Villarrica (see regional map, page 252), and arrange the walk at least the day before through Professor Ángel Aristides Troche (↘ *0544 275408*) – a former councillor and retired teacher who is dedicating himself to promoting the walk for tourists. He will arrange a guide, without whom it will be impossible to find the way through the numerous little paths up the mountain, and to whom you should pay a tip, as he will lose a day's work in the fields. (Suggested tip at least Gs30,000 or US$6.)

Professor Troche recommends setting off at 07.00, carrying with you ample water (2 litres if it is hot) and something sweet to give you energy. In Garay, turn left when you reach the old railway line and the police station, and ask for the house of Professor Troche. It has *yerba mate* trees along the edge of the garden. He will then introduce you to the guide. From there it is 10km by car up a difficult dirt road to the point where you have to leave the car behind. If you do this trip with a taxi from Villarrica you can expect to pay at least Gs400,000, to include the wait.

The ascent is being developed with some spiritual landmarks along the way: an ecological sanctuary with a replica of the Virgin of Lourdes, and a series of the mysteries of the rosary carved in stone – the work of a Paraguayan Salesian priest-artist, Gustavo Laterza. A replica of the Portiuncula chapel of Assisi is planned. A wooden hut for pilgrims – already equipped with beds and kitchen equipment – will soon be replaced by a stone retreat house for up to 30 people, possibly with a resident Franciscan priest. All of this region is historic Franciscan territory, and the Franciscans still have a house in Villarrica.

CAAZAPÁ Copaco ↘ 0542 232299; municipalidad ↘ 0542 232201

Caazapá is one of the earliest and most important of the former Franciscan Reductions, and was founded by Friar Luis Bolaños himself in 1607 (two years before the Jesuits founded their first Reduction at San Ignacio Guazú). When you arrive in Caazapá, you may gasp in delight at finding such an attractive town so deeply hidden in the countryside. At the initial little roundabout you are welcomed by a statue of Luis Bolaños, simply attired in his Franciscan habit and carrying a

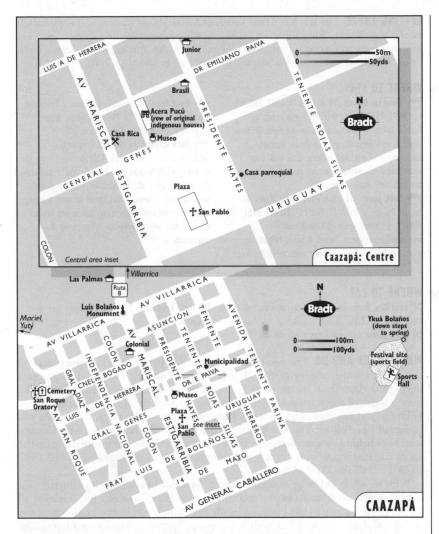

Caazapá: Centre

CAAZAPÁ

cross and a staff. From here a splendid avenue of palm trees leads to the plaza and the church, with its stunning reredos. To the right is the cemetery where there is a smaller and older chapel, also with an original reredos. And to the left the road leads on to the famous spring, Ykuá Bolaños – a name unfortunately now linked in everyone's mind with the tragic fire tragedy at the supermarket Ycuá Bolaños in Asunción in 2004, when 400 people died.

There are still very poor areas in the countryside around – four out of five families in rural Caazapá do not have electricity – but a number of better-off politicians, lawyers and businessmen have property in the area, with the result that Caazapá appears a surprisingly well-kept and well-off town. It was well off even as a Reduction, because of its excellent cotton and tobacco production, and the decoration of the church was as fine as those of the Jesuits, while the quantity of gold exceeded the Jesuit churches. (This is reported by Félix de Azara, the Spanish naturalist and military officer who was sent in 1781 to determine the border dispute between the Spanish and Portuguese colonies.)

Villarrica and Central Paraguay **CAAZAPÁ**

10

GETTING THERE The town is 51km south of Villarrica on Ruta 8, and is asphalted all the way. For reaching Villarrica on the new road, see page 260 above. The only bus that goes to Caazapá direct from Asunción is the Yuteña, which leaves eight times a day and continues, via Maciel, to Yutý (see below, page 268).

WHERE TO STAY

Hotel Las Palmas (20 rooms) ☎ 0542 232264; m 0991 951339. The first hotel you reach, on Ruta 8 before the roundabout, on the right. Modern, clean & very pleasant, good facilities. Internet, swimming pool, enclosed parking. Café next door under same management is also modern & clean but sells only basic snacks. $$

Hotel Junior (10 rooms) Presidente Hayes 437 esq Dr Paiva; ☎ 0542 232060/232321; m 0981 309777; e hotel_junior@hotmail.com; www.hoteljuniorpy.com. Tucked 1 block behind the plaza, newly decorated in smart colourful style. Wi-Fi. $$

Hotel Brasil (12 rooms) Dr Paiva y Presidente Hayes; ☎ 0542 232285. Pleasant, simple hotel. Diagonally across from Hotel Junior. $$

Hotel Colonial Av Mariscal Estigarribia; ☎ 0542 232290; m 0982 425850; e azujunisa@hotmail.com. A block and a half down the avenida after the roundabout. Traditional old building with colonial pillars, good location fronting onto the road with palm trees. Rooms set around a spacious hall which serves as b/fast room & restaurant. $

WHERE TO EAT

Casa Rica Bright new bar on the avenida, half a block from the Plaza. $
Hotel Junior Restaurant has menu del día. $

Hotel Las Palmas Typical Paraguayan fare in restaurant. $

WHAT TO SEE AND DO The two churches – the San Pablo church in the plaza and the smaller, older oratory of San Roque at the cemetery – are both kept open during the day, which means there is no hassle about seeking out key holders to have a sight of the reredos. However, if you do find them closed, then the key holder of the San Pablo church is Ña Kali, who lives on the plaza, next to the *casa parroquial* (see below). The key holder to the San Roque oratory is Doña Genara, who lives behind the cemetery, which is behind the oratory. For information on the art of the Reduction, you can talk to Sonia Espinola in the *municipalidad* (☎ 0542 232201; ⏰ 07.00–13.00 Mon–Fri).

With its white and beige octagonal tower, **San Pablo** is an elegant church, with Gothic arches inside and a brown and yellow tiled floor – not old, but rendered all the more enchanting by the birdsong inside the church and by the loveliness of the well-kept plaza outside, filled with a variety of attractive, blossoming trees. The beautiful **reredos** behind the altar is a model of the very best Franciscan design. There are six niches, set in an elaborately carved framework of plant designs, and pillars with twisted fluting on the bottom row, and with straight fluting in the row above. It is all in very good condition and mostly in the natural wood colour, with subtle colour features. The statues of saints (with the exception of St Francis, bottom right) are of the more static style usually described as Franciscan, as compared with the more exuberant postures and flowing robes of the post-Brassanelli style.

Balancing Francis, on the left, is St Dominic, carrying a church, and with a dog at his feet (emblem of the order because of the play of words on the Latin *domini canis*, dog of the Lord). Between the two is the Virgin, standing on the moon in the style so typical of the Paraguayan Reductions, carrying her Child. In the top row we have, from left to right, St Joseph with the child Jesus, St Paul, and St Blas. In all, the reredos is one of the best preserved in the country, and is a delight of harmony and skill. The tabernacle itself has a striking geometric design in red, and the altar has a chequered design of gilded wood.

The **sacristy** of the church contains a number of carved saints of the Franciscan period, including a Virgin and a St Joseph, which are taken out for display or procession on the corresponding saints' days. The *casa parroquial* or parish house (⊕ *07.00–12.00 Mon–Fri*) faces the church. It contains gold and silver items, including halos from saints, and an engraved ciborium with hanging silver bells, that were made in the workshops of the Reduction. The silversmiths of Caazapá were well known and used to export their work to many places.

Opposite the San Pablo church is a small **museum**. This is an old building, well restored, and bearing the name 'Fray Juan Bernardo'. It contains a selection of old machines, furniture, photos and war relics. To visit inside you are recommended to ring the *municipalidad* beforehand as it is often closed. Around the back of this is a well-restored row of indigenous houses from the Reduction, labelled **Acera Pucú**: *casa de indios*. (Acera means 'pavement' in Spanish, Pucú means 'long' in Guaraní; *casa de indios* means 'indian house'.)

To reach the **oratory of San Roque**, return down the avenue with the palm trees for three blocks, and when you get to the Omar supermarket on the right, turn left down Coronel Bogado. This little chapel dates back (at least in its main structure) to 1779, and is a small and simple structure, built of adobe and wood. But with its huge pitched roof, making a broad surrounding portico, it appears bigger than it really is. While the Jesuit Reductions tended to have a secondary chapel called the Capilla de Loreto, the Franciscan Reductions would typically have a secondary chapel dedicated to San Roque, but this oratory of Caazapá is the only surviving example.

Inside is an exquisite carved and painted reredos, with a magnificent San Roque in the centre, a crucifix above, and to either side paintings of Franciscan saints. With the exception of San Roque and the crucifix, these paintings are flat, which is unusual in a reredos. Not to be confused with the 17th-century Paraguayan Jesuit martyr San Roque González, San Roque was a medieval French saint who devoted his life to the care of plague victims, contracted the disease himself, and lived in the wilderness with a festering wound on his leg, where a dog would bring him food and lick his sores. In art, he is portrayed with a wound on his thigh and a dog, as we see in this example: Roque points with dignity at his wound while a black dog leaps up to lick it. Next to the oratory there are two cloisters of buildings from the Reduction: workshops, priests' houses, workshops, offices, library, etc.

Returning to the plaza, a couple of blocks to the left of the church (east) you will come to the main road that soon curves round to bring you to the sports field (*cancha*) and sports hall (*poli deportivo*). If you cross the field, in the far corner you will come to some steps that lead down to the **Ykuá Bolaños** spring. (*Ykuá* in Guaraní means 'water hole'.) It is said to be a spring miraculously created by Luis Bolaños himself with a touch of his staff on the bare rock (or, some say, by lifting a heavy stone) in response to the challenge of a *cacique*, who complained of the thirst the group was suffering, and said they would all become Christians if Bolaños could produce water, but if he could not the Franciscan would be put to death. The spring never lacks water, even in times of drought, and according to local legend brings favours to those who are in love. The saint is carved on the back wall of the spring, with his miraculous staff and surrounded by indigenous. There are stepping stones to the source of the water on the left-hand wall.

Fiesta de Ykuá Bolaños The foundation of Caazapá on 25 January is celebrated annually in magnificent style. The streets are decorated with ribbons and paintings and there are concerts every night in front of the San Pablo church. There is a *cena de gala* (grand dinner) on the Thursday night before the 25th, a festival of dance and music on the Friday night, an exhibition of craft and local produce on the Saturday, and a horse show on the Sunday. There are bullfights and rodeos. Finally on the night of 25 January, there is a mega concert attended by at least 5,000 people, with groups of traditional Paraguayan music coming from all over the country to play in the *cancha* (before the Ykuá Bolaños spring) from 21.00 to 06.00. For a confirmation of the programme each year ring the *municipalidad* or one of the hotels.

SOUTH FROM CAAZAPÁ
Estancia

 Loma Linda (45 rooms) 27km south of Caazapá, via Maciel; ✆ 021 683003; m 0981 402713; e estancia_loma_linda@hotmail.com or cstorm@conexion.com.py; www.estancialomalinda.com. From Maciel count 16.8km & it is down a little turning on the right. Horses, bike rides, swimming pool, gardens, fishing, games room. Pretty view of the tower of the Perpetuo Socorro church. Name means 'lovely hillside', as there is a gentle hill here in an otherwise flat plain. Reservations can also be made through Apatur; see *Chapter 2*, page 51. $$$

More Franciscan towns If you can bear the journey over the dirt road – do not be misled by the fact that it is called Ruta 8 – you can reach two more former Franciscan towns as you plunge south: Yutý and General Artigas.

Yutý is the end of the line for the Yuteña bus. From Caazapá on, this is a dirt road, so the 87km journey south from Caazapá is slow, taking a couple of hours. Yutý was also founded by Luis Bolaños (in 1610), but originally was further south, where San Cosme y Damián is today. Its present site is close to a hill of magnetic rock, called Itá Karú (Guaraní 'the stone that eats'). Yutý was also a former stop on the railway line. The old church no longer exists.

General Artigas, which is actually over the departmental boundary into Itapúa, used to be called Bobí, and its charming old church and wooden bell tower are still standing. For information ring the *casa parroquial* (✆ 0743 20098) or the *municipalidad* (✆ 0743 20016). From 1795 Bobí was actually a hub of communication because it was a post office stop between Asunción and Buenos Aires. But at 29km from the nearest asphalt in Coronel Bogado (see page 189), it is certainly not a hub of communication today.

You can carry on driving from Yutý right down to Coronel Bogado on Ruta 1, close to the San Cosme y Damián turn, and the Tebicuarý bus (✆ *021 558774*) covers this route. Yutý to Coronel Bogado takes 1½ hours in the best weather conditions, with General Artigas halfway between the two.

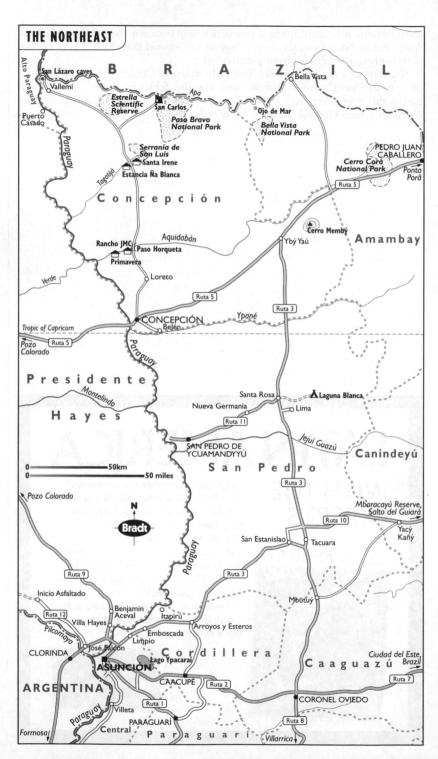

THE NORTHEAST

B R A Z I L

San Lázaro caves
Vallemí
Alto Paraguay
Puerto Casado

Estrella Scientific Reserve
San Carlos
Paso Bravo National Park
Serranía de San Luis
Santa Irene
Estancia Ña Blanca

Apa
Bella Vista
Ojo de Mar
Bella Vista National Park

PEDRO JUAN CABALLERO
Cerro Corá National Park
Ponta Porã

Concepción

Tagatijá
Paraguay

Ruta 5

Aquidabán
Rancho JMC
Paso Horqueta
Primavera
Loreto

Cerro Membý
Ybý Yaú

Amambay

Verde

Ruta 5

Ypané
Ruta 3

Tropic of Capricorn
CONCEPCIÓN
Belén

Pozo Colorado
Ruta 5

Paraguay

Presidente

Montelindo
Santa Rosa
Laguna Blanca
Nueva Germania
Lima

Hayes

Ruta 11
SAN PEDRO DE YCUAMANDYYÚ

Jejuí Guazú

Canindeyú

San Pedro

0   50km
0   50 miles

Pozo Colorado

N
Bradt

Ruta 3

Mbaracayú Reserve, Salto del Guairá

Ruta 10
Yacý Kañý

San Estanislao
Tacuara

Ruta 9

Inicio Asfaltado
Ruta 12
Villa Hayes
Benjamin Aceval
Itapirú
Emboscada
Arroyos y Esteros

Ruta 3

Mbutúy

Pilcomayo
CLORINDA
José Falcón
Limpio
Lago Ypacaraí

Cordillera

Ciudad del Este, Brazil

Caaguazú
Ruta 7

ASUNCIÓN
CAACUPÉ
Ruta 2
CORONEL OVIEDO

ARGENTINA
Villeta
Ruta 1
PARAGUARÍ

Central
Paraguay
Formosa

Paraguarí

Ruta 8
Villarrica

11

Concepción and the Northeast

Departamentos: San Pedro, Canindeyú, Concepción and Amambay

Over 97% of Paraguay's population live to the east of the Río Paraguay, but there is less of tourist interest in the northeast quarter of Paraguay than in the southeast with its old mission towns. Pedro Juan Caballero, capital of the *departamento* of Amambay, on the border with Brazil, is the largest city in the northeast, but it has a reputation for crime and holds few attractions for tourists. However, the historic park of Cerro Corá surrounded by dramatic hills is worth seeing if you can spare the time to get there.

Concepción, capital of the *departamento* of the same name, is a very different kind of town: it is sleepy but charming, with prettily painted Italianate buildings. South of Concepción is the *departamento* of San Pedro, with its capital of the same name: this is deep rural territory, but rather than sleepy it is the seat of present-day *campesino* unrest, particularly relating to land reform questions.

GETTING THERE AND AWAY

BY BUS See under the respective towns below.

BY CAR By private car, it is quicker to do the Chaco route if you are heading for Concepción, but only do it if you are confident of your vehicle, for the Chaco is a wasteland with few garages, telephones or places to eat. (See *Chapter 12*, page 296.)

Driving north up Ruta 3, through eastern Paraguay, may take an extra two hours, but the roads are good and you have the chance to see some places on the way. Start from Asunción on the Ruta Transchaco, but instead of crossing the bridge into the Chaco carry straight on through Limpio and San Estanislao on Ruta 3 – a modern, good road (though single carriageway) that cuts off the corner of the longer route through Coronel Oviedo. At 25 de diciembre (129km from Asuncion) there is a toll station that marks the entry into the San Pedro *departamento* and the rest of the north.

After passing San Estanislao you turn left for the north at Tacuara. (This is still Ruta 3.) You have now been travelling for a couple of hours or so, and after nearly three more hours you get to Ybý Yaú (which quaintly means, in Guaraní 'we eat the earth'), which is where you reach Ruta 5 and must turn either left (west) for Concepción or right (east) for Pedro Juan Caballero. Both are approximately 100km away from the turn. The whole of this route is on decent asphalt.

If you are driving, the best places to break the journey are at San Estanislao (page 272) or Santa Rosa (page 273).

BY AIR There used to be small planes that flew to Concepción, to Vallemí further north on the Río Paraguay, and to Pedro Juan Caballero, but all have been discontinued. In an emergency you can take an air taxi. (See box on chartering planes in *Chapter 2*, page 307.)

After you have left Asunción and passed through Limpio, whether by car or bus, you take Ruta 3, heading for Emboscada, which has a jewel of a church and is included in the Circuito de Oro (see *Chapter 4*, page 131). Then you pass through Arroyos y Esteros, on the way to San Estanislao.

WHERE TO STAY

San Guillermo ☎ 021 225285/446630; m 0981 410542; e marbains@hotmail.com. At only 35km from Asunción, before you get to Emboscada, this is one of the *estancias* closest to the capital, where the Río Piribebúy flows into the Río Paraguay. It has a jetty, a chapel, a pool, & is a good place for fishing or just for relaxing. Reservations can also be made through Apatur; see *Chapter 2*, page 51. $$$

Mbuni Nueva Colombia, 50km northeast of Asunción; m 0981 992491; www.mbuni.de. Calls itself a *granja de avestruz*, an ostrich farm. To get there, turn right at Emboscada, left in between Copaco & the Centro de Salud, along Profesor Méndez Mendoza,

then briefly left at the end, & right along the dirt road for 250m. You will come to a bridge over the stream to your right & then Mbuni. They have rooms for guests, pool, jacuzzi, & Wi-Fi. $$$

Hotel Olivares (4 rooms) Mariscal López 104 y 14 de mayo; ☎ 0510 272070. Excellent, small family hotel, 56km from Asunción, handy when travelling on Ruta 3. At the Copetrol station turn right (coming from Asunción) for 4 blocks, then half a block right. It is behind the hamburger bar. Attractive old building, modern bathrooms, split A/C, garden with mango tree & well, cloth napkins at b/fast. Internet in the attractive plaza, a couple of blocks away. Cheaper rooms have fans. $

An excursion can be made from Arroyos y Esteros to the **Capilla Olivares** in Itapirú, the last *compañía* of Arroyos y Esteros, on the west bank of the Río Manduvirá, close to where it joins the Río Paraguay. The chapel was built by President Carlos Antonio López and has been restored and declared a *patrimonio nacional*. There are buses that go to Itapirú, but you need to allow time for this journey.

SAN ESTANISLAO *(Copaco ☎ 043 20200; municipalidad ☎ 043 20454)*

San Estanislao, commonly known as Santaní (for Taní is Stanislaus in Guaraní), is a good place to eat or sleep on the way to the northeast. It was an old Jesuit *doctrina* (something on the way to being a Reduction) but its chief claim to fame was for being a barracks for the army of Mariscal López in the War of the Triple Alliance. There are three plazas, but the most interesting is the Plaza Bernardino Caballero, with its imposing church with colonnades on both sides in traditional style. Facing the plaza is the museum, housed in the former military barracks, and it displays military remains, a few Jesuit statues (not of the best) and the 6m-long skin of the *mbói jaguá* snake (Guaraní 'snake dog', so named because of the barking noise it makes in the mating period).

According to local legend, anyone who bathes in the River Tapiracuái will be enchanted with the desire to return to Santaní.

To get to San Estanislao by car, see page 271; any of the buses going to Pedro Juan Caballero will pass through here (see below, page 284).

There are several internet places in San Estanislao. There are cash machines at Visión and the Cooperativa, but the usual cautions apply that they may not accept cards that are not Visa. The patronal feast day is 13 November.

Where to stay

Hotel Kiko (28 rooms) 14 de mayo y Libertad 720; ☎ 043 20223. Approaching on Ruta 3 from Asunción, you reach the Plaza Mariscal López, where this hotel is, before you get to the other plaza with the church & other hotels. Friendly people, but not

quite as nice or as good value as the Hotel Safuan. Internet. $$

Hotel Safuan (12 rooms) Adolfo Mello y Defensores del Chaco; ☎ 043 20294/20096. On corner of Plaza Bernardino Caballero with church. Will do

meals if you order in advance. Pleasant b/fast room on 1st floor with balcony. Internet. Recommended. $$
🏠 **Hotel Maracaná** (18 rooms) Defensores del Chaco y Adolfo Mello; 📞 043 20282. Also overlooks

plaza but is closer to the museum. Less quality than the Safuan & only slightly cheaper. $
🏠 **Hotel Tapirakuai** Av Mariscal López 542; 📞 043 20371. Will do meals if you order in advance. $

✗ Where to eat and drink

✗ **Churrasquería Sabor Brasil** 📞 043 21095. On Ruta 3 before you get into the town, approaching from Asunción. Very basic. Another similarly basic *churrasquería* is very close, on the bend of the main road Ruta 3. $$
✗ **Restaurant Colonial** On corner near the church.

The sign Molino de Maiz is more visible, & refers to the antique maize mill in the same building. A pretty place to eat or have a drink, with tables on the portico overlooking the plaza, surrounded by greenery, & substantial old carved wooden pillars. Menu simple but typical Paraguayan fare. $

Rejoining the route north, you turn left at Tacuara to go north. This is still Ruta 3, although you feel that you are joining another main road (which goes north to Concepción and south to Coronel Oviedo).

SANTA ROSA AND SURROUNDS Continuing north up Ruta 3, about 65km after Tacuara you come to the River Jejuí, and about 25km north is the turn to Lima, which is just 3km to the east of Ruta 3. It has a pleasant diocesan retreat house and an old adobe church. And 7km further north you come to Santa Rosa.

Santa Rosa itself is an extended sprawl of buildings along the main road, and turns out to be a good stopping place for travellers. The **Hotel Cristal** (*km325; 30 rooms;* 📞 *0451 235442;* 📱 *0971 43271/0981 710489;* $$), halfway through Santa Rosa on the east side of the road, is new and well designed, with excellent facilities, including a pool, car park, football pitch and Wi-Fi. Its prices are a bargain, and it is doing such a roaring trade that booking in advance is recommended. It has recently opened the Churrasquería Cristal next door, with very cheap prices.

About 0.5km further on is a recommended restaurant, the **Boi de Oro** (📱 *0971 836950;* $$), on the west side of the road. It is run by a Brazilian and is an excellent *churrasquería*, with good fresh salad, though it can be easily missed because of its modest exterior.

One of the most beautiful natural places is close to here: a beach resort and nature reserve called **Laguna Blanca** (*270km from Asunción;* 📞 *021 424760/452506;* 📱 *0971 167600/0981 588671;* e *consulta@lagunablanca.com.py or malvinaduarte@ hotmail.com; www.lagunablanca.com.py; campers only; meals* $$). Reservations can also be made through Apatur (see *Chapter 2*, page 51) though this is not a typical *estancia*. At the southern end of Santa Rosa there is a crossroads, with no signs, but this is where you turn west if you want to go along Ruta 11 to San Pedro, 77km away (see next entry), and also where you turn east through an enchanting country landscape to reach Laguna Blanca, some 27km away along a dirt road which is due to be asphalted in 2011. After crossing four bridges you come to a water tank on stilts, and this is where you turn right and cross another bridge, then left shortly afterwards, to come to the gate of Laguna Blanca, where it says that only those with prior reservations can enter.

This is a private reserve dedicated to agriculture and tourism – one of the best of its kind in South America – and the foundation Para la Tierra is about to open a biological station here. Any birdwatcher will be enthused by the great variety of birds in this region. You can rent a tent and a hammock, or you can stay in Santa Rosa and just come in for the day. All meals are available and are cheap. You can relax on the beaches of white sand on the shores of the crystalline lake, and go rowing, paddleboating, kayaking, snorkelling or fishing. Or you can walk or go riding in the mix of low forest and grassland known as *cerrado*, which is a fragile

11

ecosystem, and characterised by scrub or grassland growing on very sandy earth – white in colour, hence the name Laguna Blanca ('white lake'). This is the most southern point of the cerrado, which stretches up into Brazil. One of the welcome characteristics of this very distinctive, sandy terrain, is that there are no mosquitoes. It is also very rich in fauna.

If you are going to Concepción or Pedro Juan Caballero, you continue going north from Santa Rosa for another 105km, to the end of Ruta 3 at Yby Yaú, where you make your choice of Concepción (left, see page 276) or Pedro Juan Caballero (right, see page 283).

SAN PEDRO DE YCUAMANDYYÚ Copaco ✎ 0342 222499; municipalidad ✎ 0342 222252

San Pedro de Ycuamandyyú (variously spelt Ycuamandiyú or Yukuamandyju in Spanish, or 'Saint Peter of the Cottonfields Spring'), was founded in 1786 by the Portuguese, and still has a number of houses of a neoclassical style from the period of the two López presidencies. (See *Chapter 4*, page 103, for the Franciscan influence in its foundation). It is sometimes said to be the poorest place in Paraguay, and until 2007 it was only accessible after two hours' determined ploughing through (rather than along) a dirt road that seemed to be composed entirely of sand dunes. If it rained you could be stranded for days, and there was only one inhabited place on the way, Nueva Germania (a 19th-century German utopian experiment).

San Pedro is identified as the approximate locality where the Portuguese explorer Alejo García was murdered by hostile indigenous in 1525: he is sometimes attributed with being the 'discoverer' of Paraguay. The town is now most famous for being the place where Fernando Lugo was bishop, before becoming president of the Republic in 2008. This popular and charismatic bishop attracted to San Pedro the Latin American Congress of Basic Ecclesial Communities in 1996, which gave the town a brief moment of glory after which it sank again into its forgotten corner.

San Pedro is also known for being the seat of the most vociferous and at times violent *campesino* discontent, particularly over the issues of land reform and the purchase of land by Brazilian planters of genetically modified crops, with all the issues of health that have arisen through the use of poisons to clear the land.

GETTING THERE Buses from Asunción (Nasa and San Pedrana) leave twice a day and do the 320km in about five hours. Buses also run directly from San Pedro to Ciudad del Este and Pedro Juan Caballero. You arrive on the Avenida Juana María de Lara, and stop at the bus terminal (✎ 0342 223017) five blocks past the plaza .

There is a little airport on the Avenida Luis María Argaña but no regular service, and now that the road is asphalted there is no longer a need for even the rich to charter a private plane. For directions on driving, see above, page 271.

WHERE TO STAY

🏠 **Hotel Santa Ana** (33 rooms) General Diaz c/ Independencia Nacional; ✎ 0342 222706. 4 blocks before you reach the central plaza, & I block to the north, near the Petropar service station. The most used & most recommended hotel. Has Wi-Fi but no computer available to guests. $$
🏠 **Hotel P L** Braulio Zelada c/ Jejuí; ✎ 0342 222043. New hotel opposite terminal. AC & cable TV. $$

🏠 **Hotel Restaurant Victorino** (15 rooms) ✎ 0342 222287. 3 blocks from the plaza, I block from the Esso station. Budget. $
🏠 **Hotel Giyoka** (7 rooms) Av Antonio Ortigoza c/ Pancha Garmendia; ✎ 042 222311; e gala_delrosario@hotmail.com. Friendly people, ask for the house of Dr Gala in barrio Fátima. Near to la Ande (electricity office). Though it is a family house the rooms have AC, private bathrooms, TV. $

✕ WHERE TO EAT

✕ **Restaurant Anamar** Eusebio Ayala esq Gral Caballero; ☎ 0342 222284. Look for low bright-red walls. The best restaurant of a limited selection. $
✕ **Pachi Pachi** ☎ 0342 222237. 1 block from the centre in a colonial building. Speciality horsemeat,

steak with onions. $
✕ **Emporio de los Alfajores** Mcal Estigarribia c/ Iturbe; ☎ 0342 222282; ⏰ 07.15–16.00 daily. Cheap restaurant, good service.

OTHER PRACTICALITIES The traditional style of this town is maintained by the use of the little horse cart for passengers, known as the sulky, and by ox carts. There is a regional hospital and a private clinic. There are not many internet facilities but there is one near the Hotel Victorino.

The patronal feast day is 29 June (feast of saints Peter and Paul) and the anniversary of the foundation is 16 March, when there are celebrations and fishing competitions.

For entertainment there is the **discotheque** Guajira Pub, and a **cinema and theatre**, Cine Teatro Juan de Dios Ramírez.

WHAT TO SEE AND DO The town centre is the **Plaza Mariscal Francisco Solano López**. Around the sides of this plaza are the cathedral, the *gobernación*, the *municipalidad*, and the Museo de Antigüedades Alejo García. The *poli deportivo* (multi-purpose sports hall) practically fronts the plaza as well, and next to it is the Casa de Cultura, a historic old building with a portico.

San Pedro has a striking, historic **cathedral** of the traditional Paraguayan style, dating from 1854 (in the presidency of Carlos Antonio López), with a double, pitched roof, a front portico supported on white pillars, and a wooden bell tower standing apart. Inside there are 18th-century wooden statues of the saints, folky in style and clothed, including of course St Peter. There is a fine, old reredos.

There is a *feria campesina* (peasant market) on Vicente Ignacio Iturbe, immediately behind the *municipalidad,* selling vegetables, meat and craft. Craft is also sold on the **Paseo de los Artistas**, a pedestrian road running to the Café Literario by the side of the *gobernación* (❧ *0342 222269*).

A rather strange monument in the **Plaza General Marcial Samaniego**, like a jigsaw piece with a hole in it, commemorates Alejo García, the Portuguese explorer who passed through this region in 1524 and is considered by some the founder of Paraguay. A nearby cross, Kurusú García, is in memory of his death at this approximate spot at the hands of the indigenous in 1525. (*Kurusú* is 'cross' in Guaraní.)

Walking around the town centre, you will find a large number of attractive old buildings, particularly in the area south of the **Avenida Braulio Zelada** and Independencia Nacional. If you walk along Zelada, every block has a house of architectural interest, and these buildings fall into two types. There are the traditional houses with pitched roofs and colonnades the length of the building, of the style built in the Jesuit-Guaraní Reductions and continued long after. One of the oldest is the house of the Salomón family (Zelada y Estigarribia), dating from around 1800, and a couple of blocks west along Zelada is an attractive corner house belonging to the Campos Ross-Cassanello family, dating from about 1850. But there are also a number of grander houses with **Italianate façades**, set on corners with the door on the angle. They have tall façades, flat roofs, and many have high rounded doorways and plaster decoration above the windows. The most grandiose of these is the Seccional Colorado (Independencia y Colón), and another attractive one is the house of the Ferreira family (Yegros y Colón), built around 1900.

San Pedro is only 3km from the Río Jejuí, just before it runs into the Río Paraguay. The road from San Pedro to **Puerto'í** (the little port on the River Jejuí) leads south, while the main asphalted road to Puerto Antequera on the River Paraguay – about 24km away – branches off to the right. When you are nearly at Puerto'i you turn right for the beach, or left for the embarkation point for going to the island Alejo García, more than 2,000m long, which is in the early stages of being presented as an **Isla de Ecoturismo**.

If you have turned right, you will come to a white-sand **beach**, and you can hire a rowing boat. At the east end of this beach is the **Restaurante** Anabar and at the west end is a Club de Caza y Pesca (hunting and fishing club). A pale pink D-shaped structure near to the river marks the spot of the *ykuá mandyjú* (cottonfields spring) which gives its name to the town.

CONCEPCIÓN Copaco ❧ *0331 242800; municipalidad* ❧ *0331 242212*

One of the most attractive Paraguayan towns and sometimes known as the Pearl of the North, Concepción is quiet, picturesque and historic. It has a number of lovely buildings constructed by Italian immigrants, typically painted yellow with white highlights, and the green cupola of the cathedral makes a welcoming sight ahead of you as you arrive.

Concepción was founded in 1773 by Agustín Fernando de Pinedo, close to the existing settlement of Belén (see below, page 280), as a centre for growing *yerba*, for

CONCEPCIÓN

Bradt

FLOW

A
Paraguay
NANAWA
Estrella del Norte
JUAN BOTAÑO
Puerto Seguro
Hotel Piscis
100m
100yds

B
CURUPAYTÝ
Museo Cuartel de Villa Real
CARLOS ANTONIO LÓPEZ
Francés
Banco de la Nación Argentina
GENERAL JOSE EDUVIGIS DÍAZ

C
TENIENTE 1°
NUESTRA SEÑORA DE LA CONCEPCIÓN
Plaza Libertad
Amistad
Cathedral

D
FLORENCIO E GOMEZ
TENIENTE 1° EUGENIO R AGUERO
MAYOR JULIO OTAÑO
PEDRO JUAN CABALLERO
BRASIL
ITURBE
CERRO CORÁ
Victoria
PRESIDENTE FRANCO
MARISCAL ESTIGARRIBIA
MARISCAL
Toninho y Jandira
Mansión Otaño
Municipalidad

E
GENERAL GARAY
El Heladero
Banco Nacional de Fomento
LÓPEZ
Teatro Municipal & Museo

F
Bus terminal (4 blocks)
14 DE MAYO
Banco Visión
Norte Cambios
Center

G
AGUSTÍN FERNANDO DE PINEDO
Monumento a la Madre
Yasy supermarket (3 blocks)
FULGENCIO YEGROS
Librería Progreso
Copaco
Banco Amambay
Banco Continental
Paiva
Ysapý
Artesanía Ren
Plaza Pinedo
Ruta 5
Librería Rocío

N

277

dominating the Mbaya indigenous, and for defence against the Portuguese who were always trying to extend the boundaries of Brazil. A century later, in 1864, Mariscal López set off from here with 2,500 soldiers to attack the Mato Grosso of Brazil. In 1884 it became a municipality.

GETTING THERE For instructions on getting to the northeast by car, see *Getting there and away* on page 271 above.

Buses take six hours to reach Concepción from Asunción, and they take a route through the Chaco, via Pozo Colorado, which is quicker for them. The companies offering this route to Concepción are Nasa, Golondrina, Pycasú, Santaniana and Ovetense. Ovetense also does the longer route to Concepción up Ruta 3 via Ybý Yaú, which takes eight hours, as does Nasa with its night buses, which leave Concepción at 23.15 and 23.45.

The bus companies that go to Pedro Juan Caballero are La Santaniana, Nasa, Cometa Amambay and Ovetense. The journey is via Ruta 3 and Ruta 5 and takes eight hours.

A lot of buses travel between Concepción and Pedro Juan Caballero, including Nasa and Cometa del Amambay, and the journey may take as long as five hours. (It is under three hours by car.) See box in *Chapter 2*, page 47, for the phone numbers of the bus companies. The phone number of the Concepción bus terminal is 0331 242744.

To get to Vallemí (further north than Concepción on the Río Paraguay) by bus is a further five hours. It is slow because you are on dirt roads. The Nasa bus leaves Concepción at 05.00 and arrives at Vallemí around 11.00. There are plans to asphalt the road between Concepción and Vallemí.

ORIENTATION Concepción spreads for about 25 blocks east to west, until it reaches the River Paraguay, and then hugs its banks. You are likely to drive in on General Bernardino Caballero, which turns into Mariscal López after crossing the Avenida Agustín Fernando de Pinedo – the big avenue that cuts the town in two, running north to south. The centre, with the *municipalidad*, the cathedral and the Plaza Libertad, are all on this road, but most hotels, as also most shops, are found on Presidente Franco, two blocks to the north. If you arrive by bus you can ask to get off in the avenida if you want to walk to your hotel, or continue to the terminal 'Yakare Valija', eight blocks north of Presidente Franco, and take a taxi. The phone number of the Concepción bus terminal is 03312 42744.

If you need a taxi while you are exploring the town and have failed to find one on the streets, try Juan Ortiz (✆ *0331 241197;* m *0971 805728*).

 WHERE TO STAY In addition to these, a large hotel is presently under construction on Mariscal López (e/ Yegros y 14 de mayo).

🏠 **Hotel Francés** [277 B3] (40 rooms) Pres Franco y Carlos Antonio López; ✆ 0331 242383; f 0331 242750. Elegant corner site & has a pool & car park. $$$

🏠 **Hotel Piscis** [277 A4] Mariscal López y Juan B Otaño; ✆ 0331 242753/243187. Large hotel with bar/restaurant right on the bank, dramatic river setting. Undergoing renovation. $$$

🏠 **Hotel Victoria** [277 D3] Pres Franco esq Pedro Juan Caballero; ✆ 0331 242826/242256; f 0331 242826. Old building of character with

colonnades & balconies, & murals in the courtyard. Owners are knowledgeable about *estancias* to the north of Concepción. Cheaper rooms have fans. $$

🏠 **Hotel Center** [277 F3] Franco c/ Yegros; ✆ 0331 242584/242360; f 0331 242360. Recently renovated. Cheaper rooms have fans. Has simple restaurant/ice-cream bar. $

🏠 **Bar Pensión Estrella del Norte** [277 A2] Nanawa c/ Pres Franco; ✆ 0331 242400. Shoestring but some rooms have bathrooms. It faces the river but there is a big fence in between so no view. $

✕ WHERE TO EAT

✕ **Hotel Francés** [277 B3] See above. Has the most ambitious food of the hotels; good value for money, if sometimes over-salted. $$

✕ **Toninho y Jandira** [277 E3] Mariscal Estigarribia, e/ Iturbe y Cerro Corá; ✆ 0331 241415/243394. Facing the *municipalidad* is a good Brazilian restaurant, where you can sit in a roofed, open area & enjoy not only excellent food but also the view of the elegant building opposite with its gardens & fountains. (Note that the muncipalidad faces two directions, & this restaurant is on the road listed above & not on Mariscal López.) $$

✕ **Hotel Victoria** [277 D3] See above. Has 2 restaurants: the lunch restaurant doubles as the b/fast room, while in the evening they open a restaurant over the road to leave the rooms quiet for guests. Sometimes has live music on Fri evenings. $

✕ **Amistad** [277 C3] Presidente Franco y Nuestra Señora de Concepción. Lively ice-cream parlour which also does meals. The notice says 'Heladería Anahi' but the locals call it the Amistad. Is full into the early hours, though the food is slow to arrive. $

✕ **El Heladero** [277 E2] Brasil y General Garay. Attractive modern café. $

✕ **Paiva** [277 G3] Avenida Pinedo e/ Presidente Franco y Mariscal Estigarribia. Good cheap restaurant where you pay by weight. $

✕ **Ysapý** [277 G3] Mariscal Estigarribia y Fulgencio Yegros. Pizzeria which produces good food quickly & cheaply. $

SHOPPING There is a corner **craft shop** called Artesanía Ren on Mariscal Estigarribia y 14 de mayo [277 F3]. It specialises in leather goods, sandals, clothes, and particularly *guampas* for *tereré*. A good **supermarket** is Yasý on Julio de Otaño y Doctor Canillas, three blocks to the east of the Avenida Agustín Fernando de Pinedo.

OTHER PRACTICALITIES The **banks** are the Banco de la Nación Argentina (*Presidente Franco y Carlos Antonio López*), the Amambay (*Presidente Franco y Avenida A F de Pinedo*), Continental (*Presidente Franco y Yegros*), Visión (*Presidente Franco, e/ Eng Garay y 14 de mayo*) and the Banco Nacional de Fomento (*Presidente Franco y Cerro Corá*). Visión and Continental have cash machines. Visión also has a Western Union office.

There are **internet cafés** on Presidente Franco (*e/ Av Pinedo y Yegros*) on Mariscal Estigarribia (*e/ Nuestra Señora de la Concepción y Pedro Juan Caballero*), and in many other places.

You might be able to get a **map** of Concepción in the form of a free calendar (if you ask nicely – they generally do one every year) from Norte Cambios (next to Visión, address above). Or you might be able to buy a similar map (expensively, for Gs100,000) from the Librería Progreso [277 G3] on Presidente Franco c/ Avenida Agustín Fernando de Pinedo, where they also sell a map of the Departamento of Concepción (for Gs50,000). There is a bigger bookshop, Librería Rocío (Av Pinedo e/ Mariscal López y Coronel Martínez), but it does not sell local maps.

The **post office** [277 B3] is on Presidente Franco on the corner of Curupaytý.

FESTIVITIES The feast of María Auxiliadora (Our Lady Help of Christians) is on 24 May, and the foundation of the city is celebrated on 25 May, which has a procession down the Avenida Agustín Fernando de Pinedo with floats relating to the history of the town. Expo Norte is a major agricultural show that comes to Concepción in the first week of September, and is held in the Campo de Exposiciones, 4.5km on Ruta 5. The feast of the Immaculate Conception of Mary is on 8 December.

WHAT TO SEE Tourist enquiries can be directed to Celso Ruiz Díaz (✆ 0331 242212; m 0981 292179), who will attend on behalf of the *municipalidad*, and arrange access to places outside their normal opening hours.

The massive white **statue of María Auxiliadora** [277 G2] dominates the Avenida Agustín Fernando de Pinedo. Situated outside the Salesian church at the junction with Mayor Julio de Otaño, it is called the Monumento a la Madre, and was inaugurated in 2002. You can climb a few stairs to a platform at the feet of the mother, for the view. At night when it is floodlit it looks even more dramatic. In general the Avenida Pinedo is lovely at night, with lights shining from inside different coloured plastic bottles. The same form of lighting is used in Presidente Franco.

The **cathedral** [277 D3] on the Plaza Libertad (Nuestra Señora de la Concepción, e/ Mariscal Estigarribia y Mariscal López) is a tall and striking building in yellow and white, not old but classical in feel and with clean elegant lines. If you find it open, you can see the altar, which is the work of the famous Paraguayan artist Carlos Colombino, who specialises in wood creations. Some large and unusual birds inhabit the small garden to the front and side, and the facing plaza is very pleasant. There is a small museum of sacred art next door: it is normally open in office hours, but in case it is not, you can enquire at the adjoining Obispado (bishop's office) or from Celso Ruiz Díaz (see above).

The **Museo Cuartel de Villa Real** [277 B3] is one block away (*Mariscal Estigarribia y Carlos Antonio López;* ⊕ *07.00–12.00 Mon–Sat & sometimes 14.00–18.00; contact Celso Ruiz Díaz for access at other times; free*), in a 19th-century building that was once the barracks for Mariscal López's army, beautifully restored in 1998. It houses the wheels of the wagon that once transported Madame Lynch's piano on the great retreat to the northeast, in the War of the Triple Alliance. There are also sabres, military pictures and trumpets, and indigenous feather headdresses, bows and arrows.

A second museum is in the **Teatro Municipal** [277 E4], on Mariscal López, an elegant yellow and grey building one block to the east of the *municipalidad*. You may or may not be lucky enough to find it open, but Celso Ruiz Díaz will open at request at any other time.

Inside the *municipalidad* [277 E4] on the Mariscal Estigarribia side there are two very large and fine oil paintings: one shows the foundation of the city by Agustín Fernando de Pinedo (with the river, the soldiers, the indigenous and a Franciscan priest); the other shows the battle of Nanawa (a victory of Paraguay over Bolivia in the Chaco War).

The **old post office** [277 B3] on Presidente Franco y Curupaytý is an elegant corner building, constructed in 1915, a couple of blocks from the port. It is marked Correos y Telegrafos, and was restored with Spanish assistance. Some of the attractive **Italianate houses** are the Mansión Otaño, Mansión Isnardi, Mansión Albertini and the Villa Ida.

The imposing bridge over the Río Paraguay is called the **Puente Nanawa**. A little to the south of the city, it carries you into the Chaco, which feels almost like another country, so different is it in terms of soil and landscape.

EXCURSION TO BELÉN Belén can be visited as a short excursion from Concepción, as it is only 21km to the southeast, along a dirt road. It is sited exactly on the tropic of Capricorn, and is a little-known Jesuit Reduction though not one of the famous group of eight in Misiones and Itapúa in the south of the country which formed part of the famous Treinta Pueblos. The Reduction of Belén tends to be forgotten, because it was founded in 1760, only seven years before the Expulsion of the Jesuits, so had little chance to establish itself, and also because it was an experimental venture among the warlike Mbaya indigenous, with none of the success of missions to the more pacific Guaraní. Though a couple of local historians have written books about Belén recently, and this is the oldest settlement in the entire area, the truth is that there is very little to see. The present school is in an original building, but it is a depressingly ramshackle affair.

If you are not under time pressure, an exploration of the vast range of land north of Concepción is an adventure. There are little-known *estancias*, extensive national parks, a remote 18th-century fort, and riverside caves. Consider going one way by boat and the other way by bus. Be careful about getting a hire car stuck in the remote dirt tracks if rain comes.

There is a Nasa bus at 05.00 from Concepción that goes all the way to Vallemí, but more buses run during the day to closer places.

LORETO Driving north from Concepción for 25km on a dirt road you come first to Loreto, which was not a Reduction although from its name it sounds as though it might have been. There are several buses per day, every hour or two, which you can take from the bus terminal. There is a rather attractive monument as you enter the town, like a mini-chapel in the middle of the road, blue and white with a tiny dome and cross. Take note too of the 10m bell tower at the church, modelled on the bell tower at Yaguarón (see page 145) but built in 2005.

ESTANCIAS These *estancias* are outside of the Apatur network, being remote from Asunción. Ring first to reserve and to get instructions: you may be able to travel by bus and be picked up at a convenient point. The Río Aquidabán, north of Concepción, has some of the finest beaches in the country, with big stretches of proper yellow sand but the best accommodation is by the stream Tagatijá Guazú.

Estancia Ña Blanca ✆ 0982 917792. 94km from Concepción. Straight up the dirt road that goes to Vallemí, crossing the Río Aquidabán & going the same distance again. When you reach the stream Tagatijá Guazú, it is on your left. Little waterfalls, crystalline water, beautiful scenery. Snorkeling, walks, camping. Also has rooms for guests, & can take groups. Visits only with prior reservation. Named after the owner, Blanca Ferreira de González. $$

Rancho JMC ✆ 0331 242722/240801/243124. The easiest to get to, with a nice run in a sulky to a good beach. Could be cleaner. $$

Estancia Primavera ✆ 0331 242045. e nievecae@hotmail.com. 46km from Concepción, on the Río Aquidabán. Simple place with 3 dormitories big enough for groups. Bunks & shared bathrooms. Isolated beaches, riding. Off the beaten track, but they can accompany you from Concepción. $$

NATIONAL PARKS There are also some national parks far to the north of Concepción – Parque Nacional Paso Bravo, Serranía San Luis and Parque Nacional Bella Vista. You are advised to first ring SEAM (Secretaria del Ambiente) (✆ *021 615804/615812; www.seam.gov.py; see page 8*), who can help facilitate your visit. They all have a park ranger who can act as a guide.

The **Serranía San Luis** reserve is a triangle of 10,0000ha to the east of the road going north from Concepción to Vallemí. It was declared protected in 1991 and is characterised by dense forest and rugged rock formations, and protects the water basins of the streams Tagatijá Guazú, Santa Isabel and La Paz. The Tagatijá Guazú has rapids, waterfalls and crystalline clear pools, with rich varieties of fish, including *boga, piký, morenita, mandi'í* and *dorado*. Three threatened varieties of macaw (hyacinth, red-and-green and blue-and-yellow) thrive in San Luis. There are also capuchin monkeys. The park ranger lives in the southern point of the reserve, and has beds for visitors.

Adjoining the fort is the extensive Parque Nacional **Paso Bravo** (93,612ha) which was formed as recently as 1998, and is named 'Wild Pass' after the stream that runs through it. It is principally savanna territory and also has caverns and hills. There is little or no visitor infrastructure.

⌂ **WHERE TO STAY** It might sound fun to stay in the 18th-century fort of **San Carlos**, now restored with Spanish aid and converted into a hotel, on the northern frontier with Brazil where there are rapids and you can take a kayak on the River Apa, but take into account the difficulty of getting there. After crossing the River Aquidabán at Paso Horqueta, drive along this dirt road for 84km and you will reach a cart track which is the turning for San Carlos del Apa. If you do not get lost in the network of tracks, you will reach San Carlos after another 40–50km. The journey can only be made by 4×4 vehicles, and you may find it a long way to go for rather little.

VALLEMÍ (*http://ciudadvallemi.tripod.com/*) Vallemí is located in the top northwest corner of this northeast section of Paraguay, right on the River Paraguay and very nearly as northerly as the Río Apa, which marks the frontier with Brazil. Vallemí is a cement producing town, and one of the striking things about it when you get off an aeroplane from the south is the totally different colour of the earth: instead of rich reddish brown it is very distinctly grey – cement-coloured in fact. There is a quarry of *piedra caliza* which is the raw material for making cement. The second striking feature is the simply enormous number of donkeys.

There is only one bus a day from Concepción (Nasa, departing 05.00). This used to be a place you flew into on the airline Arpa, and from where you could take a motorboat a short distance downriver to Puerto Casado on the Chaco side of the river (see page 308), but the flights are no longer operating.

You can have a guided visit to the **caves of San Lázaro** (*Asociación de Espeleología del Norte, Oscar Mereles;* ☏ 031 230326), which are slightly upriver and have stalactites. There are other caves in the locality too, at Cambahopo, Tres Cerros and Calera Risso (**e** *arvatur@hotmail.com*).

CRUISING THE RÍO PARAGUAY

Taking a boat up the River Paraguay is a beautiful and relaxing experience. The scenery is as wild and natural as you could possibly hope for, the time span is in another world, and the cheap boats are full of local people and local life. You may witness the hunting and preparation of capybaras. If you pass beyond the *departamento* of Concepción, on the east bank, you can go a long way further north, eventually reaching the Paraguayan Pantanal on the west bank (see *Chapter 12*, page 306). Alternatively you can take a boat to travel to Asunción. Remember that travelling upriver is slower than travelling downriver: boats go upstream at 12km/h, and downstream at 18km/h. Be patient with the relaxed Paraguayan approach to time: you may be told a boat has been cancelled and then find it leaves anyway, or that it is going to leave and then find it is cancelled, so be prepared to hang around. Sometimes travellers have been disappointed to find the boats are being repaired and are not sailing. On board you can often buy supplies from the cargo – beer and longlife milk and the like – and you are likely to find the crew helpful and friendly. The word for a 'launch' or 'motorboat' is *lancha*.

Crucero Paraguay Perú 689 c/ Juan de Salazar; ☏ 021 223217/232051; m 0981 520277; e crucero@cruceroparaguay.info; www.cruceroparaguay.info. A luxury cruiser that has been very tastefully designed, just a nice size — small enough to be intimate & big enough to have all facilities. Swimming pool, 5 decks, disco, cinema, gym. Tempting website & reality is no disappointment. Programa Pantanal offers 6 days going upriver from Concepción, as far as Fuerte Olimpo, & back to Concepción. For an extra payment you can start & end the cruise at Asunción, which gives 3 more nights on board. There is also a w/end cruise starting & ending in Asunción, which does not get as far as Concepción. One major problem is finding a sailing, as there are not enough passengers to make for a frequent service: there are w/end cruises from Asunción about once a month, but the Pantanal cruise only goes about 3 times a year & only for groups. The other problem is the price: currently US$1,980 pp for the 6-day cruise (or US$512 for a w/end starting from Asunción). More info on *Crucero Paraguay* in *Chapter 12*, page 307.

Ten Caten m 0971 819822;
e agenciaaventura@gmail.com. Fishing excursions for foreigners, departs Concepción. AC, 12 beds, diner. 4 small fishing boats with outboard motor. 8–10 passengers, US$400 per day per group, does not include food or drink. Typical excursion is 3 days. Fishing is prohibited from 15 Nov–20 Dec in Paraguayan waters & a bit longer in Brazilian waters, till end Jan.

Siete Cabrillas m 0971 800907;
e reservas@sietecabrillas.com;
www.sietecabrillas.com. Upmarket fishing boat similar to *Ten Caten* but newer: it began sailing in 2007. Snazzy website.

Aquidabán ✆ 0331 242370/242435; reservations of 4-berth cabins, Colho de Zouza agency ✆ 0331

242435 mornings. The boat the locals take. Lots of local colour & cheap. Approx US$30
Concepción–Bahía Negra return. Bahía Negra is far north – the most northerly point of Paraguay that you can reach by public boat. Departs Concepción Tue mornings; recommended arrive 08.00 to get a place. Reaches Puerto Casado & Vallemí, Wed; Fuerte Olimpo, Thu; Bahía Negra, Fri dawn; Fuerte Olimpo on journey downriver, Fri pm; Puerto Casado & Vallemí, Sat; Concepción Sun am.

Cacique II ✆ 021 492829 (Mon & Tue). Another cheap boat, that starts from Asunción but only goes as far as Vallemí. Regular journeys once a week. Cabins. Departs Asunción Wed 07.00. Arrives Concepción midday Thu. Arrives Vallemí Fri pm. Arrives back in Concepción Sun am; Asunción Mon at dawn.

Guaraní Regular journeys once a fortnight, Asunción – Vallemí – Asunción, but principally takes cargo with very little room for passengers. Departs Concepción on the journey south every other Wed 17.00, arrives Asunción Fri. Departs Asunción 17.00 every other Fri for Concepción, reaches Concepción Sun eve & then goes on to Vallemí. On the weeks when the *Guaraní* is not sailing, the **Aguapé** follows the same timetable.

PEDRO JUAN CABALLERO Copaco ✆ 0336 272299; municipalidad ✆ 0336 272212

Pedro Juan Caballero (usually known just as Pedro Juan) is a large city and the capital of the *departamento* Amambay. The city is named after one of the *Próceres* of Independence, whose statue stands in the Plaza Panchito López. This is the furthest city away from Asunción (536km), and has a reputation for poverty and all the problems associated with poverty in big cities. There are plenty of armed guards to be seen on the streets, watching over the shops.

It was founded in 1894 as a stopping point for wagons carrying *yerba* from Concepción to Brazil, and since then has profited from trade of all sorts with its larger neighbour. The **Shopping China** [286 D7] is a vast warehouse on Ruta 5 that sells everything you can think of, and serves as a prominent local landmark. There is a Paraguayan flag outside it, and that is all there is to mark the boundary with Brazil. It is typical of this crime-ridden city that the only comment on one internet tourist forum is from a Brazilian reporting the theft of his car from the Shopping China car park.

The Brazilian frontier actually runs right through the city, though the part on the Brazilian side is called by the Guaraní name Ponta Porã, which was once the name for Pedro Juan too. Ponta Porã is in the state of Mato Grosso do Sul.

Locals advise you not to cross into Brazil with your car, as the Brazilian police are vigilant and tough, charge large fines and may even confiscate your vehicle. However, the frontier is so invisible it is difficult not to cross it: one side of the road you are in Paraguay and the other you are in Brazil, with nothing to show the difference other than the change of language on the shop signs. The particular street that has the frontier running down the middle of it is called Dr Franco, and the grass strip in the middle is a no-man's land where Brazilian assassins chuck bodies at night so they can be reported as found dead in Paraguay.

11

The name of the city is spelt 'Pedro Juan Caballero' with a 'b', while the surname of the man is more correctly spelt with a 'v' – 'Cavallero' – insofar as you can talk of correct spellings in Paraguay, where the old tradition is that a legitimate variety of spellings can be used, so long as the name is pronounced the same. (In Spanish, 'b' and 'v' are pronounced the same.)

Cavallero was born in Tobatí in 1786 and as a soldier took part in the 1811 defence of Paraguay against the attempt to make it subject to Buenos Aires in the newly independent Argentina. But he is most famous for being one of the Próceres of independence on 14 and 15 May the same year (see *Chapter 1*, page 12). In the meeting of the first National Congress, Cavallero was elected as one of five members of the new junta governing Paraguay. Dr José Gaspar Rodríguez de Francia eventually became the first president of the Republic, but when he turned into a dictator his former colleague Cavallero took part in a conspiracy against him. A coup was planned for Holy Week 1820, but it was anticipated by Francia, and Cavallero was imprisoned in the house which is now the Museo Bogarín, where he chose to commit suicide on 13 July 1821 rather than suffer execution.

There is ongoing deforestation in the region, which is now principally devoted to cattle rearing. Mandioc, soya and maize are the principal crops, not to mention marihuana, of which this area is said to be the capital. Smuggling abounds.

Almost 10% of the population is indigenous – mostly from a branch of the Guaraní called Paĩ Tavyterã.

GETTING THERE AND AWAY See page 271 above for the main part of the **car** journey from Asunción. The drive from Ybý Yaú to Pedro Juan is stunning, because of the almost vertical, round-topped, red rocky hills that shoot up out of the plain, of which the most striking of all is the double-peaked Cerro Membý (Spanish 'Hill'; Guaraní 'child of a mother') only 1,000m from the road. To find your way to the city centre, turn left (northwest) at the Copetrol service station on Ruta 5. You will then be on Carlos Antonio López, and 22 blocks ahead you will come to the Plaza Panchito López. Close to the plaza you come to an Esso station on the left, which has a wall map of the city.

If you are coming by **bus**, the bus terminal (\ 0336 272708) is located on the western corner of the Laguna [286 B3] (see below, page 287). The bus companies that go to Pedro Juan Caballero are La Santaniana, Nasa, Cometa Amambay and Ovetense. The journey is via Ruta 3 and Ruta 5 and takes eight hours.

Nasa and Cometa del Amambay do the journey from Pedro Juan Caballero to Concepción.

Occasionally you hear of backpackers leaving Paraguay for Brazil by this route to Ponta Porã. The Paraguayan passport control, for your exit stamp, is at Naciones Unidas 144 (⊕ *08.00–12.00 & 13.30–19.00 Mon–Fri, 08.00–12.00 Sat*). The *aduana* (customs) is on O'Leary and Pitiantuta.

There is a little airport but there are no regular flights.

WHERE TO STAY If you are coming to Pedro Juan in your own transport and just to pass the night, there is no need to enter the city, and a couple of small hotels on the outskirts could serve well – the Bertea or Las Vegas in the San Blas barrio, on the left-hand side of Ruta 5, after you have gone under the big modern arch announcing the city.

🏠 **Hotel Casino Amambay** [286 C1] (41 rooms) Dr Francia y José Berges 01; Brazilian address for the same place is Av Internacional 3474; ✆ 0336 271140/272200/272963; e hcassino@uol.com.br; http://hcassino.sites.uol.com.br. The casino is in a huge & elegant hall with chandeliers, sofas, gaming tables. Not everyone's cup of tea but fun for those who like that kind of thing. Parking is on the street but there is a 24hr guard. $$$$

🏠 **Hotel Eiruzú** [286 C4] (60 rooms) Mariscal López esq Mariscal Estigarribia; ✆ 0336 272435/273162/+55 67 431 2555;
e interhoteis@uol.com.br;
www.grupointerhoteis.com.br. Belongs to the Brazilian hotel chain Inter Hoteis, though it is in Paraguay, 1 block away from Brazil. Seems pricey for Paraguay but in this rather seedy city you may feel the extra money is worth it. Rooms redecorated in 2007–08. Internal parking with 24hr guard, internet, sauna & swimming pool. $$$

🏠 **Porã Palace** [286 C3] (formerly La Siesta Hotel) (50 rooms) Alberdi 30 y Dr Francia; ✆ 0336 273021/272573; f 273022. Big hotel which has recently been completely renovated, catering for bank officials & commercial travelers, half from Paraguay & half from Brazil. Internet in the lobby; swimming pool & restaurant. $$$

🏠 **Hotel La Negra** [286 B5] Mariscal López 1342 c/ Curupaytý; ✆ 0336 274603/272262/270656. In the heart of the city. Simple modern rooms but good value. The best rooms are on the top floor. There is a pleasant b/fast room, a car park & it is conveniently situated right next door to a bar, a *cambio* & an internet place. $$

🏠 **Hotel Peralta** [286 C5] (8 rooms) Mariscal Lopez 1257 y Curupaytý; ✆ 0336 272017. Family hotel in the heart of the city. No meals, not even b/fast, but plenty of places to b/fast nearby, eg: Hotel La Negra. AC & TV. $$

🏠 **Hotel Victoria** [286 A3] (21 rooms) Tte Herrera 778 y Alberdi; ✆ 0336 272733. Basic but clean, & a couple of mins walk from the bus terminal. Fans, no AC. Internet close by. $$

🏠 **Hotel Bertea** (30 rooms) Ruta 5 y Rubio Ñu; ✆ 0336 271958. On Ruta 5 before you enter the city, on the north side of the road after you have gone under the big arch. A rather striking & quite agreeable hotel, with friendly people. All rooms have AC, TV & bathrooms. Internet 5 blocks away. It tends to be full Mon–Fri with commercial travellers (unless you book in advance), but there is room at w/ends. $$

🏠 **Hotel Las Vegas** (23 rooms) Ruta 5 San Blas; ✆ 0336 271575. On Ruta 5 before you enter the city, on the north side of the road after you have gone under the big arch. Modern, with less character than the Hotel Bertea, which is next door. Internet 5 blocks away. $$

✖ WHERE TO EAT

✖ **Pepe's** [286 C3] Dr Francia 758; ✆ 0336 272375. Recommended. Just round the corner from the Hotel La Siesta, a little expensive but that is to be expected since there is a live group playing traditional Paraguayan folk music every night. Portions are large. $$$

✖ **Lo de Pepe** Mariscal López c/ Mariscal Estigarribia; ✆ 0336 272796; ⏰ 11.00–14.30 & 18.00–23.30 Tue–Sun. International menu, fish is the speciality. $$

✖ **Pizza House** Mariscal López y José D Martínez. Just to the north of the Laguna. $$

A decent packed lunch suitable for picnicking can be bought at the **Copetrol service station** [286 B7] out on Ruta 5, which will serve well if you are going out to spend the day in a nature reserve (see below, page 287).

OTHER PRACTICALITIES There is a **cashpoint** in Pedro Juan, at the BBVA [286 C4] on the corner of Dr Francia and Estigarribia.

Internet can be found in various places; for example, next door to the Hotel La Negra [286 B5], or on the next corner (Carlos Antonio López y Curupaytý). Printed **maps** are impossible to buy, but you could try Norte Cambios, who do one in the form of a calendar. There are two branches, one on Dr Francia c/ Mcal Estigarribia [286 C4], and the other a couple of blocks away on Curupaytý c/ Mariscal López [286 C4].

WHAT TO SEE One of the pleasanter places within the city is the **Laguna** [286 B3–4] – the 'lake' – which is a large plaza occupying four blocks, in which an

PEDRO JUAN CABALLERO

JOSÉ BERGES

JOSÉ A BERGES

Casino Amambay

COMUNEROS

HUMAITÁ

GENERAL ROA

RUBIO ÑÚ

CARLOS ANTONIO LÓPEZ

CERRO CORÁ

REPÚBLICA DE CUBA

Hospital

TENIENTE DE CUBA

NATALICIO TALAVERA

AQUIDABÁN

GENERAL BRUGUEZ

CERRO LEÓN

CERRO HERRERO

COLÓN

Victoria

ALBERDI

MARISCAL LÓPEZ

AVENIDA CENTRAL

Pepe's
Porã Palace

B R A Z I L
(Ponta Porã)

Pizza House

JOSÉ DE MARTÍNEZ

Bus terminal

Laguna

JULIA C DE ESTIGARRIBIA

Norte Cambios
BBVA Bank

MARISCAL ESTIGARRIBIA

Lo de Pepe

Eiruzú

RUBIO ÑÚ

Perpetuo
Socorro

GENERAL DÍAZ

Municipalidad

Norte
Cambios

CURUPAYTÝ

CARLOS ANTONIO LÓPEZ

La Negra

Peralta

PERPETUO SOCORRO

Plaza
Panchito
López

Museum

N

Bradt

14 DE MAYO

Gobernación
Police station

0 ———100m
0 ———100yds

YEGROS

Plaza
Teniente Valdez

ITURBE

AVENIDA CARLOS DOMÍNGUEZ

17 Blocks omitted here

17 Blocks omitted here

JORGE CASACCIA

BRAZIL

Hotel Bertea,
Hotel Las Vegas,
Concepción

Ruta 5

Copetrol

Shopping China

Ruta 5

Ponta Porã,
Brazil

artificial lake has been created. Another square, the Plaza Panchito López [286 B5], has the **statue of Pedro Juan Cavallero** and a small **museum** situated in the middle. The museum does not have a great deal to offer, though there are old saddles and typewriters, busts and pictures of national and local figures, and a stuffed jaguar. The **church of Nuestra Señora del Perpetuo Socorro** [286 B4] has sometimes been attractively floodlit at night. But Pedro Juan Caballero is not the sort of place where people go for tourism – unless it is the commercial tourism of Brazilians, going to and fro across the border for purposes of shopping or smuggling. Pedro Juan is, however, a necessary springboard for visiting the natural sites nearby.

NATURE RESERVES CLOSE TO PEDRO JUAN Though the *departamento* of Amambay needs urgent action to stop the serious deforestation, there is still a richness of **trees**, with 442,000ha remaining wooded. The trees here are taller than in the rest of the country, and under the canopy of their branches grow long creepers and giant ferns, which have given the name to the *departamento*: Amambay (Guaraní 'fern'). The rare *peroba* tree (*Aspidosperma polyneuron; yvyraromi* in Guaraní) grows in this region. It can grow 30m high, and its pinkish wood is excellent for flooring and furniture: most of it has been exported to Brazil, usually illegally. In terms of **fauna**, you can find the marsh deer, the jaguar, the caiman, the blue-and-yellow macaw and the bell bird. The bell bird is very strongly associated with Paraguayan culture because of the famous folk song 'Pajaro campana' written by Felix Pérez Cardozo.

Because of the location of the rocky hill range (*cordillera*) down the Brazilian frontier, most of the nature reserves have cliffs that can be used for abseiling. You can picnic and go for walks in these places, but you are unlikely to find a guide, except at Cerro Corá.

Reserva San Luis 30km from Pedro Juan, a patch of virgin forest inside an *estancia* of 12,000ha. Riding & abseiling.
Reserva Y'Ambué Explorable paths, waterfalls. Abseiling. 8km away from Pedro Juan, down a dirt road. 20ha. Camping capacity for 20 people.
Reserva Fortuna Guazú Paths, waterfalls, including 1 with over 38m drop. Abseiling. 8km away from Pedro Juan, of which only 1km is on a dirt road. Natural

pools for bathing. Camping capacity for 40 people.
Parque Ecológico Sol y Luna 17km back down Ruta 5 in a place called Chirigüelo. Paths, waterfalls, pools, abseiling. Camping capacity for 60.
Granja ARA 27km from Pedro Juan, of which 7km are dirt road. The farm (*granja*) covers 100ha. Paths, waterfalls, pools, abseiling. A 50m roofed area gives protection against sun & rain. Camping capacity for 60. Holiday bungalows for 8.

But the biggest and best nature reserve to visit outside of the city is the Parque Nacional Cerro Corá. It is also the easiest to find.

PARQUE CERRO CORÁ AND SURROUNDING AREA

Because Cerro Corá is much visited, it is not necessary to follow the general rule for visiting the national parks, which is to contact SEAM (Secretaria del Ambiente) beforehand in Asunción.

This famous but remote park is best known for being the site of Mariscal López's death and the country's final capitulation in the Triple Alliance War. But in fact it includes two other attractions: a pleasant nature walk to Cerro Muralla, and the eco-archaeological reserve of Gasorý where there are cave writings. There is also a pleasant beach on the shores of the Río Aquidabán. The park covers more than 12,000ha and was declared a national park in 1976. It is visited by 9,000 people a year, of which 40% are foreigners.

GETTING THERE AND AWAY Although Cerro Corá is a household name in Paraguay, few Paraguayans have ever ventured that far. Few tourists penetrate as far as Pedro Juan, but if you do, then Cerro Corá is easy to reach, by taxi or your own vehicle, as it is only 30km or so to the west on the main road, Ruta 5. The entrance to the park is clearly marked, on the northern side of the road.

OTHER PRACTICALITIES At the national park of Cerro Corá there is a rota of park rangers or *guardabosques*, and the principal guide Hilario (m 0981 996496) is ideal – a good-humoured, easy companion, with great knowledge of his subject. (He does not speak English.) The **three tours of Cerro Corá, Cerro Muralla and Gasory** can be comfortably done in a day, but you must bring your own lunch as there is nowhere to buy food. Do not attempt to do any of these tours without a guide. High season for visits is September to November, which is when a lot of schools make trips. There is a visitor centre with a museum, and hours of attention to the public are 08.00–17.00, 365 days a year.

CERRO CORÁ The name Cerro Corá, which means 'hill circle' in a mixture of Spanish and Guaraní, is one of the most famous names in Paraguay, being the **site of the death of Mariscal Francisco Solano López**, still regarded by Paraguayans as their country's greatest hero, while outsiders more often see him as one of the world's cruellest dictators. For more information on the War of the

---

INTERPRETATIONS OF THE TRIPLE ALLIANCE WAR

Paraguayans see the Triple Alliance War as a war of genocide, under which their compatriots showed exemplary courage in the face of certain death: this consciousness is deeply engraved in the Paraguayan sense of national identity. The perception of the Brazilians, Argentinians and Uruguayans was that they were ridding the continent of a dangerous dictator, who posed a major threat to the continent, was prepared to see his country utterly destroyed rather than give up his position, and cruelly tortured and killed huge numbers of his compatriots as suspected traitors in his desperation to hang onto power. This view tends to be shared by Europeans, whose assessment is based on the reports of British men working under him as engineers and doctors. 'No surrender' was the heart of the conflict, seen by one side as supreme courage and by the other as supreme selfishness.

Mariscal López has gone down in Paraguayan history as the country's greatest hero, with the catchphrase 'un paraguayo no se rinde' (A Paraguayan does not surrender). In his final speech in Cerro Corá on the day he was to die, addressing the dozen or so crippled, starving and half-naked men who now constituted his army, he declared in grand fashion: 'The victor is not the one who remains alive on the battlefield, but the one who dies for a beautiful cause. We will be vilified by the generation that emerges from the disaster, that will carry the defeat in their souls, and in their blood, like a poison, the hatred of the victor. But other generations will come, and will do us justice, acclaiming the greatness of our immolation' (Cerro Corá, 1 March 1870). That rehabilitation of Mariscal López did in fact take place, in the aftermath of the Chaco War, when his remains were placed in the Pantéon. Every 1 March is a national holiday, the Día de los Héroes, marking the date of his death in 1870.

Meanwhile, his Irish partner, Madame Lynch, has been presented as the darling of the poor, not because she did anything for them, but because she was disliked and rejected by the society ladies of Asunción at the time.

Triple Alliance, see History in *Chapter 1*, page 12; Piribebúy in *Chapter 4*, page 138; and Humaitá in *Chapter 7*, page 222.

The historic sites are shown by the guide in ascending order of land level, beginning therefore with the **stream Aquidabaniguí** (which later becomes the Río Aquidabán as it approaches Concepción). This is where López died with the famous words 'I die with my country', or according to some 'I die for my country', after having been wounded by a lance wound in the side, a sword wound in the head and a bullet in the heart. Going up the slope you pass a row of 16 **busts** of soldiers and even priests who were among the 450 people in this final camp: most, however, were women, children and the elderly, who were starving, to the point of eating the leather soles of their shoes.

Above this on the ascent is a huge white **monument** resembling a series of white spires on a platform: this marks the site of the encampment, and there is an airstrip for receiving government representatives for the annual memorial celebration of 1 March. The surrounding hills formed a natural screen, but deserters told the allied army where López could be found.

Higher still is an avenue leading to a huge **white cross** with a hollow centre, through which the wood behind can be seen: the sensation of nature breaking through the frame of death has been movingly captured. Just beyond this is the actual site of the original grave, which Madame Lynch dug with her bare hands for her lover and one of their sons, the 16-year-old Coronel Panchito López. Panchito was shot after his father when he attacked an enemy soldier with the cry, 'A Paraguayan colonel does not surrender.' Madame Lynch is said to have wrapped herself in a Union Jack as a sign of being a non-combatant while seeking to bury the bodies, and to have paid three gold bars and some fine French cloth for the permission to do so. The rest of the army was almost naked, but she was a woman who maintained her style until the end.

A nearby **tree**, an *arbol kurañái*, has a place in the story. According to some it is where a soldier hid to watch the burial. According to others it is where Madame Lynch left a notice saying the grave was 40 paces to the east of that spot. In 1936 the grave was dug up and the remains of Mariscal López (by that time just hair and kneecaps) were transported to the Panteón in Asunción (see page 151).

CERRO MURALLA The walk to Cerro Muralla begins from a very discreet path that you would never find without a guide, a few kilometres to the east of the entrance to the park. Go to the park first, and the guide will accompany you to the path. It is a beautiful walk, through a wood, over a wooden suspension bridge, along a red earth path, turning right through white sandy terrain where there are low trunkless palm trees (*jata'í*), and cactus-like plants with thorns on the leaves (*bromelia*). Then you pass through another wood and up a short climb to a rocky peak from where there is a magnificent view over all the surrounding countryside and especially over the dramatic humps of hill-rocks: Cerro Membý, Cerro Guyrá Kuembá and Cerro Guaiguyog. The name Cerro Corá (hill corral) comes from the way these hills form a sort of circle. Allow a couple of hours maximum.

In the cracks of the rock you can see a species of orchid with a red flower only found in this *departamento*, the *sininpia amambayensis*. There are many examples of the *ficus* (common name *matapalo*) that grows in the forks of other trees; it is not a parasite but sends down long roots to the ground and eventually the mother tree dies because the ficus draws out all the nutrients from the soil. The seeds are deposited by toucans (of which there are many here) that eat the fruit.

In the area there are jaguars, mountain lions and capybaras, and other large animals that are in risk of extinction such as the marsh deer, anteater and maned wolf. Typical trees are the *palo borracho* (Guaraní *samu'ú*) which is found more

11

extensively in the Chaco, the cedar (Spanish *cedro*; Guaraní *ygarý*), the *jacaranda* (Guaraní *ka'í jepopeté*), the *palo de vino* capped with yellow flowers in January, and the beautiful, tall *lapacho* (Guaraní *tajý*) that bursts into pink blossoms in September and is such a distinctive feature of all Paraguay.

GASORÝ The ancient cave writings of Rancho Gasorý are found a little way outside the national park, on private land, but the guide Hilario has permission to take visitors there if they are accompanied. (Sadly, unaccompanied visitors cannot be trusted not to scratch their own initials in the rock.) A short walk past an indigenous settlement leads to some cliffs that slope away inwards, and here a large number of engravings or runes can be clearly seen. They are estimated as being 4,000–6,000 years old. Some are like a lot of parallel lines. Others form a divided U shape that might possibly be a female sexual symbol. Nobody knows their origin, and though the most obvious explanation is that they were carved by the indigenous peoples, none of today's indigenous know anything about their history. Another theory is that the Vikings came here and left their form of writing; yet another theory is that the Celts came.

There are other cave writings but those of Gasorý are the best ones to visit. Those at **Cerro de la Serrana** (closer to the Cerro Muralla, but south of the road on the way to Lorito Picada) can only be visited very early in the day and only then with some risk: big wasps nest under the shifting cave floor and are liable to be enraged by people walking over them. The local indigenous say they have found further cave inscriptions – more extensive and much better than either of those mentioned – but it is a full day's walk to journey there and back. Anyone keen enough to go on this expedition will need to take also a Guaraní interpreter, for the indigenous speak hardly any Spanish: ask Hilario or another guide at the Parque Cerro Corá.

THE FAR NORTH OF CERRO CORÁ A dirt road some 70km to the west of Pedro Juan Caballero on Ruta 3 leads north and eventually reaches the little town of **Bella Vista** on the Río Apa, which is simple but pretty and has nice beaches. Unfortunately it is bereft of hotels and can only be reached by driving some 75km on a dirt road, though of the superior sort known as *enripiado,* which is packed tight with gravel to make it resistant to the rain. The Río Apa forms the northern frontier with Brazil.

A little paradise called **Ojo de Mar** (Eye of the Sea) is located about 50km from Bella Vista towards the southwest, close to the Río Apa, and close to the border between the *departamentos* of Concepción and Amambay, in a place called Colonia Rinconada – a remote corner of the world if you ever want to find one. Plunging with determination through thick subtropical vegetation you reach a mysterious little round lake of clear green water which was caused by a volcanic eruption 250 million years BC and according to legend has no bottom. Locals say that people who try to cross the 100m width of the lake have found themselves swallowed up by a mysterious force from below the water. Until recently the rare white crocodile could be found here and there is still a rich variety of fish.

THE EAST-NORTHEAST

So far we have been travelling to the north-northeast of the country, up Ruta 3 and Ruta 5. If instead of going directly north up Ruta 3, you take the Ruta 10 turn 12km north of the Tacuara junction, then you pass into the Canindeyú *departamento* and reach a whole different area of the country – the east-northeast. Eventually, some

250km later, you reach the capital of Canindeyú: Salto del Guairá, on the Brazilian border. This is one of the least travelled regions of the country, though it has some of the greatest variety of fauna.

See regional map for *Chapter 9*, page 240.

BOSQUE MBARACAYÚ (*www.mbertoni.org.py*) The extensive Bosque Mbaracayú nature reserve is found in Canindeyú, tucked up by the elbow of the Brazilian border, and with its infrastructure of information and tasteful rooms for guests, this is now one of the most interesting and attractive nature reserves to visit.

The origin of the reserve was in the work of anthropologists Kim Hill and Magdalena Hurtado, from the University of Emory, Atlanta, USA, who opposed an attempt by the World Bank to sell lands of the indigenous Aché people for commercial development. The Mbaracayú reserve has now increased to 64,406ha of uninterrupted forest and provides safety for 432 species of birds, 85 species of mammals, more than 1,000 species of insects and 219 species of ants. In the huge expanses of Atlantic forest are conserved 21 botanical species in danger of extinction, including the peroba tree (*Aspidosperma polyneuron*; Guaraní *yvyraromí*) which is an important tree for furniture making. The Mbaracayú reserve is well supplied with 18 trained park rangers, of whom three come from the Aché people.

Getting there Driving to the Bosque Mbaracayú takes six hours from Asunción (375km). After passing through San Estanislao on Ruta 3, take Ruta 10 in the direction of Salto del Guairá. After 70km you pass a detachment of cavalry and here you turn left up the dirt road that goes through Curuguaty towards Ypé Hu, on the border with Paranhos, Brazil. After crossing the River Jejuí Guazú and then the River Jejuí-mí you reach the reserve, 65km after leaving Ruta 10.

The reserve cannot be reached directly by public transport, but you can take a bus (company Canindeyú) to Villa Ygatimí, and from there you can be picked up, if a vehicle is available.

The tour operator DTP Tours arranges visits (\ *021 221816;* e *info@dtp.com.py, www.dtptour.com.py*), with meals and transport included.

Where to stay and eat To stay in the Bosque Mbaracayú, contact the Fundación Moisés Bertoni who administer the reserve and have their office in Asunción (*Prócer Argüello 208 e/ Mariscal López y Boggiani;* \ *021 608740;* f *021 608741;* e *mbertoni@mbertoni.org.py; www.mbertoni.org.py;* $$$). You must apply at least two weeks in advance, and complete a form by email. You should allow at least three days at the reserve to see the principal sites. There are kitchen facilities for preparing your own meals. Prices are reasonable: Gs50,000 per person per day, Gs10,000 reservation fee, Gs10,000 entrance fee and Gs50,000 per group per day for the guide. Facilities for camping are under reconstruction.

The website has a version in English, but the best part of it – the virtual visit – is a little tricky to find: go to *www.mbertoni.org.py/What we offer/Private sector initiatives/Tourism/Virtual visit*.

What to see An observation tower 12m high gives an excellent view over lakes and forests in the Lagunita (little lake) area. Also to be visited is the Arroyo Morotῑ ('white stream' in a mixture of Spanish and Guaraní), and further north a waterfall called Salto Karapã (curved waterfall).

Animals which live in the reserve but are threatened species in other areas include jaguars, giant anteaters and tapirs. There are also mountain lions, capuchin monkeys and maned wolves. This is the only place in the country where some

11

species of birds unique to Paraguay may be commonly seen; for example, the horned screamer, the white-wedged piculet and the buff-bellied wren.

The Bosque Mbaracayú is the ancestral home of a branch of the Aché indigenous, who are hunters and gatherers and have only recently come into contact with the rest of civilisation. The forest's life was threatened along with their lives before the reserve was created. There are also a number of Guaraní communities.

SALTO DEL GUAIRÁ (*Copaco* ✆ *046 242299; municipalidad* ✆ *046 242206*)

Salto del Guairá, at the point furthest east of the Canindeyú *departamento*, is a sizeable city, but a relatively tranquil one, with little pollution, and a long way from other centres of population in Paraguay. Its income comes from forestry and from Brazilians who cross the border to do their shopping, in increasing numbers.

The city takes its name from the Saltos del Guairá (the Falls of Guairá) that in the past continued over a long distance to the point where the Río Paraná joins the Río Iguazú, some 100km to the south, just after the latter river crashes over the famous Iguazú Falls. These Saltos del Guairá had their moment of fame when the Jesuit Antonio Ruiz de Montoya led an exodus of 12,000 Guaraní in 1632 away from the attacks of slave-traders. The journey was beset by hunger, disease and natural obstacles, and only 4,000 arrived safely in what is now Misiones Argentina. All their possessions, including fantastic carved statues and musical instruments, were launched over the massive Guairá waterfalls on rafts, and were smashed to smithereens, while the Guaraní negotiated a way through the jungle on the bank. But since the formation of the hydro-electric project of the Itaipú dam, the dramatic Saltos del Guairá have been replaced by a tranquil feeder lake, and only the Iguazú Falls remain, on the Río Iguazú.

The buses that go there from Asunción are Caaguazú, Canindeyú, Ovetense and Pycasú. The journey takes eight hours via Ciudad del Este, or seven hours via Curuguaty.

Where to stay

🏠 **Hotel Tower** (28 rooms) Carlos Méndez Gonzalves y El Maestro; ✆ 046 242096/242399. At 2 blocks from Av Paraguay, which is the main street. Internet. No restaurant. $$$$

🏠 **Hotel Lago Vista** (17 rooms) Av Paraguay esq Camilo Recalde; ✆ 046 242957/242130; e lagovista-hotel@hotmail.com. $$$
🏠 **Hotel Peralta** Av Cacique Canindeyú c/ Av Paraguay; ✆ 046 242235. $$

Where to eat

🍴 **La Taberna** ✆ 046 242220; ⊕ 07.30–23.30. In the centre, 100m from the Rotunda, next door to the Galería Yasý. $$$
🍴 **Shopping America** New shopping centre 2km

from the centre, towards Brazil. Good buffets & *churrasquería*. $$$
🍴 **Neottis** Av Paraguay 688; ✆ 046 243080; ⊕ 10.30–14.00, closed eve. $$

Other practicalities Prices are a little higher in Salto del Guairá, because of the thriving business in shopping for Brazilian day trippers, who come to buy clothes, computers and electrical equipment. There are three large shopping centres and a further two were under construction at the time of going to press. There is a cash machine at the Banco Continental.

There is a beach on the river, with white sand.

12

The Chaco

Departamentos: Presidente Hayes, Boquerón, Alto Paraguay

If you like your travel to be an adventure in remote regions, you might be interested in going to the Chaco. This is a chapter for explorers rather than regular tourists.

The Chaco has been called the Green Inferno. It is a sort of desert, though that may puzzle the visitor who begins to drive through and sees green vegetation everywhere and pools of water. In the southern Chaco, the earth is a grey salty clay, unlike the red earth of eastern Paraguay, and few plants can tolerate it. What rainfall there is sits uselessly in ponds where the salt content makes it unfit for either drinking or promoting vegetation. This humid Chaco ecoregion goes up approximately to Pozo Colorado, transversed by tributaries from the Río Paraguay. Above that is the dry Chaco.

The tropic of Capricorn passes through the Chaco, at the level of Pozo Colorado, so most of the Chaco has a tropical climate, with greater heat than the more populated areas of eastern Paraguay, and with dry and rainy seasons. There is hardly any rainfall in the dry season (March–September).

The scenery is scrubland and totally flat (except for the Cerro León mountain in the north) and is used for cattle grazing, divided into huge *estancias*. The few houses you will see from the road – the Ruta Transchaco – are the poorest kind of wooden hovels, either thatched or with rusty corrugated iron roofs. Later on, in the affluent Mennonite settlements, you will see that even the mansions tend to have corrugated iron roofs: it is the best way of collecting rainwater.

In this arid and unhospitable land, almost every tree has thorns. The most distinctive trees are the *karanda'ý* and the *samu'ú* (*Chorisia insignis*). The former (*Copernicia alba*) is the Chaco palm tree, taller and more decorative than the *cocotero* of western Paraguay: the trunk, split in half, makes excellent walls – as can be observed in the Pa'í Pukú school (see page 297) – and the foliage forms a rounder circle at the top of the trunk, with a more intricate silhouette. It is not found all over the Chaco, but a couple of hours south of Filadelfia you can see plenty, down to Asunción. The *samu'ú*, or *palo borracho* in Spanish (drunken pole), sometimes known in English as the bottle tree, is a tree that stores water in its heavily swollen trunk. Thorns sit on this fat trunk, and further up the tree narrows before splaying out into delicate foliage. It is a very distinctive tree, much associated with Paraguay. During the Chaco War, the *samu'ú* was hollowed out to make a hiding place for an armed guard.

A beautiful, fragrant wood that only grows in the South American Chaco is *palo santo* (*Bulnesia sarmientoi*) or 'holy wood'– a protected tree with a slow growth rate of 200 years to develop fully. It produces a beautiful, hard, fragrant, olive-green wood that is much used in craft work. It survives in this dry climate because its leaves are small and leathery. Also distinctive to the Chaco is the white *quebracho*,

THE CHACO

BOLIVIA · Hito VII · Hito VIII · BOLIVIA
Hito VI
Cerro
Chovoreca NP
Hito V
Cabrera · Hito IX
Timane · Hito X · Paraguay
NP · Capitán · Río Negro · Tres Gigantes
Pablo Lagerenza · NP
Hito IV · Colonia Carmelo Peralta · Hito XI Tripartito
Defensores · Bahía Negra
del Chaco NP
Cerro León
Médanos
del Chaco NP · Alto · BRAZIL
Hito III · Paraguay · Puerto Leda

Teniente · Teniente
Enciso NP · Américo Picco · FUERTE
Hito II · OLIMPO

Ruta 9 · Isla · Porto Mortinho
Ruta 9 · Margarita
Boquerón · Luis María
Argaña Airport · San Lázaro
MARISCAL · Apa
Hito I · ESTIGARRIBIA · Ruta 9 · FILADELFIA · Puerto Casado · Vallemí
Pozo Hondo · Hotel de Touring · Loma Plata · Verde
Military Post · Ruta 9 · CONCEPCIÓN · Ruta 5
Neuland · Eastern
Boquerón · Verde · Ruta 9 · Paraguay
Tropic of Capricorn · Presidente · Ruta 5
N · Buffalo Bill
Pilcomayo · POZO COLORADO
Bradt · Montelindo · Hayes
Tinfunque · Teniente
NP · Esteban Martínez · Ruta 9
Escuela Pa'i Puku

ARGENTINA · General Bruguez · Benjamín
Bermejo · Aceval
Ruta 12
0 ——— 100km · José Falcón · Villa Hayes
0 ——— 100 miles · ASUNCIÓN

popularly known in English as the break-axe tree. The indigenous eat the purple
fruit of the cactus, and *poroto del monte* (wild beans). Another Chaco fruit that is
good to eat is the *nistol*, which is like a small apple.

Until a few decades ago, the Chaco was inhabited only by indigenous, and it was
not entirely clear whether it belonged to Paraguay or to Bolivia: both countries
believe that it had always been theirs, and a variety of interpretations can be seen
in maps of the time. The situation changed when the US Standard Oil company,
which was working in Bolivia, announced that there was oil in the Chaco.
Meanwhile Royal Dutch Shell encouraged Paraguay to hold on tightly to its
territory. It suddenly became important for both countries to confirm their claim
to the land, and Bolivia also had the motivation of needing access to the River
Paraguay, to have a route to the sea for exporting it.

In 1925 Bolivia began to build forts in the Chaco to stake their claim, and a bitter
war was fought in appalling conditions of drought – the War of the Chaco, or as
Paraguay prefers to say, the War for the Defence of the Chaco, 1932–35. Paraguay

basically won the war, though was disappointed in being obliged by international pressure to cede some land back to Bolivia in the final settlement. In total, about 100,000 men had lost their lives in the war.

The oil, if it exists, has never materialised (though as recently as May 2009 the British CDS Oil and Gas Group declared that there were an estimated 243 million barrels of crude oil and 161 thousand million cubic feet of gas in the northwest *departamento* of Boquerón). But winning the war had huge symbolic importance for Paraguay, as a sign of national dignity after being so extensively destroyed in the earlier War of the Triple Alliance. But blame is also laid on Britain and the USA for encouraging a conflict to protect their respective economic interests.

The Chaco covers almost 300,000km², and accounts for 61% of Paraguay's territory, but only includes 3% of its population. It would be even more uninhabited had it not been for the arrival of the **Mennonites**, a Christian pacifist church originating in Switzerland which has been wandering the earth for 400 years seeking a land where they can live out their beliefs apart, without being absorbed into the local population. In 1927 they began to arrive in the Chaco, in a migration they describe as 'unsurpassed by anything in history since the Pilgrims sailed from Delft Haven'. Although they were arriving during the tensions immediately leading up to the Chaco War, they had no fear because their pacifism kept them safe from reprisals, and a Paraguayan government charter granted them exemption from military service. Since then they have been turning the desert into a land of fertility and plenty, so that today the Mennonite towns of Filadelfia, Loma Plata and Neuland are attracting internal immigration of Paraguayans from eastern Paraguay, looking for work.

TRAVELLING ALONG THE RUTA TRANSCHACO

Most of the traffic that crosses the bridge Puente Remanso over the Río Paraguay, immediately to the north of Asunción, turns sharp left, and takes a short stretch of Ruta 12 to the frontier with Argentina. On the Paraguayan side of the border there is Puerto José Falcón (close to Nanawa), and on the Argentinian side Clorinda, and then, 200km south, the more substantial town of Formosa. This is the most frequent route by which Paraguayans go to Buenos Aires – by bus. (The alternative bus route to Buenos Aires via Posadas is used by Paraguayans who live further south, in Misiones or Itapúa.) The border post is at the Río Pilcomayo, and is open 24 hours.

If you turn north just before Falcón, Ruta 12 will take you parallel to the Río Pilcomayo, as far as the Parque Nacional Tinfunque, which is a nature reserve of the humid Chaco ecoregion. Beware, however, that only the first stretch of this road is asphalted, and when you get to Tinfunque there are no provisions for visitors.

If, however, you want to visit the central Chaco, you turn right and go up Ruta 9, known as the **Ruta Transchaco**.

BY BUS Once it has passed Villa Hayes (12km) and Benjamín Aceval (11km), the Ruta Transchaco continues for miles and miles with no civilisation in sight. After about an hour you will notice it is a rarity to pass a vehicle coming in the opposite direction. The road plunges straight ahead till it narrows to a tiny gap on the horizon, in which you will occasionally see the distant dot of another vehicle coming towards you. The advantage of going by **bus** on this deserted road rather than by car is not only that it is cheap, but that if the vehicle breaks down it is somebody else's problem.

The bus companies that serve the towns up the Ruta Transchaco are Nasa/Golondrina (✆ *021 551731*) and Stel Turismo (✆ *021 551680*): for more

12

details see below under the different towns. See also the section on arriving by bus from Bolivia, in *Chapter 2*, page 34.

BY CAR Though the drive through the Chaco is exceedingly long, there are often opportunities to see interesting fauna. In addition to having a rich bird life, the Chaco is the habitat for many mammals too, and as you drive along the Ruta Transchaco, you may see foxes, deer and armadillos.

Here is a list of where you can find food, drink and a bed on the Ruta Transchaco.

🏠 Bar-Parador Tacuara km101 $
🏠 Bar-Parador Río Negro km170 $
🏠 Bar-Parador Montelindo km210 $
✖ Restaurant Pirahú km240; m 0991 700683 $
🏠 Bar-Parador Ka'i km243 $
🏠 Restaurant-Parador Touring Pozo Colorado, km270 (see opposite)

🏠 Hotel-Restaurant Bufalo Bill km283. Lake & mini-zoo. $$
🏠 Hotel-Restaurant Los Pioneros ✆ 0491 432170; km415 $$
🏠 Hotel de Touring km423 (see page 299)
🏠 Parador Aramí Mariscal Estigarribia, km530 (see page 304)

After that, you are on your own, and you still have another 300km or so to go to the frontier. The usual crossing point is from the military outpost of Infante Rivarola, Paraguay, which brings you to Villa Montes, Bolivia. This involves swinging west from La Patria, from where there is another road, not yet asphalted, going in a more northerly direction to cross the frontier at Hito III, after the military outpost of General G E Garay. You are strongly advised to take the asphalted road.

Until a very few years ago, the asphalt ran out somewhere in the middle of the road to Bolivia, and if you were crossing in the rainy season you were liable to be stuck in the mud for several days on end, without access to food or water. One traveller said this was the best bit of his journey, because he forged such strong friendships with the other stranded passengers. Be that as it may, the road is now asphalted all the way to Bolivia, but not the side roads – except for the one leading to Concepción.

If you want to **drive** your own vehicle, and to leave the main road to go on dirt roads, then you will need to hire a 4×4 from the Touring y Automovil Club Paraguayo (*25 de mayo y Brasil;* ✆ *021 210550/53; www.tacpy.com.py*). Unlike the car-hire companies, their insurance covers journeys on dirt roads – but at a price: you can expect to pay over well over US$1,000 for a week of unlimited mileage on earth and asphalt.

The advice of the local Paraguayan guidebook, *La Magia de Nuestra Tierra*, should be taken to heart before you plunge into the terrain of interminable dirt tracks: 'Remember, before you try to have an adventure in the Chaco, that it is a inhospitable, desert territory, where many people have died of thirst. It is easy to get lost because it is flat and lacks points of reference.' For this reason no details are given here of the dirt road that takes you to the border at Hito IV, or of the bridge into Argentina at Pozo Hondo, which crosses the Río Pilcomayo near the triple frontier of Paraguay, Argentina and Bolivia.

OTHER PRACTICALITIES

Chaco schools within reach of Asunción The first towns you come to as you go north after the Puente Remanso are Villa Hayes, and then Benjamín Aceval, which has the **Escuela Agrícola San Francisco**. This agricultural school functions as a **hotel** (*Ruta Transchaco km46.5;* ✆ *0271 272223;* e *nelvadiaz@fundacionparaguaya.org.py; www.fundacionparaguaya.org.py;* $$), with double and triple rooms, and dormitories. The school is 500m off the main road. You can spend a day with the students, in their activities of organic cultivation, and rearing pigs, chickens and rabbits. It has internet, and craft from Toba Qom (Guaicurú) indigenous community.

After 2½ hours of hard driving, you come to the **Escuela Pa'í Pukú** (*Ruta Transchaco km156;* ✆ *0891 8033*) immediately on the right of the highway. If you get a chance to visit this educational establishment, take it: it has been beautifully and simply constructed, with a chapel built from tree trunks and full-throated birdsong in the garden painstakingly constructed by the pupils, with fertile earth and water transported in buckets. The school is run for the children of poor families in far-flung *estancias*, and the furniture made by the pupils is highly sought after. It can be ordered through the Asunción office of the foundation (*Defensa Nacional 846;* ✆ *021 226699;* e *fundacionpaipuku@rieder.net.py*).

Pozo Colorado Pozo Colorado is some 250km northwest of Asunción and is where you can find petrol, a mechanic to mend your car and a hotel to stay the night. If you are travelling to Concepción via the Ruta Transchaco (whether by bus or car) you will turn sharp east at Pozo Colorado. Work is currently under way to improve that 138km of poor asphalt from Pozo Colorado across the Chaco to the Nanawa bridge and Concepción.

⌂ **Parador del Touring** Ruta 9 km270;
m 0971 395750. Run by the national motoring
organisation TACPy (see page 67). $$

FILADELFIA Copaco ✆ *0491 432012; municipalidad* ✆ *0491 433374/6*

Filadelfia (about 70km further north than Boquerón), Loma Plata and Neuland are three Mennonite towns, sited close to each other right in the middle of the Chaco. Filadelfia is 13km north of the Ruta Transchaco. Loma Plata is also to the north (21km), and Neuland is 20km to the south.

In Filadelfia there are recognised groupings of other nations and races, although the Mennonites run the town through their *cooperativa* and comprise 30% of the population. There are three indigenous communities – the Nivaclé, the Guaraní and the Lengua – who account for 60% of the population. The remaining 10% are Latinos – that is, Paraguayans who are neither Mennonites nor indigenous – Argentinians and Brazilians. Each grouping lives in its own barrio, like a self-enclosed colony.

The economy of Filadelfia is based in big companies producing dairy products, and peanuts for export.

GETTING THERE Filadelfia is the easiest of access of the Mennonite towns and has most to see. You would be advised to use it as a base, from where you can visit the other towns if you wish. Some **buses** to Fildelfia go on to Loma Plata, and others do not. The main bus company serving the area is Nasa (✆ *021 551731 in Asunción;* ✆ *0491 432492 in Filadelfia*), which also uses the name Golondrina. Nasa buses leave the Asunción Terminal at 06.00, 14.30, 21.15, 22.00 and 23.00, and the journey takes around six hours. Buses from Stel Turismo (✆ *021 558051*) leave the Terminal in Asunción at 19.00 every day and go to Loma Plata as well as Filadelfia, but their buses, though good in quality, have more stops and arrive in Filadelfia at 02.00 (*Gs70,000*). The return journey is made from Filadelfia at the same time, ie: 19.00, arriving 02.00.

If you are driving **your own vehicle**, you can find petrol at the Shell station on the corner of the turn to Filadelfia, and in Filadelfia itself there are four petrol stations, of which one is open 24 hours.

12

Contrary to expectations in this remote and arid land, the towns founded by the Mennonites are modern cities, where many things work as well as, or better than, they do in Asunción. It is difficult to imagine a starker cultural contrast than that of Germanic peoples and Paraguayan Latinos, and the Germanic influence here produces a different kind of culture. Phones work, electricity does not fail, window frames fit, and schools open like clockwork even in the torrential rain. Large supermarkets are better stocked than in most other parts of the country, even though it is a six-hour hard drive to their source of supply in Asunción.

The Mennonites were given the most difficult of all terrains to farm, but in the course of a few decades they have turned it around to the point where Paraguayans are flocking in, in search of work – indigenous from the rest of the Chaco, and Latinos from the east of the country. But the Mennonites keep a tight control on the positions of power: only those who can establish their Mennonite ancestry can gain a place in their barrios, which are full of mansions and fruit trees, and the financial bonuses of the cooperativa (the civic organisation that runs everything) are reserved for Mennonites alone. While the other races live better here than in the places they came from, they also feel they are locked forever into being second-class citizens. They receive at least the legal minimum wage, but the cost of living is double here what it is in the rest of the country.

Loma Plata was the first Mennonite town, founded in 1927 by settlers from Canada, who in turn had come from Russia (where they had gone to in 1789, after a time in Prussia, from 1535, and in Holland, from 1530). Filadelfia was founded in 1930 by Mennonites coming more directly from Russia, fleeing the Stalinist regime and the repression of peasants. Neuland was not founded until after World War II.

There are also Mennonites in eastern Paraguay, where they hold onto their group identity by conservative practices that mark them out as different: the men wear black dungarees, and the women flowery, gathered dresses and headscarves. The Chaco Mennonites, by contrast, are culturally and economically progressive, and look like an ordinary group of modern, educated Germans.

GETTING AROUND You can buy a map of Filadelfia in the post office on Avenida Hindenburg. The town is composed of wide, long avenues of grey clay, but the two principal *avenidas*, Hindenburg and Trébol, are asphalted. They cross at the point where there is the Second Monument (see below), close to the Hotel Florida.

Here is the sequence of the streets on the usual grid system. Going south of Trébol you come to in order: Unruh, Industrial, Chaco Boreál, Boquerón, Palo Santo, Amistad and Carayá. Heading north from Trébol: Bender, Asunción, and several more streets, going into Mennonite territory. From Hindenburg, if you go east you come to: Miller, Gondra, Harbiner-Strasse, Quebracho, etc. Finally, going west from Hindenburg: Estigarribia, 25 de noviembre, Urundeý and Concordia.

If you are staying in Filadelfia's Hotel Golondrina or the Hotel Florida, the **bus** will take you to the door. Otherwise, the principal bus stop is known as the Parada de Nasa (or as Agencias), which is on Chaco Boreal, three blocks south and half a block east from the Second Monument. There is a **taxi** rank around the corner on Hindenburg. If you want to ring for a taxi, try Señor Arzamendia (m *0981 111233*). The Hotel Los Delfines (❧ *0491 432376*) also has a taxi service.

The **bus** journey from Filadelfia to Loma Plata takes half an hour, and can be done with the company Nasa (❧ *0491 432492*). It leaves Filadelfia at 07.00, and returns from Loma Plata either late morning or early afternoon, depending on the day.

Exploring Filadelfia and the surrounding area has recently become easier thanks to a new company, Gran Chaco Turismo (*Hindenburg 247 e/ Unruh y Industrial;* ✆ *0491 432944;* m *0981 223974;* e *info@granchacoturismo.net; www.granchacoturismo.net*). They have an office where you can use the internet, and speak German, Spanish and English. They offer tours of Filadelfia and also a wide range of ecotours all over the Chaco, from the Tinfunque national park in the southwest to Bahía Negra in the northeast. This company is particularly useful for facilitating the more local expeditions such as to Boquerón (see page 301) or the salt lakes (see page 303).

🏠 WHERE TO STAY

🏠 **Hotel Florida** (40 rooms) Av Hindenburg e/ Unruh y Trébol; ✆ 0491 432151/5; e hotelflorida@fernheim.com.py; www.hotelfloridachaco.com. Generally agreed to be the best hotel. Opposite the museum. Excellent food, good service, pool & a pleasant inside courtyard. Rooms in old building are cheaper. $$$

🏠 **Hotel del Touring** (16 rooms) Cruce Filadelfia, Ruta 9 km423; ✆ 0493 240611. Not in Filadelfia itself, but on the Ruta Transchaco. Opened in 2006, pool, restaurant. $$$

🏠 **Hotel Golondrina** (50 rooms) Av Hindenburg 635-Sur; ✆ 0491 432643/43111;

e info@hotelgolondrina.com; www.hotelgolondrina.com. The next recommendation after the Florida, 5½ blocks south of the Second Monument, & 1½ north of the Third Monument. White tiled floors, TVs, restaurant (closed Sat eve). There are cheaper rooms with fewer facilities. $$

🏠 **Los Delfines** Unruh esq Miller; ✆ 0491 432376. This place 1 block south & 1 block east of the Second Monument is more modest, with a more Latin feel. Plebeian, slightly seedy, bit of a motel, but a nice buzz of the kind you do not find in the German establishments. They have a **campsite** as well as hotel rooms, and run a taxi service. $

🍴 WHERE TO EAT

🍴 **Hotel Florida** See above. Has good reputation for food. $$

🍴 **Girasol** Calle Unruh c/ Hindenburg 126-E; ✆ 0491 432078. Considered one of the best restaurants. $$

🍴 **El Rincón** ✆ 0491 432496. In the shopping centre Portal del Chaco, at the entrance to the town, next to the monument where the Ruta Transchaco meets the town. Extensive menu & even a simple hamburger & salad is excellent. On Sat night & Sun lunchtime they offer *asado* & a buffet. $$

🍴 **Shopping Boquerón** Boquerón c/ Miller. This new shopping centre 1 block to the south from the Parada de Nasa has a *patio de comidas* with excellent quality food at cheap prices. $

🍴 **Restaurant Estrella** Calle Unruh; m 0981 890992; ⊕ Mon–Sat. More popular clientele, nice patio & has a zip to it. Closed Sun. $

🍴 **Restaurant Remi** Calle Unruh e/ Gondra y Miller. More modest restaurant & ice cream parlour, mostly for young people. Same management as Boquerón. $

OTHER PRACTICALITIES Next door to the Hotel Florida is El Mensajero – a **bookshop** that sells indigenous crafts as well as books and postcards. There is an **Interbanco** bank in the Portal del Chaco shopping centre (at the entrance to town), with a cash machine. There is an internet café on Av Hindenburg e/ Unruh y Industrial. The **post office** is on the corner opposite the museum. Mennonite businesses observe strict opening hours: 07.00–11.30 and 14.30–18.00. By 20.00 it is a dead city, apart from inside the restaurants.

WHAT TO SEE The **Jakob Unger Museum** (✆ *0491 432211;* ⊕ *07.00–11.30 Mon–Sat*), occupies two adjacent buildings, on Avenida Hindenburg e/ Calle Unruh y Trébol. Jakob Unger had been the first of the pioneers to propose a scientific study of the fauna of the Chaco. One of the buildings is an original house of the colony. On the ground floor it contains a collection of Mennonite bits and pieces, including a butter churn, and the printing press for the Mennonite paper *Mennoblatt*, which is still published today. In the second building (which was previously a primary school) is the natural history section, with many stuffed animals, including a jaguar, armadillo, coati, puma, anteater, wolf, tapir, tree sloth, skunk and boa constrictor. There are also 210 out of the 250 bird species in the Chaco, and a large section devoted to insects. The museum has a pleasant garden – the Plaza de los Recuerdos – and the **First Monument** erected in town, a small obelisk, placed in 1955, on the 25th anniversary of the foundation of the town.

The **Second Monument** was put up on the 50th anniversary, and is not far away, in the centre of the junction of Avenida Hindenburg and Avenida Trébol. The **Third Monument** (erected on the 75th anniversary) is a more ambitious affair at the entrance to the town (Hindenburg y Carayá): five figures of varying heights hold up a ring with a cross in the middle. It looks its best at night when it is floodlit, and resembles a crown.

The **Parque Eirene** is a zoo and is well worth visiting, four blocks to the west of the junction of Avenida Hindenburg and Avenida Trébol, on the left. The animals it has in enclosures are all native to the Chaco and include foxes, giant tortoises, deer and two different kinds of wild boar or peccary. The *kure'í* is commonly found, while the *jabalí*, which looks very similar, is dangerous and is prone to attack people. The *kure'í* has a white collar but the *jabalí* has a white beard. There is a third kind of peccary, the *taguá*, which was in the park until recently: it is so rare that it was believed for many years to be extinct until it was sighted again in the Chaco. It looks like the *kure'í* except that the hair on its shoulder sticks up almost like the spikes of a porcupine.

There are three principal **Mennonite churches** in town, and the one on Avenida Hindenburg (two blocks north of the Librería El Mensajero) includes an old church, now used as a dining room, as well as the modern ramped church they use today, with simultaneous translation for visitors.

It is not recommended to visit the indigenous communities unless you have an introduction: the people do not like being gazed at like animals in cages. However, there is an opportunity at carnival time, when the **Guaraní** in Filadelfia issue a general invitation over the radio for anyone to join them in their annual festival, the Areté Guasú, with the condition that you must join in the dancing – which can be quite energetic, and may include being rolled in mud. They wear long costumes and masks – of tigers, pigs or frightening faces of dead ancestors. The tradition is to dance three days and nights without stopping (in teams) and to drink *chicha*, a drink of the fermented fruit of the *algarroba* – a tree that grows only in the Chaco. The Guaraní in Filadelfia now speak the same Guaraní as the rest of Paraguay, though originally the dialect was distinct.

The **Lengua**, also known as the Enxet (variously spelt Enlhet) are a little shorter and have rounder faces. They moved to Filadelfia in the early 1980s, when they came (like the other indigenous peoples) to seek work for the men in the construction industry, and for the women in domestic work. They are now losing touch with their traditional communities in the *campo*. The married Lengua women wear long skirts covering their ankles.

The **Nivaclé** are known for the beauty of their women. In the old system of leadership the leader would be someone who had fought tigers or showed similar physical prowess, but with the move to urban life, leaders are now elected who can read and write. The Nivaclé tend to be Catholic, evangelised by the Oblates (order of priests) who came out to the Chaco in 1925, and the Sisters of St Joseph of Cluny are working with them now. (The other principal evangelisation in the Chaco was initiated by the Salesians, in the north reaches of the River Paraguay.)

The Nivaclé come out in force for a monthly mass in the **church of San Eugenio de Macenod**, which has a vividly painted back wall behind the altar showing a surprisingly feminine Christ crucified and a balanced pair of male and female Christian evangelists. The Nivaclé all sit on the right of the church, while the Guaraní sit on the left with the other racial groupings that make up this lively Catholic congregation, principally Brazilians and Germans.

BOQUERÓN

Boquerón is a little to the south of Filadelfia, just off the Ruta Transchaco to the west, but you will probably want to go to Filadelfia first and do Boquerón as an excursion. It is the site of the most famous battle of the Chaco War, and the victory of Boquerón is a national feast day celebrated on 29 September. (The other national holiday relating to that war is the Paz del Chaco, the declaration of Peace, on 12 June.)

In 1928 the fort of Boquerón was taken by Bolivia, but then taken back by Paraguay. In July 1932 Bolivia took the fort again, and in September the same year it was retaken by Paraguay, in a costly and bloody siege that marked a decisive victory for Paraguay. The fort was considered important because it had a small lake, in this dry terrain. It still took Paraguay another three years to push the Bolivians right out of the Chaco, and the peace settlement was not signed until 1938.

GETTING THERE It is worth the effort to visit the site: it is tasteful, respectful, informative, and tragic. However, it is not easy to find as there are no road signs, and no people around to ask. The safest way to get there is to go with Gran Chaco Turismo (see page 299): they offer a day that includes an indigenous village and a few other places on the way, and they have English-speaking guides. Failing that, take a **taxi** for the 70km from Filadelfia, which will cost around Gs350,000, or at least to get someone from the locality who knows the roads to accompany you if you are in a **hire car**.

But if you want to try to get there on your own, it would be a good idea to take a compass, and ask for directions at the Hotel del Touring (⟍ *0493 240611*) which is on Ruta 9 between Filadelfia and Boquerón: as this is run by the motoring organisation TACPy, they ought to be able to help you. Failing that, ask the military at the next crossroads north from the Hotel del Touring.

WHAT TO SEE The Boquerón site (⏰ *07.00–17.00 Wed–Sun; foreigners/Paraguayans US$1/Gs3,000*) is officially closed on Monday and Tuesday but it is still possible to visit if you walk in: the gate will be closed to vehicles. The guide Carlos Aguero lives at the site and is well informed. There are no facilities for English-speakers. The site is mostly visited by Paraguayan school parties. Sadly it is not yet visited by Bolivian groups.

Triumphalism is kept to a minimum, perhaps because the site is owned by the pacifist Mennonites. Inside the museum of rusty battle relics there is a tribute of 'Eternal gratitude to the heroes of the Chaco!' from a Paraguayan school, but alongside it is a text that reads: 'Paraguay, America and the World should learn from their history that wars impoverish populations and sow hatred amongst people. No more war and violence between brothers!'.

On a hillside facing the museum is the memorable figure of a stainless steel soldier running, the work of artist Herman Guggiari. The soldier has a large hole in his chest where his heart should be, but the hole is the shape of the map of Paraguay: it makes a powerful point. The monument that most expresses the idea of reconciliation was placed in 2004 by the presidents of both Paraguay and Bolivia. Two huge stainless steel leaves ripple in parallel, not touching, representing the two countries at war, and a plaque renders 'homage to the fallen, who in offering their blood constructed the foundations of peace and confraternity that today unite our peoples'.

The fort was surrounded by a 4km circle of trenches, with lookout posts every 5m from where the Bolivians shot down the approaching Paraguayan troops. Some 1,200 Bolivians guarded the fort, and 8,000 Paraguayans attacked. Their only way of taking the fort was by crossing a field where there was no cover, other than by piling up in front of them the gunned-down bodies of their companions. With huge carnage over 20 days, the Paraguayans inched forward behind walls of flesh three bodies high, and took the fort on 29 September 1932.

The Paraguayan cemetery is placed in this field, where most of them died, and a mass of tightly spaced white crosses indicate where there was a huge common grave. The Bolivian cemetery is placed inside the trenches, where they died. Next to the Bolivian cemetery is a twin grave with a simple tree-trunk headstone where a Paraguayan and a Bolivian lie buried together. Captain Tomas Manchego of Bolivia and First Lieutenant Fernando Velázquez of Paraguay became friends when Manchego was a prisoner in Paraguay, prior to the formal outbreak of war, and they met again in a Bolivian hospital, when both men were wounded and dying. They left instructions that their bodies were to be buried in a joint grave.

LOMA PLATA Copaco ✆ 0492 253240; municipalidad ✆ 0492 252254/252163

Loma Plata has less of a mixed community than Filadelfia, and there is a much more German feel to the town. The streets are all called *Strasse*. Some people do not speak any Spanish, and most speak it hesitatingly and with a strong accent. If you are not a Mennonite, you feel an outsider – except that any fair-skinned person is assumed to speak German and is liable to be addressed in that language.

The big Trébol factory in Loma Plata supplies good-quality milk products to all over the country. There is an Escuela Agricola (agricultural school) run by the *cooperativa*.

GETTING THERE AND AROUND The **bus** company Nasa (or Golondrina) (✆ 0492 252521; ✆ 021 551731 in Asunción) goes to Loma Plata once a day, leaving the Terminal in Asunción at 23.00. The journey from Filadelfia to Loma Plata takes half an hour, and can be done also with Nasa. There is a service that leaves Filadelfia around 07.00, and for the return journey to Filadelfia, the bus leaves Loma Plata at 11.00, so you can get there and back comfortably within the day.

A detailed city plan, marking every building but with very small print and nothing marked on it that you might want to visit, can be bought from the *cooperativa* (upstairs from the supermarket).

Loma Plata has even less of a **taxi** service than Filadelfia. The best option – if you arrive in the morning – is to get off the bus at the *cooperativa* and look for the office of information and tourism (✆ 0492 52301/52401/52501; m 0981 202200; f 0492 52406; e turismo@choritzer.com.py; www.choritzer.com.py) to the left of the *cooperativa* and to the right of the museum. Someone from there will probably offer to act as a guide and driver, probably Walter Ratzlaff, who principally deals with tourists. You should cover the costs of the petrol at least. Failing that, the Hotel Mora offers a good quality taxi service (✆ 0492 252255), though if you are staying in a different hotel, it might be awkward to ask for it.

WHERE TO STAY

Loma Plata Inn (22 rooms) ✆ 0492 253235/6. Hotel built around 2006, shimmering white. Spacious rooms, the closest hotel to the Nasa bus terminal. $$$

Hotel Mora (38 rooms) Calle Sandstrasse 803; ✆ 0492 252255; m 0981 213040. Not far from the Hotel Palace, pleasant front courtyard with a private, family feel. You are expected to speak

German but the manager has a little Spanish. Variety of rooms at variety of prices. Taxi service. $$$
🏠 **Hotel Palace** (9 rooms) Fred Engen Strasse & Elim Strasse; ➑ 0492 252180/53190. Further away but has an attractive feel to it & has big rooms

with frigobar, TV & phone. Most distinctive is its indoor swimming pool, set in the midst of the bar & TV area, & with bedrooms opening off the same space. The food is good & hygienic. $$$

✘ WHERE TO EAT

✘ **Chaco Grill** Calle sin nombre c/ Manuel Gondra; ➑ 0492 252166. Adjoins the Loma Plata Inn. Has a Chopp Haus (a German pub) as well as a restaurant section, & a good outside area for eating. Comfortable walking distance from bus terminal. $$

✘ **Restaurant Norteño** Calle 3 Palmas 990; ➑ 0492 252447; m 0981 202447. A Latin place, constructed of airbricks, with relaxed atmosphere & good variety of meat dishes. Slow service, clean bathrooms. Comfortable walking distance from bus terminal. $

OTHER PRACTICALITIES The only bank is the Banco Nacional de Fomento, which does not have a cash machine that accepts foreign cards.

WHAT TO SEE There is little to see in Loma Plata apart from a small **museum** of photographs showing the tough history of the 70 years of Mennonite colonisation – hoes and watering cans and horse carts, and a group of the first nurses. The visitors' book shows that travellers do make it here from Japan, Canada, Australia and Europe.

To the north of Pozo Colorado and the southeast of Loma Plata is an area of **salt lakes**, known as Riacho Yacaré (Spanish and Guaraní 'Caiman Creek') which is a paradise for herons and flamingoes, and also attracts migratory birds such as plovers. The origin of the salt lakes is that this part of South America used to be sea, 60 million years ago. Guyrá (see page 9) have more information. Gran Chaco Turismo (see page 299) can do a daytrip here – either to Chaco Lodge, which is a Ramsar site, or to Campo María; both have coscoroba swans and flamingos.

MARISCAL ESTIGARRIBIA *Copaco ➑ 0494 247397; municipalidad ➑ 0494 247201 .*

Further northwest of the group of Mennonite towns on Ruta 9 you come to Mariscal Estigarribia, which is not Mennonite. This really is a remote town: coming north from Asunción you feel you have reached the furthest outposts of human existence. On the other hand, coming south from Bolivia you feel you have finally arrived at civilisation and are on the home run. It has a population of 1,000.

Named after a famous general in the Chaco War, Mariscal Estigarribia's chief claim to fame is its vast but unused jet airport, an extraordinary white elephant in the middle of nowhere (see below).

A moment of recent history when people went to Mariscal Estigarribia was during the visit of Pope John Paul II in 1988. He had a big rally with the indigenous in Santa Teresita, a barrio on the outskirts of the town, to which native people came from all over the Chaco.

GETTING THERE AND AROUND You can get to Mariscal Estigarribia with the **bus** company Nasa/Golondrina (➑ 021 551731 in Asunción; ➑ 0494 247282 in Mariscal Estibarribia), which currently has buses leaving Asunción at 14.30 and at 22.00 which pass through Filadelfia first. If you go to Mariscal by **taxi** from Filadelfia, it will cost around Gs400,000 for the 80km.

There is no taxi service in Mariscal Estigarribia, but you need transport to get around the surprisingly spread-out town. To the west of the Ruta are the extensive military quarters, the old cathedral (which was built in the midst of them) and the

12

lake. The civilian town is to the east of the Ruta, and is a long thin town with a couple of kinks along its length as it follows the line of Ruta 9. The bus terminal is near the beginning of the town. There is a roundabout at each kink, allowing access to and from the Ruta. The *municipalidad* serves as a point of reference, and it is close to the roundabout at the first kink.

WHERE TO STAY

Hotel Campo'i (13 rooms) Book through Hotel Florida, see page 299. This new & well-equipped hotel, 70km north of Filadelfia & slightly to the east of Mariscal Estigarribia, is in a former *estancia* of the Mennonites. It includes 2 separate houses as well as rooms in the main building. $$$

Parador Arami 0494 247230. Not in the town but on Ruta 9 – & distances here are huge, so this is more for travellers taking a break from driving than for visitors to Mariscal Estigarribia. AC, TV, en-suite bathrooms. $$

Hotel Laguna (25 rooms) m 0985 779088. Simple hotel behind the *municipalidad*, run by a French woman, rooms have little furniture, but there is a nice feel to the place. No b/fast, but there is a small café next door. Rooms vary in price depending on whether they have a bathroom, fan or AC. $

The Hotel de Transito is not open to the public, but is only for official delegations to the military or to the airport.

WHERE TO EAT

Restaurant Italiano Close to the bus terminal; 0494 247231; 09.00–midnight every day. Attractive dining room with windows on 3 sides. $

WHAT TO SEE AND DO The **airport** Luis María Argaña is worth going to gaze at, as a huge, unused enigma constructed in 1988 by the USA. The local people are quite proud of it, but will tell you that they do not want the US army moving in: there was an attempt to bring in 1,000 US troops around the end of 2005 and the local people blocked the plan. The runway is 3.5 km long – the longest runway in the country – but is used more for car racing (in the annual Chaco Rally, see below) than for actual aeroplanes. The base is capable of housing 16,000 troops, has an enormous radar system, huge hangars and an air traffic control tower. It has never been used, other than fleetingly, and (as a surprise bonus) for Pope John Paul II to meet the indigenous in 1988. You have to get out of your car and enter on foot if you want to pass the gate. The official US line is that they have no plans to open a base here, and that the airport 'was constructed at a time when the Paraguayan government envisioned developing a free-trade zone in its northern Chaco region to help develop the area'. With a population of only 1,000 and no local industry looking for air freight, something is fishy here.

Other than the airport you should visit the **cathedral and the museum** adjoining it. The **cathedral** is modern and was opened in 2000. Do not miss the fine, striding figure of Mary carved in wood by Miguel E Romero of Tobatí (one of the artesan towns famous for woodcraft, see page 133). The museum (*ask at the Oblate house next to the cathedral for access;* 0494 247217; f 247218) has a big copy of the Virgin of Guadalupe as you go in. (This dark-skinned Madonna is a painting in Mexico that has become the principal Marian icon for the whole of Latin America.) The museum houses a strange mixture of items considered to be of interest: craftwork by the Nivaclé, a poncho, an enormous cooking pot, old saddles, vestments and items of early technology such as a sewing machine, telephone, radio, camera and typewriter. There are also bullets from the Chaco War.

The **old cathedral** (*la antigua catedral*) is in another part of town. It is a substantial and attractive red-brick building, whose principal fault was its location:

sited in the midst of the military camp, it was inaccessible for the civilian population. One of its features is the tomb of the much loved Pa'í Pukú (Guaraní 'tall priest'): Monsignor Pedro Shaw OMI. He was the Apostolic Vicar of the Pilcomayo region and died in 1984 at the age of 59. He was known for his love of the people, his travel round the Chaco on horseback, and a number of development projects, most especially the Pa'í Pukú school (see page 297 above). The diocesan radio station is also named after him.

Rally Transchaco This annual motor-racing event (*www.transchacorally.com.py*) is centred around Mariscal Estigarribia, though the exact route varies every year. It attracts huge media attention as well as crowds of followers on, who unfortunately have got a bad name for the event, leaving behind their debris of beer cans and motor oil containers, while the cars plough up the dirt roads and make them unusable for the local population. It happens in mid-September. For information consult the website above or the motoring organisation Touring y Automovil Club Paraguayo (*25 de mayo y Brasil;* ↘ *021 210550/53; www.tacpy.com.py*).

Pigeon shooting 'Paraguay is synonymous with the world's best pigeon shooting', says the brochure of one US agency specialising in shooting tours (*www.frontierstravel.com*). 'It has the largest wild pigeon population in South America', says another (*www.wingssafari.com*). This surprising, specialist area of tourism is centred on the central Chaco, and shooters stay either in the Florida Hotel of Filadelfia, or in one of the *estancias*, such as Estancia Palo Santo S A (*4 rooms & 7 bungalows;* ↘ *0493 240690;* e *denisdbertrand@gmail.com*), 80km south of Neuland, run by a Belgian, a Frenchman and a Canadian, or Estancia Faro Moro, which is run by North Americans. The pigeons descend when the Mennonite farmers harvest their sesame, sunflowers, sorghum or peanuts, and the shooting season is mid-February to May/June. The great majority of the shooters come from the USA, and this is big business.

Within Paraguay, you can get information on pigeon shooting from:

DTP ↘ 021 221816; e info@dtp.com.py   **Global Travel** ↘ 021 296245;
Faro Moro Tours Service ↘ 021 755832   e globaltrading@mmail.com.py

NORTH OF MARISCAL ESTIGARRIBIA Adjoining the Ruta Transchaco in its most northerly stretch is the national park Médanos del Chaco, which belongs to the Dry Chaco Ecoregion – what they call the green desert. The *médanos* are sand hills, which carry a fragile covering of vegetation. On the other side of it is another national park, the Defensores del Chaco, which is the largest conservation area in Paraguay (780,000ha). It includes the only near-mountain for hundreds of miles around, Cerro León. Strictly speaking this is a grouping of about 46 hills over an area of just 40km, rising to a maximum height of 604m above sea level. If you want to go there, Gran Chaco Turismo, in Filadelfia (see page 299) can take you: it is 263km each way, on dirt roads, and will take three days, in a 4×4 vehicle, and you will have to camp when you get there.

Cerro León has tapirs, peccaries, jaguars and (true to its name) mountain lions or pumas. The jaguar, which is a threatened species, illegally hunted, needs at least 3,500ha of wild to survive in.

It is possible to stay in this region, in the Campo Iris reserve, organising your visit through Guyrá Paraguay (see page 9). The Teniente Enciso National Park has a lodge and the Defensores del Chaco National Park also has a simple lodge that can receive groups. Again, Gran Chaco Turismo can take you from Filadelfia. For the location of the National Parks see map on page 8.

12

Going up the Ruta Transchaco is not the only way of exploring the Chaco, though it does take you through the centre of the region. You can also go north of Asunción up the Río Paraguay, which borders the Chaco to the east, so the places on the Río Paraguay form another area of the Chaco that can be visited. You may reach these Chaco river towns by boat, which is slow, but you are more likely to arrive by bus, overland from the Ruta Transchaco, or in some cases by plane. If you go far enough north up the Río Paraguay you reach the Pantanal – perhaps the most gloriously exciting excursion anyone can make anywhere in Paraguay.

Fuerte Olimpo is the gateway to the Paraguayan Pantanal. Getting to that point is quite feasible, though it takes a little time. Beyond Fuerte Olimpo is where you really get inside the Pantanal, and also where travel becomes difficult.

More than 60 million years ago, the centre of South America was a sea. This explains why there are still expanses of salt lakes in the Chaco (see above). Movements of the earth's surface led to the formation of the Andes, and the north–south depression to the east of that range is the Pantanal. It is the flat land around the Río Paraguay, of which 70–80% floods in the rainy season, from December on, raising the water level by some 5m. This makes it become enormously fertile territory for flora and fauna, but very inhospitable for human beings. The average temperature is 32°C in summer and 21°C in winter. In the time of the Jesuit missions the Pantanal was called simply La Laguna. The Pantanal is principally associated with Brazil, but in fact 5% of this territory is in Paraguay.

The Pantanal is considered one of the most important and beautiful ecological sanctuaries of the planet. The tall *karanda'y* palm with its fan-like leaves abounds, and the *karaguatá* is a low-growing bromelid with bright-red, thorned leaves and white flowers. The pink *ipés* blossoms on trees, the *aguapé* (Spanish *camalote*) fills the waters with a green carpet and keeps the waters fresh, and the huge 30cm wide flowers of the Victoria Regia open at night. There are water hyacinths, water lilies and water lettuces.

The Pantanal has the largest faunal concentration in the Americas, and has been estimated to contain 650 species of birds, 260 of fish, 160 of reptiles, 80 of mammals and 6,000 of insects, not to mention 1,800 species of plants. Emblematic of this paradise of flora and fauna is the jabiru stork which has a black head and neck and a red collar, and a wingspan of 2m. It feeds richly on the fish, frogs and insects left behind by the floods.

The marsh deer has long, wide hooves with a membrane between its toes, so it can run on the swampy ground. There are caimans, lizards and iguanas, tapirs, wild pigs (or peccaries), coati, the paca rodent, eight species of armadillo, and all five species of Paraguayan monkey. The handsome and dangerous jaguars are the most striking of all the animals. The bird life is spectacular, with herons, ducks, cormorants, scarlet ibis, spoonbills and toucans, and there is the world's largest population of blue hyacinth macaws. The early hours of the morning and the last hours of daylight are when there is most activity from the birds.

The density of human population in the Pantanal is only 0.14 per km²; the population includes a small number of Chamakoko indigenous (also known here as the Ishir).

GETTING THERE

By air If you do not have a lot of time, you can get to the upper reaches of the Panatanal by plane. Although the scheduled service was discontinued in the early years of this century, a new service began hesitantly in 2009, travelling to Vallemí (on the east bank; see *Chapter 11*, page 282), Fuerte Olimpo, Puerto Leda and Bahía Negra. Fuerte Olimpo is the gateway to the Pantanal, and Puerto Leda and Bahía Negra are firmly within it (see below), so this is your quickest route in, if the date of the flight is convenient. The aeroplane goes about once a week but the day varies according to the weather and the number of passengers.

This new air service is called Transporte Aereo Militar and should not be confused with the international airline TAM. There is no website or email, and booking is only by mobile phone to the co-ordinator, Sonia Suárez (m *0983 454486*). The flight costs Gs350,000 to tourists, Gs250,000 to local residents. The aeroplane takes a maximum of 26 passengers, and needs a minimum of 17 for the flight to leave. It takes off at 07.00 from the *aeropuerto militar* on the way to the international airport of Asunción, Pettirossi, and returns there by about 13.00 the same day. There are also landing strips at Puerto Casado and Concepción where the plane can land.

You can also charter a **private plane**, but it is very expensive (see box above).

By bus It is a long way to go to the upper reaches of the Río Paraguay by bus. You will be travelling over dirt roads, and the buses are infrequent. However, if the day the bus travels coincides with the day you want to travel, it is faster than going by boat. Stel Turismo (☎ *021 558051*) goes to Puerto Casado once a week, and to Fuerte Olimpo twice a week. A small company called Turismo goes to Bahia Negra once a week. Details of these buses are found under the respective towns, below.

By car If you really want to drive so far on such unmarked terrain without asphalted roads, you will need to hire a 4×4, for which see page 66 above.

By boat

Crucero Paraguay Very expensive (but you get more for your money than chartering a plane) is a Pantanal trip on the *Crucero Paraguay* (*Nuestra Señora de la Asunción, 1102 esq Jejui, Asuncion;* ☎ *021 447710/440669;* e *crucero@cruceroparaguay.info; www.cruceroparaguay*). The *Crucero* offers journeys on the Río Paraguay from Concepción, for groups at luxury prices (US$1,980 per person for a six-day cruise). It is a lovely ship, tastefully designed with five decks, a swimming pool, a discotheque, a cinema and a gymnasium, and lots of comfy sofas. It can take 50 passengers. They may offer on-board cultural lectures, dinner parties, folk music and performances by a chamber orchestra.

The drawback is not only the price, but the fact that it only makes this cruise north from Concepción about three times a year, and only for groups, and only **as far as Fuerte Olimpo**, which is where the Pantanal starts. You can get to Fuerte

The Chaco **THE PANTANAL**

12

Olimpo without too much trouble anyway, by cheap boat or bus, and your problem will be how to get beyond that gateway.

Halfway between Puerto Casado and Fuerte Olimpo the Paraguayan boats stop at the Brazilian port of Porto Mortinho. So this is a backdoor into Paraguay and onto the Río Paraguay. But remember the difficulties that may afflict you on your way out of the country if your passport was not stamped when you entered.

Aquidabán If you do not want to pay for a flight, but want to be a pioneer in exploring the Paraguayan Pantanal beyond Fuerte Olimpo, then take your mosquito net, your hammock (you can buy one in the open-air market behind the Pantheon in Asunción), a couple of good ropes, your first-aid kit, insect repellent, sun hat, camera, and a very long novel, and take the *Aquidabán*, which leaves Concepción on Tuesday at 11.00 and goes to Puerto Casado, Fuerte Olimpo, Puerto Leda and **as far as Bahía Negra** (Gs100,000/US$20 sgl; Gs80,000/US$15 bunk if you do not bring a hammock), arriving at dawn on Friday. (See *Chapter 11*, page 283, for full details of the *Aquidabán*, and page 278 for how to get to the starting point of Concepción).

If you want to, you can do the journey by boat all the way upriver, from Asunción to Concepción (four days, plus several days waiting for a boat to leave Asunción) and then onto the *Aquidabán* from Concepción to Bahía Negra (another four days, plus any more waiting time for it to leave). But you save a lot of time if you go to Concepción by bus: it will take around six hours and you can do the journey overnight (Gs 70,000).

This is a great trip for an adventurer with time to spare, because of the beauty of the scenery, the sense of freedom and release from time pressures, the personal space and comfort of your own hammock strung taut and high over the boat's cargo, the support from the tight community of the boat's crew, the novelty of seeing them hunt capybaras and gut them on the deck before chucking them whole into a massive freezer. Some basic provisions can be bought on board, but you should complement it with your own food, and enough water for several days. Some boats have kitchen facilities you can use.

Beyond Bahía Negra But what do you do if you want to go beyond Bahía Negra? The only way is by river, but there are no scheduled boats. You would have to get private boat transport, with one of the tour operators who travel to this remote area. Note that you cannot get there with the tour operator DTP (contact details in *Chapter 3*, page 67), in their eight-day tour to the 'Chaco and Pantanal by water', because they only go as far as Fuerte Olimpo.

Guyrá Paraguay This non-profit organisation has opened a new research station, called Tres Gigantes, which is as far north as you can get on the river without leaving Paraguay. They will take you in their motorboat from Bahía Negra up to Tres Gigantes. (For contacts, & details of the visit, see the end of this chapter, page 310). **Paraguay Natural Ecoturismo** General Santos y 18 de Julio, Asunción; ☏ 021 302027; e ecoturismo@paraguaynatural.com.py; www.paraguaynatural.com.py. Offers a tour to the Pantanal which takes at least 6 days (to allow time to get you there & back). It includes crossing the border into Brazil – to Fuerte Coimbra, where there is a colonial fort. **Agyr** ☏ 021 201244; e info@agyrsa.com; www.agyrsa.com. Also have means to take you beyond Bahia Negra – onto the Río Negra, which is deep into the Pantanal – on a 7-day tour called 'Chaco & Pantanal'. Like Paraguay Natural Ecoturismo, they also take you to Fuerte Coimbra in Brazil.

PUERTO CASADO (*Copaco* ☏ *0351 230693/230696; municipalidad: ring Copaco & ask to be put through*)
Puerto Casado, halfway between Concepción and Fuerte Olimpo, is not itself in

the Pantanal, but it is the most southerly town of this riverside region, on the way to the Pantanal. It is a delightful but dying place on the west bank of the Río Paraguay, shortly before eastern Paraguay comes to an end, with the town of Vallemí and the caves of San Lazaro on the opposite bank (see *Chapter 11*, page 282). On some maps Puerto Casado is marked as La Victoria.

Once economically thriving with the tannin industry of the now defunct firm Carlos Casado SA, it has something of the feel of a ghost town, with the old factory, and the unused railway station once built by the company, falling into disrepair. Mariscal José Félix Estigarribia, a hero of the Chaco War, had a house here, and an ancient carob tree (*algarrobo*) in his garden, beneath which he used to sit, is marked with a plaque. The town served as a gathering point for the troops in the Chaco War, before they were sent to the front.

In 2000 the local people were roused into panicked demonstrations, when they suddenly discovered that their town had been bought up by the Moonies, as part of a 400,000ha purchase of land in the region, for purposes unknown. Years of legal and parliamentary wrangling followed to recover the independence of the town.

There is one **bus** a week to Puerto Casado with the company Stel Turismo (✆ *021 558051*), which leaves Asunción from the corner diagonally opposite the Terminal on República Argentina y Fernando de la Mora at 19.00 on Friday and arrives at Puerto Casado midday Saturday. It leaves Puerto Casado at 13.00 Saturday and arrives back in Asunción early on Sunday morning. The fare is currently Gs110,000. To get there by plane or boat, see above: Vallemí is only a short motor-boat ride away, if you want to arrive by plane.

There is a small *hospedaje* at the Bar Coelho but it has no landline. There should be no problem about turning up unannounced.

FUERTE OLIMPO (*Copaco* ✆ *0497 281000; municipalidad* ✆ *0497 281155*)
With hills rising behind it, and the attractive cathedral of Maria Auxiliadora, there is a pleasant, airy feel to this town, which is capital of the *departamento* of Alto Paraguay and known as the gateway to the Pantanal. It is 782km from Asunción by road, beginning with the Ruta Transchaco for 415km up to Cruce de Pioneros, then a dirt road for 367km.

Fuerte Olimpo is halfway between Puerto Casado and Bahía Negra. It has a number of tourist attractions, including the **Fuerte Borbón**, built in 1792: the name of the place was changed from Borbón to Olimpo by President Carlos Antonio López, who wanted to break the old colonial ties. There is a Centro de Información Ambiental y Turística in the town centre (✆ *0497 281117).* Young people have been trained to be guides. A good person to talk to is Profesora Cristina González de Méndez (✆ *0497 281229*).

The **bus** Stel Turismo does the journey once a week, leaving at 17.00 on Friday from outside the company's office, opposite the Terminal on República Argentina (✆ *021 558051*). It leaves Fuerte Olimpo on Monday at 07.00, and the journey takes about 18 hours. The fare is currently Gs150,000. Another and more pleasant way to arrive is by **boat** from Concepción: the *Aquidabán* arrives from the south at about midday on Thursday, and from the north at about 20.00 on Friday. See above for details and for getting there by plane.

The **indigenous museum** has items by the Ayoreo, Chamokoko and Maskoy. There are slings for honey pots and for babies, feather headdresses, stone tools, lances, arrows, wooden shoes, a stone pipe for smoke-making, etc. A **visit to the Chamokoko** (or Ishir) community of Virgen Santísima can be arranged, which may include a display of craft for sale, a welcome from the *chamán* and a trip in a boat.

The **Tres Hermanos hill** has 535 steps up, and from the summit you have a magnificent view over both Paraguay and Brazil. There are opportunities for all-day **motorboat trips** to see flora and fauna, particularly caimans, or for going in a rowing boat or a *piragua*, which is slightly broader than a *kayak*.

If you carry on north from Fuerte Olimpo, you are seriously into the Pantanal. If adventure tourism in one of the most remote spots of the planet is what you want, then this is it.

⌂ Where to stay and eat

⌂ **Hotel AA** ↘ 0497 281017. Beautiful & atmospheric with its river-facing rooms along a wooden balcony on stilts. Simple rooms, some with AC, others with fans, very cheap. Total capacity for 42 people. Excellent home-cooked food. $

⌂ **Hotel Chaco Pantanal** ↘ 0497 281027. A second choice of a more solid terrestrial variety. $

PUERTO LEDA You will probably reach Puerto Leda (halfway between Fuerte Olimpo and Bahía Negra) in the middle of the night. This is where Japanese Moonies are carving out of the wild a beautiful city for their adherents, with plantations and swimming pool, and are now planning to build a university. Before them, there was nothing, except a police station, in the midst of most inhospitable territory inhabited by mosquitoes, jaguars and caimans. You are now properly into the Pantanal. At some times of year you may need a special helmet to stop the mosquitoes flying into your mouth when you speak. See above for how to get there.

BAHÍA NEGRA This is a town that only has electricity up till midnight, and where an overland bus penetrates only once a week. The bus from the company Turismo (↘ *021 931826;* m *0982 328342*) leaves Asunción at 18.00 Tuesday and arrives around 15.00 Wednesday. It leaves Bahía Negra at 09.00 Friday and gets back to Asunción in the early hours of Saturday morning. The fare is currently Gs190,000. The bus does not leave from the Asunción Terminal, but from Cuatro Mojones, which is on Fernando de la Mora, under the viaduct of Madame Lynch. The agency is by the stop for the number 15 bus (*línea 15*) and by the supermarket Curva de Oro, and it has a notice saying 'Romería Bahía Negra'. To get there by plane or by boat, see above.

The *Aquidabán* goes no further than Bahía Negra. If you want to carry on north into wilder and wilder country, then the people of Guyrá Paraguay will come and fetch you in their motorboat. There is a Paraguayan naval base here (and another further south at Isla Margarita, halfway between Fuerte Olimpo and Puerto Casado).

⌂ Where to stay

⌂ **Pensión Hombre y Naturaleza** m 0982 898589/862543. Small guesthouse with 10 beds in 3 rooms, often booked out. $

TRES GIGANTES About 20km north of Bahía Negra is a junction of rivers at a point called Hito XI Tripartito, which is where the three countries of Paraguay, Brazil and Bolivia meet. If you take the Río Negro from there (the smaller river, going more directly north) you will continue along the Paraguayan border, until you reach Hito X, which is a little over 40km further north, and is as far as you can go without leaving Paraguay. The west bank is Paraguay, and the east bank is a tongue of Bolivia that pokes down between Paraguay and Bolivia to Bahía Negra. (The Hitos, one to ten, are boundary markers between the Río Pilcomayo and the Río Paraguay, and straight lines drawn from one to the next mark the frontier between Paraguay and Bolivia.)

The river is called Río Negro because of algae that give a black tinge to the water. Just before the confluence of the Río Negro and the Río Paraguay is Colonia Carmelo Peralta, where you can hire a 'hotel boat' called *Sueño del Pantanal* with

The Tropic of Capricorn passes through the southern Chaco, at 23.4° of latitude, and marks the most southerly point at which the sun can be seen directly overhead at noon: this occurs at the December solstice, when the southern hemisphere is tilted towards the sun to its maximum extent. The name was chosen because the constellation of Capricorn rises above it at the summer solstice. This line runs immediately south of Pozo Colorado in the Chaco, and Concepción in eastern Paraguay. When you are north of the Tropic people tend to talk of the dry season and the rainy season (December to April, approximately), rather than winter and summer.

four cabins and four bunks in each, a living room, dining room, bathroom and air conditioning (*contact Luis Penayo;* \ *+55 67 9 6033580;* m *0984 152682*). If you are planning to leave the country by this route, there is a customs office and passport control in Carmelo Peralta, open 07.00–19.00.

On the Paraguayan bank is the **Parque Nacional Río Negro**, covering 30,000ha, which protects the Pantanal against damage from deforestation, water contamination and uncontrolled fishing and hunting. Apart from anything else, the wetlands of the world are essential for storing over 40% of the earth's carbon monoxide, and their degradation releases a large amount of carbon dioxide.

Just before Hito X you come to the Estación Biológica Tres Gigantes, which is the research station run by Guyrá Paraguay, inaugurated only in 2008. It is so named because this is the only place in the world where you can see the giant armadillo, the giant anteater and the giant nutria. They can be observed taking the sun on the shore or walking through the woods. The tours on offer have walks along jungle tracks, including at dawn, fishing, boat trips after nightfall with lights to see the caimans and capybaras, and navigating the streams in a rowing boat or a flat-bottomed aluminium boat called a *deslizador.* The iguana hangs from the trees, the caiman patrols the water, and the yellow anaconda slithers silently through this natural paradise.

Tour operators Guyrá Paraguay specialises not only in birdwatching (*guyrá* is 'bird' in Guaraní), but the preservation of the entire ecosystem. You contact them through their Asunción office (*Gaetano Martino, fomerly José Berges, 215 esq Tte Ross;* \ *021 229097/223567;* e *alistair@guyra.org.py* or *birding.paraguay@gmail.com; www.guyra.org.py*) and you can email or talk on the phone in English. The same organisation also offers tours in Campo Iris, by Ruta 9, just before you get to Bolivia, and in the Parque San Rafael (see *Chapter 6,* page 209).

The tours are a way of financing the conservation work of Guyrá, so you will get a good welcome and a tailor-made tour. They have **beds** for 12 people in a surprisingly comfortable house with solar panels. They charge US$55 per person per day, plus US$30 for the motorboat to collect you from Bahía Negra, plus US$80 for the cost of the fuel. They can provide an English-speaking guide as an extra. This must count as one of the most wild and remote holidays in the world.

The Chaco THE PANTANAL

12

Appendix I

LANGUAGE
SPANISH
Pronunciation

Consonants are as in English, except that *b* and *v* are pronounced the same (in Paraguay, aim more for a *v* sound). There is no *w* except for foreign words like *whisky*. The *h* is silent. The *j* is pronounced (in Paraguay) like an English *h*. The *t* and *d* are pronounced very lightly.

If *c* is followed by *i* or *e* it is pronounced like an *s* (in Paraguay); otherwise it is hard. The same with *g*: if it is followed by *i* or *e* it is pronounced like an *h*; otherwise hard. To make an English *qu* sound you use *cu* in Spanish. The Spanish *qu* is pronounced like a *k*.

The *r* is lightly rolled, and the *rr* strongly rolled. The *ll* is pronounced *l-y* but the *l* bit almost disappears. There are very few double consonants in Spanish. The *ñ* is also pronounced with a *y* sound: *n-y*.

Vowels are pronounced short and each one is separate. A *y* at the end of the word is pronounced like the vowel *i*.

Examples:
prohibido (forbidden) = pro-i-bi-do
cada (each) = ka-da
cielo (sky) = see-eh-low
aceite (oil) = a-say-ee-tay
causa (cause) = cow-za
gato (cat) = ga-to
Jorge (George) = hor-hay
cuesta (it costs) = ques-ta
que (that) = ke
caballo (horse) = ka-val-yo
niño (child) = nin-yo
ley (law) = le-ee

The **word stress** falls on the penultimate syllable unless the last syllable ends in a consonant other than *n* or *s*, in which case it falls on the last syllable. Exceptions to this have an acute accent on the stressed syllable.

Examples:
cocotero (palmtree) is said *cocotéro*
ciudad (large town) is said *ciudád*
viernes (Friday) is said *viérnes*
miércoles (Wednesday) is written with an accent

Basic grammar

Nouns have masculine and feminine forms. eg: *el sol* (the sun); *la luna* (the moon).
Adjectives agree with the nouns and are usually placed after them. There are forms for the masculine singular, feminine singular, masculine plural and feminine plural, eg: *los pueblos antiguos* (the old towns); *las casas blancas* (the white houses).
Adverbs normally have *–mente* on the end of the feminine form of the adjective.
Verbs conjugate as in most other European languages, into 1st, 2nd and 3rd person singular, and 1st, 2nd and 3rd person plural. In Paraguayan Spanish the usual 2nd person singular pronoun is *vos* rather than *tú* as in Spain, but it is quite acceptable to use *tú*. The *vosotros* form (2nd person plural) of Spain is never used, except when reading texts written in Spain: even for friends and family the word used is *ustedes*.

Vocabulary
Essentials

Good morning	*buen día/*	How are you?	*¿Cómo estás?*
	buenos días	Pleased to meet you	*Mucho gusto*
Good afternoon	*buenas tardes*	thank you	*gracias*
Good evening	*buenas noches*	Don't mention it	*De nada*
Hello	*hola*	Cheers!	*!Salud!*
Goodbye	*chau/adios*	yes	*sí*
My name is...	*Me llamo …*	no	*no*
What is your name?	*¿Cómo te llamas?*	I don't understand	*no entiendo*
	¿Cómo se llama	Please would you	*¿Podría hablar más*
	usted?	speak more	*despacio por favor?*
I am from England/	*Soy de Inglaterra/*	slowly	
America/	*los Estados Unidos/*	Do you understand?	*¿Entiende?*
Australia	*Australia*		

Questions

how?	*¿cómo?*	when?	*¿cuándo?*
what?	*¿qué?*	why?	*¿por qué?*
where?	*¿dónde?*	who?	*¿quién?*
what is it?	*¿qué es?*	how much?	*¿cuánto?*
which?	*¿cuál?*		

Numbers

1	*uno*	17	*diecisiete*
2	*dos*	18	*dieciocho*
3	*tres*	19	*diecinueve*
4	*cuatro*	20	*veinte*
5	*cinco*	21	*veintiuno*
6	*seis*	30	*treinta*
7	*siete*	31	*treinta y uno*
8	*ocho*	40	*cuarenta*
9	*nueve*	50	*cincuenta*
10	*diez*	60	*sesenta*
11	*once*	70	*setenta*
12	*doce*	80	*ochenta*
13	*trece*	90	*noventa*
14	*catorce*	100	*cien*
15	*quince*	1,000	*mil*
16	*dieciseis*		

Time

What time is it?	*¿qué hora es?*	tomorrow	*mañana*
its…am/pm	*son las ….am/pm*	yesterday	*ayer*
today	*hoy*	morning	*mañana*
tonight	*esta noche*	evening	*tardecita*

Days

Monday	*lunes*	Friday	*viernes*
Tuesday	*martes*	Saturday	*sábado*
Wednesday	*miércoles*	Sunday	*domingo*
Thursday	*jueves*		

Months

January	*enero*	July	*julio*
February	*febrero*	August	*agosto*
March	*marzo*	September	*setiembre*
April	*abril*	October	*octubre*
May	*mayo*	November	*noviembre*
June	*junio*	December	*diciembre*

Public Transport

I'd like…	*me gustaría …*	bus station	*terminal*
…a one-way ticket	*pasaje de ida*	railway station	*estación de ferrocarril*
…a return ticket	*pasaje de ida y vuelta*	airport	*aeropuerto*
		port	*puerto*
I want to go to…	*quiero ir a …*	bus	*colectivo/omnibus*
How much is it?	*¿cuánto cuesta?*	local town bus	*colectivo/linea*
What time does it leave?	*¿a qué hora sale?*	train	*tren*
		plane	*avión*
What time is it now?	*¿qué hora es ahora?*	boat	*barco*
		ferry (across river)	*balsa*
The bus has been…	*El colectivo está …*	motorboat	*lancha*
…delayed	*atrasado*	rowing boat	*canoa*
…cancelled	*suspendido*	car	*auto*
economy class	*común*	4×4	*cuatro por cuatro*
with reclining seats ('half-bed')	*semi cama*	taxi	*taxi*
		minibus	*minibus*
with fully reclining seats ('bed car')	*coche cama*	motorbike/moped	*moto*
		bicycle	*bicicleta*
platform	*plataforma*	arrival/departure	*llegada/salida*
ticket window	*ventanilla*	here	*acá/aquí*
timetable	*horario*	there	*allá/allí*
from	*de*	bon voyage!	*!buen viaje!*
to	*a*		

Private transport

Is this the road to…?	*¿es éste el camino a …?*	I'd like… litres	*quiero … litros*
		diesel	*gasoil/diesel*
Where is the service station?	*¿dónde queda la estación de servicios/ el surtidor?*	unleaded petrol	*nafta sin plomo*
		I have broken down	*mi auto se descompuso*
Please fill it up	*tanque lleno, por favor*		

Road signs

give way	*ceda el paso*	oneway	*contramano*
danger	*peligro*	toll	*peaje*
entry	*entrada*	no entry	*prohibido el paso*
detour	*desvío*	exit	*salida*

Directions

Where is it?	*¿dónde queda?*	south	*sur*
Go straight ahead	*siga derecho/adelante*	east	*este*
turn left	*doble a la izquierda*	west	*oeste*
turn right	*doble a la derecha*	behind	*detrás de ...*
...at the traffic lights	*... al semáforo*	in front of	*delante de ...*
...at the roundabout	*... a la rotonda*	near	*cerca de ...*
north	*norte*	opposite	*en frente de ...*

Street signs

entrance	*entrada*	toilets –	*baños/sanitarios*
exit	*salida*	men/women	*caballeros/damas*
open	*abierto*	information	*información*
closed	*cerrado*		

Accommodation

Where is a cheap/ good hotel?	*¿dónde se encuentra un hotel barato/bueno?*	...a room with two beds	*... una habitación con dos camas*
Could you please write the address?	*¿podría escribirme la dirección por favor?*	...a room with a bathroom	*... una habitación con baño privado*
Do you have any rooms available?	*¿tiene habitaciones disponibles?*	How much it is per night/person?	*¿cuánto cuesta por persona/por noche?*
I'd like ...	*me gustaría ...*	Where is the toilet/ bathroom?	*¿dónde está el baño?*
...a single room	*... una habitación simple*	Is there hot water?	*¿tiene agua caliente?*
...a double room	*... una habitación doble*	Is there electricity?	*¿hay luz?*
		Is breakfast included?	*¿está incluido el desayuno?*
		I am leaving today	*salgo hoy*

Food

Do you have a table for...people?	*¿Tiene mesa para ... personas?*	Please bring me...	*Por favor, tráigame ...*
...a children's menu?	*... menu de niños?*	...a fork/knife/ spoon	*... tenedor/cuchillo/ cuchara*
I am a vegetarian	*Soy vegetariano/-a*	Please may I have the bill?	*La cuenta, por favor.*
Do you have any vegetarian dishes?	*¿Tiene algún plato vegetariano?*		

Basics

bread	*pan*	pepper	*pimienta*
butter	*manteca*	salt	*sal*
cheese	*queso*	sugar	*azúcar*
oil	*aceite*		

Fruit

apples	*manzanas*	mango	*mango*
bananas	*bananas*	oranges	*naranjas*
grapes	*uvas*	pears	*peras*

Vegetables

carrot	*zanahoria*	[green/red] pepper	*locote/moron*
garlic	*ajo*	potato	*papa*
onion	*cebolla*		

Fish

tuna	*atún*	fish	*pescado*

Meat

beef	*carne (de vaca)*	pork	*chancho/cerdo*
chicken	*pollo*	sausage	*chorizo*

Drinks

beer	*cerveza*	tea	*té*
coffee	*café*	water	*agua*
fruit juice	*jugo de fruta*	wine	*vino*
milk	*leche*		

Shopping

I'd like to buy...	*me gustaría comprar ...*	Do you accept...?	*¿Se acepta ...?*
		credit card	*tarjeta de crédito*
How much is it?	*¿cuánto cuesta?*	travellers' cheques	*cheques viajeros*
I don't like it	*no me gusta*	more	*más*
I'm just looking	*sólo estoy mirando*	less	*menos*
It's too expensive	*es demasiado caro*	smaller	*más pequeño/chico*
I'll take it	*lo voy a llevar*	bigger	*más grande*
Please may I have...	*¿Podría darme ...?*		

Communications

I am looking for...	*estoy buscando*	...embassy	*embajada*
bank	*banco*	exchange office	*cambio*
post office	*correo*	telephone centre	*Copaco*
church	*iglesia*	tourist office	*oficina de turismo*

Health

diarrhoea	*diarrea*	contraceptive	*anticonceptivos*
nausea	*náusea*	sun block	*protector/bloqueador solar*
doctor	*doctor*		
prescription	*receta*	I am ...	*soy ...*
pharmacy	*farmacia*	...asthmatic	*asmático/-a*
paracetamol	*paracetamol*	...epileptic	*epiléptico/-a*
aspirin	*aspirina*	...diabetic	*diabético/-a*
antibiotics	*antibióticos*	I'm allergic to...	*soy alergico/-a a ...*
antiseptic	*antiséptico*	...penicillin	*penicilina*
tampons	*tampones*	...nuts	*nueces*
condoms	*preservativos/ condones*	...bees	*abejas*

Help!	!socorro!/!ayuda!
Call a doctor	llame al doctor
There's been an accident	ha ocurrido un accidente
I'm lost	estoy perdido/-a
Go away!	!váyase! !fuera!
police	policía
fire	incendio
ambulance	ambulancia
thief	ladrón
hospital	hospital
I am ill	estoy enfermo/-a

Travel with children

Is there a...?	¿Hay ...?	nappies	pañales
Do you have...?	¿Tiene usted ...?	babysitter	niñera
...infant milk formula?	leche en polvo para bebé?	Are children allowed?	¿se permiten niños?

Other

my/mine/ours/yours	mi/mis	that (close)	ese/esa/eso
your (sing)	tu/tus	that (far)	aquel/aquella/
his/her	su/sus		aquellos/aquellas
our	nuestro/-a/-os/-as	expensive/cheap	caro/barato
your (pl)	su/sus	beautiful/ugly	lindo/feo
their	su/sus	old/new	viejo/nuevo
and	y	good/bad	malo/bueno
but	pero	early/late	temprano/tarde
some	algún/alguna/	hot/cold	caliente/frío
	algunos/algunas	difficult/easy	difícil/fácil
this	este/esta/esto	boring/interesting	aburrido/interesante

GUARANÍ

Accents Words in Guaraní are regularly accented on the final syllable. This means that accents are only marked when the stress falls somewhere other than on the last syllable, eg: *ndaipóri* (there is not). In Spanish, however, words are regularly accented on the penultimate syllable, and accents are marked when the stress falls somewhere else, eg: *fotógrafo* (photographer). When including a Guaraní word in a Spanish text, therefore, the Spanish rule is followed, and accents are put on the final syllable of a Guaraní word, eg: *Se fueron a Caacupé* (They went to Caacupé). In this guide the same practice has been followed in order to help pronunciation: accents have been put on the final syllables of Guaraní words (even though in pure Guaraní they would not be marked), to help the reader remember how to pronounce them. This can be particularly helpful in the case of *jopará* terms (mixed language) like *sombrero pirí*. An accent on a final 'y' is often omitted, probably because of the difficulty of finding it on a Spanish keyboard.

Translation In the many instances of compound phrases using both Guaraní and Spanish words, I have given a translation that distinguishes the language of each, eg: *pelota tatá* (Spanish 'ball', Guaraní 'of fire'). Where the language of the original is not specified, it is Spanish.

Spelling Another consequence of *jopará* is that Guaraní words are sometimes spelt in the Spanish way (eg: *yacaré* for *jakaré* – caiman) and Spanish words sometimes in the Guaraní way (eg: *kandil* for *candil* – torch). This guide tries to be consistent but there are moments when consistency has to give way to general usage. It is useful, also, to be aware that you will come across a variety of spellings in Guaraní. Attempts at standardisation of Guaraní spelling have replaced the hard 'c' with a 'k', the 'z' with an 's', the 'y' with a 'j' and the 'x' with a 'ch'. Proper names have not kept up with the changes: we write Caacupé and not Ka'akupé; the Argentinians write Puerto Iguazú but the Paraguayans write San Ignacio Guasú; the usual spelling of the dam shared with Argentina is Yacyretá and not Jasyretá; but we have always written Che Guevara and not Xe Guevara. You will also find a variation between the use of the 'v' and the 'b' (which sound the same when pronounced by Spanish-speakers) and the 's' and the soft 'c'. The same street in Asunción has one street sign saying 'Tabapy' and another saying 'Tavapy'.

The sixth vowel In addition to a, e, i, o and u, Guaraní has a sixth vowel written 'y' and pronounced a bit like 'oo' and a bit like 'ugh': really, it cannot be explained without demonstration. In addition to this, all vowels have nasalised forms, and this is marked with a tilde. So there are 12 vowels in all: a, ã, e, ẽ, i, ĩ, o, õ, u, ũ, y and ỹ. A Guaraní speaker will wrinkle his or her nose when pronouncing ỹ.

Consonants A number of consonants are missing from the Guaraní language – b, c, d, f, q, w, x and z. But there are a number of extra consonants not used in the Latin alphabet, though they are written in the Latin form with two letters – mb, nd, ng, nt and rr. Finally there is abundant use of the glottal stop, which is called the *puso* and written as an apostrophe '; it is treated as a consonant and put at the end of the alphabet. A common word with the *puso* is *mba'e* (thing).

Greetings Learning a language that has no European roots is difficult but intriguing, as so many things are completely different from the expectation. Since this is one of the delights of discovering Paraguay, a few of the most basic points of grammar are included here. It is a surprise to find that there is no word for 'hello' or 'goodbye', but the regular greeting is *mba'éichapa* (how are you?), and the most common dismissal is to say *jahá* (let's go), and *jajetopáta* (we'll see each other), which is in any case a *jopará* word.

Plurals You do not add 's' to form a plural, and indeed, there is no plural form, either of nouns or of verbs. Sometimes the word *kuéra* is put after a noun to indicate a plural, and *hikuái* is sometimes put after verbs. Otherwise, the context indicates a plural.

Verb 'to be' Continuing with the surprises of a non-European language, there is no verb 'to be', but this is indicated by saying 'I [am] the one', 'you [are] the one', etc: *che ha'e, nde ha'e*, etc.

Question marks There are no question marks written in Guaraní.

Numbers In strict Guaraní numbers only go up to five: *peteĩ, mokõi, mbohapý, irundý, po*, the last being the word for 'hand'. Then there is 'many' *hetá*, and 'few' *mbový*. In practice, the number you most frequently hear is 'one', *peteĩ*, and for the rest the Spanish numbers are often used. But further numbers in Guaraní have been constructed out of combinations of the first five, and they are used by speakers trying to avoid *jopará*: eg: *poteĩ* (6), *pokõi* (7), *poapy* (8), *porundy* (9), *pa* (10), *pateĩ* (11), *mokõipa* (20), etc.

First person plural There are two words for 'we', the inclusive and the exclusive, and corresponding conjugative forms; *ñande* means 'me and you (and perhaps others)', while *ore* means 'me and others but not you'. For example, when talking about God to other people, you say *Ñandejára* (Our Lord) because God is the Lord of the people you are talking to, but when addressing God you say *Ore Ru* (Our Father) because God is not the Father of himself.

Conjugating Verbs are conjugated at the beginning of the word rather than at the end, eg: *apuká, repuká, opuká, japuká, ropuká, pepuká*: 'I laugh', 'you (s) laugh', 's/he laughs', 'we (incl) laugh', 'we (excl) laugh', 'you (pl) laugh'. *Japuká* corresponds to the pronoun *ñande*, and *ropuká* corresponds to the pronoun *ore*. There is no third person plural form, because the third person singular form is used.

Prepositions In Guaraní the prepositions come after the noun and so are called *pospociones*, eg: *kokuépe* (in the field), where *-pe* means 'in' or 'at'.

Prefixes and suffixes There are a host of prefixes and suffixes that subtly modify the meaning, so that a line of poetry in Guaraní may consist of two or three words, and need ten or 12 words to capture its sense in Spanish or English. The word 'hallowed' in the Lord's Prayer, *toñembojeroviákena*, has four prefixes and two suffixes added to the verb *(a)roviá* (believe). The prefixes express the sense of the optative, the reflexive, the idea of making something happen, and the first person plural. The suffixes express the sense of command and of politeness in making the command.

Appendix 2

GLOSSARY

See also box on *Craft*, page 21.

almacen	store, corner shop
aó po'í	(Guaraní) a traditional form of embroidery
arroyo	stream
bandeirantes	lit. flag-bearers, used of Brazilians who invaded the Reductions to hunt for slaves
baño moderno/baño común	flushing toilet/latrine
barrio	neighbourhood
bombilla	metal straw for drinking *tereré* or *mate*
bosque	wood
cabildo	(colonial) representatives who administer the town; the building they use
cabinas	telephone boxes
cacique	indigenous leader
camino de tierra	dirt road
camioneta	jeep, van
campesino	person living in the *campo*, peasant
campo	countryside
candiles	candles made from animal fat in an *apepú* (bitter orange) skin
carpincho	capybara
casa parroquial	parish house
celular	mobile phone
cerro	hill
chip	SIM card, microchip
chipa, chipa guasú, chipa so'ó	(Guaraní) see *Food glossary*, below
chipería	shop that sells *chipa*
choza	hut of indigenous
churrasquería	Brazilian-style restaurant where a lot of roast meats are served
coche cama	sleeper (on bus)
cocotero	Paraguay's most typical palm tree
colegio	secondary school
compañía	a small village in the countryside, attached to a larger town or *pueblo*
común	'common' or ordinary, eg: a third-class bus
cooperativa	1) credit union; 2) firm run by its workers, eg: of craft workers, or of Mennonites

Copaco	(Compañía Paraguaya de Comunicaciones) state telephone network, previously called Antelco
copetín	small café
correo	post, email address
criollo	born in Latin America, but of Spanish parents
cucaracha	cockroach
departamento	political division of country, like a province
deposito	left luggage, storeroom
diferencial	of buses, a superior class
Don	term of respect for a man, like *Señor*
ejecutivo	of buses, a superior class
empedrado	road covered with small stones, cobbled
empresa	company, particularly of bus company
encomienda	packet sent by bus instead of through the post; hard labour for indigenous in colonial times
enripiado	road covered with smaller stones or fine gravel
encaje ju	(Spanish, Guaraní) traditional Paraguayan lace
estancia	country estate
festival	show of music and dance
fiesta	party
fiesta patronal	feast day of a town, on the day of its patron saint
Fray	Friar (of Franciscans)
frigobar	minibar
gaseosa	fizzy drink
gobernación	regional government office, at the level of the *departamento*
guampa	cup for *tereré* or *mate* (different for each), see *Chapter 1,* page 22
guarania	form of Paraguayan traditional music, in minor key
guardabosque, guardaparque	park ranger
H	*Hermano* ie: Brother (religious)
Hna	*Hermana* ie: Sister (religious)
heladería	ice-cream parlour
hospedaje	small hotel, hostel
iglesia	church
imagen	statue
intendente	mayor
interno	extension (of telephone)
IVA (impuesto de valor agregado)	Value Added Tax
jopará	(Guaraní) mixture of Guaraní and Spanish
kotý guasú	(Guaraní, in Reductions) house for widows and orphans
lapacho	large tree with beautiful pink (or yellow) blossom, used a lot in building
librería	stationery shop, bookshop
linea baja	landline
maraca	instrument to shake, like a rattle
mate	hot tea-like infusion made with *yerba*
mburucuyá	national flower of Paraguay, much sculpted in the Reductions; corresponding fruit
mensú	(Guaraní) late 19th-century and early 20th-century agricultural worker, in the region around Hernandarias, whose work conditions especially

	on the *yerbales* made him a slave
mestizo	mixed race, with Spanish and indigenous blood
mini carga	putting some credit onto a mobile phone
mirador	viewpoint, lookout point
monte	wild wood
motel (Cupido, del Bosque, Pasión, etc)	hotel for amorous liaisons, renting rooms by the hour
Municipalidad	town council, town hall, area of jurisdiction of same
Ña	(Guaraní) term of respect for a woman, like *Señora*
ñandutí	(Guaraní) traditional spiderweb lace
P or *Padre* or *Pa'i*	Father (ie: priest)
palo santo	fragrant hardwood used for small carvings
parrilla	grill, barbecue
patio de comidas	group of restaurants in one food hall
peatonal	pedestrian precinct
pesebre	crib
plaza	square
polka	form of traditional dance music, in major key
poli deportivo	or just *poli* for short; multi-use sports hall, a large roofed area with semi-open walls
Próceres	the people who effected the independence of Paraguay
propina	tip
pueblo	town or village
puente	bridge
quincho	roofed area without walls, especially with a barbecue
rancho	small country house
reducciones	reductions (as in Jesuit-Guaraní Reductions)
remedios	herbs with medicinal qualities used in *mate* or *tereré*, or in infusions like tea
remise	taxi, especially Argentinian
retablo	reredos, the decorative setting on the wall behind the altar, that in the Reductions acted as a frame for statues
río	river
ruta	main road
selva	wild wood
semáforo	traffic lights
Semana Santa	Holy Week, especially Maundy Thursday to Easter Sunday
sombrero	broad brimmed hat
sulky	horse cart for tourists
tatakuá	(Guaraní) traditional brick oven, shaped like igloo (almost every house in the *campo* has one in the garden)
telefax	joint telephone and fax line
tenedor libre	restaurant where you can eat all you want for a fixed price
tereré	iced tea-like infusion made with *yerba*
tigre	literally tiger, but used for jaguar
ventilador, aire	fan, air conditioning
yerba	plant used for *tereré* and *mate*
yerbal	plantation of *yerba* trees

FOOD GLOSSARY These are traditional foods, such as are served all over the country (but less so in the cosmopolitan restaurants of Asunción). Some of these names are in Guaraní, others in Spanish.

albóndigas	meatballs usually made with breadcrumbs
apepú	bitter oranges
arrollado	strip of meat rolled up
asado	the favourite meal of Paraguayans – a barbecue. It can include beef, chicken, pork and sausages, or any combination.
asado a la estaca	more special kind of *asado* cooked on long wooden spits stuck in the ground next to an open fire. It is generally offered at big, public events, but you need to take your own sharp knife, plates and cutlery.
asado a la olla	pot roast
batata	not potato, but sweet potato. It is eaten as much as or more than ordinary potatoes.
batiburrillo	a delicious speciality of Misiones, made by stewing together all the beef innards
bife	beef steak
butifarra	sausage made of chopped pork
caldo	soup or broth
caña	Paraguayan spirit made from sugar cane, similar or identical to rum. The cheapest *caña* is very rough but the fine Aristocrata or Tres Leones – Etiqueta Negra, at the top end of the market, still costs barely more than US$2.
carnaza	meat without bones
carne	literally 'meat', but in fact used to mean 'beef', the principal meat of Paraguay
chicharõ trenzado	traditional dish in which strips of meat are plaited together and then fried
chipa	sold as a snack on the streets and in buses, this roll is not made of bread but of maize flour and cheese
chipa guasú	a great favourite: like *sopa paraguaya* but made with fresh, tender maize instead of maize flour.
chipa so'ó	a kind of *chipa* with a meat filling
chancho	pig, and so, pork
choclo	corn on the cob, when it is fresh and tender as opposed to dried and hard
chorizo	sausage
clérico	a cross between a dessert and a drink, made from fruit cut up and served in wine. It is served only at Christmas.
cocido	a tea-like drink made by caramelising the *yerba* leaf; Paraguay is neither a tea country or a coffee country, but *cocido* is a delicious alternative. It can be served with milk or without.
dorado	a large river fish, usually grilled, and considered to be the finest fish on the market
dulce de leche	a sweet spread for putting on bread

empanada	very common snack or light meal, like a Cornish pasty but filled with a beef and egg mixture, or with other fillings
guiso	meat stew usually cooked with rice
kavuré	a pastry mixture with egg and cheese, wrapped around wooden spits and cooked by an open fire, coming out in a long cylindrical shape
leche de vaca	literally 'cow's milk', the term is used to distinguish fresh milk from longlife milk bought in cartons
locro	a variety of white maize generally cooked in a meat stew
lomo	flank of beef used for steak
mandioca	white root vegetable, in English 'mandioc' or 'yucca', peeled, boiled and served with most meals like bread or potatoes, eaten with the hands
mamón	papaya, usually served as a jam, and usually heavily sweetened to appeal to the Paraguayan palate
mate	see above
mbejú	delicious breakfast dish or snack like a firm pancake but made from mandioc flour, maize flour, pork fat and cheese
media luna	croissant
miel de abeja	honey
miel negro	treacle, a side-product of sugar processing
milanesa	an escalope of beef or chicken coated in breadcrumbs and fried
ñoqui	what Italians call *gnocchi*
pastel mandi'ó	*empanada* made with minced mandioc
poroto	beans, kidney beans
queso paraguayo	Paraguayan cheese, excellent for cooking, but not designed to be eaten on its own
rorá	a savoury dish made of boiled maize flour, usually a breakfast or a supper dish
so'ó apuá	meatballs usually formed with maize flour
sopa paraguaya	a maize cake eaten as accompaniment to a dinner or on its own, and made from milk, maize flour, pork fat, onion, cheese and eggs. It has its origin in a soup that turned out too thick, made by the cook of President Carlos Antonio López: she put it in the oven and so created a new dish.
surubí	the most common fish, with firm white flesh and no bones
tallarín	what the Italians call *tagliatelle*, often served with a chicken sauce
tortilla	a Paraguayan *tortilla* (quite different from a Spanish *tortilla*) is a savoury pancake, sometimes fried with green vegetables inside, particularly *acelga* (chard); a common supper dish.
tereré	see above
vorí vorí	a stew, often of chicken, with dumplings
yacaré	crocodile (or, strictly, speaking) caiman. Now a protected species, but Paraguayans pay no attention to the law. However, restaurants can no longer serve it.

Appendix 3

SELECTIVE LIST OF FAUNA

In most cases, the Guaraní name is the one that Paraguayans will be most familiar with.

ENGLISH	LATIN	SPANISH	GUARANÍ
BIRDS			
bellbird, bare-throated	*Procnias nudicollis*	*pájaro campana*	*guyrá campana*
duck	(various)	*pato*	*ypé*
cormorant, neotropical	*Phalacrocorax brasilianus*	*biguá*	*mbiguá*
eagle, crowned	*Harpyhaliaetus coronatus*	*águila coronada*	*taguató hový apiratí*
eagle, harpy	*Harpia harpyja*	*harpia*	*taguató ruvichá*
egret, snowy	*Egretta thula*	*garcita blanca*	*itaipyté*
flamingo, Chilean	*Phoenicopterus chilensis*	*flamenco austral*	*guarimbó pytã*
heron	(various)	*garza*	*hokó*
hummingbird	(various)	*picaflor*	*mainumbý*
kingfisher, ringed	*Ceryle torquita*	*martín pescador grande*	*javatĩ*
lapwing, southern	*Vanellus chilensis*	*tero tero*	*tetéu*
macaw, hyacinth	*Anodorhynchus hyacinthinus*	*papagayo azul*	*gua'á hový*
macaw, blue-and-yellow	*Ara ararauna*	*paraguayo amarillo*	*gua'a sa'yjú*
macaw, red-and-green	*Ara chloropterus*	*guacamayo rojo*	*gua'á pytã*
owl	(various)	*lechuza/buho*	*suindá*
piculet, ochre-collared	*Dryocopus galeatus*	*carpintero cara canela*	*ypekũ*
potoo	*Nyctibius griseus*	*guaimingue*	*urutaú*
rhea, greater	*Rhea americana*	*avestruz*	*ñandú guasú*
screamer, southern	*Chauna torquata*	*chajá*	*chahã*
seriema, black-legged	*Chunga burmeisteri*	*saria patas negras*	*saria hũ*
seriema, red-legged	*Cariama cristata*	*saria patas rojas*	*saria pytã*
spoonbill, roseate	*Platalea ajaja*	*espátula rosada*	*ajajai*
stork, jabiru	*Jabiru mycteria*	*tuyuyú cuartelero*	*jabirú*
stork, maguari	*Ciconia maguari*	*cigüeña*	*mbaguarí*
stork, wood	*Mycteria Americana*	*tuyuyú*	*tujujú kangý*
tinamou, brushland	*Nothoprocta cinerascens*	*perdiz de monte*	*ynambú sĩsĩ*

toucan, toco	*Ramphastos toco*	*tucán grande*	*tukã guasú*
woodpecker	(various)	*carpintero*	*ypekũ*

REPTILES

anaconda, yellow	*Eunectes notaeus*	*anaconda del sur*	*kurijú*
boa constrictor	*Boa constrictor*	*boa*	*mbõi ro'ý*
caiman	(various)	*jacaré*	*jakaré*
iguana, common	*Iguana iguana*	*iguana*	*tejú*
lizard	(various)	*lagartija*	*tejú*
snake	(various)	*culebra/serpiente*	*mbõi*
tortoise/turtle	(various)	*tortuga*	*karumbé*

AMPHIBIANS

frog	(various)	*rana*	*ju'í*
toad	(various)	*sapo*	*kururú*

MAMMALS

anteater, giant	*Myrmecophaga tridactyla*	*oso hormiguero*	*jurumí*
armadillo	(various)	*armadillo*	*tatú*
armadillo, giant	*Priodontes maximus*	*armadillo gigante*	*tatú carreta*
capybara	*Hydrochaeris hydrochaeris*	*carpincho*	*capi'í yvá*
coati, South American	*Nasua nasua*	*coati*	*koatí*
deer, grey brocket	*Mazama gouazoupira*	*corzuela parda*	*guasú virá*
deer, marsh	*Blastocerus dichotomus*	*ciervo de los pantanos*	*guasú pucú*
deer, pampas	*Ozotoceros bezoarticus*	*ciervo de las pampas*	*guasutí*
jaguar	*Panthera onca*	*jaguar*	*jaguareté*
lion, mountain/puma	*Puma concolor*	*puma*	*jaguá pytã*
monkey, brown capuchin	*Cebus paella*	*mono capuchino*	*ka'í paraguay*
monkey, howler	*Alouatta caraya*	*mono aullador*	*karajá*
nutria	*Myocastor coypus*	*nutria*	*kyjá*
nutria, giant	*Pteronura brasiliensis*	*nutria gigante*	*kyjá guasú*
peccary, Chacoan	*Catagonus wagneri*	*quimilero*	*taguá*
peccary, white-lipped	*Tayassu pecari*	*jabali*	*tañykatí*
tapir, South American	*Tapirus terrestris*	*tapir*	*mboreví*
wolf, maned	*Chrysocyon brachurus*	*lobo de crin*	*aguará guasú*

Appendix 4

FURTHER INFORMATION

GUIDEBOOKS If you would like to supplement this guidebook with a local guidebook, there are a few (very few) that have been published within Paraguay, and that can be bought in a few (very few) places in the country. They are in Spanish, and do not have as much information as your Bradt Guide, but they have some nice pictures, and also some reference details that are not in this guide.

Jaha (Guaraní 'Let's go'), first published 2009 and regularly updated. This leaflet is a fairly comprehensive list of tourist facilities all over the country, with a wealth of contact details but no other kind of text. It is in Spanish only, and in tiny print so it fits onto one large fold-out sheet or a 16-page leaflet. Excellent reference tool, but not designed to be read through. Distributed free by Senatur (*Palma 468 e/ Alberdi y 14 de mayo;* ✆ *021 494110;* f *021 491230;* e *senator@pla.net.py; www.senatur.gov.py;* ⊕ *07.00–19.00 daily including Sun & holidays*). Also available as a pdf file, downloadable from the Senatur website.

La Magia de Nuestra Tierra, Fundación en Alianza, 2007. No ISBN. This is the top choice: A4 size, 266 pages, all with colour pictures. (The first 2003 edition was just in black and white.) It manages to say something about practically every town in Paraguay. Well planned and laid out, accurate in its information. With its large number of photographs it makes an excellent souvenir even if you cannot read Spanish. Its weak point is its maps, which have very little detail. The problem, as always with books in Paraguay, is to know where to get hold of a copy – even in the capital city where it is published – but if you have failed to pick one up at the airport in the Los Nietos shop, it can be bought from the offices of the Fundación (*Juan de Salazar 486 e/ San José y Boquerón;* ✆ *021 222215; www.enalianza.org.py;* ⊕ *08.00–17.30 Mon–Fri*), or from the bookshop called Books (see page 77), or from Petrobras service stations. Only Gs50,000.

Paraguay: Guía Turística TACPy, Touring y Automovil Club Paraguayo, 2007. No ISBN. This is the second choice, and again is just in Spanish. Handy size (13 x 24.5cm) and extensively illustrated in colour, with every other page entirely photos. In contrast to *La Magia de Nuestra Tierra*, its strong point is its maps: it has 22 fold-out maps at the back (though it lacks an overall map to find your way among them). Its weak point is that it has very little text on each place, and is more like an annotated catalogue of places with map references. It is a little better distributed than *La Magia*, and can be found in some service stations, as well as direct from the office of the motoring organisation Touring (*Brasil c/ 25 de mayo, up a ramp to the right of the service station;* ✆ *021 210550;* ⊕ *08.00–17.00 Mon–Fri, 08.00–12.00 Sat*). Gs70,000.

TAP Guia: Paraguay Westfalenhaus Verlag SA, second edition 1999. ISBN: 99925 3 000 6. The first serious attempt at a guidebook to the country, but now superseded by more recent books. The same dimensions as a Bradt Guide but much heavier, because of the glossy paper used. Written in Spanish, German and

English, the amount of information that fits into this heavy book is scanty, the colour photos are poor quality and the information is now dated. However, it does have a useful Itinerario de Transporte Público Metropolitano (the route of each bus line). Available from the Hotel Westfalenhaus (*Sgto 1° M Benitez 1577 c/ Santísima Trinidad;* ↘ *021 292374/292966*). US$15.

NATURAL HISTORY

Clark, Peter T *Guia de los Parques Nacionales y Otras Areas Silvestres Protegidas del Paraguay – Guide to Paraguay's National Parks and other Protected Wild Areas* Paraguay, Servilibro, 2004. ISBN: 99925 3 298 X. Bilingual edition, in Spanish and English.

Kohn Patiño, Celia Edith and 5 other authors *Fauna Silvestre del Paraguay – Wildlife of Paraguay* Paraguay, 2007. ISBN: 99925 913 1 5. Bilingual edition, in Spanish and English.

Lowen, James *Pantanal Wildlife: A Visitor's Guide to Brazil's Great Wetland* Bradt Travel Guides, 2010. ISBN: 978 1 84162 305 4. A comprehensive introduction to the best place to watch wildlife in South America, and beautifully illustrated throughout, this Bradt guide is the only portable book to cover all the main wildlife groups while focussing exclusively on the Pantanal. Includes both Brazil and Paraguay.

Narosky, Tito and Yzurieta, Dario *Guia para la Identificación de las Aves de Paraguay* Buenos Aires, Vazquez Mazzini, 2006. ISBN: 987 9132 13 0. In Spanish. Illustrated with clear, coloured line drawings, this is the most comprehensive printed guide available, and is easy to use because the index includes the Latin, Spanish and Guaraní name of each bird.

JESUIT–GUARANÍ REDUCTIONS

Abou, Selim *The Jesuit 'Republic' of the Guaranís (1609–1768)* New York, UNESCO/Crossroad Herder, 1997. ISBN: 0 8245 1706 7. A coffee table book with not only good pictures but excellent, reliable text.

Caraman, Philip *The Lost Paradise* London, Sidgwick and Jackson, 1975. ISBN: 0 283 98212 8. Also published by Seabury in the USA in 1976. Still regarded by many as the classic history in English of the Jesuit-Guaraní Reductions. Author was a Jesuit and drew heavily on Cunninghame Graham's book below.

Cunninghame Graham, R B *A Vanished Arcadia* London/Melbourne/Auckland/ Johannesburg, Century, 1988. ISBN: 0 7126 1887 2. Re-publication with introduction by Philip Healy of work originally published by Century in 1901. Opened up the Jesuit-Guaraní Reductions to the English-speaking world, after Cunninghame Graham returned enthused from a trip to Paraguay in 1871.

Gott, Richard *Land without Evil: Utopian journeys across the South American Watershed* London/New York, Verso, 1993. ISBN: 0 86091 398 8. A travel book with a solid study of the old Jesuit history woven in, but more about Bolivia than Paraguay.

Jaenike, William F *Black Robes in Paraguay: the success of the Guaraní missions hastened the abolition of the Jesuits* Minneapolis, Kirk House, 2007. ISBN: 1 933794 04 6. A detailed historical study.

McNaspy, Clement J *The Lost Cities of Paraguay: art and architecture of the Jesuit Reductions* Chicago, Loyola 1982. Old book but still a staple reference by this US Jesuit who became a leading expert on the Reductions and lived in Paraguay for many years. Black-and-white photographs by José María Blanch, also available in Spanish.

McNaspy, Clement J *Una Visita a las Ruinas Jesuíticas* Paraguay, CEPAG, 1987. First edition was in 1981. Slim travel guide in Spanish to the Paraguayan Jesuit-Guaraní Reductions, plus San Ignacio Miní and São Miguel. Very dated.

Montoya, Antonio Ruiz de *The Spiritual Conquest: a personal account of the founding and early years of the Jesuit Paraguayan Reductions* St Louis, Institute of Jesuit Sources, 1993. ISBN: 1 880810 02 6. Translated by Clement J McNaspy and others. An excellent modern English translation of Montoya's great work of 1639, with useful notes. Recommended, if you can get hold of a copy.

TRIPLE ALLIANCE WAR AND MADAME LYNCH

Cawthorne, Nigel *The Empress of South America: the true story of Eliza Lynch, the Irishwoman who destroyed Latin America's wealthiest country and became its national heroine* London, Heinemann, 2003. ISBN: 0 434 00898 2. See Rees below.

Lillis, Michael and Fanning, Ronan *The Lives of Eliza Lynch: scandal and courage* Dublin, Gill & Macmillan, 2009. ISBN: 978 07171 4611 6. A new exploration of Madame Lynch and the reasons for her bad reputation. Something of a reply to the four books published only a few years earlier by Rees and Cawthorne, Enright and Tuck.

Masterman, George Frederick *Seven Eventful Years in Paraguay: a narrative of personal experience amongst the Paraguayans* USA, Kessinger. ISBN: 978 781432 699109. Facsimile edition of book published in 1870 by the once Chief Military Apothecary of Mariscal López.

Rees, Sian *The Shadows of Elisa Lynch: how a nineteenth-century courtesan became the most powerful woman in Paraguay* London, Hodder Headline, 2003. ISBN: 0 7553 11140. This and Cawthorne's book, above, are fairly similar – readable, historical studies.

Schofield Saeger, James *Francisco Solano López and the Ruination of Paraguay: Honor and Egocentrism* New York/Toronto/London, Rowman & Littlefield, 2007. ISBN: 978 0 7425 3755 2. A serious study by the Professor of History at Lehigh University.

Washburn, Charles Ames *The History of Paraguay Volume 1* USA, Elibron Classics, 2005. ISBN: 978 1402 161414 90000. Facsimile edition of 2-volume work published in 1871 by the once US Minister to Paraguay 1863–68.

FICTION

Bolt, Robert *The Mission* England, Penguin, 1986. ISBN: 0 14 009869 0. A novel surrounding the episodes that became the screen play.

Enright, Anne *The Pleasure of Eliza Lynch* London, Jonathan Cape, 2002. ISBN: 0 224 06269 7. Not dissimilar to the Rees and Cawthorne histories, but this one is a novel. It is well done.

Grisham, John *The Testament* USA, Doubleday, 1999. ISBN: 0 385 49380 2. Compelling thriller set partly in the Pantanal, actually on the Brazilian side of the river, but similar to Paraguay on the other bank.

Trower, Philip *A Danger to the State: a historical novel* San Francisco, St Ignatius Press, 1998. ISBN: 0 89870 674 2. A novel of the political intrigue leading up to the Expulsion of the Jesuits.

Tuck, Lily *The News from Paraguay* USA/London, HarperCollins, 2004/2005. ISBN: 0 00 720799 9. Yet another book about Madame Lynch, which might have been omitted from this bibliography had it not won the US National Book Award.

OTHER BOOKS

Berrigan, Daniel *The Mission: a film journal* San Francisco, Harper & Row, 1986. ISBN: 0 14 009869 0. Daniel Berrigan, Jesuit and peace activist, played the part of a Jesuit in the film.

Caravias, José Luis *Vivir como Hermanos: reflexiones bíblicas sobre la hermandad* Paraguay, CEPAG, 2003. ISBN: 99925 849 6 3. Republication of a pioneering book on liberation theology first published in 1971 in Spain (because of the dictatorship of Stroessner in Paraguay). Caravias was expelled by Stroessner. Only in Spanish. Available from Librería de Ediciones Montoya/CEPAG, see page 78.

Gimlette, John *At the Tomb of the Inflatable Pig: Travels through Paraguay* London, Hutchinson, 2003. ISBN: 0091794331. Riddled with little errors, but a good read. The author's friends seem to be all well-off people in Asunción, which leads to a slightly one-sided perspective.

Ivereigh, Austen, ed *Unfinished Journey: The Church 40 Years after Vatican I* New York/London, Continuum, 2003. ISBN: 0 8264 7100 5. Includes chapter on Paraguay's Christian Agrarian Leagues by Margaret Hebblethwaite.

Nickson, R Andrew *Paraguay* Oxford/Santa Barbara/Denver, Clio Press, 1987. ISBN: 1 85109 028 2. A bibliography, now rather out of date. Volume 84 in the World Bibliographical Series.

Nickson R Andrew *Historical Dictionary of Paraguay* Scarecrow Press, 1993. ISBN: 081082 643 7/978 0 81082 643 4. Major reference book, but not cheap. Revised, enlarged and updated.

O'Shaughnessy, Hugh *The Priest of Paraguay* London/New York, Zed Books, 2009. ISBN: 978 1 84813 313 6. The background to the election of President Fernando Lugo.

Van Houten, Lynn *Flavors of Paraguay: 101 authentic Paraguayan recipes* Petaluma CA USA, Anteater Press, 1997. ISBN: 0 9659173 9 8. Simple spiral-bound book with the families of adopted Paraguayan children in mind.

BOOKSHOPS Books in Spanish have been kept to a minimum, but inevitably some of the titles in this bibliography are only available in Paraguay, and even then, may be out of print. For bookshops in Asunción where you may be able to pick up some new or second-hand books from this list, see *Chapter 3*, page 76.

DVD
The Mission film, written by Robert Bolt, directed by Roland Joffé, starring Robert de Niro and Jeremy Irons, 1986.

WEBSITES
www.oanda.com/currency/converter and **www.xe.com/ucc/full** Two websites showing the Guaraní exchange rate. In English.

www.senatur.gov.py The Paraguayan government tourist office. In Spanish.

www.dgeec.gov.py For up-to-date statistics on Paraguay. In Spanish.

www.abc.com.py *ABC-Color* newspaper online.

www.ultimahora.com *Ultima Hora* newspaper online.

www.seam.gov.py For Paraguay's nature reserves in the National Parks. The letters stand for *Secretaria del Ambiente*. In Spanish.

www.guyra.org.py For eco-tours. Click top right for the site in English.

www.birdlist.org/paraguay Check list of birds in Paraguay. In English, Spanish and other languages.

www.faunaparaguay.com In English and Spanish. A wealth of information on wildlife, but some of the links do not work, and some of the opportunities offered are more in the aspiration than the reality. Invaluable for detailed data on wildlife (click the image gallery).

www.faunaparaguay.com/listbirds.html For birds. (This page is listed separately as it is not clear how to reach it from the home page.)

www.faunaparaguay.com/butterflies.html For butterflies. (This page is listed separately as it is not clear how to reach it from the home page.)

www.artesania.gov.py For craft. In Spanish.

www.mca.gov.py The city of Asunción website, with many links to museums etc. In Spanish.

www.jma.gov.py A web map of Asunción, which you can enlarge or compress, move around, and print.

www.mca.gov.py/webtermi.html The website of the Asunción bus terminal, full of out-of-date information, but gives you something to start from. In Spanish.

www.uninet.com.py Various interesting and useful links to cultural sites in Paraguay. In Spanish.

www.yagua.com A portal much used by Paraguayans, with a lot of useful links, and always up to date. In Spanish.

For visiting San Ignacio Miní and other Reductions in **Argentina** (all in Spanish):
www.turismo.misiones.gov.ar
www.misiones-jesuiticas.com.ar
www.elbastion.com/ruinas

Not within the scope of this book, but here are the key websites you need if you want to travel by bus from Paraguay to visit the Jesuit-Guaraní Reductions in **Brazil** (all in Portuguese):
www.reunidas.com.br for buses from Posadas to Santo Ângelo.
www.rotamissoes.com.br for the Jesuit route in Brazil.
www.saomiguel-rs.com.br for information about São Miguel.
www.missoesturismo.com.br for information on visiting the Reductions in Brazil.
www.caminhodasmissoes.com.br for pilgrimage walks from Reduction to Reduction.

Bolivian sites where you can order sheet music of what was once played in the Paraguayan Reductions, including many Zipoli pieces: Bolivian Chiquitos book order.
www.festivalesapac.com In Spanish.
www.verbodivino-bo.com In Spanish. This is the publisher of the books distributed by APAC.

Index

Page numbers in **bold** refer to major entries; those in *italics* indicate maps